1993

Educating Children
with Multiple Disabilities

Educating Children with Multiple Disabilities

A Transdisciplinary Approach

Second Edition

by
Fred P. Orelove, Ph.D.
Executive Director
Virginia Institute for Developmental Disabilities
Virginia Commonwealth University
Richmond

and
Dick Sobsey, R.N., Ed.D.
Professor
Department of Educational Psychology
University of Alberta
Edmonton, Alberta, Canada

with invited contributions

·P·A·U·L·H·
BROOKES
PUBLISHING CO

Baltimore • London • Toronto • Sydney

Paul H. Brookes Publishing Co.
P.O. Box 10624
Baltimore, Maryland 21285-0624

Copyright © 1991 by Paul H. Brookes Publishing Co., Inc.
All rights reserved.

Typeset by Brushwood Graphics Inc., Baltimore, Maryland.
Manufactured in the United States of America by
The Maple Press Company, York, Pennsylvania.

Library of Congress Cataloging-in-Publication Data

Orelove, Fred P., 1951–
    Educating children with multiple disabilities : a transdisciplinary
approach / by Fred P. Orelove and Dick Sobsey.—2nd ed.
        p.   cm.
    Includes bibliographical references and index.
    ISBN 1-55766-077-8
    1. Handicapped children—Education. 2. Handicapped children—
Care.   I. Sobsey, Richard.
LC4015.068   1991
371.9–dc20
                                                          91-12364
                                                             CIP

Contents

Contributors

Irene H. Carney, Ph.D.
Director of Program Development
Virginia Institute for Developmental
  Disabilities
Box 3020
Virginia Commonwealth University
Richmond, Virginia 23284

Ann W. Cox, R.N., M.N.
Director of Program Support
Virginia Institute for Developmental
  Disabilities
Box 3020
Virginia Commonwealth University
Richmond, Virginia 23284

Winnie Dunn, Ph.D., OTR, FAOTA
Professor and Chair
Occupational Therapy Education
  Department
University of Kansas Medical Center
4013 Hinch Hall
39th and Rainbow Boulevard
Kansas City, Kansas 66103

Fred P. Orelove, Ph.D.
Executive Director
Virginia Institute for Developmental
  Disabilities
Box 3020
Virginia Commonwealth University
Richmond, Virginia 23284

Beverly Rainforth, Ph.D., P.T.
School of Education and Human
  Development
Division of Education
State University of New York-
  Binghamton
P.O. Box 6000
Binghamton, New York 13902-6000

Dick Sobsey, R.N., Ed.D.
Professor
Department of Educational Psychology
University of Alberta
6-102 Education North
Edmonton, Alberta T6G 2G5
CANADA

**Enid G. Wolf-Schein, Ed.D.,
  CCC-SLP**
1703 Andros Isle, Suite J-2
Coconut Creek, Florida 33066

Jennifer York, Ph.D., P.T.
Assistant Professor of Special Education/
  Interdisciplinary Training Director
Institute on Community Integration
University of Minnesota
6 Pattee Hall
150 Pillsbury Drive, S.E.
Minneapolis, Minnesota 55455

Preface

The first edition of this book, published in 1987, was based on the belief that a transdisciplinary model of service delivery has much to offer school-based teams that work with individuals with multiple disabilities. Since then this belief has been strengthened. Many school districts have caring and competent teachers, administrators, and related services staff. In many places, the concept of functional assessment and instruction has gained a solid footing. Moreover, there is increasing commitment to integrated education.

Despite advances in curriculum, instructional technology, and inclusive education, however, we have seen many instances in which professionals feel frustrated, not necessarily by their students, but by their own inability to work together harmoniously and efficiently to do what is best for their students. We do not suggest that the job is a simple one. Children with multiple disabilities present many challenges, and educators and related services personnel must be knowledgeable across many areas, in addition to being creative, dedicated, and tireless, among the many qualities found in any professional working in school programs. We do suggest, however, that the challenges presented by students with multiple disabilities demand that professionals employ a model of services that respects and takes advantage of their different fields of expertise.

Thus, the second edition continues to advocate for a transdisciplinary service delivery model, arguing that the increased presence of children with special health care needs makes this model even more valuable. Indeed, this edition has added two chapters (5 and 6) that examine issues concerning maintaining optimal health, in addition to prevention of and intervention for health care problems in children. Some topics, such as child abuse and HIV infection, are new in this edition. Others, such as seizures and medications, have been updated and revised.

This edition also continues to present a practical array of techniques useful in educating children with multiple disabilities. Therefore, some areas traditionally covered in textbooks for students with severe disabilities (e.g., assessment) are omitted here in favor of rather specialized topics (e.g., mealtime skills) treated in greater detail.

Educating Children with Multiple Disabilities continues to infuse a variety of values into the material in its 13 chapters. We have a strong commitment to family, children, and teamwork. This commitment translates into support for nonaversive medical or behavioral interventions and for integrated school programs. New material on these topics has been added to this edition. The final chapter, on trends and issues, also has been expanded to explore a greater range of current controversial topics.

Despite these additions and updates, this edition retains the basic format of the original book. Chapter 1 examines teamwork models, specifically focusing on trans-disciplinary teams. Chapters 2–6 present basic terminology; information on physical, medical, and sensory characteristics and development; and basic techniques for handling and positioning. Readers are advised to complete these chapters as a basis for appreciating the remainder of the book.

Chapters 7–11 discuss general principles in curriculum and instruction, as well as specific strategies for developing adaptations and for teaching communication, mealtime, and self-care skills. Suggestions are provided within each chapter for working within transdisciplinary teams.

The final two chapters are issue-oriented, rather than focusing on intervention. Chapter 12 deals with issues related to understanding and working with families. Chapter 13 discusses current issues, such as guidelines for treating newborns with disabilities and individuals in a persistent vegetative state, and presents a rationale and strategies for establishing integrated school programs.

This edition continues to avoid using jargon; where this was not possible or desirable, we have tried to define or describe terms within the text. We hope that this approach will appeal to a broad readership, spanning a wide variety of disciplines and laypeople.

The ultimate test for this book, of course, is whether it contributes to the information and skills of the reader and whether, in turn, this translates into improved education and services for children. We hope this book contributes to these outcomes at least in part, and we wish all readers the very best success in meeting their own needs and those of the children with whom they work and whom they love and care for.

Acknowledgments

We wish to thank the following individuals for their help and advice on specific chapters:

Chapter 2. Bonnie Danley for her expertise in producing the text, tables, and figures; and Debra Cook, M.S. OTR, for her thoughtful feedback regarding content

Chapter 3. Amy Atherton, her parents, Linda and Bob, and her sister, Wendy, for graciously allowing photographs of Amy and for providing opportunities to learn about integrating positioning, handling, and mobility strategies into homes and neighborhoods

Chapter 8. Nancy Caldwell, Renee Reif, Alice Udvari-Solner, and Kathy Zanella Albright of the Madison, Wisconsin, Metropolitan School District; Jane Barry, Rod Ivey, Cheryl Moran-Behrens, and Jo-Ann Schaidle, formerly of the East Central Cooperative Educational Program in Urbana, Illinois; and Debra Kohrs and Barbara Williams of the EAST CONN Cooperative, Willimantic, Connecticut, for contributing many creative adaptations

Chapter 9. Louise Correia for useful suggestions

Chapter 12. Edmund Carney, for the hard lessons he has had to learn and to teach about having a child with multiple disabilities

Thanks also go to Don Wells and Sheila Mansell, University of Alberta, for their comments, suggestions, library research, and miscellaneous help; and to Mary Beers, Cecial Culley, Joel Diambra, Johnna Elliott, Paul Gerber, Rachel Janney, Alan McLeod, Paul Rupf, and Kathie Wolff, Virginia Commonwealth University, for their continued advice, support, and patience.

We also would like to thank the many students, professionals, and reviewers who responded to the first edition of this book. The reinforcement gave us the impetus to work on a second edition, and the critical feedback has, we believe, made for a better book.

A special "thank you" to Melissa Behm, Vice President, and Natalie Tyler, Production Editor, Paul H. Brookes Publishing Company, for their expertise and, especially, their unflagging support and understanding throughout the development and production of the book.

Finally, each of us owes a great debt to those families, students with disabilities, and team members who have provided knowledge, support, and training opportunities that were truly transdisciplinary and that have resulted in our personal and professional growth. We hope that this book reflects at least some of their inspiration and strength.

*To our children
Emma and Samuel Orelove
and
Ananta, Constance, and David Sobsey,
with love.*

Chapter 1

Designing Transdisciplinary Services

This chapter focuses on a system of providing services to individuals with multiple disabilities that has proved successful—the transdisciplinary model. Major features of the model are discussed, with particular emphasis given to team decision-making and implications for providing school-based services. Problems in implementing a transdisciplinary model are also presented. This chapter begins, however, by: 1) discussing the needs of students with multiple disabilities, 2) surveying professionals who work with the students, and 3) describing educational teaming approaches.

NEEDS OF CHILDREN WITH MULTIPLE DISABILITIES

As used throughout the book, the phrase "children with multiple disabilities" refers to individuals with: 1) severe to profound mental retardation, and 2) one or more significant motor or sensory impairments and/or special health care needs. These individuals are an important subgroup of students commonly referred to as "severely handicapped" by the federal government and in the professional special education literature. Because of their combinations of physical, medical, educational, and social/emotional needs, children with multiple disabilities present an immense challenge to professionals responsible for their education. The remainder of this section highlights the varied needs these children bring to the educational setting.

Physical and Medical Needs

The increased frequency of physical and medical problems in individuals with severe disabilities has been well documented (e.g., Mulligan-Ault, Guess,

1

Struth, & Thompson, 1988; Thompson & Guess, 1989). Within this larger group, the individual with multiple disabilities almost always presents two or more of the characteristics described below.

Restriction of Movement   The single largest identifiable organic cause of multiple disabilities is cerebral palsy. The hallmark of cerebral palsy (see Chapter 2) is disordered movement and posture. Because of the damage to or improper development of the brain that causes cerebral palsy, the vast majority of children with multiple disabilities are unable to walk. Many of these children, in fact, have voluntary movement that is limited both quantitatively and qualitatively, making it difficult or impossible for them to move freely about their environment or to change their positions (Campbell, 1987). Proper positioning and handling (see Chapter 3) are vitally important in facilitating proper movement and posture and in preventing secondary deformities.

Skeletal Deformities   Many children with multiple disabilities are born with or, more commonly, develop physical disabilities secondary to their primary disability as a result of brain damage (Campbell, 1989). Such problems typically include: 1) scoliosis (curvature of the spine) and other back and spinal disorders, 2) contractures (permanent shortening of muscles and tendons), 3) partial or total dislocation of the hips, and 4) disorders of the foot and ankle. These and other problems within the bones, joints and connecting muscles, tendons, and ligaments not only cause discomfort and interfere with movement, but actually can be life-threatening in severe cases.

Sensory Disorders   In addition to experiencing difficulty in movement, students considered to have multiple disabilities are more likely than other persons with severe handicaps to have vision and hearing loss. While the number of children considered to be truly "deaf-blind" is relatively small (Fredericks & Baldwin, 1987), it is not uncommon to find children with one or more impaired sensory systems.

Seizure Disorders   As is examined further in Chapter 6, almost one-third of individuals with severe disabilities experience seizures (Spooner & Dykes, 1982). Although seizures frequently are controlled with medication, many students with multiple disabilities present a challenge to the physician trying to regulate seizure activity. Moreover, the medication itself can result in adverse physiological and behavioral side effects.

Lung and Breathing Control   Largely because of their muscle and skeletal disorders, children with multiple disabilities are at greater risk of incurring breathing and lung problems. Such problems often occur during mealtimes, when the student may have trouble handling food in the mouth and swallowing. Other children may accumulate excessive amounts of mucus or other secretions in the airway and lungs, obstructing normal breathing. Still others may have an underdeveloped respiratory system, requiring dependence on mechanical respirators.

Other Medical Problems   In general, children with multiple disabilities

are less healthy than other children (Thompson & Guess, 1989). Their problems range from ear and bladder infections to skin ulcers and constipation. They are more likely to take a variety of medications, from antibiotics to anticonvulsants to stool softeners. Certainly, proper attention to such matters as physical activity, diet, positioning, and medical referrals can reduce students' discomfort, enhance their education, and improve the overall quality, if not length, of their lives. (Chapter 5 discusses health care issues in greater detail.)

Educational Needs

Many of the educational needs of students with multiple disabilities are similar to those of any individual with severe handicaps. The loss of or decrease in function within sensory or motor systems, however, makes more urgent the demand for organized, systematic instruction and management.

Appropriate Positioning and Handling   It was suggested earlier that good positioning and handling of children with multiple disabilities could reduce their pain and prevent further complications of their structural impairments. Because of their possible lack of voluntary control and sensory impairments, it is equally important that these students be positioned to allow them to see, to hear, to reach, and to otherwise become engaged with individuals and materials. Appropriate positioning is essential for efficient movement in all activities.

Appropriate Methods of Communication   Most children with multiple disabilities are unable to communicate through speech. Almost all, however, can express basic wants and needs if given appropriate training and if staff are attuned to students' individual behaviors and personalities. Communication is a basic need of any human being, and it certainly is critical for those individuals who are physically unable to retrieve or seek what they want, including food, drink, and the bathroom.

Means to Choose   Because children with severe disabilities usually cannot say what they want or make the movements necessary to reach it, adults often choose for them. There has been an increasing emphasis on facilitating choice for all learners (Guess & Siegel-Causey, 1985) as an essential catalyst for reducing dependence and the sense of "learned helplessness" that can accrue from lack of control over the environment (Campbell, 1989).

Other Educational Needs   Some of the medical and physical characteristics of children with severe disabilities described earlier impinge on their educational programs. Examples include: 1) the child with seizures who cannot go swimming, 2) the child on anticonvulsant medication who sleeps half the day, 3) the student whose lungs must be cleared of secretions before he or she eats lunch, and 4) the student in the body cast to correct scoliosis who needs community instruction. The challenge for the team is to determine how to work with and around the students' medical and physical needs to provide an appropriate education, rather than turning the school day into an extended therapy session. Therapy and specialized health care procedures should *facilitate*, not replace, instruction.

Social/Emotional Needs

Children with multiple disabilities are more than conglomerations of educational and medical problems. They are, first of all, children; they are the sons and daughters of parents who care about their well-being. Like all other individuals, children with disabilities need affection and attention. They should never become mere passive recipients of services. If you can imagine what it would be like to be trapped physically by your own body and to be unable to tell anyone how you felt or what you wanted, then you can begin to understand how you might interpret and respond to a child's crying or "noncompliant" behavior.

Professionals, no matter how skillful or caring, are unable to provide all of the emotional support children need. Children with multiple disabilities need opportunities to interact with, and, especially, to develop friendships with other children (Forest & Lusthaus, 1989; Strully & Strully, 1989). Professionals can, and should, facilitate those opportunities, not as a "frill," but as an essential part of a student's educational and emotional life.

IMPORTANCE OF A VARIETY OF DISCIPLINES

It is probably evident from the preceding description of the needs of children with multiple disabilities that a range of expertise is necessary in educating these children. Skills are needed from fields as diverse as special education, nursing, social work, and physical therapy (and sometimes from fields less traditionally associated with education, such as rehabilitation engineering, dietetics, and respiratory therapy). It should be clear that no one or two individuals can possibly meet all the needs that these children have. Whitehouse recognized the need for interdependence among professionals as far back as 1951:

> We must understand that there are no discrete categories of scientific endeavors. Professions are only cross-sections of the over-all continuum of human thought. Fundamentally no treatment is medical, social, psychological, or vocational—all treatment is total. Yet members of each profession within the narrowness of their own training and experience will attempt to treat the whole person. Obviously, no one profession can do this adequately under present conditions. (p. 45)

Although Whitehouse was speaking of the rehabilitation field, his words are equally true today for educating students with multiple disabilities. The remainder of this section briefly explores the nature of the disciplines that work with these children.

This book emphasizes the importance for persons representing different disciplines to work together and to share some of their skills. It may seem odd, therefore, to parcel out descriptions of individual fields. Nevertheless, it is essential to recognize that different professions do have distinct training backgrounds, philosophical and theoretical approaches, experiences, and specialized skills. Moreover, the success of an educational team depends in part on the competence of the individual team members and on a mutual understanding and respect for individuals' skills and knowledge.

The roles of those persons who are typically part of the school-based educational team are described first. The roles of other valuable professionals found less commonly within the school setting are then described.

Persons on Educational Teams

Special Educator   Gaylord-Ross and Holvoet (1985) summarized five major roles of a teacher of students with severe handicaps: 1) educator of learners with severe handicaps, 2) liaison between the parents and school district, 3) supervisor and teacher of paraprofessionals, 4) member and coordinator of a team of professionals who will work with the students, and 5) advocate for the students. The specific skills required in each of those roles are too numerous to be described here. As the profession continues to define itself, and to reach a consensus on best practices, the teacher's role becomes more complex, encompassing a broad spectrum of concerns. More on the special educator's role, in terms of being part of the team, of particular interest here, appears in the "Transdisciplinary Model of Delivering Services" section of this chapter.

Associate   Sometimes referred to as a teacher's aide or a paraprofessional, the associate in a classroom for students with multiple disabilities frequently plays a vital role in the daily functioning in the classroom. In addition to helping to conduct instructional activities, the associate often is heavily involved in handling and positioning students and in providing for their physical health and comfort.

Physical Therapist   The physical therapist is trained to prescribe and supervise the following types of activities: gross motor activity and weight-bearing, positioning, range of motion, relaxation, stimulation, postural drainage, and other physical manipulation and exercise procedures (Fraser, Hensinger, & Phelps, 1987). An essential member of the team, the physical therapist often provides information and direct instruction to team members on appropriate positioning and handling and on the use and construction of adaptive equipment (Copeland & Kimmel, 1989).

Occupational Therapist   Occupational therapy generally is oriented toward the development and maintenance of functions and skills necessary for daily living. Accordingly, occupational therapists in school programs attempt to prevent deterioration of those functions and help remediate deficits that impair performance (Lansing & Carlsen, 1977). These professionals often have special expertise in prescribing and constructing adaptive devices (especially for fine motor activities) and in conducting mealtime activities for individuals with physical involvement.

Communication Therapist   Because a large percentage of students with multiple disabilities not only are nonverbal, but also lack any systematic means of communicating, language or communication therapists play a specialized and important role. They are responsible for assessing and training students directly on methods of communicating, teaching other staff these methods, and monitoring students' communication progress (Stremel-Campbell, 1977). Communication therapists also may consult with audiologists when an individual experiences hearing loss. Finally, because of the anatomical and functional relationship between eating and speech, many therapists are trained in assessing and facilitating mealtime skills.

Family Member   Although not typically present in the school on a regular basis, a parent or other family member should be recognized as a central part of an educational team. Apart from parents' rights to participate in assessment and planning, it simply makes good sense to invite their participation as individuals with the most knowledge of their child and the greatest stake in the child's future. The degree to which individual parents are able to or choose to participate will vary. (Chapter 12 examines this and other issues concerning families in greater detail.)

Professionals Who Serve Students with
Multiple Disabilities Usually Outside of the School Setting

The daily contact that individuals described in this section have with children varies with the size and organization of the school division and the degree of specialization of the professions. In some cases, involvement of professionals (e.g., social worker, psychologist, nurse) may be extensive and ongoing. Other persons (e.g., audiologist, dietitian) may be consulted on an as-needed basis.

Psychologist   The role most often associated with school psychologists is that of evaluator of a child's intellectual and adaptive abilities. The child with multiple disabilities, however, presents significant obstacles to traditional psychometric instruments and procedures. Thus, psychologists in some cases have taken increasingly more visible roles in designing strategies for reducing excess behaviors. They could be particularly instrumental in working with teaching staff to develop alternative, long-term adaptive behaviors in students who lack key social or self-regulatory skills (Meyer & Evans, 1989). Additionally, psychologists can be helpful in working with families (and professionals) in times of stress and grief, such as at the death of a child.

Social Worker   School social workers serve as facilitators of access to services and advocates for the child and family (West, 1978). They are trained in communicating with and gaining access to community resources. Some programs employ individuals with specialized training to coordinate services between school and home and community.

Administrator   Administrators include those persons responsible for policy, decision-making, and implementation in areas such as placement, transition, curriculum development, transportation, related services, equipment, and scheduling. The administrator is also responsible for ensuring compliance with local, state, and federal regulations. It is clear that the administrator (e.g., principal, program director, special education supervisor) is highly influential in the quality of students' educational programs.

Vision Specialist   A large number of children with multiple disabilities experience loss in visual function; therefore, the vision specialist has come to play a more important role. These professionals are equipped to assess students' vision, and to adapt activities and materials to make full use of each child's residual vision. The orientation and mobility specialist is a professional with specialized training in vision in relation to mobility across environments. Along with the communication, occupational, and physical therapists, the vision specialist provides vital information related to alternative communication systems.

Audiologist   The audiologist is trained to identify type and degree of hearing loss and to provide guidelines on equipment and procedures to help students compensate for their impairment (Gaylord-Ross & Holvoet, 1985). The audiologist who works with individuals who experience a combination of cognitive, physical, and sensory impairments must be knowledgeable about a variety of alternative, nontraditional assessment strategies.

Nurse   The school nurse is often the best source of readily available information regarding the physical well-being of children with multiple disabilities. This information covers a range of needs from seizure control to medication to emergency first aid. Nurses also are invaluable for helping students (and teaching staff) who require specialized procedures such as catheterization, suctioning, and nasogastric tube feeding, as well as routine procedures, such as skin care and cast care (cf. Graff, Ault, Guess, Taylor, & Thompson, 1990 and Chapter 5 of this book).

Nutritionist/Dietitian   Nutritionists and dietitians can help with increasing students' caloric intake, minimizing the side effects and maximizing the effectiveness of medications, and designing special diets for individuals with specific food allergies or health care needs (Crump, 1987; Worthington, Pipes, & Trahms, 1978). Unfortunately, nutritionists and dietitians are not included on most school teams, which is probably attributable to a general lack of information about their skills and about the relevance of diet and nutrition to the physical and instructional needs of students (McCamman & Rues, 1990).

Physician/Pediatrician   The physician can help the school team by revising effects of medications and screening for and treating common medical problems. This professional is most effective when engaged in ongoing communication with school staff.

Other Medical Specialists   School staff and parents are also likely to need the services of one or more of the following specialists: dentist (teeth), ophthalmologist or optometrist (eyes), otorhinolaryngologist (ear, nose, and throat), orthopedist (bones and muscles), neurologist (nervous system), physiatrist (physical medicine and rehabilitation), and urologist (urinary system).

Other Nonmedical Specialists   In interviews with teachers who work effectively with children with the most severe disabilities, Thompson and Guess (1989) reported that numerous disciplines were perceived as critical for team input. Those disciplines not already mentioned above include: respiratory therapy, pharmacology, rehabilitation engineering, and computer science. Clearly, individuals with multiple disabilities impose upon teams the need to think creatively and across the range of traditional, school-based disciplines.

EDUCATIONAL TEAMING
MODELS FOR PERSONS WHO
SERVE CHILDREN WITH MULTIPLE DISABILITIES

The preceding section described the roles of individuals who work directly with children with multiple disabilities or who otherwise provide them with services. How well children are served in educational settings depends, of course, on many factors, including the skill and care of each professional. Individual competence itself, however, while essential, is not sufficient to guarantee a good program. Perhaps more than any other group of individuals, students with severe disabilities require a team of professionals who can work together effectively. The manner in which teams are formed and the way in which they operate greatly influence both the process and outcomes of education for children. Although there are numerous ways teams can be designed, this section briefly describes three teaming models: multidisciplinary, interdisciplinary, and transdisciplinary. Most school programs for students with multiple disabilities operate within some variation of one of these models.

Multidisciplinary Team Model

Organization   Through the multidisciplinary model professionals with expertise in different disciplines work with the child individually. In contrast to more coordinated models, however, individuals within the multidisciplinary model work in isolation from other professionals to evaluate and serve children. Thus, no formal attempt is made to allocate resources by setting priorities for childrens' needs or to consider the overlap among disciplines (McCormick & Goldman, 1979). Best characterized by coexistence (Sparling, 1980), the multidisciplinary model was designed to meet the needs of patients within medical settings (Hart, 1977) whose problems are typically isolated within one particular domain. In fact, because individuals work independently of one another, they may not even think of themselves as belonging to a team. Figure 1.1 depicts the model's organization.

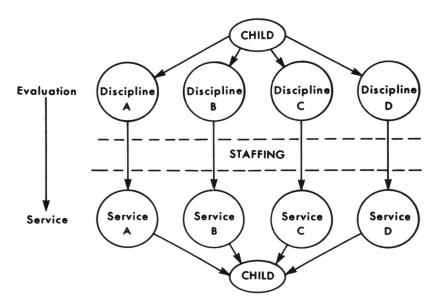

Figure 1.1.   Organization of a multidisciplinary model of service delivery. (From McCormack, L., & Goldman, R. [1979]. The transdisciplinary model: Implications for service delivery and personnel preparation for the severely and profoundly handicapped. *AAESPH Review, 4*[2], 154; reprinted with permission.)

Disadvantages   The multidisciplinary model has at least two major disadvantages as applied to serving children with multiple disabilities: insufficient assessment and difficult educational planning (Peterson, 1980).

Assessment   The more team members work in isolation, the greater the likelihood they will generate information that fails to address the child's needs holistically. As noted previously, students with multiple disabilities often have motor, sensory, and communication impairments, but professionals rarely are trained to be proficient in all areas. When four or five professionals, each representing a different discipline, evaluate a child's needs and submit recommendations, the chance of opposing suggestions is great (Hart, 1977). The likelihood of inaccurate and inconsistent recommendations also increases.

Educational Planning   Recommendations from multidisciplinary teams often are numerous and complicated, making their implementation extremely difficult (Peterson, 1980). As with assessment information, suggestions for educational programs may also result in conflicting ideas. For example, an educator may recommend a specific program to teach a motor skill that the physical therapist feels should be inhibited. Moreover, team members often end their responsibilities by making recommendations, leaving actual implementation to the classroom teacher (Hart, 1977).

Interdisciplinary Team Model

Organization   Representing a higher order of evolution on the scale of team models, the interdisciplinary model provides a formal structure for interaction and communication among team members that encourages them to share information (Garland, McGonigel, Frank, & Buck, 1989). Although programming decisions are made by group consensus, assessment and implementation remain tied to each discipline (Hart, 1977; McCormick & Goldman, 1979). Thus, while program planning is more collaborative than in the multidisciplinary model, program implementation remains isolated.

Disadvantages   The interdisciplinary model improves on the strict isolationism of the multidisciplinary model but suffers from the same problems. As McCormick and Goldman (1979) observed, the interdisciplinary model supports group decision-making and greater opportunity for interactions across disciplines in theory only; in actual practice, responsibility is usually diffused.

Both the multidisciplinary and interdisciplinary models have been termed "discipline-referenced" models (Giangreco, York, & Rainforth, 1989), in which decisions about assessment, program priorities, planning, intervention, evaluation, and team interactions are driven by the orientations of each discipline. Giangreco et al. (1989) caution that such structures "are more likely to promote competitive and individualistic professional interactions resulting in disjointed programmatic outcomes" (p. 57). The authors further note that discipline-referenced approaches "have perpetuated the misguided notion that students with severe handicaps attend school primarily to receive therapy, rather than the notion that therapy is provided to support the educational program" (p. 57).

An additional problem with the multidisciplinary and interdisciplinary models is their total reliance on therapy services that are direct and isolated (Giangreco, 1986; Sternat, Messina, Nietupski, Lyon, & Brown, 1977). Direct services represent hands-on intervention by therapists, rather than the therapists serving as consultants to other team members. Isolated services imply a separate, "pull-out" model, in which students receive therapy away from the flow of on-going activities, often in separate rooms or even in clinics or hospitals outside the school.

There are several problems with a direct, isolated therapy approach (Albano, Cox, York, & York, 1981; Giangreco, 1986; Giangreco et al., 1989; Sternat et al., 1977; York, Rainforth, & Giangreco, 1990). First, because skills are not assessed in the student's natural environments, the outcomes may not be representative of what the student actually can do in those settings. Second, assessments often test specific, isolated skills instead of clusters of skills used in everyday activities. Third, the assessments frequently result in diagnostic labels and descriptions of students' performances, but fail to include suggestions to help teachers and other professionals to remediate skill deficits. Fourth, when team members work in isolation, it is difficult to collaborate on performance of individual students in natural situations. Fifth, because of limited staff and time, children may receive small amounts of practice on such vital areas as movement and communication. Sixth, limited resources have led some administrators to create centralized service delivery systems, in which students with multiple disabilities are grouped together, preventing or minimizing interactions with nondisabled peers.

Transdisciplinary Team Model

Originally designed to serve high-risk infants (Hutchison, 1978; United Cerebral Palsy, 1976), the transdisciplinary model has been embraced by programs serving children with multiple disabilities. The model is characterized by a sharing, or transferring, of information and skills across traditional disciplinary boundaries. In contrast to the multidisciplinary and interdisciplinary approaches, the transdisciplinary model incorporates an indirect model of services, whereby one or two persons are primary facilitators of services and other team members act as consultants (Albano et al., 1981). Figure 1.2 depicts the organization of a transdisciplinary model.

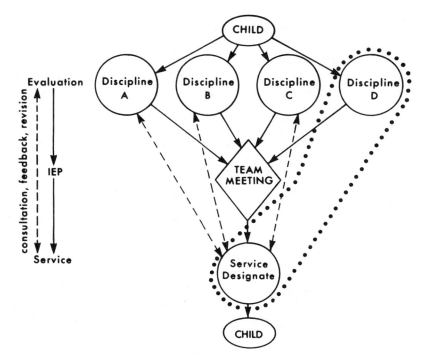

Figure 1.2. Organization of a transdisciplinary model of service delivery. (From McCormack, L., & Goldman, R. [1979]. The transdisciplinary model: Implications for service delivery and personnel preparation for the severely and profoundly handicapped. *AAESPH Review, 4*[2], 156; reprinted with permission.)

Although simple in concept, implementation of a transdisciplinary model can be initially difficult because it represents a significant departure from most models of service delivery to which professionals are accustomed. The remainder of this chapter examines in greater detail the features of the model.

TRANSDISCIPLINARY MODEL OF DELIVERING SERVICES

The team structure and approach to services known as the transdisciplinary model has gained increasing acceptance by members of many disciplines: occupational therapy (Dunn, 1988; Ottenbacher, 1982; 1983); physical therapy (Giangreco et al., 1989; York et al., 1990); special education (Campbell, 1987); early childhood education (Woodruff & McGonigel, 1988); nursing (Hutchison, 1978); and medicine (Bennett, 1982). This section details: 1) the major features of a transdisciplinary model, 2) applications of this model, 3) aspects of team dynamics, and 4) challenges to implementing the model and strategies for overcoming these difficulties. (Table 1.1 compares the three team models across several dimensions.)

Major Features of a Transdisciplinary Model

Indirect Therapy Approach   One of the criticisms of the multidisciplinary and interdisciplinary models is that they rely on a direct service approach, that is, *all* therapy services are provided directly by therapists, often in isolation. York (1984) gave an example of a direct service practice:

> A developmental therapist pushes Mike (a student) in a wheelchair from his classroom to the "therapy" room (or, as is often the case, a classroom staff member delivers him to the therapy room, then picks him up when therapy is completed). In the therapy room, the therapist assists the student to get out of his wheelchair, facilitating the desired weight-bearing, weight-shifting, and trunk rotation movement components. Next, they work on balancing and protective responses in a tall-kneeling position. Then, they work on improving the way in which Mike walks using the assistance of parallel bars. Finally, he is assisted back into his chair again emphasizing the performance of desirable weight-shifting and rotation movement components. Once in his wheelchair, he is returned to his classroom. (p. 4)

(It should be noted that terms such as "weight-bearing" and "protective responses" are part of technical language used by therapists. Concern about use of professional terminology to convey information is raised later in this chapter under "Differences in Philosophy and Orientation.")

Through an *indirect* approach, in contrast, therapists involve themselves to a greater extent as consultants to the teacher and other team members (Giangreco, 1986; Nietupski, Scheutz, & Ockwood, 1980). The transdisciplinary model *does not*, however, presume that therapists cease to provide direct services to children. In fact, therapists who ceased hands-on interactions would become less effective professionals, both to the children as well as to other team members. Moreover, as York et al. (1990) observed, "there may be circum-

Table 1.1.   Comparison of three team models

	Multidisciplinary	Interdisciplinary	Trandisciplinary
Assessment	Separate assessments by team members	Separate assessments by team members	Team members and family conduct a comprehensive developmental assessment together
Parent participation	Parents meet with individual team members	Parents meet with team or team representative	Parents are full, active, and participating members of the team
Service plan development	Team members develop separate plans for their discipline	Team members share their separate plans with one another	Team members and the parents develop a service plan based upon family priorities, needs, and resources
Service plan responsibility	Team members are responsible for implementing their section of the plan	Team members are responsible for sharing information with one another as well as for implementing their section of the plan	Team members are responsible and accountable for how the primary service provider implements the plan
Service plan implementation	Team members implement the part of the service plan related to their discipline	Team members implement their section of the plan and incorporate other sections where possible	A primary service provider is assigned to implement the plan with the family
Lines of communication	Informal lines	Periodic case-specific team meetings	Regular team meeting where continuous transfer of information, knowledge, and skills are shared among team members

(continued)

Table 1.1.   (*continued*)

	Multidisciplinary	Interdisciplinary	Trandisciplinary
Guiding philosophy	Team members recognize the importance of contributions from other disciplines	Team members are willing and able to develop, share, and be responsible for providing services that are a part of the total service plan	Team members make a commitment to teach, learn, and work together across discipline boundaries to implement unified service plan
Staff development	Independent and within their discipline	Independent within as well as outside of their discipline	An integral component of team meetings for learning across disciplines and team building

From Woodruff, G., & McGonigel, M.J. (1988). Early intervention team approaches: The transdisciplinary model. In J.B. Jordan, J.J. Gallagher, P.L. Hutinger, & M.B. Karnes (Eds.), *Early childhood special education: Birth to three,* p. 166. Reston, VA: Council for Exceptional Children.

stances that warrant short-term or long-term frequent and direct services by a therapist. For example, a learner may present such complex movement difficulties that the therapist needs to spend large amounts of individual time with the learner to perform assessment and to determine effective intervention procedures" (p. 76). Therapists use the analogous terms of *direct therapy, monitoring,* and *consultation* to differentiate among strategies for delivering therapy services (Dunn, 1988, 1991). Clearly, each mode of service delivery has a place in educating children with multiple disabilities. Decisions to use a particular approach at a particular moment need to be made by teams on the basis of appropriate outcomes for the student being served.

To appreciate the differences between direct and indirect therapy approaches, contrast the direct service approach to Mike described earlier to the following indirect therapy approach with the same student:

> The therapist meets Mike and his teacher in his classroom just before it is time to go to the cafeteria for lunch. The therapist explains to the student that he is going to learn to walk part of the way to the cafeteria instead of using his wheelchair for the entire distance. She also explains that she and the teacher will need to determine the best way to assist him and then the teacher will assist him in the same manner every day on their way to lunch. The therapist proceeds to model and give instructions as to how to get Mike out of his wheelchair, transfer to his walker, and walk in therapeutically desirable ways. She is careful to emphasize *where* she holds Mike, *how* she physically assists him, *what* responses she is looking for, the *rate* of

the movements involved, and the most efficient sequence to follow. The teacher then assists Mike as the therapist coaches and provides the feedback. After this training session, the therapist writes a detailed task analysis of the steps involved, including both student and trainer behaviors. At a later time, the therapist and teacher go over the sequence together, discuss questions, practice on each other how to physically assist Mike, and decide what data should be taken on his performance to monitor progress. The teacher carries out the program with Mike each day before lunch. On a weekly, or as needed basis, the therapist participates in the session by observing, providing feedback, or performing the activity to recommend changes in the type of physical assistance provided. (York, 1984, pp. 4–5)

Note in the preceding scenario that the therapist's services were indirect, but the student's educational needs clearly were being addressed directly. The teacher in this case was acting in a role of facilitator or synthesizer (Bricker, 1976). (In some applications of the transdisciplinary model, teachers also serve at times in a consultative capacity.) The scenario also incorporates four basic assumptions of an indirect therapy model (Sternat et al., 1977):

1. Assessment of motor abilities can be conducted best in natural environments.
2. Students should be taught clusters of motor skills through games and functional activities (those needed in everyday living).
3. Therapy should be provided throughout the day and in all the settings in which the student functions.
4. Skills must be taught and verified in the settings in which they occur naturally.

Three concerns are often raised with regard to an indirect therapy model. The first concern is that therapists have special training and expertise that teachers do not have and cannot (or should not) acquire. However, a transdisciplinary model does not involve teachers' total takeover of the therapists' role (Nietupski et al., 1980; York et al., 1990). In fact, it is because of the need for the therapists' expertise that the model has become so popular.

A second concern about an indirect therapy approach is that students with multiple disabilities are easily distracted and need quiet settings in which to work. Unfortunately, students with multiple disabilities do not remain in quiet, distraction free settings forever, and it is therefore important to give them the opportunity to cope with real situations whenever possible. In addition, when therapy not only is physically isolated, but also disconnected from the student's educational goals, one could question whether that therapy qualifies as related services under the law (Giangreco et al., 1989).

The third concern is that indirect therapy would cause therapists to lose their professional identity. The reality, however, is that transdisciplinary models that operate effectively result in *enhanced* professional identity among therapists. There is at least anecdotal evidence that teachers valued and understood the importance of therapists to a greater degree after working within a transdisciplinary model and that therapists also felt more valued within the team (Albano, 1983). The rationale for implementing an indirect therapy approach should *not* be to reduce the number of therapists within a given setting, thereby increasing case loads. As York et al. (1990) noted, "Learners for whom a transdisciplinary model is appropriate usually have intense and comprehensive related service needs. . . . Caseloads of 60 students across three counties or schedules that allow 1 hour of consultation per student per month are unlikely to be effective in any service delivery model!" (p. 78).

Role Release   It is probably obvious that for staff to serve in consulting positions and for some services to be delivered indirectly, traditional roles of teachers, therapists, and other team members must become more flexible. Role release refers to a sharing and exchange of certain roles and responsibilities across team members (Lyon & Lyon, 1980). The term more specifically implies a *releasing* of some functions of one's primary discipline to other team members (United Cerebral Palsy, 1976).

Woodruff and McGonigel (1988) described a process, *role transition,* through which transdisciplinary teams can teach and learn across disciplinary boundaries. Role transition consists of six separate but related processes, organized sequentially. (Role release, as defined within this model, is one of the six processes.) Table 1.2 briefly describes each of the six processes and provides an example of each process. Table 1.3 lists several practices that can be carried out daily to support some facets of role transition.

It should be noted that sharing or releasing roles occurs in two directions across all team members; each person has unique skills and information to impart. Personnel must keep in mind that parents and other family members should be considered an important part of the team.

Applications of a Transdisciplinary Model

There are three major areas within educational programs upon which the choice of a team model has a direct influence: assessment, development of instructional goals, and delivery of instruction and therapy. This section examines each of these applications.

Assessment   The method an instructional team elects to obtain initial information on a student's performance will directly affect all other aspects of the student's program. It is important, therefore, that team members devote as much attention to assessing skills as they do to teaching those skills. There are at least three different types of assessment information (York et al., 1985).

General Background Information   One or more team members can compile information from the student's family, previous service providers, and the child's cumulative file. This process yields information on past and current educational goals, individuals' preferences for what skills should be taught first, special learning characteristics, medical problems, and so forth. It is particularly important that the parents be consulted. They can provide valuable infor-

Table 1.2.   Role transition processes and examples

ROLE EXTENSION: Self-directed study and other staff development efforts to increase one's depth of understanding, theoretical knowledge, and clinical skills in one's own discipline or area of expertise

Example: An occupational therapist who is an expert on mealtime skills attends a workshop on new feeding techniques.

ROLE ENRICHMENT: Team members being well versed in their own disciplines and developing a general awareness and understanding of the terminology and basic practices of other disciplines

Example: The pediatrician conducts an in-service session on medical terminology.

ROLE EXPANSION: Acquiring sufficient information from disciplines represented on the team to allow a team member to make knowledgeable observations and program recommendations outside his or her own discipline

Example: The special education teacher determines that a child needs her visual acuity tested and makes a referral to the vision specialist.

ROLE EXCHANGE: Learning the theory, methods, and procedures of other disciplines and beginning to implement the techniques learned by practicing them under the observation of the team member from the relevant discipline

Example: A parent demonstrates to the physical therapist an activity to increase a child's capacity to bear weight on his arms.

ROLE RELEASE: Putting newly acquired techniques into practice with consultation from the team member from the discipline that is accountable for those practices

Example: The social worker teaches a father a simple carrying technique for a child for whom he is the primary service provider.

ROLE SUPPORT: Informal encouragement from other team members and, when necessary, backup support and help by the team member from the appropriate discipline

Example: The audiologist tests the child's hearing.

Adapted from Garland, McGonigel, Frank, and Buck (1989).

mation on such things as the child's preferences of food, objects, and activities; medical precautions; ways in which the child communicates; and family activities (York, 1984). This general information should be shared among all team members.

Observations of the Student   Traditional assessment is performed individually by each professional on a team. Within a transdisciplinary model, however, several team members jointly plan for and conduct the assessment, in which the student functions in several natural environments and activities. Referred to as an ecological inventory (Brown et al., 1979), this assessment strategy consists of the following steps:

1.   Determine the environments in which the student currently functions or is likely to function.

2. Determine the activities necessary to perform in those environments and the skills necessary to engage in those activities.
3. Determine the professionals who should be involved in the assessment. For example, a physical therapist might be called upon to help assess a student who has difficulty walking on uneven terrain and negotiating stairs.
4. Conduct the environmental assessment by: a) going to the actual environments with the student, b) recording the student's responses, and c) making notes to indicate activities that need further assessment.

Discipline-Specific Information   Sometimes individual team members can obtain useful information through traditional assessment strategies within their own disciplines (e.g., communication, movement). Most of this information, however, can be assessed in the context of naturally occurring situations (Rainforth & York, 1987; York et al., 1990). It is important to recall that the main purpose of assessment is to determine relevant educational goals. As York et al. (1990) observed, the emphasis should be on assessment conducted in priority educational environments on activities identified by the team. This should not imply a decrease in sophistication or quality of assessments conducted by therapists.

Development of Instructional Goals   Once assessment is complete, the team must: 1) establish priorities for the skills to be taught to each student, and 2) write goals that address those skills deemed appropriate.

Content Priorities   Determining which skills to teach in a given year is a difficult task. The decision takes into account such diverse considerations as the student's preferences, the parents' preferences, the skills' social significance,

Table 1.3.   Practices to support role transition

Role extension
Read current journals and texts
Join professional organizations
Attend local, regional, and national conferences
Request current in-service training and technical assistance
Take university courses

Role enrichment
Create reference library of conference notes and professional journals
Use one-to-one exchange to teach colleagues basic terms and concepts

Role expansion
Share information with colleagues during assessment
Conduct regular meetings to discuss programming ideas

Role exchange
Explore team teaching
Engage in regular case consultation
Conduct periodic shared home visits

Adapted from Garland, McGonigel, Frank, and Buck (1989).

the student's age, and so forth. In general, teaching content should be organized around naturally occurring *activities,* rather than isolated skills or tasks (Ford et al., 1989). Moreover, teams should *not* select activities on the basis of whether students will perform them independently; most children with multiple disabilities will require assistance on some or all parts of activities. Rather, activities should be selected based on such criteria as: 1) whether performing the activity will make a real difference in the quality of the student's life, and 2) whether performance will increase the student's likelihood of interacting with peers.

Finally, students with the most severe disabilities, who have quite limited repertoires of behaviors, may profit from learning *effective* behaviors, those that produce an effect upon the social environment (Evans & Scotti, 1989). Selecting these behaviors might be done by surveying the caregivers and other significant individuals in the student's life, rather than relying on an ecological inventory approach (Orelove, 1991).

Writing Educational Goals   The goals and objectives on students' individualized education programs (IEPs) dictate the schedule, the physical organization of the classroom, and the choice of instructional materials and strategies. In short, the IEP drives the flow of the entire day. Therefore, the way in which educational goals are developed is absolutely critical to the success of operating within a transdisciplinary model.

Unfortunately, many people believe that an IEP developed by a team is simply goals and objectives written from individual disciplines and compiled into a single document, with the individual team members responsible for implementing and evaluating progress on their individual goals (York et al., 1990). Having separate sections of IEPs for each discipline, however, is incompatible with the philosophy of a transdisciplinary approach and runs counter to best practices for children with multiple disabilities. A separatist approach promotes: 1) the development of segregated goals that have no real function in the real world (e.g., "Will increase relaxation," "Will visually track from left to right 180 degrees"); and 2) the exclusion of critical objectives related to movement, communication, and so forth across school and community environments.

An alternative approach is to develop goals that identify educationally relevant priority environments and activities where performance is desired. The corresponding objectives specify the priority skills for the student to acquire so that participation in each environment is improved. (Chapter 7 provides examples of goals developed in this manner.)

Delivery of Instruction and Therapy   It was stated earlier that a key feature of a transdisciplinary approach is its incorporation of indirect therapy, in which therapists serve in part in consulting roles to other team members. It was also noted that direct therapy is often characterized by delivery of services in isolation. However, the location of services does not in itself determine whether a model is transdisciplinary. A therapist who practices one-to-one therapy in the back of the student's classroom is still engaging in a direct, nonintegrated approach (York et al., 1990).

For a model to be truly transdisciplinary, therapy needs to be *integrated*. An integrated approach is characterized by two features: "(a) planning is referenced to a common set of goals and needs whereby each team member applies his or her disciplinary skill to the shared goals, and (b) therapeutic techniques are implemented in concert with other instructional methods in the context of functional activities. . ." (Giangreco et al., 1989, p. 61).

Putting a process in place for accomplishing these transdisciplinary goals, however, is not a simple task. Campbell (1987) presents a model for doing so, which she terms an "integrated programming team." These teams, organized around the needs of individual students, consist of professionals (teachers and therapists), who are involved in some form of ongoing service delivery for the students, as well as parents. The administrator acts to support and facilitate team programming. Figure 1.3 presents the steps necessary to implement team programming for an individual student. In Figure 1.3, Step 6 states "Team members train each other in integrated methods." York et al. (1985) described the intricacies of accomplishing such a task:

> When teaching other team members how to perform skills and techniques and how to integrate information from one's own discipline, a variety of teaching strategies may need to be used. For example, when teaching an assistant how to instruct a student to perform a pivot transfer from her wheelchair to the toilet seat in a community restroom stall, the skill sequence may need to be specifically outlined, the assistant may practice the transfer sequence with the physical therapist in a simulated situation at the school, and/or a series of stick figure drawings of the most critical steps may be provided. . . . The primary point here is that the team member who is teaching *and* the instructor who is learning new information and skills must take equal responsibility for successful transfer of skills from one person to the other. . . . It would behoove those doing the training to recall their first attempts at learning the information they are now expected to teach others. (not paginated)

Dynamics of Teams

As Hutchison (1978) observed, "Calling a small group of people a team does not make them so; team relationships are forged over time" (p. 70). It is particularly easy to see the truth in this statement relative to transdisciplinary teams, whose success depends on close cooperation of their members and a relinquishing of individual power. To appreciate the difficulty of organizing truly effective educational teams and to learn how to avoid or overcome some of the common problems teams experience, it is important to understand their dynamics. This section briefly examines team process and some of the factors influencing teams' effectiveness.

Team Process   Bailey (1984) proposed a triaxial model for understanding the process within teams that work with individuals with disabilities. His model is based on three premises:

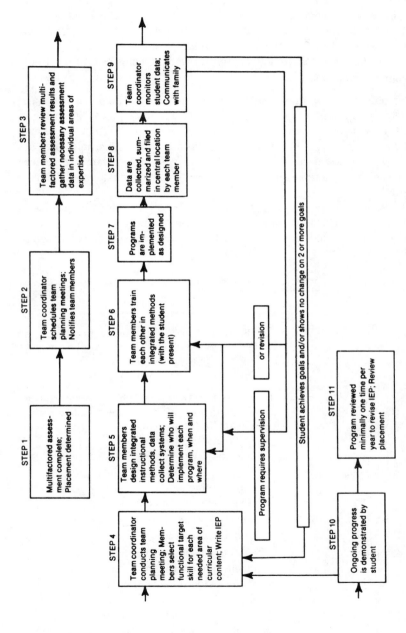

Figure 1.3. Steps to implementing team programming for an individual student. (From Campbell, P.H. [1987]. The integrated programming team: An approach for coordinating professionals of various disciplines in programs for students with severe and multiple handicaps. *Journal of The Association for Persons with Severe Handicaps, 12*[2], 114; reprinted with permission.)

STEP 1
Multifactored assessment complete; Placement determined

STEP 2
Team coordinator schedules team planning meetings; Notifies team members

STEP 3
Team members review multifactored assessment results and gather necessary assessment data in individual areas of expertise

STEP 4
Team coordinator conducts team planning meeting: Members select functional target skill for each needed area of curricular content; Write IEP

STEP 5
Team members design integrated instructional methods, data collect systems; Determine who will implement each program, when and where

STEP 6
Team members train each other in integrated methods (with the student present)

STEP 7
Programs are implemented as designed

STEP 8
Data are collected, summarized and filed in central location by each team member

STEP 9
Team coordinator monitors student data; Communicates with family

STEP 10
Ongoing progress is demonstrated by student

STEP 11
Program reviewed minimally one time per year to revise IEP; Review placement

or revision

Program requires supervision

Student achieves goals and/or shows no change on 2 or more goals

1. Team growth is a developmental process; thus, some problems in team functioning can be attributed to the stage a team is in at a given point.
2. Teams are composed of individuals; some problems may result from interpersonal problems or subsystems within the team.
3. Teams themselves are functional units; some problems result from whole team dysfunction.

Examining the first premise, Bailey summarized the model of Lowe and Herranen (1982), who proposed six stages in team development, as shown in Table 1.4. As with any developmental model, each team will not necessarily experience every stage, nor will teams go through each stage in a fixed sequence. It does seem clear, however, that virtually every team experiences growing pains as a normal part of the process of evolving into a smoothly operating unit.

In the second premise of the triaxial model, Bailey (1984) asserted that in the ideal team: 1) a leader is present but acts as one member of the team, 2) each member is about equal in power and influence, and 3) conflicts and disagree-

Table 1.4.   Six-stage process of team development of Lowe and Herranen (1982)

Stage	Features
I. Becoming acquainted	Hierarchical group structures Autocratic leadership Polite and impersonal interactions Low overall team productivity
II. Trial and error	Begins to work together toward common goal Team members align themselves with one or two other team members Factions sometimes occur Role conflict and ambiguity arise
III. Collective indecision	Attempts to avoid direct conflict and achieve equilibrium No group norm for accountability
IV. Crisis	Members realize importance of mission Emotion expressed
V. Resolution	Effort to work together as team Open communication Shared leadership, decision-making, and responsibility
VI. Team maintenance	Client's needs major driving force Conflict management, client-team relationships important

ments are based on substantive issues, not personality conflicts. Problems that can arise within the team subsystem include dominant leaders, dominant and inferior team members, and specific conflicts between two members or between one member and the others.

The third facet of Bailey's model focuses on the team as a whole. Teams can experience problems of being underproductive, overstructured, disorganized, or having ambiguous roles.

Factors Influencing Team Effectiveness Group process and decision-making have been the subjects of countless theories and research. Despite everything known about communication and working in groups, however, there remains no simple recipe that a team can follow to ensure success. Regardless, the quality of the educational program for children with multiple disabilities depends largely upon the degree to which team members can work together and communicate. This section summarizes several of the factors that typically operate within successful small groups; these factors can be subsumed under three broad categories: 1) intrapersonal factors, 2) interpersonal factors, and 3) group identity factors (Fisher, 1980).

Intrapersonal Factors Since a group is composed of individuals, individual team members must monitor themselves for continued constructive contribution to team functioning. Following are several attitudes and values that are typical of members of successful groups:

1. Individuals' attitudes toward the group reflect open-mindedness about possible outcomes and a sensitivity toward the feelings and beliefs of other group members. The individual is committed to the group and to the process. The individual also has a sense of responsibility to the group and is willing to expend time and energy for the benefit of the group.
2. Individuals who are committed to a group participate actively, share responsibility for the group's decisions, and express feelings and ideas, even at the risk of being proved wrong.
3. Individuals demonstrate creativity, proposing numerous ideas, especially during the group's early stages.
4. Individuals take stands and defend them, even if they leave themselves open to criticism. In addition, they constructively criticize others, and try to do so at appropriate moments in the group process.
5. Individuals express themselves honestly; they say what they mean.

Interpersonal Factors The ability to understand and relate to others in the group is a second key area governing success. Some of these specific interpersonal factors follow:

1. All members must participate for group decision making to be effective; members who remain forever silent do not contribute.
2. Groups in which members are more skilled at the art of communicating are more effective.

3. Members engage in supportive, not defensive, communication. Supportive communications evaluate problems or issues, not other members, thus creating a climate of mutual trust.
4. Members make sure they understand one another and they are clearly understood by others; they do this by checking others' reactions, being specific in describing an idea, and being descriptive, rather than judgmental, in response to others' ideas.

Group Identity Factors   The identity of a group flows directly from the intrapersonal and interpersonal factors just described. Several of these group identity factors are presented below:

1. Members are sensitive to the group process; they sense *when* to communicate a particular idea.
2. Members who fail to contribute—and, hence, are uncommitted to the group or the task—should consider quitting the group. Having uncommitted members reduces the group's effectiveness.
3. Members who understand the group process exhibit patience at the slowness of change, particularly in the early stages. Allowing time to think through ideas is important to creative and effective decision-making.
4. Successful groups avoid unrealistic formula answers to difficult problems.

Carney (1988) has summarized many of the factors described in this section in checklist form. Tables 1.5 and 1.6 present these checklists, which individual team members can use to evaluate their own contributions and reactions to groups in which they participate.

Table 1.5.   Checklist on personal dynamics related to team performance

Did you contribute more to the task orientation or the emotional orientation of the group?

Did you show enthusiasm and give positive feedback for other members' ideas?

Did you assert your preferences and opinions? If not, why?

Did you paraphrase or ask for clarification when you had a question or felt uncertainty or a strong reaction to another's comments?

Did you identify for the group any concerns you had about the process or outcome of the decision?

Did you feel generally trusting of other group members?

If you asked questions, were they open ended or closed ended?

What did your facial expression and body language communicate?

If you had to do it again, would you behave or interact differently?

Adapted from Carney (1988).

Table 1.6.   Checklist on group dynamics related to team performance

Who assumed responsibility for getting the job done?

Who assumed responsibility for the emotional climate of the group?

Did the group have all the information it needed to proceed?

Did group members disagree with one another? How did that feel to the disagreeing members? To other members?

Did the group have a shared frame of reference for how the decision should be reached? Did it help? Would it have?

Did one or two people assume leadership or was leadership shared among all group members?

Did the meeting progress show a balance of permissiveness and control?

Did group members appear to accurately understand one another's questions and comments or did they jump to conclusions?

How would you describe the general atmosphere of the group?

Did you notice any nonverbal communication that influenced communication in the group?

Adapted from Carney (1988).

Challenges to Implementing a Transdisciplinary Model

Professionals who try to implement a transdisciplinary model frequently encounter a variety of challenges along the way. None of these obstacles is insurmountable, and most are grounded in a lack of understanding or a general resistance to change. However, it is important to appreciate others' views; failing to do so typically results in failure to reach agreed upon goals, which ultimately harms the students for whom the group is working. Challenges in implementing the model can be divided into three categories: philosophical and professional, interpersonal, and administrative.

Philosophical and Professional Challenges

Differences in Philosophy and Orientation   A problem that team members confront quickly is the difference in their own training and philosophy (Courtnage & Smith-Davis, 1987; Geiger, Bradley, Rock, & Croce, 1986). Therapists, for example, are usually taught within a medical model, whereby one uncovers the underlying cause of a behavior and then directs therapy toward the presumed cause. Special educators, however, especially those who work with children with multiple disabilities, are taught to emphasize functional assessment and skills. This fundamental difference in orientation can result in significantly different approaches to instruction and therapy. The problem is further exacerbated by the preparation of professionals in isolation, preventing therapists, teachers, nurses, and others in training from learning about and valuing other professionals. In addition, professionals often use jargon, which is

,47, 44

appropriate as shorthand and when technical clarity is essential. Unfortunately, other team members, including parents, often do not understand what is being said or written in jargon about a child, which frustrates efforts at solving common problems (Rainforth, 1985; Sears, 1981).

Diminishment of Professional Status   Related to professionals' training and orientation is the status that they acquire or seek. As Bassoff (1976) clearly stated, "The assumption that different disciplines on teams gather together as equals, while an overt statement of a desired state, cloaks the reality that some team members are more equal than others" (p. 224). Releasing part of one's role does threaten the status that some professionals perceive themselves as having. However, as was described earlier in this chapter, transdisciplinary teams that operate smoothly actually can *enhance* the status of team members by fostering greater respect and interdependence (York et al., 1990).

Isolation of Parents   Some individuals (Bennett, 1982; Holm & McCartin, 1978) have expressed a concern that parents may become confused by a transdisciplinary model, since the line between therapy and education becomes blurred. It is essential to explain the model clearly to parents, demonstrating the ways in which integrated therapy services result in better learning for the children. Perhaps more important, an effectively operating transdisciplinary model should provide more opportunities for involving parents at all levels—assessment, program planning and delivery, and evaluation—thereby *reducing* parents' feeling of estrangement.

Interpersonal Challenges

Threat of Training Others and Threat of Being Trained   At the core of the transdisciplinary model is the need for team members to teach others and to accept other members' skills and information. Meeting this need can be quite threatening, because it places the team members' skills under close scrutiny (Peterson, 1980). It calls into question an individual's own competence and confidence, as well as evoking his or her feelings toward fellow team members. In short, a transdisciplinary team, like any other decision-making group, requires its members to trust each other and to risk themselves.

Role Conflict or Ambiguity   A common source of interpersonal problems is a lack of clear differentiation of responsibilities among team members (Butler & Maher, 1981). Since functions often blur within a transdisciplinary approach, it is essential throughout the life of the team to clarify people's roles. It may also be difficult for some professionals to release themselves from traditional service roles (Sparling, 1980).

Administrative Challenges

Failure To Understand the Approach   The transdisciplinary model is complex in its subtleties and logistical demands. As a result, it is often misunderstood and implemented improperly. The model does not advocate that any team member should do anyone else's job or that the amount of therapy services

should be reduced. It is important for program administrators to understand the approach, particularly its enhanced benefits for the children. Administrators can be very helpful in supporting the professionals who serve the students. Table 1.7 lists several steps administrators can take to facilitate implementation of a transdisciplinary model in their programs.

Resistance to Change   Implementing a new service delivery model takes time and concerted effort, as well as administrative support and technical assistance. Any significant change will be met with resistance by at least one team member. This resistance must be anticipated and confronted; left unchecked, it can be destructive. It is critical for the team to have jointly developed, common goals that benefit the children.

Professional Ethics and Liability   Some have expressed concern that a model based heavily on indirect services may foster negligent behavior by not ensuring sufficient supervision by appropriately licensed or certified professionals (Geiger et al., 1986). This concern should be taken seriously and appropriate steps taken to ensure the health and safety of all students. However, as Giangreco (1986) observed, "one reason indirect models are necessary is because therapists can not be available 24 hours a day" (p. 24). Clearly there are certain highly specialized, or potentially risky, procedures that only specifically designated, trained professionals (or parents) should perform. In all cases, prudence and common sense should prevail.

Table 1.7.   Steps administrators can take to facilitate implementation of a transdisciplinary program

Encourage individuals to view themselves as responsible to the team.

Encourage the team to view itself as responsible to the student and the family.

Encourage involvement of parents at whatever level they choose to participate.

Arrange school schedules to allow for formal, regular staff meetings.

Model appropriate behavior in team meetings: active listening, support.

Arrange the school building to maximize interaction between students with disabilities and typical students.

Arrange the building and schedule to avoid reliance on separate therapy rooms.

Encourage teachers and related services personnel to work together to assess students' strengths and needs and to develop goals and objectives.

Encourage a data-based model of instruction.

Encourage use of clear, simple language in meetings, IEPs, reports, and discussions.

Do not prevent conflict, but help resolve it as it arises.

Give the model time to work.

CONCLUSION

The challenges described in the preceding section should be viewed as just that—challenges. When professionals act in good faith—toward one another and toward children and families—and make a commitment to better educational services for students with multiple disabilities, no barrier is permanent. Teams should not be fooled into believing that implementing the techniques and principles described in this chapter will be easy; the work is difficult. But the outcomes, both for children and professionals, justify the effort.

REFERENCES

Albano, M.L. (1983). *Transdisciplinary teaming in special education: A case study.* Unpublished doctoral dissertation, University of Illinois at Urbana-Champaign.

Albano, M.L., Cox, B., York, J., & York, R. (1981). Educational teams for students with severe and multiple handicaps. In R. York, W. Schofield, D. Donder, D. Ryndak, & B. Reguly (Eds.), *Organizing and implementing services for students with severe and multiple handicaps* (pp. 23–34). Springfield: Illinois State Board of Education.

Bailey, D.B. (1984). A triaxial model of the interdisciplinary team and group process. *Exceptional Children, 5*(1), 17–25.

Bassoff, B.Z. (1976). Interdisciplinary education for health professionals: Issues and directions. *Social Work in Health Care, 2*(2), 219–228.

Bennett, F.C. (1982). The pediatrician and the interdisciplinary process. *Exceptional Children, 48*(4), 306–314.

Bricker, D. (1976). Educational synthesizer. In M.A. Thomas (Ed.), *Hey, don't forget about me!* (pp. 84–97). Reston, VA: Council for Exceptional Children.

Brown, L., Branston-McClean, M., Baumgart, D., Vincent, L., Falvey, M., & Schroeder, J. (1979). Using the characteristics of current and subsequent least restrictive environments in the development of content for severely handicapped students. *AAESPH Review, 4,* 407–424.

Butler, A.S., & Maher, C.A. (1981). Conflict and special service teams: Perspectives and suggestions for school psychologists. *Journal of School Psychology, 19*(1), 62–70.

Campbell, P.H. (1987). The integrated programming team: An approach for coordinating professionals of various disciplines in programs for students with severe and multiple handicaps. *Journal of The Association for Persons with Severe Handicaps, 12*(2), 107–116.

Campbell, P.H. (1989). Dysfunction in posture and movement in individuals with profound disabilities: Issues and practices. In F. Brown & D.H. Lehr (Eds.), *Persons with profound disabilities: Issues and practices* (pp. 163–189). Baltimore: Paul H. Brookes Publishing Co.

Carney, I.H. (1988). *Team membership self-assessment checklist.* Unpublished manuscript, Virginia Commonwealth University, Richmond.

Copeland, M.E., & Kimmel, J.R. (1989). *Evaluation and management of infants and young children with developmental disabilities.* Baltimore: Paul H. Brookes Publishing Co.

Courtnage, L., & Smith-Davis, J. (1987). Interdisciplinary team training: A national survey of special education teacher training programs. *Exceptional Children, 53,* 451–458.

Crump, M. (Ed.). (1987). *Nutrition and feeding of the handicapped child.* Boston: College-Hill.

Dunn, W. (1988). Models of occupational therapy service provision in the school system. *The American Journal of Occupational Therapy, 42*(11), 718–723.

Dunn, W. (1991). Integrated related services. In L.H. Meyer, C.A. Peck, & L. Brown (Eds.), *Critical issues in the lives of people with severe disabilities* (pp. 353–377). Baltimore: Paul H. Brookes Publishing Co.

Evans, I.M., & Scotti, J.R. (1989). Defining meaningful outcomes for persons with profound disabilities. In F. Brown & D.H. Lehr (Eds.), *Persons with profound disabilities: Issues and practices* (pp. 83–107). Baltimore: Paul H. Brookes Publishing Co.

Fisher, B.A. (1980). *Small group decision making* (2nd ed.). New York: McGraw-Hill.

Ford, A., Schnorr, R., Meyer, L., Davern, L., Black, J., & Dempsey, P. (Eds.). (1989). *The Syracuse community-referenced curriculum guide for students with moderate and severe disabilities.* Baltimore: Paul H. Brookes Publishing Co.

Forest, M., & Lusthaus, E. (1989). Promoting educational equality for all students: Circles and maps. In S. Stainback, W. Stainback, & M. Forest (Eds.), *Educating all students in the mainstream of regular education* (pp. 43–57). Baltimore: Paul H. Brookes Publishing Co.

Fraser, B.A., Hensinger, R.N., & Phelps, J.A. (1987). *Physical management of multiple handicaps: A professional's guide.* Baltimore: Paul H. Brookes Publishing Co.

Fredericks, H.D.B., & Baldwin, V.L. (1987). Individuals with sensory impairments: Who are they? How are they educated? In L. Goetz, D. Guess, & K. Stremel-Campbell (Eds.), *Innovative program design for individuals with dual sensory impairments* (pp. 3–12). Baltimore: Paul H. Brookes Publishing Co.

Garland, C., McGonigel, M., Frank, A., & Buck, D. (1989). *The transdisciplinary model of service delivery.* Lightfoot, VA: Child Development Resources.

Gaylord-Ross, R.J., & Holvoet, J.F. (1985). *Strategies for educating students with severe handicaps.* Boston: Little, Brown.

Geiger, W.L., Bradley, R.H., Rock, S.L., & Croce, R. (1986). Commentary. *Physical and Occupational Therapy in Pediatrics, 6*(2), 16–21.

Giangreco, M.F. (1986). Delivery of therapeutic services in special education programs for learners with severe handicaps. *Physical and Occupational Therapy in Pediatrics, 6*(2), 5–15.

Giangreco, M.F., York, J., & Rainforth, B. (1989). Providing related servines to learners with severe handicaps in educational settings: Pursuing the least restrictive option. *Pediatric Physical Therapy, 1*(2), 55–63.

Graff, J.C., Ault, M.M., Guess, D., Taylor, M., & Thompson, B. (1990). *Health care for students with disabilities: An illustrated medical guide for the classroom.* Baltimore: Paul H. Brookes Publishing Co.

Guess, D., & Siegel-Causey, E. (1985). Behavioral control and education of severely handicapped students: Who's doing what to whom? And why? In D. Bricker & J. Filler (Eds.), *Severe mental retardation: From theory to practice* (pp. 230–244). Reston, VA: Council for Exceptional Children.

Hart, V. (1977). The use of many disciplines with the severely and profoundly handicapped. In E. Sontag, J. Smith, & N. Certo (Eds.), *Educational programming for the severely and profoundly handicapped* (pp. 391–396). Reston, VA: Council for Exceptional Children.

Holm, V.A., & McCartin, R.E. (1978). Interdisciplinary child development team. Team issues and training in interdisciplinariness. In K.E. Allen, V.A. Holm, & R.L. Schiefelbusch (Eds.), *Early intervention: A team approach* (pp. 97–122). Baltimore: University Park Press.

Hutchison, D.J. (1978). The transdisciplinary approach. In J.B. Curry & K.K. Peppe (Eds.), *Mental retardation: Nursing approaches to care* (pp. 65–74). St. Louis: C.V. Mosby.

Lansing, S.G., & Carlsen, P.N. (1977). Occupational therapy. In P.J. Valletutti & F. Christoplos (Eds.), *Interdisciplinary approaches to human services* (pp. 211–236). Baltimore: University Park Press.

Lowe, J.I., & Herranen, M. (1982). Understanding teamwork: Another look at the concepts. *Social Work in Health Care, 7*(2), 1–11.

Lyon, S., & Lyon, G. (1980). Team functioning and staff development. A role release approach to providing integrated educational services for severely handicapped students. *Journal of The Association for the Severely Handicapped, 5*(3), 250–263.

McCamman, S., & Rues, J. (1990). Nutrition monitoring and supplementation. In J.C. Graff, M.M. Ault, D. Guess, M. Taylor, & B. Thompson. *Health care for students with disabilities: An illustrated medical guide for the classroom* (pp. 79–117). Baltimore: Paul H. Brookes Publishing Co.

McCormick, L., & Goldman, R. (1979). The transdisciplinary model: Implications for service delivery and personnel preparation for the severely and profoundly handicapped. *AAESPH Review, 4*(2), 152–161.

Meyer, L.H., & Evans, I.M. (1989). *Nonaversive intervention for behavior problems: A manual for home and community.* Baltimore: Paul H. Brookes Publishing Co.

Mulligan-Ault, M., Guess, D., Struth, L., & Thompson, B. (1988). The implementation of health-related procedures in classrooms for students with severe multiple impairments. *Journal of The Association for Persons with Severe Handicaps, 13*(2), 100–109.

Nietupski, J., Scheutz, G., & Ockwood, L. (1980). The delivery of communication therapy services to severely handicapped students: A plan for change. *Journal of The Association for the Severely Handicapped, 5*(1), 13–23.

Orelove, F.P. (1991). Educating all students: The future is now. In L.H. Meyer, C.A. Peck, & L. Brown (Eds.), *Critical issues in the lives of people with severe disabilities* (pp. 67–87). Baltimore: Paul H. Brookes Publishing Co.

Ottenbacher, K. (1982). Occupational therapy and special education: Some issues and concerns related to P.L. 94-142. *American Journal of Occupational Therapy, 36,* 81–84.

Ottenbacher, K. (1983). Transdisciplinary service delivery in school environments: Some limitations. *Physical and Occupational Therapy in Pediatrics, 3*(4), 9–16.

Peterson, C.P. (1980). Support services. In B. L. Wilcox & R. York (Eds.), *Quality education for the severely handicapped: The federal investment* (pp. 136–163). Washington, DC: Bureau of Education for the Handicapped.

Rainforth, B. (1985). *Collaborative efforts in the preparation of physical therapists and teachers of students with severe handicaps.* Unpublished doctoral dissertation, University of Illinois at Urbana-Champaign.

Rainforth, B., & York, J. (1987). Integrating related services in community instruction. *Journal of The Association for Persons with Severe Handicaps, 12*(3), 190–198.

Sears, C.J. (1981). The transdisciplinary approach: A process for compliance with Public Law 94-142. *Journal of The Association for the Severely Handicapped, 6*(1), 22–29.

Sparling, J.W. (1980). The transdisciplinary approach with the developmentally delayed child. *Physical and Occupational Therapy in Pediatrics, 1*(2), 3–16.

Spooner, F., & Dykes, M.K. (1982). Epilepsy: Impact upon severely and profoundly handicapped persons. *Journal of The Association for the Severely Handicapped, 7*(3), 87–96.

Sternat, J., Messina, R., Nietupski, J., Lyon, S., & Brown, L. (1977). Occupational and physical therapy services for severely handicapped students: Toward a naturalized public school service delivery model. In E. Sontag, J. Smith, & N. Certo (Eds.),

Educational programming for the severely and profoundly handicapped (pp. 263–278). Reston, VA: Council for Exceptional Children.

Stremel-Campbell, K. (1977). Communication skills. In N.G. Haring (Ed.), *Developing effective individualized education programs for severely handicapped children and youth* (pp. 139–182). Washington, DC: Department of Health, Education, and Welfare, Office of Education, Bureau of Education for the Handicapped.

Strully, J.L., & Strully, C.F. (1989). Friendships as an educational goal. In S. Stainback, W. Stainback, & M. Forest (Eds.), *Educating all students in the mainstream of regular education* (pp. 59–68). Baltimore: Paul H. Brookes Publishing Co.

Thompson, B., & Guess, D. (1989). Students who experience the most profound disabilities: Teacher perspectives. In F. Brown & D.H. Lehr (Eds.), *Persons with profound disabilities: Issues and practices* (pp. 3–41). Baltimore: Paul H. Brookes Publishing Co.

United Cerebral Palsy, National Organized Collaborative Project to Provide Comprehensive Services for Atypical Infants and Their Families. (1976). *Staff development handbook: A resource for the transdisciplinary process.* New York: United Cerebral Palsy Association.

West, M.A. (1978). The social worker specializing in handicapped children. In K.E. Allen, V.A. Holm, & R.L. Schiefelbusch (Eds.), *Early intervention—A team approach* (pp. 269–285). Baltimore: University Park Press.

Whitehouse, F.A. (1951). Teamwork—A democracy of processions. *Exceptional Children, 18*(2), 45–52.

Woodruff, G., & McGonigel, M.J. (1988). Early intervention team approaches: The transdisciplinary model. In J.B. Jordan, J.J. Gallagher, P.L. Hutinger, & M.B. Karnes (Eds.), *Early childhood special education: Birth to three* (pp. 164–181). Reston, VA: Council for Exceptional Children.

Worthington, B.S., Pipes, P.L., & Trahms, C.M. (1978). The pediatric nutritionist. In K.E. Allen, V.A. Holm, & R.L. Schiefelbusch (Eds.), *Early intervention—A team approach* (pp. 199–218). Baltimore: University Park Press.

York, J.L. (1984). *A transdisciplinary model of service delivery for educational teams who serve students with severe and multiple handicaps: Implications for developmental therapists.* Unpublished manuscript, University of Wisconsin-Madison.

York, J., Long, E., Caldwell, N., Brown, L., Zanella Albright, K., Rogan, P., Shiraga, B., & Marks, J. (1985). Teamwork strategies for school and community instruction. In L. Brown, B. Shiraga, J. York, A. Udvari-Solner, K. Zanella Albright, P. Rogan, E. McCarthy, & R. Loomis (Eds.), *Educational programs for students with severe intellectual disabilities* (Vol. 15, pp. 229–276). Madison, WI: Madison Metropolitan School District.

York, J., Rainforth, B., & Giangreco, M.F. (1990). Transdisciplinary teamwork and integrated therapy: Clarifying the misconceptions. *Pediatric Physical Therapy, 2*(2), 73–79.

Chapter 2

The Sensorimotor Systems
A Framework for
Assessment and Intervention

Winnie Dunn

The sensory and motor systems form a definitive network through which individuals experience and act on the environment. Information produced through sensory and motor exploration form the foundation for developmental experiences (Rogers & D'Eugenio, 1981; Short-DeGraff, 1988). For example, while learning how to reach and grasp objects in the environment (a motor skill), the young child also acquires cognitive information such as object distance, spatial relationships, and weight. The child who puts on a shirt receives sensory input as the shirt moves across the body surface, and the child also uses motor functions to accomplish the task. The sensory input and motor responses necessary for this and other self-care tasks develop accurate and reliable maps of one's body (called body scheme), which one becomes accustomed to making use of; this leads to greater independence. When young children are deprived of typical sensory and motor experiences, due to either environmental or biological variables, there is a risk that other areas of development may also be affected.

The sensory and motor systems are intimately linked within the nervous system; in fact, many refer to them as the sensorimotor systems (e.g., Moore, 1980; Short-DeGraff, 1988; Weeks & Ewer-Jones, 1983). The sensory systems provide an interface between the environment and the individual for incoming information. Each sensory system receives, transmits, and interprets specific environmental stimuli for the nervous system, creating maps of oneself and one's environment that identify spatial and temporal qualities of body and environment; as more information is gathered from experiences, the maps become more complex (Dunn, 1991c). The motor system uses these maps of self and environment to plan, organize, and execute movements in response to environmental demands. The motor response itself then produces sensory feedback regarding the event, which enhances the maps for the next time they need to be used. Figure 2.1 summarizes these relationships.

For example, when a person reaches for a cup, the sensory receptors in the joints and muscles provide information about the arm's location in space; the visual receptors report on the closing distance between the cup and the person's hand; and the tactile system sends information regarding the texture and weight of the cup (sensory input). These data are incorporated into maps of self and environment, producing accurate current movement (interpretation of sensory

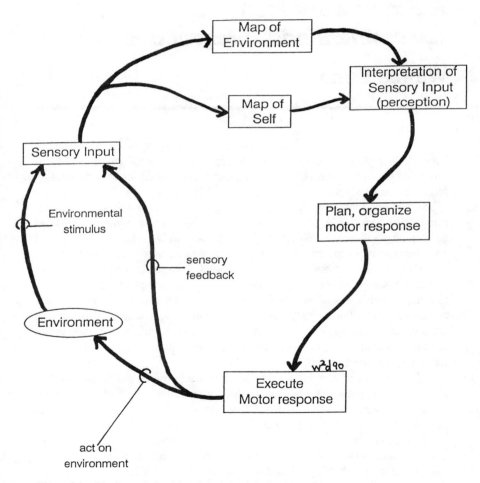

Figure 2.1. The interrelationships of the sensory and motor systems.

input leading to organizing and executing a motor response) and enabling the next reaching task to be more routine. When errors occur in the motor action (as determined by sensory feedback), the nervous system adjusts its maps to improve performance the next time. Therefore, any discussion about motor systems must acknowledge dependence upon sensation for information and guidance.

Knowledge of the operation and interdependence of the sensory and motor systems can be an advantage when planning interventions for children with multiple disabilities. Portions of the sensory or motor systems are involved in all disabilities; knowledgeable professionals can recognize the variations in performance that indicate both intact and involved systems. Professionals can then facilitate functional performance through intact systems and create strategies that minimize the effects of involved systems.

The first purpose of this chapter is to introduce the basic principles of sensorimotor skill acquisition and use as they apply to students with multiple disabilities. The second purpose is to explore assessment and intervention strategies that incorporate this knowledge to enhance the functional abilities of students with multiple disabilities.

TYPICAL SENSORIMOTOR SKILL ACQUISITION AND USE

The Sensory Systems

Physical stimulation from the environment (e.g., a noise, a light, a tap on the arm) activates the receptors of the sensory systems to create a nervous system impulse. Stimulus thresholds (the strength needed for the stimulus to be noticed) and ranges (upper and lower limits for noticing the stimuli) are specific both to humans as a species and to particular individuals based on their life experiences. For example, dogs hear a range of high pitched sounds that are inaudible to the human ear. One person may comment on a sound in the environment (e.g., a car driving past the house) that another person does not hear. A person who has never tasted lemonade will have a lower threshold for the tart taste, and would therefore have more visible response to it; a person who has had lemonade before can anticipate the taste (has developed a higher threshold) and responds accordingly.

Sensation arouses and alerts the individual and provides information for discrimination of salient features of the stimuli (Dunn, 1991c). Certain characteristics of each sensory system's input are more likely to produce either alerting or discrimination. Arousal/alerting stimuli tend to generate noticing behaviors. The individual's attention is at least momentarily drawn toward the stimulus (commonly disrupting ongoing behavior). These stimuli enable the nervous system to become oriented to stimuli that may require a protective response. In some situations, an arousing stimulus can become part of a functional behavior pattern (e.g., when the arousing somatosensory input from putting on a shirt becomes predictable, a discriminating/mapping characteristic). Discriminatory/mapping stimuli are those that enable the individual to gather information that can be used to support and generate functional behaviors. The information identifies spatial and temporal qualities of body and environment (the content of the maps), which can be used to create purposeful movement. These stimuli are more organizing for the nervous system. Table 2.1 provides examples of the stimuli characteristics that fall into each category. When planning programs for children with multiple disabilities, team members can use this information to create activities that include an optimal combination of sensory inputs. (The "Application of Knowledge of Sensorimotor Systems to the Needs of Children with Multiple Disabilities" section of this chapter describes planning strategies.)

Most milestones associated with the sensory systems occur prior to the preschool period, when the child learns to explore the environment and begins building maps of self and environment for more complex interactions. The brain combines information from all sensations to build multidimensional maps of self and environment; for example, a young child combines movement with visual and tactile information to determine how to retrieve a favorite stuffed animal. Multiple experiences provide the underlying information to facilitate development of motor, perceptual, cognitive, and language relationships (Dunn, 1991c).

The Somatosensory System   The somatosensory system responds to touch input through receptors on the surface of the skin. Somatosensory receptors respond to light touch (e.g., tickling), touch-pressure (e.g., firm rubbing or pressing), pain, and temperature. The input from these receptors forms a map of self; they tell where the individual ends and the world begins (Dunn, 1991c). Somatosensory input triggers many of the early motor reflexes that enable infants to react to environmental stimuli. For example, the rooting reflex occurs when one touches the infant's lower face, and results in head movement toward the stimulus to suckle; the grasp reflex occurs when one touches the infant's palm, with the result that the infant grips the object. These early experiences initiate the process of sensory input→motor response→sensory feedback (see Figure 2.1), which will facilitate the development of an accurate body map.

There are many somatosensory receptors on the face and in the mouth, enabling the child to develop a very clear map of the oral-motor structures for eating and talking. Textures and tastes of foods can play an important role in early oral-motor exploration. There are also many receptors on the hand; the information gathered from object manipulation and exploration promotes functional hand use and cognitive development. Children with multiple disabilities cannot generate the volume of independent tactile exploration observed during typical child development. They must rely on skilled care providers to create situations that enable exploration to occur.

Table 2.1.   Arousal/alerting and discrimination/mapping descriptors of the sensory system

Sensory system	Arousal/alerting descriptors[a]	Discrimination/mapping descriptors[b]
For all systems	*Unpredictability:* The task is unfamiliar; the child cannot anticipate the sensory experiences that will occur in the task	*Predictability:* Sensory pattern in the task is routine for the child, such as with diaper changing—the child knows what is occurring and what will come next
Somatosensory	*Light touch:* Gentle tapping on skin; tickling (e.g., loose clothing making contact with skin) *Pain:* Brisk pinching; contact with sharp objects; skin pressed in small surface (e.g., when skin is caught in between chair arm and seat) *Temperature:* Hot or cold stimuli (e.g., iced drinks, hot foods, cold hands, cold metal chairs) *Variability:* Changing characteristics during the task (e.g., putting clothing on requires a combination of tacticle experiences) *Short duration stimuli:* Tapping, touching briefly (e.g., splashing water) *Small body surface contact:* As when using only fingertips to touch something	*Touch pressure:* Firm contact on skin (e.g., hugging, patting, grasping); occurs both when touching objects or persons, or when they touch you *Long duration stimuli:* Holding, grasping (e.g., carrying a child in your arms) *Large body surface contact:* Includes holding, hugging; also holding a cup with the entire palmar surface of hand

(continued)

Table 2.1.   *(continued)*

Sensory system	Arousal/alerting descriptors[a]	Discrimination/mapping descriptors[b]
Vestibular	*Head position change:* The child's head orientation is altered (e.g., pulling the child up from lying on the back to sitting) *Speed change:* Movements change velocity (e.g., the teacher stops to talk to another teacher when pushing the child to the bathroom in a wheelchair) *Direction change:* Movements change planes (e.g., bending down to pick up something from the floor while carrying the child down the hall) *Rotary head movement:* Head moving in an arc (e.g., spinning in a circle, turning head side to side)	*Linear head movement:* Head moving in a straight line (e.g., bouncing up and down, going down the hall in a wheelchair) *Repetitive head movement:* Movements that repeat in a simple sequence (e.g., rocking in a rocker)
Proprioceptive	*Quick stretch:* Movements that pull on the muscles (e.g., briskly tapping on a belly muscle)	*Sustained tension:* Steady, constant action on the muscles, pressing on or holding the muscle (e.g., using heavy objects during play) *Shifting muscle tension:* Activities that demand constant changes in the muscles (e.g., walking, lifting, and moving objects)
Visual	*High intensity:* Visual stimulus is bright (e.g., looking out the window on a bright day) *High contrast:* Great difference between the visual stimulus and its surrounding environment (e.g., cranberry juice in a white cup)	*Low intensity:* Visual stimulus is subdued (e.g., finding objects in the dark closet) *High similarity:* Small differences between visual stimulus and its surrounding environment (e.g., oatmeal in a beige bowl)

(continued)

Table 2.1.   *(continued)*

Sensory system	Arousal/alerting descriptors[a]	Discrimination/mapping descriptors[b]
Visual *(continued)*	*Variability:* Changing characteristics during the task (e.g., a television program is a variable visual stimulus)	*Competitive:* The background is interesting or busy (e.g., the junk drawer, a bulletin board)
Auditory	*Variability:* Changing characteristics during the task (e.g., a person's voice with intonation)	*Rhythmic:* Sounds repeat in a simple sequence/beat (e.g., humming; singing nursery songs)
	High intensity: The auditory stimulus is loud (e.g., siren, high volume radio)	*Constant:* The stimulus is always present (e.g., a fan noise)
		Competitive: The environment has a variety of recurring sounds (e.g., the classroom, a party)
		Noncompetitive: The environment is quiet (e.g., the bedroom when all is ready for bedtime)
		Low intensity: The auditory stimulus is subdued (e.g., whispering)
Olfactory/ Gustatory	*Strong intensity:* The taste/ smell has distinct qualities (e.g., spinach)	*Mild intensity:* The taste/ smell has nondistinct or familiar qualities (e.g., cream of wheat)

[a]Tend to generate "noticing" behaviors; the individual's attention is momentarily drawn toward the stimulus, and away from ongoing behavior. Can become part of a functional behavior sequence. (See text for example.)

[b]Create temporal and spatial qualities of body and environments (maps created), which can be used to create goal-directed movement. (See text for example.)

Touch also contributes to a psychosocial experience through natural interactions with others. Although a person's cultural experience partially dictates the amount and type of human touch and contact that occurs, touching among humans is critical to survival. Young children who do not receive physical love and contact can "fail to thrive." They do not initiate contact and express little interest in eating or interacting with persons or the environment.

The Proprioceptive System   The receptors of the *proprioceptive system* are housed in the muscles, joints, and surrounding tissues. They respond to the ongoing repositioning of body parts in space; stretching and compressing the muscles and tendons at the ends of muscles sends information into the nervous system. Proprioceptive input contributes to the map of the body, but through internal mechanisms. While touch input often triggers movement, proprioceptive input occurs during the movement to support the movement and to keep the nervous system apprised of body status. Weight bearing tasks such as kneeling, standing, and walking activate proprioceptors in the legs; propping on forearms provides that same type of input to the arms. Bouncing, jumping, pushing, pulling, and lifting activate proprioceptors by stretching and compressing joints during a task. Thus, many of the exploratory activities of toddlers and preschoolers stimulate the proprioceptive system, and create maps of the body as it moves about in space. Children with multiple disabilities often receive too much (children with high muscle tone) or too little (children with low muscle tone) proprioceptive information from their muscles and tendons, making it difficult for them to modulate muscle actions to support particular movements.

The Vestibular System   The vestibular system's primary task is orientation of the head in space. The vestibular receptor is housed in the inner ear; it is constructed so that any head position or movement can be detected. The eye muscles and the vestibular system are connected to coordinate head and eye movements; body receptors and motor systems are connected to the vestibular system to coordinate head and body movements. The vestibular system forms an interfacing map, one that coordinates the map of self with the map of the environment, to produce organized, sequenced, and well-timed body adjustments and movements. Balance and equilibrium tasks activate the vestibular receptors; the vestibular system then generates muscle actions to hold the person upright when equilibrium is upset. Since many children with multiple disabilities have a difficult time moving independently, they rely on caregivers to provide movement experiences that produce vestibular information.

Biobehavioral state (the condition of the individual in relation to the ability to notice and respond to information from the environment) is altered with vestibular system input (Guess et al., 1988; Short-DeGraff, 1988). Certain forms of movement stimulate arousal (e.g., spinning, moving the head into the upside-down position), while others are calming and organizing to the nervous system (e.g., rhythmic movements, such as rocking). Knowledge of these effects can aid in the proper structuring of activities for young children. This relationship can easily be seen during a preschooler's bedtime. If a parent begins to roughhouse with a child, bouncing, swinging, and so forth, the child has a more difficult time going to sleep than if the parent uses rhythmic rocking and cuddling.

Taste   Taste is a response to chemical receptors in the mouth, specifically in the taste buds on the tongue. Descriptions of tastes are derived from four basic qualities: bitter, sour, sweet, and salty. Taste is a significant variable to consider when one examines the development of eating skills. Specific oral-motor responses are associated with eating (e.g., sucking, chewing, and swallowing) and can be facilitated with the use of taste and texture in the mouth. The movements needed to move food about in the mouth are also needed for the production of language, although language must also be specifically taught. When children with disabilities have been restricted from eating a full range of foods for health risk reasons (e.g., fear of choking; inability to swallow properly), they may also have limited experiences with tastes. This can sometimes lead to difficulty learning to accept new foods when the medical issues have been resolved.

Smell   Smell is a distance sense that also uses chemical receptors. Researchers have tried unsuccessfully to categorize odors, but the importance of the olfactory system for human behavior is not questioned (Coren, Porac, & Ward, 1984). Smells can signal familiarity of persons, places, or things. Potential danger, pleasure, and fear can all be triggered with the introduction of an odor into one's environment. The smell of bread baking or a familiar cologne reminds us of past experiences and our feelings about them. Young children recognize family members by their distinctive odors. Children with multiple disabilities may use their sense of smell to map out their environment, especially when other sensory input is more difficult to obtain.

Hearing   The auditory receptor is housed in the inner ear. The structure of the ear and ear canal facilitates the movement of sound waves into the middle and inner ear for processing. Sound is used to map the environment, and is frequently coordinated with movement as the child searches for the source of the sound. As children grow older, the sound of voices directs movement when children give and follow directions. The auditory system also supports the development of communication systems, as one begins to understand and describe sensorimotor experiences.

Vision   The visual system is the last sensory system to mature. The receptors are housed in the eyeball. Some of them react to light and dark, while others pick up color stimuli. The receptors identify form by transmitting information about contrasting images, creating a map of the environment. This environmental map must be updated constantly as the child moves about in space and alters the relationships between self and objects; this requires continuous coordination with the map of self. As discussed earlier, this interface is provided by the vestibular system. Children are often motivated to move and learn by seeing interesting objects and persons in the environment.

One specific form of movement, object use, depends heavily on the visual system for refinement. As the child reaches for, grasps, and manipulates objects, visual guidance supports and refines these actions. Gross forms of this sequence can occur with very little visual input, but in order to develop more refined movements, coordination of visual regard of the task and necessary hand movements (which produce somatosensory and proprioceptive feedback as the child manipulates the objects) must occur. Eating with a spoon and using a communication board are examples of visual-motor integration tasks for children with multiple disabilities.

The Motor Systems

The motor systems operate to enable the individual to interact with the environment. Even early movements of infancy, which are random and automatic, are in response to sensory stimuli. When one touches an infant's face, the infant turns toward the stimulus (the rooting reflex); the infant grasps objects that are placed into the palm of the hand (grasping reflex); when the infant moves its head to the right or left (providing vestibular input), the muscles in the arms and legs move in particular patterns (the asymmetrical tonic neck reflex). Children develop control and organization over these automatic or reflexive movements as they grow. Young children also move in response to visual and auditory stimuli; they turn their heads when they hear their names being called; they reach or move toward interesting objects when they see them.

Approaches to Motor Development Typically, professionals have viewed motor development from a skill acquisition perspective (Gesell, 1954). This perspective organizes motor skills according to the typical time they emerge in the behavioral repertoire. Although this framework provides a general guideline for emergence of developmental skills, individual children can vary quite a bit from this standard. Developmental scales do not incorporate a method for recording descriptive information about emerging skills, or the level of control over acquired skills (e.g., the length of time the child takes to perform the skill correctly). There is also an implication that skills of an earlier age must be present (i.e., are prerequisites) in order for the later skills to emerge; it is more characteristic for the child to demonstrate interest in and experimentation with several skill components well before mastering the motor skills.

The developmental perspective is not useful for programming with children with multiple disabilities; these children frequently do not have the motor control necessary to explore independently, and have a different sensorimotor experience when they do move. Typical children display a great deal of variability in movement patterns; for children with disabilities this variability is frequently a central problem (Scherzer & Tscharnuter, 1982). It is more useful for professionals to describe motor performance in relation to its usefulness for function and its efficiency for present and future performance desires (Campbell, 1990; Dunn, 1991a, 1991c).

A functional approach is more useful when considering children with multiple disabilities. Within a functional skills approach, it is important to identify those motor skills that are *essential* to task performance, particularly tasks that are important for adult life. Campbell (1987a) suggests that looking, vocalization, functional reach, simple manipulation, and combined manipulation are the essential skills for performance of daily life tasks. These simple behavioral forms are useful in themselves, but are also necessary components of more complex forms of interaction. The actions that these behavioral forms create can also be built into many opportunities throughout the day, across many types of activities, providing multiple opportunities for practice.

Purposes for Movements   Campbell (1990) delineates three primary purposes for movements. First, movements occur to restore equilibrium when the body has been displaced in relation to gravity. Typically, these movements become automatic during the first years of life, such that persons do not need to think about the need to reorient the body when it is displaced. When people are riding in a car, and it turns sharply, the passengers readjust their body positions quickly and spontaneously to accommodate themselves to the turn. Second, persons combine movements with ideas to create desired actions; this conceptualization and organization process is called motor planning or praxis (the ability to organize and conceptualize a new motor act)(Ayres, 1980). The child sees a favorite toy in the vicinity, and moves in an organized way to obtain the toy. Cognitive and motor systems function in concert to achieve desired actions. The third purpose of movement is to increase and refine skills. Although a child may be able to move toward a desired toy, the child may not be able to pick up or explore the toy properly without refined motor skills. Younger children use the same few movements to explore objects (e.g., grasping and releasing objects), while older children can move an object within their hands to discover additional qualities and properties (Exner, 1989).

Component Parts of Movements   Movements have component parts (i.e., the form of the movement)(Campbell, 1989). The components of movement can create an efficient motion, one that expends a great deal of effort, or one that does not produce the desired outcome at all. Skilled observations are used to analyze movement qualities and their effectiveness for desired performance. Young children who are learning to eat with a spoon initially use ineffective movements. For example, a child will dump the contents of the spoon before it reaches the mouth because the child cannot coordinate the necessary wrist, hand, and arm movements with the utensil position. After practicing, the child discovers a way to keep food on the spoon and get it to the mouth, but movement qualities are poor. The child may miss the mouth, hold the spoon in a primitive manner, or may use excessive head movement to get the food off the spoon. After experimenting with various patterns of movements, the child creates an efficient method for eating with a spoon, and relies on this pattern when eating all meals. This adaptability of form is a hallmark of typical skill acquisition and use but is a significant barrier for many children with multiple disabilities. (See the "Atypical Sensorimotor Skill Acquisition and Use" section of this chapter for a discussion of these barriers.)

Reaching, grasping, manipulating, and releasing objects with the hand are significant components of the exploration process. This sensorimotor sequence enables a person to locate objects within the immediate environment and discover their properties (Exner, 1989). Most functional tasks require a combination of arm and hand movements to achieve the desired outcome. For example, a child uses simple reaching patterns to put on a shirt, but a complex pattern of arm and hand movements is necessary to button it. Muscle tone and postural control problems inhibit the evolution of this sequence for children with multiple disabilities.

Movement and Cognitive Skill Acquisition   It is important to remember the relationship between movement abilities and the acquisition of cognitive skills (Campbell, 1990). Children explore objects and persons in their environment to learn their characteristics, qualities, and functions; children must move to explore the environment. Functional movement is a combination of sensorimotor and cognitive systems operations. There must be a reason for the individual to move (a motivating factor), and the child must have sensorimotor capabilities to act on the environment. This is a key focus of attention when working with children who have multiple disabilities. Professionals must acknowledge the potential for sensorimotor impairments to affect cognitive skill acquisition and use, and provide intervention to minimize this possibility.

Acquisition of Postural Control

Postural control is the ability to manage one's body parts with and against the forces of gravity. Postural control begins when an infant can hold the body still to focus on a particular stimulus (Gilfoyle, Grady, & Moore, 1981). The infant proceeds to experiment with many postural control patterns, which incorporate combinations of holding one body part still while moving another body part to meet a functional goal. Postural control is observable in all body positions: supine (on the back), prone (on the stomach), sitting, and standing. In each position, the child initially moves toward gravity, and eventually the child can move against the force of gravity.

Young infants depend on adults to provide the stable base for simple movements; for example, the adult commonly holds the child in the upper trunk so the child can hold up his or her head. As the child grows and develops better control, the adult provides less external support and the child establishes internal stability to support exploratory movements. Internal support generally occurs within the central trunk initially, to support the head and then to provide a stable base for limb movements (Campbell, 1989). The child also learns to use objects in the environment to provide support when experimenting with new postures and movements. For example, when a child is learning to stand up, he or she holds onto furniture for support. The child experiments with movements against gravity by moving only briefly at first, increasing the length of time the posture can be maintained, and finally by developing control over the movements (Campbell, 1989). Ultimately the child can move with and against the force of gravity independently; exploratory movements and postural control for stability become fluid with each other, so that the child can engage in complex motor sequences for problem-solving. The child learns to move away from the furniture and walk across the room, and eventually he or she can play with a toy while standing or walking.

Although professionals discuss the emergence of postural control from a head-to-foot, and trunk-to-extremities direction, it is clear from watching young children that they experiment with postural control in all directions simultaneously. A child might hold his or her trunk against the high chair to reach for the fruit chunks on the tray (proximal stability for distal mobility), and later that day might place hands and knees on the floor and rock the shoulders and pelvis back and forth (distal stability for proximal mobility). Children with multiple disabilities frequently lack balance between stability and mobility; this is a significant barrier to the acquisition of postural control for functional performance.

Functional Importance of Typical Sensorimotor System Evolution

The sensorimotor systems support the individual's ability to experience and interact with the environment. The sensory systems transmit information from the environment; this information forms maps of the individual and the surrounding environment. The motor systems use sensory maps to create accurate, smooth, and well-timed movements in response to environmental demands. As the child acquires information, ideas and interests guide sensorimotor experiences; problem-solving activities build the cognitive repertoire but continue to rely on the sensorimotor systems to carry out the intended activities. Typical children acquire and use sensorimotor and cognitive skills systematically through ongoing experimentation with sensory input, movements, and their consequences.

The ongoing experimentation processes of young children enable them to learn to socialize, communicate, eat, dress, complete personal hygiene, learn, and play. The sensorimotor systems support these functional life tasks by providing the mechanisms through which the child experiences and acts on the environment in specified ways (Dunn, 1991a). When the sensorimotor systems are disrupted due to disease or trauma, the child has difficulty developing the ability to perform functional life tasks because the experimentation process is disrupted.

ATYPICAL SENSORIMOTOR SKILL ACQUISITION AND USE

Major Features of Atypical Skill Acquisition and Use

Children with multiple disabilities must acquire functional skills even though their sensorimotor systems operate differently. Although each child demonstrates an individual pattern of performance strengths and deficits, several characteristics of atypical sensorimotor skill acquisition and use are commonly observed.

Muscle Tone Is Abnormal   Muscle tone is the underlying tension of muscles; due to insults to the central nervous system (CNS), it is common for children with multiple disabilities to display abnormal muscle tone (Campbell, 1987a). Tone can be lower or higher than the expected range (see the following section). Since muscle tone underlies the capacity of muscles to act (Campbell, 1987a), abnormal tone interferes with task performance.

Primitive Reflexes Persist   Primitive reflexes are those movement patterns that occur automatically when a particular stimulus is present. For example, the asymmetrical tonic neck reflex is generated by movement of the head to the side (chin to shoulder) and causes increased extensor muscle tone in the limbs on the face side, and increased flexor tone in the limbs on the skull side. Many reflexes act on the sensorimotor system in the first months of life; their purpose is to provide a mechanism through which the infant can begin having experiences in the environment.

It is common for primitive reflexive patterns of movement to continue in children with multiple disabilities (Scherzer & Tscharnuter, 1982). Instead of the child gaining control over his or her own movement patterns, these primitive patterns of movement frequently persist. This means that attempts at functional performance can be interrupted by an obligatory reaction from a primitive reflex pattern. For example, a child is working to pick up objects and place them in a container in front of him. The influence of the asymmetrical tonic neck reflex may cause the child to knock the materials off the table when he looks to the side to find out who is laughing in the room. Interruptions in task performance such as these can be difficult to manage, because the child may become discouraged or lose interest. When primitive reflexes tend to predominate, tasks can be structured to minimize their interference with task performance.

Postural Control and Movement Are Difficult   Postural control depends on the ability to grade movements across the entire range of joint and muscle capacity. Children with multiple disabilities do not have the sensorimotor resources to experiment with body adaptations to environmental demands. They become fixed in particular positions and are held there either by the force of gravity or by the tension in the muscles. Movement quality is also limited by these same factors, which decrease efficiency or effectiveness of movements. Since postural control underlies the ability to interact with objects and persons in the environment, learning experiences sometimes become limited when postural control is poor.

Early Positioning and Handling Problems Can Lead to Orthopedic Changes   The limitations in the repertoire of movements and positions the child can acquire and use independently can also lead to constitutional changes in the child's body. Joints and muscles can become stiff, and ultimately be unable to move in the full range possible. Bony prominences can be present due to lack of muscle and tissue bulk, and can themselves become sources of skin breakdown and infection. Many of the intervention techniques that facilitate postural control for functional movement also serve to prevent or limit the effects of these orthopedic changes on the child's ability to function.

Functional Skill Development Is Interrupted The most important global characteristic of children with multiple disabilities is their difficulty acquiring and using functional life skills. They require specific and individually designed strategies to learn to use their sensorimotor and cognitive systems for functional performance. The goals set for other children are equally applicable to these children, and include participation in daily care routines such as attention to personal hygiene, dressing, eating, and in interactional activities such as those related to socialization and communication.

Classification Systems for Children with Disabilities

There are several ways to classify the problems of children with multiple disabilities. They may be classified by the particular systems that are affected, by medical diagnoses, by intellectual status, or by functional limitations. When considering a sensorimotor perspective, classifications are most frequently based on particular diagnoses and functional issues.

Classification of Cerebral Palsy Cerebral palsy is the most common medical diagnosis for children with multiple disabilities. Cerebral palsy is a nonprogressive central nervous system (CNS) disorder that affects motor performance. Specific patterns of motor performance have characteristic behavioral manifestations and are associated with particular areas of the brain. Other disabilities are frequently present with cerebral palsy, including visual abnormalities, hearing and speech difficulties, seizures, mental retardation, learning disabilities, and socioemotional problems (Scherzer & Tscharnuter, 1982).

Classically, cerebral palsy has been categorized by motor characteristics and by involved body parts (Scherzer & Tscharnuter, 1982). Table 2.2 presents general definitions of the terms for each. Motor characteristics include spasticity, athetosis, ataxia, rigidity, and hypotonia (Campbell, 1990). Spastic cerebral palsy is the most common type of motor dysfunction; *spasticity* can be defined as increased muscle tone or stiffness in the muscles, sometimes referred to as hypertonus (hyper means high; tonus means tone). *Athetosis* is characterized by continuous, uncontrolled movements of the limbs, hands, and feet. Athetoid movements have a writhing quality, and are usually visible both during activity and at rest. *Ataxia* refers to movements characterized by poor balance and coordination. The individual with ataxia has more pronounced difficulty when trying to perform a specific movement (e.g., taking a step, reaching for a glass) than when at rest. An individual might also display *rigidity,* in which muscle tone is severely rigid, that is hypertonic, interfering with any movement by the individual or by a caretaker. *Hypotonia* is characterized by decreased muscle tension, which interferes with postural alignment; the joints are excessively mobile (i.e., hypermobile in range of motion), and it is difficult

Table 2.2.   Terms used in the diagnosis of cerebral palsy

Term	Definition
Muscle status	
Spasticity	Stiffness or constant tension in the muscles; sometimes called hypertonus
Athetosis	Writhing movements within the muscles; movements can be seen during tasks and at rest
Ataxia	Uncoordinated movements, especially during activities requiring balance and equilibrium; most noticeable during task performance
Rigidity	Extremely high muscle tone (hypertonicity); it is even difficult for caregivers to move body parts
Hypotonia	Low muscle tone; difficulty moving body parts against the force of gravity
Limb involvement	
Quadriplegia	Involvement of all four extremities
Hemiplegia	Involvement of the arm and leg on one body side
Diplegia	More serious involvement of the legs than the arms

for the individual to move against gravity because the weight of the body part is much greater than the power of the muscle.

Professionals also refer to particular patterns of limb involvement in cerebral palsy. The term plegia means paralysis, or loss of functional ability. *Quadriplegia* refers to involvement of all four limbs. *Hemiplegia* refers to involvement of the arm and leg on one side of the body; hence, a child can have a right or left hemiplegia. *Diplegia* applies to more serious involvement in the lower extremities than in the upper extremities. Because the motor involvement and the body part involvement refer to different characteristics of the same disorder, a child's diagnosis typically includes both references (e.g., a child has spastic quadriplegic cerebral palsy).

Classification for Intervention Planning   Campbell and Forsyth (1990) have created a system for classifying impaired or delayed posture and movement skill acquisition and use in young children with CNS dysfunction. Rather than relying on particular medical diagnoses, their system addresses problems that are the focus of the intervention planning process. They consider the following factors when creating their classification system: integrity of muscle tone, the relationship between body alignment and performance of motor skills, patterns of delayed skill acquisition, and atypical performance of posture and movement skills. Three of the classifications (Type I: hypotonia present in combination with genetic disorders, prematurity, or other medical complications; Type V: spastic diplegia; and Type VI: hemiplegia) describe children who are *not* candidates for programs serving individuals with severe and multiple disabilities. The other four classifications include children who *are* likely candidates for these programs.

Type II includes children with severe hypotonia. These children have a very difficult time moving any body parts against the force of gravity, and so are unable to move with any frequency. Lack of movement leads to significant delays in skill acquisition, and eventually can contribute to other problems such as contractures (the tissues surrounding the joints become shortened and inflexible, preventing movement or change in position). Professionals who work in the area of multiple disabilities will have children with severe hypotonia in their programs. It is important to create intervention strategies that compensate for the child's inability to move body parts (e.g., through good positioning, see Chapter 3) so that the child can engage in cognitive and language tasks.

Children who are characteristic of Type III classification have decreased muscle tone in the trunk, and increased muscle tone in the extremities. Because of the increased muscle tone in the extremities, these children can position themselves, but their positioning prohibits other interactions (e.g., if the child uses arms to hold up in sitting, then the child cannot play with a toy or eat because the arms and hands are occupied). Children in this category may display ataxia, athetosis, or overall spasticity as they grow older. These children are also likely to develop deformities due to lack of functional movement patterns. Intervention planning for this group facilitates functional performance by providing external support for certain body parts so that other body parts can be used to engage persons and objects in the environment. For example, a seat can be designed to support the trunk and head so the child can reach for a communication board.

Type IV includes children who have hypertonia throughout the body (spastic quadriplegia). It is difficult for these children to move; when they do move, spasticity is involved in the movement, so their condition affects both the rate and the quality of movement. Skill acquisition is delayed and these children frequently develop compensatory patterns of movement. They can develop contractures and deformities as they grow older. Children with spastic quadriplegia can also have other complications. Intervention addresses the ability to move body parts in functional patterns. As these children grow, intervention also includes compensatory strategies to minimize the interference of spasticity, so they can use acquired movements to interact with the environment.

Type VII includes children with severe and multiple disabilities. They may have significantly increased or decreased tone, and have additional visual and/or auditory problems (see Chapter 4) or other disabilities. These children have difficulty with producing and using movement to engage the environment, which also results in poor rates of performance, additionally affecting skill acquisition. Because these children are unable to engage the environment with even simple movement schemata (e.g., looking, reaching), cognitive and language areas can also be affected due to lack of experiences. Intervention planning must be multifaceted and must address functional performance within naturally occurring opportunities; this facilitates skill acquisition, which is supported by environmental cues.

Functional Manifestations of
Atypical Sensorimotor Skill Acquisition and Use

When serving children with multiple disabilities, caregivers must focus attention on the many factors that contribute to the pattern of their performance. Their difficulties with sensorimotor functions interfere with both caregiver routines and the children's ability to participate in daily life tasks, including handling, diaper changing, bathing, eating, dressing, and personal hygiene. Each of these activities requires variability and adaptability of movement in response to environmental demands, and this is the central problem for children with multiple disabilities. Team members recognize the components of these tasks, and create interventions that maximize functional performance and minimize the interference of the sensorimotor problems. The cognitive components of the above tasks are also a factor in successful performance. Socialization and communication are cognitive processes that rely heavily on the sensorimotor systems for both information and mechanisms to respond. As with other daily life tasks, plans are created to address all aspects of the activity and the children's skills and limitations.

APPLICATION OF KNOWLEDGE OF SENSORIMOTOR SYSTEMS TO THE NEEDS OF CHILDREN WITH MULTIPLE DISABILITIES

Service Provision Models and Approaches Used by Therapists

Service Provision Models   Educationally related and early intervention services require a wide range of service provision options to meet the divergent needs of children and their families (Dunn, 1988, 1989, 1991b). Historically, occupational and physical therapists have employed a *direct service* model of providing services to address sensorimotor needs. In this situation, the therapist creates an individualized intervention plan and carries out the programming with the individual in a one-to-one interaction. In addition to a direct service model, therapists can provide monitoring and consultation (American Occupational Therapy Association, 1990).

In a *monitoring* model of service provision, the therapist creates an intervention plan to meet the child's needs and supervises someone else in the routine implementation of the plan (American Occupational Therapy Association, 1989; Dunn & Campbell, 1991). The therapist remains responsible for the plan, adaptations that are necessary, and program outcomes. The therapist and the teacher meet regularly to ensure that procedures are carried out in a safe, consistent manner and to answer questions. This is a useful service provision option since many therapeutic opportunities occur throughout the week, and therapists are not available to be with a specific child all the time to take advantage of these opportunities. It is most common for monitored (or supervised) programs to address positioning, handling, carrying, eating, self-care, and other activities of daily living. For example, a team has determined that eating independently is a goal for a particular student. The occupational therapist determines that a physical guidance procedure will enable the child to move the spoon to the mouth, and oral motor activities will improve the child's ability to eat the food off the spoon. The therapist and teacher meet during mealtime so that the teacher can learn the procedures, and then they meet twice a month to adjust programming strategies and refine procedures as the child acquires eating skills.

Consultation occurs when the therapist uses discipline expertise to address the needs of another adult on the intervention team (e.g., teacher) (American Occupational Therapy Association, 1990). The therapist and the teacher create intervention plans using their collective knowledge of the child and the situation. The therapist provides consultative services when he or she adjusts task demands to enable task performance, adapts environmental conditions to improve integration, alters materials to address specific strengths and needs, creates optimal postural conditions, establishes movement parameters within the educational environment, and instructs the classroom personnel about specific methods that can be used to improve learning (Dunn & Campbell, 1991).

When teachers work on teams with occupational and physical therapists, they can expect to see all service provision models in operation within their classrooms. Children with multiple disabilities require multifaceted strategies to produce successful outcomes; this includes the expertise of many disciplines. A wider range of service provision options ensures that the children's entire environment is therapeutic, instead of providing therapy during only isolated portions of the day. Many of the services provided by therapists will be incorporated into the curriculum routine; this provides opportunities for practice and reinforcement in naturally occurring situations. It is sometimes necessary to isolate children from the natural environment (e.g., when a child needs to concentrate on acquiring a new skill, or when the procedure is disruptive to ongoing classroom activities). In these situations, therapists provide a specific rationale for isolating children from the natural environment for services (Dunn & Campbell, 1991).

Service Provision Approaches A therapist may also choose various service provision approaches, including prevention intervention, remediation, and compensation (Dunn et al., 1989). The therapist considers the child's status, environmental conditions, and team priorities when selecting an approach to a particular problem.

A *prevention intervention* approach is used when the team wishes to intervene to prevent problems that may arise in the future. For children with multiple disabilities, a prevention intervention approach might be used to prevent the occurrence of later orthopedic deformities. The therapist might design positioning strategies to be implemented throughout the day, and teach the classroom staff to work on range of motion prior to particular activities.

The therapist selects a *remediation* approach when the problem can be at least partially corrected, and the intervention results in improved functional performance. Therapists have chosen a remedial approach in working with children to develop head control, trunk control, reach, and grasp. These basic motor patterns underlie all functional activities; if they can be at least partially corrected, the child will have increased independence. Therapists have particular expertise to address sensorimotor skill acquisition and use, and they contribute this knowledge to team strategies.

Children with multiple disabilities also have problems that persist and interfere with functional performance. In these cases, a *compensatory* approach is appropriate. The therapist designs strategies that neutralize the effects of the problem, and therefore enable the child to engage in activities. For example, a child with severe hypotonia is unable to hold body parts up against gravity; this problem interferes with the child's ability to interact with persons and objects in the environment. The therapist creates strategies that provide external support for the head and trunk (to compensate for excessively low muscle tone) so the child can see others easily for communication and so that the arms and hands are in a proper position to play with toys on the table.

Therapists may select all the service provision approaches within a comprehensive program for a child with multiple disabilities. It is important for the team to discuss these possibilities so that everyone is working toward the same outcomes; approaches that are at cross purposes are not in the child's best interests. Table 2.3 presents examples of activities using these service provision models and approaches.

Typical Intervention Strategies Used by Therapists

Occupational and physical therapists employ many strategies when they create interventions for children with multiple disabilities. These strategies are based on theories and frames of reference developed within their respective fields, knowledge from other fields, and interventions originally designed for different populations that are adapted to meet particular needs. It is useful for all team members to understand the bases for these intervention choices, so that more collaborative strategies can be created. The primary tenets of the most common intervention strategies are introduced here, with a discussion of their application to the needs of children with multiple disabilities.

Neurodevelopmental Treatment (NDT)   Neurodevelopmental treatment (NDT) addresses the movement problems of children with neurological dysfunction. The therapist identifies the posture and movement problems and implements procedures to decrease the effects of abnormal muscle tone, and to increase the normal, balanced actions of muscles for functional movement (Bobath, 1963; Campbell, 1990). Campbell (1990) summarizes the goals of NDT: to analyze dysfunction in order to identify primary problems with posture and movement; to implement facilitation and inhibition procedures to es-

Table 2.3. Combined use of service provision models and approaches

	Direct	Monitor	Consult
Remedial	Improve head control for looking.	Supervise all adults to facilitate tone for reaching.	Identify heavy objects that can be incorporated into classroom tasks to increase proprioceptive input.
Compensatory	Fabricate a splint to enable grasp.	Supervise feeding program that minimizes time required to eat so student can socialize with peers.	Provide an adapted seat that controls trunk position so child can socialize.
Prevention intervention	Facilitate upright posture to prevent delays in standing and walking.	Supervise teacher in use of oral facilitation techniques when feeding the preschooler, to prevent difficulties in lip closure during eating and talking.	Teach staff a range of motion program to prevent deformities.

Adapted from Dunn, W., & Campbell, P. (1991). Designing pediatric service provision. In W. Dunn (Ed.), *Pediatric occupational therapy: Facilitating effective service provision*. Thorofare, NJ: SLACK, Inc., p. 146; used with permission.

tablish postural stability and functional movement; to teach sensorimotor procedures to others so problems are managed across situations; to select and use equipment that will support postural control and functional movement; and to prevent abnormal patterns from persisting and creating secondary changes (e.g., tightness, deformities).

The therapist identifies posture and movement problems by observing the child in various situations. Stern and Gorga (1988) suggest that one observe to determine the child's response to dynamic interactions (e.g., Is the child frightened? Does the child stiffen with movements?) with a critical eye for the child's ability to change. The therapist records the motor characteristics, with particular attention to the postural stability patterns used, and the form and function of the movements (Campbell, 1990). For example, a child with hypertonicity may sit without support, but the therapist may notice that the pelvis is poorly positioned to support an aligned trunk and head. Proper alignment of the trunk and head enables the child to see objects and persons in front and facilitates interactions. This child might also reach for food on the plate (movement with a function), but may take a long time, and have poor wrist and hand position for picking up the food (form of the movement). In this example, the child has the functional aspects of the movement, but lacks the form to succeed. Proper form within functional movement might be obtained with the application of NDT techniques. Therapists guard against the attainment of proper form without corresponding functional application of the movement.

The therapist uses a wide range of facilitation and inhibition techniques when working from an NDT frame of reference. These techniques are applied to affect muscle tone and improve patterns of postural control and movement. The sequence begins with preparation (Campbell, 1990) to establish body alignment and to decrease interfering muscle tension (i.e., hypertonicity). During this phase, the therapist applies deep pressure to body surfaces, either with hands, or via the supporting surface (pushing the body into the mat, floor, or chair also produces pressure on the body part touching the surface) to obtain and maintain proper relationship of body parts. This provides an optimal base of support for functional movements.

Next, the therapist provides intervention to facilitate desired muscle actions and inhibit unwanted patterns (Campbell, 1990). Since the children who are the primary focus of NDT cannot move independently, the therapist moves the child through small, subtle movement patterns such as body rotation to facilitate adaptations to postural demands. The therapist then incorporates these patterns into functional routines. For example, if the child has achieved rotational postural shifts with the arms forward, the team then uses this skill to begin using an augmentative communication board.

Therapists have primarily used NDT within a direct service model. However, NDT contains many useful principles that can be applied to all aspects of the child's life. It is important that children with multiple disabilities be positioned, handled, and moved in consistent ways to minimize the effects of their sensorimotor problems on their ability to function. Therapists who are trained in the use of NDT principles can apply these principles to school routines. A therapist might supervise the classroom staff as they facilitate an upright, aligned posture before a cognitive task. The therapist could also consult with classroom staff to create functional positioning and handling strategies for the child throughout the school day (see Chapter 3 for examples).

Although therapists have reported clinically that NDT produces positive changes in children's performance, research has not supported these claims (Harris, 1988; Stern & Gorga, 1988). Research is needed that includes both adequate amounts of intervention and appropriate outcome measures to document the clinical reports of therapists.

Sensory Integration (SI)   Sensory integration is a neurobiologically based theoretical model used by occupational and physical therapists. Sensory integration theory hypothesizes that individuals develop skills through a process of receiving and interpreting sensory stimuli from the environment and creating adaptive responses to those stimuli (Ayres, 1980). An adaptive response is an appropriate action toward or reaction to an environmental stimulus. Adaptive responses themselves create additional sensory information (feedback) that the CNS assimilates for future task performance. When occupational and physical therapists use a sensory integrative approach to problem-solving, they consider the sensory qualities of the tasks, the environment, and the child's interactions with others and objects. They examine those sensory qualities that are enabling or blocking the production of an adaptive response.

Intervention using a sensory integrative approach can incorporate all of the service provision models listed earlier. In a consultative model, the therapist and the consultee (usually the teacher) create environmental conditions and intervention strategies that increase the chances that an adaptive response will occur. The therapist and the teacher may collaborate to design a learning activity that incorporates sensory integrative knowledge into the task. For example, the therapist has learned from assessment that a certain child pays attention to tasks longer when receiving a more intense form of vestibular input. The teacher and therapist decide to place the child in a prone position during a small group activity because this will increase vestibular input (and the new head position will provide additional input).

The therapist can address the sensory aspects of movement and interaction with the environment when using a direct service model of intervention. For example, the team has determined that functional performance will be enhanced if the child can sit independently. The therapist places the child in prone (face down), supine (face up), and sitting positions on a large inflated ball; they work on looking and reaching to the front and sides while the therapist slowly rocks the ball in various directions. These activities enhance vestibular, proprioceptive, and tactile input for body scheme and improved postural control. As the child acquires particular skills, the therapist incorporates these skills into classroom routines.

In some cases, the child may benefit from consistent implementation of a specific intervention strategy, but the therapist cannot be present consistently to provide the intervention. In these cases, the therapist may need to use a monitoring model of intervention to ensure that the process of intervention is carried out in a consistent manner. For example, the team determines that the child can learn to eat independently; the child has hypersensitivity to textures in and around the mouth, which interferes with eating. The therapist can contribute to the daily eating routine by designing an intervention strategy to decrease the child's sensitivity (e.g., by using firm touch pressure around the mouth), and to increase oral-motor control simultaneously. The therapist shows the teacher and aide how to implement the procedure, and observes during lunchtime to ensure that the procedures are carried out safely and consistently. The classroom staff carry out the program daily as part of the child's routine. The therapist might also teach parents the same technique to make home mealtime less stressful.

Sensory integrative approaches were originally designed for children with educational handicaps such as learning disabilities. Since its core principles are based upon nervous system functions that are well-documented in the neuroscience literature (Cool, 1987; Dunn, 1988, 1991a, 1991c), many professionals have clinically extended the use of this theory to persons with other disabilities, including children with multiple disabilities. There is face validity to this practice, since the need for nervous system information is universal to all human beings. Studies are needed to clearly validate that it is acceptable to apply sensory integration principles to the needs of persons with clearly documented CNS problems. For example, it is still unknown whether significant insults to the CNS change the operation of the sensorimotor processes in some primary way such that the application of these principles to these persons' needs becomes inappropriate.

Developmental Frame of Reference   Professionals understand the typical evolution of skills from a developmental perspective (Rogers & D'Eugenio, 1981). Persons who use a developmental frame of reference operate under the assumption that skill acquisition occurs in children with disabilities in a way similar to that in typical children. Interventions are designed to facilitate the acquisition of the predetermined set of skills found in developmental tests and curriculum materials. Skills at earlier levels in development are considered general prerequisites to skills at later levels. Interventions address mastery of earlier skills for the ability to then acquire the later skills.

It is difficult to employ a developmental perspective with children who have multiple disabilities. These children do not have the abilities of typical children to interact with the environment, and so cannot acquire skills in the same manner. If one were to work with a child with multiple disabilities on a skill, remaining at one developmental level until the child used the skill in a typical manner, this child would never learn functional skills. Other approaches are better suited to the needs of children with multiple disabilities. Significant adaptations in tasks and performance standards are necessary to enable children to engage in functional tasks.

Adaptive Approaches   It is also common for therapists to select adaptive strategies in intervention planning for children with multiple disabilities. Adaptation occurs when the professionals identify the child's limitations and create alternative strategies that will support successful task performance (Rainforth & York, 1987; York & Rainforth, 1987). Baumgart et al. (1982) suggest that there are four types of adaptations: 1) personal help, 2) skill/activity modification, 3) use of an adaptive device, and 4) environmental modification.

Teachers and therapists participate in adaptive approaches when they create programs for children with multiple disabilities. It is important for persons with divergent expertise to join forces, because one frame of reference will not provide adequate information to create the wide range of adaptations necessary to facilitate participation. Chapter 8 discusses the adaptive strategies in detail.

Joint Mobilization Techniques Joint mobilization techniques have been documented in the literature for many centuries. They include passive movements applied to the joint and surrounding soft tissues in a specific manner to restore active range of motion to the joint (Saunders, 1985). Therapists apply joint mobilization techniques to those joints that are hypomobile (i.e., the joint is tight, unable to move through the normal range of motion). The intimate connection between the joint space and the muscles makes it important to consider intervention to both structures (Cyriax & Cyriax, 1983; Saunders, 1985; Wadsworth, 1988). Saunders (1985) states "a muscle cannot be fully rehabilitated if its joint is not free to move, and conversely, a muscle cannot move a joint which is not free to move . . ." (p. 196). The therapist employs a combined mechanical and neurophysiological approach to relieve pain, produce relaxation, increase joint range, and gain muscle control when reflexive activity predominates.

These techniques most commonly have been applied to acute injuries, but some therapists will use joint mobilization in their overall programs for children with multiple disabilities. The techniques are generally incorporated into the direct service components of the programs, since the techniques require special knowledge and skills. As with any of the traditional therapeutic interventions, therapists also design strategies to incorporate the improved joint integrity into functional daily tasks.

Myofascial Release Techniques Myofascial release is a therapeutic technique that relies on the therapist's skills to stimulate the muscles and related tissues in a specified manner (Manheim & Lavett, 1989; Travell & Simons, 1983). The techniques and mechanisms of myofascial release are not completely understood, but clinical trials have shown improvements in specific cases (Travell & Simons, 1983). Proponents suggest that myofascial release is safer and more comfortable for the individual than traditional stretching techniques used by therapists in the past (Manheim & Lavett, 1989). The goal of myofascial release is to remove restrictions to movement and enable effective postural alignment.

The therapist trained in myofascial release techniques palpates (feels the integrity of muscles, skin, and joint tissues) the body areas to determine where restricted movements may be occurring. Then the therapist gently stretches along the lines of the muscle fibers, and through this process, the muscles and related tissues (i.e., fascia-tissue that surrounds body structures) let go, or relax (Manheim & Lavett, 1989). Application of the techniques looks like massage. This then allows the therapist to align or realign body parts for better postural positioning and control.

Myofascial release techniques are applied by therapists who have had special training; the therapist selects a direct service provision model and a re-medial approach. It is important to remember, however, that myofascial release only prepares the system; the therapists and teachers must always incorporate this preparedness into functional life tasks for children with multiple disabili-ties. Postural alignment alone is not an adequate goal for a child's program; postural alignment enables the child to have opportunities to interact and to develop basic movement sequences.

Craniosacral Therapy   The craniosacral system is described as a phys-iological system of membranes that connects the bones and related structures (Upledger & Vredevoogd, 1983). Proponents of craniosacral therapy believe that these structures form an internal hydraulic system that either supports or prohibits movements. Typically there is thought to be a craniosacral rhythm affecting the entire body; when this rhythm is disrupted, restricted physiologi-cal motion is said to be present (Upledger & Vredevoogd, 1983).

Upledger and Vredevoogd (1983) describe the typical craniosacral therapy techniques as "non-intrusive and indirect" (p. 21). They are not referring to service provision models as described above; they use the terms direct and indi-rect to describe the particular methods used to address the craniosacral prob-lem. The therapist uses light touch to assist the hydraulic system and therefore improve the body's internal environment. It is most common for the application of this technique to occur in the neck or pelvis regions. At this writing this approach is being used less frequently in pediatric practice, but increasingly therapists are pursuing training in this specialized set of techniques. They are applied in a direct service model of service provision, most often with a remedi-ation approach. As with myofascial release, this is a preparatory technique, and must be used in combination with functional skill acquisition and use.

APPRECIATION FOR ALTERNATIVE
FRAMES OF REFERENCE IN INTERVENTION

It is sometimes confusing to other professionals that therapists have a variety of frames of reference for assessment and intervention. However, this range of viewpoints is comparable to the approaches used in education. Some educators advocate the use of behavioral approaches to address children's needs, while others prefer cognitive or developmental approaches. As in education, multiple viewpoints are not incompatible with each other; they offer alternative ways of solving problems, and frequently can be combined to create integrated assess-ment and intervention strategies (Campbell, 1987a; Dunn, 1991b). When edu-cators and therapists combine their viewpoints, many more options present themselves. Therapists have expertise that enables the student to perform the skills properly, while teachers contribute knowledge about the functional use of the skills in selected activities (Campbell, 1987a).

For example, a child may need to learn to grasp a cup, bring it to the mouth, and take a drink. There are several ways of viewing this situation to determine an effective strategy. Table 2.4 provides an example of the issues that team members with various perspectives might raise when assessing this child. None of these perspectives addresses the situation completely, yet each contrib-

Table 2.4. Parameters considered by various team members for a child who needs to learn to drink from a cup independently

Frame of reference/ perspective	Factors considered within the various perspectives
Neurodevelopmental	What is the status of muscle tone (e.g., hypertonus; hypotonus)?
	Does muscle tone interfere with movement (e.g., tightness restricts movement; low tone prohibits child from moving)?
	What is the base of support (e.g., legs, pelvis, back supporting body weight when sitting)?
	How is the trunk aligned for the task?
	How can I support functional movement (e.g., use facilitation or inhibition)?
Sensory integrative	Does the child notice the stimulus (e.g., voice command, cup of liquid)?
	How does the child respond to positioning (e.g., light touch, touch pressure)?
	What are characteristics of cup surface?
	How does the child respond to the surface (on hand; on lips)?
	Will the grasping pattern further enable adaptive responses, or will it interfere with movement (e.g., the tension for gripping may enhance extensor muscle tone; then the child cannot get the cup to the mouth)?
Behavioral	Is the child interested in drinking from cup?
	Does the child like the liquid being used?
	Is the child thirsty?
	How does the child know it's time to drink (e.g., what cues are used—verbal prompt, physical prompt)?
Cognitive	Does the child understand what he is supposed to do?
	Does the child have the perceptual skills to accomplish the task (e.g., can he find the cup on the table with other eating utensils)?
	Can the child generalize skills from one cup to another, from one setting to another?

utes vital information for the intervention planning process. Team members would consider all of these issues in light of multiple observations and data sources to determine the best approach for the particular child.

Team members can use a hypothesis testing approach to program planning for children with multiple disabilities. In this approach, the team members analyze the problem situation, determine all possible barriers to successful performance, and then create a plan based on only one factor at a time. This process enables the team members to discover successful and unsuccessful adaptations; this information is useful for future intervention planning and environmental design.

A teacher observes that a particular child is more successful scooping chocolate pudding than vanilla pudding onto the spoon. The teacher and the therapist hypothesize that either the chocolate pudding is easier to see on the beige plate, or the child may prefer chocolate. To test their hypotheses, they serve vanilla pudding on a red plate at the next meal and discover that the child scoops the vanilla pudding easily. In this example, the team members created a plan based on one characteristic of the activity—the contrast between the colors of the food item and the plate. If they had changed both the visual contrast and the flavor at the same time, they still would not have known which variable was causing the problem, nor would they have been able to generalize their knowledge about this student to other situations. However, having tested their hypotheses systematically, they have discovered information that can be used in future program plans. For example, the teacher now selects brightly colored objects to place on the child's white lap tray when they practice reaching and grasping, and other team members have designed highly contrasting plates for the child's augmentative communication board.

ANALYZING LEARNING SITUATIONS FROM A SENSORIMOTOR PERSPECTIVE

A sensorimotor perspective expands the problem-solving possibilities for educational tasks. Therapists and teachers can collaborate to enrich the life experiences of children with multiple disabilities. This section provides examples of how to apply sensorimotor knowledge to children's needs within natural environments. (See also Chapters 3 and 8 for additional information, especially in regard to motor issues.)

Creating Interventions Based on Sensory Qualities

Therapists and other team members can use several methods to identify the child's sensory processing abilities. When children have multiple disabilities, it is best to rely on skilled observations to obtain information. Professionals infer the integrity of the sensory systems by observing and recording motoric behaviors (Dunn, 1991a). Professionals identify the child's tolerance, preference, and need for particular sensory experiences during routine life tasks and while interacting with the child. For example, while lifting and moving a child across the room for a new activity, the teacher has a natural opportunity to determine the child's response to vestibular stimulation (the child's head will be changing position, direction of movement, and speed of movement during this experience) and tactile stimulation (the teacher will be touching the child's skin with his hands and body as he carries her). The teacher can note the child's response to these experiences; the child may smile when being moved, indicating pleasure, or may become irritable when touched. Table 2.5 provides examples of observations that can be made during routine life tasks that may indicate the integrity of the sensory system.

The professionals accumulate information across many activities to confirm the meaning of the responses. In the previous example, the child who smiles may be responding to the movement, may be happy to be held by the teacher, or may have been bored with the past activity and is anticipating a new task. Irritability may indicate fear of change of any sort, displeasure with movement rather than touch, or unhappiness about being interrupted from an interesting task. Professionals must make multiple observations to determine the relationship between responses and situational characteristics. The team can then systematically test the hypotheses in additional situations.

Sensory processing can also be inferred by examination of the sensory qualities of tasks and environments. Figure 2.2 provides a worksheet to assist professionals as they examine the sensory properties of functional tasks. Each sensory system is listed in the first column; the second column contains key descriptors for each sensory system. Refer to Table 2.1 for additional information about these descriptors.

When using the worksheet, select a task or routine and write the selection in the upper left hand section. Next, consider how a typical individual under typical circumstances would perform the task in a routine manner. Mark the sensory qualities that would be activated during task performance in the third column of the worksheet. If the task or routine is more complex, it is helpful to break it down into components. Three columns (A, B, C) are provided for this possibility; the task components can be listed at the bottom left of the worksheet.

One then considers the specific environment in which the task will take place in the next section of the worksheet. Although typical performance of face washing occurs in one's bathroom at home, children who are learning to wash their faces at school frequently perform this task in the classroom or school bathroom with other children and adults present. These changes can affect particular children, and so must be considered in the analysis. If the environment is a familiar one, the boxes can simply be marked; brief descriptions can be written for less familiar environments. Figure 2.3 displays a completed form for face washing.

Table 2.5.   Examples of observable behaviors that indicate difficulty with sensory processing during daily life tasks

Sensory system	Personal hygiene	Dressing	Eating	Homemaking	School/work	Play
Somatosensory	Withdraws from splashing water Pushes washcloth/towel away Cries when hair is washed & dried Makes face when toothpaste gets on lips, tongue Tenses when bottom is wiped after toileting	Tolerates a narrow range of clothing items Prefers tight clothing More irritable with loose textured clothing Cries during dressing Pulls at hats, head gear, accessories	Tolerates food at only one temperature Gags with textured food or utensils in mouth Winces when face is wiped Hand extends & avoids objects & surfaces (finger food, utensils)	Avoids participation in tasks that are wet, dirty Seeks to remove batter that falls on arms	Cries when tape or glue gets on skin Overreacts to pats, hugs; avoids these actions Tolerates only one pencil, one type of paper, only wooden objects Hands extend when attempting to type	Selects a narrow range of toys, textures similar Can't hold on to toys/objects Rubs toys on face, arms Mouths objects

62

Proprioception	Can't lift objects that are heavier (a new bar of soap) Can't change head position to use sink & mirror in same task	Can't support heavier items (belt with buckle, shoes) Fatigues prior to task completion Misses when placing arm or leg in clothing	Uses external support to eat (propping) Tires before completing meal Can't provide force to cut meat Tires before completely eating foods that need to be chewed	Drops equipment (broom) Uses external support (leaning on counter to stir batter) Difficulty pouring a glass of milk	Drops books Becomes uncomfortable in a particular position Hook limbs on furniture to obtain support Moves arm, hand in repetitive patterns (self-stimulatory)	Unable to sustain movements during play Tires before game is complete Drops heavy parts of a toy/game

(continued)

Table 2.5. (continued)

Sensory system	Personal hygiene	Dressing	Eating	Homemaking	School/work	Play
Vestibular	Becomes disoriented when bending over the sink Falls when trying to participate in washing lower extremities	Gets overly excited/distracted after bending down to assist in putting on socks Cries when moved around a lot during dressing	Holds head stiffly in one position during mealtime Gets distracted from meal after several head position changes	Avoids leaning to obtain cooking utensil Becomes overly excited after moving around the room to dust	Avoids turning head to look at persons; to find source of a sound After being transported in a wheelchair, more difficult to get on task Moves head in repetitive pattern (self-stimulatory)	Avoids play that includes movement Becomes overly excited or anxious when moving during play Rocks excessively Craves movement activities

Visual					
Can't find utensils on the sink	Can't find buttons on patterned or solid clothing	Misses utensils on the table	Can't locate correct canned item in the pantry	Can't keep place on the page	Trouble with matching, sorting activities
Difficulty spotting desired item in drawer	Overlooks desired shirt in closet or drawer	Has trouble getting foods onto spoon when they are a similar color to the plate	Has difficulty finding cooking utensils in the drawer	Can't locate desired item on communication board	Trouble locating desired toy on cluttered shelf
Misses when applying paste to toothbrush	Misses armhole when donning shirt			Attends excessively to bright or flashing objects	

(continued)

Table 2.5. (continued)

Sensory system	Personal hygiene	Dressing	Eating	Homemaking	School/work	Play
Auditory	Cries when hair dryer is turned on Becomes upset by running water Jerks when toilet flushes	Distracted by clothing that makes noise (crisp cloth, accessories)	Distracted by noise of utensils against each other (spoon in bowl, knife on plate) Can't keep eating when someone talks	Distracted by vacuum cleaner sound Distracted by TV or radio during tasks	Distracted by squeaky wheelchair Intolerant of noise others make in the room Overreacts to door closing Notices toilet flushing down the hall	Play is disrupted by sounds Makes sounds constantly
Olfactory/ Gustatory	Gags at taste of toothpaste Jerks away at smell of soap	Overreacts to clothing when it has been washed in a new detergent	Tolerates a narrow range of foods Becomes upset when certain hot foods are cooking	Becomes upset when house is being cleaned (odors of cleaners)	Overreacts to new person (new smells) Intolerant of scratch-n-sniff stickers Smells everything	Tastes or smells all objects before playing

ROUTINE/TASK SENSORY CHARACTERISTICS		WHAT DOES THE TASK ROUTINE HOLD?			WHAT DOES THE PARTICULAR ENVIRONMENT HOLD?	WHAT ADAPTATIONS ARE LIKELY TO IMPROVE FUNCTIONAL OUTCOME?
		A	B	C		
Somatosensory	light touch (tap, tickle)					
	pain					
	temperature (hot, cold)					
	touch- pressure (hug, pat, grasp)					
	variable					
	duration of stimulus (short, long)					
	body surface contact (small, large)					
	predictable					
	unpredictable					
Vestibular	head position change					
	speed change					
	direction change					
	rotary head movement					
	linear head movement					
	repetitive head movement -rhythmic					
	predictable					
	unpredictable					
Proprioceptive	quick stretch stimulus					
	sustained tension stimulus					
	shifting muscle tension					
Visual	high intensity					
	low intensity					
	high contrast					
	high similarity (low contrast)					
	competitive					
	variable					
	predictable					
	unpredictable					
Auditory	rhythmic					
	variable					
	constant					
	competitive					
	noncompetitive					
	loud					
	soft					
	predictable					
	unpredictable					
Olfactory/ Gustatory	mild					
	strong					
	predictable					
	unpredictable					

Task _____

Components: A = _____
B = _____
C = _____

Figure 2.2. Form for analyzing sensory characteristics of task performance.

ROUTINE/TASK SENSORY CHARACTERISTICS	Washing face	WHAT DOES THE TASK ROUTINE HOLD?			WHAT DOES THE PARTICULAR ENVIRONMENT HOLD? (classroom sink)	WHAT ADAPTATIONS ARE LIKELY TO IMPROVE FUNCTIONAL OUTCOME?
		A	B	C		
Somatosensory	light touch (tap, tickle)	X				Turn water off to decrease splashing
	pain					
	temperature (hot, cold)	X				Try alternative water temperatures
	touch-pressure (hug, pat, grasp)	X				Pat face instead of rubbing cloth on face
	variable	X				Pat large face area
	duration of stimulus (short, long)	L				
	body surface contact (small, large)	L				Try washing one part only; begin with chin area
	predictable	X				
	unpredictable					(NOTE: make sure routine is consistent day to day)
Vestibular	head position change	X				Alter water source so don't have to bend head down (e.g., in a pan or rub)
	speed change					Keep head up so don't have the down-up pattern
	direction change	X				
	rotary head movement					
	linear head movement	X				Keep head up; if need arousal, place items on counter to encourage more head turning
	repetitive head movement -rhythmic					
	predictable					
	unpredictable					
Proprioceptive	quick stretch stimulus					
	sustained tension stimulus	X				Move objects to decrease head control requirements
	shifting muscle tension	X				
Visual	high intensity					
	low intensity					
	high contrast					
	high similarity (low contrast)	X			X Other objects	Use dark wash cloths & light soap; use dark containers on light counter; remove extra items from counter
	competitive	X			X on sink	
	variable				X Counter changes day to day	
	predictable	X				
	unpredictable				X	If arousal is needed, vary placement of items
Auditory	rhythmic	X				Prepare wet cloth; don't have running tap water
	variable	X				Use tub of water instead of running water
	constant					
	competitive					
	noncompetitive	X			X Other students	Move child to the bathroom alone
	loud					
	soft				X Teacher's voice	Provide physical prompts and decrease talking
	predictable	X				
	unpredictable				X Unplanned	
Olfactory/ Gustatory	mild					
	strong	X				If arousal is needed, use strong smelling soap
	predictable	X				
	unpredictable					

Task ____
Components: A = ____
B = ____
C = ____

Figure 2.3. Sample completed form for analyzing sensory characteristics of face washing.

The last column is used to create intervention planning strategies for children who have been unable to engage in the task or routine successfully. Team members consider alterations in task qualities that may facilitate the child's ability to perform the task. For example, a child may react negatively to the terry cloth washcloth; the terry cloth texture may be providing too much arousal/alerting input, causing disruption in task performance. The team may consider other fabrics that would elicit a better discrimination/mapping response during face washing (e.g., cotton cloth or cotton knit).

Table 2.6 summarizes the reasons for targeting various sensory qualities during the intervention process, and provides examples to illustrate their coverage in integrated programming. There is a strong interrelationship among the various sensory qualities. A certain level of arousal is necessary for a child to engage in a functional task, and arousing stimuli can be used to generate an appropriate level of alertness for activities. However, arousal/alerting stimuli can also be disruptive to ongoing task performance; a child who is intent on placing an object into a container can lose postural and movement control when distracted by a slamming door. Discriminating/mapping stimuli are very useful both for facilitating the child's ongoing involvement in a task, and for calming the child who has been overstimulated. However, too much calming input can lead to lethargy and listlessness, prohibiting the child from interacting with others and the environment. Team members collaborate to determine the optimal balance for particular children.

After considering all possible modifications, the team initiates one change at a time (hypothesis testing) to determine which change is most effective. This hypothesis testing model is important for future planning as well; as the child begins to demonstrate a pattern of preferences across activities that facilitate function, those preferences can systematically be built into all classroom tasks and routines to support the child's learning. In the face washing example, team members may generalize their knowledge about textures to clothing selection.

Creating Interventions Based on Motor Qualities

Campbell (1990) suggests that observations of movement qualities include an assessment of muscle tone, postural alignment, the use of compensatory strategies, and identification of present deformities and limitations related to the sensorimotor systems. Although the therapists may evaluate the child for specific motoric involvement, observations within naturally occurring situations is also important. For example, it is only partially useful to know that a child has hypertonia, has poor ability to sit up independently, and can hold his or her head up when supported in sitting. The picture is more complete when the team knows that the hypertonia interferes with the child's attempts to crawl across the room (e.g., the legs become very stiff and extended). It is also helpful to know that positioning adaptations significantly reduce the effects of poor trunk and head control and hypertonus in the arms, enabling the child to both see and

Table 2.6.   Reasons for incorporating various sensory qualities into integrated intervention programs

Sensory system	Arousal/alerting descriptors	Discrimination/mapping descriptors
For all systems	*Unpredictability:* To develop an increasing level of attention to keep the child interested in the task/activity (e.g., change the position of the objects on the child's lap tray during the task).	*Predictability:* To establish the child's ability to anticipate a programming sequence or a salient cue; to decrease possibility to be distracted from a functional task sequence (e.g., use the same routine for diaper changing every time).
Somatosensory	*Light touch:* To increase alertness in a child who is lethargic (e.g., pull cloth from child's face during peek-a-boo). *Pain:* To raise from unconsciousness; to determine ability to respond to noxious stimuli when unconscious (e.g., flick palm of hand or sole of foot briskly). *Temperature:* To establish awareness of stimuli; to maintain attentiveness to task (e.g., use hot foods for spoon eating & cold drink for sucking through a straw). *Variability:* To maintain attention to or interest in the task (e.g., place new texture on cup surface each day so child notices the cup). *Short duration:* To increase arousal for task performance (e.g., tap child on chest before giving directions). *Small body surface contact:* To generate & focus attention on a particular body part (e.g., tap around lips with fingertips before eating task).	*Touch pressure:* To establish & maintain awareness of body parts & body position; to calm a child who has been overstimulated (e.g., provide a firm bear hug). *Long duration:* To enable the child to become familiar, comfortable with the stimulus; to incorporate stimulus into functional skill (e.g., grasping the container to pick it up & pour out contents). *Large body surface contact:* To establish & maintain awareness of body parts & body position; to calm a child who has been overstimulated (e.g., wrap child tightly in a blanket).

(continued)

Table 2.6.   *(continued)*

Sensory system	Arousal/alerting descriptors	Discrimination/mapping descriptors
Vestibular	*Head position change:* To increase arousal for an activity (e.g., position child prone over a wedge). *Speed change:* To maintain adequate alertness for functional task (e.g., vary pace while carrying the child to a new task). *Direction change:* To elevate level of alertness for a functional task (e.g., swing child back & forth in arms prior to positioning him at the table for a task). *Rotary head movement:* To increase arousal prior to functional task (e.g., pick child up from prone [on stomach] facing away to upright facing toward you to position for a new task).	*Linear head movement:* To support establishment of body awareness in space (e.g., carry child around the room in fixed position to explore its features). *Repetitive head movement:* To provide predictable & organizing information; to calm a child who has been overstimulated (e.g., rock the child).
Proprioception	*Quick stretch:* To generate additional muscle tension to support functional tasks (e.g., tap belly muscle of hypotonic muscle while providing physical guidance to grasp).	*Sustained tension:* To enable the muscle to relax, elongate, so body part can be in better position for function (e.g., press firmly across belly muscle while guiding a reaching pattern; add weight to objects being manipulated). *Shifting muscle tension:* To establish functional movement patterns that contain stability & mobility (e.g., prop & reach for a toy; reach, fill, & lift spoon to mouth).

(continued)

Table 2.6.   (continued)

Sensory system	Arousal/alerting descriptors	Discrimination/mapping descriptors
Visual	*High intensity:* To increase opportunity to notice object; to generate arousal for task (e.g., cover blocks with foil for manipulation task). *High contrast:* To enhance possibility of locating the object & maintaining attention to it (e.g., place raisins on a piece of typing paper for prehension activity). *Variability:* To maintain attention to or interest in the task (e.g., play rolling catch with a clear ball that has moveable pieces inside).	*Low intensity:* To allow the visual stimulus to blend with other salient features; to generate searching behaviors, since characteristics are less obvious (e.g., find own cubby hole in back of the room). *High similarity:* To establish more discerning abilities; to develop skills for naturally occurring tasks (e.g., scoop applesauce from beige plate). *Competitive:* To facilitate searching; to increase tolerance for natural life circumstances (e.g., obtain correct tools from equipment bin).
Auditory	*Variability:* To maintain attention to or interest in the task (e.g., play radio station after activating a switch). *High intensity:* To stimulate noticing the person or object; to create proper alerting for task performance (e.g., ring a bell to encourage the child to locate the stimulus).	*Rhythmic:* To provide predictable & organizing information for environmental orientation (e.g., sing a nursery rhyme while physically guiding motions). *Constant:* To provide a foundational stimulus for environmental orientation; especially important when other sensory systems (e.g., vision, vestibular) do not provide orientation (e.g., child recognizes own classroom by fan noise & calms down).

(continued)

Table 2.6. *(continued)*

Sensory system	Arousal/alerting descriptors	Discrimination/mapping descriptors
Auditory *(continued)*		*Competitive:* To facilitate differentiation of salient stimuli; to increase tolerance for natural life circumstances (e.g., after child learns to look when her name is called, conduct activity within busy classroom).
		Noncompetitive: To facilitate focused attention for acquiring a new & difficult skill; to calm a child who has been over stimulated (e.g., move child to quiet room to establish vocalizations).
		Low intensity: To allow the auditory stimulus to blend with other salient features; to generate searching behaviors since stimulus is less obvious (e.g., give child a direction in a normal volume).
Olfactory/ Gustatory	*Strong intensity:* To stimulate arousal for task (e.g., child smells spaghetti sauce at lunch).	*Mild intensity:* To facilitate exploratory behaviors; to stimulate naturally occurring activities (e.g., smell of lunch food is less distinct, so child is encouraged to notice texture, color).

reach for objects in front. Figure 2.4 provides a framework for analyzing the motor components of the performance, which will then facilitate effective program planning.

Motor problems are best addressed within the context of daily activities and with the combined expertise of multiple disciplines (Campbell, 1987a; Rainforth & York, 1987; York & Rainforth, 1987). There are several important considerations in creating integrated programs (Campbell, 1987a). First, the child should be positioned so that the best possible postural alignment is attained. This enables the child to have access to environmental cues and opportunities. Second, the level of support or interference provided by muscle tone should be determined. Both low and high muscle tone can interfere with task performance, as discussed above. Team members must also consider the effects of the child's tone during the activity, because muscle tone can change as the child intends to accomplish a goal. Therapists provide specialized expertise for this consideration (Campbell, 1987a). Third, physical guidance and therapeutic facilitation of the proper movement should be provided (Campbell, 1987b). The first two considerations provide information that is helpful in creating these facilitation strategies. The goal is to provide input to the muscles, joints, and limbs so the child experiences the sensorimotor sequence and can rely on this information to perform the action with decreasing assistance over time. This is an important step because children with multiple disabilities do not know what it feels like to move in and interact with the environment, and so may not be motivated to move or may not understand what the verbal prompt means.

Finally, team members must consider the environmental variables and the context of the task. Children with multiple disabilities may also have visual and/or auditory problems, and so may require objects with a bright color or with a unique sound (refer to Table 2.1 to review the characteristics of each sensory system); children with very low vision may rely more heavily on the somatosensory aspects of objects. When a particular reaching or manipulation pattern is desired, the target objects can be placed in regions in front of or to the side of the child to encourage the optimal motor pattern (see Campbell, 1987a, for good examples). The context also includes knowledge about the child's interests, to ensure that selected activities not only are therapeutic from a sensorimotor and cognitive perspective, but also will keep the child's attention to persisting in acquiring and using the desired skills. There is a delicate balance in programming between therapeutic benefit and the child's interest in the task. A well-designed intervention in which the child will not participate is not going to yield effective outcomes. The final aspect of the context is the reinforcement the child receives for engaging in the task. Activities are graded both to provide an adequate challenge and to ensure success to encourage the child to continue.

Since some of the problems of children with multiple disabilities will prohibit performance of functional tasks or even the essential skills necessary for

Routine/Task Motor Characteristics		General Status of Individual	Status During This Task	What adaptations are likely to improve functional outcome?
Muscle tone	Hypertonic			
	Hypotonic			
	Other Pattern			
	Reflexive Patterns			
Physical Capacity	Strength			
	Endurance			
	Range of Motion			
	Structural limitations			
Postural Control	Accomplishes alignment			
	Maintains alignment			
	Adaptability (e.g., restore equilibrium)			
Movement Characteristics	Efficient			
	Effortful but functional			
	Ineffective			
	Use of compensatory actions			
Essential Skills	Looking			
	Vocalizing			
	Reaching			
	Manipulating			
Cognition Requirements				

Figure 2.4. Form for analyzing motor characteristics or task performance.

functional task performance, adaptations can be constructed to minimize the interference of the particular problems. Chapters 3 and 8 provide many excellent examples of positioning, handling, and environmental adaptations that acknowledge and accommodate for motoric problems and therefore will not be elaborated upon here.

CONCLUSION

The sensorimotor systems provide a vital link between the individual and the environment. Environmental conditions are noticed and observed via sensory system input. Responses to environmental demands are carried out by the motor systems. The sensorimotor systems are an interdependent network that enable the individual to acquire increasingly complex skills and use them in functional tasks. Children with multiple disabilities have difficulty with certain aspects of the sensorimotor systems. These problems interfere with the acquisition and use of sensorimotor skills for functional performance. When the sensorimotor problems diminish the adaptability, frequency, and form of interactions, the child can also miss the cognitive opportunities that facilitate growth in problem-solving skills. Effective intervention acknowledges all of these relationships and serves to minimize the effects of the disability while maximizing function.

REFERENCES

American Occupational Therapy Association. (1990). *Guidelines for occupational therapy services in the schools:* Second Edition. Rockville, MD: Author.

Ayres, A.J. (1980). *Sensory integration and the child.* Los Angeles: Western Psychological Services.

Baumgart, D., Brown, L., Pumpian, I., Nisbet, J., Ford, A., Sweet, M., Messina, R., & Schroeder, J. (1982). Principle of partial participation and individualized adaptations in educational programs for severely handicapped students. *Journal of The Association for the Severely Handicapped, 7*(2), 17–27.

Bobath, B. (1963). A neurodevelopmental treatment of cerebral palsy. *Physiotherapy, 49*(8), 242–244.

Campbell, P.H. (1987a). Integrated programming for students with multiple handicaps. In L. Goetz, D. Guess, & K. Stremel-Campbell (Eds.), *Innovative program design for individuals with dual sensory impairments* (pp. 159–188). Baltimore: Paul H. Brookes Publishing Co.

Campbell, P.H. (1987b). Programming for students with dysfunction in posture and movement. In M. Snell (Ed.), *Systematic instruction of persons with severe handicaps* (3rd ed., pp. 188–211). Columbus, OH: Charles E. Merrill.

Campbell, P.H. (1989). Posture and movement. In C. Tingey (Ed.), *Implementing early intervention* (pp. 189–208). Baltimore: Paul H. Brookes Publishing Co.

Campbell, P.H. (1990). *A guide to neurodevelopmental treatment with infants: A family-centered approach.* Unpublished manuscript. Family and Child Learning Center, Children's Hospital Medical Center of Akron.

Campbell, P.H., & Forsyth, S. (1990). *A system for classifying impaired or delayed posture and movement skill development.* Unpublished manuscript. Family and Child Learning Center, Children's Hospital Medical Center of Akron.

Cool, S.J. (1987). A view from the "outside": Sensory integration and developmental neurobiology. *Sensory Integration Specialty Section Newsletter, 10*(2), 2–3.

Coren, S., Porac, C., & Ward, L.M. (1984). *Sensation and perception* (2nd ed). Orlando: Academic Press.

Cyriax, J.H., & Cyriax, P.J. (1983). *Illustrated manual of orthopaedic medicine.* London: Butterworths, OM Publications.

Dunn, W. (1988). Basic and applied neuroscience research provides a basis for sensory integration theory. *American Journal of Mental Retardation, 92*(5), 420–422.

Dunn, W. (1989). Occupational therapy in early intervention: New perspectives create greater possibilities. *American Journal of Occupational Therapy, 43*(11), 717–721.

Dunn, W. (1991a). Assessing sensory performance enablers. In C. Christiansen & C. Baum (Eds.), *Occupational therapy: Overcoming human performance deficits.* Thorofare, NJ: SLACK.

Dunn, W. (1991b). Integrated related services. In L.H. Meyer, C.A. Peck, & L. Brown (Eds.), *Critical issues in the lives of people with severe disabilities* (pp. 353–377). Baltimore: Paul H. Brookes Publishing Co.

Dunn, W. (1991c). Dimensions of performance. In C. Christiansen & C. Baum (Eds.), *Occupational therapy: Overcoming human performance deficits.* Thorofare, NJ: SLACK.

Dunn, W., & Campbell, P.H. (1991). Designing pediatric service provision. In W. Dunn (Ed.), *Pediatric occupational therapy: Facilitating effective service provision* (pp. 140–159). Thorofare, NJ: SLACK.

Dunn, W., Campbell, P., Oetter, P., Hall, S., & Berger E. (1989). Guidelines for occupational therapy services in early intervention and preschool services. Rockville, MD: American Occupational Therapy Association.

Exner, C.E. (1989). Development of hand functions. In P.N. Pratt & A.S. Allen (Eds.), *Occupational therapy for children* (2nd ed.) (pp. 235–259). St. Louis: C.V. Mosby.

Gesell, A. (1954). The ontogenesis of infant behavior. In L. Carmichael (Ed.), *Manual of child psychology* (pp. 335–373). New York: John Wiley & Sons.

Gilfoyle, E.M., Grady, A.P., & Moore, J.C. (1981). *Children adapt.* Thorofare, NJ: SLACK.

Guess, D., Mulligan-Ault, M., Roberts, S., Struth, J., Siegel-Causey, E., Thompson, B., Bronicki, G.J.B., & Guy, B. (1988). Implications of biobehavioral states for the education and treatment of students with the most profoundly handicapping conditions. *Journal of The Association for Persons with Severe Handicaps, 13*(3), 163–174.

Harris, S. (1988). Early intervention: Does developmental therapy make a difference? *Topics in Early Childhood Special Education, 7*(4), 20–32.

Idol, L., Paolucci-Whitcomb, P., & Nevin, A. (1987). *Collaborative consultation.* Austin: PRO-ED.

Idol, L., & West, J.F. (1987). Consultation in special education (Part II): Training and practice. *Journal of Learning Disabilities, 20,* 474–494.

Manheim, C.J., & Lavett, D.K. (1989). *The myofascial release manual.* Thorofare, NJ: SLACK.

Moore, J. (1980). Neuroanatomical considerations relating to recovery of function following brain lesions. In P. Bach-y-Rita (Ed.), *Recovery of function: Theoretical considerations for brain injury rehabilitation* (pp. 9–90). Baltimore: University Park Press.

Rainforth, B., & York, J. (1987). Handling and positioning. In F.P. Orelove & D. Sobsey, *Educating children with multiple disabilities: A transdisciplinary approach*. Baltimore: Paul H. Brookes Publishing Co.

Rogers, S.J., & D'Eugenio, D.B. (1981). *Developmental programming for infants and young children: Assessment and application*. Ann Arbor: The University of Michigan Press.

Saunders, H.D. (1985). *Evaluation, treatment and prevention of musculoskeletal disorders*. Minneapolis: H. Duane Saunders.

Scherzer, A.L., & Tscharnuter, I. (Eds.). (1982). *Early diagnosis and therapy in cerebral palsy: A primer on infant development problems*. New York: Marcel Dekker.

Short-DeGraff, M.A. (1988). *Human development for occupational and physical therapists*. Baltimore: Williams & Wilkins.

Stern, F.M., & Gorga, D. (1988). Neurodevelopmental treatment (NDT): Therapeutic intervention and its efficacy. *Infants and Young Children, 1*(1), 22–32.

Travell, J.G., & Simons, D.G. (1983). *Myofascial pain and dysfunction: The trigger point manual*. Baltimore: Williams & Wilkins.

Upledger, J.E., & Vredevoogd, J.D. (1983). *Craniosacral therapy*. Seattle: Eastland Press.

Wadsworth, C.T. (1988). *Manual examination and treatment of the spine and extremities*. Baltimore: Williams & Wilkins.

Weeks, Z.R., & Ewer-Jones, B. (1983). Assessment of perceptual-motor and fine motor functioning. In K. Paget & B. Bracken (Eds.), *A psychoeducational assessment of preschool children* (pp. 261–291). Orlando: Grune & Stratton.

West, J.F., & Idol, L. (1987). School consultation (Part I): An interdisciplinary perspective on theory, models, and research. *Journal of Learning Disabilities, 20*, 388–408.

York, J., & Rainforth, B. (1987). Developing instructional adaptations. In F.P. Orelove & D. Sobsey, *Educating children with multiple disabilities: A transdisciplinary approach*. Baltimore: Paul H. Brookes Publishing Co.

Chapter 3

Handling and Positioning

Beverly Rainforth and Jennifer York

Throughout daily activities people skillfully position and move their bodies to perform a variety of functions. Even the simple task of face washing, which most people can perform without being fully awake, requires a series of complex motor actions. By practicing this task thousands of times, however, people increase proficiency to the extent that they can execute the motor components of face washing on a subconscious level. Analysis of this task discloses several forms of positioning and movement activity that are essential to all types of independent functioning. These positioning and movement components include the following:

1. Selecting a position that matches the practical and movement demands of the task
2. Assuming and balancing the body in that position
3. Coordinating the movements required to engage in the task

Each component is discussed below.

Prior to performing any task, a person selects a position in which the task can be performed easily. For example, standing at a sink is ideal for face washing. When a person is standing, both hands are free to perform the task. One can also shift forward, backward, and sideways to look in the mirror, reach the wash cloth or towel, adjust the faucets, confine drips to the sink basin, and so forth. In turn, one has constructed the environment so that access to the sink, towel bar, and mirror is easy and comfortable when standing. Other positions, such as sitting, usually are not chosen for face washing since they restrict reaching and body-shifting, which interferes with the practical and movement demands of the activity. Once an efficient position is selected, balance and comfort must be achieved before the task can be performed. For face washing, people generally stand at the sink with the feet and legs separated and the muscles throughout the legs and back contracted slightly to maintain a stable up-right position. Some people also might lean their hips against the front of the sink or rest one hand on top of the sink to increase balance or support (sta-bility). Throughout the activity, one makes minor postural adjustments in the ankles, knees, hips, and back to maintain balance.

Once balance and comfort are achieved, the arm movements required for the task of face washing can begin. One must coordinate the muscles around the various joints to provide adequate support (stability) and to execute efficient movements. For example, simply bringing a wash cloth to the face requires complex coordination between joint stability and mobility. First the shoulder blade is stabilized on the back to provide a base of support for moving the arm. Then, simultaneously, one rotates the forearm so the palm of the hand faces upward, straightens the wrist and fingers, bends the elbow, and brings the el-bow slightly forward and out to the side (see Figure 3.1). For this movement to be coordinated, however, there also must be some motion at the shoulder blade

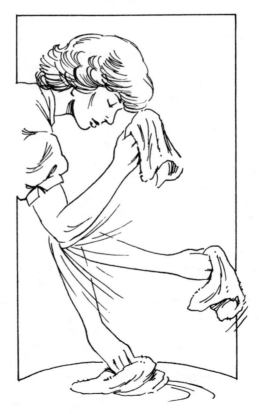

Figure 3.1.   Arm position when bringing a wash cloth to the face.

and shoulder joint (mobilization) and some stabilization at the other joints. Each step of the face washing task requires one to combine joint stability and mobility in a similar manner to produce efficient patterns of arm movement.

In summary, accomplishment of even the simplest daily activity requires a sophisticated combination of positioning and movement skills. It is important for educational team members, including family members, to recognize the complex motor demands of such simple tasks. These positioning and movement activities often present challenges for children with physical disabilities such as cerebral palsy. For example, a child who is unable to stand at a sink may sit in a wheelchair, but this position restricts access to the sink and face washing materials. Another child might be capable of standing at the sink, but only when using both hands for support. Efforts to use either hand for face washing reduce the child's balance, and in turn, eliminate the stable foundation needed to use the hands. A different child may have adequate balance, but still may be unable to coordinate arm movement sufficiently to perform the task. Efforts to flex (bend) the elbow may elicit uncontrolled muscle contractions (spasticity) through the arm, causing: 1) the child's arm to pull close to the body; 2) the elbow, wrist, and fingers to bend excessively; and 3) the palm of the hand to turn downward (see Figure 3.2). The arm position prevents the child from completing the task.

Because children with neuromotor disabilities often encounter the types of problems described above, they may find it difficult or impossible to participate in tasks such as face washing. When they do perform such tasks, these children often develop postures and movement patterns that appear abnormal and limit skill development. Continued practice of such abnormal patterns can decrease rather than increase proficiency in task performance (Bobath, 1980). To minimize the influence of these abnormal postures and movement patterns, educational team members can apply a variety of handling and positioning techniques (Bergen, Presperin, & Tallman, 1990; Bobath & Bobath, 1972; Connor, Williamson, & Siepp, 1978; Finnie, 1975; Fraser, Hensinger, & Phelps, 1990; Jaeger, 1987; Levitt, 1982; Morris & Klein, 1987). Because occupational and physical therapists have developed these techniques and have used them extensively, handling and positioning sometimes are considered specialized treatment provided by therapists. Episodic intervention is inadequate, however, because: 1) children need extensive practice to learn new movement patterns (Kottke, Halpern, Easton, Ozel, & Burrill, 1978); and 2) poor positioning generally has a deleterious effect on performance, even among children who do not have motor impairments (Sents & Marks, 1989). Furthermore, most children with disabilities are handled, moved, and positioned each day by numerous people, including parents, teachers, and assistants, regardless of whether these people know appropriate methods. When therapists delineate methods and provide systematic instruction, other team members can learn to use handling and positioning methods effectively (cf. Inge & Snell, 1985).

Figure 3.2.   A child with cerebral palsy attempting to bring a wash cloth to his face.

It is essential that all team members provide consistent handling for children with neuromotor disorders. Successful implementation of a transdisciplinary approach to service provision (Hart, 1977; Hutchison, 1978) promotes this consistency. Within the transdisciplinary model, therapists teach the principles of handling and positioning to other team members. Parents, teachers, and therapists also share information about the methods each has found effective with individual children. Finally, the entire team works together to establish a full set of handling and positioning procedures for each student. Within this model, handling and positioning become integral components of the daily routine for children with multiple disabilities. To enhance a transdisciplinary approach, this chapter discusses theory, research, and practices relevant to handling and positioning children with cerebral palsy and similar neuromotor impairments.

HANDLING CHILDREN WITH CEREBRAL PALSY

Children with cerebral palsy display a variety of posture and movement problems, which were discussed thoroughly in Chapter 2. It may be recalled that these children typically have too much or too little tension (tone) in their muscles, resulting in problems with positioning and movement. The term *handling*, as used here, applies to techniques intended to improve these impairments. The following are the goals of handling:

1. To elicit more normal muscle tone
2. To facilitate upright positions with normal posture
3. To facilitate normal movement patterns, including:
   a. Automatic movements that maintain balance
   b. Locomotion for independent mobility
   c. Arm and hand movements for task performance
   d. Oral movements for eating and speech

Methods to achieve each goal are discussed below. Teachers are encouraged to confer with an occupational or physical therapist regarding which methods are appropriate for individual children.

Normalizing Tone

The presence of too much, too little, or fluctuating muscle tone is symptomatic of damage to the child's brain. Although the damage itself cannot be repaired, there are a variety of ways to influence muscle tone. One way to normalize muscle tone is through the postural and movement strategies that comprise handling. For handling techniques to be effective, however, certain health, emotional, and environmental factors may require attention.

Health, Emotional, and Environmental Factors When children become excited or irritated, their muscle tone tends to increase. These responses may result from: 1) physical conditions such as pain, 2) personal interactions producing overenthusiasm or apprehension, or 3) stimulating environments with high levels of noise and activity. In contrast, children who are subdued tend to have lower muscle tone. This situation may result from: 1) conditions such as fatigue or illness, 2) personal interactions producing complacency or depression, or 3) environments that are quiet or languid. Medications often have side effects of irritability or lethargy, with a corresponding influence on muscle tone (Gadow, 1986). Theoretically then, children with excessive tone (spasticity or hypertonia) would benefit from being somewhat subdued, while children with very low tone (hypotonia or floppiness) would benefit from greater stimulation and excitement. Children's responses to various health conditions, personal interactions, and environmental stimuli vary tremendously, however, and each child must be assessed as an individual. For example, children with severe spasticity have demonstrated the ability to eat as well in a bustling cafeteria as in a quiet classroom, whereas children with hypotonia sometimes withdraw when they encounter stimulating environments.

Educational team members should be cognizant of how health, emotional, and environmental factors might influence a child's muscle tone. Of course, health care problems and unsatisfactory relationships need resolution, regardless of their effect on the child's muscle tone. Furthermore, when a child shows strong negative responses to the varied levels of stimulation encountered in natural environments, there must be conscious efforts to control the type and amount of stimulation. A balance must be sought, however, between protecting the child from undesirable stimulation and systematically teaching the child to develop the tolerance required for successful participation in normal life activities.

Posture and Movement Factors   Rapid or jerky movements tend to stimulate muscle contractions, much like when the physician taps the patellar tendon at a person's knee joint. Conversely, slow, smooth, rhythmic movement, like rocking in a rocking chair, promotes relaxation. These principles apply as much to children with cerebral palsy as they do to other people. Therefore, spasticity often can be reduced by an adult slowly rocking the child in a rocking chair, slowly rotating the child's hips and shoulders in opposite directions, or slowly bending or straightening a limb while gently moving the limb side to side. A floppy child's low tone often can be increased by an adult bouncing the child on the lap, applying vibration to a group of muscles, or quickly tapping a body part in the direction of a desired movement.

Children with ataxic and athetoid cerebral palsy have muscle tone that fluctuates between high and low. For these children, the procedures described above are alternated as necessary to reduce or increase the tone demonstrated at a particular moment. As noted previously, each child with cerebral palsy must be handled individually, with the particular type and intensity of motion determined by its effectiveness for that particular child. For some children, it may be necessary to experiment with numerous techniques before discovering one that is effective to normalize tone. Many children with cerebral palsy also have primitive reflexes, which result in obligatory postures and movement patterns and concurrently interfere with normal muscle tone. When these reflexes are present, avoidance of reflex stimulating positions is essential to normalize tone.

Unfortunately, hypotonia often prevents children from experiencing the positions that stimulate postural control. Also, spasticity increases as children attempt to move, preventing adequate movement experience. These situations illustrate that normal muscle tone is both the prerequisite for and the result of normal postural control and movement. For this reason children with cerebral palsy derive the greatest benefit from relaxation and facilitation procedures when the procedures are applied to posture and movement activities in which the children are active participants (e.g., sitting, reaching, rolling).

Facilitating Normal Postures and Movement Patterns

Although the specific methods to achieve various positions and movements vary, three general principles remain the same—normalizing tone (discussed above), "breaking up" abnormal postures, and using "key points of control" (Bobath & Bobath, 1972). Children with cerebral palsy often become "locked" into abnormal postures that interfere with or completely prevent functional movement. For example, a child with flexor spasticity would tend to hold many or all joints in flexion, as depicted in Figure 3.3a. To break up this flexed posture, an opposite posture of greater extension must be achieved. It is not sufficient, however, simply to extend the hip, knee, and elbow joints, where flexion is most obvious. A closer look at Figure 3.3a reveals that there is not just an abnormal degree of flexion at many joints, but that the hips, shoulders and other joints are also rotated into abnormal positions. Therefore, breaking up the flexed posture requires the child's arms and legs to be both extended and rotated in the opposite direction (see Figure 3.3b), while using the relaxation techniques described in the previous section. Frequently rotation is more influential than either flexion or extension alone to break up abnormal postures.

The key points of control are those parts of the child's body where the facilitator can most effectively break up abnormal postures and elicit more normal postures and movement patterns. These key points of control are usually at

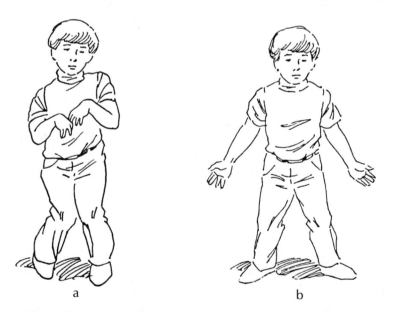

a   b

Figure 3.3.   A child with increased muscle tone (a) standing with excessive flexion and internal rotation, and (b) standing with the pattern reversed to increase extension and external rotation.

the head, trunk, shoulders, and hips, with preference for the area of the body closest to the trunk where normal patterns can be elicited most effectively. The principles and methods of normalizing tone, breaking up abnormal postures, and using key points of control cannot be isolated from one another. Examples of how these principles are integrated and applied to achieve the goals of therapeutic handling are presented below.

Facilitating Upright Positions and Normal Posture   The child depicted in Figure 3.4a has severe spasticity and cannot assume or maintain a sitting position independently. Note that the child's neck is extended and rotated, and that the shoulders are extended, and the elbows, wrists, and fingers are flexed. The hips and knees are flexed slightly and pulled together (adducted). To position the child for instruction, the teacher first rolls the student from his back to his side, a position that is less likely to stimulate extension. The teacher uses the

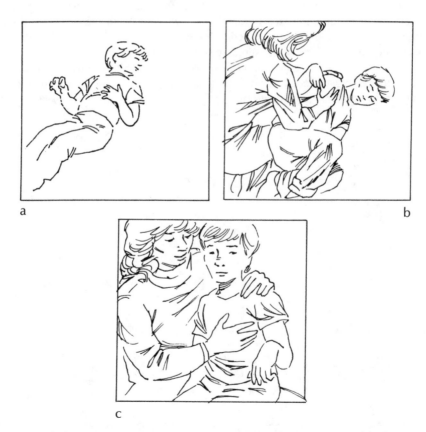

a   b

c

Figure 3.4.   A child with spasticity (a) in an undesirable resting posture, (b) relaxed and positioned on his side, and (c) seated on the teacher's lap with the muscle tone controlled.

student's head, shoulders, and hips as key points of control, flexing and rotating his neck, bringing his arms together, and further flexing his hips and knees. At the same time the teacher gently rocks the student and rolls him onto his side (see Figure 3.4b). With the student in this position, the teacher lifts the student and seats him on her lap. The teacher keeps one hand behind the student's head and around his shoulders to keep his shoulders and arms forward and neck slightly flexed. When the student begins to extend his neck and push his head backward, the teacher tips his head forward with her elbow while pressing in and down on his breast bone and gently rocking the student side to side (see Figure 3.4c). Because the student continues to push into extension periodically, this *dynamic* positioning offered by the teacher is somewhat more effective in maintaining normal sitting posture than the *static* positioning offered by the student's adapted chair. Every effort is made to adapt the student's chair to provide the same type of control at the head, shoulders, and hips as the teacher provides, since sitting in a chair has both social and instructional advantages for the student.

The child in Figure 3.5a has low muscle tone (hypotonia), and cannot assume or maintain sitting independently. To position this student for instruction, the teacher will help him roll to the side and then push up to sitting. Using the student's shoulders as the key point of control, the teacher slowly turns the student's shoulders toward sidelying. The teacher uses a series of short, quick pushes to the shoulder to stimulate muscle tone in the student's trunk and to elicit his participation in rolling (see Figure 3.5b). With the student on his side, the teacher helps him use his arms to push upward (Figure 3.5c) to sidesitting, resting on his hands (Figure 3.5d), and finally, to longsitting (Figure 3.5e). The teacher continues to use short, quick, upward pushes to stimulate muscle tone in the student's arms and trunk, and to elicit his participation in pushing up to sit. In sitting, the student's legs are positioned to give him a wide base of support, and his arms are positioned so he can continue to lean on them. The teacher keeps her hands on the student's shoulders to prevent falling and to give more quick pushes down through the back and arms, which increases the student's awareness of his position and stimulates his muscle tone (Figure 3.5e).

Although the two examples above use therapeutic handling to achieve and maintain normal upright sitting postures for instruction, numerous positions (e.g., sidelying, kneeling, standing) have therapeutic and instructional value for students with multiple impairments. Table 3.1 presents the advantages and disadvantages of various positions that might be used in educational programs for students with severe and multiple disabilities.

Facilitating Automatic Movements that Maintain Balance   When children learn to sit, kneel, or stand, they maintain their upright positions using automatic reactions such as protective reactions and righting reactions (Fiorentino, 1963). These automatic reactions were described in Chapter 2. Righting reactions, in which a person positions and maintains the head and trunk upright

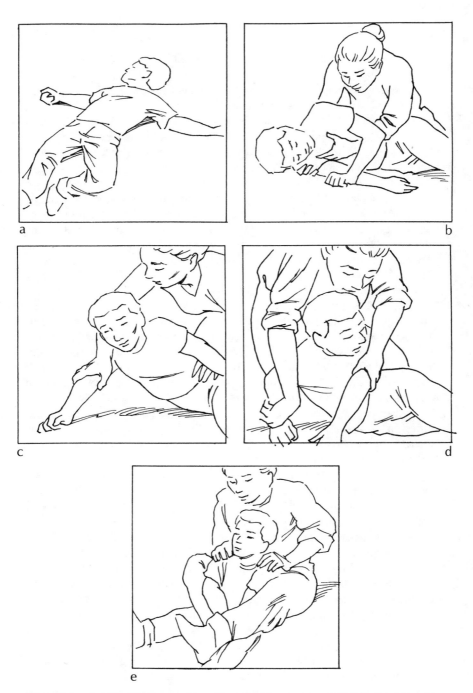

Figure 3.5. A child with hypotonia (a) unable to sit without assistance, (b) being taught to roll to his side, (c) pushing up to semisitting, (d) then sidesitting, (e) with pressure applied through the spine and shoulders to increase muscle tone and position awareness in the trunk and arms.

Table 3.1.   Positions for students with physical disabilities

Position	Advantages	Disadvantages
Prone	Normal resting position; requires no motor control; promotes trunk and hip extension	Possibility of suffocation; stimulates asymmetry if head turned to side; may stimulate flexor tone; functional activities limited
Supine	Normal resting position; requires little motor control; no danger of suffocation; symmetry can be maintained	May stimulate extensor tone; prolonged position inhibits respiration; possibility of aspiration; ceiling view; functional activities limited
Prone on elbows	Encourages head, arm, and trunk control; allows improved view	May stimulate flexor tone; may stimulate excessive extension; tiring position; limits hand use
Sidelying	Normal resting position; usually does not stimulate abnormal tone; improves alignment, brings hands together at midline	May require bulky equipment; sideward view; few functional activities; pressure on bony prominences (hips)
Side sitting	Easy to assume from lying, hands and knees, kneeling; promotes trunk rotation, range of motion in hips, trunk if sides alternated	May reinforce asymmetry; may require one or both hands for support; difficult with tight hips or trunk
Indian or ring sitting	Wide base of support; symmetrical position; easier to free hands	Difficult transition to/from other positions; may reinforce flexed posture
Long sitting	May provide wide base of support; may prevent hamstring contractures	Impossible with tight hamstrings; may stimulate trunk flexion, flexor spasticity
Heel or W-sitting	Easy transition to/from other positions; stable base of support; frees hands	Reinforces hip, knee, and ankle deformity; reduces reciprocal movement, weight shifting, and trunk rotation
Chair sitting— standard chair	Normal position and equipment; easy transition to/from other positions; minor adaptations can be added to improve position	May not provide adequate position for feet, trunk, hips; may be overused

(continued)

Table 3.1.   (*continued*)

Position	Advantages	Disadvantages
Chair sitting— bolster chair	Reduces scissoring at hips; may increase anterior pelvic tilt	Bulky equipment; difficult transition to/from other positions
Chair sitting— corner chair	Inhibits extensor tone in trunk and shoulders	May encourage excessive flexion; may rotate trunk and pelvis
Chair sitting— wheelchair	Allows for positioning and mobility simultaneously; adaptations can control most postural problems	Chairs may be expensive, complicated, easily maladjusted; may become over-reliant on chair
Kneeling	Promotes trunk and hip control; improves hip joint; possible despite knee flexion contractures; stabilizes hip joint	May cause bursitis at knees
Standing prone	Promotes trunk and hip control; standing stabilizes hip joint; allows access to normal work surfaces (e.g., counters)	May stimulate flexor tone; may stimulate excessive extension; may need hands for support; requires bulky equipment
Standing supine	Promotes trunk and hip control; stabilizes hip joint; hands free for work; head supported	May stimulate extensor tone; may not reach work surfaces; requires bulky equipment
Standing upright	Promotes greater trunk and hip control and balance	May require bulky equipment

in space, are first seen when an infant lifts its wobbling head off a parent's shoulder. For children with multiple disabilities, experiencing upright positions is an important aspect of developing righting reactions. These reactions can be strengthened further by seating the child on an adult's lap, a stool, or the floor and gently tipping the child from the upright position. The key point of control might be at the child's head, shoulders, trunk, hips, or even the thighs, depending on the child's head and trunk control. Protective reactions, in which a person extends the arms to break a fall, start developing when a child bears weight on the arms in sitting and hands-and-knees positions (see Figure 3.6a). When a child with cerebral palsy can use the arms for the basic function of propping, facilitating more advanced protective reactions can involve holding the child's arm with wrist and elbow extended, gently pulling the child off balance, and positioning the arm to break the fall (see Figure 3.6b). In this example, the child's hand and elbow are the key points of control.

Facilitating Locomotion for Independent Mobility   Children move

 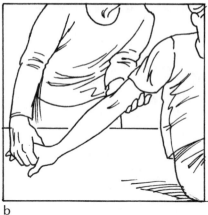

a   b

Figure 3.6. (a) A young child using his arms to break a fall and resume sitting; (b) assisting a child with cerebral palsy to extend and bear weight on his arm as part of a sequence for teaching protective reactions.

around their environments by rolling, crawling on their stomachs, creeping on hands and knees, knee-walking, and walking. Children may also move by driving a wheelchair or by riding a tricycle or bicycle. Teaching any means of mobility to children with cerebral palsy requires them to maintain relatively normal postures while coordinating smooth movements of the arms, legs, and trunk. Although commando-crawling and creeping on hands and knees are considered basic locomotor patterns, encouraging their use is counterproductive for many children with cerebral palsy. The prone position and the movements themselves may stimulate so much flexor tone in the trunk and limbs that effective movement is impossible. Rolling, riding an adapted tricycle, or driving an electric wheelchair are more successful alternatives for children with severe cerebral palsy.

The movement requirements for independent mobility can be analyzed much like those of any task. (This type of analysis requires the teacher's skills in task analysis to be combined with the therapist's knowledge of normal movement patterns, and offers an excellent opportunity for collaboration between teacher and therapist.) Table 3.2 presents a task analysis for rolling, showing both the movements to be performed by the student and the key points for facilitation by the teacher. The task analysis for another student might have different components, depending on the type and extent of that student's independent movement and abnormal postures. The movements required for other forms of independent mobility can be analyzed in the same way.

Facilitating Arm and Hand Movements for Task Performance The previous sections have offered examples of facilitating arm movement for weight-bearing functions. Although it had been believed that proximal control and

Table 3.2.   Task analysis for rolling

Student movements	Staff key points[a]
Supine lying, extend right arm overhead	Move at right upper arm
Rotate head and shoulders to face right	Stabilize at right upper arm; move at left shoulder
Swing left leg over and forward	Stabilize at left shoulder; move at left thigh (Prevent trunk, hip and knee flexor pattern)
Extend left arm over head and roll to prone	Move at left upper arm (Prevent pushing up on elbows)
Plant right hand next to right shoulder	Stabilize at left upper arm; move at right elbow
Rotate head and push right shoulder up to face right	Stabilize at left upper arm; move at right upper arm
Swing right leg over and backward	Stabilize at left upper arm; move at right thigh (Prevent trunk, hip, and knee flexor pattern)
Roll supine, bring head to midline, and bring left arm down to side	Move at left forehead and left upper arm

[a]Parentheses indicate postures the student tends to assume during rolling, which the staff must be prepared to inhibit if necessary.

weightbearing were prerequisites for skillful hand use, research suggests that these abilities evolve simultaneously with distal control and reach, grasp, and object manipulation skills (Case-Smith, Fisher, & Bauer, 1989; Loria, 1980). Furthermore, since children with cerebral palsy tend to use total patterns of movement (e.g., they are unable to isolate elbow or finger movement), it is useful to facilitate patterns of movement that involve the entire upper limb: shoulder, elbow, wrist, and fingers. The only essential prerequisites for trying to facilitate functional arm and hand movement (e.g., for reach, grasp, manipulation) are: 1) that the student be positioned with sufficient support so the hands are not needed to stabilize the body, and 2) that the student's position promote normalization of tone throughout the trunk and limbs.

The student depicted in Figures 3.7a and 3.7b has flexor spasticity, which interferes with reaching for the wash cloth, grasping it, or bringing it to his face. To facilitate these movements, the teacher provides control at the student's upper arm, forearm, and hand. The teacher first normalizes the student's tone by slowly rotating his arm inward while moving his arm down and away from his body. When the teacher feels the student participating in these movements, she repeats the same pattern, helping the student pick up the wash cloth and bring it to his face (see Figures 3.7c and 3.7d). If the student's tone starts to

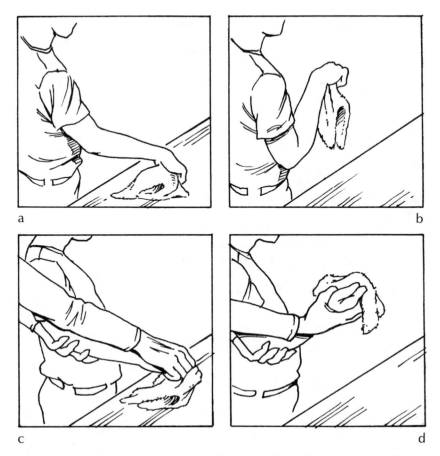

Figure 3.7.   (a) and (b) A child with increased flexor tone trying to bring a wash cloth to his face; (c) and (d) a teacher facilitating more typical and efficient movement for picking up and bringing the wash cloth to his face.

increase, the teacher resumes the rhythmic pattern of arm movement. The student is encouraged to participate in the activity to the greatest extent possible while maintaining functional movement. Using the principle of key points of control, the teacher facilitates at the part of the arm closest to the trunk where normal movement patterns can be elicited. Generally, the key point is at or just below the joint to be moved. One exception to this rule occurs when opening a fisted hand. The anatomy of the hand makes it possible (and easier) to open a fisted hand by flexing the wrist joint, which automatically extends the fingers. Then the teacher can hold the student's fingers extended while gently extending the wrist (see Figure 3.8), and proceed with the activity. It must be recalled,

Figure 3.8.   Opening a fisted hand by changing the wrist position.

however, that efforts to open the student's hand and facilitate hand use will not be successful if the student's entire posture is not addressed.

Facilitating Oral Movements for Eating and Speech   The methods used to facilitate oral movement are discussed thoroughly in Chapter 8. It is appropriate to emphasize here the importance of normalizing overall postural tone and positioning the student upright with sufficient support to the trunk and head to allow concentration on oral activity. Without addressing these prerequisites, no oral facilitation techniques will be powerful enough to overcome the resulting abnormalities.

Validity of Therapeutic Handling

According to neurodevelopmental treatment theory, handling provides the experience with normal postures and movement through which children with cerebral palsy learn to control their muscle tone (Bobath, 1980). Unfortunately, research on the effects of neurodevelopmental treatment has demonstrated significant improvement for only very few of the children studied (DeGangi, Hurley, Linscheid, 1983; Lilly & Powell, 1990; Noonan, 1984). Whereas Noonan noted that treatment effectiveness is correlated with (not necessarily determined by) children's intelligence, others have concluded that intelligence strongly influences treatment outcomes for children with cerebral palsy (Goldkamp, 1984; Parette & Hourcade, 1984). The interaction between treatment outcomes and other variables, such as frequency, duration, context, and goals of treatment, have not been studied however. With up to 60% of children with cerebral palsy having mental retardation (Batshaw & Perret, 1981), greater attention must be given to methods to improve treatment results for children with multiple disabilities.

Although research is limited, more encouraging results have been reported when aspects of systematic instruction and neurodevelopmental treatment have been combined. In studies by Campbell, McInerney, and Cooper (1984) and Giangreco (1986), four children with multiple disabilities all improved significantly when therapeutic handling techniques were combined with frequent practice in meaningful contexts (e.g., reaching for microwave oven door) and when movement immediately elicited desirable consequences (e.g., lunch from the microwave oven). In these applications, handling might be viewed as a specialized form of physical prompting that applies to posture and movement disorders. Such an integration of handling and systematic instruction procedures concurrently addresses the cognitive, movement, and motivational needs of children with multiple disabilities. This comprehensive approach currently offers the greatest possibilities to evaluate therapeutic handling techniques adequately and to teach children with multiple disabilities effectively.

POSITIONING STUDENTS WITH CEREBRAL PALSY

Therapeutic positioning is the placement of body parts in postures to achieve the following goals:

1. To maintain normalized muscle tone
2. To maintain alignment of body parts
3. To maintain stabilization of body parts
4. To promote active participation in meaningful activity

While the first three goals are critical, they are not ends in themselves; rather, they are means to achieve the ultimate goal of preparing a person to perform functional activities. Proper positioning is an essential prerequisite for effective instruction of students with multiple disabilities.

Positioning can be either *static* or *dynamic*. Dynamic positioning is achieved and maintained entirely through therapeutic handling; static positioning is maintained through use of adapted equipment. Static positioning is considered a supplement to rather than a substitute for dynamic positioning. Prior to positioning a child in an adapted chair, for example, therapeutic handling techniques are applied to place the child in a sitting position with tone normalized and the body properly aligned. Without performing this dynamic positioning first, it becomes difficult to achieve any of the four goals listed above through static positioning. There are advantages, however, to providing static positioning with adapted equipment. These include: 1) making the student more mobile, 2) freeing the student from a one-to-one relationship with parents or educational staff, 3) freeing staff hands from positioning to provide instruction and to facilitate other types of student performance, and 4) enabling students with disabilities to participate in activities with typical peers without constant adult presence.

In addition to the therapeutic benefits of positioning, researchers have identified several functional benefits for providing children with physical disabilities with adapted equipment for positioning. Benefits include the following:

1. Children at school maintained upright postures longer, attended to and participated in more instruction, and learned to perform academic and self

care tasks more quickly and more independently (Trefler, Nickey, & Hobson, 1983).

2. Children at home spent less time lying in their bedrooms, spent more time sitting and less time lying down, maintained better alignment in upright postures, improved abilities to eat and drink, increased abilities to grasp objects and feed themselves, and spent more time interacting with others (Hulme, Poor, Schulein, & Pezzino, 1983; Hulme, Shaver, Acher, Mullette, & Eggert, 1987).

When positioning equipment also provided a means of mobility (e.g., wheelchair), the following additional benefits were demonstrated:

1. Children went more places outside of their homes (Hulme et al., 1983).
2. Children (and their families) engaged in more social activities, had more contact with peers outside of school,increased activities in school, and had greater independence in all environments (Kohn, Enders, Preston, & Motloch, 1983).
3. Children engaged in more positive social interactions, became more curious about the environment, and became interested in other activities involving movement (e.g., playing baseball, going hiking) (Butler, 1986; Butler, Okamoto, & McKay, 1983).

To achieve therapeutic positioning for children with multiple disabilities, team members should understand the purpose of the various types of equipment and procedures for effective positioning. The following sections provide information on positioning with chairs, braces and splints, and other pieces of equipment.

Positioning in Adapted Chairs

Sitting is a traditional and therefore a "normal" position for children in educational settings. Sitting in adapted chairs allows children with physical disabilities to be in the same upright position, to be at the same eye level, and to use the same work surfaces as their nondisabled peers. Sitting in wheelchairs has the added benefit of providing children with a means of mobility that is a commonplace alternative to walking. Studies of use of wheelchairs and other adapted seating reveal that children with physical disabilities spent 2–4 hours per day in wheelchairs at the ages of 2 and 3 years (Butler et al., 1983), and 4–6 hours per day at a somewhat older age (Hulme et al., 1983), increasing to an average of 9 hours per day by adolescence (Kohn et al., 1983). Despite such extensive use and ongoing technological developments, adapted chairs do not always meet the needs of children with neuromuscular disabilities. Problems may result from poor selection (design and/or measurement) by rehabilitation professionals, poor acceptance by the child or family, or poor placement of the child in the seat by caregivers (Hundertmark, 1985; Kohn et al., 1983). Considering the amount of time many children spend in adapted chairs, it is essential that educators understand and execute principles of effective seating to minimize the problems resulting from the situations identified above, and to maximize therapeutic and functional benefits. Table 3.3 provides a checklist to assess application of these principles to seating students with physical disabilities. The items on the checklist were derived from an analysis of efficient seated positioning of individuals who do not have physical disabilities. The principles outlined above for positioning children in adapted chairs apply directly to positioning in other types of equipment. Similar checklists can be developed to guide positioning in other equipment. The checklist is meant to

Table 3.3.   Checklist for seated positioning

PELVIS AND HIPS
_____   Hips flexed to 90°
_____   Pelvis tilted slightly forward
_____   Pelvis centered in the back edge of seat
_____   Pelvis not rotated forward on one side

THIGHS AND LEGS
_____   Thighs equal in length
_____   Thighs slightly abducted (apart)
_____   Knees flexed to 90°

FEET AND ANKLES
_____   Aligned directly below or slightly posterior to knees
_____   Ankles flexed to 90°
_____   Feet supported on footrest
_____   Heel and ball of feet bearing weight
_____   Feet and toes facing forward

TRUNK
_____   Symmetrical, not curved to the side
_____   Slight curve at low back
_____   Erect upper back, slight extension

SHOULDERS, ARMS, AND HANDS
_____   Relaxed, neutral position (not hunched up or hanging low)
_____   Upper arm flexed slightly forward
_____   Elbows flexed in midrange (about 90°)
_____   Forearms resting on tray to support arms and shoulders if necessary to maintain alignment
_____   Forearms neutral or rotated downward slightly
_____   Wrists neutral or slightly extended
_____   Hand relaxed, fingers and thumb opened

HEAD AND NECK
_____   Midline orientation
_____   Slight chin tuck (back of neck elongated)

From York, J., & Wiemann, G. (1991). Accommodating severe physical disabilities. In J. Reichle, J. York, & J. Sigafoos. *Implementing augmentative and alternative communication: Strategies for learners with severe disabilities*. Baltimore: Paul H. Brookes Publishing Co., p. 247; reprinted with permission.

serve only as a guide, however, and there may be individuals for whom specific items on the checklist are inappropriate.

   Positioning the Pelvis   When a child with physical disabilities is positioned in an adapted seat, the pelvis becomes the key point of control. The pelvic bones in the lower trunk are attached to the backbone, the thigh bones (femurs), and the trunk and leg muscles. The hips provide the base of support for the trunk and therefore influence trunk alignment and posture, head position, and arm use. To provide the proper base of support, the right and left side of the pelvis must be level so the child sits evenly on both hips (see Figure 3.9). When the pelvis is not level, lateral pelvic tilt and curvature of the spine (scoliosis) interfere with normal digestive and respiratory functions and may contribute to dislocation of the hip (Kalen & Bleck, 1985). The top of the pelvis should also be tipped forward slightly to maintain the normal arch in the low back (lumbar lordosis), and to prevent spasticity in the low back muscles (Hundertmark, 1985). A lumbar roll inserted in the low back area may help produce this position (see Figure 3.10).

   Therapists have observed that seating children upright with hips and knees flexed to 90° often minimizes the influence of primitive reflexes and spasticity while providing a functional work position. Bringing the trunk forward with an additional 15° of hip flexion reduces spasticity in the low back extensors of children with cerebral palsy (Nwaobi, Brubaker, Cusick, & Sussman, 1983; Nwaobi, Hobson, Eng, & Taylor, 1988). The appropriate hip angle generally is determined at the time the child is fitted with a chair, and then is built into the chair. This therapeutic hip angle in the chair is only effective, however, when the child's hips are properly flexed prior to placement in the chair. With some children, it is helpful to tip the chair backward during positioning so gravity aids rather than interferes with placing the hips back in the chair. Tipping a

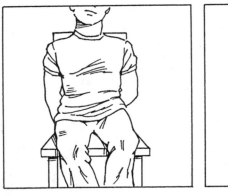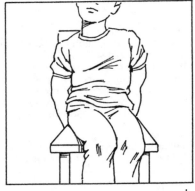

a   b

Figure 3.9.   Alignment of the hips in a seated position (a) with the pelvis symmetrical, and (b) with the pelvis tilted, causing poor alignment of the trunk, shoulders, head, and legs.

chair 30° has been found to increase tone in low back extensors, hip adductors, and ankle plantar flexors (Nwaobi, 1986), so the benefit of tipping the chair needs to be assessed for each child. Once the child's hips are well-aligned and positioned in the chair, a seat belt maintains the position. The seat belt crosses the bend in the hip joint (see Figure 3.10) and is tightened as necessary to allow the child freedom of movement in the hips while still holding the therapeutic position of the pelvis. The seat belt should not be placed across the child's abdomen since it will put pressure on internal organs and tip the top of the pelvis backward. Figure 3.9 illustrates the correct positions and Figure 3.10 illustrates the incorrect positions for the pelvis and seat belt.

Positioning the Thighs With the hips stabilized in the chair, the child's base of support is improved further by positioning the thighs. The preferred position is with the legs symmetrical and the thighs slightly separated. If the student's thighs pull together, a wedge may be necessary to position them (see Figure 3.11). Less frequently, children pull their thighs far apart, which requires pads to push them closer together. If one or both hips are dislocated, it may be difficult to keep the thighs in a symmetrical position. In this event, first consideration is given to the position of the pelvis in relation to the child's back and the back of the wheelchair. (Positioning the trunk is discussed in a later section.) The thighs are positioned the best way possible without disturbing the position of the pelvis. Some older children have such serious deformity of the hips and back that they develop a difference in leg length or a deviation of both legs to one side in a "windblown" deformity. When this occurs, the chair seat might be extended forward on one side so that the full length of both thighs is supported (see Figure 3.12). To provide good support for the thighs, the seat should extend to approximately one inch from the back of the calf. A deeper

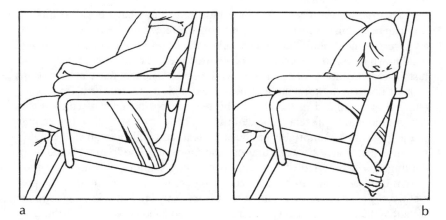

a   b

Figure 3.10. Sitting in a chair (a) with a seatbelt keeping hips flexed and lumbar roll supporting the low back and (b) with the seatbelt improperly positioned across the abdomen.

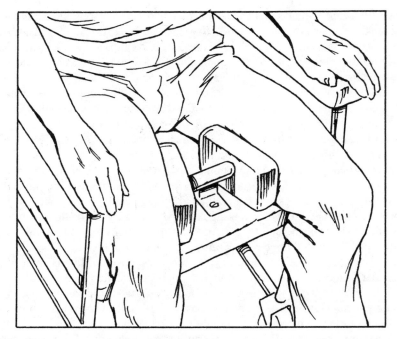

Figure 3.11. A wedge positioned between the thighs to keep them separated and aligned for a stable seating base. (Note that the wedge is not placed against the pelvis. It must not be used to keep the child from sliding forward.)

seat puts pressure on the blood and nerve supply behind the knee and pulls the hips forward in the chair.

Positioning the Feet Once the hips and thighs have been positioned, they can be stabilized further by positioning the feet. The feet are supported by a footrest, which should be directly below the knees. If the child has a severe windblown deformity or knee flexion contractures, it may be necessary to adjust the foot position to one side or toward the rear. The foot rest can have straps or built up sides to keep the feet positioned and to prevent them from being bumped or entangled in the chair. The feet are positioned flat with the toes straight forward to prevent ankle deformity. The footrest should be low enough so the thighs rest comfortably on the chair seat, and high enough so the child's weight is distributed between the seat and footrest. If the footrest is too high, the thighs will be lifted off the seat, decreasing stability, shifting the child's weight back onto the hip bones, decreasing comfort, and increasing the possibility of pressure sores. If the footrest is too low, the feet will hang, and the weight of the legs will create pressure on the blood and nerve supply behind the knees. If the child has knee extension contractures or poor circulation, it may be necessary to elevate the feet and legs. In this situation, attention is given to

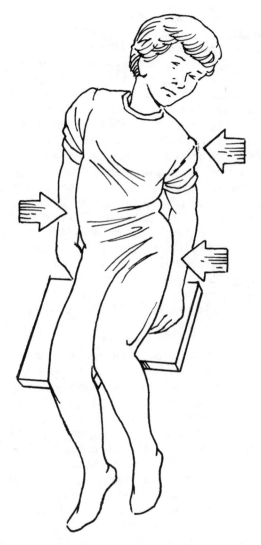

Figure 3.12.   A child with severe scoliosis and leg length difference, resulting from hip dislocation. The seat is lengthened on the right side to support the right leg without putting pressure on the
back of the left knee. The arrows indicate where lateral supports would be placed to provide counter
pressures to achieve optimal alignment.

supporting the calves and feet, and to preventing ankle deformity, excessive
rotation of the legs, or localized pressure on the heels. Although the foot position reinforces the hip and thigh position, only quick and temporary foot placement may be possible before the trunk and head are stabilized, especially if the

child has poor trunk and head control. Once the upper body is positioned properly, attention is redirected to the feet.

Positioning the Trunk and Head   For best alignment of the trunk, the shoulders should be directly over the hips. A child with poor trunk control may wear a harness, secured at the hips with a lap belt, and secured at the shoulders to the back of the chair. If the child falls to the side, lateral supports may be necessary. The lateral supports may come forward from the back of the chair at the level of the rib cage, or may be attached to the child's tray. Children with scoliosis or other back deformity require more specialized adaptations. The back of the chair may be built up in some areas and cut out in others to provide support to areas of the child's back that curve inward and relieve pressure from areas that curve outward. Lateral supports are most effective when placed at the extreme points of the curve, providing counterpressure to straighten the curve or to prevent increased deformity (see Figure 3.12). To provide comfortable and effective positioning for children with very severe back and hip deformity, it may be necessary to mold a plastic or foam seat to the child's body. Some children move about independently in spite of severe scoliosis or other deformity. For these children, scoliosis pads and other types of chair adaptations are not as effective for long-term positioning as braces, which are discussed later.

The stable and well-aligned trunk provides a good base of support for the student's head. Achieving and maintaining an appropriate head position, with the head erect and chin tucked, remains one of the greatest challenges when positioning children with equipment. Children with poor head control may benefit from pads placed behind and/or beside the head. In some situations, it may be necessary to use a "halo," which surrounds the head and provides anterior as well as lateral support. Even more control can be gained with an overhead sling that provides support under the chin, at the base of the skull, and on both sides of the head. While simply having the child in an upright position tends to stimulate head control (Trefler et al., 1983), positioning combined with sensory feedback (Cantanese & Sandford, 1984; Leiper, Miller, Lang, & Herman, 1981) and contingent reinforcement (Murphy, Doughty, & Nunes, 1979) can further improve head control and decrease the need for head supports.

Positioning the Arms   Students with adapted chairs often have trays, both to provide a work surface and to provide additional support. The tray should be high enough to allow the student to rest both elbows and forearms on the tray without bending the trunk forward. For children with poor head and trunk control, leaning on the tray provides greater voluntary control of the shoulders, and in turn, more stability for the trunk and head. As noted previously, lateral trunk supports can be mounted on the tray. Other pads, straps, or pegs also can be attached to the tray to facilitate arm positioning. Naturally, the tray must be large enough to accommodate the various adaptations and the student's work materials, while remaining small enough to fit through doorways. If the only purpose of the tray is to provide a work surface, it may be preferable to dispense with the tray and position the student at a table. This alternative would provide the students with a more normalized work situation and opportunities for more interactions with teacher and peers. Students who do not need extensive chair adaptations can transfer from their wheelchairs to regular classroom chairs for table work, increasing their normalization. With regular furniture, students still need their feet positioned flat on the floor or on a footrest. The table should be just high enough to allow the students to rest their elbows and forearms.

Determining the Need for Positioning Adaptations   When positioning children with physical impairments, the dangers of providing too much or too little control must be considered. The obvious danger of providing too little control is that this does not maintain proper positioning, and so it fails to offer experience in aligned and upright postures, allows deformity, and hampers participation in instructional activities. In fact, research conducted with preschool-age children showed that poor positioning lowered their performance on IQ tests, *even though the children had no motor impairments* (Sents & Marks, 1989). Providing too much support is also potentially dangerous, however, because some children will rely on whatever support they are given, using their own motor skills as little as possible, and eventually losing rather than gaining abilities. Maintaining too much external control also limits opportunities to improve motor skills and to develop internal control. Maintaining adaptations and monitoring their use is a time-consuming responsibility that should be eliminated if the adaptations are not necessary. Furthermore, chair adaptations increase the time and difficulty of seating the child for work or transportation, and removing the child for repositioning or emergencies. Finally, the presence of numerous adaptations on a chair may elicit undesirable reactions, such as pity or apprehension, which should be minimized. While unnecessary adaptations can be completely eliminated from chairs, even essential controls or supports might be removed at certain times of the day. For example, a student might need a headrest during transportation, but not when listening to a story. During eating, the static positioning offered by the headrest might be less beneficial than dynamic positioning, in which the teacher puts one hand on the student's head only when stabilization is needed.

When positioning children with multiple disabilities in adapted chairs or other equipment, it is necessary to view each child as an individual. An adaptation that is necessary or effective for one child may be neither for another child. Many minute adjustments may be necessary before a chair adaptation has the desired effect. Once the desired effect is attained, change in the child's size or condition may necessitate more modifications. These warnings are not meant to be discouraging; they emphasize that positioning equipment is not a quick cure, but a tool to be used skillfully. In the same way, chair positioning has many advantages for children with multiple disabilities, but it cannot meet all the positioning needs of any child. Therefore, a variety of positioning options should be considered for each child. Selecting the proper pieces of equipment requires knowledge of what equipment is available or technologically feasible, and how that matches therapeutic, functional, and social needs and goals of the individual child and family (Taylor, 1987). It is often helpful to include an adaptive equipment specialist on teams of children with multiple disabilities.

Alternative Positions

In selecting a variety of positions for a student with physical disabilities, the educational team addresses each of the following questions:

- What postures should be reinforced?
- What postures should be avoided?
- What functions must be performed?
- What are the social contexts?
- What positioning alternatives are possible in the course of the day?

The postures to be reinforced may be any in which the child is currently developing greater control. The postures to be avoided are those that reinforce primitive reflexes, deformities, abnormal postures, or abnormal movement patterns. (These considerations were outlined in Table 3.1.) Analysis of the function to be performed requires evaluation of the postural and movement demands of the tasks involved. A good frame of reference for this analysis is to consider how people without disabilities perform the task. To perform the task of face washing, discussed earlier in this chapter, a student must be able to see the task area and reach the materials (e.g., water, soap). While a basin of water might be placed on a table or tray where the student sits, it is awkward to put both hands in a basin at chest height and it may be difficult to see to perform the task. Removing the child from the sink also eliminates the possibility of performing important steps in the task, such as turning the water on and off. Children with physical disabilities may be unable to use the "normal" position of standing unsupported at the sink for face washing. Many children can perform the task while standing in a prone stander or parapodium stander, either of which gives postural support, frees the hands sufficiently to perform the task, provides a clear view and good access to the necessary materials, and approximates the normal position for the activity. Figures 3.13a and b show a child performing a similar task, washing dishes at home while standing at the sink in a prone stander. This child is also pictured lying on her side to watch television (see Figure 3.13c) and with her sister prone over a wedge strumming a guitar (see Figure 3.13d). These positions accommodate the performance demands of the activities and simultaneously facilitate normal postures and movements. Of equal importance, the child's daily routine provides natural opportunities to use a variety of therapeutic positions.

Another consideration in determining appropriate positions is the social context in which activities will be performed, both currently and in the future.

Figure 3.13a.   Therapeutic positions are matched with normal daily living activities for this girl with cerebral palsy. In this picture she stands in a prone stander to wash her lunch dishes.

The child in Figures 3.13a and b is engaged in activities at home, using positions that are suitable for the social context of her home. Within a self-contained special education classroom, these positions might still meet the social norm. If this child attends integrated classes, however, sitting may be preferable to enhance social integration, since other students sit in chairs for many of their classes. Experiences in integrated elementary and secondary schools have shown that typical students are extremely accepting of less traditional positioning, especially when they understand the reason for alternative positions.

Finally, the educational team must consider the various positions available to the students over the course of the day. Medical professionals have long recognized that immobility has adverse effects on motor, cardiovascular, respiratory, gastrointestinal, urinary, and metabolic functions (Olson, 1967). Prolonged sitting invites hip and knee flexion contractures and other deformities, particularly for children who cannot independently assume other positions (Fulford & Brown, 1976). Some muscles will develop contractures unless the muscle is in a lengthened position for a minimum of 5 hours per day (Tardieu, Lespargot, Tabary, & Bret, 1988). Sitting motionless creates circulatory problems underneath the hip bones, with noticeable changes occurring after just 30 minutes, and pressure sores developing in as little as 1–2 hours (Garber, 1985). Intense pressure, friction on the skin, or irritation from urine all increase the possibility of skin breakdown over bony areas when children with severe physical disabilities remain in the same position for long periods. Immobility and

Figure 3.13b.   Here is another view of her using a prone stander to assume the common position for dishwashing.

lack of weightbearing on the legs contribute severely to osteoporosis (Kaplan, 1983). Immobility and poor positioning interfere with pulmonary function, and are directly related to shortened life expectancy for people with profound disabilities (Eyman, Grossman, Chaney, & Call, 1990; Nwaobi & Smith, 1986). For these reasons, it is important that children experience a variety of positions. A good rule of thumb is for students to have at least two different positions between which they can alternate, and that positions be changed at least once an hour, preferably every 30 minutes. Table 3.4 presents a list of positions, equipment that might be used to achieve positions, and activities that typically would be performed in those positions. (Resource lists for locating and purchasing adapted equipment can be found in Fraser et al., 1990.) It is useful to develop a positioning plan to ensure that each student's positioning matches daily activi-

Figure 3.13c.   Recumbent positions are natural for leisure activities at home. She lies on her side to watch television.

ties while alternating between positions in which: 1) the head and trunk are upright, then reclined; 2) the hips and knees are flexed, then extended; and 3) weightbearing is on the hips and thighs, then on other body parts (preferably on the feet). The relative importance of each of these considerations depends on the student's risk for the health and therapeutic concerns identified earlier. A

Figure 3.13d.   For leisure activity, she lies on her stomach over a small wedge to strum her guitar.

Table 3.4.   Activities and equipment for alternative positions

Position	Typical activities	Standard equipment
Lying prone or supine	Resting, sunbathing	Mat or bed, pillow, wedges, rolls, sandbags
Sidelying	Resting, looking at books, listening to music or stories	Sidelying board, pillow
Prone on elbows	Watching television, looking at books	Wedge, roll, sandbags
Kneeling	Playing at low table, gardening, washing tub, cleaning cupboards	Kneeling box, adapted prone stander, tray or table
Sitting	Eating, playing board games, watching television, clerical work, needlework, toileting, riding in car	Wheelchair, corner chair, standard chair, stool, adapted toilet seat, carseat, tray or table
Standing	Grooming at sink or mirror, washing dishes, cooking, ironing, house cleaning, sports, locomotion	Prone stander, supine stander, parapodium stander, standing box, tray or table, walkers
Miscellaneous		Small cushions, belts

positioning plan is presented in Table 3.5 for a 14-year-old boy with severe physical disabilities who attends an integrated middle school program.

Braces and Splints

Braces and splints are prescribed: 1) when other positioning is not effective to maintain normal posture or alignment, 2) when children are too active to remain in static positions, and 3) when external control of a particular joint enhances more normal posture or movement patterns for the entire limb. Braces or splints may be worn on the trunk, leg, or arm. One type of brace, a plastic corset, has been used successfully in the treatment of scoliosis (Laurnen, Tupper, & Mullen, 1983), preventing further curvature of the spine but not necessarily reversing the process. For children with cerebral palsy, scoliosis, and poor head control, plastic corsets with chin and skull supports have controlled the scoliosis, increased the ease of handling and positioning the children, and simultaneously facilitated development of head control (Fulford, Cains, & Sloan, 1982). Although problems can arise when children have sensitive skin, when corsets are worn in warm climates, and when fit is not adjusted during growth, children with scoliosis typically wear corsets 23 hours per day with no detrimental effects (Keim, 1983).

For the leg and foot, splinting and casting have been used to reduce defor-

Table 3.5. Positioning plan for middle school student with multiple disabilities

Period	Activity	Position
Home room	Arrival routine (integrated)	Sitting in adapted wheelchair
1	Work in cafeteria	Standing in supine stander
2	Science (integrated)	Sitting in adapted wheelchair
3	Hygiene and break (grooming, changed in nurse's office, then rest)	Sitting, then supine lying with legs positioned
4	Lunch	Sitting in adapted wheelchair
5	Art (integrated) (M–Th)	Sidelying
	Music (integrated) (T–F)	Prone over wedge
	Community-based instruction (CBI) (W)	Sitting in adapted wheelchair
6	Language arts (integrated) (CBI) (continued) (W)	Sitting in adapted wheelchair
7	Technology (M–Th) Home and careers (T–F) (both integrated)	Standing in supine stander
	CBI (continued) (W)	
8	Hygiene and break (same as 3rd period)	Sitting, then supine lying
Home room	Departure routine (integrated)	Sitting in adapted wheelchair

mity, reduce spasticity, maintain stable joint positions during rest and standing, and ultimately reduce the need for surgery (Barnard et al., 1984; Booth, Doyle, & Montgomery, 1983; Sankey, Anderson, & Young, 1989; Sussman, 1983; Zachazewski, Eberle, & Jeffries, 1982). When children with cerebral palsy wear ankle-foot orthoses while walking, they typically increase their speed and decrease their energy consumption (Mossberg, Linton, & Friske, 1990). Although plastic splints have almost replaced metal braces, some children with severe spasticity or excessive weight require the more traditional high-top shoe and short leg brace. There is little evidence that orthopedic shoes alone prevent flat feet or deformities associated with physical disabilities; nevertheless, all children should enjoy the safety and cosmetic benefits of wearing shoes.

Splinting and casting have also been used to reduce deformity, reduce spasticity, and increase stabilization during functional use of the arm and hand. Although some practitioners believe that splinting masks spasticity in the hand and increases the abnormal tone in the rest of the arm, studies of electrical activity in the arm muscles do not support this contention (Mills, 1984). In fact, children with cerebral palsy have developed and maintained better bilateral hand use, grasp, and arm-hand posture after treatment with hand splints (Exner & Bonder, 1983). There are numerous types of orthokinetic, functional, and resting arm splints, however, and the attributes of each type must be understood for use to be effective (Exner & Bonder, 1983; McPherson, Kreimeyer, Aalderks, & Gallagher, 1982).

Currently the majority of splints are made of heat-molded plastics. Therapists have started experimenting with soft splints, made of polyurethane and neoprene (Anderson, Snow, Dorey, & Kabo, 1988; Casey & Kratz; 1988). Soft splints hold promise for greater comfort, function, and decreases in deformity than rigid splints. No matter what type of splint is used, splinting arms or legs can be expected to improve function only when muscle tone, posture, and movement in other parts of the body are normalized using therapeutic handling and positioning methods.

BODY MECHANICS

A discussion of handling and positioning would not be complete without attention to the body mechanics used by team members. The term *body mechanics* refers to the way caregivers position themselves and move when lifting and positioning children. Although adults have sustained back strain or more serious injuries when moving children with multiple disabilities, these problems usually can be avoided by using principles of body mechanics. Employing these principles also ensures greater safety and security for the children being moved.

Planning the Transfer

Prior to actually lifting the child, the adult arranges the environment, determines the extent to which the child can assist in the transfer, considers the position in which the child will be lifted, and determines whether assistance is needed to lift the child. The environment is arranged to minimize the distance the adult must carry the child. When positioning equipment can be moved easily, it is brought to the child rather than the child being carried to the equipment. Belts and other equipment needed for positioning are collected and placed nearby for quick application. The path between the child and positioning device is cleared to ensure a safe transfer.

Children are lifted and carried only when other more independent transfers and mobility cannot be facilitated. Most children with physical disabilities can roll, crawl on hands and knees, or walk within their home and classroom. Often they can be taught to climb in and out of their chairs as well. Although it is easy to lift young children, it is important that they learn to actively participate in transfers while they are small. Waiting until the child is older means the child will have to manage increased size, weight, and possibly contractures while working to develop the coordination needed for transfers and mobility. Even when children must be lifted and carried, their participation is enlisted. For one child, participation may be reaching for and holding the adult's shoulders. For another child, it may be staying relaxed or moving the head forward slightly when the adult reaches toward the child. The practice of soliciting the child's participation serves to maximize opportunities to teach children with multiple impairments and to further protect adults from unnecessary physical strain.

The next consideration is the position in which the child will be lifted. Children with extensor spasticity, flexor spasticity, and hypotonia (floppiness) are handled differently to normalize their tone. Therefore, they are positioned, lifted, and carried in somewhat different ways. It is helpful to physically orient the child to the next position, prior to lifting. This protects the adult from having to change the child's position during the transfer, when adult and child are most precarious.

The final consideration in planning the transfer is how many adults are needed to lift the child. While adults frequently lift small children independently, assistance should be enlisted to lift larger children. A good rule of thumb is to seek assistance when a child's weight is more than one quarter of one's own. To lift heavier children it may be necessary to have a third or even a fourth person. While these guidelines may seem unnecessarily restrictive, and therefore impractical, they serve to protect both children and adults from injury.

Lifting the Child

When all aspects of the lift have been planned, the adult prepares to lift the child. If the child is on the floor, the adult will squat or kneel on the floor facing the child and as close as possible. If the child is not on the floor, the adult will stand facing the child, with weight evenly distributed over both legs. If it is necessary to reach downward for the child, the adult will squat slightly by bending the knees. The trunk is not bent or twisted since these positions tend to cause back injuries. The adult then informs the child of the move to be made and requests the child's assistance. The adult takes hold of the child and brings the child close to the trunk to keep the child's weight over the adult's hips. When the child is positioned securely in the adult's arms, the adult can proceed to lift or lower the child. The essential rules for lifting and lowering are: 1) position the feet to provide a stable base of support, 2) keep a slight arch in the low back, 3) tighten and hold the abdominal muscles (but continue breathing), and 4) bend and straighten the hips and knees rather than the trunk. McKenzie (1985) recommends arching the back five or six times immediately before and after lifting to relieve pressure on the disks in the spine, thereby decreasing the chance of injury. Figure 3.14 illustrates the proper body position for lifting a small child. When two people lift a child, the same principles apply. Usually one adult holds the child's arms while the other adult holds the child's legs. One adult coordinates the lift, verbally rehearses the plan for the transfer, informs the child, and signals the other adult when to lift or lower the child. Figure 3.15 illustrates one way to hold a large child for lifting. Although the adults shown

Figure 3.14.   Correct handling and body mechanics for lifting a small child.

are handling the child securely, their own positions are precarious. Note that their backs are rounded, making them prone to back injury, and their foot position is unstable, increasing the chance of falling off balance. These poor body mechanics also increase the probability of injury to the child. Preventing injuries and ensuring safety requires that team members consistently apply the principles listed above.

DEVELOPING AND IMPLEMENTING HANDLING AND POSITIONING PROGRAMS IN EDUCATIONAL SETTINGS

All members of the educational team can provide important information about handling and positioning techniques that enhance the performance of students

Figure 3.15.   Correct handling for two people to lift a large child, but with *incorrect* body mechanics.

with multiple disabilities. For this reason, decisions on these matters are *team* decisions. Occupational and physical therapists offer the team particular expertise in therapeutic handling and positioning, current technological developments, and fitting equipment. Therefore an occupational or physical therapist on each student's team takes primary responsibility for developing procedures for normalization of tone, dynamic positioning, and positioning in equipment. Therapists also develop procedures to facilitate normal movement patterns and sequences, such as rolling, rising to stand, or walking. Once these procedures are developed, therapists create task analyses or checklists that become the basis for staff training. Therapists have used these tools successfully to train teachers in handling and positioning (Inge & Snell, 1985), and to monitor positioning, application of splints, and functions of various pieces of adapted equipment (Stephens & Lattimore, 1983; Venn, Morganstern, & Dykes, 1979). Checklists, pictures of proper positioning, and schedules of positioning and mobility for each activity and transition can be posted on bulletin boards and adapted equipment as reminders for educational team members. Using these simple systems to train staff and promote proper ongoing implementation of procedures, educational team members can ensure that each student derives the greatest benefit from therapeutic handling and positioning.

REFERENCES

Anderson, J., Snow, B., Dorey, F., & Kabo, J.M. (1988). Efficacy of soft splints in reducing severe flexion contractures. *Developmental Medicine and Child Neurology, 30*(4), 502–508.

Barnard, P., Dill, H., Eldredge, P., Held, J., Judd, D., & Nalette, E. (1984). Reduction of hypertonicity by early casting of a comatose, head-injured individual. A case report. *Physical Therapy, 64*(10), 1540–1542.

Batshaw, M.L., & Perret, Y.M. (1981). *Children with handicaps: A medical primer.* Baltimore: Paul H. Brookes Publishing Co.

Bergen, A., Presperin, J., & Tallman, T. (1990). *Positioning for function: Wheelchairs and other assistive technologies.* Valhalla, NY: Valhalla Rehabilitation Publications, Ltd.

Bobath, K. (1980). *The neurophysiological basis for the treatment of cerebral palsy* (2nd ed.). Philadelphia: J.B. Lippincott.

Bobath, K., & Bobath, B. (1972). Cerebral palsy. In P. Pearson & C. Williams (Eds.), *Physical therapy services in the developmental disabilities* (pp. 31–185). Springfield, IL: Charles C Thomas.

Booth, B., Doyle, M., & Montgomery, J. (1983). Serial casting for the management of spasticity in the head injured adult. *Physical Therapy, 63*(12), 1960–1966.

Butler, C. (1986). Effects of powered mobility on self-initiated behaviors of very young children with locomotor disability. *Developmental Medicine and Child Neurology, 28*(3), 325–332.

Butler, C., Okamoto, G., & McKay, T. (1983). Powered mobility for very young disabled children. *Developmental Medicine and Child Neurology, 25*(4), 472–474.

Campbell, P., McInerney, W., & Cooper, M. (1984). Therapeutic programming for students with severe handicaps. *American Journal of Occupational Therapy, 38*(9), 594–602.

Cantanese, A., & Sandford, D. (1984). Head position training through biofeedback: Prosthetic or cure. *Developmental Medicine and Child Neurology, 26*(3), 369–374.

Case-Smith, J., Fisher, A., & Bauer, D. (1989). An analysis of the relationship between proximal and distal motor control. *American Journal of Occupational Therapy, 43*(10), 657–663.

Casey, C., & Kratz, E. (1988). Soft splinting with neoprene: The thumb abduction supinator splint. *American Journal of Occupational Therapy, 42*(6), 395–398.

Connor, F., Williamson, G., & Siepp, J. (1978). *Program guide for infants and toddlers with neuromotor and other developmental disabilities.* New York: Teachers College Press.

DeGangi, G., Hurley, L., & Linscheid, T. (1983). Toward a methodology of short term effects of neurodevelopmental treatment. *American Journal of Occupational Therapy, 37*(7), 479–484.

Exner, C., & Bonder, B. (1983). Comparative effects of three hand splints on bilateral use, grasp, and arm-hand posture in hemiplegic children: A pilot study. *Occupational Therapy Journal of Research, 3*(2), 75–92.

Eyman, R., Grossman, H., Chaney, R., & Call, T. (1990). The life expectancy of profoundly handicapped people with mental retardation. *The New England Journal of Medicine, 323*(9), 584–589.

Finnie, N. (1975). *Handling the young cerebral palsied child at home.* New York: E.P. Dutton.

Fiorentino, M. (1963). *Reflex testing methods for evaluating CNS development.* Springfield, IL: Charles C Thomas.

Fraser, B.A., Hensinger, R.N., & Phelps, J.A. (1990). *Physical management of multi-*

ple handicaps: A professional's guide (2nd ed.). Baltimore: Paul H. Brookes Publishing Co.

Fulford, G., & Brown, J. (1976). Position as a cause of deformity in children with cerebral palsy. *Developmental Medicine and Child Neurology, 18*(3), 305–314.

Fulford, G., Cains, T., & Sloan, Y. (1982). Sitting problems of children with cerebral palsy. *Developmental Medicine and Child Neurology, 24*(1), 48–53.

Gadow, K. (1986). *Children on medication, Volume II: Epilepsy, emotional disturbance, and adolescent disorders.* San Diego: College-Hill Press.

Garber, S. (1985). Wheelchair cushions: A historical review. *American Journal of Occupational Therapy, 39*(7), 453–459.

Giangreco, M. (1986). Effects of integrated therapy: A pilot study. *Journal of The Association for Persons with Severe Handicaps, 11*(3), 205–208.

Goldkamp, O. (1984). Treatment effectiveness in cerebral palsy. *Archives of Physical Medicine and Rehabilitation, 65*(5), 232–234.

Hart, V. (1977). The use of many disciplines with the severely and profoundly handicapped. In E. Sontag, J. Smith, & N. Certo (Eds.), *Educational programming for the severely and profoundly handicapped* (pp.391–396). Reston, VA: Council for Exceptional Children.

Hulme, J., Poor, R., Schulein, M., & Pezzino, J. (1983). Perceived behavioral changes observed with adaptive seating devices and training programs for multihandicapped, developmentally disabled individuals. *Physical Therapy, 63*(2), 204–208.

Hulme, J., Shaver, J., Acher, S., Mullette, L., & Eggert, C. (1987). Effects of adaptive seating devices on the eating and drinking of children with multiple handicaps. *American Journal of Occupational Therapy, 41*(2), 81–89.

Hundertmark, L. (1985). Evaluating the adult with cerebral palsy for specialized adaptive seating. *Physical Therapy, 65*(2), 209–212.

Hutchison, D. (1978). The transdisciplinary approach. In J. Curry & K. Peppe (Eds.), *Mental retardation: Nursing approaches to care* (pp. 65–74). St. Louis: C.V. Mosby.

Inge, K.J., & Snell, M.E. (1985). Teaching positioning and handling techniques to public school personnel through inservice training. *Journal of The Association for Persons with Severe Handicaps, 10*(2), 105–110.

Jaeger, L. (1987). *Home program instruction sheets for infants and young children.* Tucson: Therapy Skill Builders.

Kalen, V., & Bleck, E. (1985). Prevention of spastic paralytic dislocation of the hip. *Developmental Medicine and Child Neurology, 27*(1), 17–24.

Kaplan, F. (1983). Osteoporosis. *Clinical Symposia, 35*(5).

Keim, H. (1983). Fundamentals and basic principles of scoliosis. *Orthopedic Review, 12*(3), 31–40.

Kohn, J., Enders, S., Preston, J., & Motloch, W. (1983). Provision of assistive equipment for handicapped persons. *Archives of Physical Medicine and Rehabilitation, 64*(8), 378–381.

Kottke, F., Halpern, D., Easton, J., Ozel, A., & Burrill, C. (1978). The training of coordination. *Archives of Physical Medicine and Rehabilitation, 59*(11), 567–572.

Laurnen, E., Tupper, J., & Mullen, M. (1983). The Boston brace in thoracic scoliosis. A preliminary report. *Spine, 8*(4), 388–395.

Levitt, S. (1982). *Treatment of cerebral palsy and motor delay* (2nd. ed.). Boston: Blackwell Scientific.

Leiper, C., Miller, A., Lang, J., & Herman, R. (1981). Sensory feedback for head control in cerebral palsy. *Physical Therapy, 61*(4), 512–518.

Lilly, L., & Powell, N. (1990). Measuring the effects of neurodevelopmental treatment on the daily living skills of 2 children with cerebral palsy. *American Journal of Occupational Therapy, 44*(2), 139–145.

Loria, C. (1980). Relationship of proximal and distal function in motor development. *Physical Therapy, 60*(2), 167–172.

McKenzie, R. (1985). *Treat your own back.* Lower Hutt, New Zealand: Spinal Publications Ltd.

McPherson, J., Kreimeyer, D., Aalderks, M., & Gallagher, T. (1982). A comparison of dorsal and volar resting hand splints in the reduction of hypertonus. *American Journal of Occupational Therapy, 36*(10), 664–670.

Mills, Y. (1984). Electomyographic results of inhibitory splinting. *Physical Therapy, 64*(2), 190–193.

Morris, S., & Klein, M. (1987). *Pre-feeding skills: A comprehensive resource for feeding development.* Tucson: Therapy Skill Builders.

Mossberg, K., Linton, K., & Friske, K. (1990). Ankle-foot orthoses: Effect on energy expenditure of gait in spastic diplegic children. *Archives of Physical Medicine and Rehabilitation, 71*(7), 490–494.

Murphy, R., Doughty, N., & Nunes, D. (1979). Multielement designs: An alternative to reversal and multiple baseline evaluation strategies. *Mental Retardation, 17*(1), 23–28.

Noonan, M. (1984). Teaching postural reactions to students with severe cerebral palsy. *Journal of The Association for Persons with Severe Handicaps, 9*(2), 111–122.

Nwaobi, O. (1986). Effects of body orientation in space on tonic muscle activity of patients with cerebral palsy. *Developmental Medicine and Child Neurology, 28*(1), 41–44.

Nwaobi, O., Brubaker, C., Cusick, B., & Sussman, M. (1983). Electromyographic investigation of extensor activity in cerebral palsied children in different seating positions. *Developmental Medicine and Child Neurology, 25*(2), 175–183.

Nwaobi, O., Hobson, D., Eng, P., & Taylor, S. (1988). Mechanical and anatomical hip flexion angles on seating children with cerebral palsy. *Archives of Physical Medicine and Rehabilitation, 69*(4), 265–267.

Nwaobi, O., & Smith, P. (1986). Effect of adaptive seating on pulmonary function of children with cerebral palsy. *Developmental Medicine and Child Neurology, 28*(3), 351–354.

Olson, E. (1967). The hazards of immobility. *American Journal of Nursing, 67*(4), 780–797.

Parette, H., & Hourcade, J. (1984). How effective are physiotherapeutic programs with young mentally retarded children who have cerebral palsy? *Journal of Mental Deficiency Research, 28*(3), 167–175.

Sankey, R., Anderson, D., & Young, J. (1989). Characteristics of ankle-foot orthoses for management of the spastic lower limb. *Developmental Medicine and Child Neurology, 31*(4), 466–470.

Sents, B., & Marks, H. (1989). Changes in preschool children's IQ scores as a function of positioning. *American Journal of Occupational Therapy, 43*(10), 685–688.

Stephens, T., & Lattimore, J. (1983). Prescriptive checklist for positioning multihandicapped residential clients: A clinical report. *Physical Therapy, 63*(7), 1113–1115.

Sussman, M. (1983). Casting as an adjunct to neurodevelopmental therapy for cerebral palsy. *Developmental Medicine and Child Neurology, 25*(6), 804–805.

Tardieu, C., Lespargot, A., Tabary, C., & Bret, M. (1988). For how long must the soleus muscle be stretched each day to prevent contracture? *Developmental Medicine and Child Neurology, 30*(1), 3–10.

Taylor, S. (1987). Evaluating the client with physical disabilities for wheelchair seating. *American Journal of Occupational Therapy, 41*(11), 711–716.

Trefler, E., Nickey, J., & Hobson, D. (1983). Technology in the education of multiply handicapped children. *American Journal of Occupational Therapy, 37*(6), 381–387.

Venn, J., Morganstern, L., & Dykes, M. (1979). Checklists for evaluating the fit and function of orthoses, prostheses, and wheelchairs in the classroom. *Teaching Exceptional Children, 11*(2), 51–56.

York, J. & Wieman, G. (1991). Accommodating severe physical disabilities. In J. Reichle, J. York, & J. Sigafoos. *Implementing augmentative and alternative communication: Strategies for learners with severe disabilities.* Baltimore: Paul H. Brookes Publishing Co.

Zachazewski, J., Eberle, E., & Jeffries, M. (1982). Effect of tone inhibiting casts and orthoses on gait. A case report. *Physical Therapy, 62*(4), 453–455.

Chapter 4

Sensory Impairments

Dick Sobsey and Enid G. Wolf-Schein

Most people who see and hear without difficulty cannot imagine life without these abilities. Vision and hearing are vital to survival, health, and quality of life. With the loss of only one of these senses, mobility, communication, and learning become much more difficult. When both senses are impaired or additional disabilities are present and one is unable to use functional alternatives, all aspects of life are affected.

This chapter presents basic information about disorders of hearing and vision as they affect children with multiple disabilities. It identifies suitable assessment procedures that can provide the intervention team with a clear picture of the nature and extent of sensory deficits. It describes methods of prevention and treatment, discusses the educational implications of sensory impairment for children with multiple disabilities, and explores the roles of transdisciplinary team members in maximizing functional performance by the child.

SENSORY IMPAIRMENT AMONG CHILDREN WITH MULTIPLE DISABILITIES

Prevalence

Estimates of the numbers of children with multiple disabilities who also have impaired hearing and/or vision are notoriously inconsistent and inaccurate. Inconsistencies result from differences in the definitions used for various disabilities as well as the differences in sampling procedures. According to the Annual Survey of Hearing Impaired Children and Youth (Wolff & Harkins, 1986), 30.2% of the students with hearing impairments reported on had additional handicapping conditions, with 9.5% of those having two or more additional disabilities. However, they acknowledge that two groups are grossly under-represented in the survey: children with significant disabilities who have a hearing impairment and children with mild hearing impairments who are mainstreamed with hearing children. For example, a high rate of hearing impairment has frequently been observed in institutions for people with developmental disabilities (Moores, 1987), but because institutions do not generally participate in the Annual Survey, these children are undercounted. A New York State study of the "frail/severely handicapped" found that 22% of the children in the community and 23% of the children in institutions had impaired hearing (Jacobson & Janicki, 1985). This means that 100% of these people with hearing impairments who were excluded from the Annual Survey had at least one additional disability! If they, and similar populations, were counted in the Annual Survey, the percentage of children and youth with hearing impairments who have additional disabilities obviously would be much greater.

Kirchner (1985) examined data collected in the 1977 Health Interview Survey prepared by the U.S. National Center for Health Statistics, which defined "Severe visual impairment" as the "inability to see well enough to read ordinary newsprint even with glasses," and he found that 59% of respondents with visual impairment also had other disabilities. Furthermore, having multiple impairments frequently meant having two or more types of impairment besides visual impairment. Other surveys conducted in Scandinavia and the United States suggest that blind children with mental retardation outnumber those with unimpaired cognitive abilities (Brett, 1983). Some research suggests that as many as 75%–90% of the people with severe or profound disabilities also have visual impairments (Cress et al., 1981). The New York State study of the "frail/ severely handicapped" found that 43% of the children in the community and 42% of the children in institutions had impaired vision (Jacobson & Janicki, 1985). It also has been suggested that the number of children with visual impairments may be increasing because of medical advances that have made survival possible for many infants who are premature and/or have low birth weight and health problems (Leung & Hollins, 1989).

The number of children with both hearing and visual impairments is also difficult to estimate accurately. In 1986, Dantona reported a total population of 6,117 deaf-blind children in the United States. A projection of data from the Jacobson and Janicki (1985) study suggests a figure of 12,000 or more children with visual and hearing impairments in addition to other developmental disabilities. A study of the size and characteristics of the United States deaf-blind population conducted by the Department of Education (Wolf-Schein, 1989) divides the population into four groups: Deaf-Blind, Deaf and Severely Impaired Visually, Blind and Severely Impaired Auditorily, and Severely Impaired Auditorily and Visually. A combination of noninstitutionalized and institutionalized people who are Deaf-Blind showed a prevalence of 45,310. The combined prevalence of all four groups was 747,457. This provides a strong indication that the number varies depending on the way the group is defined and that even when the most stringent definition was used, the numbers were greater than generally assumed. Other findings indicate that females were represented in each group at a higher rate than males, that the highest prevalence rate in each of the categories was for the 65-and-over group, and that there was considerable difference depending on geography.

Regardless of which estimates are eventually validated, it is clear that impairment of vision and/or hearing occurs many times more frequently among children with multiple disabilities than among other children. Approximately one child with multiple disabilities in five can be expected to have impaired hearing, and two in five can be expected to have impaired vision. Every teacher of children with severe and multiple disabilities can expect to encounter these students and should be prepared to meet their special needs. Program planners should also be aware that prevalence rates for any disability vary according to location and that rates calculated for one period of time will not hold for another period, even in the same locale (Schein, 1987).

The Nature of Sensory Impairments

Vision   There are degrees of blindness: some blind people are unable to see at all, others can see a little, while still others can see enough to recognize another person using physical cues. The definition of legal blindness involves measures of acuity, the visual system's ability to perceive detail, and visual field. Visual acuity is typically measured with an eyechart placed 20 feet away from the person being tested and is typically described as a fraction with its numerator representing the actual distance (20 feet) of the chart from the person and its denominator representing the distance (e.g., 20, 40, 200 feet) at which the smallest letters that the individual can read at 20 feet should be readable (i.e., would be readable to a person with unimpaired vision). The person with unimpaired vision can read letters a certain size at 20 feet and is said to have 20/20 vision. The worse the person's visual acuity, the larger the denominator. Individuals are considered *legally blind* when, with the best visual correction, their visual acuity is 20/200 or worse. This is 10 times poorer than that of a person with unimpaired vision. A person may also be legally blind because of a restricted visual field. Anyone whose visual field is less than 20 degrees in diameter qualifies as being legally blind, regardless of acuity in the region of the field that remains (Hollins, 1989). Being *partially sighted* is defined as having vision of 20/70–20/200 after correction (Batshaw & Perret, 1986). The term *low vision* is now sometimes used to describe the vision of individuals who have a serious visual impairment but still have some functional vision.

Visual impairment is much more complex than indicated by these simple numbers or categories of acuity. The visual system is highly sophisticated with many components, as illustrated in Figure 4.1. Defects in any of these components may result in visual impairment. The muscles that control the eye may lack mobility or coordination. The *cornea,* which covers the pupil, may be mis-

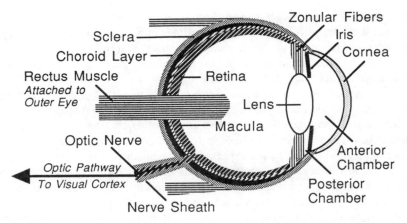

Figure 4.1.   Some of the structures of the eye frequently involved in visual impairment.

shapen, distorting the light that enters the eye. The *iris*, which opens and closes to control the amount of light entering the eye, may be damaged and let in too much or too little light. The *lens*, which focuses light as it enters the eye, may become opaque, preventing light from entering. All or part of the *retina*, which transforms the pattern of light to chemical-electrical impulses, may be damaged in ways that create blind spots or limit the field of vision. Weak receptors in the retina may require extra light for vision. *Optic pathways*, which carry visual impulses to the brain, may be damaged, limiting vision severely. The *visual cortex*, an area at the back of the brain that translates visual images, may be damaged, restricting or eliminating vision (Bach-y-Rita, 1972). Even when all of these visual components are working properly, higher brain centers may have difficulty using visual information. It is important that all transdisciplinary team members understand the specific nature of a child's impairment and its implications for intervention. For example, two students may have 20/180 vision, but one may have impaired vision as a result of *aniridia* (congenital lack of the iris), and the other as a result of *optic atrophy* (degeneration of the optic nerve). The former student will see better with increased illumination and the latter with lowered illumination (Sims-Tucker & Jensema, 1984). Because the various visual defects require specific interventions, the vision specialist plays an important role in preparing other team members to best meet the needs of each child.

Hearing   Hearing loss may be classified by the degree of loss, age at onset, cause of impairment, or structures affected. Of course factors such as environmental demands, the individual's other senses, and often several additional factors have an impact on hearing impairment, resulting in specific capabilities and needs. For example, the ability to understand speech may differ for two children with identical hearing loss, depending on their visual and cognitive skills, and the social environment that they experience.

Degree of Loss   When a person is *deaf,* the hearing is impaired to the extent that he or she cannot understand speech through the ear alone, with or without the use of a hearing aid. When a person is *hard of hearing* the hearing is impaired to an extent that makes difficult but does not preclude the understanding of speech through the ear alone, with or without a hearing aid (Moores, 1987). Degree of loss may be classified according to sound frequency (Hertz or Hz [cycles per second]) and intensity levels (Decibels or dB) that the individual requires to hear speech or other sounds (Moores, 1987). The degree of hearing loss may differ across frequencies, but particular attention is usually paid to losses in the 500–2000 Hz range because this range is critical for discrimination of speech.

Individuals with *mild hearing loss* (Level I, 35–54 dB) can hear most speech and many other sounds in their environment, but generally benefit from classroom modifications, including amplification in many cases. Speech-language therapy and auditory training will also be helpful for these students. Although some will benefit from nonspeech language alternatives, partially depending on the nature and extent of other concurrent disabilities, speech is a viable receptive and productive language alternative for many. Students with *moderate hearing loss* (Level II, 55–69 dB) require special speech, hearing, and language assistance and amplification unless the nature of the hearing loss precludes benefit (e.g., some types of neural hearing loss are not helped with amplification). Speech can still be an important part of communication for these students. Individuals with *severe hearing loss* (Level III, 70–89 dB) and other disabilities will require special speech, hearing, language, and educational assistance. Some will benefit from amplification, but many will not. Most will benefit from the use of nonspeech language alternatives. Individuals with *profound hearing loss* (Level IV, 90 dB or greater) require intensive language and educational assistance. With this level of impairment, nonspeech language alternatives are almost always necessary, but careful assessment of individuals by speech and hearing professionals is important to determine the most appropriate intervention.

Age at Onset   Individuals are considered to have prelingual deafness when their deafness was present at birth or occurred prior to the development of speech and language. Persons with postlingual deafness are those whose deafness occurred after they had acquired speech and language. Students with multiple disabilities who have been exposed to speech and learned some basic receptive and productive speech skills will have a better chance of acquiring useful speech with any given degree of loss than students with prelingual deafness.

Cause   Deafness can result from many causes. For example, it may be due to environmental factors such as infections or injury before, during, or after birth or exposure to loud noise over a period of time. It may also be of genetic origin. Often when deafness is genetic in origin, parents and siblings are also deaf. Deaf children who grow up in homes where sign language is used often learn this language alternative with greater ease, so this may be a factor in selecting a language alternative. The full extent of the hearing loss may be present from birth or it may be progressive. The frequency with which deafness occurs is also influenced by sickness, disease, and the quality of health care. A dramatic example is the rubella epidemic of 1963–1965, which tripled the number of children born deaf in the United States over that period. Since then there have been several epidemics in North America resulting in increased numbers of individuals with hearing loss in specific years.

Structures Affected   Hearing losses are usually categorized as either *conductive, sensorineural, mixed,* or *central auditory disorders.* Conductive impairments result from interference in the pathway from the ear canal to the inner ear. They may be caused by wax, a hole in the eardrum, middle ear infection (otitis media), bony growth of the small bones (ossicles) in the middle ear, or a birth abnormality. Sensorineural (nerve damage) hearing loss occurs in the inner ear or along the eighth cranial (vestibulocochlear) nerve, which is the auditory pathway. This may result from such maternal infection as rubella (German measles), or from inherited conditions, early childhood problems (e.g., anoxia, meningitis), ototoxic (harmful to hearing) drugs, or other causes, some of which may be unknown. Mixed impairments are those in which both the conductive and sensorineural systems are impaired. Conductive loss is often medically or surgically correctable, while a sensorineural loss is not. Figure 4.2 depicts some of the structures that may be involved in hearing loss.

Individuals are considered to have central auditory disorders when they cannot respond meaningfully to sound due to central organic dysfunctions. Remediation is accomplished through language therapy and educational intervention. Often this diagnosis is made as a result of the elimination of other possible causes rather than clear identification of damage to the central auditory system, and it is particularly difficult to make this diagnosis with certainty in students with multiple disabilities.

There is no such thing as a "typical" hearing impaired (HI) student with additional disabilities. Service providers face a challenge in dealing with the diversity of characteristics found among HI students with developmental disabilities (Karchmer, 1985). Even when two individuals have identical degrees of hearing impairment, the effects may differ (Schein, 1988). One student may benefit from a hearing aid, while the other will not be helped by amplification. The audiologist and communication therapist can play important roles in helping all transdisciplinary team members understand the nature of the child's hearing loss and how best to provide intervention.

Vision and Hearing   Children who are both visually impaired (VI) and

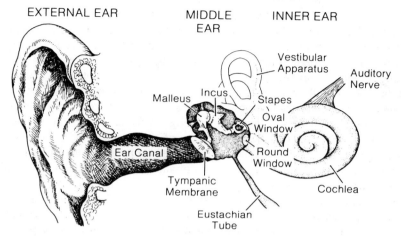

EXTERNAL EAR   MIDDLE   INNER EAR
                        EAR

Vestibular
Apparatus   Auditory
                   Nerve
Malleus   Incus   Stapes
                   Oval
                   Window
Ear Canal   Round
                   Window
Tympanic   Cochlea
Membrane
Eustachian
Tube

Figure 4.2.   Components of the auditory system. (From Batshaw, M.L., & Perret, Y.M. [1986]. *Children with handicaps: A medical primer* [2nd ed.], p. 225. Baltimore: Paul H. Brookes Publishing Co.; reprinted with permission of author.)

hearing impaired (HI) require special consideration. For the individual with only one of these sensory impairments, the ability to compensate often depends on increased dependence on the unimpaired sense; if the other sense is also impaired, alternatives are greatly reduced. Obviously, this problem is greatly compounded when children also have motoric and cognitive disabilities. Depending on the nature and degree of the impairments, students with this dual disability have often been placed in a hierarchy of programs:

1. A regular classroom with special devices, attention, and support
2. A classroom for either VI or HI children
3. A noncategorical special education program with specialized educational procedures provided for the VI/HI student
4. A self-contained program for deaf-blind students, with all activities geared toward their special needs
5. A highly protective environment with the focus primarily on self-help skills

Any placement should be monitored so that the student will have opportunities for movement to a more normalized setting. As with placements for students with other types of disabilities, the setting may not always be as important as the skill of the teacher, the specialized support that is available, and the technical aids that can be provided. It is also important to consider that the degree of the visual or hearing impairment may not be as important in determining a placement as the motivation of the student to learn, the nature and extent of socially unacceptable behavior, and the motivation of others to accept and meaningfully integrate the child.

Many children who have other multiple disabilities and are deaf-blind have serious emotional or behavioral problems (Chess, Korn, & Hernandez, 1971). Some of these children also engage in a high degree of self-stimulation (Moersch, 1977). The function of some of the self-stimulation, such as eye gouging and screaming, appears to be either an attempt to intensify visual and auditory input to their impaired senses or to provide a general tactile-kinesthetic stimulation. Unfortunately, these behaviors are often socially unacceptable, and many of them are self-injurious, making it difficult to place these children in mainstream social and educational environments where more socially acceptable behavior is likely to be learned. The best approach to elimination of these behaviors is to provide less harmful and more socially acceptable substitute activities. These must be incorporated in the educational process because many of these students do not have the ability to determine what is or is not acceptable, or the skills to develop an alternative behavior. For example, body-rocking may be viewed as deviant behavior, but an exercise program providing similar stimulation may be socially valued.

Etiology   The high correlation between sensory impairments and other handicapping conditions is probably due to six factors. First, any of the same factors that cause sensory impairments can also cause other defects. For example, *Haemophilus influenzae B* can cause otitis media (middle ear infection), which may lead to impaired hearing, and also can cause meningitis, which may lead to cognitive and motor deficits.

Second, the same syndromes that cause other developmental disabilities may be associated with sensory impairments (Efron, 1981). For example, children with Down syndrome often have *keratoconus* (a malformation of the cornea that distorts vision); decreased resistance to middle ear infections; and narrow, easily blocked ear canals. In the fragile X syndrome, which is now considered second only to Down syndrome as a genetic cause of mental retardation, a connective tissue disorder may facilitate a tendency toward ocular problems (e.g., myopia, strabismus), as well as a malfunction of the eustachian tube, which can result in an increased number of middle ear infections (Wolf-Schein, 1990).

Third, attempts to treat another disability may result in a sensory deficit. For example, high oxygen levels given to premature infants may cause retrolental fibroplasia producing severe visual impairment. Toxic reactions to some antibiotics may also produce hearing impairment.

Fourth, failure to recognize early signs of illness or disability among children with multiple disabilities may result in permanent sensory impairment. For example, middle ear infections may go untreated when children are unable to communicate that they are experiencing discomfort, and the resulting delay can cause permanent hearing loss.

Fifth, although it should never occur, treatment has sometimes been withheld from children with severe or multiple disabilities. For example, Cress et al.

(1981) point out that corrective lenses may not be prescribed because it is believed that vision is "adequate for the learner's needs." Of course, they go on to urge that no such discriminatory criterion be applied and that corrective intervention be considered according to the same criteria as for children who do not have disabilities.

Sixth, there can be decreased expectations for performance of individuals with mental disabilities. Negative expectations sometimes result in reduced stimulation during the developmental period and the lack of adequate stimulation may lead to functional impairment of vision, hearing, and related functional skills. For example, lack of sensitivity to nonintentional communicative behavior may hinder emergence of intentional communication (Siegel-Causey & Downing, 1987).

ASSESSMENT OF SENSORY DEFICITS

Team members who need sensory assessment data on children with multiple disabilities often meet with obstacles. They may be told that because of the severity of the disability the child's hearing or vision cannot be tested. Or, after inadequate assessment , they may be told that the child is totally and irrevocably deaf or blind and no remediation will be of value. Fortunately, neither of these situations needs to occur. Adequate assessment of both hearing and vision can be carried out for every child. There is no longer any justification for placing loosely applied labels (e.g., cortical blindness) on a child without clear and objective evidence of pathology (Harden, 1983). Furthermore, increasing evidence suggests that even children who lack hearing or vision at a given point may develop or recover it in time. For example, some children who have been blind for several months after birth have shown the first signs of vision at 6–8 months and developed normal vision by 2 or 3 years of age (Harel, Holtzman, & Feinshod, 1985). This means that no diagnosis should be viewed as a "life sentence" for the young child.

Typically, evaluation procedures are categorized as *screening,* which is used to identify increased risk of sensory deficits, or *clinical assessment,* which is used to determine the exact nature and extent of sensory abilities and deficits (Atkinson, 1985). Since children with multiple disabilities are already identified as being at risk for sensory deficits and typically require individualized testing procedures rather than the standard screening procedures, all children with multiple disabilities should have a complete clinical assessment of vision and hearing (Cress et al., 1981).

Assessing Vision

Assessing the vision of children with multiple disabilities requires two main areas of evaluation: 1) tests of physiological function, and 2) evaluation of functional use of vision. Each type of evaluation supplies valuable information, and neither can substitute completely for the other.

Tests of Physiological Function   The testing of vision can be a highly technical process, employing a large number of tests and sophisticated equipment. Only a few of these tests will be discussed here. Those selected for discussion are tests that are often well suited to assessing children who cannot or will not actively participate in more traditional tests.

Modified Subjective Acuity Tests   Students who do not have disabilities usually take subjective acuity tests in which they are typically shown a Snellen chart and asked to read letters of various sizes. The smaller the letter the student can read, the better his or her vision. Of course, most children with multiple disabilities will not be able to read letters at any distance, making commonly used charts inappropriate for testing them.

One approach to solving this problem is to replace the letters with various objects or pictures. From 20 feet away, a child with 20/20 vision should be able to recognize an item ⅜ inch long and with details as small as ¹⁄₁₆ inch. A child with 20/200 vision should be able to recognize an item 3.5 inches long with details as small as ¹³⁄₁₆ inch, and so forth. For children capable of recognizing and labeling familiar items, a chart replacing the standard letters with items of similar size provides a good alternative, but for many others, such a task goes far beyond their current skills (Cress et al., 1981).

Forced-Choice Preferential Looking   Forced-choice preferential looking (FPL) requires a simpler response. In the FPL procedure, two screens lit with the same average illumination intensity are projected. As illustrated in Figure 4.3, one has no pattern, and the other is striped, checkered, or has lines that wiggle. Most children will consistently look at the patterned screen. If the child demonstrates a preference for the patterned screen, repeated pairings are presented, with the patterned side alternated and with increasingly finer patterns. When the individual units in the pattern become too small to be discriminated by the individual, the square appears gray and cannot be discriminated from the other item in the pair. Therefore, no pattern preference occurs. The smallest pattern size for which the child demonstrates consistent preference indicates visual acuity (Atkinson, 1985). Such tests of visual acuity are extremely important because they test the function of the entire visual system rather than its individual parts; even so, the FPL procedure may be extremely difficult for some students.

Optokinetic Nystagmus (OKN)   Another test that can be useful in estimating visual acuity, but with further reduced response requirements, is the optokinetic nystagmus test (Hall & Jolly, 1984). Optokinetic nystagmus refers to the natural reflex response in which the eyes follow a moving stimulus. Repetitive stimuli are projected on a moving drum so that they move across the child's entire visual field at a rate of 20–30/second (Atkinson, 1985). (See Figure 4.4.) If the child tracks the stimuli, the eyes, visual pathways, and some basic cortical processing must be functioning (Taylor, 1983). When line size is too small to be seen, the observer no longer perceives rotation and the eyes

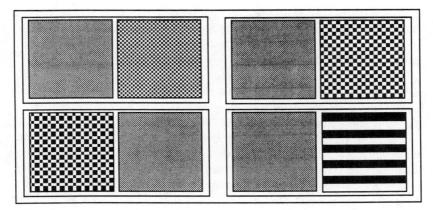

Figure 4.3. Four stimulus pairs used in a Forced Choice Preferential Looking test. All are 50% black and 50% white.

cease to follow. Although more work is needed to determine the accuracy and reliability of these estimates, the smallest size component in the moving patterns tracked by the student allows the examiner to estimate visual acuity (Taylor, 1983). OKN is also useful for assessing movement patterns of the eyes and how well the right and left eyes are coordinated (Atkinson, 1985).

Orthoptic Tests   Tests of alignment of the eyes are known as orthoptic tests. Severe *strabismus* (misalignment of the eyes, which makes it difficult or impossible to point them toward the same target) can typically be detected by casual observation, but milder or transient forms of misalignment may require examination. Often, these misalignments are given a diagnostic label that indicates the type of deviation. *Esotropia* (an eye pointing inward), *exotropia* (an

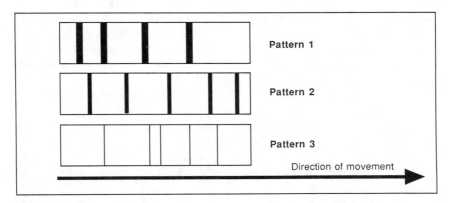

Figure 4.4. Optokinetic Nystagmus (OKN) Test. Lines move on rotating drum and eyes follow direction of rotation. When line size is too small to be seen, the observer no longer perceives rotation and eyes cease to follow.

eye pointing outward), *hypertropia* (an eye pointing upward), and hypoptropia (an eye pointing downward) all result in difficulty integrating visual images from the two eyes and are generally correctable through simple surgical procedures.

Tests to detect alignment problems examine eye alignment during a number of visual tasks and when covered eyes are suddenly uncovered (Atkinson, 1985). Symmetrical or asymmetrical reflections of a lighted stimulus in the child's eyes also provide valuable data.

Retinoscopy   An objective method of assessing refractive error of an eye, called *retinoscopy* or *skiascopy,* allows for diagnosis of *myopia* (nearsightedness), *hyperopia* (farsightedness), or *astigmatism* (irregular refractive error), all of which can be corrected with the appropriate corrective lenses (Atkinson, 1985). Since the lenses of the eyes permit light to travel in either direction, their refractive power can be measured by the examiner looking in and focusing the retina. The amount of correction required to attain focus indicates the type and degree of refractive error without requiring any response from the child (Cress et al., 1981).

Isotropic Photorefraction   Using the same principle, *isotropic photorefraction* uses a series of at least three flash photographs with the camera focused in front of, on, and behind the child's eyes. White blur circles over the child's pupils indicate where the child's eyes were focused. Misshapen reflections indicate astigmatism (Atkinson, 1985).

Electrical Discharge Tests   In *electroretinography* (ERG), electrodes attached near the eyes allow measurement of the retina's general ability to produce electrical discharges in response to stimulation by light (Batshaw & Perret, 1986). *Visual evoked potentials* (VEP), also known as *visual evoked response* (VER), measure electrical activity from the visual cortex at the back of the brain in response to flashes of light (Baine, 1985). Although much remains to be learned regarding exactly how much this test can reveal, patterns responded to can provide a rough estimate of acuity (Atkinson, 1985). Careful placement of electrodes is essential since poor data that result from badly placed electrodes can easily be misinterpreted as indicating visual defects (Longo, Rotatori, Heinze, & Kapperman, 1982).

Harden (1983) points out that VEP and ERG are most useful when used together and along with other tests. For example, a poor or absent ERG with a normal VEP might indicate that peripheral vision is lost but that central vision is intact. A normal VEP in a child who has a severely abnormal electroencephalogram (EEG) may indicate that vision is unimpaired but that the child has difficulty processing visual information, a condition that may be reversible, especially with training.

VEP procedures also have been used to assess orientation-selective cortical function. Since sub-cortical visual mechanisms do not react to orientation,

VEP responses to sequenced changes in orientation of line edges superimposed on circular patterns specifically indicate cortical function (Atkinson, 1989).

Other Visual Assessment The tests discussed above represent only a few of the many evaluation procedures appropriate for use with children with multiple disabilities. Ultrasound, X-ray, reflexes, eye preference, pupillary response, and many more can provide additional, useful information (Jose, Smith, & Shane, 1980). The vision specialist plays an important role in planning and conducting evaluation suited to the child and in helping the other transdisciplinary team members understand the assessment results and their implications for intervention. Tests of physiological function play an important role in this process, but much more information is required to understand the child's functional use of vision.

Evaluation of Functional Use of Vision In order to evaluate functional use of vision, the team can: 1) obtain information about the child's history from existing records; 2) request information from parents, caregivers, or others who have spent significant time with the child; 3) observe the child in natural environments; or 4) attempt to elicit responses related to visual skills. Functional assessment must be individualized on the basis of the child's abilities and disabilities; degree of cooperation given; reaction to reinforcers available; previous learning history; past, current, and future environments; and objectives for learning. Some of the information that might be important to review from the four sources includes:

1. What was the age at onset and type and degree of problem?
2. Has the visual problem been improving or worsening?
3. Does the environment or activity seem to have an effect on the child's ability to see?
4. Is the child taking medication that is known to have visual side effects? For example, phenobarbital may cause double vision, impaired visual pursuit, and many other visual problems; other anticonvulsants and tranquilizers also can have very significant visual effects (Fraunfelder, 1976).
5. Does the child show signs of any other condition that could affect vision either temporarily or permanently?
6. What kinds of visual skills are required for current objectives?

Parents and other informants can also provide information based on their daily experiences. While their reports may lack precision, they are based on a variety of experiences over a period of time and may be more sensitive than a limited observation by a professional, particularly if the child is not very cooperative. Also, parents as well as the teacher or other prominent caregivers, are able to report behavior that occurs only occasionally, and obtaining information from these knowledgeable sources may be much faster than other methods. The most effective evaluation process usually combines all four methods. Reviewing records and interviewing family and significant others first may provide information about the best times and places for natural observation. Information from natural observation may suggest important stimuli to present or responses to look for in an elicited behavior sample.

Together, review of history, interview, natural observation, and elicited observation can help provide answers to many important questions (Cote & Smith, 1983; Jose et al., 1980). Does the child orient himself or herself toward light? Does the child move easily around the environment without bumping into things? Does the child exhibit visual discrimination? Does the child recognize faces? Does the child look directly at things? Do the child's eyes track moving objects with smooth and coordinated movements? Does the child demonstrate interest in visual stimuli? Does the child walk with a shuffling gait, arms extended in front, or head shifted back? The answers to these questions must be considered along with data on the child's physiological functioning when planning and intervention are carried out by the transdisciplinary team.

Assessing Hearing

A variety of procedures can be used to assess the hearing of people with severe disabilities who have been characterized as difficult to test. These procedures may be divided into two groups: 1) tests of physiological function that determine if all or a specific part of the auditory system is functioning properly, which include behavioral test procedures and objective hearing tests, and 2) evaluation of functional use of hearing.

Behavioral Test Procedures

Behavioral Observation Audiometry (BOA)   Behavioral observation audiometry depends upon the observation of change in a child's behavior and activity upon presentation of test stimuli. Behavioral responses can take several forms and are often subtle, requiring the observations of experienced examiners.

Visual Reinforcement Audiometry (VRA)   Visual reinforcement audiometry is a test procedure that, in its most commonly employed form, involves the presentation of an auditory signal from a loudspeaker, a head-turn response toward the sound source, and the presentation of an attractive visual stimulus (such as an animated toy) as reinforcement for appropriate responses (Thompson, Thompson, & Vethivelu, 1989). This procedure has limitations when children have visual impairments, are uninterested in the toys, are unable to turn their heads from side to side, or are able to hear but not to localize sounds.

Conditioned Play Audiometry (CPA)   Conditioned play audiometry is a procedure in which a child is conditioned, using instruction or demonstration, to complete a specific play activity, such as dropping blocks into a bucket, in response to presentation of an auditory signal (Friedrich, 1985).

Tangible Reinforcement Operant Conditioning Audiometry (TROCA)   Tangible reinforcement operant conditioning audiometry is a procedure that uses a tangible reinforcer (e. g., food, drink, toy) to reinforce a child's response to an auditory stimulus. It was originally developed by Lloyd, Spradlin, and Reid (1968) for use with children with developmental disabilities, but it has since been adapted for many difficult-to-test populations. The technique requires the use of specially designed equipment that will dispense the reinforcer to the child after he or she presses a lighted bar or button. Once the child is able to respond to the auditory stimulus and lighted button without assistance, the light is faded until only the auditory stimulus cues the response. Both CPA and TROCA require voluntary motor responses, which may be difficult to train in some people with severe or multiple disabilities.

Northern and Downs (1984) provide more detailed descriptions of these and other methods of modified pure tone audiometry, including methods using conditioned avoidance rather than reinforcement. If initial testing reveals a problem, audiometry procedures can also be used with bone conduction, which helps discriminate middle ear from inner ear dysfunction.

Objective Hearing Tests

Modified Pure Tone Audiometry   Pure tone audiometry typically identifies the lowest intensity of sound that can be heard at various frequencies. Performance at 500, 1000, and 2000 Hz (cycles per second) is particularly important because most speech is in this range. A range of -10 to $+25$ dB is considered within normal limits (Baine, 1985). Usually, the person being tested is asked to push a button or otherwise signify when a tone is heard; however, as noted previously, many children with multiple disabilities cannot or will not perform tasks requiring voluntary responses. One solution has been to develop objective tests of auditory function. Following are brief descriptions of some of the more commonly used procedures.

Auditory Brainstem Response (ABR)   This testing is appropriate when one desires a benign approach for testing auditory function in very young infants and children, or adults with severe or multiple disabilities who cannot participate in voluntary audiometry (Berlin & Hood, 1987). This procedure measures changes in electrical brain wave activity that occur when auditory stimuli are presented. This testing requires an individual to sit or lie motionless for 30–45 minutes with electrodes attached to the scalp. For children who are difficult to test, sedation is necessary and sometimes even general anesthesia is required. This is a medical procedure and must be done with proper safeguards and supervision. In applying this procedure to people with multiple disabilities, the presence or absence of central nervous system pathology can affect the outcome of the evaluation. Once this limitation is considered, the ABR remains the best measure available to date for objectively evaluating the auditory status of this population (Worthington & Peters, 1984) since the threshold for electrical discharge is typically very close to the threshold identified by traditional audiometry (Sohmer, 1989).

Impedance Audiometry   By measuring changes in air pressure in the ear canal that occur in response to a tone, *impedance* or *immittance audiometry* provides useful information about the condition of the eardrum, mobility and continuity of bones in the middle ear, acoustic reflexes, and eustachian tube function. It can be used to estimate hearing sensitivity when audiometry cannot be performed satisfactorily (Northern & Downs, 1984). It cannot identify many sensorineural hearing problems and is difficult to carry out with an actively uncooperative or continuously vocalizing child. Sedation can be used if necessary, but it may influence acoustic reflex (Northern & Downs, 1984).

Heart Rate Response Audiometry (HRRA) Changes occur in electrocardiograms as an unconditioned response to auditory stimuli. These changes are related to sound intensity and have been used to determine auditory thresholds (Schulman & Wade, 1970). Some disagreement still remains regarding the accuracy of this procedure and what physical conditions may influence responses (Northern & Downs, 1984)

These and other tests of physiological functioning can provide valuable information, especially when interpreted by the audiologist. Assessment of functional hearing also provides essential information to the transdisciplinary team.

Evaluation of Functional Use of Hearing The audiological tests described above typically require carefully controlled testing conditions and cannot provide direct information about children's hearing in the educational, domestic, leisure, and community environments where they typically spend time. (Kenworthy, 1982). As with vision, the child's history, interviews with significant others, natural observation, and elicited responses can provide this valuable information. Children's responses to speech and other naturally occurring sounds in the environment are particularly significant. It is important to remember that even when hearing acuity in speech frequencies is known to be present, it is only a rough predictor of the child's ability to understand speech, which depends on many additional factors.

There are some informal observations that can be made about the hearing responses of most children. Does noise wake them from sleep? Do noises of various intensities startle them? Do they look toward the source of sounds? Do they respond to voices? Do they recognize voices? Do they imitate vocalizations? Do they demonstrate recognition of any words? Do they seem to comprehend better when they are looking directly at the face of the person who is speaking? Do they often ask for words to be repeated? Does the voice seem to have an unusual quality? Do they respond to music?

Instruments that provide a standard set of items and attempt to grade responses, such as the Auditory Behavior Index for Infants discussed by Northern and Downs (1984, p. 135), are available. Unlike the less formal observations suggested above, these assessments may specify that sounds be a certain loudness and that testing be done in a sound controlled room. While these instruments may need to be modified for children with multiple disabilities, they can be extremely useful in suggesting possible items and providing a framework for interpreting responses.

Often, there will be considerable overlap between functional assessment of hearing and of communication skills. The entire team may play a role in the assessment process, with the audiologist and communication therapist taking major roles in developing, implementing, and interpreting results.

It is important to remember that hearing function changes over time; consequently, a single evaluation has limited value. In order to reflect changes in learning and physiological function, assessment must be an ongoing process (Stromer & Miller, 1982).

INTERVENTION

Educational experiences and expectations for children with sensory disabilities should be no different from those available for children with unimpaired vision and hearing. The use of environmental modifications or sensory enhancements that allow a child equal access to information should always be considered. The number and extent of modifications and enhancements required for any child depends not only on the nature and extent of the sensory impairment, but also on the child's other abilities and disabilities and on environmental conditions. With this in mind, a number of possible interventions are presented below.

Intervention for Children with Impaired Vision

Intervention for children with impaired vision may occur in at least seven areas:

1. Restoration of vision to the greatest extent possible
2. Use of adaptive equipment to help compensate for problems with visual acuity
3. Modification of environmental conditions and training to help children make maximum use of any residual vision
4. Training to enhance use of other senses to compensate for visual loss
5. Modifying tasks to reduce visual requirements
6. Orientation and mobility training
7. Behavioral and social intervention to aid children's integration into social settings

Visual Restoration   Children should never be denied access to corrective treatment for visual disorders simply because they have multiple disabilities (Cress et al., 1981). Of course, not every visual defect can be corrected, but medical treatment, surgery, and corrective lenses can help many individuals. A few examples are discussed below.

Misalignment of the eyes often can be treated with surgery (Harcourt, 1983). Although surgical procedures vary in complexity, depending on the type and severity of strabismus, they typically involve simple reattachment or shortening of ocular muscles. This surgery is not merely cosmetic—it allows for properly functioning binocular vision.

Lens implants can replace lenses that are missing or damaged. Although not typically recommended for young children because the implanted lens will not grow with them, the procedure has been used with great success with many individuals with severe and multiple disabilities. Vision often can be restored to near normal, and implanted lenses cannot be lost or broken as can eyeglasses or contact lenses. Implants are frequently used as treatment for cataracts. Old lenses may be frozen for easy removal (*cryoextraction*) or liquefied with an ultrasonic probe (*phacoemulsification*) before the fluid that fills the eye is replaced with new, clear fluid. Lenses are then easily inserted through a small incision (Clayman, Jaffe, & Galin, 1983). Although the implanted lens is not adjustable and will not focus on very close objects (just as a fixed-focus camera is more limited than an adjustable focus camera), this procedure has restored near-normal vision to many who were previously blind.

These surgical procedures are only two of many. Often, misshapen corneas can be reshaped, and detached retinas can be reattached. Excessive pressure in the eye can sometimes be relieved. Medical treatment is also useful, particularly in prevention of visual defects. Early detection and prompt medical treatment of infections, injuries, pressure, and other eye problems greatly reduce the chances of permanent damage. In addition to the student having regular checkups, changes in appearance of the eyes, signs of changes in vision, drainage or tearing, pain or itching, or any other sign of possible eye disease should be assessed immediately by an ophthalmologist.

Eyeglasses can be used to help compensate for a variety of visual impairments. Contact lenses are inappropriate for most children with multiple disabilities because they are tolerated poorly and because these children have difficulty caring for the lenses and coping with displaced, poorly hydrated, or irritating lenses. An extra pair (or two) of eyeglasses is often advisable to ensure continuity of use for children who lose or break them frequently; in some cases, it is recommended that an extra set be kept in school. Many children with disabilities require specific reinforcement to aid in adjustment to glasses during the first days or weeks of use. The transdisciplinary team should develop a reinforcement plan *before* introducing the glasses. The best reinforcement plans allow the child to participate in a highly reinforcing visually directed task (e.g., find the food) while the glasses are on. Sessions begin with fairly short periods and gradually increase as tolerance increases. In time, the ability to see better and consequently have better control over the environment becomes a natural reward.

Adaptive Equipment   A great deal of highly sophisticated equipment is available to people with visual impairments. Electronic magnification systems allow for greater use of residual vision. Sound and vibration patterns have been used to provide "visual" information in alternative formats (Bach-y-Rita, 1972). However, in the case of students with multiple disabilities, special attention must be paid to readiness levels. A student cannot perform with a low vision device beyond his or her functional ability to manipulate and care for devices (Watson, 1989). More research is needed to determine exactly who might benefit from which aids. In the meantime, teams should carefully consider potential benefits and functional requirements for use on an individual basis, and they should *require* sales representatives to provide a sample for use in evaluating the appropriateness for the child prior to purchase.

Maximizing Use of Residual Vision   Making the best possible use of any residual vision can include modifying environmental conditions to suit the child's individual needs, and training the child to use existing vision most effectively. It is recommended that a team who is familiar with the individual determine the most effective interventions, but some examples are provided here for consideration.

Lighting is a major environmental factor. As noted earlier, depending on the visual defect, particularly high or particularly low illumination may be required. Tasks may require additional illumination, but they should not be excessively brighter than their background (Kirk, 1981). Backlighting generally should be avoided except when used to show up the outline of an object that the child is expected to discriminate. Print, symbols, pictures, and other critical visual features often can be enlarged. Desks and tabletops with adjustable heights and angles assist optimal viewing. Highly reflective surfaces should be avoided in the classroom. In implementing these or other general guidelines, it is important to evaluate the response of each individual and to identify the optimal working conditions for each child.

Visually directed skills are typically acquired by nondisabled children with little formal instruction, but children with multiple disabilities, including visual impairments, typically require carefully structured training to learn these skills. Many of the sensorimotor skills outlined by Robinson and Robinson (1983) are visually directed, and methods for teaching these skills are clearly described by these authors. Very basic objectives may be as simple as teaching the child to indicate whether or not a light source is present and to visually track the light source. One caution is that the light source should not be distressing to the child; for example, it is better to ask the student to follow a light spot moving across a wall than to shine the light directly in his or her face.

Three principles should be considered in providing visual training to individual children. First, mere visual stimulation is not adequate. Contingent control of the visual stimulation or an associated reinforcer is critical for learning (Utley, Duncan, Strain, & Scanlon, 1983). Second, specific visual skills must serve a meaningful function for the child and, whenever possible, training should occur during functional activities. Third, to the maximum extent possible, these activities should be appropriate to the child's chronological age.

Using Other Senses   Training should also encourage children to use their other senses to compensate for lost visual abilities. While it is not true that blind people have more sensitive hearing or extra senses, they can learn to use hearing, touch, and smell to *substitute* for some functions that vision normally serves. Tactile and auditory skills should be taught in specific training sessions and then generalized to use in functional activities. Similarly, the sense of smell can be developed through a series of identification and discrimination exercises; following these, the use of olfactory cues may be introduced to identify various significant others by such features as distinctive perfume or aftershave.

   Modifying Task Requirements   Task requirements may be altered to take advantage of other senses or to require less visual acuity. Some functional modifications may include:

1.   Enlarging materials
2.   Making the outlines bolder
3.   Reducing irrelevant stimulus characteristics
4.   Covering that part of the stimulus not currently relevant
5.   Putting heavy lines between task stimuli
6.   Giving the student more time to examine the material
7.   Supplementing visual information with auditory or tactile information
8.   Providing alternative materials that require less visual skill

   These modifications work well with a variety of appropriate stimulus materials, including paper and pencil or materials used in teacher-developed assessments; however, in standardized testing, if the number and extent of modifications required for students with multiple disabilities is so great that tests bear little resemblance to their original form, interpretation of results becomes less valid. For this reason, use of standardized tests should be minimized, and comprehensive individualization of educational programming in accordance with the principles presented in Chapters 7 and 8 is suggested for all children with multiple disabilities.

   Orientation and Mobility Training   Although orientation and mobility (O&M) training has long been recognized as critical for blind children, children with severe, multiple disabilities often were excluded because they were considered unable to benefit or they failed to meet the entrance criteria (Brady, 1985). Without modification of training methods and content, traditional O&M training probably requires skills beyond the current functioning level of most children with multiple disabilities (Uslan, 1979), but when O&M programs are tailored to the individual needs of children with multiple disabilities, meaningful gains can be achieved. Gee, Harrell, and Rosenberg (1987) developed a model of O&M training specifically for individuals with multiple disabilities that stresses training in natural environments; interspersed training trials; functional, contextual cues; and operant training procedures.

   Geruschat (1980) stresses the importance of: 1) conducting appropriate initial evaluation of vision, medications, and restrictions; mode of communication; and body and environmental awareness; 2) establishing rapport; 3) establishing a consistent routine to help the student feel comfortable and secure;

4) setting relevant and realistic goals; 5) providing instruction in the use of senses, body awareness, spatial concepts, and route travel; and 6) collecting data to show progress. The Peabody Mobility Scale is a criterion-referenced evaluation instrument and program of instruction in O&M designed for children who are blind and have multiple impairments, with subscales in the areas of motor, sensory, conceptual, and O&M skills (Harley, Wood, & Merbler, 1980). It has been tailored for use with children with low vision who have multiple impairments, with some revisions and a new area for developmental vision and visual integration (Harley & Merbler, 1980). Some children with multiple disabilities have been successfully taught to use a cane as a navigational aid (Morse, 1980). In addition to acting as a simple walking aid, the cane helps the person keep his or her balance, provides advance warning of danger, and samples the path of travel for changes in terrain (Uslan,1979).

Electronically controlled auditory cues at key locations have been useful in some environments (Uslan, Malone, & De l'Aune, 1983), but care should be taken not to overuse such external, instructional cues because they may encourage dependency and interfere with generalization to natural environments where these prompts are not available. An ecological approach that identifies landmarks (dominant environmental features), techniques (methods of traveling across or between landmarks), and orientations (methods of maintaining direction) in the natural environment is extremely useful (Geruschat, 1980).

Motor skills play an important role in O&M (McDade, 1969), so occupational therapy, physical therapy, and physical education are important disciplines to involve in O&M programs. While the entire transdisciplinary team should participate in these programs, the O&M specialist is an extremely important resource for the team. On a practical level, keeping in mind that their students are less able and inclined to engage in even ordinary day-to-day activities involving movement in space such as walking, running, or riding a bicycle, caregivers must ensure that the classroom routine includes time for gross motor activity and that special attempts are made to take the children outside for walks and play, even if they are in wheelchairs.

Behavioral and Social Intervention Another important area of intervention for many children with severe visual impairment is behavioral and social intervention. Poor mobility skills sometimes lead to social withdrawal. Lack of vision may restrict available reinforcing activities. Habitual self-stimulation involving visual or ocular sensation (sometimes called "blindisms") may increase the deviancy of these children's image (Sims-Tucker & Jensema, 1984). Most of these concerns are best approached through reinforcement of more appropriate forms of behavior. Mobility and communication skills should be emphasized to minimize isolation. Reinforcing physical contact can be very helpful. Rather than merely trying to suppress "inappropriate" self-stimulation, caregivers should provide appropriate activities that allow learners to use their other senses and residual vision.

Providing services in the most normal, age-appropriate environment in the individual's natural community is a key concern. Service provision has sometimes involved clustering individuals with visual impairments in residential settings or self-contained classrooms in an attempt to make special resources and modified programs more accessible (Sacks & Reardon, 1989). Unfortunately, such segregated alternatives often interfere with social adjustment and make return to the natural environment more difficult. Since children with multiple disabilities who have visual impairments require highly individualized programs, the advantages of clustering are minimized. Since these same students typically have more difficulty generalizing skills from the training environment to the setting in which those skills are naturally functional, the disadvantages of segregation will likely be greater. Therefore, mainstream educational, residential, recreational, and social environments should be considered the top priority environments for training.

Nevertheless, integration by itself is not a substitute for carefully planned and structured programs tailored to the unique abilities and needs of individual students and implemented by competent professional staff. The placement of students with complex educational needs in mainstreamed settings without adequate planning and support to ensure optimal learning is a form of educational neglect and can never be justified in the name of integration. In an ideal world, no one should be forced to choose between powerful interventions applied in isolated, inappropriate settings and inadequate education in fully integrated settings. Unfortunately, this ideal is achieved rarely in contemporary schools. Even though some compromise may be unavoidable, the goals of educational planners must include *both* the best available educational methods *and* the most mainstream educational environment appropriate.

The interventions discussed here are only a small representation of the available alternatives for children with multiple disabilities who have visual impairments. The transdisciplinary team must review alternatives, considering every aspect of the child and the requirements of current and future environments.

Intervention for Children with Impaired Hearing

Intervention for children with impaired hearing attempts to:

1. Restore hearing to the greatest degree possible
2. Improve residual hearing using equipment
3. Develop oral and manual communication skills
4. Adapt assessment and training in all content areas
5. Maximize use of residual hearing
6. Maximize social and behavioral adjustment

The manner of application of any or all of these goals to any individual child requires careful consideration by the entire transdisciplinary team.

Hearing Restoration   In some cases, surgical treatment can restore or improve hearing. Broken eardrums can often be repaired. Delicate bones in the middle ear cavity can sometimes be repaired or replaced. New procedures, such as implanted auditory prostheses and cochlear implants, require more refinement, but they have good potential for future applications. Most hearing losses, however, cannot be corrected by surgery.

Improved Residual Hearing Using Equipment   The use of suitable hearing aids should always be considered when developing comprehensive habilitation programs for children with hearing impairment. Both parents and teachers need to understand that use of amplification not only may accelerate the development of receptive and expressive communication skills, but also may minimize academic difficulties (Matkin, 1984). Despite wide acceptance of this concept, some problems exist. First, many children who would benefit from wearable amplification, particularly those with mild and profound hearing losses, are not aided or they are not aided early enough to prevent delays in the development of language. Second, some children do not receive optimal amplification because they need more powerful or more appropriate aides. Third, many children are wearing hearing aids that are in poor condition. Reichman and Healey (1989), examining the status of monitoring and maintenance of amplification systems used in schools, found that 54.1% of the sample had not achieved the level that would ensure that hearing aids were consistently functioning properly. Fourth, not all children are introduced to their aids with a period of auditory training that enables them to adjust to and use their aids properly and at all appropriate times.

One factor that has deterred some audiologists from recommending hearing aid use is the fear that the introduction of wearable amplification may result in either temporary or permanent threshold shifts in cases of mild hearing loss. The probability of further damaging a child's sensorineural auditory mechanism can be substantially minimized by first limiting the maximum output of the hearing aid and then by ongoing monitoring of auditory status (Matkin, 1984). In the case of children with profound losses, even when discrimination of words is not possible, an aid can help the individual respond to and localize environmental sounds and also to perceive other elements of speech, such as tempo and intonation. In the fitting of hearing aids for children, audiologists now recommend a hearing aid for each ear (Northern & Downs, 1984). The reasons for this are that improved localization should assist the child in quick and accurate location of the speaker, which is a prerequisite to adequate speechreading, and that binaural-aided hearing improves speech recognition in adverse listening situations since one aided ear is always favorably placed with respect to the person who is talking. This concept should also be kept in mind when the child has a monaural loss. Often, it is felt that the one unimpaired ear is sufficient. It is not. If hearing in the impaired ear can be improved, then it is important for the child to be given the advantage of binaural hearing. In any case, there needs to be a realistic understanding that the use of personal amplification is to enable the child to communicate better (Northern & Downs, 1984).

Great care must be taken in selecting, fitting, and maintaining the aid, as well as training the child to use it. It is essential that the audiologist participate not only in the initial selection and fitting of the aid, but also in the ongoing monitoring of its function and the child's response to it and in the training of other team members to participate in this monitoring. A daily check of the aid is especially important for children who may not recognize or inform others of problems. A check-up routine can be learned easily by the teacher, and many simple problems can be corrected immediately. A lack of amplification, fluctuating sound levels, whistling, squealing, or other noises may signal damaged equipment, a poor fit, run down batteries, or a number of other problems. A child with problems that are not easily corrected should be referred immediately to a specialist (Holvoet & Helmstetter, 1989).

Children often require specific training to use aids. Reinforcing activities using auditory stimuli are often useful. Short initial periods of use should be gradually lengthened. Excessive prompting and attempting to stop the child from removing the aid should be avoided because this often reinforces attempts to remove it. Since static, overamplification, or an otherwise malfunctioning aid can be aversive to the student, ensuring that the aid is working properly and is properly adjusted also help improve tolerance for the hearing aid.

There are two major classifications of personal hearing aids: 1) body-type hearing aids, and 2) ear-level hearing aids, which include behind-the-ear models, eyeglass models, and all-in-the-ear aids. Whenever possible, an ear level type is the aid of choice for a child (Northern & Downs, 1984). This is because the instrument's microphones are located at each ear and clothing noise as well as other common problems encountered with body aids (e.g., food in microphones and broken cords) are eliminated. Body aids are typically reserved for use with infants and toddlers whose small external ears do not provide sufficient stability to keep behind-the-ear-aids in place, children with malformations of the outer ear or ear canal or with recurrent ear disease requiring bone conduction amplification, and for older children with motor impairments and limited manual dexterity who can more easily use and care for a body aid.

The most common equipment used to enhance the signal-to-noise ratio (S/N) or the ratio between the teacher's voice and background sounds in classrooms is the FM system. The teacher wears a microphone that broadcasts a signal directly to the child's ear, eliminating a significant amount of background noise. This also allows for child-to-child communication. A promising new type of FM technology, soundfield amplification, amplifies the teacher's voice for all children in the classroom (Flexer, 1990). Another type of technology, infrared systems, offers the transmission of signals by means of infrared

light. While currently used primarily in public facilities, they have potential for use in schools.

Developing Communication Skills   The three primary variables of the overall process of communication for students with hearing impairment are degree of hearing loss, level of speech intelligibility, and mode of expressive communication. The relationships between these three variables are highly significant. A student's degree of hearing loss is the strongest and most consistent correlate to intelligibility of the student's speech. The greater the intelligibility the more likely the student is to rely on speech for communication (Wolk & Schildroth, 1986). A student's use of manual communication is closely related to whether that student attends an educational program where signing is used for instruction. In the 1982–1983 Annual Survey of Hearing Impaired Children and Youth, 98% of the students who signed were also in education programs in which signing was used (Jordan & Karchmer, 1986).

Because of the major hindrance that lack of hearing presents to language learning, any educational system should recognize the deaf child's need for early natural language competence and for communicative access to curricular material. Fewer than 10% of children with prelingual deafness come from families in which there are deaf parents, siblings, or other deaf near relatives. This means that those closest to most deaf children have had no experience with deafness (Schein, 1988). Thus, it is difficult for these children to acquire a natural language such as American Sign Language (ASL) and thereby to acquire the information that is critical for those aspects of normal socio-emotional development founded in family interaction. Typically, a deaf child is the first deaf person whom other members of the family have ever encountered. In addition to the trauma this creates, family members seldom have the communication skills or the knowledge and experience required to provide these children with an optimal context for the acquisition of either a natural language or the cultural understandings and experiences available to hearing children (Johnson, Liddell, & Erting, 1989). A major goal should be to provide educational and emotional support for the families of deaf children so they can provide the environment their children need for enhanced linguistic and developmental experiences. This would include the use of early auditory stimulation, vocal practice, amplification as required, and constant exposure to language whether signed or spoken.

Adapting Assessment and Training   Most assessment and training relies heavily on verbal instructions and cues. When doing so is not possible, alternatives must be used. These alternatives may require considerable learning on the part of parents, caregivers, and all other team members. If alternative languages (e.g., a gestural language) are used, communication partners must become sufficiently proficient in these languages to provide a rich language environment. Use of standardized tests of cognitive and developmental skills may produce *poor* results strongly influenced by lack of auditory skills. While selecting the most appropriate test to compensate for the hearing loss may overcome some of this problem (Gill & Dihoff, 1982), the presence of other specific disabilities must also be taken into account. Criterion-based assessment directly related to training objectives is typically more valuable.

Maximizing Use of Residual Hearing Most children with hearing impairments have some remaining auditory sensation. Training can help them use residual hearing to better advantage. Simple exercises to teach sound awareness, sound discrimination, and sound localization are valuable (Sims-Tucker & Jensema, 1984). Information about the child's current auditory skills can help suggest which stimuli and tasks might be appropriate. Whenever possible, these exercises should be taught during functional activities in the child's natural environment.

Maximizing Social and Behavioral Adjustment Social adjustment is an important overall goal for all children with multiple disabilities. Concerns about social adjustment have become particularly complex and intermingled with controversy over oral versus *manual* approaches for children with hearing impairment. Maximizing speech reception and production is sometimes considered a key to entering the mainstream of society. Some persons feel that individuals with significant hearing impairment will always be at a disadvantage in a "vocal society," but they can become fully functioning members of a "signing society" and so should be encouraged to develop the skills for which they have the greatest potential. Since children with multiple disabilities typically encounter difficulty with acceptance among either group, regardless of their predominant communication mode, this controversy may seem moot, but it does point out the general importance of communication skills for acceptance in either group. Undoubtedly, functional communication skill training in realistically available environments is a major factor in social adjustment.

Self-stimulating behaviors producing auditory feedback (sometimes called "deafisms") are common among children with multiple disabilities and hearing impairment. Rather than attempting to suppress this behavior, intervention should be aimed at developing more suitable behavior and replacing inappropriate stimulation with more fitting auditory input.

No aspect of educational integration has been as controversial as the education of students with severe hearing impairments. While integration with hearing students generally improves social adjustment in the mainstream (e.g., Esposito & Koorland, 1989), difficulty with speech as the primary method of communication typically leaves the deaf individual at a disadvantage. Within the deaf community, however, the relevance of speech is vastly diminished, and the deaf individual can be a fully functioning member of this vital community. Thus, some individuals view integration as pushing children toward adult roles as second-class members of the hearing community and depriving them of the opportunity to develop into first-class members of the deaf community. Ideally, the deaf individual should develop the skills that allow maximum adjustment to both communities and permits free choice and easy movement between the deaf community and the hearing community. Unfortunately, only a few individuals seem to achieve this and difficult choices are often necessary in educational planning. This issue may be less relevant to deaf children with multiple disabilities because their other disabilities often interfere with the acquisition of a common alternative language (e.g., ASL) and make their inclusion in the deaf community as complex as their inclusion in the hearing community. An assessment of social adjustment and communication development may provide useful data for guiding decisions regarding integration for these individuals. As a rule, the community, age-appropriate, natural environment should be considered the best educational environment. Nevertheless, contact with other deaf individuals should be encouraged, and ASL or an appropriate, commonly used alternative taught whenever possible through bilingual and bicultural education (Reiman & Bullis, 1987). If social adjustment to the deaf community and non-speech communication skills are developing at a rate that suggests the individual may adjust better to the deaf community, this choice should be encouraged.

Intervention for Deaf-Blind Children

Although the principles of intervention for both children with hearing impairments and children with visual impairments can generally be applied to deaf-blind children, the unique nature and needs of these children require special consideration (Orlansky, 1980). Deaf-blind children with additional handicapping conditions require further program modification, particularly in the area of communication.

Most alternatives to vocal communication depend upon vision as a functional alternative to hearing. For children who are both deaf and blind, the visual alternative is unavailable. Van Dijk (1986) suggests that the establishment of communication and rapport is a prelude to progress in all educational and social areas. This must begin at a very basic level, using physical contact to develop an attachment to others and to begin interaction routines. Van Dijk's program to stimulate attachment and develop interaction patterns that serve as a foundation for communication includes:

1. *Co-active movement and responsiveness*—Co-active movement means that the teacher joins in with the activity of the child. This has been described as a hands-on method because often one has to lead the child's hands through the activity.
2. *Structuring the child's daily routine*—The most fruitful approach is to build the day around some important activities to build up a chain of expectancies.
3. *Characterization*—Helping the bonding process can involve having the person assigned to the child come to be recognized by a special charac-

teristic, such as a teacher's earring. When the child has residual vision, as many deaf-blind children do, one can use drawings or photographs of the favorite person as an object of reference.

Sternberg, Pegnatore, and Hill (1983) also have recommended slightly modified versions of these procedures for developing skills prerequisite to communication in students with profound disabilities who are not deaf and blind.

Some deaf-blind children have enough residual hearing or vision to use speech, symbols, or gestures without special modification; others may require amplification or enlargement. For those with severely limited vision and hearing, it may be necessary to use more specialized materials, such as object or texture boards, or some other tactile modality. These materials include various forms of an alphabet code or adaptations of lipreading and sign language. Criteria for sign selection (including iconicity) appear to be similar for deaf-blind children and their sighted peers (Griffith, Robinson, & Panagos, 1983). However, size and speed of signs and gestures need to be adapted to the individual student. Among the more common techniques used are the American one-hand alphabet; the British two-hand alphabet; alphabet gloves; the Lorm alphabet; block printing (on the palm or other part of the body); visual or tactile one-to-one signing; and Tadoma, a method in which the deaf-blind person places his or her thumb on the speakers lip with his or her palm and remaining fingers touching the speaker's throat. Alphabet methods, which also include Braille, are useful only when the individual has sufficient cognitive level and sensitivity of touch to comprehend abstract symbols (Wolf, 1986).

Awareness of self and self-concept development are areas of significant delay for children with severe disabilities, and in particular, body awareness develops very gradually in the absence of visual exploration and observation (Jones, 1988). Tactile stimulation and sensory exploration using other senses, such as smell and residual hearing, must be substituted. Adults must make the child aware that they are paying attention and provide some cue as to whether the attention is negative or positive. Leisure, recreational, and physical activities, which are so readily available for other children, require special consideration when children who are deaf-blind are involved. Play skills are very slow in developing and must be specifically taught, often with the adult providing a great deal of physical guidance. Physical education can help develop exteroceptive (touch), proprioceptive (muscle position), and vestibular (equilibrium) senses (Silberman & Tripodi, 1979), which are valuable for functional motor behavior. Adults can adapt these and other recreation and leisure programs for individuals who are deaf-blind by enhancing sensory input, matching motor and speed requirements to the child's skills, increasing tactile cues, and stabilizing materials to limit changes in their position (Hamre-Nietupski, Nietupski, Sandvig, Sandvig, & Ayres, 1984).

The development of appropriate social behavior also requires special con-

sideration for children with dual sensory impairments. Stereotypic, self-abusive, autoerotic, and ritualistic-perseverative behaviors are common. With the possible exception of behavior that is severely and immediately damaging to the child or others, efforts should be geared toward developing more acceptable forms of behavior, rather than suppressing current behavior. Some forms of self-stimulation are acceptable at appropriate times and places, and training may be aimed at teaching the child to discriminate these times and places, rather than at eliminating the behavior. Such decisions must be made by the transdisciplinary team, considering each child and the child's environment.

Educational programs for individuals who are deaf-blind may afford little opportunity for students to develop self-sufficiency and autonomy and to learn necessary skills that range from home management to work skills. At some point, it is important to increase independent learning skills if students are to make transitions from school to adult life (Ven & Wadler, 1990). This factor is critical for all children with multiple disabilities since at some point they will leave the relatively sheltered school and home environment, and the better prepared they are, the better their chances for a fulfilling life.

THE TRANSDISCIPLINARY TEAM

A well-coordinated transdisciplinary team is essential for providing optimal service to all children with multiple disabilities, particularly those with sensory impairments. Two levels of team professionals need to be considered. The first level includes teachers, school administrators, and other permanent school staff, such as social workers, counselors, and therapists, who are involved not only in assessment and planning, but also in the ongoing teaching and monitoring of progress. The second level involves team members who are available on an as needed basis. These include specialists with particular professional competence who also have the belief that positive changes can occur as a result of their intervention (Murphy, 1983).

The *ophthalmologist* (or *oculist*) is a physician specializing in detection and treatment of eye diseases. The *optometrist* is a nonmedical professional trained to measure refractive errors and fit lenses to the individual's eyes. The *optician* grinds lenses and fits frames according to prescription by the ophthalmologist or optometrist. All three of these professionals can have important roles in the delivery of transdisciplinary services, but it is essential to select the appropriate person for the services required. Every child with multiple disabilities and known or potential visual impairment should be evaluated by an ophthalmologist to determine if eye disease exists. Once eye disease has been ruled out, regular visual examinations and prescription of corrective lenses can be carried out by an optometrist. The specialized nature of assessing the vision of children with multiple disabilities requires more than basic professional competence in ophthalmologists and optometrists. They must be willing and interested. They must be knowledgeable about specialized procedures and resourceful in applying them. They often will require specialized equipment. As professional training expands to consider the special needs of individuals with disabilities and as specialized equipment becomes more readily available, appropriate services become easier to find. In locating vision professionals to examine and treat children with multiple disabilities, it is important to discuss the child's special needs and ask if the professional is prepared to meet them. If not, the professional may be able to refer the child to a colleague who is better prepared to serve children with multiple disabilities.

The *orientation and mobility specialist* is another important member of the team serving children with visual impairment, and can be very useful in teaching O&M skills to children with multiple disabilities. Unfortunately, few trained O&M specialists are available, and only very few of those are trained to work with clients with multiple disabilities (Uslan, 1979). While an O&M specialist with training and experience relevant to children with multiple disabilities is desirable, even one without this specific background will be a valuable consultant to the team, advising them on the principles of O&M, while learning more about the population from other team members.

The *otologist and audiologist* play important roles on teams serving children with known or suspected hearing impairments. The role of the otologist is to determine the medical cause of the problem and provide any treatment that would alleviate or improve the condition. Even an acute middle ear infection that creates a temporary hearing loss can have a permanent effect on the child's language development, and chronic problems, including such easily cured conditions as impacted wax, can have major consequences. Children with Down syndrome are particularly vulnerable to middle ear problems, which, if left untreated, can result in permanent hearing loss. It is also important to involve an otologist when surgery is an option. The role of the audiologist is to provide an ongoing measure of the individual's hearing acuity. An isolated test producing an audiogram in the child's record is not adequate (Kenworthy, 1982). While acting as a consultant to team members, interpreting the implications of test findings for training, the audiologist could also suggest and monitor amplification equipment both for classroom and individual use. It is important to modify hearing aids as changes in hearing occur over time or as more useful modes of amplification become available. Speech-language or hearing therapists can also provide expertise in interpreting test results and have specialized knowledge about communication systems and adaptive equipment. Their input is extremely valuable for team decisions about communication systems and programs. In addition, these therapists should be available for ongoing assessment and training in their specialized areas. Unlike eyeglasses, hearing aids require a significant amount of auditory training and training in care and use if they are to be optimally used.

These specialists must work closely with teachers, parents, and all other transdisciplinary team members. The specialists depend on other team members to provide vital assessment information, determine appropriate objectives, and integrate sensory-related program components with all other areas of training.

Teachers working with these students need specialized training and materials to do the best job possible. A survey of teachers serving children with visual impairments who have multiple disabilities (Erin, Daugherty, Dignan, & Pearson, 1990) indicated that a substantial number felt inadequately prepared. These researchers conclude that there is a need to improve teacher preparation at the pre-service and in-service levels, a need that has also been identified by others (Wolf, 1986). Several excellent resources are available to assist in training teachers of students with both sensory impairments and multiple disabilities (e.g., Hamre-Nietupski, Swatta, Veerhusen, & Olsen, 1986; Helmstetter, Murphy-Herd, Roberts, & Guess, 1984; Roberts, Helmstetter, Guess, Murphy-Herd, & Mulligan, 1984). Such specialized training makes it possible for teachers to apply their instructional skills more effectively as members of transdisciplinary teams.

SUMMARY

This chapter has presented some of the special concerns in educating children with multiple disabilities that include sensory impairments. It was stressed that every child's vision and hearing can be meaningfully assessed. Some interventions designed to maximize residual vision and hearing and to compensate for lost vision and hearing through the use of other senses were suggested. The involvement of specialized professionals who play major roles in assessment and intervention of these children was also discussed.

REFERENCES

Atkinson, J. (1985). Assessment of vision in infants and young children. In S. Harel & N.J. Anastasiow (Eds.), *The at-risk infant: Psycho/socio/medical aspects* (pp. 341–352). Baltimore: Paul H. Brookes Publishing Co.

Atkinson, J. (1989). New tests of vision screening and assessment in infants and young children. In J.H. French, S. Harel, & P. Casaer (Eds.), *Child neurology and developmental disabilities* (pp. 219–227). Baltimore: Paul H. Brookes Publishing Co.

Bach-y-Rita, P. (1972). *Brain mechanisms in sensory substitution.* New York: Academic Press.

Baine, D. (1985). *Selected topics in special education.* Delhi, India: Allied Publishers and Utkal University.

Batshaw, M.L., & Perret, Y.M. (1986). *Children with handicaps: A medical primer* (2nd ed.). Baltimore: Paul H. Brookes Publishing Co.

Berlin, C.I., & Hood, L.J. (1987). Auditory brainstem response and middle ear assessment in children. In F.N. Martin (Ed.), *Hearing disorders in children* (pp. 151–167). Austin: PRO-ED.

Brady, M.P. (1985). Orientation and mobility for severely multiple handicapped individuals: A developing technology. *DPH Journal, 8*(1), 32–41.

Brett, E.M. (1983). The blind retarded child. In K. Wybar & D. Taylor (Eds.), *Pediatric ophthalmology: Current aspects* (pp. 113–122). New York: Marcel Dekker.

Chess, S., Korn, S.J., & Hernandez, P.B. (1971). *Psychiatric disorders of children with congenital rubella.* New York: Brunner /Mazel.

Clayman, H.M., Jaffe, N.S., & Galin, M.A. (1983). *Intraocular lens implantation: Techniques and complications.* St. Louis: C.V. Mosby.

Cote, K.S., & Smith, A. (1983). Assessment of the multiply handicapped. In R.T. Jose (Ed.), *Understanding low vision* (pp. 379–401). New York: American Foundation for the Blind.

Cress, P.J., Spellman, C.R., DeBriere, T.J., Sizemore, A.C., Northam, J.K., & Johnson, J.L. (1981). Vision screening for persons with severe handicaps. *Journal of The Association for the Severely Handicapped, 6*(3), 41–50.

Dantona, R. (1986). Implications of demographic data for planning of services for deaf-blind children and adults. In D. Ellis (Ed.), *Sensory impairments in mentally handicapped people* (pp. 69–82). San Diego: College-Hill.

Efron, M. (1981). Vision assessment and implications. In S.R. Walsh & R. Holzberg (Eds.), *Understanding and educating the deaf-blind/severely and profoundly handicapped* (pp. 73–84). Springfield, IL: Charles C Thomas.

Erin, J., Daugherty, W., Dignan, K., & Pearson, N. (1990). Teachers of visually handicapped students with multiple disabilities: Perceptions of adequacy. *Journal of Visual Impairment and Blindness, 84*(1) 16–21.

Esposito, B.G., & Koorland, M.A. (1989). Play behavior of hearing impaired children: Integrated and segregated settings. *Exceptional Children, 55,* 412–419.

Flexer, C. (1990). Audiological rehabilitation in the schools. *Asha, 32,* 44–45.

Fraunfelder, F.T. (1976). *Drug-induced ocular side effects and drug interactions.* Philadelphia: Lea & Febiger.

Friedrich, B. (1985). The state of the art in audiologic evaluation. In E. Cherow (Ed.), *Hearing impaired children and youth with developmental disabilities* (pp. 122–153). Washington, DC: Gallaudet University Press.

Gee, K., Harrell, R., & Rosenberg, R. (1987). Teaching orientation and mobility skills within and across natural opportunities for travel: A model designed for learners with multiple severe disabilities. In L. Goetz, D. Guess, & K. Stremel-Campbell (Eds.), *Innovative program design for individuals with dual sensory impairments* (pp. 127–157). Baltimore: Paul H. Brookes Publishing Co.

Geruschat, D.R. (1980). Orientation and mobility for the low functioning deaf-blind child. *Journal of Visual Impairment and Blindness, 74,* 29–33.

Gill, G., & Dihoff, R. (1982). Nonverbal assessment of cognitive behavior. In B. Campbell & V. Baldwin (Eds.), *Severely handicapped/hearing impaired students: Strengthening service delivery* (pp. 77–113). Baltimore: Paul H. Brookes Publishing Co.

Griffith, P.L., Robinson, J.H., & Panagos, J.H. (1983). Tactile iconicity: Signs rated for use with deaf-blind children. *Journal of The Association for the Severely Handicapped, 8*(2), 26–38.

Hall, D.M.B., & Jolly, H. (1984). *The child with a handicap.* Oxford: Blackwell Scientific Publications.

Hamre-Nietupski, S., Nietupski, J., Sandvig, R., Sandvig, M.B., & Ayres, B. (1984). Leisure skills instruction in a community residential setting with young adults who are deaf/blind severely handicapped. *Journal of The Association for Persons with Severe Handicaps, 9*(1), 49–54.

Hamre-Nietupski, S., Swatta, P., Veerhusen, K., & Olsen, M. (1986). *Teacher training modules related to teaching students with sensory impairments*. Cedar Falls: University of Northern Iowa.

Harcourt, B. (1983). Guidelines for the management of incominant strabismus in children. In K. Wybar & D. Taylor (Eds)., *Pediatric ophthalmology: Current aspects.* New York: Marcel Dekker.

Harden, A. (1983). Electrodiagnostic assessment in infancy. In K. Wybar & D. Taylor (Eds.), *Pediatric ophthalmology: Current aspects.* New York: Marcel Dekker.

Harel, S., Holtzman, M., & Feinshod, M. (1985). The late visual bloomer. In S. Harel & N.J. Anastasiow (Eds.), *The at-risk infant: Psycho/socio/medical aspects* (pp. 359–362). Baltimore: Paul H. Brookes Publishing Co.

Harley, R.K., & Merbler, J.B. (1980). Development of an orientation and mobility program for multiply impaired low vision children. *Journal of Visual Impairment and Blindness, 74,* 9–14.

Harley, R.K, Wood, T.A., & Merbler, J.B. (1980). An orientation and mobility program for multiply impaired low vision children. *Exceptional Children, 46,* 326–331.

Helmstetter, E., Murphy-Herd, M.C., Roberts, S., & Guess, D. (1984). *Individualized curriculum sequence and extended classroom models for learners who are deaf and blind.* Lawrence: University of Kansas.

Hollins, M. (1989). *Understanding blindness.* Hillsdale, NJ: Lawrence Erlbaum Associates.

Holvoet, J.F., & Helmstetter, E. (1989) *Medical problems of students with special needs: A guide for educators.* Boston: College-Hill.

Jacobson, J.W., & Janicki, M.P. (1985). Functional and health status characteristics of persons with severe handicaps in New York State. *Journal of The Association for Persons with Severe Handicaps, 10*(1), 51–60.

Johnson, R.E., Liddell, S.K., & Erting, C.J. (1989). *Unlocking the curriculum: Principles for achieving access in deaf education.* Gallaudet Research Institute Working Paper 89-3, Washington, DC: Gallaudet University.

Jones, C.J. (1988). *Evaluation and educational programming of deaf-blind/severely multihandicapped students: Sensorimotor stage.* Springfield, IL: Charles C Thomas.

Jordan, I.K., & Karchmer, M.A. (1986). Patterns of sign use among hearing impaired students. In A.N. Schildroth & M.A. Karchmer (Eds.), *Deaf children in America* (pp. 125–139). San Diego: College-Hill.

Jose, R.T., Smith, A.J., & Shane, K.G. (1980). Evaluating and stimulating vision in the multiply impaired. *Journal of Visual Impairment and Blindness, 74,* 2–8.

Karchmer, M. (1985). A demographic perspective. In E. Cherow (Ed.), *Hearing impaired children and youth with developmental disabilities* (pp. 36–59). Washington, DC: Gallaudet University Press.

Kenworthy, O.T. (1982). Integration of assessment and management processes: Audiology as an educational program. In B. Campbell & V. Baldwin (Eds.), *Severely handicapped/hearing impaired students: Strengthening service delivery* (pp. 49–76). Baltimore: Paul H. Brookes Publishing Co.

Kirchner, C. (1985). *Data on blindness and visual impairment in the U.S.* New York: American Foundation for the Blind.

Kirk, E.C. (1981). *Vision pathology in education.* Springfield, IL: Charles C Thomas.

Leung, E.H.L., & Hollins, M. (1989). The blind child. In M. Hollins (Ed.), *Understanding blindness* (pp. 139–170). Hillsdale, NJ: Lawrence Erlbaum Associates.

Lloyd, L.T., Spradlin, J.E., & Reid, M.J. (1968). An operant audiometric procedure for difficult-to-test patients. *Journal of Speech and Hearing Disorders, 33,* 236–245.

Longo, J., Rotatori, A.F., Heinze, T., & Kapperman, G. (1982). Technology as an aid in assessing visual acuity in severely/profoundly retarded children. *Education of the Visually Handicapped, 14*, 21–27.

Matkin, N. (1984). Wearable amplification: A litany of persisting problems. In J. Jerger (Ed.), *Pediatric audiology* (pp. 123–145). San Diego: College-Hill.

McDade, P.R. (1969). The importance of motor development and mobility skills for the institutionalized blind mentally retarded. *New Outlook for the Blind, 63*, 312–317.

Moersch, M. (1977). Training deaf-blind. *The American Journal of Occupational Therapy, 3*, 425–431.

Moores, D.F. (1987). *Educating the deaf: Psychology, principles, and practices* (3rd ed.) Boston: Houghton Mifflin.

Morse, K.E. (1980). Modifications of long cane for use by multiply impaired children. *Journal of Visual Impairment and Blindness, 74*, 15–18.

Murphy, K. (1983). The educator-therapist and deaf, multiply disabled children: Some essential criteria. In G.T. Mencher & S.E. Gerber (Eds.), *The multiply handicapped hearing impaired child* (pp. 13–26). New York: Grune & Stratton.

Northern, J.L., & Downs, M.P. (1984). *Hearing in children* (3rd ed.). Baltimore: Williams & Wilkins.

Orlansky, M. (1980). Appropriate educational services for deaf-blind students. *Education of the Visually Handicapped, 12*, 122–128.

Reichman, J., & Healey, W.C. (1989) Amplification monitoring and maintenance in schools. *Asha, 31*, 43–47.

Reiman, J. W., & Bullis, M. (1989). Integrating students with deafness into mainstream public education. In R. Gaylord-Ross (Ed.), *Integration strategies for students with handicaps* (pp. 105–128). Baltimore: Paul H. Brookes Publishing Co.

Roberts, S., Helmstetter, E., Guess, D., Murphy-Herd, M.C., & Mulligan, M. (1984). *Programming for students who are deaf and blind.* Lawrence: University of Kansas.

Robinson, C.C., & Robinson, J.H. (1983). Sensorimotor functions and cognitive development. In M.E. Snell (Ed.), *Systematic instruction of the moderately and severely handicapped* (2nd ed.) (pp. 237–268). Columbus, OH: Charles E. Merrill.

Sacks, S.Z., & Reardon, M.P. (1989). Maximizing social integration for students with visual handicaps. In R. Gaylord-Ross (Ed.), *Integration strategies for students with handicaps* (pp. 77–104). Baltimore: Paul H. Brookes Publishing Co.

Schein, J.D. (1987). The demography of deafness. In P.C. Higgins & J.E. Nash (Eds.), *Understanding deafness socially* (pp. 3–27). Springfield, IL: Charles C Thomas.

Schein, J.D. (1988). Effects of hearing loss in adults. In P.W. Alberti & R.J. Ruben (Eds.), *Otologic medicine and surgery* (pp. 885–910). New York: Churchill Livingstone.

Schulman, C.A., & Wade, G. (1970). The use of heart rate in the audiological evaluation of non-verbal children; II. Clinical trials on an infant population. *Neuropaediatrica, 2*, 197–205.

Siegel-Causey, E., & Downing, J. (1987). Non-symbolic communication development: Theoretical concepts and educational strategies. In L. Goetz, D. Guess, & K. Stremel-Campbell (Eds.), *Innovative program design for individuals with dual sensory impairments* (pp. 15–48). Baltimore: Paul H. Brookes Publishing Co.

Silberman, R.K., & Tripodi, V. (1979). Adaptation of project "I CAN": Primary skills physical education program for deaf-blind children. *Journal of Visual Impairment and Blindness, 73*, 270–276.

Sims-Tucker, B.M., & Jensema, C.K. (1984). Severely and profoundly auditorially/ visually impaired students: The deaf-blind population. In P.J. Valletutti & B. Sims-Tucker (Eds.), *Severely and profoundly handicapped students: Their nature and needs* (pp. 269–317). Baltimore: Paul H. Brookes Publishing Co.

Sohmer, H. (1989). Contributions of auditory nerve-brain stem evoked responses to the diagnosis of pediatric neurological and auditory disorders. In J.H. French, S. Harel, & P. Casaer (Eds.), *Child neurology and developmental disabilities* (pp. 229–232). Baltimore: Paul H. Brookes Publishing Co.

Sternberg, L., Pegnatore, L., & Hill, C. (1983). Establishing interactive communication behaviors with profoundly mentally handicapped students. *Journal of The Association for the Severely Handicapped, 8*(2), 39–46.

Stromer, R., & Miller, J. (1982). Training parents of multiply handicapped/hearing impaired children. In B. Campbell & V. Baldwin (Eds.), *Severely handicapped/hearing impaired children: Strengthening service delivery* (pp. 199–218). Baltimore: Paul H. Brookes Publishing Co.

Taylor, D. (1983). Clinical visual assessment in infancy. In K. Wybar & D. Taylor (Eds.), *Pediatric ophthalmology: Current aspects* (pp. 5–9). New York: Marcel Dekker.

Thompson, M., Thompson. G., & Vethivelu, E. (1989). A comparison of audiometric test methods for 2-year-old children. *Journal of Speech and Hearing Disorders, 54*(2), 174–180.

Trief, W., Duckman, R., Morse, A.R., & Silberman, R.K. (1989). Retinopathy of prematurity. *Journal of Visual Impairment and Blindness, 83*(10), 500–504.

Uslan, M.M. (1979). Orientation and mobility for severely and profoundly retarded blind persons. *Journal of Visual Impairment and Blindness, 73,* 53–58.

Uslan, M.M., Malone, S., & De l'Aune, W. (1983). Teaching route travel to multiply handicapped blind adults: An auditory approach. *Journal of Visual Impairment and Blindness, 77,* 213–215.

Utley, B., Duncan, D., Strain, P., & Scanlon, K. (1983). Effects of contingent and noncontingent vision stimulation on visual fixation in multiply handicapped children. *Journal of The Association for the Severely Handicapped, 8*(3), 29–42.

van Dijk, J. (1986). An educational curriculum for deaf-blind multi-handicapped persons. In D. Ellis (Ed.), *Sensory impairments in mentally handicapped people* (pp. 374–382). San Diego: College-Hill.

Ven, J.J., & Wadler, F. (1990). Maximizing the independence of deaf-blind teenagers. *Journal of Visual Impairment and Blindness, 84*(3), 103–108.

Watson, G. (1989). Competencies and a bibliography addressing students' use of low vision devices. *Journal of Visual Impairment and Blindness, 83*(3), 160–163.

Wolf, E. (1986). Deaf-blind. In J. VanCleve (Ed.), *Gallaudet encyclopedia of deaf people and deafness* (pp. 226–252). New York: McGraw-Hill.

Wolff, A.B., & Harkins, J. E. (1986). Multihandicapped students. In A.N. Schildroth & M.A. Karchmer (Eds.), *Deaf children in America* (pp. 55–83). San Diego: College-Hill.

Wolf-Schein, E.G. (1989). A review of the size, characteristics, and needs of the deaf-blind population of North America. *The ACEHI Journal, 15*(3), 85–100.

Wolf-Schein, E.G. (1990, May). *Fragile X syndrome: Association with autism and other severe disabilities.* Paper presented at Shaping Alternative Futures: Strategies for Effective Integration, Edmonton, Alberta, Canada.

Wolk, S., & Schildroth, A.N. (1986). Deaf children and speech intelligibility: A national study. In A.N. Schildroth & M.A. Karchmer (Eds.), *Deaf children in America* (pp. 139–160). San Diego: College-Hill.

Worthington, D.W., & Peters, J.F. (1984). Electrophysiologic audiometry. In J.Jerger (Ed.), *Pediatric audiology* (pp. 95–125). San Diego: College-Hill.

Chapter 5

Integrating Health Care and Educational Programs

Dick Sobsey and Ann W. Cox

As noted in Chapter 1, many students with multiple disabilities have significant health care needs. Intervention that is carefully coordinated with the students' educational programs is the best method for meeting those needs. This chapter includes a discussion of some issues that affect the coordination of health care with educational services and provides some practical strategies for planning and implementing services.

Local and state education agencies have been struggling with the definition of "school health services" as it pertains to the "related services" clause in PL 94-142, the Education for All Handicapped Children Act, 1975. The distinction between "medical services," which are to be provided for diagnostic and evaluation purposes only, and school health related services, which are to be provided to students who qualify under the provisions of PL 94-142, has been tested in the courts. It has become clear through litigation and grievance petitions (e.g., *Bevin H. by Michael H. v. Wright*, 1987; *Department of Education, State of Hawaii v. Dorr*, 1983; *Detsel by Detsel v. Board of Education of Auburn*, 1986; *Irving Independent School District v. Tatro*, 1984) that variability exists in the interpretation of the definition of school health services.

THE CHILDREN WHO NEED SERVICES

In spite of this variability, however, students with special health care needs are entering public school systems in increasing numbers. Lehr and Noonan (1989) suggested that the presence of this new group of students can be attributed to three factors: 1) improvements in medical technology, 2) development of early childhood programs, and 3) application of the principle of normalization.

Advances in medical technology have increased the survival rates for low birth weight infants and children with chronic conditions (Cohen, 1990; Gittler & Colton, 1987; Koop, 1987). The result is often assumed to be that more children survive with health care needs, including those who depend upon technology such as respirators, monitoring equipment, and nutritional support (Moskop & Saldanha, 1986). The U.S. Congress, Office of Technology Assessment (1987) estimates that 27% of babies admitted to neonatal intensive care units will die, 57% will develop normally, and 16% will survive with severe disabilities. This increase in survivors with severe disabilities may be more than offset, however, by the increase in the number of children who avoid disability or experience milder disabilities because of the same or closely related medical advances (Sobsey, 1989a), as illustrated in Figure 5.1. Actually, a growing body of research supports the notion that the total number of children with disabilities is *decreasing,* not increasing, because of advances in perinatal care (Haas, Buchwald-Saal, Leidig, & Mentzel, 1986; Hagberg, Hagberg, & Olow, 1982; Marlow, D'Souza & Chiswick, 1987; Robertson & Etches, 1988; Shapiro, McCormick, Starfield, & Crawley, 1983), as well as advances in genetic counseling, control of communicable disease, and other preventive strategies (Menolascino & Stark, 1988).

More research is needed to understand the real effects on distribution of various types and severities of disabilities occurring in infants receiving perinatal care. Whether the number of children with disabilities is increasing or decreasing, the nature of the health related services they require is changing as the relative frequency of occurrence of various disabilities changes. Furthermore, many more of these children, who once would have been cared for in hospitals or special residential care facilities, are receiving health care services from their families and school personnel in the least restrictive environments of their

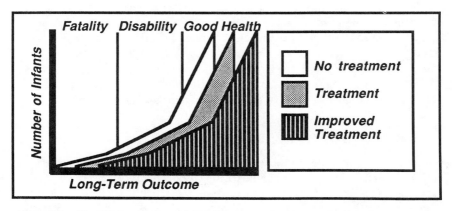

Figure 5.1.   The shift in mortality and disability as a result of improved perinatal care.

homes and neighborhood schools (Palfrey, Singer, Walker, & Butler, 1986). For example, massive and immobile hospital respirator units of the past have been replaced almost completely by portable and self-contained ventilator units, allowing mobility for individuals dependent on ventilators.

The passage of PL 99-457, the Education of the Handicapped Act Amendments of 1986, heralded an increased commitment to the younger population by mandating special educational services to children beginning at age 3, with incentives to agencies providing services to infants and toddlers (birth to 3 years). These younger children have been the beneficiaries of technological advancements in medicine and the values of community-based health care. Therefore, there are a growing number of children with special health care needs in this group of preschoolers receiving special education services in the public schools (Lehr & Noonan, 1989).

POLICY, ADMINISTRATIVE
GUIDELINES, AND ROLE DELINEATION

The principle of normalization (Wolfensberger, 1972) provides the rationale from which the least restrictive environment (LRE) requirement of PL 94-142 evolved. The least restrictive, most normalized environment for special education services is in regular schools with nonhandicapped peers. For students with special health care needs who are receiving health care in community-based, family-centered systems, the natural extension of the LRE requirement is that special educational services be provided in community schools with the supports necessary from school health services.

The result is that younger students with new and often different health service needs are entitled to participate in special education in the least restrictive, most integrated manner. This has particular relevance for students with multiple disabilities, because it is likely that the prevalence of complex health care needs is higher in this student group (Abromowicz & Richardson, 1975).

Many complex issues surround the provision of health related services in educational settings. Most states have either: 1) nursing practice acts that restrict the administration of health care procedures to nurses and members of other health related disciplines, with no provision for delegating responsibilities or training others, or 2) ambiguous laws regarding what nursing functions, if any, can be carried out by others (e.g., New York State Department of Education, 1988; Statutes of Alberta, 1990). Moreover, few states have developed clear guidelines for carrying out health related procedures in the classroom (Wood, Walker, & Gardner, 1986), and local school divisions frequently are left to determine policies and procedures without guidance. Nevertheless, many local education agencies, with or without state level involvement, are beginning to develop their own guidelines regarding educational programming, placements, personnel training, and management policies for various school health services that support the education and integration of students with special health care needs (e.g., Heller et al., 1990).

In response to requests for assistance from educators, health care providers, and administrators, representatives of five professional organizations in the United States convened a Task Force in 1988 to examine and make recommendations regarding role delineation for personnel who care for children with special health care needs in educational programs (Joint Task Force for the Management of Children with Special Health Needs, 1990). The five organizations included the National Association of School Nurses, National Education Association Caucus for Educators of Exceptional Children, Council for Exceptional Children, American Academy of Pediatrics, and the American Federation of Teachers. While the guidelines recommended are consistent with law in most states, they prohibit many transdisciplinary practices that frequently are carried out in schools. For example, teachers would not be permitted to administer oral medication, feed a child with a gastrostomy or nasogastric tube, or perform clean intermittent catheterization. To conform to these guidelines would require a massive influx of health care personnel into the schools, or the clustering of students with disabilities into segregated settings, or both. For example, of 1424 teachers responding to a survey (about 80% regular classroom teachers and 20% special education teachers), 49.6% had at least one child in their classrooms receiving oral medication, and teachers (30.7%), secretaries (15.2%), and teaching associates (12.3%) were more likely to administer medications than nurses (8.1%) (Orelove & Sobsey, 1990). Most of the remainder of medications taken were self-administered or administered by parents.

A few states have allowed for more transdisciplinary service delivery in their legislation. Kansas, for example, provides the following specific exemption for school health care:

(k) performance in the school setting of selected nursing procedures, as specified by rules and regulations of the board, necessary for handicapped students; or
(l) performance in the school setting of selected nursing procedures, as specified by rules and regulations of the board, necessary to accomplish the activities of daily living and which are routinely performed by the student or student's family in the home setting. (Kansas Nurse Practice Act, 1988 revised)

Other states may follow the lead of this progressive legislation, but, currently, most states have significant discrepancies between law, policy, and practice.

A survey of state guidelines regulating the administration of medications and eight common nursing care procedures (Wood et al., 1986) found that only 13 of 50 states had guidelines for delivery of medication and only 6 of 50 had guidelines for the other health care procedures. Sciarillo, Draper, Green, Burkett, and Demetrides (1988) suggest that "clear and thorough guidelines and regulations are not likely to be forthcoming" (p. 83) because of the complex licensing, liability, administrative, legal, and training issues that remain unresolved.

In this fragmented and changing legislative and administrative climate, it is difficult to recommend universally applicable practices. Therefore, the methods and strategies suggested in this chapter are based on the principles of best transdisciplinary practice, individualization, and the overall welfare of the student, and not any specific legal or administrative framework. Professionals are advised to consult local legislation and policy to determine the best application of these practices to their own students. It is important to remember in developing or revising law and policy that legal and administrative decisions regarding the sharing of professional responsibility and the blurring of traditional roles should always be guided by the students' best interests and never become a rationale for service provision that threatens the quality of services to students with disabilities.

DELIVERY OF HEALTH CARE SERVICES THROUGH A TRANSDISCIPLINARY MODEL

The transdisciplinary coordination of health care and education has at least three major advantages. First, training and expertise of the direct service providers is tailored more to the individual needs of the student receiving services than to inflexible procedure. Teachers, parents, and other team members become experts in meeting the needs of individual students with the specific care that each student requires. Parents of the students who require these procedures thus are often recommended as the best people to train school-based personnel to perform them (Schwab, Brown, & Grant, 1990).

Second, decisions regarding the best person to carry out a specific procedure also are based on the individual needs of students rather than general rules. For example, according to the Joint Task Force for the Management of Children with Special Health Care Needs (1990), teachers should be allowed to feed students orally, but not by nasogastric or gastrostomy tubes, correctly implying that tube feedings normally require more specialized skills. For some students, however, oral feedings require extremely sophisticated training and skill, while for others tube feedings are relatively trouble-free. Such decisions should be carefully evaluated by the entire team to decide how each procedure can be best administered to meet the needs of the individual.

Third, the administrative arrangements required to ensure that specific health care procedures are performed only by appropriately licensed or certified personnel often result in social, educational, and sometimes even health care disadvantages. Since most schools lack adequate nursing personnel to perform the health care procedures currently required by students, attempts to restrict administration of these procedures to allied health personnel typically leads to inappropriate clustering of students with physical disabilities, hurried performance of procedures that threatens the quality of care, and rescheduling of procedures to conform to the schedule of busy health care personnel rather than the times ideal for maintaining the health of the student.

The need to provide more and better health care services outside hospital environments and the challenges presented in doing so have been recognized through increasing emphasis on home care (Kaufman & Hardy-Ribakow, 1987). Kohrman (1984) suggests that quality will be best ensured if programs "empower the formal and informal caretakers of the child to assess the effectiveness" (p. 103). A narrow focus on home care as opposed to community care, however, would fail to serve the underlying principle of the best quality care in the most natural setting. School-based care providers also should be empowered through training and support to provide health related services.

Challenges and opportunities exist for those responsible for providing comprehensive services for students with special health care needs and their families. Unique challenges surface regarding the delineation of roles and responsibilities of parents, educators, health care providers, and students in partnerships to achieve the goal of educational services that are integrated, normalized, and provided in the least restrictive environments. Opportunities exist for collaboration among parents, health care agencies, and education agencies, and among various support services within the educational setting. The opportunity to practice a transdisciplinary model for the integration of students with multiple disabilities, including those with special health care needs, into the public school system requires appropriate planning that involves the student, parents, physician, teachers, therapists, school administrators, and school nurse. Before addressing a transdisciplinary model related to school health services, however, it is important to discuss the scope of health related services for students with multiple disabilities.

COMMON MEDICAL CONDITIONS

All children have health care needs. Some of these needs are addressed by school health services. Other students may have health care needs that require a broader range of services. Students with multiple disabilities are at greater risk for developing certain health impairments that may adversely affect their education program. These students also may have ongoing conditions requiring attention during the school day.

It is important to remember that the need for health related services in school settings is not unique to children with multiple disabilities or to students in special education programs. In a survey of teachers in North Carolina, for example, 76% had taught at least one child with health care needs for chronic conditions (Johnson, Lubker, & Fowler, 1988). It is important to note that this survey included regular and special education teachers in their natural proportions. Only 7% of the North Carolina teachers surveyed felt they had been adequately prepared by their preservice education to meet the health care needs of the students they served. Similarly, only 5% of teachers surveyed in Alberta,

Canada felt adequately prepared to meet the health care needs that they encountered in their students (Orelove & Sobsey, 1990).

A basic knowledge of common medical conditions is necessary for education professionals, especially those serving students with multiple disabilities. This section briefly addresses some health conditions to which students with multiple disabilities may be more susceptible. It is important for school personnel to be aware of the causes of common health impairments so that measures may be taken to prevent complications and children can be referred for appropriate medical follow-up.

Anemia

Anemia is due to a combination of factors that contribute to inadequate ingestion of foods high in iron, folic acid, or vitamin B-12; poor gastrointestinal absorption; or excessive loss of these nutrients (Healy, 1990). Students receiving anticonvulsants are particularly at risk for folic acid anemia (Truman, 1984). In addition, some syndromes associated with multiple disabilities (e.g., Fanconi's anemia) also produce anemia. Since anemia interferes with the oxygen-carrying capacity of the blood, the student with anemia may be less active and more irritable. Mild anemia is not visibly detected. Moderate to severe and prolonged anemia can be visibly detected by pale skin and loss of the pink coloration of the gums, lips, and conjunctiva.

Chewing and swallowing difficulties that may be associated with students with multiple disabilities tend to cause children or those selecting foods for them to avoid foods such as meats, poultry, and dried fruits—foods that are high in iron. A diet that contains other iron rich foods such as fortified bread; cereal (e.g., cream of wheat); peanut butter; dark vegetables (e.g., spinach and broccoli); and dried beans may be more easily tolerated. To help the body use folic acid found in foods, the diet also should be rich in vitamin C. Vitamin C sources include oranges, berries, broccoli, cabbage, grapefruit, melons, and citrus juices. School personnel who become concerned that a student is acting unduly lethargic or irritable should speak with the family. Anemia can be diagnosed by a physician sampling a small amount of blood. If anemia is detected, appropriate intervention at home and school can be planned. More about diet and nutrition is included in Chapter 10, Mealtime Skills.

Otitis Media

Otitis media is an inflammatory disease of the middle ear and is common in children under 6 years of age. There are two types. Acute otitis media is related to a bacterial or viral infection and is characterized by a red, bulging eardrum, ear pain, and pus in the middle ear. Serous otitis media, a more chronic condition, may have similar symptoms but is characterized by accumulation of fluid in the middle ear. The eustachian tube connects the middle ear space with the nasal cavity and equalizes pressure between the middle ear and the atmosphere. This promotes drainage of secretions. If the tube becomes blocked because the nasal tissues become swollen, fluid may accumulate in the middle ear. This trapped fluid becomes an excellent medium for the growth of bacteria and viruses and results in an infection (acute otitis media). Even after the infection has been treated, the fluid may persist for many weeks (serous otitis media). The recurrence of otitis media can be a major problem because it affects hearing and, therefore, language development and learning. Recurrent otitis media may place great stress on the family, the child, and the educational process (Blackman, 1990).

Students spending a large amount of time in a recumbent position are more susceptible to otitis media. To facilitate drainage of the middle ear, these students should be positioned in a more upright position, particularly during eating. Educators of students with multiple disabilities can note changes in the behavior of students at risk for ear infection. By noting, recording, and bringing changes to the attention of the school nurse and parent, educators may help in the identification of otitis media and prompt early treatment. Students with poor resistance to infection or chronic upper respiratory infections, including many students with Down syndrome, have increased risk of experiencing otitis media. Treatment of otitis media may include antibiotics, decongestants, myringotomy tube insertion, dietary regulation, or a combination of any of the above under the supervision of a physician. It is important to note that since there is an accumulation of fluid in the middle ear, hearing is affected and teaching strategies need to account for this.

Dehydration

Dehydration occurs when the output of fluids from the body exceeds intake. Intake refers to the amount of fluid taken, usually through feeding (i.e., drinking or eating foods high in liquid). Output includes the fluid excreted in urine, through perspiration, vomiting, and defecation, particularly diarrhea. The cells of the body can carry out their normal functions when there is a relative balance between intake and output. When imbalance occurs, as in dehydration, the body attempts to compensate in a variety of ways. Dehydration classifications go from mild to severe.

Young students, students with decreased mobility, and students with certain ongoing medical conditions are susceptible to developing dehydration. In these students, simply missing a meal or refusing fluid during the school day may lead to mild dehydration or a change from mild to moderate degrees quickly. Fortunately there are several warning signs of dehydration. The skin will appear pale and may feel cool to cold. The turgor (elasticity) of the skin is reduced. One may test this by slightly pinching the back of the hand. If the child is moderately dehydrated, the skin does not snap back into position quickly. The mucus inside the mouth does not glisten because it is dry. Tearing of the eyes also diminishes. Mild dehydration is best treated with frequent, small amounts of liquid. Parents should be informed of the condition so that they may evaluate the student at home. Moderate to severe dehydration must be evaluated by a physician to determine the cause and appropriate treatment. To help prevent dehydration, fluids should be offered regularly, especially during warm weather or after exertion.

Skin Irritation

Students with multiple disabilities are especially prone to skin irritation because of limited mobility, the need for bracing, and lack of bladder control. In each of these situations, the skin must be inspected regularly for irritated, reddened, and ulcerated areas. Repositioning students who are unable to move their body parts is essential. The exact frequency varies depending on individual needs, but many students require repositioning at least four times per hour (see Chapter 3, Handling and Positioning). Padding around prominent bony areas may be necesssary for the child with braces. Light massage to the affected area will stimulate blood supply. For the student in diapers or one who may dribble urine, the groin area should be washed with mild soap and warm water and dried thoroughly each time the student becomes soiled. Some students can be encouraged to do all or part of this cleansing activity independently. To promote home monitoring, parents should be informed about any irritated areas. Skin ulcerations that are not healing will require medical follow-up.

SPECIAL HEALTH RELATED PROCEDURES

Public school systems are experiencing an increase in the number of students requiring special health related procedures (Mulligan-Ault, Guess, Struth, & Thompson, 1988). These special health related procedures may include a variety of tasks ranging from the administration of medications to assistance with mechanical ventilation. The following sections address three health care procedures: clean intermittent catheterization, tube feeding, and administration of medication. Each section identifies the principles and issues surrounding the integration of special health care procedures into the individualized education program (IEP) provided for by PL 94-142. The sections include a description of each procedure and a discussion of when the procedure is required, the necessary safeguards, the individuals responsible for administering the procedure, and a review of the issues. This is followed by a discussion of planning procedures and the role of the school nurse in the delivery, supervision, and evaluation of the effectiveness of the plan.

Clean Intermittent Catheterization

Clean intermittent catheterization (CIC) is required because of either the temporary or permanent inability to empty the bladder. A catheter is a slender, hollow tube that is inserted into a cavity to provide for drainage. When the catheter is inserted periodically, it is considered an intermittent process. Intermittent urinary catheterization is performed to provide for the periodic drainage of urine from the bladder for those individuals who, otherwise, are unable to excrete urine efficiently. Intermittent urinary catheterization can be performed by sterile or nonsterile, clean technique.

When the bladder is not properly emptied it can become overdistended. An overdistended bladder slows the circulation of blood through the bladder walls and weakens its resistance to infection (Altshuler, Meyer, & Butz, 1977). Residual urine in the bladder provides an excellent medium for the growth of bacteria, thus resulting in infection. The infection may remain confined to the bladder (cystitis) or may ultimately lead to a kidney infection (nephritis). Thus, the primary medical goal of CIC is to decrease the likelihood of infection within the urinary tract system by providing periodic draining of urine from the bladder for those students unable to do so independently.

Some students with myelomeningocele (a form of spina bifida) or spinal cord injury have little or no control over urination. Some of these students may dribble urine or be unable to empty the bladder completely. In other students the bladder may overdistend to the point that urine is forced up the ureters back into the kidneys. This ultimately may lead to significant kidney damage. To prevent serious infections, the bladder must be drained by CIC frequently (as often as every 3–4 hours), at prescribed times throughout the day. Therefore, CIC will need to be completed at school according to a time schedule ordered by a physician.

CIC is a procedure that can be safely and effectively carried out independently by some students once they are adequately trained. Skill training can begin as early as 6–7 years of age if the student has sufficient motor and cognitive ability. More than likely, the student has already been involved with helping during the procedure at home. It is important to ask the parent or student about the previous level of involvement. There are many advantages to the student performing CIC, including greater independence, self-esteem, and privacy. If appropriate, training typically involves a process of task analysis of the skill, instruction, demonstration, and return demonstration. However, before embarking upon teaching the skill to the student, the team (school personnel, parents, student, physician) must all agree to the plan and the timing.

It is important to consider several issues as part of the planning process regarding performing CIC at school. One issue involves training regarding aspects of administering the procedure. The training must include the primary caregiver and alternative caregivers. Areas of content include the purpose of the procedure, risks, safeguards, and emergency measures. Although printed materials are helpful (e.g., Taylor, 1990), skill in performing the technique of CIC is best acquired through demonstration and return demonstration. The parent, if willing, can demonstrate the procedure on the student, and, with the supervision of a health professional, the designated caregiver can then demonstrate the skill. The involvement of all these individuals sets the tone for subsequent cooperation and collaboration among the parents, health professionals, and teacher. CIC is classified as a skilled nursing procedure under some state laws, regulations, or guidelines. Therefore, determining responsibility for carrying out CIC is among the complex issues discussed previously in this chapter under "Policy, Administrative Guidelines, and Role Delineation."

Another issue is communication, both written and verbal. A record-keeping system for recording the administration of the procedure and the student's response is needed. For instance, it would be important to document and verbally report to the parent that the urine drained by CIC during the school day appeared cloudy or had a foul odor. Both might be indicators of infection. Furthermore, one should record the color and general amount of urine. If the amount significantly decreases, one might become concerned about whether the student is receiving adequate fluids. Typically, the teacher, nurse, and parent work out a system for telephone and written communication that allows each to update the other as needed. Also, it is helpful to identify in advance an effective way to communicate with the physician. Except in an emergency, the student's physician usually is updated by the parent or through written communication from the school. A survey of physicians' involvement with schools indicates direct communication is relatively uncommon; Palfrey et al. (1986) found that parents reported any history of contact between school personnel and the physician for only 13.8% of special education students.

Finally, the issue of legal responsibility is addressed during the planning process. Local and state guidelines regarding training, health related procedural techniques, and who is qualified to carry out the procedures must be reviewed. Staff should follow these guidelines for their own protection and for the safety of the student. If not in place, guidelines should be developed. A system for initial training, supervision, follow-up support, and retraining will help to diminish apprehension. Adequate training and systematic documentation are important safeguards.

Tube (Gavage) Feeding

The purpose of tube (gavage) feeding is to provide fluid and nutrients for the student who otherwise is unable to take in adequate amounts. Also, oral medications may be given through a feeding tube. Students with conditions that cause severe central nervous system dysfunction, such as cerebral palsy with oral-motor difficulties, head trauma with resultant muscular and nervous system impairment, craniofacial or structural conditions, or hypersensitivity of the mouth or throat, are the most likely to require tube feeding for a prolonged period. Because providing adequate nutrition and fluids by tube requires frequent administration in small amounts, especially during warm weather, these procedures must be provided during the school day.

Placement Feeding tubes may be placed through the nose (nasogastric tube) or, occasionally, through the mouth (orogastric tube) and allowed to descend through the esophagus into the stomach. One must exercise caution to be certain that the tube is placed correctly before feeding begins, since improper placement may introduce food or fluids into the airway. Nasogastric (NG) tubes are usually temporary and either may be removed and replaced with each feeding or may be allowed to remain in place from several days to a few weeks. The decision will be made by the physician, parents, and student, and depends upon the type, size, and material of the feeding tube and the condition and individual response of the student. As explained in Chapter 10, NG tube feedings should be used only as a short-term method of feeding, normally less than a few weeks. Nevertheless, these tubes may become dislodged during the school day, necessitating reinsertion by a trained caregiver.

Feeding tubes that are inserted through the skin of the abdomen directly into the stomach (gastrostomy tube) or into the small intestine (jejunostomy tube) typically are considered permanent or long-term placements. They too may become accidentally dislodged or obstructed and must be replaced. Students with more permanent tube placements may have a gastrostomy button. This device is made of silicon and is put into place by the physician. The button is inserted under the skin through the abdominal cavity. One end is inserted into the stomach or intestine, while the other end comes through the abdominal cavity and appears as an opening on the skin of the abdomen. A dome is inflated around the middle of the button to prevent it from slipping. A feeding tube is attached to the end of the button during feeding. After the feeding, the tube is removed and a cap is placed on the button. Advantages to this method include: 1) less frequent changes of the feeding system, 2) reduced incidence of accidental displacement of the tube and the need to reinsert during the school day, 3) more freedom of movement for the student without fear of dislodging the tube, and 4) more normalized appearance of the student during other activities.

Methods   Three basic methods may be followed to meet the nutritional requirements of students requiring tube feedings. The specific method for a given student will be prescribed by the physician. The *tube syringe,* or *gravity,* method is intermittent feeding that is given by a liquid being poured into a receptacle, either a syringe or a funnel, attached to a feeding tube. The rate of flow is regulated as the receptacle is raised or lowered. The higher the receptacle above the level of the stomach, the faster the liquid will flow by gravity from the receptacle through the tube into the stomach. The flow is slowed when the receptacle is lowered. Care must be exercised to avoid too much pressure in the tube or too rapid a flow since the feeding and other contents of the stomach may be pushed up the esophagus and may enter the airway and cause irritation.

An alternative intermittent feeding method is the *slow-drip* method. A clamp is introduced along the tubing of the feeding system to allow the flow to be regulated by how far one opens or closes the clamp. The advantages to the slow-drip method include decreased vomiting, abdominal cramping, and reflux (contents of the stomach moving back into the airway). The disadvantage is the need for the student to be connected to the feeding apparatus for longer periods of time.

Tube feeding may be given continuously throughout the school day. To regulate the slow flow needed for this method, a mechanical infusion pump may be required. The person who spends the most time with the student must become familiar with operating the pump. Issues include how to set and regulate the rate, the capacity of the battery to operate the system, the length of time to recharge, and trouble-shooting as problems arise. Like CIC, tube feeding may be classified as a skilled nursing procedure, and the qualifications of a person administering tube feedings may be regulated by law, policy, or guidelines.

Requirements for Administering and Monitoring Tube Feedings   The following requirements apply to all methods of administering and monitoring tube feedings:

1. Tubing should be checked for placement and patency. The parent or health professional (physician or nurse) can provide invaluable information regarding techniques. The tube must be in the proper location and be unobstructed to avoid complications.
2. The student should be fed in an upright (i.e., elevated at least 30–40 degrees) or sitting position. If the student is fed in a reclining position, there is increased chance of reflux and aspiration.
3. Generally, the liquid fed should be given at room temperature and should always be refrigerated between feedings to prevent contamination from bacteria. Some students may require slightly warmed liquid. Parents can provide information regarding the temperature best tolerated by the student.
4. Equipment must be clean. Keeping the feeding tube clean requires washing with warm water and soap between feedings or flushing with a small amount of water to remove liquid residue following feeding.
5. Speed of the flow of liquid should be that which has worked well for the student in the past. Parents and health professionals can be helpful with relevant information. This information typically is provided by the physician when tube feeding is first recommended. Generally, one should avoid giving the liquid too fast in order to avoid possible abdominal distension, cramping, reflux, and vomiting.
6. Contamination of the feeding system must be prevented. The end of the feeding tube should be sealed when not in use. A cap usually is available; if not, the end may be covered with gauze and held in place with a rubber band.
7. The procedure should be integrated into the education program for the student in a way that provides opportunities for student decision-making, participation, and normalized social interaction during eating activities with other students.
8. Appropriate training for all individuals who provide tube feeding is essen-

tial. Periodic clinical supervision also must be provided to ensure quality control.

Administering Medication

In general terms, as used here, medication, drug, or medicine is used to describe any substance ingested by (or applied to) an individual intended primarily to influence subsequent behavior, development, or healing. Almost every person in this society uses some of the thousands of available medications at some time, but this chapter emphasizes the few categories of medication commonly used to treat children with severe or multiple disabilities. These include: 1) anticonvulsants, used to control seizures; 2) tranquilizers, used to control undesirable behavior; 3) stimulants, used to control hyperactivity, treat depression, or increase activity level; and 4) muscle relaxants, used to decrease excess muscle tone. Of course, only a small amount of the information available on these drugs can be included here, so emphasis will be placed on the purposes for which drugs are prescribed, common side effects of the drugs, and methods of evaluating response to treatment. More detailed information about specific drugs can be found in *Physicians' Desk Reference* (Barnhart, 1990); the Canadian counterpart, *Compendium of Pharmaceuticals and Specialties* (Canadian Pharmaceutical Association, 1989); or a variety of other reference materials (e.g., Karb, Queener, & Freeman, 1989; Malseed, 1985). Therefore, the information provided here should be considered an overview of selected topics and not a substitute for more specific information or training.

Anticonvulsants   One of the most common uses for anticonvulsant medications with children who have multiple disabilities is for epilepsy. Anticonvulsants do not cure epilepsy, but they can reduce the frequency and severity of seizures (Karb et al., 1989). Although the effectiveness of anticonvulsants varies with the type of epilepsy, environmental factors, and the individual, Gadow and Poling (1988) reported that medication allows 50% of individuals with epilepsy to be seizure-free and another 25% to have significantly fewer and less severe seizures. About 15% are not helped by medication. Unfortunately, the benefits provided must be carefully balanced against other undesirable effects of treatment. Often these include impaired learning and physical and mental performance, in addition to changes in behavior and health problems (Wardell & Bousard, 1985). Since 1968, reliable methods have been available to measure anticonvulsant levels in the blood (Sands & Minters, 1977). Because blood levels may vary independently from dosage levels, these tests have been extremely useful in the regulation of treatment of convulsions.

Although the use of a single drug (monotherapy) is generally recommended and has been associated with a number of advantages, using two or more drugs (polypharmacy) remains a common practice (Gadow & Poling, 1988; Reynolds & Shorvon, 1981). Shreeve (1983) reported that monotherapy provides: 1) more rapid establishment of therapeutic blood levels, 2) easier maintenance of those blood levels, 3) better patient compliance (medication is taken more with better regularity), and 4) fewer problems caused by drug interactions. In a related study, Thompson and Trimble (1982) found that reducing polypharmacy and switching some patients to carbamazepine (Tegretol) improved memory, concentration, mental speed, and motor speed with no loss of seizure control. In spite of these findings, however, Gadow and Poling (1988) reported that 50% of children in early childhood special education programs who receive drugs to control seizures receive two or more anticonvulsants. They also reported that 64% of children in self-contained special education classes who receive drugs to control seizures receive two or more anticonvulsants.

Table 5.1 lists some of the anticonvulsant drugs commonly used with chil-

Table 5.1.   Some commonly used anticonvulsant drugs

Drug	Seizures Typically Treated	Untoward Reactions/ Side Effects
Carbamazepine *Tegretol*	Complex partial Tonic-Clonic	•Confusion, incoordination, speech disturbances, rash, blood abnormalities, frequent urination, loss of appetite, impaired liver function, changes in blood pressure. •Educational impairment often less severe than with other drugs, but blood and liver problems may be serious. Sore throat, loss of appetite, or easy bruising may be early signs of serious problems.
Dextroamphetamine *Dexedrine*	Absence Sleep	•Dry mouth, diarrhea, loss of appetite, headache, hyperactivity, increased blood pressure, irritablility, aggression, psychotic episodes. •May increase the frequency of some types of seizures.
Diazepam *Valium*	Myoclonic	•Drowsiness, fatigue, lethargy, coordination problems, depression, constipation, weight gain.
Ethosuximide *Zarontin*	Absence	•Gastric irritation, drowsiness, coordination problems, dizziness, irritability, hyperactivity, impaired concentration, insomnia, blurred vision, blood abnormalities, rash, hair loss, vaginal bleeding • May increase aggressive behavior.
Mephobarbital Mebaral	Tonic-Clonic	•Lethargy, dizziness, irritability, nausea, diarrhea, blood abnormalities, rash • Often used if phenobarbital causes hyperactivity.
Methsuximide *Celontin*	Absence	•Blood abnormalities, liver damage, nausea, diarrhea, vomiting, loss of appetite, drowsiness, coordination and balance problems, confusion, headache, insomnia, rash.
Phenobarbital *Luminal*	Tonic-Clonic	•Hyperactivity, sedation, impaired learning, dizziness, rash, nausea, diarrhea, blood abnormalities, loss of calcium, bone weakness.
Phenytoin *Dilantin*	Tonic-Clonic	•Overgrowth of gums, coarsening of facial features, drowsiness, impaired coordination, loss of calcium, bone weakness, slurred speech, nausea, diarrhea, vomiting, difficulty swallowing, rash, increased facial and body hair, joint pain, liver damage, blood abnormalities •May worsen partial seizures.
Primidone *Mysoline*	Complex partial	•Folic acid anemia, sedation, impaired learning, rash, nausea, drowsiness, hyperactivity, dizziness, coordination problems.
Valproic Acid *Depakene*	Myoclonic Tonic-Clonic	•Nausea, vomiting, indigestion, lethargy, liver damage, eye damage, dizziness, coordination problems, tremor, loss of hair, hyperactivity, aggression, weakness, •Irritation of mouth and throat are likely if capsules are not swallowed whole.

dren. Drugs are listed by generic names, with brand names below in italics. Of course, only the pharmacist, physician, and other appropriately trained health care professional should be directly involved in substitution of equivalent drugs or calculating dosage. Information provided under "Seizures Typically Treated" indicates which types of seizures each type of medication typically is recommended to treat. Typically, anticonvulsants that are not recommended for the specific type of seizure that a child exhibits will not help and often can increase severity or frequency of seizures. "Untoward Reactions/Side Effects" lists some of the more common and more serious undesirable effects of each drug. Many of these can seriously affect behavior, growth, and learning. For example, Gadow (1982) reported that one third of children receiving medication for epilepsy were reported as drowsy by peers and teachers. Hahn and Avioli (1984) reported studies that show that up to 70% of patients receiving anticonvulsants have lowered blood calcium levels, which can lead to weakened bones, deformities, and frequent fractures. Therefore, although these drugs are extremely valuable in controlling seizures, they must be used conservatively to minimize undesirable effects. Although anticonvulsants remain the primary treatment for epilepsy, other interventions also can be useful. Some of these other approaches to controlling epilepsy are discussed in Chapter 6.

Tranquilizers   Gadow and Poling (1988) estimate that 20% of school-age children classified as "severely and profoundly mentally retarded" receive tranquilizers. These are generally divided into two categories: 1) antipsychotic drugs (major tranquilizers), and 2) antianxiety drugs (minor tranquilizers) (Malseed, 1985). These two groups are compared in Table 5.2. In this table the "Examples" list drugs by generic names, with brand names in parentheses.

Considerable controversy exists regarding the appropriate use of tranquilizers, especially for children with severe disabilities. For example, the Court of Appeals of Iowa upheld a lower court decision awarding $785,165 to a person who developed chronic movement problems after being treated with antipsychotic drugs in a state institution for individuals with mental retardation (*Clites v. State of Iowa*, 1982). The court found that the use of these drugs was not properly monitored, was not part of a therapeutic program, and was not appropriate for the symptoms displayed.

While some studies suggest clinical improvement in the behavior of children with disabilities treated with tranquilizers, many of these studies have four significant problems (Sobsey, 1989b). First, while some children improve, others do not. There is little information to help predict who will improve, and, often, the absence of an appropriate control group leaves doubt that the number improving is much greater than it would be in the absence of treatment. Second, improvements generally are measured as a simple decrease in undesirable behavior. Since tranquilizers may depress all behavior, however, this so-called improvement may merely reflect the incapacitating effects of the medication. Third, many of these studies have design flaws related to the lack of random

Table 5.2.   Tranquilizer categories

	Antianxiety drugs (minor tranquilizers)	Antipsychotic drugs (major tranquilizers)
Examples	Chlordiazepoxide (Librium) Diazepam (Valium) Hydroxyzine (Atarax, Vistaril) Meprobamate (Equanil, Miltown) Oxazepam (Serax)	Chlorpromazine (Thorazine) Chlorprothixene (Taractan) Fluphenazine (Prolixin) Halperidol (Haldol) Mesoridazine (Serentil) Prochlorperazine (Compazine) Perphenazine (Trilafon) Promazine (Sparine) Thioridazine (Mellaril) Trifluoperazine (Stelazine)
Common side effects	(Typically less severe) Drowsiness, fatigue, lethargy, coordination problems, rash, dry mouth, weight gain, impaired learning	(Typically more severe) Drowsiness, low blood pressure, dry mouth, blurry vision, constipation, stuffy nose, palpitations, weight gain, impaired learning
Potentially serious reactions	Confusion, disorientation, slurred speech, hyperactivity, constipation, difficulty swallowing, dizziness, headache, depression, vomiting, increased incidence of grand mal seizures	Lowered seizure threshold, hyperactivity, confusion, insomnia, depression, tremor, movement disorders, blood abnormalities, incontinence

assignment of subjects and the use of post hoc analysis instead of true experimental control. Fourth, most published studies compare treatment with tranquilizers to no treatment at all rather than comparing it to alternative forms of treatment. When Lennox, Miltenberger, Spengler, and Erfanian (1988) compared drugs to other forms of intervention (e.g., role playing, overcorrection, reinforcement of more appropriate behavior), they found medication to have a very low mean rate of effectiveness. In view of this questionable support for improved function in response to tranquilizers and the severe side effects often associated with long-term use, tranquilizers should be used extremely rarely, if ever, with children who have multiple disabilities. They should be considered only if *all* of the following 10 conditions apply:

1. A specific, observable, measurable behavior problem has been identified.
2. The identified problem presents a risk to the individual's physical health or social adjustment more serious than potential drug effects.
3. A thorough functional analysis of behavior has been completed to determine the function that the undesirable behavior serves for the individual. Some children, for example, develop noncompliant or other inappropri-

ate behavior in response to abuse (Sobsey, 1990). Treating the behavioral symptom without addressing the abuse is both unethical and unlikely to succeed.

4. A thorough medical examination has been completed to find any illness or condition that may be contributing to the behavior problem. The pain associated with otitis media (middle ear infection) or toothaches, for example, sometimes precipitates aggressive or self-injurious behavior, particularly in individuals who cannot discuss their problem or seek help in other ways.

5. Less dangerous and intrusive alternatives for controlling the undesirable behavior have been exhausted.

6. Tranquilizers are used as part of—not in place of—a comprehensive program for behavior change.

7. Tranquilizers are used for a limited, prespecified period.

8. The behavior requiring intervention is observed and recorded before and during drug treatment.

9. A specific, minimum criterion for behavioral improvement is specified and achieved (otherwise, use of tranquilizers is discontinued).

10. A plan is implemented to observe, record, and evaluate health, behavior, and learning side effects.

Stimulants   Another category of drug used to control behavior in children with multiple disabilities is stimulants. A survey of elementary schools in four areas of the United States found that, although the overall rate of use of stimulants was less than 2% of all students, usage tended to be significantly higher in some school districts, particularly in urban areas and with students with disabilities (Frankenberger, Lozar, & Dallas, 1990). Although these drugs have been demonstrated as effective in reducing hyperactivity in some children, group studies involving subjects with severe and multiple disabilities have failed to show positive effects (Gadow, 1986). Other studies involving subjects with moderate and mild mental disabilities have shown inconsistent results. When stimulants proved effective, they were combined with other educational and behavioral treatment approaches, which led Mira and Reece (1977) to conclude, "The use of medication alone or as primary treatment, although a common practice, is not warranted on the basis of what we know about the complexity of problems of hyperactivity" (p. 63). Unfortunately, stimulants are rarely used as an adjunctive treatment; when used, they are typically the sole therapy (Bosco & Robin, 1980).

Stimulants also have negative side effects, most frequently insomnia, loss of appetite, and depression or agitation on withdrawal (Cohen, 1980; Karb et al., 1989). Although recovery from growth retardation tends to occur after withdrawal from treatment (Levitsky, 1984), long-term treatment may result in permanent losses. In view of this information, stimulants should be considered rarely and used only as a partial intervention, not the whole treatment. Although these drugs have different effects, the differences usually exist primarily in degree and are therefore spoken of here in general terms for convenience.

Muscle Relaxants Children with excess muscle tone are sometimes treated with muscle relaxants, although this treatment remains relatively rare (Gadow & Poling, 1988). Often, minor tranquilizers (e.g., Diazepam, Meprobamate) are used to reduce tone in muscles affected by cerebral palsy, but their general sedative effects make them undesirable for many children, and, generally, benefits are limited (Gadow & Poling, 1988). Dantrium (dantrolene sodium) continues to be used for some children, especially those in whom spasticity results in discomfort (Karb et al., 1989). Like stimulants, muscle relaxants can have a number of undesired effects. Drowsiness, impaired memory and learning, depression, dizziness, weakness, and vomiting are common side effects. Careful measurement of the drugs' benefits must be considered along with risks to each individual.

Team Roles Related to Medication   While major responsibility for decisions about medication rests with the physician, pharmacist, and other health care professionals, all transdisciplinary team members must be involved in medical treatment. Three major areas require specific consideration: 1) observing treatment effects, 2) observing side effects and adverse reactions, and 3) providing alternatives to treatment with drugs.

Observing Treatment Effects Any drug prescribed should be directed toward a specific goal (e.g., to reduce seizures or to improve learning). To evaluate the effectiveness of the drug, the transdisciplinary team should develop a specific criterion and continue careful observation and record keeping. Teachers, therapists, and other team members should help develop goals and criteria. For example, if Dantrium is given to reduce spasticity, the physical therapist should determine an appropriate measure of spasticity and measure it repeatedly before treatment. Once the level and variability of spasticity is known, the therapist, physician, and other team members should decide how much improvement would be required to justify the use of medication. They should then conduct ongoing evaluation during treatment to determine whether the criterion is met.

Observing Side Effects   Since side effects and adverse reactions are difficult to predict, observing them is more complex than observing treatment effects. All team members should be acquainted with potential side effects and be alerted to medication changes to maximize the chance of early recognition of any developing problems. It should be pointed out that side effects may take a long time to develop, so they can occur at any time.

Providing Treatment Alternatives   Possibly the most valuable thing that the team can do regarding medication is to provide effective programming that does not require the use of medication. Physicians are criticized frequently for using drugs to treat behavior problems, but, if the physician is not communicating adequately with other team members, he or she might assume that all other educational and behavioral approaches were exhausted before a medical referral was made. Careful implementation of well-designed programs will eliminate the need for treatment with medication in most problems with behavior. Many children treated with drugs do as well or better with behavioral therapy (Duckham-Shoor, 1980).

Storing and Dispensing Medication   Many children with multiple disabilities receive medication at school. This creates significant concern about procedures used to store and administer these medications. Gadow and Kane (1983) pointed out that only 16 states have laws regulating administration of medications in school, and clear guidelines are unavailable generally (Wood et al., 1986). Many drugs used (especially stimulants and many anticonvulsants) are controlled substances (Malseed, 1985). In hospitals these drugs require tight security (e.g., must be kept in a locked box inside a locked drug cabinet, every pill counted between shifts). This kind of security is not typically provided in schools. Laws and policies require trained nurses to dispense drugs in hospitals; however, teachers, associates, and secretaries dispense them in some schools (Gadow & Kane, 1983).

School personnel who administer medication must be appropriately trained and have a set of procedures to follow that has administrative approval and complies with relevant law. These procedures must specify: 1) who can dispense medications; 2) an appropriate system for storing medications; 3) labeling requirements (including simple language, without codes or abbreviations); 4) recording procedures; and 5) a method of communication between the person administering medication and the physician.

Communication with the Physician

As suggested earlier, lack of communication between the physician and other team members is a common and serious problem. While there may be many methods of improving communication, one simple method is the use of a concise communication form that shows relevant behavioral observations, areas of concern, and the physician's response (Brulle, Barton, & Foskett, 1983).

General Guidelines for Administration of Health Related Procedures

Specific guidelines for performing a variety of health related procedures can be found in many excellent manuals. Still, one must exercise caution to avoid assuming that reading alone is adequate preparation for performing these procedures. Most of the procedures are skill-based and require, besides reading, opportunities for performance under the supervision of a well-trained parent or health professional.

The more thorough the planning and preparation, the easier it is to integrate the procedure into the daily routine for the student in the classroom. Essential elements of a well-designed program of special, health related school services include thorough knowledge of the purpose for which a procedure is to be performed, policies and guidelines for performing the procedure, individualized methods, monitoring student reactions to the procedure and learning how to handle them, and where and how to record performance of the procedure.

Planning for Health Related Procedures

Upon receiving a request to provide special health related procedures during the school day, the school administrator must decide whether the resources within the system are sufficient to ensure the safety of the student while providing the educational opportunities that the student is entitled to. New and different health care procedures may cause fear and apprehension, especially for individuals unfamiliar with them. The tendency in the past has been to meet the student's education needs in home programs or segregated schools, yet it is recognized that such action limits the opportunities of these students to have the benefits of educational services within the context of the most normalized, integrated classroom environment. A systematic, planned approach can alleviate much of the concern. Such an approach should address the following phases.

Initial Planning Phase   The initial planning phase begins with selection of a student coordinator. This individual should be familiar with the implications of the health procedure and knowledgeable about the school resources. Where available, the school nurse is an ideal candidate to establish and maintain effective communication between the school, physician, and parents throughout this initial phase and to serve as student coordinator. A few school districts employ physicians to serve this function (Sobsey, Orelove, Sehring, & Todaro, 1989). As the student proceeds through program eligibility, the coordinator is responsible for facilitating the process by ensuring that all the necessary forms are completed, evaluation sessions are attended, consents are received, and issues are addressed.

After student evaluation, the school team, parents, physician, student, and personnel from other community resources indicated hold a planning meeting to identify issues from a variety of perspectives that must be addressed in the individualized education program. Particularly when a special health related procedure is required, questions regarding the nature and extent of the procedure (e.g., who will be responsible for administration, the safety issues, the responsibilities of the parents, and whether other support services are indicated) can and should be addressed during this planning meeting. The result should be the development of an IEP that is reasonable, supportive of the student's education program, integrative, and nonrestrictive. Another outcome of this planning meeting is the enhancement of collaborative decision-making and the clarification of expectations of those involved. Such collaborative decision-making will lead to a transdisciplinary service model.

Physicians rarely participate directly in IEP meetings. In a study of five nationally dispersed urban school districts, Palfrey et al. (1986) found that physicians attended only 1.8% of IEP meetings. With or without direct participation, however, it is essential that physicians be aware of and contribute to school-based health care programs, and it is important that they have the opportunity to contribute to other components of the IEP.

The team develops the IEP with parents and appropriate health care professionals as full partners in the decision-making process. Decisions regarding placement are made during development of the IEP. It is important for educational placement decisions to be made for provision of services in the most appropriate setting in the least restrictive environment for each individual student; decisions should not be based primarily on the need for health care. During the IEP development meetings, the team should define and discuss what must take place during the next phase of planning, the pre-entrance phase. A school health care plan may be developed as a component of the IEP. The school health care plan should specify the health care procedures required by the student; who will carry out the procedures; any training that is required; who will provide clinical supervision; and any documentation, equipment, or resources that are necessary. Figure 5.2 illustrates a page from a sample school health care plan. While a separate school health care plan may not be necessary for every child, the categories of information illustrated in the sample plan should be addressed for each procedure required by a student and incorporated in some manner in that child's IEP.

Pre-entrance Phase   After development of the IEP, the second phase, pre-entrance, includes those activities that are necessary for implementing the education program, including providing health related procedures. The team will need to identify whether there are guidelines or protocols in place within the local or state education agency to provide guidance regarding the health related procedures required for the student. If not, these must be developed. Guidelines generally include the purpose of the procedure, safeguards, equipment needs, training, supervision, and a record-keeping system. If adaptation or modification of the procedure is indicated, approval by the physician and parent must be obtained in writing.

Most of what occurs during this phase includes identifying who will administer the procedure and how training will be completed. Five areas of training must be considered: 1) training in the specific procedures, 2) emergency measures, 3) back-up equipment and supply needs, 4) precautions, and 5) record-keeping. It is helpful to identify one person to be responsible for all aspects of training. The school nurse, other community nurse, physician, and parent may all be involved. The important issue is that the person providing training must be competent in the procedure and available for support following training. Collaboration between the parent, who is uniquely qualified in understanding what works best for the student, and a health professional, ideally the school or community nurse, who is licensed, generally works well. For professionals to become familiar with individual students and their unique needs, it is helpful

| School Health Care Plan | Name: John Doe | Date: December 20, 1991 | Page 1/5 |

Procedure: Administer oral anticonvulsants (as ordered by physician)
Goal/ Rationale: Seizure control
Schedule: Daily/ after lunch
Duration: Allow ten minutes for set-up, administration, and recording
Staff: Classroom teacher after training
Backup: Trained teacher from another classroom
Required Training: 18 hour medication course
Clinical Supervision: Direct observation by RN at least once in each 60 day period
Clinical Supervision Dates: 9/15/1992 Jane Goe, RN \ 11/11/1992 Jane Goe, RN \
Evaluation: Physician reviews orders once per month, blood tests as required, school
nurse visits at least every two weeks
Target Date: On-going, consider reduction on reviews if seizure free
Review Dates: Every 30 days
Documentation: Sign medication record, maintain seizure observation records
Contacts: Parents' Home 555-1234, Work 555-4321, Dr. Poe 555-9876
Resources: Physician's Desk Reference in Principal's Office; Drug administration form
Equipment: Locked medicine cabinet in classroom
Precautions: Contact school nurse for advice before giving meds if John appears quite
drowsy. Parents must notify school immediately if medication orders are changed.
Other: See Drug Administration Form for additional information

| Teacher: A. Boe | Principal: B Coe | Parent: C. Doe | Nurse: J. Goe | Physician: K. Poe |

Figure 5.2. A sample page from a school health care plan, a component of an IEP.

177

for parents to bring their children to the school for demonstration and practice of procedures (Schwab et al., 1990).

Other issues to be addressed during the pre-entrance phase include the identification and training of support personnel. A back-up system of qualified personnel is essential for times when the primary caregiver is absent or unable to perform the procedure. Anticipating the training needs of individuals involved in transportation, playground supervision, and emergency services must be addressed before the student enters school.

Finally, some attention must be given to whether the environment is supportive of completion of the procedure in a manner that is safe and that accommodates right to privacy. The classroom environment must be equipped with hot and cold water for washing hands and equipment. Refrigeration may be required for storing feeding liquids and medications. An area equipped with a cot that is shielded somewhat from other activity in the room may be useful not only during certain procedures but also when a student becomes ill. The school nurse and teacher can discuss what environmental supports will be needed. The time and effort spent during the pre-entrance phase is crucial to ensure the safety of the student, confidence and legal protection of school personnel, and clarification of roles and responsibilities.

Monitoring Procedures   The third phase involves monitoring procedures and begins when the student enters the classroom. The student coordinator will need to evaluate the effectiveness of the planning and training. The monitoring of procedures will be most intensive during the first several weeks. Questions that must be answered during this phase include:

1.   Is the procedure being provided in a safe and effective manner?
2.   Is the record-keeping system sufficient without being cumbersome?
3.   Are staffing needs adequate?
4.   Is the process supportive of the student's education program?
5.   Are the parents comfortable with and supportive of the plan?
6.   Is communication between the school and home ongoing and effective?

If the answer to any of these questions is no, then certain modifications may be required. However, with adequate time and appropriate support, some issues may be resolved. It is important to recognize that the integration of certain health related procedures into the education program is a new and different set of responsibilities for educators and support personnel in public schools.

NURSING ROLE ON TRANSDISCIPLINARY TEAMS

Effective transdisciplinary team members share a common purpose, compatible personal qualities, and values and a belief system that are suitable underpinnings for the decisions regarding student programs (Giangreco, York, & Rainforth, 1989). As members of these teams, nurses recognize that their contribution must extend beyond a competent, purely unidisciplinary perspective. Like all other team members, they must be willing to share and learn information and skills across traditional disciplinary boundaries. This willingness supports the view of one's role from a perspective of reciprocal, collaborative interaction in which the release of traditional roles is valued.

Nurses typically share in the belief that health care practices should be least restrictive for the student, and they will try to provide services in a manner consistent with maximizing integration. For example, a student requiring intermittent tube feeding does not need to be removed from the classroom and taken to an office for the procedure. It may be more appropriate to provide the feeding in the classroom, or even better, in the cafeteria. The more the procedure is treated as a normal experience, the better the student's peers will accept the student and the procedure.

Optimizing the health status of students is an important element in achieving educational progress. Frequent absences from school, distraction resulting from discomfort, and drowsiness associated with illness are several ways in which poor health threatens educational success. Also, health care service delivery should be supportive of the education program in a manner that emphasizes educational outcomes. Additionally, a health care procedure should be integrated with other instructional methods within the context of the functional activities of the instructional environment. This is particularly relevant for students requiring clean intermittent catheterization. The educational goal for these students might be to develop independence in activities of daily living to the greatest extent possible. In addressing this goal, the teacher, parent, and school nurse may use the activities involved in CIC as an opportunity to foster independence. They may begin by assessing the current level of involvement in the procedure and follow by deciding, with the student, how acquisition of the skill must gradually develop for greater independence in performing the procedure. The involvement of the parent in the decision-making process at the outset will provide for consistency in approach between home and school. The participation of the student will encourage motivation and communication.

Provision of services must foster the belief that students with severe and multiple disabilities can be educated in the least restrictive environment of classrooms with non-handicapped peers. The concept of integration has particular relevance for nurses assuming responsibility for planning, providing, and supervising school health related services and procedures that support the education program.

Nurses may provide direct care to students, conduct pre-intervention and progress evaluations, and provide technical assistance and consultation to other team members. Technical assistance may include: 1) health information and referral services, 2) workshops and other forms of in-service training, and 3) on-site consultation and training individualized to the student and setting (Sciarillo et al., 1988). Nurses often provide a primary channel of communication between the education and medical communities (Holvoet & Helmstetter, 1989).

Limitations on Realizing Transdisciplinary Team Nursing Roles

The role of school nursing services as part of a transdisciplinary team service model in planning for and providing health related services for students may be confounded by restrictions imposed by a given state's Nurse Practice Act. Typically, these acts specify the dependent and independent activities in which the licensed nurse can legally engage. The importance of full knowledge regarding the implications of these acts must be stressed because they provide state policies that may affect whether school nurses are permitted to function with regard to health related procedures within the school setting. For example, a state Nurse Practice Act may restrict the nurse from training a teacher or paraprofessional in performing tracheal suctioning unless the nurse assumes supervisory responsibility. The nurse may be reluctant to delegate responsibility for the procedure if the nurse can be available only one time a week for supervision, especially during the early weeks of skill monitoring. Clear, written consents from the physician and the student's parents and guidelines and policy at the local level will support the nurse in her or his supervisory role. Likewise, a somewhat flexible schedule that is adaptable to the particular needs in the schools at any given period will support the nurse as she or he addresses particular supervisory functions.

The role of the school nurse may involve actually performing a procedure, training others to perform the procedure, supervising and coordinating the management of a procedure in the classroom, or serving as a consultant and providing support for the classroom teacher. Mulligan-Ault et al. (1988) revealed that teachers of students with severe disabilities in Kansas were willing to assume the responsibility for implementing many health related procedures. Still, they felt that the school nurse should assume responsibility for implementing others. It is notable that the mix of procedures designated as the responsibility of teachers was as complex as those that teachers believed the school nurse should assume. Complicating the delineation of the roles of teachers and school nurses is the reality that school nurses may be unfamiliar with some health related procedures and require training themselves. Training others, performing health related procedures, monitoring outcomes, consulting, and evaluating are new responsibilities for many school nurses. As school systems serve more students with multiple disabilities who have health care needs, the role of the school nurse must be more clearly defined and supported.

Collaborative Service Delivery

For students requiring special health care procedures during the day, opportunities to receive transdisciplinary services are enhanced through reciprocal, collaborative teamwork among parents, school nurses, and educators. As those most familiar with the health care needs of their own children, parents have the primary responsibility for providing their health care. To the maximum extent possible, health care procedures should be carried out before and after school. However, it is recognized that certain health care procedures will be required during the school day. Families of students with multiple disabilities that create special health care needs should be full partners in the decision-making process necessary for the transition into the school environment.

The school nurse brings a traditional, holistic approach to providing health care services to the student within the context of the family and community. The teaching role of the nurse is deeply entrenched within the discipline. The nurse is responsible for teaching the family various interventions, procedures, and monitoring protocols in preparation for a child's discharge from the hospital. Community health nurses have particular knowledge about community resources that may be of assistance to the student and family. The nurse is in the unique position of having an understanding of the interactive nature of the various physiological systems of the body and being able to combine this with sound clinical judgment. Most important, perhaps, the nurse has a strong family orientation and values time spent working with parents. In concert with the primary physician, the nurse can serve as a student coordinator in the education system for students with special health care needs.

Parents and nurses can gain valuable perspectives from the special educator through collaborative planning. In particular, the special educator's focus on enhancing the functional abilities of the student places the education program within the context appropriate for approaching the student as a learner, not a patient. The special educator's knowledge of the student's unique learning characteristics is invaluable. Finally, the special educator's emphasis on the ideas and values inherent in integration and normalization shape the direction and intent of activities regarding educational opportunities.

Together the parent, nurse, and special educator can plan, implement, and evaluate the response of the student with special health care needs better than each can individually. With full communication and support of the physician and the school administrator, decisions can be reached collaboratively regarding how to modify health care for and adapt it to an integrated school setting; when and how to implement procedures to attain the desired educational outcomes; and how and to whom to provide training, monitoring, and evaluation.

REFERENCES

Abromowicz, H.K., & Richardson, S.A. (1975). Epidemiology of severe mental retardation in children: Community studies: *American Journal of Mental Deficiency, 80*, 18–39.

Altshuler, A., Meyer, J., & Butz, M.K.J. (1977). Even children can learn to do self-catheterization. *American Journal of Nursing, 77*(1), 97–101.

Barnhart, E.R. (1990). *Physician's Desk Reference* (44th ed.). Oradell, NJ: Medical Economics Co.

Bevin, H. by Michael H.v. Wright, 666 F. Supp. 71 (W.D. Penn. 1987).

Blackman, J.A. (1990). Middle ear disease. In J.A. Blackman (Ed.), *Medical asepcts of developmental disabilities in children birth to three* (pp. 191–196). Rockville, MD: Aspen Publishers, Inc.

Bosco, J.J., & Robin, S.S. (1980). *Parent, teacher and physician in the life of the hyperactive child: The coherence of the social environment.* Rockville, MD: National Institute of Mental Health. (ERIC Document No. ED 244 498)

Brulle, A.R., Barton, L.E., & Foskett, J.J. (1983). Educator/Physician interchanges: A survey and suggestions. *Education and Training of the Mentally Retarded, 18,* 313–317.

Canadian Pharmaceutical Association. (1989). *Compendium of pharmaceuticals and specialties* (25th ed.). Ottawa: Canadian Pharmaceutical Association.

Clites v. State of Iowa, 322 N.W.2d 917 (Iowa Court of Appeals, 1982).

Cohen, L. (1990). *Before their time: Fetuses and infants at risk.* Washington: American Association on Mental Retardation.

Cohen, M.W. (1980). Medications. In J. Umbreit & P.J. Cardullias (Eds.), *Educating the severely physically handicapped: Treatment and management of medically related disorders* (Vol. 2, pp. 1–7). Columbus, OH: Special Press.

Department of Education, State of Hawaii v. Dorr. U.S. District Court, 727 F. 2d 809 (D.H. Cir. 1983).

Detsel by Detsel v. Board of Education of Auburn, 637 F. Supp. 1022 (N.D.N.Y. 1986).

Duckham-Shoor, LA. (1980). *Behavioral alternatives to stimulant medication in treating childhood hyperactivity: Effects on school and home behavior.* Final report. Washington, DC: Office of Special Education and Rehabilitation Services. (ERIC Document No. ED 244 503)

Frankenberger, W., Lozar, B., & Dallas, P. (1990). The use of stimulant medication to treat attention deficit hyperactive disorder in elementary school children. *Developmental Disabilities Bulletin, 18*(1), 1–13.

Gadow, K.D. (1982). Problems with students on medication. *Exceptional Children, 49,* 20–27.

Gadow, K.D. (1986). *Children on medication: Volume 1: Hyperactivity, learning difficulties and mental retardation.* San Diego: College-Hill.

Gadow, K.D., & Kane, K.M. (1983). Administration of medication by school personnel. *The Journal of School Health, 53,* 178–183.

Gadow, K.D., & Poling, A.G. (1988). *Pharmacotherapy and mental retardation.* Boston: Little, Brown.

Giangreco, M.F., York, J., & Rainforth, B. (1989). Providing related services to learners with severe handicaps in educational settings: Pursuing the least restrictive option. *Pediatric Physical Therapy, 1*(2), 55–63.

Gittler, J., & Colton, M. (1987). *Alternatives to hospitalization for technology dependent children: Program models.* Iowa City: National Maternal Child Health Resources Center, University of Iowa.

Haas, G., Buchwald-Saal, M., Leidig, E., & Mentzel, H. (1986). Improved outcome in very low birth weight infants from 1977 to 1983. *European Journal of Pediatrics, 145,* 337–340.

Hagberg, B., Hagberg, G., & Olow, I. (1982). Gains and hazards of intensive neonatal care: An analysis from Swedish cerebral plasy epidemiology. *Developmental Medicine and Child Neurology, 24,* 13–19.

Hahn, T.J., & Avioli, L.V. (1984). Anticonvulsant-drug-induced mineral disorders. In

D.A. Roe & T.C. Campbell (Eds.), *Drugs and nutrients: The interactive effects* (pp. 409–427). New York: Marcel Dekker, Inc.

Healy, A. (1990). Anemia. In J.A. Blackman (Ed.), *Medical aspects of developmental disabilities in children birth to three* (pp. 1–7). Rockville, MD: Aspen Publishers.

Heller, K.W., Alberto, P.A., Schwartzman, M.N., Shiplett, K., Pierce, J., Polokoff, J., Heller, E.J., Andrews, D.G., Briggs, A., & Kana, T.G. (1990). *Suggested physical health procedures for educators of students with special needs.* Atlanta: Georgia State University.

Holvoet, J.F., & Helmstetter, E. (1989). *Medical problems of students with special needs: A guide for educators.* Boston: Little, Brown.

Irving Independent School District v. Tatro, 468 U.S. 883, 82 L. Ed. 2d 664, 104 S. Ct. 3371 (1984).

Johnson, M.P., Lubker, B.B., & Fowler, M.G. (1988). Teacher needs assessment for the educational management of children with chronic illnesses. *Journal of School Health, 58,* 232–235.

Joint Task Force for the Management of Children with Special Health Needs. (1990). *Report on the delineation of roles and responsibilities for the safe delivery of specialized health care in the educational setting.* Reston, VA: Council for Exceptional Children.

Kansas Nurse Practice Act, Revisions of 1988, §65-1124 (1988).

Karb, V.B., Queener, S.F., & Freeman, J.B. (1989). *Handbook of drugs for nursing practice.* St. Louis: C.V. Mosby.

Kaufman, J., & Hardy-Ribakow, D. (1987). Home care: A model of a comprehensive approach for technology-assisted chronically ill children. *Journal of Pediatric Nursing, 4,* 244–249.

Kohrman, A.F. (1984). *Criteria for admission to programs for funding. Home care for children with serious handicapping conditions.* Houston: Proceedings of the Association for the Care of Children's Health Conference.

Koop, C.E. (1987). *Surgeon General's report: Children with special health care needs* (DHHS Publication No. HRS/D/MC 87-2). Rockville, MD: U.S. Department of Health and Human Services.

Lehr, D.H., & Noonan, M.J. (1989). Issues in the education of students with complex health care needs. In F. Brown & D.H. Lehr (Eds.), *Persons with profound disabilities: Issues and practices* (pp. 139–160). Baltimore: Paul H. Brookes Publishing Co.

Lennox, D.B., Miltenberger, R.G., Spengler, P., & Erfanian, N. (1988). Decelerative treatment practices with persons who have mental retardation: A review of five years of literature. *American Journal on Mental Retardation, 92,* 492–501.

Levitsky, D.A. (1984). Drugs, appetite and body weight. In D.A. Roe & T.C. Campbell (Eds.), *Drugs and nutrients: The interactive effects* (pp. 375–408). New York: Marcel Dekker.

Malseed, R.T. (1985). *Pharmacology: Drug therapy and nursing considerations* (2nd ed.). Philadelphia: J.B. Lippincott.

Marlow, N., D'Souza, S.W., & Chiswick, M.L. (1987). Neurodevelopmental outcome in babies weighing less than 2001 g at birth. *British Medical Jurnal, 294,* 1582–1586.

Menolascino, F.J., & Stark, J.A. (Eds.). (1988). *Preventive and curative intervention in mental retardation.* Baltimore: Paul H. Brookes Publishing Co.

Mira, M., & Reece, C.A. (1977). Medical management of the hyperactive child. In M.J. Fine (Ed.), *Principles and techniques of intervention with hyperactive children* (pp. 47–76). Springfield, IL: Charles C Thomas.

Moskop, J.C., & Saldanha, R.L. (1986, April). The Baby Doe rule: Still a threat. *Hastings Center Report,* 8–12.

Mulligan-Ault, M., Guess, D., Struth, L., & Thompson, B. (1988). The implementation of health-related procedures in classrooms for students with severe multiple impairments. *Journal of The Association for Persons with Severe Handicaps, 13*(2), 100–109.

New York State Department of Education. (1988, December). *Nursing handbook*. Albany: Author.

Orelove, F.P., & Sobsey, D. (1990, December). *Who should deliver health care services to children with severe disabilities in public schools?* Paper presented at the Sixteenth Annual Conference of The Association for Persons with Severe Handicaps, Chicago.

Palfrey, J.S., Singer, J.D., Walker, D.K., & Butler, J.A. (1986). Health and special education: A study of new developments for handicapped children in five metropolitan communities. *Public Health Reports, 101*, 379–388.

Reynolds, E.H., & Shorvon, S.D. (1981). Monotherapy or polytherapy for epilepsy? *Epilepsia, 22*, 1–10.

Robertson, C.M.T., & Etches, P.C. (1988). Decreased incidence of neurological disability among neonates at high risk born between 1975 and 1984 in Alberta. *Canadian Medical Association Journal, 139*, 225–229.

Sands, H., & Minters, F.C. (1977). *The epilepsy fact book*. Philadelphia: F.A. Davis.

Schwab, W., Brown, L., & Grant, L. (1990, December). *Parent-professional collaboration in planning services for children with special health care needs*. Paper presented at the Sixteenth Annual Conference of The Association for Persons with Severe Handicaps, Chicago.

Sciarillo, W.G., Draper, S., Green, P., Burkett, K., & Demetrides, S. (1988). Children with specialized health care needs in the special education setting: A statewide technical assistance approach. *Infants and Young Children, 1*, 74–84.

Shapiro, S., McCormick, M.C., Starfield, B.H., & Crawley, B. (1983). Changes in infant morbidity associated with decreases in neonatal mortality. *Pediatrics, 72*, 408–415.

Shreeve, C. (1983, May 11). Treating epilepsy. *Nursing Mirror, 156*, 20–21.

Sobsey, D. (1989a). Are we preventing mental retardation? *Newsletter of the American Association on Mental Retardation, 2*(2), 2,8.

Sobsey, D. (1989b). Issues in the use of medications. *Newsletter of the American Association on Mental Retardation, 2*(4), 2,8.

Sobsey, D. (1990). Modifying the behavior of behavior modifiers: Arguments for counter-control against aversive procedures. In A.C. Repp & N.N. Singh (Eds.), *Perspectives on the use of nonaversive and aversive interventions for persons with developmental disabilities* (pp. 421–433). Sycamore, IL: Sycamore Publishing Company.

Sobsey, D., Orelove, F., Sehring, M., & Todaro, A. (1989, December). *Health care and education*. Paper presented at the Fifteenth Annual Conference of The Association for Persons with Severe Handicaps, San Francisco.

Statutes of Alberta. (1990, September 1). *Nursing Profession Act* (Chapter N-14.5). Edmonton.

Taylor, M. (1990). Clean intermittent catheterization. In J.C. Graff, M.M. Ault, D. Guess, M. Taylor, & B. Thompson. *Health care for students with disabilities: An illustrated medical guide for the classroom* (pp. 241–252). Baltimore: Paul H. Brookes Publishing Co.

Thompson, B.J., & Trimble, M.R. (1982). Anticonvulsant drugs and cognitive function. *Epilepsia, 23*, 531–544.

Truman, J.T. (1984). The blood. In M. Ziai (Ed.), *Pediatrics* (3rd ed., pp. 387–410). Boston: Little, Brown.

U.S. Congress, Office of Technology Assessment. (1987). *Technology-dependent children: Hospital v. home care—A technical memorandum* (OTA-TM-H-38). Washington, DC: U.S. Government Printing Office.

Wardell, S.C., & Bousard, L.B. (1985). *Nursing pharmacology: A comprehensive approach to drug therapy.* Monterey, CA: Wadsworth Health Sciences Division.

Wolfensberger, W. (1972). *Normalization: The principle of normalization in human services.* Toronto, Canada: National Institute on Mental Retardation.

Wood, S.P., Walker, D.K., & Gardner, J. (1986). School health practices for children with complex medical needs. *Journal of School Health, 56*(6), 215–217.

Chapter 6

Health Care Problems
Prevention and Intervention

Any child can experience an injury or contract an illness that requires special care and treatment and that may become life-threatening. Typically, children with multiple disabilities are more susceptible to many illnesses and tend to experience more injuries than children who do not have disabilities. Illness and injury make life generally more difficult. Specifically, illness and injury can interfere with learning and place additional demands on service resources. This chapter describes some of the more common health care problems that often affect children with multiple disabilities. It also suggests some strategies for intervention and, perhaps more important, for prevention of these problems.

This chapter includes some practical suggestions for responding to emergencies. These are presented with two important cautions. First, this book is not intended to provide training in first aid. All teachers, especially those working with students with multiple disabilities, should take a practical course in first aid. Second, individualization is a fundamental principle of quality in health care and education. The general rules discussed here will not always be the best for every individual or every situation. When the health care team has made individual plans based on a particular student's needs, those plans, rather than more general rules, should be used with that individual. For example, having more than one seizure in any single day is normally considered to be a sign of a potentially serious problem, and immediate notification of the family or the physician is advisable. For some individuals, however, two or more seizures in a day may be common and not associated with any serious problem. Although the greater frequency of seizures does not indicate the need for special concern in these individuals, a change in seizure frequency, duration, or pattern may be cause for legitimate concern, and individualized warning criteria need to be identified for these children.

COMMUNICABLE DISEASE

Susceptibility and Effects

Communicable disease is a general term that includes all of the illnesses that can be transmitted directly or indirectly from person to person and are caused by viruses, bacteria, or parasites. Some diseases, like the common cold, are extremely common and generally not serious. Other diseases may be much less common and/or likely to be much more dangerous. Communicable disease is a particular concern for many individuals with multiple disabilities for two reasons: First, many individuals with multiple disabilities are particularly likely to contract some communicable disease. Second, once infected, these individuals are likely to suffer more severe symptoms and to be ill longer than people who do not have disabilities.

Although not every child with disabilities exhibits an increased risk for contracting communicable diseases or for suffering serious effects from illness, many appear to be more vulnerable because of one or more factors. Some of these children have genetic and metabolic anomalies that reduce their resistance to infection. For example, children with Down syndrome often have such severe problems with respiratory infections that survival until adulthood was considered to be exceptional before antibiotics became available. Reduced levels of physical activity and nutritional problems also contribute to the vulnerability of children with multiple disabilities. Also, many medications that are frequently used by children with disabilities can inhibit the body's natural defenses against infection. Some of these children have not learned sanitary self-care skills, a situation that might contribute to their risk of contracting a communicable disease (e.g., by putting soiled objects in their mouths). The crowded conditions often found in institutions certainly contribute to increased illness among people with disabilities who live in group residences. For example, delta hepatitis, which is commonly found in some third world countries is also found "in institutions for the developmentally disabled" (Benenson, 1990, p. 209). While crowded conditions have become less common with improvements in services, many children and adults with multiple disabilities continue to live under such conditions. Children with multiple disabilities also are more likely to experience more severe illness because diagnosis is often delayed until the illness becomes more serious. Although changes in behavior, lethargy, or irritability might be early signs of illness, they may not be recognized as such by caregivers in the absence of the more specific signs because of the child's inability to communicate the nature of the distress. Finally, some children with multiple disabilities acquired their disabilities as a result of an ongoing illness. For example, 20%–40% of children born to mothers who carry the HIV virus will be infected before, during, or shortly after birth (UNICEF, 1991). Most of the children who are affected will have physical and developmental disabilities along with AIDS (acquired immunodeficiency syndrome) (Rowitz, 1989; Ultman et al., 1985). AIDS is an extremely serious communicable disease in itself, but it also damages the body's natural system of immunity, which increases susceptibility to other communicable diseases.

Some of the factors that contribute to increased risk for contracting communicable diseases are beyond the control of current caregivers, and, even if as many sources of increased risk as possible were controlled, one still could expect to find communicable disease among children with multiple disabilities as frequently as it is found in other segments of the general population. Therefore, it is important to minimize risk for students and staff whenever possible, to detect illness as soon as possible, and to take appropriate action when illness occurs.

Controlling Communicable Diseases

The control of communicable disease has been an ongoing challenge throughout the history of civilization. Although the challenge remains, much progress has been made. Almost all of this progress resulted from improvements in personal hygiene and sanitation, new and better immunization agents, more effective treatment of infected individuals, epidemic control measures such as quarantines, and improved living conditions. As a result of these measures, polio, smallpox, rubella (German measles), pertussis (whooping cough), and many other diseases have been eliminated or significantly reduced in occurrence. The United Nations reports that "after smallpox eradication in the 1970s, polio is likely to be the next major disease to be eliminated" (UNICEF, 1991, p.14) and points out that over 1.5 million cases of polio have been prevented in third world countries during the 1980s.

Professionals working with children with multiple disabilities have a responsibility to do their part in protecting the children they serve (and themselves) from the spread of communicable disease. The children they serve typically experience the same risks as all other children, and, generally, they require the same precautions. Some children with multiple disabilities, however, experience greater risk because they have poor resistance to infection, their own behavior puts them at risk, or environmental factors increase their risk. Table 6.1 lists some examples of communicable diseases that can be found among children with multiple disabilities along with their modes of transmission and some control measures. (For more complete information about the control of these and other communicable diseases, see *Control of Communicable Diseases in Man* [Benenson, 1990]. This book should be available in every school, day care center, and other facility serving significant numbers of children.)

Sanitation and Hygiene   Arguably, clean food and water, sanitation

Table 6.1. Some communicable diseases found among children with multiple disabilities

Communicable Disease	Type	Source	Control Measures
AIDS Acquired Immunodeficiency Syndrome	HIV-1 virus HIV-2 virus	Blood Sexual contact Contaminated needles	Report to public health; careful handling of blood and body fluids that may contain blood (e.g., saliva; control sexual contact and biting)
Hepatitis A Infectious Hepatitis	Hepatitis A virus	Feces Fecal contamination	Prevent fecal contamination of food, hands, and any other objects that may be put in mouth.
Note: Exposed individuals may transmit the disease from several weeks before symptoms appear usually until several days after the onset of jaundice. Incubation period is 15-50 days. Most cases are probably not infectious after the first week of jaundice			
Hepatitis B Serum Hepatitis	Hepatitis B virus	Blood, saliva, semen, and vaginal fluid	Vaccination recommended if exposure risk is high; report to public health; careful handling of blood and body fluids that may contain blood
Note: Exposed individuals may transmit the disease from many weeks before symptoms appear and throughout acute stage. Incubation period is 45-180 days. Some individuals can be asymptomatic carriers of Hepatitis B. Certain syndromes (e. g., Down syndrome) increase risk of being an asymptomatic carrier.			
Scabies Sarcoptic itch	Sarcoptes scabiei (a parasitic mite)	Skin, less frequently undergarments or bedding	Identify and treat cases quickly, avoid contact with infected skin, launder undergarments and bedding, thorough washing; treat all cases in cohort group concurrently
Pediculosis Lice	Pediculus captis (head) humanus (body), or pubis (pubic area)	Physical contact, undergarments or bedding	Identify and treat cases quickly, avoid contact with infected skin, launder undergarments and bedding, thorough washing; treat all cases in cohort group concurrently
Common Cold Acute viral rhinitis	Various rhinoviruses	Airborne droplets, contaminated hands	Handwashing, proper disposal of contaminated materials, keeping fingers out of nose
Influenza	Influenza virus (Type A, B, or C)	Airborne droplets, contaminated hands	Handwashing, proper disposal of contaminated materials, keeping fingers out of nose; immunization of those most vulnerable

sewers, and modern cooking and hygiene practices have done more to extend the life of people in contemporary society than all the other developments in science and medicine. Children with disabilities usually benefit from these developments in public health to the same extent as all other members of our society; however, in some cases, they may not receive the full benefit from these developments because they live in substandard environments or because they have not adequately learned personal hygiene skills.

Children with multiple disabilities who live in institutions or crowded group residences are almost always exposed to greater risk of contracting a communicable disease (Benenson, 1990). Many diseases that are exceptional in community settings are endemic to institutions housing people with developmental disabilities. The best remedy for this problem is moving people out of these facilities to more normal community living arrangements. Until this happens, increased emphasis on sanitation and immunization programs may help to control the excessive risk associated with institutional living.

Children who pick up discarded food, soiled items, or even body wastes and put them in their mouths obviously experience increased risk of infection. The best method for eliminating this source of excess risk is teaching improved personal hygiene skills. These skills should be reflected in the goals of all students who require them and be among the highest priorities for training. Extra emphasis on environmental cleanliness is essential. Keeping the environment free of any potentially contaminated materials can prevent the cycle of transmission even if students do not exhibit personal hygiene skills.

Immunizations Immunity against some infections can be produced through the use of vaccines. The devastating effect of smallpox, polio, rubella, and whooping cough on previous generations has been greatly reduced through the introduction of vaccinations. The risk of contracting serum hepatitis, influenza, some forms of meningitis, and a number of other diseases can also be substantially reduced by vaccination. Nevertheless, vaccinations also involve some risk (though typically much less risk than contracting the disease) and discomfort; therefore, the decision as to whether or not to vaccinate any individual against any specific disease requires evaluation of potential risks and benefits. For example, influenza vaccination is typically not recommended for most healthy children, but it may be advisable for a child who is medically fragile since a respiratory infection would be more dangerous to this child. Also, children living in group residences with active cases or known carriers of hepatitis B should be considered for vaccination.

Many schools require proof of vaccination against some diseases for all students as a method of preventing the spread of disease. School personnel should have current immunization records for each student and should work along with public health agencies to provide parents with accurate information about the benefits and risks of immunization. Parents should be told to inform teachers when a child is vaccinated since adverse reactions to vaccination may develop at any time for several days after a vaccination. In some cases, these reactions can develop rapidly, and immediate detection and treatment can be important.

Classroom staff should work closely with parents, their physicians, the school health team, and public health staff in order to determine which immunizations are appropriate for each child. These decisions should consider the needs and welfare of both the individual and the group since each child who is not immunized increases the risk for others.

Diagnosis and Treatment of Communicable Diseases   The primary responsibility for the diagnosis and treatment of communicable disease rests with the family and their physician. Nevertheless, teachers and other program staff can play an important role in detection and treatment of communicable diseases, and they have a specific responsibility to their students to fulfill this role.

The symptoms of a communicable disease may be noticed first in the classroom for at least two reasons: First, many infectious diseases are cyclical. This means that the symptoms may be more apparent at certain times of day, and in some cases, they may be more obvious during school hours. Second, program staff have the opportunity to observe all their students. This can provide additional information unavailable to parents. For example, a particular child may be predisposed to noncommunicable rashes, but, if several children in close contact with this child begin developing similar rashes, more careful evaluation is required. When communicable diseases are discovered among students, efforts to treat the child and to protect other students and staff from exposure should be coordinated among the school, the family, and health professionals. In most cases, treating the individual who has the illness as soon as possible is essential not only for his or her recovery, but also for protecting others from becoming infected.

Information regarding how and when the illness may be spread is essential in determining other appropriate precautions (Holvoet & Helmstetter, 1989). For example, chicken pox is infectious for no more than 5 days after the appearance of the first outbreak of a rash. Thus, children returning to school after this time who still have visible signs of a rash cannot give chicken pox to other children. However, children who have never had chicken pox but have been exposed should be considered potentially infectious 10–21 days after exposure. Therefore, requiring these children to stay home from school for more than 5 days will provide little or no extra protection for classmates. Careful handling of items that are soiled with nasal and respiratory secretions from children who are potentially infectious can help provide additional protection. Since 95% of all people contract chicken pox before they reach adulthood, and since chicken pox during pregnancy creates serious risks for babies born with the infection, exposure in childhood may be difficult to prevent but less risky than entering adulthood without being exposed. Nevertheless, children with leukemia or other health problems that compromise their abilities to fight the disease may suffer prolonged and sometimes fatal effects and need special protection. A vaccine has been used successfully in Japan to protect children with leukemia (Benenson, 1990), and it is hoped that a safe and effective vaccine will be available universally in the future. Although individual factors must be considered in each case, students and staff fall into three basic categories of risk, requiring three different approaches to immunization. First, those who have already had this disease are at little or no risk and probably need no prevention plans, since normally they are immune to reinfection. Second, those who have not yet had the disease are at greater risk and require moderate precautions. Third, children with leukemia, AIDS, or other conditions that increase the risk of contracting the disease, and women who are pregnant and have not yet had chicken pox, require a much more complete protection plan because of their greater risk. As this example of chicken pox suggests, accurate information is vital to the development of any plan to limit the spread of communicable diseases.

Occasionally, classrooms serving children with multiple disabilities, like any other classroom, may experience epidemics of parasites or other infectious diseases. The term *epidemic* simply refers to the occurrence of more than the normal number of cases among a particular group of individuals. Often, the control of epidemics in the school requires careful coordination of home- and school-based efforts to eliminate the problem. Concurrent disinfection is typically a key element in controlling these outbreaks. *Concurrent disinfection* requires simultaneous treatment of all members of the group and simultaneous eradication of other sources of infection from the environment. Head lice (pediculosis capitas), for example, are a fairly common problem among children and adults and are transmitted directly from person to person through direct, typically prolonged contact. Head lice can also be spread through clothing and bedding. While treatment with medicated shampoo is generally effective in treating the problem, failure to eliminate sources of reinfection often leads to recurrence. If several children in a classroom have head lice, it may be important to identify all of them and coordinate the treatment in order to prevent a recurrence. Often, however, nonsymptomatic adults (who may be classroom staff or family members), siblings or other children in close contact outside of school, or even clothing may lead to reinfection, even if every child in the classroom is successfully treated. Laundering in hot water or drycleaning possibly contaminated clothing at the same time that all infected individuals are treated is essential to the successful eradication of lice. Successful treatment may be possible only with careful coordination of home and school efforts.

Children with Increased Vulnerability   All children are vulnerable to communicable diseases, but some children may be more likely to become infected and suffer more severe illness of infection. Many factors can contribute to increased vulnerability, and the degree of risk varies. Acquired immunodeficiency syndrome (AIDS), genetically transmitted immunodeficiency syndromes, leukemia and some other forms of cancer, Down syndrome, certain medications, nutritional imbalances, and a number of other factors can greatly increase the risk associated with communicable disease for some children. These children will require enhanced protection from exposure and special treatment if they become infected.

For example, children with AIDS, ARC (AIDS-related complex), or asymptomatic HIV (human immunodeficiency virus) infections served in school settings require special consideration and precautions. Individuals who are *HIV positive* have been exposed to and have contracted the virus. In the ARC stage, nonspecific symptoms appear (e.g., swollen glands, fever, fatigue). Any of several unusual opportunistic infections and cancers may lead to an actual diagnosis of AIDS (Benenson, 1990). Thus, AIDS is not diagnosed until late in the disease process, but the virus is present and may be transmitted long before the diagnosis of AIDS. For this reason, much of the attention given to preventing the spread of AIDS must be focused on the earlier HIV positive and ARC stages (McCormick, 1989).

Ironically, although children with AIDS experience a much greater risk of being fatally infected by their schoolmates with a common childhood disease, most attention has been given to protecting their schoolmates from them. A well-designed program considers both of these concerns rationally when making team decisions about the best health care and educational program components for each child. Because blood and other body fluids from an infected child could infect others, attention to preventing exposure of these fluids is essential (Caldwell, Todaro, & Gates, 1991). It is important to recognize that sexual contact, sharing contaminated needles, transfusions (especially prior to 1985 testing procedures), and congenital infection of newborns account for the greatest majority of transmissions. "Routine social or community contact with an HIV-infected person carries no risk of transmission" (Benenson, 1990, p. 3). While the virus has occasionally been found in saliva, tears, urine, and other body secretions, there is no record of transmission of the HIV virus through these fluids (Benenson, 1990).

Children with AIDS are very vulnerable to viral and bacterial infections. Efforts to minimize exposure to infections are important. The educational and social advantages of inclusion, however, must be carefully weighed against any potential health advantages of isolation. Since it is almost impossible to fully protect the susceptible individual from every source of infection, isolation may be justified only when an unusual risk is present. Special precautions with vaccinations are also essential. Some vaccines, especially many using live viruses, should not be given to children with AIDS because they may do serious harm and little good. Other immunizations are essential since they carry little additional risk for the child with AIDS and can protect the child from life-threatening illnesses. Some vaccines may be used at the HIV or even the ARC stage, but not once the AIDS stage begins. Careful consultation with the physician and public health officials is essential to ensure that decisions regarding immunization are made on the basis of the most current research. However, health specialists cannot make the best decisions in all cases without information from parents and the educational team regarding the environment and potential risks for exposure.

Summary All children encounter communicable diseases, and they require the best protection and treatment available. Some children with multiple disabilities have increased risk for contracting communicable diseases and are likely to suffer more severe consequences if infected. The educational team and the health care team must join forces to determine and implement appropriate prevention and treatment strategies. Adequate control of communicable disease is an important component of health care that improves the quality of life for students and provides a better environment for educating children with multiple disabilities. Management of other health-related concerns can also contribute to an improved context for learning.

SEIZURE DISORDERS

Epilepsy is not a specific disease; it is a group of symptoms characterized by recurrent, sudden, transient, and intense disturbances in the activity of the central nervous system (Hauser & Hesdorfer, 1990). The term *epilepsy* is often limited to *unprovoked* seizures that are not known to be secondary to another primary diagnosis (e.g., low blood sugar, disturbances of heart rhythm), while *seizure disorders* is a broader category that includes both primary and secondary seizure symptoms (Hauser & Annegers, 1989). Since the manifestations of these episodes of abnormal electrical discharge in the brain can vary greatly, and the frequency of recurrence required for diagnosis of epilepsy is not uniformly specified, individual diagnosis depends greatly on the physician's judgment. Statistics on incidence and prevalence vary greatly, depending on the particular diagnostic criteria used for inclusion. In general, estimates of the prevalence of epilepsy in the U.S. population range from 0.5% to 2.0% (Yousef, 1985). Epilepsy occurs much more frequently among children with multiple disabilities, and as many as 31% of people with severe disabilities have been reported to have epilepsy (Spooner & Dykes, 1982). Mental retardation is often accompanied by epilepsy, and the more severe an individual's disability, the greater the chance of epilepsy (Richardson, Koller, & Katz, 1981). Cerebral palsy is also commonly associated with epilepsy. Keats (1965) suggested that about 35% of children with cerebral palsy will develop seizures. Although epilepsy can first manifest itself at any time during a person's lifetime, 75% of cases first occur before age 20 (Sands & Minters, 1977). Symptomatic epilepsy (epilepsy for which a specific cause has been identified) accounts for only 30% of cases, while idiopathic epilepsy (epilepsy for which no underlying cause has been identified) accounts for the remaining 70% (Yousef, 1985). Still, a number of potential causes have been identified.

Etiology

Many of the known causes of epilepsy are also potential causes of cerebral palsy and mental retardation, and many children have more than one of these disabilities. Typically, these causes are divided into three major categories: 1) prenatal (occurring before the child's birth), 2) perinatal (occurring during or very close to birth), and 3) postnatal (occurring later in life).

Prenatal Causes A number of events before a child's birth can result in epilepsy. Exposure to radiation, toxic substances, or infectious diseases (e.g., German measles) during pregnancy can damage the developing nervous system of the fetus (Sands & Minters, 1977). Fetal anoxia (lack of sufficient oxygen) can occur for a variety of reasons (e.g., a poorly attached placenta) and damage the child's brain. Despite the excellent natural protection provided, trauma can occur as a result of accidents before birth. Undoubtedly, the most controversial prenatal cause of epilepsy is genetic inheritance. The once widespread belief that epilepsy was commonly inherited contributed to stigma and repressive laws. Although more enlightened attitudes have reversed the trend, three states (Delaware, Mississippi, and South Carolina) still have laws allowing involuntary sterilization of individuals with epilepsy (Epilepsy Foundation of America, 1985). Still, some genetic transmission does appear to occur. Siblings and children of individuals with idiopathic epilepsy appear to be about twice as likely to be affected as siblings and children of individuals without epilepsy (Gumnit, 1983), but the risk remains low (4%–5%) in this group. When two or more family members are affected, this risk increases to 6%–8% (Gumnit, 1983). Except where specific inherited syndromes have been identified, these differences probably have little practical predictive value (Newmark, 1983a). Some studies suggest that an increased susceptibility to epilepsy as a result of trauma exists in some individuals, and a genetic factor appears more clearly for generalized seizures than for partial seizures (Newmark, 1983a).

Perinatal Causes Epilepsy may also occur as a result of trauma or insufficient oxygen during the birth process (Sands & Minters, 1977). Incompatible blood types (most often Rh factor) between mother and fetus may result in erythroblastosis neonatorum (a disease characterized by the clumping and breakdown of red blood cells) shortly after birth, but the frequency of these problems has decreased rapidly since the advent of preventive medication and the trend toward having fewer children (there is little risk of Rh problems with a first pregnancy and risk increases with subsequent pregnancies). Brain damage and epilepsy may subsequently occur if exchange transfusions do not bring the effects of antibodies rapidly under control (Sands & Minters, 1977). Fortunately, much of this risk has been eliminated through treatment of mothers to prevent antibody production.

Postnatal Causes   Head injuries and childhood diseases (e.g., encephalitis, measles, whooping cough) can also cause epilepsy (Yousef, 1985). Brain tumors and strokes are also implicated (Sands & Minters, 1977). It should be pointed out that the occurrence of seizures may not immediately follow a causal event, and therefore, certainty regarding the cause for any individual's seizures generally is not possible. Regardless of the cause, however, the physiological process that produces seizures remains the same.

Seizure Mechanisms   The central nervous system is a complex network of individual neurons (i.e., cells that transmit electrochemical information). Each time a neuron fires, it depolarizes its electrical charge and allows electrolytes to pass through its membrane. These electrochemical changes signal other nearby neurons to fire (Batshaw & Perret, 1986). To carry out any of its complex functions, the nervous system must selectively control which neighboring neurons are stimulated, ensuring that information follows specific neural pathways. Chemical inhibitors and facilitators help mediate this process. Sometimes something goes wrong, and rather than following orderly pathways, neurons begin to fire in an uncontrolled chain reaction with rapid, repeated, synchronous discharges. When this malfunction occurs in as few as 7 of the 10 billion neurons in the central nervous system, a seizure may result (Sands & Minters, 1977).

International Classification System

Although seizures are often classified by the age of the person or the symptoms observed during a seizure, the International Classification System is generally more useful to physicians, because knowing where and how localized the abnormal discharges are helps the physician determine the most appropriate treatment. Seizures that begin with an abnormal discharge in a localized area of the brain are called partial seizures. Elementary partial seizures do not result in loss of consciousness. Complex partial seizures cause an alteration in or loss of consciousness (Gastaut, 1970). Seizures with apparent bilateral, symmetrical, nonlocalized abnormal discharges are called generalized seizures. Although generalized seizure activity may follow and result from localized discharges, these episodes are classified and treated as partial seizures because they begin as localized discharges (Gastaut, 1970). Seizures that are generalized to only one half of the brain are called unilateral seizures. They are rare compared to partial or generalized seizures. Often, inadequate information is available to place seizures in any of these categories; consequently, these are considered unclassified (Gastaut, 1970).

Diagnostic Procedures

Epilepsy is diagnosed primarily on the basis of symptoms and history and by the process of elimination. In some cases, response to trial treatment is considered in making a diagnosis. For example, a physician may suspect that the frequent falls of a patient are the result of epileptic seizures, but inadequate data are available to confirm this diagnosis. If falling episodes decrease during a trial period of antiepileptic medication, the diagnosis of epilepsy may follow. In the 1980s, several tools were used increasingly to help make more precise diagnoses.

Electroencephalogram (EEG)   In 1929, Hans Berger demonstrated that the electrical impulses within the human brain can be measured on the outside of the skull and recorded (Sands & Minters, 1977). The shape, voltage, and frequency of waves from specific sites help determine if a patient has epilepsy and, if so, which type of epilepsy. Many individuals with epilepsy have abnormal brainwave patterns between seizures. When these exist, they will show up with a single EEG in 40%–50% of cases. A second or third EEG will raise the probability that disturbances will be found to 70% or 90%, respectively (Riley & Massey, 1979). Still, certain diagnosis cannot always be made by EEG. The EEG procedure takes 45 minutes to 1 hour and requires the patient to remain reasonably still during this time (MacDougall, 1982). Sedation may be used, if required, but using sedation may influence the results obtained.

Computerized Axial Tomography (CAT Scan)   The gross structure of the brain can be viewed via CAT Scan (a series of X rays taken through a 180° arc assembled into a three-dimensional image by computer). The procedure takes about 5 minutes and is not affected by sedation. Most epilepsy cannot be diagnosed by this method, but some specific causes of seizures can be identified (MacDougall, 1982).

Echoencephalogram (Echogram)   The positions of some of the structures deep inside the brain can be determined by echoencephalogram, a procedure that pulses ultrasound waves through both sides of the head and records echoes. A tumor or other gross abnormality deep in the brain may be suspected if the midline structures are shifted more than 2.5 mm (MacDougall, 1982). Once identified, some of these conditions can be corrected surgically or otherwise treated. Successful treatment of the condition often eliminates seizures or reduces their frequency or intensity.

Types of Seizures

Although the International Classification System is generally most useful for diagnosis and treatment of epilepsy, this system provides little descriptive information about seizures. Therefore, seizures are still most commonly described by their symptoms. In considering these descriptions, it is important to remember that they are prototypes, not descriptions of real, specific seizures. Real seizures vary in duration, severity, and symptoms, but often, they approximate the symptoms of a specific category and are thus classified. The seizures described in this chapter are presented by their common names, but proper names are also provided.

Grand Mal Seizures   Grand mal seizures are also called generalized tonic-clonic seizures (Lechtenberg, 1990). They are the most common (about 60% of cases) epileptic convulsions (Yousef, 1985). Before the seizure, some individuals experience an aura (an unusual sensation) or prodrome (a change in appearance or behavior) that provides warning, but the onset of the seizure is sudden. The person immediately loses consciousness and becomes rigid, often falling at this time. During this tonic (rigid) phase, breathing does not occur, and the person may begin to turn blue. The following clonic (shaking) phase is characterized by alternating, involuntary contraction and relaxation of muscles that results in undirected movement throughout the body, usually most notice-able in the arms and legs. The person remains unconscious during this phase, and breathing is very inefficient, which may lead to additional cyanosis (turn-ing blue). Often, individuals urinate and/or defecate involuntarily while uncon-scious. They may injure themselves while falling or by their flailing move-ments. Sometimes they bite their tongues. The entire seizure rarely lasts more than 5 minutes. During the postictal (after seizure) phase, the individual has no recollection of the seizure, may be confused or irritable, and almost always is drowsy and requires rest (Batshaw & Perret, 1986). Sometimes, the individual may remain unconscious after the seizure and require positioning to maintain an open airway.

Petit Mal Seizures   Petit mal seizures are also called generalized absence seizures or sometimes called minor motor seizures (Lechtenberg, 1990). Al-though less common than grand mal, petit mal seizures are also common, espe-cially in children, and individuals often outgrow them before adulthood. The individual suddenly loses consciousness for a brief period (usually 5–30 sec-onds) and does not become rigid, shake, or fall usually, but typically stares into space without moving. Some petit mal episodes produce clonic movements of eyelids, head, or (rarely) arms. Others produce repeated chewing, swallowing, or lip-smacking movements. Most petit mal seizures, however, produce none of these involuntary movements. When the seizure is over, the child typically re-sumes previous activities unaware of any interruption (Howard, 1980). These seizures may be frequent and, if so, disruptive to learning and other activities. When occurring infrequently, petit mal seizures generally cause few problems and may go unnoticed much of the time.

Other Generalized Seizures   Although grand mal and petit mal are the most common types of generalized seizures, others have also been identified. Tonic seizures are similar to the tonic phase of grand mal seizures but without a clonic phase. Conversely, clonic seizures are similar to the clonic phase of a grand mal seizure but without a tonic phase. Atonic seizures (sometimes called drop attacks) are characterized by a loss of muscle tone, while akinetic seizures are characterized by a loss of muscle movement (Sands & Minters, 1977).

Psychomotor Seizures   Psychomotor seizures are also called partial complex seizures and sometimes referred to as temporal lobe seizures (Lechtenberg, 1990). Since psychomotor seizures involve the temporal lobe of the brain, a child may exhibit a change in behavior or emotional state just prior to the seizure (Gold, 1974). Odor, tastes, colors, or sounds may also be vividly imagined (Batshaw & Perret, 1986). Consciousness may be impaired or lost during the seizure, and the individual might perform automatisms, which are coordinated complex actions without purpose (Sands & Minters, 1977). Generally, these actions are fairly simple (e.g., smacking the lips, rubbing the hands, turning the head). The duration of psychomotor seizures is highly variable (from a few seconds to hours). Following the seizure, the individual rarely remembers the episode clearly, if at all. Drowsiness and sleep typically follow, but it is not uncommon for a psychomotor seizure to generalize to a grand mal seizure.

Jacksonian Seizures   Jacksonian seizures are also called partial simple motor seizures (Lechtenberg, 1990). During Jacksonian seizures, consciousness is not typically altered, but involuntary movement or, rarely, rigid paralysis begins in part of the body (usually a finger or toe) and gradually proceeds up the extremity. Sometimes the arm and leg on the same side of the body are affected and subsequently the same side of the face. This is often followed by a grand mal seizure (Sands & Minters, 1977).

Sensory-Evoked Seizures   Environmental stimuli have been known to trigger seizures in some individuals (Dreisbach, Ballard, Russo, & Schain, 1982). Although this phenomenon has been given considerable attention, it is important to note that only 5%–6% of persons with epilepsy report that sensory stimulation triggers or exacerbates seizure activity (Newmark, 1983b). In a survey of mothers, 2.5% reported sensory-evoked seizures in their children with epilepsy (Verduyn, Stores, & Missen, 1988). Of those sensitive to external stimuli, most individuals are sensitive to various types and amounts of stimulation, but a small subgroup is sensitive to very specific stimuli. Therefore, people with epilepsy need not be restricted from stimuli unless their personal histories indicate that a specific stimulus affects them. For example, photic-induced seizures (triggered by flickering lights, headlights, helicopter blades, or other visual stimulation) have been reported in some individuals. Newmark (1983b), however, reported a study indicating that only 25 of 20,000 persons with epilepsy had photic-induced seizures, and these were usually only susceptible to one or two (not all) of these stimuli. For the other 99.9% of individuals with epilepsy, restriction from all of these stimuli is an unnecessary intrusion. It is not surprising that the suggested relationship between fluorescent lights and seizures has not been supported by research (Binnie, deKorte, & Wisman, 1979). Similarly, auditory-evoked, movement-evoked, startle-evoked, and even language-evoked epilepsy have been found, but these cases are very rare. Some individuals have even been found to be selectively sensitive to card games or other highly specific stimuli (Senanayake, 1987). Restrictions on stimulation should occur only if justified by demonstrable benefits to the specific child. When sensory-evoked seizures do occur, they may be grand mal, psychomotor, or any other type of seizure.

Pseudoseizures Sometimes, what appears to be a seizure may be a good imitation. Riley and Massey (1979) found that the behavior problem of pseudoseizures occurred frequently among patients referred to them for epilepsy, and Lechtenberg (1990) reported that "as many as 36 percent of the patients diagnosed and treated as epileptic have factitious seizures rather than or as well as true seizures" (p. 51). Pseudoseizures also may occur among children with severe disabilities. Although pseudoseizures may look very much like the real thing, breathing rarely stops, and a tonic phase rarely precedes the convulsive stage. Riley and Massey (1979) suggested careful evaluation of anyone able to make a voluntary movement during a seizure. Lechtenberg (1990) suggested that grunting, moaning, sobbing, speaking, coughing, intentional or semi-intentional movements, or avoidance behavior during seizures and rapid return to full alertness after seizures may be signs of pseudoseizures. EEG studies and analysis of the context in which the seizure episode occurs may also be useful. It is important to remember that none of these signs is conclusive, and atypical seizures may easily be mistaken for counterfeit ones. Evaluation should include diagnostic procedures and behavioral assessment, but this process is far from foolproof. Pseudoseizures may be particularly difficult to detect in a child who also has genuine seizures, and the dangers of misdiagnosis may be just as great (or greater) if real seizures are mistaken for pseudoseizures. A matter-of-fact (nonreinforcing) attitude toward all seizures that minimizes social reaction may make discrimination of pseudoseizures from real seizures unnecessary. Nonaversive behavior management procedures may be used if pseudoseizures are causing serious problems.

Seizure Management

Seizure management refers to prevention, protection, and first aid measures applied by the transdisciplinary team. Since every child is an individual, seizure management must be tailored to the specific needs of the child, and none of the management provisions discussed here will be appropriate for every child. Rather, these provisions should be thought of as general recommendations to be considered for each individual.

Prevention Although complete control over seizures is not possible with every child with epilepsy, reduction in the frequency and/or severity of seizures can be accomplished through a program of prevention. In most cases, the primary prevention method is the careful maintenance of medical treatment. Unless presented with evidence to the contrary, most physicians will assume that the level of medication prescribed is actually the amount received. Unfortunately, many intervening factors can influence the actual amount of medication that reaches the bloodstream. Failure to take prescribed medication is a major cause of difficulty in controlling epilepsy (Schmidt & Leppik, 1988). Some children with multiple disabilities refuse medications and may conceal them in their mouths for later disposal. This may result in an inadequate dosage. Also, the resulting low blood levels of medication may influence the physician to increase the dosage prescribed; subsequently, if the child begins to accept the medication consistently, an overdose may result. When administering medications, it is essential to be certain that they are accepted by the child. The manner in which drugs are given also affects maintenance levels. For example, some anticonvulsants are given in suspension form. Unless the suspension is thoroughly mixed before each administration, dosage will be unreliable (Gumnit, 1983). Some doses will be too strong, others too weak. Mixing medications in food can also affect dosage, especially if not all the food is eaten. Some drugs will be absorbed differently if tablets are crushed or chewed or capsules opened before swallowing (Gumnit, 1983). When these or other factors influence dose maintenance, careful consultation among pharmacist, physician, and individuals administering the medication can develop suitable strategies for ensuring accurate and consistent dosage. The benefits of taking any particular type and amount of medication must be carefully balanced with the negative effects and risks of taking the medication. Freeman (1987) advocates using less medical treatment for seizures, pointing out that the major risks from additional seizures for most children are psychosocial and that anticonvulsants often cause behavior problems and learning difficulties in addition to negative health effects.

Avoiding factors that may precipitate seizures is another important component of seizure prevention for some children with epilepsy (Svoboda, 1979). As discussed earlier, specific environmental stimuli that trigger seizures may be identified for some children through careful observation. When they occur, they may be eliminated or controlled in the child's environment. Other factors can lower the threshold for seizure triggers. These factors may be internal or external to the central nervous system (Shreeve, 1983). External factors can often be identified and sometimes controlled. These factors vary among individuals, but some common ones are stress, fatigue, metabolic changes (e.g., lowering of blood pressure as a result of missing meals), effects of drugs (e.g., some tranquilizers), and electrolyte imbalances (e.g., excessive fluid or salt intake). Careful recording of events that precede seizures can help identify contributing factors for a specific child. Once identified, these factors can often be eliminated or controlled.

Intervention during the prodrome can also help prevent seizures. Zlutnick, Mayville, and Moffat (1975) found that specific behavioral chains could be identified in some individuals prior to seizures, and interrupting these chains of behavior could reduce the frequency of seizures. For example, careful observation may reveal that a child frequently stares out the window and hums prior to seizures. Interrupting this behavior prior to a seizure may prevent some seizures. Biofeedback has achieved some success controlling epilepsy that has responded poorly to medication or when the dosage required to control seizures has had undesirable side effects (Lechtenberg, 1990). The application of bio-feedback to control seizures in children with multiple disabilities needs further exploration, but could prove valuable.

Protection When seizures cannot be prevented, protection against injury during the seizure may be important. Protective measures, like other interventions, need to be individualized to meet the needs of the specific child. For example, petit mal seizures typically do not require special risk-reduction procedures, but some activities (e.g., riding a bicycle) can be hazardous if periods of unconsciousness are long and/or frequent. In determining the suitability of any potential measure for a specific child, it is important to recognize that unnecessary restrictions and overprotectiveness can become greater problems than the risks they are intended to reduce (Yousef, 1985). The team must carefully consider the following before placing restrictions on the child: 1) the nature of the risk, 2) the extent of the risk, 3) the extent of risk reduction that can be expected as a result of the proposed measure, and 4) the intrusiveness of the risk-reduction measure.

There are many possibilities for methods of risk reduction. One method is environmental modification. Architectural decisions made during building design stages may greatly influence environmental hazards. For example, long, steep, straight staircases present much greater hazards than stairs interrupted by large landings. Many simple modifications can be made in existing buildings. Padded carpeting will greatly reduce the risk of head injury for some children with epilepsy. Furniture with rounded corners also reduces the risk of injury during a fall. These and other modifications can be achieved, when required, within the standards of normal classroom environments. Another common risk-reduction measure is the use of protective clothing, most commonly helmets (Spooner & Dykes, 1982). For individuals experiencing frequent, injurious falls, helmets can be extremely useful. The potential benefit to the wearer, however, must be weighed against the intrusiveness of the intervention. Wearing a helmet may contribute to the perception of the wearer as abnormal, may restrict the child's movements, and/or may be uncomfortable (especially in warm weather) and poorly tolerated. If protective headgear is required, it should be lightweight, well-fitting, and as normal to the social environment as possible. For example, a hockey helmet is much lighter than a football helmet and is not very abnormal apparel for a school-age child at play. A knit or other type of thick hat will provide considerable protection and will appear more normal in many environments than a helmet. The thick hair typically found on the human scalp provides significant natural protection. Hairstyles that are thick over frequently injured areas of the scalp can also provide significant protection without abnormal appearance. Another strategy for risk reduction involves the restriction of hazardous activities. Again, weighing the risk-reduction potential against the restriction of the activity requires careful judgment on the part of the team, and, regardless of communication and cognitive skill level, the child's input should be included in the decision-making. Restricting a child from a favorite or highly prized activity should occur only if great risk is present and restriction substantially reduces the risk. Swimming is a common example of an activity that many children with multiple disabilities (including epilepsy) enjoy. It can be dangerous if the individual has a seizure while in the water. Gumnit (1983) recommends that a person with poorly controlled seizures not swim, but a person with well-controlled seizures may swim providing someone is nearby to assist if necessary. The nature of the seizures, size of the person, and other factors may also need consideration. For example, during a tonic phase, water cannot normally enter the lungs. This provides a brief period for a rescuer to remove a person from the water. A heavy individual may be more difficult to bring out of the water, and, once the clonic phase begins, removing the individual from the water without allowing water to get into the lungs is extremely difficult. Also, chlorinated water and salt water pose special hazards since even small amounts in the lungs are potentially fatal.

First Aid Measures   When seizures occur, simple first aid measures may be required. These are summarized in Table 6.2. In most cases, little intervention is required, and misguided efforts are potentially harmful. First aid measures are aimed at preventing injury and generally involve simply using common sense.

Grand mal and other major motor convulsions often cause injury as a re-

Table 6.2   First aid of seizures

Type of seizure	Do	Do not
Grand mal	During 　　Ease to floor 　　Remove hazards 　　Cushion vulnerable body 　　　parts After 　　Allow for rest 　　Position for airway, if 　　　required 　　Check for injury	Put anything in mouth Move, unless absolutely 　required Restrain movements Give food or fluids, until 　fully conscious
Psychomotor	Remove hazards from area 　and/or pathway Supervise until fully 　conscious	Restrain movements Approach, if agitated, unless 　necessary Give food or fluids, until stu- 　dent is fully conscious
Petit mal	Protect from environmen- 　tal hazards	Give food or fluids, until stu- 　dent is fully conscious

sult of falling or from powerful involuntary movements. Often, the onset is too sudden for the individual to be eased to the floor, but sometimes (e.g., often when the child is sitting in a chair) the person does not fall immediately. Easing the person to the ground can prevent serious injury. Furniture with hard or sharp edges and other hazardous objects should be removed from the area, if possible. Only if a hazard cannot be moved (e.g., stairwell, swimming pool) should the child be moved away from it. Placing a soft object (e.g., cushion, sweater) under the head or other vulnerable body parts can also prevent injury.

One must not attempt to put anything in a person's mouth during a seizure. Although some injuries may occur from biting the tongue, these are not as frequent or severe as injuries caused by items placed in the mouth. Items placed in the mouth could: 1) force jaws out of joint due to unequal pressure, 2) break teeth, 3) obstruct the airway, or 4) spear oral structures if the person flips over on his or her face. Since the child is unconscious and anything given by mouth may enter the airway, it is also essential to refrain from giving food or fluid.

During the seizure, it is not normally useful to attempt to open or clear the airway, but it may be necessary after the seizure is over. If the child remains unconscious, it is desirable to position him or her on the right or left side, with the neck in slight extension and the head slightly lower than the midline of the body to encourage saliva or any other secretions to run out of the mouth and not back into the throat. The child should then be examined for signs of injury.

Observation should continue until the child is fully conscious, but it is not generally necessary to call for medical help unless one or more of the following occurs: 1) breathing does not resume (start mouth-to-mouth resuscitation), 2) one seizure follows another, 3) the person sustains a significant injury (Gumnit, 1983), 4) the seizure lasts more than 5 minutes, 5) the child has no history of epilepsy, or 6) the seizure appears substantially different from previously known seizures.

Other types of seizures typically require no first aid procedures. Only general precautions, such as removing dangerous objects, are necessary to protect the child from hazards that he or she might come into contact with. For example, a child with psychomotor epilepsy might walk off the edge of a porch, or a child with petit mal epilepsy might not be conscious of an approaching car.

Prolonged or repeated seizures, as previously mentioned, require immediate medical attention. This situation occurs most often when serum levels of medication drop suddenly from failure to take prescribed medication, metabolic changes (e.g., fever), or interactions with other medications (Gumnit, 1983). Other physiological changes (e.g., head injury, illness) can also contribute to prolonged or repeated seizures. Some individuals routinely have two or more grand mal seizures in a day or have seizures that last as long as 7 or 8 minutes, but, unless the observer is certain that this represents normal behavior for the child, immediate medical assistance should be requested. In a case of uncertainty, it is better to request assistance when it is not required than to fail to request it when needed. Whether or not a seizure is reported immediately, it should be carefully observed and recorded for the planning of care and treatment.

Observing and Recording   Since most physicians rarely have the opportunity to observe their patients over extended periods of time and seizures generally are unpredictable, physicians must treat most of their patients with epilepsy without ever observing their seizures. Therefore, they depend on parents, teachers, and others who directly observe seizures for accurate descriptions to guide their diagnosis and treatment.

Reports of seizures should be descriptive, not diagnostic (Sobsey, 1982). Using diagnostic descriptions may mislead the physician and/or fail to provide important details required for appropriate treatment. For example, a seizure reported as grand mal may be briefly preceded by focal seizure symptoms (e.g., a shaking right arm). This may be treated more effectively as a partial seizure since its origin is probably localized, but it will likely be considered a generalized seizure if merely described as grand mal. Careful observation and recording of the events that precede and follow seizures are also important. A record of antecedent events can help to identify seizure triggers or prodromal symptoms. These events can be useful in providing warning and even preventing seizures. A record of subsequent events can be helpful in determining a recovery pattern, the severity of the seizure, and whether an injury has occurred. No special form is required for reporting seizures, but the use of a form may help ensure uniform reporting and speed the recording process. Figure 6.1 shows an example of a form. Copies of seizure reports should be sent home to parents and kept on file for team consideration, and they should be made available to the physician whenever the child's seizure history is reviewed.

Treatment of Epilepsy

The primary treatment for epilepsy is the administration of anticonvulsant drugs. This was considered in Chapter 5. Three other types of treatments are considered here: 1) surgery, 2) behavioral intervention, and 3) dietary control.

Since the 1950s, when Penfield and the Montreal Neurological Institute popularized it, surgical treatment for uncontrollable cases of epilepsy has continued to increase in use (Dreifuss, 1983). Four major categories of procedure have been identified by Dreifuss (1983). First, prophylactic surgery can prevent epilepsy through removal of bone fragments, prevention of infection, and relief of pressure after head injury. Second, when seizures can be traced to a specific lesion, the lesion can be removed or inactivated (often by freezing). Third, even when no specific lesion can be identified, seizure foci (areas of origin) can be removed. Commonly, this involves removal of a section of the temporal lobe. This is probably the most frequently used surgical treatment for epilepsy. Fourth, surgical procedures can obstruct the spread of abnormal electrical activity in the brain. (Frequently, this involves severing part—usually the ante-

·· SEIZURE RECORD ··

Student's Name: _____   Date: _____

Time (of occurrence): _____   Classroom: _____

———————————————————————————— ANTECEDENTS

Student's location: _____

Student's activity: _____

Warning signs ☐ No Yes ☐ *If "Yes," describe:* _____

———————————————————————————— SEIZURE BEHAVIOR

Duration *(If approximate, state it):* _____

Did student's body stiffen?   ☐ No   ☐ Yes   **Parts of Body Involved :**

Did student's body shake?   ☐ No   ☐ Yes   Arms ☐ Left Right ☐

Did the student fall?   ☐ No   ☐ Yes   Legs ☐ Left Right ☐

Any apparent injury?   ☐ No   ☐ Yes   Other: _____

Describe: _____

Did the student appear to become unaware of the environment?   ☐ No ☐ Yes

Was there a change in color of the student's lips, nailbeds, etc.?   ☐ No ☐ Yes

Describe: _____

Did student wet or soil?   Urine: ☐ No ☐ Yes   Feces: ☐ No ☐ Yes

Did student have difficulty breathing?

  Before ☐ No ☐ Yes   During: ☐ No ☐ Yes   After: ☐ No ☐ Yes

Other/*Describe:*_____

_____

_____

———————————————————————————— SUBSEQUENCES

Describe first aid given: _____

_____

Describe student's activity after seizure: _____

_____

Notifications: ☐ None required   ☐ Parents   ☐ Physician

            ☐ Other (Specify): _____

Reported By:_____   Date/ Time Filed:_____

Figure 6.1.   A behavioral seizure observation record. (Based on Sobsey [1982].)

rior two-thirds—of the corpus callosum [a connecting tissue between the right and left hemispheres].) In spite of the fact that surgical intervention is well tolerated by many patients, it is still considered intrusive and risky. Therefore, surgery is performed on only a small percentage of individuals whose seizures do not respond to other treatment but can be traced to specific areas of the brain (Dreifuss, 1983). Developmental disabilities are still generally considered to contraindicate surgical treatment of epilepsy by many physicians, but decisions about the appropriateness of such treatment should be made on the basis of risks and benefits to individuals, not on the basis of diagnostic labels. Since some procedures require patients to remain conscious and to describe their sensations during surgery, patients who cannot participate in this manner may be difficult or impossible to accommodate.

Behavioral intervention has also proven useful in treating some individuals with epilepsy. Parrino (1971) demonstrated that, for some persons with epilepsy with identified seizure triggers, systematic desensitization (gradual exposure) to triggering stimuli reduced seizures. Wright (1973) showed that self-induced seizures could be reduced through punishment of the seizure-inducing behavior. Certainly, similar results could be achieved with non-aversive behavior management techniques. Zlutnick et al. (1975), as reported previously, found that seizures could be reduced when prodromal behavior chains were interrupted. Each of these approaches has enormous potential for some persons. They provide alternatives or supplements to medications, which often have deleterious side effects. Children with epilepsy should be considered good candidates for behavioral intervention if they have one or more of the following: 1) self-induced seizure activity, 2) identifiable preseizure behavior patterns, or 3) identifiable environmental seizure triggers. Careful evaluation and planning by the entire transdisciplinary team is required to determine appropriateness of behavioral intervention and evaluate its success.

Dietary intervention is also used to treat epilepsy in some individuals. The *ketogenic* diet (which accumulates byproducts of fat metabolism in the blood) has been used since the 1940s to control seizures, primarily in children (Palmer & Kalisz, 1978). As awareness of problems related to high fat intake increased, and better drug therapy became available, ketogenic diets became less frequently used. In the 1970s, however, the MCT (medium-chain triglyceride) ketogenic diet came into use, which reduced some concern over high intake of saturated fats. Dietary intervention should be considered when drugs are ineffective or have serious side effects and when decreased seizure activity can be demonstrated during a trial period. A dietitian or nutritionist should be part of the transdisciplinary team considering and monitoring dietary intervention.

Educational Implications

Many of the topics already discussed greatly affect the provision of education for children with epilepsy (e.g., observing and reporting seizures in the classroom, behavioral intervention), but a few specific educational concerns are addressed here: 1) the effects of epilepsy on learning and behavior, 2) social implications of epilepsy, and 3) some specific roles of the transdisciplinary team.

Learning and Behavior   Although epilepsy is only weakly correlated with intelligence, it may influence learning in a number of ways (Dreisbach et al., 1982). Drugs, intense and frequent seizures, brain damage, related behavior problems, and attention deficits have all been identified as impediments to learning for some children with epilepsy (Yousef, 1985). Postictal (after seizure) effects such as confusion, mental impairment, headache, or fatigue may interfere with learning in some children (Dreisbach et al., 1982). It is important to remember, however, that not all children who experience seizures are affected equally by these factors, and some are not affected by any of these factors. Team decisions must be reached through careful consideration of effects on specific children. For example, there have been reports of attention deficits as a result of subclinical seizure activity (Dreisbach et al., 1982). Although these deficits may be controlled by medication, the medications may occasionally result in sluggishness, lethargy, depression, irritability, or behavior problems that also interfere with learning. Careful evaluation of both liabilities and benefits of treatment must be undertaken by the team based on clear and complete records of the child's social, learning, and seizure behavior.

The role of epilepsy in violence, aggression, and lack of impulse control remains controversial. Although Solomon, Kutt, and Plum (1983) reported that 25%–35% of patients with psychomotor epilepsy show excessive aggressive behavior or episodic dyscontrol (a loss of normal inhibition), Lechtenberg (1984) pointed out that the results of such studies have been inconsistent. Intervening social factors make it extremely difficult to interpret any correlational studies (e.g., Taylor, 1972). The Epilepsy Foundation of America (1985) reported that epilepsy was three times more common among prison inmates, but it also pointed out that stigma associated with epilepsy and increased risk of head injury (as well as other factors) may account for these figures. Regardless of the interpretation of these statistics, however, it is clear that the majority of persons with epilepsy exhibit no special behavior problems. Therefore, behavior problems should not be anticipated simply because a child has epilepsy. When behavior problems do occur in children with epilepsy, they should be treated exactly like behavior problems in any other child. In the rare instances in which behavior problems appear to be direct results of seizure activity, medical treatment with anticonvulsants may be considered.

Social Implications of Epilepsy   Epilepsy has a long history of social stigma that continues to be a major problem for individuals with epilepsy (Lindsay, 1983). In one study (Dreisbach et al., 1982), parents of 36% of children with epilepsy reported stigma, lack of social acceptance, and negative public opinion as their children's greatest problems. Fortunately, public attitudes toward epilepsy are improving. Caveness and Gallup (1980) found that public attitudes became progressively more favorable over 30 years. For example, in 1949, 57% of respondents indicated they would not object to their children playing with a child with epilepsy. By 1979, the percentage indicating no objection had grown to 89% (Caveness & Gallup, 1980). Another encouraging finding of the Caveness and Gallup (1980) study was that responses became more favorable as educational level and exposure to individuals with epilepsy increased. This suggests further improvement through public education and integration efforts.

It might be argued that the stigma associated with severe and multiple disabilities is more prevalent and intense than the stigma associated with epilepsy, and therefore, improved attitudes toward children with epilepsy have little benefit to the child with multiple disabilities. If such severe stigma does exist toward persons with multiple disabilities, the improved attitudes toward epilepsy provide a hopeful note on how such attitudes may change. In addition to public opinion, attitudes about epilepsy within the child's family are a special concern.

Many parents have serious misconceptions about their children's seizures (e.g., death is likely to occur during a seizure) or epilepsy in general (Ford, Gibson, & Dreifus, 1983). Parents of children with epilepsy have reported lowered self-esteem and difficulty with communication within the family (Ferrari, Matthews, & Barabas, 1983). Parents' attitudes toward their children's epilepsy became more positive as mothers adjusted to their child's epilepsy (Austin, McBride, & Davis, 1984). These findings suggest that intervention to teach families about epilepsy and to encourage acceptance of their child's condition can be valuable components of the child's program.

Specific Transdisciplinary Team Roles   Since control of seizures and learning are closely interrelated, decisions affecting either must consider both. The physician should be part of the team making decisions, along with parents, teachers, and other staff. Unfortunately, direct communication between teacher and physician regarding children with epilepsy is extremely rare (Gadow, 1982). It is essential that strategies for communication be put in place. Sending seizure records with a brief summary of educational performance to the physician and providing a form for a brief report back is one method of encouraging communication. Education and training of all team members and other school staff are essential to ensure that they are prepared to handle seizures. Workshops have been demonstrated to be effective in imparting information about epilepsy, improving teacher attitudes toward epilepsy, and building teachers' confidence in their ability to cope with seizures (Rassel, Tonelson, & Appolone, 1981). Nurses may play a central role in providing training for other team members as well as administering medications and maintaining health records.

Education of families is also important. MacDougall (1982) suggests six major goals for training: 1) understanding the nature of seizures, 2) understanding the basis for diagnostic procedures, 3) knowing what to do when a seizure occurs, 4) recognizing effects and side effects of medications, 5) knowing how to control seizure triggers (when appropriate), and 6) enhancing self-esteem. Decisions regarding behavioral intervention for seizure control should include the entire team. Even when treatment is solely medical, team members must participate in the evaluation of treatment by carefully recording the effects of treatment. Similarly, decisions regarding restrictions of activity or protective equipment must include the entire team. Daily activity schedules may require modification to take advantage of peak learning times, especially when medication side effects reduce responsiveness during specific parts of the day. Careful planning and scheduling by the team can work around some of these side effects, and, by allowing some flexibility in scheduling, it becomes possible to compensate, at least partially, for unpredictable changes.

SELF-INJURIOUS BEHAVIOR

Some students with severe or multiple disabilities harm themselves through their own repetitive, stereotypic, or intense episodic behavior. These students may bang their heads, poke their eyes, scratch or tear their skin, bite their arms or fingers, or engage in one or more other self-damaging behaviors. The effects of this behavior range from transient irritation to severe and permanent injury. In addition, self-injurious behavior is often very disruptive to activities and demoralizing to parents, staff, and others.

Causes

A variety of possible causes and contributing factors for self-injurious behavior have been proposed, and many appear to provide at least a partial explanation (Meyer & Evans, 1989). Some organic conditions appear to predispose individuals to self-injurious behavior. For example, children with Lesch-Nyhan syndrome often exhibit severe and intractable forms of self-injurious behavior. Other hypotheses with organic components suggest that self-inflicted pain may help block other more aversive sensations, may increase the production of natural opiates in the system and thus be reinforced, or may be used by the individual to raise the general level of arousal (much in the way that a tired driver sometimes turns up the car radio, opens the car window to let in cold air, or even slaps his or her own cheeks to try to stay alert). Other explanations are more behavioral, suggesting that the behavior is developed, maintained, and strengthened as the individual learns that it is associated with reinforcement or escape from aversive stimuli. For example, individuals may learn that self-injurious behavior quickly attracts the attention of caregivers; distracts caregivers, thereby providing the individual with the opportunity to escape from demands of a task; or both. Behavioral and organic explanations are not mutually exclusive, and it is likely that these and other factors interact in at least some individuals (Meyer & Evans, 1989). Approaches to management of and intervention for self-injurious behavior include one or more of the following: 1) medication to reduce frequency of the behavior, 2) restraint to prevent the individual from self-harm, 3) first aid and treatment to promote healing, 4) aversive procedures to reduce the frequency of the behavior, and 5) educative or nonaversive procedures to teach less harmful and more acceptable behavioral alternatives.

Intervention

There are a wide variety of drugs used to reduce or eliminate self-injurious behavior. Tranquilizers, opiate antagonists, beta-blockers, stimulants, and anticonvulsants are sometimes used (Gadow & Poling, 1988). Although many of these drugs have been at least partially successful in achieving some reduction for some individuals, they often suppress other more appropriate behavior to a greater or equal extent, interfere with learning, have deleterious side-effects, and create chronic dependency since any improvement achieved typically is reversed when use of the drug ceases. Therefore, drugs should not be considered as a primary resource for treating self-injurious behavior. They may be considered a time-limited component of intervention if the behavior puts the individual in immediate danger and their application meets the conditions for their use presented in Chapter 5.

Another common approach to managing severe self-injurious behavior is restraint. One may apply restraint by holding the individual in a manner that prevents movement or injury. It can also be applied in the form of elbow or knee splints, camisoles (straight jackets), restraint nets, support belts, or a number of other devices. Occlusive bandages that keep the individual from further damaging the part of the body that is the preferred target for injury is another form of restraint. The advantage of restraint is that if it is applied successfully it can prevent further injury immediately and for as long as the restraint remains in place. Like medical intervention for self-injurious behavior, however, restraint cannot cure the problem, which often reappears as soon as restraint is removed. Restraint also can cause injury, and the use of restraint has been shown to reinforce the self-injurious behavior in some individuals (Favell, McGimsey, & Jones, 1978). Therefore, restraint should be used only as a last resort on a time-limited basis to prevent imminent and potentially severe injury. It should never be used to take the place of a more appropriate program. Measures such as removing dangerous objects from the environment or keeping the fingernails of those who scratch themselves well-trimmed may be justified in some cases as part of a risk-reduction program.

First aid and other forms of treatment are often important elements of a total program for individuals with self-injurious behavior. Methods for controlling bleeding and other first aid measures are discussed in the "Classroom Emergencies" section of this chapter. Other treatments (e.g., sterile dressings, surgery to repair detached retinas) may be required in some cases. The health care team should work closely with the educational team in determining appropriate treatments. Since the care and attention associated with a treatment may reinforce the self-injurious behavior of some individuals, it is essential that their treatment be provided in a neutral manner that minimizes reinforcement. It is also essential to remember that even the best treatment can be expected only to slow down the rate of damage if severe self-injurious behavior continues; therefore, treating the injuries should be considered a necessary component of the individual's care, but primary emphasis should be placed on eliminating the self-injurious behavior.

Elimination of self-injurious behavior has been accomplished through aversive and nonaversive means. *Aversive* treatment typically attempts to eliminate unacceptable behavior through punishment procedures. *Nonaversive* treatment attempts to eliminate unacceptable behavior through teaching more appropriate alternatives or through other methods that do not require punishment. Considerable controversy exists among proponents of aversive and nonaversive intervention for this and other severe behavior problems (Repp & Singh, 1990). Those who favor the use of aversive intervention suggest that it has been proven to be more effective and it is justified since brief punishment frees the individual from chronic self-injury (Axelrod, 1990; Coe & Matson, 1990). Proponents of nonaversive approaches suggest that research demonstrates that nonaversive intervention is as effective or more effective than aversive alternatives (Donellan & LaVigna, 1990; Sobsey, 1990a). An extensive meta-analysis of the research on methods of intervention for problem behavior suggests that more aversive forms of intervention result in no more improvement than nonaversive intervention (Scotti, Evans, Meyer, & Walker, in press). While controversy continues, nonaversive approaches appear to be making headway as more questions are raised regarding the research supporting aversive approaches and more research becomes available demonstrating the effectiveness of nonaversive alternatives.

The authors of this book strongly recommend the use of nonaversive procedures to address self-injurious behavior. More information on how to design and implement nonaversive programs is included in Chapters 7 and 9. Many other sources are also available (for complete information on assessment and design of these programs, see LaVigna & Donnellan, 1986, and Meyer & Evans, 1989).

Nonaversive intervention requires a functional analysis of the behavior along with its temporal, social, and physical contexts. Antecedents and consequences of the behavior are carefully examined to determine the function of the behavior for the individual. For example, two individuals may have episodes of hitting their heads, but one may hit herself when she is left alone and the other may do so when he is asked to carry out a difficult task. For the former, hitting herself may function as a means of attracting attention from caregivers. For the latter, hitting himself may function as a means of escaping from task demands. Since the behavior of the two students is almost identical, one can make and test hypotheses regarding the function only by considering the specific contexts and effects of each behavior. Once the function of the behavior has been identified, intervention is designed to provide training in a more so-cially appropriate and less dangerous method of serving the function. It is im-portant to remember that requesting attention or protesting a demand are not the problems. Everyone has a right and a need to carry out these functions at times. It is the method of carrying out these functions that needs to change. Unfortu-nately, caregivers often ignore appropriate requests for attention and protests, but find inappropriate behavior more difficult to ignore. Effective transfer of the behavioral function to a more appropriate form of behavior requires care-givers to respond to the new form of behavior as quickly and as enthusiastically as they responded to the less appropriate form. More information on methods of teaching communication functions is presented in Chapter 9.

CLASSROOM EMERGENCIES

General Strategies

Every person who works with children in a day care, school, or other group setting should be prepared to prevent health related emergencies whenever pos-sible and to treat emergencies when necessary. A practical course in safety and first aid with periodic refresher classes should be included in the training of all staff. Staff working with students with multiple disabilities also need specific training related to the special needs of the children they serve. For example, staff who serve students with tracheostomies need to be familiar with modifica-tions of the resuscitation procedures required for these children in respiratory emergencies (Holvoet & Helmstetter, 1989).

Every classroom needs a plan for handling emergencies, and it is impor-tant that all staff be familiar with the plan in advance. For example, staff need to know whether to call the school nurse, the principal, the parent, or an ambu-lance in case of a serious emergency. They should have all important telephone numbers available. In cities with 911 emergency service coordination numbers, this task is greatly simplified, but in other cities, separate numbers may be re-quired for an ambulance service, the police, a hospital, the poison control cen-ter, and other vital services. Staff must be able to reach parents or guardians quickly during the day since medical treatment may be delayed if parents can-not be notified. For some students, particularly those with highly individu-alized health care needs, there should also be a plan in place (and approved by parents) to contact the child's physician directly. Any health care information that is likely to be relevant in an emergency situation (e.g., current medica-tions, blood type, allergies) should be kept in a file with easy access that can be taken with the child if he or she needs to be transported to a hospital or other setting for treatment. It may be useful to keep general consents for emergency treatment in this file, although the value of this type of consent is questionable. Since these consents are made in advance and not after being informed of a current situation and the specific risks and potential benefits of treatment, they cannot substitute for the normal informed consent to permit medical treatment. Since first-aid measures that are necessary to prevent the death of or serious harm to a child are permitted if the parent or guardian is unavailable, general consents are not required for these purposes. Nevertheless, there often remains a large area of uncertainty regarding what treatments are essential and how long a delay is justifiable. Some health care team members suggest that general consents may be helpful, because knowing the general intentions of the parents helps physicians determine how far to take the limits of justifiable emergency procedures.

Some Specific Emergencies

Airway Obstruction Preventing and treating airway obstruction are probably the most important emergency health care skills for teachers of students with multiple disabilities. These skills are essential for four important reasons. First, airway obstruction is a major cause of accidental death of children in schools (Torrey, 1983). Second, the risk of airway obstruction is greater for children with disabilities. Third, if complete obstruction of the airway occurs, treatment must be given immediately; there is rarely enough time to obtain outside help to save a child. Fourth, simple prevention and treatment methods could save almost every choking victim. Although the exact extent of the increased risk for children with multiple disabilities is unknown, a number of risk factors have been identified in the general population (Dailey, 1983) that indicate substantially increased risk for children with disabilities: 1) decreased gag reflex, 2) incomplete chewing, 3) use of medication, 4) missing teeth, and 5) altered consciousness.

Food asphyxiation occurs when food enters the airway or when it becomes stuck in the upper part of the throat, preventing the epiglottis from opening. Four specific foods (hot dogs, candy, nuts, and grapes) account for more than 40% of choking deaths in young children (Harris, Baker, Smith, & Harris, 1984). About 15% of deaths are caused by soft, loosely textured foods that become compressed upon swallowing (Dailey, 1983). This is probably more common in older children and adults with multiple disabilities. Bread and similar compressible foods have been found trapping the epiglottis (which closes the airway) at autopsy of a number of victims with disabilities.

Prevention One simple prevention measure is to eliminate some of the high-risk foods from meals or to alter them to reduce the risk. For young children with small airways, peanuts and hard candies should be eliminated. Hot dogs and sausages (which together constitute the single largest threat category) should be included only if ground up. Grapes should be cut in half. Bread and similarly compressible foods should be given in small installments that do not permit a large bolus to collect in the mouth and be swallowed at once. Bread with sticky spreads (e.g., peanut butter, marshmallow spread) should not be given to children who are at risk. While the completely pureed food diets have sometimes been used to reduce the risk of choking, they are not typically justifiable since these diets cause other health problems and increase the risk of aspiration, which may also be life-threatening.

Several other measures can be taken to decrease the risk of choking. First, children must be properly positioned in an upright position for eating. Second, slight flexion of the neck assists proper swallowing (Logemann, 1983) and helps encourage closure of the epiglottis before food approaches. Also, since flexion narrows the throat, it allows the throat to widen through extension if obstruction occurs. Third, children must not be allowed to eat too fast or to attempt to swallow large amounts of food that have accumulated in their mouths. Fourth, adequate fluids must be provided with dry foods to lubricate them adequately for swallowing. Fifth, rapid attention should be given to any health problem (e.g., reduced alertness as a side effect of medication) that might increase the risk of choking. Sixth, good dental care and appropriate training to chew will help prevent choking.

Signs and Symptoms   In spite of the best prevention efforts, choking incidents will continue to occur from time to time. Parents, teachers, and other mealtime caregivers must be adequately trained to recognize and treat airway obstruction. Early symptoms of complete airway obstruction are nonspecific. In the first 1–3 minutes, the child is likely to remain conscious but indicate distress through agitated movement and possible clutching of the throat or tears in the eyes. The child attempts to breathe, but no air can be felt entering or leaving the nose or mouth. Since no air can enter or leave, the child cannot vocalize. Pulse and blood pressure increase rapidly. Color gradually begins to change to a deep red or purple; this condition is called cyanosis (Dailey, 1983). During the next phase, which lasts approximately 3 minutes, the child loses consciousness. Cyanosis deepens to a mottled blue or purple. Pulse and blood pressure drop rapidly. Attempts at respiration weaken. About 5 minutes (often less) after the initial obstruction, the child enters a third phase, deep coma. Blood pressure, pulse, and attempts at respiration are absent. Pupils become dilated. Brain damage and death will ensue rapidly unless the airway is cleared and pulse and respiration restarted (Dailey, 1983).

Treatment   The rapidity of these events demands immediate action. Available time is often further restricted by failure to notice a problem until the second stage or by the mistaken belief that an epileptic seizure or other problem is the cause. Attempting mouth-to-mouth resuscitation and finding that air will not go in or come out confirms airway obstruction.

The best training requires direct instructor-to-student contact, which can be obtained in first aid courses or specialized training programs, but some general discussion of these procedures is included below. While considerable controversy existed during the 1980s over the best choice of treatment for airway obstruction (i.e., back blows versus Heimlich maneuver) (Day, Crelin, & Du-

Bois, 1982), in July of 1985, agreement was reached among all major first aid groups that the Heimlich maneuver, already credited with saving thousands of lives, should be the sole treatment in choking emergencies (American Heart Association, 1985). Heimlich (1982) urged the use of the subdiaphragmatic thrust (Heimlich maneuver) as treatment for choking. He stated that back blows are less effective and may convert a partial obstruction into a complete one or a treatable obstruction into an untreatable one.

Following is the procedure for performing the subdiaphragmatic thrust (Figure 6.2): 1) place arms around the victim from the rear, 2) grasp one wrist with the other hand, 3) make a fist with the empty hand, 4) press the fist against the victim's upper abdomen just below the tip of the sternum (breastbone), and 5) hug forcefully while pressing the fist upward and into the abdomen (Heimlich & Uhley, 1979). This procedure forces the abdomen upward and compresses the air in the lungs, which pushes out the obstruction. If the mouth is full, it is desirable to clear it carefully (so that nothing is pushed further into the throat or airway) before carrying out the subdiaphragmatic thrust. If the rescuer cannot position himself or herself behind the victim, an alternative pro-

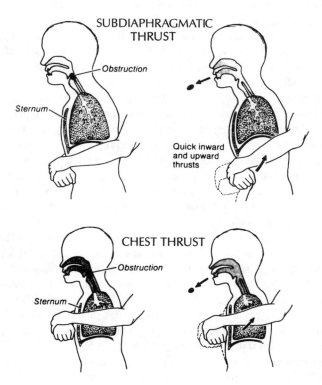

Figure 6.2.   Subdiaphragmatic thrust and chest thrust.

cedure positions the victim supine on the floor or firm surface and the rescuer kneeling over the victim, facing the victim's head. The rescuer applies the thrust by positioning the hands just below the sternum (as described above) and leaning rapidly and forcefully forward. Chest thrusts (Figure 6.2) are similar to the subdiaphragmatic thrusts, except that pressure is applied directly to the middle of the sternum (breast bone). They may be necessary to use if the choking victim is quite obese or in the advanced stages of pregnancy. Chest thrusts may be applied with two fingers and the infant-in-supine position for children less than 1 year old (St. John Ambulance, 1988).

A finger sweep of the mouth and upper throat also may remove obstructions. This method is sometimes effective when other methods fail, but cannot be recommended as an initial measure because of the danger of pushing obstructions farther into the airway or compacting the obstruction, which makes the obstruction more difficult to remove. These difficulties are especially likely to occur with a young child with a small oropharyngeal space to work in. The finger sweep is recommended while the victim is still conscious (Dailey, 1983) or after subdiaphragmatic thrust has been attempted repeatedly without success. Performance involves the rescuer positioning the victim supine (on a sloping surface with head lower than feet if possible) with head extended back. The rescuer inserts an index finger into the mouth with the back of the finger pressed against the obstruction; this can allow removal of all or part of the obstruction. If part of the obstruction is removed, the procedure is repeated only after a check reveals that the airway remains obstructed.

Head Injury   This section includes some basic information about some common signs of head injury and the appropriate response when head injury is suspected. Some of the special considerations related to recognizing and treating head injury in children with severe disabilities are also discussed. Head injury is frequently classified as *concussion* (a temporary disturbance in brain function as a result of an impact) and *compression* (pressure on some part of the brain caused by a fracture of the skull, swelling, or the collection of fluid in an area of the brain). While compression is typically more serious, differentiating between the two is difficult, and first aid measures discussed here are the same. Therefore, the two types of injury are discussed jointly here. Table 6.3 lists some of the common signs of concussion and compression along with some special considerations for people with multiple disabilities and basic first aid measures. As shown in this table, signs of concussion and compression overlap, and the distinction between the two is more difficult to make if the individual sustaining the injury has epilepsy, a movement disorder, or impaired communication. Many medications used by people with disabilities can also mask symptoms. Since the rapid diagnosis and treatment of head injury is essential to the best treatment, and accurate diagnosis may be impossible without careful evaluation by a physician using sophisticated tests and equipment, it is better to

Table 6.3
Signs of head injury and treatment

•Concussion•
- •Partial loss of consciousness
- •Shallow breathing
- •Weak pulse
- •Pale appearance
- •Headache
- •Confusion

- •Complete loss of consciousness
- •Rapid pulse
- •Cool skin
- •Vomiting
- •Loss of memory (especially for recent events)
- •Potentially injurious event (may have been seen)

•Usually these signs begin immediately or shortly after injury

---

•Compression•
- •Partial loss of consciousness
- •Seizures (mild to severe) may occur
- •Slowing of pulse
- •Raised body temperature
- •Dilated pupils
- •Coordination problems
- •Confusion

- •Complete loss of consciousness (more common)
- •Irregular breathing
- •Flushed face
- •Unequal pupils
- •Weakness (may affect one side more than the other)
- •External injury may or may not be present
- •Potentially injurious event (may have been seen)

•These signs may begin immediately or shortly after injury but may be delayed significantly

---

•Special Considerations for Individuals with Multiple Disabilities•
- •Many of these signs can be masked if they are present prior to injury.
- •Seizures are more common in concussion among people with preexisting seizure disorders.
- •Seizures sometimes produce many of the same signs as head injury.
- •Seizures may also result in head injury.
- •Medications (e.g., anticonvulsants, tranquilizers) may mask symptoms.

•First Aid Treatment and Response•
- •Assess consciousness, observe for breathing difficulties, keep under constant observation.
- •Maintain open airway, provide assisted breathing, if required.
- •Give no food or fluids.
- •Protect area of injury from any further trauma (and from contamination if open wound).
- •Keep victim calm and inactive if possible (do not use excessive restraint).
- •Avoid nose blowing if possible.
- •Avoid pressure to area of injury.
- •Unless bleeding is so severe that it must be stopped, do not use direct pressure to skull injuries.
- •Call for medical assistance.

---

err on the side of safety and have the child evaluated if signs of injury are ambiguous.

First aid measures often consist only of keeping the individual safe and calm until help arrives (St. John Ambulance, 1988). No food or fluids should be given because intake may increase swelling in the brain, and creates the risk of aspiration since swallowing may be difficult. The danger of vomiting is also increased. This is particularly problematic since vomiting is likely to increase pressure on the brain and creates further risk of aspiration. Since persons sustaining head injury are likely to lose consciousness or have a seizure, they should be protected against falls. If bleeding from the a head wound is not too severe, it is better to allow bleeding than to apply pressure. One should keep the person calm and comfortable, observing continuously for changes, particularly any difficulty with breathing. If the person will lie down quietly, he or she should be encouraged to do so, but it is important that the person avoid restraint or struggling, which may aggravate the injury.

Poisoning Children with multiple disabilities sometimes ingest potentially toxic substances. These may include medications, cleaning products, herbicides, pesticides, certain household and garden plants, and a variety of other substances. Often this problem can be prevented, and prevention efforts should be practiced carefully by everyone who works with children with multiple disabilities. These efforts include: 1) keeping all household cleaners, pesticides, drugs, and other dangerous substances safely locked away; 2) being certain that no poisonous plants are kept in areas frequented by children; 3) discarding old or excess medication, pesticides, cleaners, and so forth in a safe manner; 4) keeping all dangerous substances in childproof containers; and 5) never transferring toxic materials to old food containers (St. John Ambulance, 1988).

Fortunately, the development of a network of poison control centers across North America has greatly simplified the basic first aid protocol for ingestion of toxic substances. If a telephone is available, one should contact the poison control center immediately, be prepared to give complete information regarding the substance, and follow the instructions provided. Staff of the poison control center will need to know what substance was ingested, how much, and how long ago. They should also be told the child's age, approximate weight, any available information regarding special medical conditions, and what medications, if any, the child normally takes.

Poison control staff may recommend immediate first aid measures and will often suggest that the child be brought in for examination. When the child goes for examination the container that held the substance, any labeling material available, and any remaining sample of the substance should be brought. If the toxic was a plant, one should bring it or part of it for identification. If the child vomited, one should try to bring the vomitus or at least a sample for examination. It is essential to note the time of the ingestion and bring along any records available regarding health conditions, allergies, and medications.

In the rare case that contacting the poison control center it is not possible, one should check the label of the substance for directions on how to treat ingestion. Several glasses of water may help to dilute the substance and may induce vomiting. Syrup of ipecac also is commonly used to induce vomiting. Inducing vomiting may be difficult in some children with multiple disabilities because of medications (particularly Thorazine) that they are receiving. Inducing vomiting is not recommended, except under specific medical instructions, if the victim is drowsy or unconscious, under 1 year old, has ingested a petroleum product (since these would be much more dangerous in the lungs than in the stomach), or has ingested a corrosive substance that may do additional damage to the mouth, throat, and esophagus on the way out. Children with motor impairments are at greater risk for aspiration, and inducing vomiting should not be attempted in them unless the ingested substance poses a serious risk and medical help is unavailable.

Bleeding   External bleeding is easily recognized and easily treated. Almost all bleeding, including that resulting from severe injuries, can be controlled by direct pressure. If available, a sterile bandage or clean cloth can be pressed over a wound. When those items are unavailable, pressure applied with the bare hand works quite satisfactorily. The person who is injured should be encouraged to rest and stay calm and the injured body part should be elevated in relation to the rest of the body if possible. If the injury appears to be severe, medical advice and assistance must be sought. If internal bleeding is suspected, the injured person should be at rest. If possible, the individual should lie down with the legs slightly elevated. One should prevent the person from becoming chilled and should seek medical advice and assistance as quickly as possible (St. John Ambulance, 1988).

Efforts to prevent classroom emergencies can greatly reduce the frequency and severity of these episodes. Despite even the best prevention efforts, emergencies sometimes occur, and all staff working with children with multiple disabilities must be prepared to respond to them.

ABUSE

Child abuse is a terrible reality for too many children in contemporary society. A significant proportion of children from all segments of society are subjected to physical, sexual, or emotional abuse or neglect (Sobsey, Gray, Wells, Pyper, & Reimer-Heck, 1991). Increasing awareness of the extent of these problems and of the degree of harm suffered by victims of abuse has resulted in the development and implementation of programs to prevent and detect abuse in addition to intervention programs for victims of abuse (e.g., West Contra Costa Rape Crisis Center, 1986).

The connection between disability and abuse is well established, but the precise nature of the relationship remains obscure. Even so, abuse is recognized as a significant cause of disability. As diagnostic techniques improve, the role of abuse in causing disability becomes clearer and appears more extensive than previously believed (Sobsey, 1989). For example, improved brain imaging techniques have helped to identify many cases of whiplash shaken infant syndrome, which likely would have been diagnosed only as "brain damage of undetermined origin" in previous years (Sobsey, 1989). Different factors can contribute to both abuse and disability. For example, excessive use of alcohol within families has been found to be associated with physical and sexual abuse of children within these families and to fetal alcohol syndrome (FAS), which causes disability (O'Sullivan, 1989). Even when the cause of disability appears to be unrelated to abuse, children with disabilities are more frequently the targets of abuse than are children who do not have disabilities. Furthermore, while children with disabilities suffer the same effects of abuse as other children, they are often excluded from intervention programs that serve other children. Even when programs are accessible to children with disabilities, rarely are they appropriately individualized to meet the needs of children with severe or multiple disabilities.

The Nature and Extent of Abuse

Increased Risk   No one really knows what percentage of children with multiple disabilities are victims of abuse. Even in studies of the general population, differences in definitions and reporting criteria for abuse, inclusion or exclusion of unconfirmed cases, and the covert nature of the phenomenon of abuse have resulted in great variability in the estimates of actual frequency of abuse. Nevertheless, many studies reveal increased incidence of physical and sexual abuse and neglect among children with disabilities when the criteria for inclusion, the distribution of ages, and the gender of the subjects are held constant. The extent of the increase varies from study to study, but the risk for abuse of children with disabilities is at least one and one half times as high as that for other children (Sobsey & Varnhagen, 1989). Most children with multiple disabilities will experience abuse before reaching adulthood, and in many cases, the abuse will be severe and prolonged (Sobsey, in press).

An Ecological Model   The traditional explanations for the increased abuse of children with disabilities are inadequate. Much emphasis has been placed on a model that suggests that with increasing severity of disability the individual becomes more dependent. As dependency increases, family stress also increases, and this increase in family stress precipitates abuse. While this model appears to have gained some general acceptance, available research strongly contradicts it (Sobsey, 1990b). The level of severity of disability or dependency is a poor predictor of abuse and much of the abuse occurs from sources outside the family. The willingness of researchers and professionals to accept a model that ultimately places the cause of abuse with the victim not only is ethically worrisome, but also shows little potential for producing solutions. However well-intentioned, research that attempts to identify characteristics of people with disabilities that supposedly provoke abuse (e.g., Rusch, Hall, & Griffen, 1986) will have limited value for solving the problems of abuse and may help to perpetuate the victim-blaming attitudes that encourage abuse.

An alternative explanation for the abuse of people with disabilities suggests that "it may not be the disability that contributes to the increased risk, but rather a function of society's expectations and treatment of disabled people" (Sobsey & Varnhagen, 1989, p. 202). Based on this principle and considerable clinical and research evidence, a multifactorial ecological model has been proposed (Sobsey, in press). This model includes factors within the victim and offender, but it considers these within the context of the interaction between the two (microsystem), the setting (exosystem), and the social and cultural milieu (macrosystem). For example, excessive compliance has been identified in many victims of abuse who have disabilities, but this may result from the "educational focus" on compliance training for people with disabilities (in a world where people who do not have disabilities receive assertiveness training) and not from any inherent trait in the victims.

The ecological model provides a framework for examining the individual characteristics of abusers and victims along with their interaction patterns within a family or other environmental setting, and the broader social context. It also provides a framework for the identification of prevention and intervention methods.

Prevention and Intervention

Detecting and Reporting Abuse   Most states require educational and health care professionals to report suspected abuse to police or child protection agencies, and some states require any individual to report suspected abuse (Holvoet & Helmstetter, 1989). Nevertheless, abuse frequently goes undetected, and when detected, it often goes unreported (Sobsey, in press).

Several reasons contribute to poor detection (Holvoet & Helmstetter, 1989). First, offenders generally hide their abusive behavior well. They select times and places that provide privacy, and they often select victims who cannot tell what has happened to them. Offenders also may go to great lengths to construct alternative explanations for unexplained injuries or other signs of abuse. Many children with severe disabilities cannot communicate clearly about their mistreatment and may not know that they have a right to better treatment. For example, when one mother asked her 5-year-old daughter why she never told about the frequent sexual assaults she had endured, her daughter replied simply, "I thought you knew." Even when they understand that they are being mistreated and are capable of telling about the abuse, many victims are intimidated by the offenders. Most signs of abuse are inconclusive and may easily be attributed to other causes. Symptom masking, the attribution of a particular symptom to a known pre-existing condition rather than its real cause, often occurs when the victim of abuse has a disability. For example, behavioral changes, withdrawal, fearfulness, and frequent bruises or even fractures that result from abuse may be attributed to the child's disability rather than mistreatment. Finally, team members may be reluctant to accept evidence that their colleagues and coworkers are abusing the children they serve. In spite of these problems, knowledge of the signs of abuse can be very useful in detecting it. Signs of abuse are summarized in Table 6.4.

Many of these signs are ambiguous, and it is often an overall pattern or impression that is more powerful than any single sign. Each school or agency should have a protocol in place for reporting *suspected* abuse. Since there is rarely direct or overwhelming evidence at the time of the initial report, it is

Table 6.4
Signs of abuse

		•All Forms of Abuse•	
Direct observation	Disclosure	Sleep disturbances	Stoical responses to discomfort
Withdrawal	Escape behavior	Passivity	Inappropriate behavior
Resistance to touch	Hypervigilance	Reenactment	Behavioral regression
Fear of specific caregivers		Fear of specific environments	
Poor self-esteem		Self-abuse	
Victimization of others			

		•Physical Abuse•	
Frequent injury	Unexplained injury	Atypical injury	Patterned injury
Unexplained coma	Threats	Aggression	Temporally dispersed injuries
Noncompliance	Grab marks	Unreported fractures	

		•Sexual Abuse •	
Genital irritation	Noncompliance	Threats	Inappropriate sexual behavior
Aggression	Gender specific fear	Sexual precocity	Unexplained pregnancy
Resistance to touch	Promiscuity	Sexually transmitted disease	

	•Neglect•
Low affect	Poor nutritional status
Dehydration	Stoical responses to discomfort
Indifference to other people	Untreated illness or injuries
Unusual need for attention	

	•Abusive Caregiver Traits•
Authoritarian behavior	Unusual concern for privacy
Seeks isolated contact	Use of alcohol or disinhibiting drugs
History of violence or coercion	Problems with self-control
Dehumanizing attitudes	Negative evaluation of child
Difficulty relating to authority	Failure to support abuse control measures
Hostility toward reporters	Expression of myths of devaluation
Abusive counter-culture in setting	Subverts investigation
Fearful of victim	Blames victim
Grooming behavior	Limit testing behavior
Competition with child	Self-reports of stress

important that staff understand that they must report suspected abuse, and that many of these reports will prove unfounded or lack sufficient evidence for confirmation. Child abuse is a crime, and reporting suspected abuse to police or a child welfare agency is mandatory in most states. In schools and agencies that have protocols requiring internal reporting, there should also be provisions mandating external reporting. No report should be dismissed arbitrarily; thorough investigation is essential.

Preventing Abuse   Abuse prevention efforts cannot eliminate all risk of abuse, but they can significantly reduce those risks. Effective prevention methods may involve efforts directed toward the child, potential offenders, other program staff and family members, administrative reform, legislative reform, and cultural attitude change (Sobsey & Mansell, 1990).

Education is a powerful intervention against abuse. Teaching children that they have a right to be treated decently and how to assert those rights helps to reduce their risk for abuse. Communication skill training is vital to abuse prevention. Children who can express their feelings and indicate when they feel that they are being mistreated are less likely to be abused and exploited. Appropriate social and sex education is also important to prevention of sexual abuse and exploitation. Children who do not receive appropriate sex education from parents and teachers are likely to accept inappropriate sex education from an abuser. Program staff, parents, and advocates also need to learn to recognize and report abuse. Early recognition and response to problems is an essential element of abuse prevention because most abuse begins in milder forms and escalates to more severe forms.

Learning to recognize and respond to one's own difficulty in responding to a situation may be among the most difficult things to learn. Family members and caregivers should learn to recognize early signs of difficulty that they are experiencing and know where they can go for advice or counseling. While stress may play a smaller part in precipitating abuse than previously believed (Sobsey, 1990b), helping individuals though periods of stress may avert some abuse. Even more important, since family homes generally appear safer than institutional care, family support may help to hold families together and keep the child in a safer environment.

Administrative reform is also useful in preventing abuse. Careful screening of staff is essential. Individuals with known histories of perpetrating physical or sexual abuse or other violent crimes should not be hired to provide care to children with disabilities. Administrative reform is also essential to demonstrate an unequivocal commitment to protecting the children served by an agency. Criminal behavior must be treated as such and not as an employee relations problem or, perhaps worse, as a public relations problem. DiLionardi and Kelly's (1989) study of children in group care suggested that "some institutions have a high tolerance for child abuse and need to develop a low threshold culture for child abuse" (p. 253). In another study, Hass and Brown (1989) asked agencies serving people with disabilities if they would report crimes committed against their clients by staff; not a single agency indicated that they "would report the sexual assault of a client without fail" (p. 46). Some even admitted that the "impact of reporting on the agency" (p. 46) would be considered in the filing of reports. These findings suggest that much more can and needs to be done to ensure that agencies place a high priority on protecting the children they serve. Clustering both vulnerable and aggressive people with disabilities together without adequate safeguards to prevent injury to the vulnerable individuals is another form of abuse.

Further integration of children with disabilities into mainstream services and reduction of isolated services is also an essential component of abuse prevention. The risk of abuse in institutional settings appears to be two to four times as high as in community settings. Serving more children in community settings helps to reduce the risk they experience (Sobsey & Mansell, 1990).

Legal reform is also essential. Many states and some Canadian provinces have introduced protection and advocacy programs for children with disabilities (Sobsey & Mansell, 1990). More can be expected to follow. Some specific provisions that may serve as useful deterrents to abuse include: 1) allowing victims of abuse to testify in a manner most appropriate to their communication skills, 2) guaranteeing that employees who report abuse will not be administratively harassed, 3) guaranteeing that victims of abuse who have disabilities and their families will not have services disrupted in retaliation for reporting abuse, and 4) ensuring that all reports of abuse go to an impartial advocate outside of the agency involved.

Attitude change is also essential to preventing abuse. The powerful role of attitudes in facilitating abusive behavior cannot be ignored (Shaman, 1986). Perceptions of people with disabilities as less than fully human, "damaged merchandise," incapable of suffering, dangerous, or helpless have all been identified as factors in abuse. In the abuser, these myths become full blown and provide the rationale that abusers may use in disinhibiting aggressive and sexual drives (Sobsey & Mansell, 1990).

Intervention for Victims of Abuse   Children with multiple disabilities suffer the same negative effects of abuse as other children who are victimized. Physical harm can be significant and may add to a child's existing disability. Emotional, behavioral, and social harm may be even more serious. The best general intervention is ending the abuse and ensuring a supportive environment that can begin to nurture some positive growth in the child. Medical treatment is required for some children. Teaching self-protection skills may reduce the chances for repeated victimization.

Counseling is typically an important component of the intervention children receive to minimize or reverse the effects of abuse. Counseling will often require significant modification to be appropriate for children with severe communication impairments. Nevertheless, individualized programs developed through consultation between generic abuse counselors and specialists in areas related to the child's disability are probably the most effective approach to providing services to abused children with multiple disabilities. A number of resources are available for those who wish to develop such programs (e.g., Brown & Craft, 1989).

The Transdisciplinary Team and Abuse Issues   All members of the transdisciplinary team should be actively involved in abuse prevention. Signs of physical abuse, sexual abuse, and neglect must be watched for carefully. Protocols must be in place for how to respond to potential incidents of abuse. The health care team should be skilled in recognizing patterns of abuse. Administrators should exercise careful screening procedures in hiring staff. Social workers, child protection workers, and sometimes police can be a part of the team that plans prevention or responds to suspected abuse. Psychologists, counselors, and sex educators may also play valuable roles in prevention programs and in providing services to victims if abuse occurs.

SUMMARY

This chapter has presented some of the common health care problems experienced by children with multiple disabilities and presented some basic information about methods of prevention and intervention. Communicable disease, seizure disorders, self-injurious behavior, classroom emergencies, and abuse are among health concerns that have particular implications for children with multiple disabilities. The education and health care teams must work together to determine individual needs in these areas and develop individual prevention and intervention strategies.

REFERENCES

American Heart Association. (1986). Transcript of National Conference on Standards and Guidelines for CPR and Emergency Care (cassette recording). Dallas: Author.

Austin, J.K., McBride, A.B., & Davis, H.W. (1984). Parental attitude and adjustment to childhood epilepsy. *Nursing Research, 33*(2), 92–96.

Axelrod, S. (1990). Myths that (mis)guide our profession. In A.C. Repp & N.N. Singh (Eds.), *Perspectives on the use of nonaversive and aversive intervention for persons with developmental disabilities* (pp. 59–72). Sycamore, IL: Sycamore Publishing Co.

Batshaw, M.L., & Perret, Y.M. (1986). *Children with handicaps: A medical primer* (2nd ed). Baltimore: Paul H. Brookes Publishing Co.

Benenson, A.S. (Ed.). (1990). *Control of communicable diseases in man* (15th ed.). Washington, DC: American Public Health Association.

Binnie, C.D., deKorte, R.A., & Wisman, T. (1979). Fluorescent lighting and epilepsy. *Epilepsia, 20,* 725–727.

Brown, H., & Craft, A. (1989). *Thinking the unthinkable: Papers on sexual abuse and people with learning difficulties.* London: FPA Education Unit.

Caldwell, T.H., Todaro, A.W., & Gates, A.J. (1991). Special health care needs. In J. L. Bigge (Ed.), *Teaching individuals with physical and multiple disabilities* (3rd ed.) (pp. 50–74). New York: Macmillan.

Caveness, W.F., & Gallup, G.H. (1980). A survey of public attitudes toward epilepsy in 1979 and an indication of trends over the past thirty years. *Epilepsia, 21,* 509–518.

Coe, D.A., & Matson, J.L. (1990). On the empirical basis for using aversive and nonaversive therapy. In A.C. Repp & N.N. Singh (Eds.), *Perspectives on the use of nonaversive and aversive intervention for persons with developmental disabilities* (pp. 465–475). Sycamore, IL: Sycamore Publishing Co.

Dailey, R.H. (1983). Acute upper airway obstruction. *Emergency Medicine Clinics of North America, 1,* 261–277.

Day, R.L., Crelin, E.S., & DuBois, A.B. (1982). Choking: The Heimlich abdominal thrust vs. backblows: An approach to measurement of enteral and aerodynamic forces. *Pediatrics, 70,* 113–119.

DiLionardi, J., & Kelly, E. (1989). Preventing and managing child abuse in group care: Report and recommendations of a report on practice. In E.A. Balcerzak (Ed.), *Group care of children: Transitions toward the year 2000* (pp. 239–253). Washington, DC: Child Welfare League of America.

Donnellan, A.M., & LaVigna, G.W. (1990). Myths about punishment. In A.C. Repp & N.N. Singh (Eds.), *Perspectives on the use of nonaversive and aversive intervention for persons with developmental disabilities* (pp. 33–57). Sycamore, IL: Sycamore Publishing Co.

Dreifuss, E.E. (Ed.). (1983). *Pediatric epileptology.* Boston: John Wright—PSG Inc.

Dreisbach, M., Ballard, M., Russo, D.C., & Schain, R.J., (1982). Educational intervention for children with epilepsy: A challenge for collaborative service delivery. *Journal of Special Education, 16*(1), 111–121.

Epilepsy Foundation of America. (1985). *The legal rights of persons with epilepsy* (5th ed.). Landover, MD: Author.

Favell, J., McGimsey, J., & Jones, M. (1978). The use of physical restraint in the treatment of self-injury and as positive reinforcement. *Journal of Applied Behavior Analysis, 11,* 225–241.

Ferrari, M., Matthews, W.S., & Barabas, G. (1983). The family and the child with epilepsy. *Family Process, 22,* 53–59.

Ford, C.A., Gibson, P., & Dreifus, F.E. (1983). Psychosocial considerations in childhood epilepsy. In F.E. Dreifuss (Ed.), *Pediatric epileptology* (pp. 277–295). Boston: John Wright—PSG Inc.

Freeman, J.M. (1987). A clinical approach to the child with seizures and epilepsy. *Epilepsia, 28* (Supplement 1), 103–109.

Gadow, K. (1982). School involvement in treatment of seizure disorders. *Epilepsia, 23,* 215–224.

Gadow, K.D., & Poling A.G. (1988). *Pharmacotherapy and mental retardation.* Boston: Little, Brown.

Gastaut, H. (1970). Clinical and encephalographical classification of epileptic seizures. *Epilepsia, 11,* 103–113.

Gold, A.P. (1974). Psychomotor epilepsy in childhood. *Pediatrics, 53,* 540–542.

Gumnit, R.J. (1983). *The epilepsy handbook: The practical management of seizures.* New York: Raven Press.

Harris, C.S., Baker, S.P., Smith, G.A., & Harris, R.M. (1984). Childhood asphyxiation by food: A national analysis and overview. *JAMA, 251,* 2231–2235.

Hass, C.A., & Brown, L. (1989). *Silent victims: Canada's criminal justice system and persons with mental handicap.* Calgary: The Calgary Sexual Assault Committee.

Hauser, W.A., & Annegers, J.F. (1989). Epidemiologic measurements for the determination of genetic risks. In G. Beck-Mannagetta, V.E. Anderson, H. Doose, & D. Janz (Eds.), *Genetics of the epilepsies* (pp. 7–12). New York: Springer-Verlag.

Hauser, W.A., & Hesdorfer, D.C. (1990). *Epilepsy: Frequency, causes and consequences.* New York: Raven Press.

Heimlich, H.J. (1982). First aid for choking children: Back blows and chest thrusts cause complications and death. *Pediatrics, 70,* 120–125.

Heimlich, H.J., & Uhley, M.H. (1979). The Heimlich maneuver. *Clinical Symposia, 31*(3), 1–32.

Holvoet, J.F., & Helmstetter, E. (1989). *Medical problems of students with special needs: A guide for educators.* Boston: Little, Brown.

Howard, J. (1980). Seizures. In J. Umbreit & P.J. Cardullias (Eds.), *Educating the severely physically handicapped: Treatment and management of medically related disorders* (Vol. II, pp. 8–15). Columbus: Special Press.

Keats, S. (1965). *Cerebral palsy.* Springfield, IL: Charles C Thomas.

LaVigna, G.W., & Donnellan, A.M. (1986) *Alternatives to punishment: Solving behavior problems with non-aversive strategies.* New York: Irvington.

Lechtenberg, R. (1984). *Epilepsy and the family.* Cambridge, MA: Harvard University Press.

Lechtenberg, R. (1990). *Seizure recognition and treatment.* New York: Churchill Livingstone, Inc.

Lindsay, M. (1983, May 11). Never mind the label. *Nursing Mirror, 156,* 18–19.

Logemann, J. (1983). *Evaluation and treatment of swallowing disorders.* San Diego: College-Hill Press.

MacDougall, V. (1982, April). Teaching children and families about seizures. *The Canadian Nurse, 78,* 30–36.

McCormick, K. (1989). *Reducing the risk: A school leader's guide to AIDS education.* Alexandria, VA: National School Boards Association.

Meyer, L.H., & Evans, E.M. (1989). *Nonaversive intervention for behavior problems: A manual for home and community.* Baltimore: Paul H. Brookes Publishing Co.

Newmark, M.E. (1983a). Genetics of epilepsies. In F.E. Dreifuss (Ed.), *Pediatric epileptology* (pp. 89–116). Boston: John Wright—PSG Inc.

Newmark, M.E. (1983b). Sensory evoked seizures. In F.E. Dreifuss (Ed.), *Pediatric epileptology* (pp. 199–219). Boston: John Wright—PSG Inc.

O'Sullivan, C.M. (1989). Alcoholism and abuse: The twin family secrets. In G.W. Lawson & A.W. Lawson (Ed.), *Alcoholism & substance abuse in special populations* (pp. 273–303). Rockville, MD: Aspen Publishers.

Palmer, S., & Kalisz, K. (1978). Epilepsy. In S. Palmer & S. Ekvall (Eds.), *Pediatric nutrition in developmental disabilities* (pp. 61–72). Springfield, IL: Charles C Thomas.

Parrino, J. (1971). Reduction of seizures by desensitization. *Behavior Therapy and Experimental Psychiatry, 2,* 215–218.

Rassel, G., Tonelson, S., & Appolone, C. (1981). Epilepsy workshop for public school personnel. *Journal of School Health, 51,* 48–50.

Repp, A.C., & Singh, N.N. (Eds.). (1990). *Perspectives on the use of nonaversive and aversive intervention for persons with developmental disabilities.* Sycamore, IL: Sycamore Publishing Co.

Richardson, S.A., Koller, H., & Katz, M. (1981). A functional classification of seizures and distribution in the mentally retarded population. *American Journal of Mental Deficiency, 85,* 457–466.

Riley, T.L., & Massey, W. (1979, Nov. 15). Pseudoseizures versus real. *Emergency Medicine, 11,* 122–129.

Rowitz, L. (1989). Developmental disabilities and HIV Infection: A symposium on issues and public policy (Special Issue). *Mental Retardation, 27,* 197–262.

Rusch, R.G., Hall, J.C., & Griffen, H.C. (1986). Abuse-provoking characteristics of institutionalized mentally retarded individuals. *American Journal of Mental Deficiency, 90,* 618–624.

St. John Ambulance. (1988). *First aid: Safety oriented.* Ottawa: Author.

Sands, H., & Minters, F.C. (1977). *The epilepsy fact book.* Philadelphia: F.A. Davis.

Schmidt, D., & Leppik, I. (Eds.). (1988). *Compliance in epilepsy.* New York: Elsevier.

Scotti, J.R., Evans, I.M., Meyer, L.H., & Walker, P. (in press). A meta-analysis of intervention research with problem behavior: Treatment validity and standards of practice. *American Journal on Mental Retardation.*

Senanayake, N. (1987). Epileptic seizures evoked by card games, draughts, and similar games. *Epilepsia, 28,* 356–357.

Shaman, E.J. (1986). Prevention for children with disabilities. In M. Nelson & K. Clark (Eds.), *The educator's guide to preventing sexual abuse* (pp. 122–125). Santa Cruz, CA: Network Publications.

Shreeve, C. (1983, May 11). Treating epilepsy. *Nursing Mirror, 156,* 20–21.

Sobsey, D. (1982). Behavioral observation and recording of seizures. *DPH Journal, 6*(1), 14–19.

Sobsey, D. (1989). Whiplash shaking syndrome. *Newsletter of the American Association on Mental Retardation, 2*(6), 2, 8.

Sobsey, D. (1990a). Modifying the behavior of behavior modifiers: Arguments for countercontrol against aversive procedures. In A.C. Repp & N.N. Singh (Eds.). *Perspectives on the use of nonaversive and aversive intervention for persons with developmental disabilities* (pp. 421–433). Sycamore, IL: Sycamore Publishing Co.

Sobsey, D. (1990b). Too much stress on stress? Abuse and the family stress factor. *Quarterly Newsletter of the American Association on Mental Retardation, 3*(1), 2, 8.

Sobsey, D. (in press). Sexual abuse of individuals with intellectual disabilities. In A. Craft (Ed.), *Practice issues in sexuality and intellectual disability*. London: Routledge.

Sobsey, D., Gray, S., Wells, D., Pyper, D., & Reimer-Heck, B. (1991). *Disability, sexuality, and abuse: An annotated bibliography*. Baltimore: Paul H. Brookes Publishing Co.

Sobsey, D., & Mansell, S. (1990). The prevention of sexual abuse of people with developmental disabilities. *Developmental Disabilities Bulletin, 18*(2), 61–73.

Sobsey, D., & Varnhagen, C. (1989). Sexual abuse of people with disabilities. In M. Csapo & L. Gougen (Eds.), *Special education across Canada: Challenges for the 90's* (pp. 199–218). Vancouver: Centre for Human Development & Research.

Solomon, G.E., Kutt, H., & Plum, F. (1983). *Clinical management of seizures: A guide for the physician (2nd ed.)*. Philadelphia: W.B. Saunders.

Spooner, F., & Dykes, M.K. (1982). Epilepsy: Impact upon severely and profoundly handicapped persons. *Journal of The Association for the Severely Handicapped, 7*(3), 87–96.

Svoboda, W.B. (1979). *Learning about epilepsy*. Baltimore: University Park Press.

Taylor, D.C. (1972). Mental state and temporal lobe epilepsy: A correlative account of 100 patients treated surgically. *Epilepsia, 13,* 727–765.

Torrey, S.B. (1983). The choking child—A life threatening emergency. *Clinical Pediatrics, 22,* 751–754.

Ultman, M.H., Belman, A.L., Ruff, H.A., Novick, B.E., Cone-Wesson, B., Cohen, H.J., & Rubinstein, A. (1985). Developmental abnormalities in infants and children with acquired immune deficiency syndrome (AIDS). *Developmental Medicine & Child Neurology, 27,* 563–571.

UNICEF. (1991). *The state of the world's children 1991*. New York: Oxford University Press.

Verduyn, C.M., Stores, G., & Missen, A. (1988). A survey of mothers' impressions of seizure precipitants in children with epilepsy. *Epilepsia, 29,* 251–255.

West Contra Costa Rape Crisis Center (1986). *Disabled children's prevention program*. San Pablo, CA: Author.

Wright, L. (1973). Aversive conditioning of self-induced seizures. *Behavior Therapy, 4,* 712–713.

Yousef, J.M. (1985). Medical and educational aspects of epilepsy: A review. *DPH Journal, 8*(1), 3–15.

Zlutnick, S., Mayville, W.J., & Moffat, S. (1975). Modification of seizure disorders: The interruption of behavioral chains. *Journal of Applied Behavior Analysis, 8,* 1–12.

Chapter 7

Curriculum and Instruction

Deciding *what* to teach students with multiple disabilities and *how* to teach them may seem to be insurmountable tasks. Some children have so many things to learn that team members may find it difficult to choose among the scores of possible goals. Other children may have such limited response repertoires and so many sensory and motoric impairments that professionals may wonder where to begin.

Until the late 1970s, practititioners in special education and the allied professions had virtually no guidelines for working with students with severe disabilities. Fortunately, this is changing rapidly, and a variety of excellent textbooks and professional readers have emerged that describe curricular and teaching approaches for this population (e.g., Brown & Lehr, 1989; Falvey, 1989; Ford et al., 1989; Gaylord-Ross & Holvoet, 1985; Goetz, Guess, & Stremel-Campbell, 1987; Horner, Meyer, & Fredericks, 1986; Snell, 1987; Wilcox & Bellamy, 1987).

This chapter draws upon research, curricular models, and demonstration to describe successful approaches to determining content and teaching skills. Particular emphasis is given to those strategies that appear to have merit for the learner with multiple disabilities. It should be noted that many curricula and models for the student with severe disabilities have not been designed specifically for, and have not been validated on, those children with profound mental retardation and significant medical, sensory, and motoric involvement. Nevertheless, much of the work can be translated, at least in part, to individuals with the most severe disabilities. Subsequent chapters treat several key curricular areas in greater detail: communication skills (Chapter 9), mealtime skills (Chapter 10), and self-care skills (Chapter 11). In addition, Chapter 8, which is devoted specifically to adapting instructional materials and environments, should be viewed as a companion to the present chapter.

CURRICULUM

The curriculum is, strictly speaking, the *content* to be taught. It would be rather simple to obtain agreement on some general skill areas in which most students with multiple disabilities need training: motor, self-care, communication, and so forth. Beyond this gross categorization, however, it becomes extremely difficult to determine exactly what skills all children need. Therefore, it is imperative that any approach to determining content be based on a determination of each child's current and future needs, abilities, and interests. This section describes several models that have been used to develop curricula for students with severe disabilities. The focus is on strategies team members can use to determine priority skills to be taught to a given student.

Models for Determining Content

Developmental Model

Major Features The developmental model relies on the sequences of development of children who do not have disabilities (Sailor & Guess, 1983; Wilcox & Bellamy, 1982). Proponents argue that instructional content for children with multiple disabilities should be based on the development of children who do not have disabilities and that skills should be taught in the same sequence as they are demonstrated by children who do not have disabilities. Thus, curriculum content is determined through the administration of informal checklists or developmental tests that are based on the capabilities of children who do not have disabilities (e.g., Behavior Characteristics Progression, Learning Accomplishment Profile). Items that students fail are then rewritten as instructional goals (Snell, 1987). Often, content is specified within broad domains, such as gross motor, fine motor, social, and self-help.

Advantages There are several advantages to the use of developmental assessment instruments. First, some of them may provide a global picture of a child's abilities, thus giving direction for more specific, informal assessment (Snell, 1987). Second, some developmental scales do a good job of breaking down complex skills into their component parts. Third, developmental checklists and curricula are commonly used with infants and toddlers, providing a common ground for comparing the early development of children who do and those who do not have disabilities. Finally, since many professionals are familiar with developmental theory for children who do not have disabilities, using developmental scales may facilitate communication across disciplines (Brown, 1987).

Disadvantages Despite its apparent advantages, the developmental model presents some serious problems when used with students with multiple disabilities. First, the items on developmental scales are based on the development of children who do not have disabilities. Children with severe disabilities, however, do not necessarily develop or acquire skills in a "normal" sequence. (Some of these children will never demonstrate some of these skills because it is physically impossible for them.) Second, the focus of many developmental assessment instruments is on the specific *form* of the behavior (e.g., "grasps pellet"), rather than its *function* (White, 1980, 1985). Many individuals with multiple disabilities can achieve certain ends using means that are different from those used by persons who do not have disabilities (e.g., they move from one place to another using a wheelchair, rather than by walking). It is important to understand the *reason* for assessing a particular item. The mere presence of an item on a checklist does not make it instructionally meaningful. Third, the specific materials and situations prescribed by many developmental scales do not relate to those materials and situations needed by persons with multiple disabilities in the real world. Not only is there insufficient time allotted to learn the artificial tasks, but students have a difficult time transferring or generalizing their skills to different situations (Gaylord-Ross & Holvoet, 1985). Fourth, skills within or across curricular domains may be seen in isolation and, therefore, remain unrelated to each other (Brown, 1987). Teaching isolated or splinter skills is less effective, less efficient, and less enjoyable than teaching in the context of meaningful activities.

Environmental Model

Major Features   An environmental or ecological model of curriculum development is designed to determine those skills needed for a particular individual in his or her current and future environments (Brown, Branston, et al., 1979; Helmstetter, 1989; Nietupski & Hamre-Nietupski, 1987). The five major components of an ecological inventory are as follows:

1. *Dividing the curriculum into **domains**:* These domains have most commonly included domestic (i.e., skills performed in and around the home), leisure-recreation (i.e., skills used to participate in or to watch such activities), community (i.e., skills needed to move about in the community and to use stores and services), and vocational (i.e., skills used to acquire and maintain work). These four domains are assumed to include major arenas in which individuals with multiple disabilities are expected to function as adults. Critical skill areas, such as motor functioning and communication, are subsumed under each domain.

2. *Determining the **environments** in which the student presently functions or might function in the future:* These environments should represent the various domains. Thus, environments for a particular child might include the school, the neighborhood pool, his or her home, and a public bus.

3. *Dividing each environment into **subenvironments**:* This step allows activities to be targeted and taught. Subenvironments for the home might include

the bedroom, bathroom, and kitchen. The pool environment could be sub-divided into the wading area, vending area, locker room, and so forth.

4. *Determining the relevant **activities** within each subenvironment:* The person completing the inventory lists major clusters of behaviors (e.g., "clears table," "goes to toilet," "plays with toys") that are likely to be performed by the student within each subenvironment.

5. *Determining the **skills** necessary to engage in each activity:* Through a process of task analysis, each activity can be divided into teachable units or skills. "Going to the toilet," for example, may include indicating need, adjusting clothing, and transferring to the commode. Naturally, skills can be further subdivided, as necessary, to facilitate instruction. Professionals are encouraged, however, not to lose the context of the activity in the process of teaching small aspects of it. For example, it is not very meaningful or fun for a child to spend 30 minutes a day for several weeks practicing components of making a milkshake before having the chance to see and sample the results.

After the five steps described above have been completed, team members perform a *discrepancy analysis* to determine what necessary skills are not currently in the student's repertoire. Based on the discrepancy analysis, possible individual adaptations for performing the activities can be determined and instructional programs developed. (Chapter 8 presents examples of this approach; also, see Falvey [1989].)

Parts of an ecological inventory for a 6-year-old with severe disabilities are presented in Figure 7.1. It is important to underscore that this model demands an individualized approach. While similarities across various students' inventories are inevitable, the final products are not transferrable.

Advantages   The environmental model to determining content resolves most of the disadvantages of the developmental model. First, because the inventory is based on an individual child's environments, the content is highly individualized and relevant to his or her life skill needs. Second, the approach is top-down, rather than bottom-up. Critical skills needed by the student later in life are taught, thus preventing him or her from becoming mired down in readiness activities. Third, since the skills selected for instruction are already known to be relevant, the model avoids a heavy reliance on generalization from isolated tasks and situations to natural contexts. Fourth, the ecological approach is designed to prevent instruction of numerous splinter skills. Rather, it focuses on *activities* that have meaning in the child's life.

Disadvantages   There are three possible difficulties with the environmental model. First, it is time-consuming, particularly for those team members who have never completed inventories or for those who have several new students. (Of course, it is argued here that the time is well-spent, since it significantly reduces time that otherwise would have been spent later on meaningless

I. Current environments

    A. Grandmother's home

        1. Bedroom

           a. Preparing for sleep

               i. Locating bedroom
               ii. Entering bedroom
               iii. Removing clothes
               iv. Putting dirty clothes in appropriate place
               v. Locating pajamas
               vi. Putting on pajamas
               vii. Locating bed
               viii. Pulling down sheets/blankets
               ix. Getting in bed
               x. Pulling up sheets/blankets

           b. Waking up/dressing

               i. Getting out of bed
               ii. Locating and selecting clothes
               iii. Removing pajamas
               iv. Placing pajamas in appropriate place
               v. Putting on clothes
               vi. Making bed
               vii. Leaving bedroom

        2. Bathroom

           a. Toothbrushing

               i. Locating bathroom
               ii. Entering bathroom
               iii. Locating sink
               iv. Identifying toothbrush and locating toothpaste
               v. Brushing teeth
               vi. Putting toothbrush and toothpaste in appropriate place
               vii. Leaving bathroom

           b. Brushing/combing hair

               i. Locating bathroom
               ii. Entering bathroom
               iii. Locating brush/comb
               iv. Brushing/combing hair
               v. Putting brush/comb away in appropriate place
               vi. Leaving bathroom

    B. School

        1. Cafeteria

           a. Eating lunch

               i. Walking to cafeteria with class
               ii. Locating cafeteria
               iii. Entering cafeteria
               iv. Locating lunch line

Figure 7.1. Sample section of an ecological inventory for a 6-year-old with severe disabilities.

tasks.) Second, the approach by itself yields hundreds of possible skills, with no indication of which to teach first or how to combine them, leading to a potential smorgasbord effect in selecting goals. (This concern is addressed under the "Determining Priorities" section of this chapter.) Third, for students with the most severe disabilities, ecological inventories may result in a list of skills that need to be analyzed so minutely that they begin to lose any real purpose or function (Orelove, 1991).

Individualized Curriculum Sequencing (ICS) Model

Major Features   The individualized curriculum sequencing (ICS) model was designed, in part, to take advantage of the relationship among skills in performance of tasks. To maximize generalization, the student is taught concurrent responses across content domains, or skill clusters (Guess & Helmstetter, 1986). The ICS model actually extends beyond the developmental and environmental models, by tying itself closely to teaching strategies. The model is linked to two principal instructional practices: distributed-trial presentation and concurrent task sequencing. Briefly: Distributed trials refers to presenting trials from a given program or content area between repeated trials from another program (Mulligan, Guess, Holvoet, & Brown, 1980). Concurrent task sequencing refers to the teaching of two or more content domains within a training session.

An individualized curriculum sequence is prepared once the skills to be taught are identified. This involves completing an activities/skills matrix. The matrix lists materials and events with which to teach each skill during daily activities. A sample completed matrix is presented in Figure 7.2. Additional information on the ICS model may be found in Brown, Holvoet, Guess, and Mulligan (1980), Guess and Helmstetter (1986), Guess et al. (1978), Helmstetter and Guess (1987), Helmstetter, Murphy-Herd, Roberts, and Guess (1984), and Holvoet, Mulligan, Schussler, Lacy, and Guess (1982).

Advantages   Holvoet et al. (1982) cited several advantages of the ICS model: 1) students learn somewhat faster than with traditional models; 2) generalization of skills is encouraged without specific generalization training; 3) communication among school staff is encouraged; 4) the model allows students to learn relationships among skills; and 5) there is a high compatibility with a transdisciplinary approach.

Disadvantages   The major disadvantages of the ICS model seem to lie in the logistics of the system, particularly in designing data sheets and summarizing data. Because students are being taught multiple skills, often in group situations, the professional needs to be well prepared.

Structured Approaches to Curriculum

Philosophy   Several structured curriculum guides have been developed since the later 1980s that draw upon the ideas rooted within the ecological and

ICS models. These guides differ sharply from the early curricula published in the 1970s and early 1980s, which tended to focus on having students acquire long lists of skills, some functional, but most not. The later approaches rely on professional team members working with each other and with families to develop a plan to meet the needs of each student based on his or her current needs and interests. Thus, they are, in the true sense, *guides,* rather than prescriptive recipes.

In addition, all of the curriculum guides described in this section are governed by a clear philosophy about children, their families, and how individuals learn best. Neel and Billingsley (1989) based their curriculum on the following six assumptions:

1. Increasing control over the environment is the major goal of instruction.
2. Communication/social skills are the most important skills a child can learn.
3. Motivation is achieved by ensuring that instruction produces desired results for the student.
4. Functional skills are best taught in their natural context.
5. Instructional priorities come from the individual and his or her environment.
6. Parent participation is the crucial component of the instructional process. (pp. 15–17)

In addition to these six assumptions, the *Syracuse Curriculum Guide* (Ford et al., 1989) includes two more principles: 1) "Social integration is an essential element of an appropriate education;" and 2) "Interdependence and partial participation are valid educational goals" (p. 3).

Determining Priorities With a clear philosophical underpinning, the task of determining priorities becomes clearer. Ferguson and Wilcox (1988) stipulated nine decision rules for selecting IEP (individualized education program) goals and objectives, rules that support the assumptions articulated by Neel and Billingsley (1989) and Ford et al. (1989). They are listed below:

Select activity goals and supporting objectives that:

1. Increase participation in activities and use of materials typically engaged in and used by nonhandicapped age peers.
2. Increase participation across a variety of activities and environments, including the domains of Personal Management, Leisure, and Jobs and Chores, across Classroom, School/Community and Home Environments.
3. Maximize the repertoire of each student, increasing the variety of activities while also facilitating longitudinal skill development.
4. Contribute to the outcome of the activities. Parts of activities targeted for either acquisition or participation should make a difference to the completion of the entire activity.
5. Enhance image and appeal, resulting in the student being perceived by others as a more valuable, less different, contributing, striving, and productive member of society.
6. Increase opportunities for interaction with nonhandicapped peers.
7. Focus on establishing a functional communication system that is maximally

Skills to be taught

Activity (Location)	Time / Instructor	Head up	Indicate desire for more	Segment at waist	Toilet regulation	Reach across midline	Localize to sound	Track horizontally	Drink from cup	Hands out of mouth
Arrival (Bus)	Time 8:15 / Instructor Kay					To shake hands, hang coat	To name by teacher, peer	Teacher, peer		X
Toileting (Bathroom)	Time 8:30 / Instructor Kay	On toilet		During rolling, in sidesit	X	To sidesit	To name			X
Grooming (Bathroom)	Time 9:00 / Instructor Kay	In standing table		To hang towel		For faucet, soap, towel	To name	Soap, towel		X
Group 1 (Table)	Time 9:15 / Instructor Sally	In chair, in sidesit	Caps for syringe, paper for collate	During rolling, in sidesit	Pants check	For cap, paper, cereal	To name	Cap, paper, cereal		X
Group 2 (Mat)	Time 9:45 / Instructor Sally	Prone on mat	Music, story	During rolling	Pants check	For sidesit, tape, book	To name, music	Cassette tape, book		X
Snack (Dining area)	Time 10:15 / Instructor Nena	In chair, in sidesit	Juice, cookie	During rolling, in sidesit	Pants check	Juice, cookie, napkin, sidesit	To name	Juice, cookie	Juice for snack	X
Toileting (Bathroom)	Time 10:30 / Instructor Nena					(See 8:30 Toileting)				
Grooming (Bathroom)	Time 11:00 / Instructor Nena					(See 9:00 Grooming)				

238

Activity	Time / Instructor									
Group 3 (Mat)	Time 11:15 Instructor Nena	Prone on mat	Caps for syringe, paper for collate	During rolling	Pants check	For cap, paper, cereal	To name	Cap, paper, cereal		X
Lunch (Lunchroom)	Time 11:45 Instructor Sally	In chair, in sidesit	Food, drink	During rolling, to throw away napkin	Pants check	For spoon, cup, napkin	To name	Spoon, cup	Milk at lunch	X
Toileting (Bathroom)	Time 12:45 Instructor Sally					(See 8:30 Toileting)				
Grooming (Bathroom)	Time 1:15 Instructor Sally					(See 9:00 Grooming)				
Group 4 (Table)	Time 1:30 Instructor Kay	In chair, in sidesit	Music, story	During rolling, in sidesit	Pants check	For cassette tape, book	To name, music	Cassette tape, book		X
Departure (Bus)	Time 2:15 Instructor Kay	Supine for coat on, in sidesit		During rolling	Pants check	For coat	To name	Coat		X

Figure 7.2. Sample activities/skills matrix. (From Guess, D., & Helmstetter, E. [1986]. Skill cluster instruction and the individualized curriculum sequencing model. In R. H. Horner, L. H. Meyer, & H. D. B. Fredericks [Eds.], *Education of learners with severe handicaps: Exemplary service strategies* [pp. 228–229]. Baltimore: Paul H. Brookes Publishing Co.; reprinted with permission.)

accessible to any nonhandicapped person, not just persons who are familiar to the student. If not yet achieved, communication objectives should be developed for all possible activity goals.

8. Increase efficient mobility and movement across all activities and domains and include a range of mobility alternatives as well as movement goals that contribute to improved body mechanics. If not yet achieved, motor/mobility objectives should be developed for all possible activity goals.

9. Increase ease in providing for a student's basic needs including eating, dressing, and hygiene. Goals might target direct skill building and/or improving the assistance the student can provide to a caregiver. (From Ferguson, D.L., & Wilcox, B.L. [Eds.]. [1988]. *The elementary/secondary system: Supportive education for students with severe handicaps: Module I: The activity-based IEP.* Eugene: Specialized Training Program, University of Oregon, p. 33; reprinted with permission.)

The decision rules by themselves, of course, are of little practical value in generating potential IEP goals. In their activity-based approach, therefore, Ferguson and Wilcox (1988) have developed a clear process for determining content, based on the needs and interests of the child and his or her family. A modified version of an ecological inventory, termed a "Home Activities Interview," is used to determine current home and community activities and the level of the child's current and desired participation. An example of a completed interview form for the leisure/recreation domain is presented in Figure 7.3.

Based in part upon the interview and in part upon other strategies, potential goals (based on *activities,* not isolated skills) are discussed between staff and parents in the IEP meeting. Parents should be given the opportunity to propose their goals first. Undoubtedly, there will be areas of disagreement. This should be expected and is not to be viewed as negative. If reasonable discussion does not succeed, team members may want to use a more structured approach to resolving differences, such as principled negotiation (described in Chapter 12). Ferguson and Wilcox (1988) proposed several strategies for facilitating consensus on the final list of IEP goals:

1. Focus discussion on one domain at a time and identify the final list of goals before moving to another domain.

2. Defer to parent and student selections when the activity is targeted for home. . . .

3. Combine activities that are similar . . . to reduce the overall number of goals . . . . (p. 48)

It is difficult to overestimate the importance of parents and caregivers in helping to select priority goals. In thinking about possible objectives for learners with multiple disabilities, team members might consider what the effect of students learning certain skills could have on facilitating the caregiver's life. Readers desiring other samples of home surveys in specific domains are encouraged to consult Wuerch and Voeltz (1982) (leisure domain) and Klein et al. (1981) (communication domain).

Finally, increasing attention is being directed to giving students them-

Home Activities Interview
AGES [13–15]

Student: Sheila Chandler
Interviewer: Sara Mason
Domain: Leisure/Recreation

Date 9/8/88
Initial
Year 2
Year 3

Activity	How does he/she currently do or participate?	How often? Community?	What kind of support?	A high preference activity? Student	A high preference activity? Family	Do you want to increase participation?	Update year 2	Update year 3
2.4.8 Fan Clubs	Never	—	—	No	No	No		
2.4.9 Parties	Family Get-Togethers	Once in a while	Too many people get Sheila upset	"	"	Small Class Party		
2.4.10 Going to Performing Arts Center	Never	—	—	"	"	No		
2.4.11 Going to Ball Game	Just watches on TV	Once in a while on TV	—	"	"	Maybe go to school game		
2.5.1 Car-Camping	Never	—	—	"	"	No		
2.5.2 Going to Zoo	"	—	—	"	"	Field trip OK		
2.5.3 Going to the Museum	"	—	—	"	"	"		
2.5.4 Going to the Park	Walks around and watches others play	1x/week	Needs to rest often	"	"	Does enough w/Family		
2.5.5 Going to the Library	Went to School Library last year	In School 1x/week	Assistance handling Magazine	"	"	Go to Library w/class		
2.5.6 Visit Relatives	Goes with Family	During holidays	Small groups	"	Yes	No		

Figure 7.3. Sample Home Activities Interview form. (From Ferguson, D.L., & Wilcox, B.L. [Eds.]. [1988]. *The elementary/secondary system: Supportive education for children with severe handicaps. Module I: The activity-based IEP.* Eugene: Specialized Training Program, University of Oregon, p. 16; reprinted with permission.)

241

selves a greater voice in selecting activities (Guess, Benson, & Siegel-Causey, 1985; Guess & Siegel-Causey, 1985; Shevin & Klein, 1984). One of the problems, of course, is that most learners with multiple disabilities have not been taught reliable means to communicate their needs or to express their choices. Some work in this area (e.g., Mirenda & Smith-Lewis, 1989; Reichle, York, & Eynon, 1989) shows great promise.

Commercial Curriculum Guides　It is nearly impossible to assemble a curriculum that could be used for every student with multiple disabilities. The differences among students, their needs, and their environments demand a high degree of individualization. Nevertheless, there is some benefit to consulting (not relying upon) commercially available curricula. At the very least, many have performed basic analyses of hundreds of tasks. Although task analyses are not transferable from student to student, sometimes it is helpful to have a starting point. Several curricula also provide ideas about adapting the task and materials to allow the learner to participate at least partially. The reader is strongly cautioned, however, that using predetermined goals, criteria, and isolated tasks from commercial curricula makes for poor instruction.

Gaylord-Ross and Holvoet (1985) summarized seven important criteria for evaluating curricula:

1. Is the curriculum specific to a disabling condition? This is a question even for those curricula designed for "the severely handicapped." Students with multiple disabilities often are unable to perform many tasks that curricula consider basic.
2. Does the curriculum have curriculum objectives? What is the benefit to the students who are taught from the curriculum?
3. Does the curriculum have long- and short-term objectives that can be included in students' IEPs?
4. Is the curriculum data based? Many even provide sample data sheets or suggestions regarding measuring student performance.
5. Is the curriculum sequenced? Of course, all curricula follow some sequence; the better curricula state theirs explicitly and base them on some reasonable model.
6. Does the curriculum have teaching strategies that provide information about prompting, reinforcing, and so forth? This criterion exceeds the minimal standards for a basic curriculum. Actually, the most a curriculum can do is to suggest possible strategies in this area.
7. Does the curriculum provide implementation strategies? This includes step-by-step suggestions for teaching.

INSTRUCTION

Determining *what* to teach solves the first problem. What remains is figuring out how best to reach the objectives. This half of the chapter describes some of the principles and strategies for teaching individuals with multiple disabilities.

Principles of Effective Teaching

Numerous elements go into effective teaching, ranging from the broad and value-oriented (e.g., To what degree do staff members view children as educable?) to the specific and technical (e.g., Are data on student performance for each IEP objective collected at least weekly?). A list of such "program quality indicators" determined to represent the most promising practices for individuals with severe disabilities has been generated and validated (Meyer & Eichinger, 1987; Meyer, Eichinger, & Park-Lee, 1987). It is not practical to list the more than 100 indicators in this chapter. Instead, this section briefly describes several of the established principles that underlie effective instruction for learners with multiple disabilities. The emphasis is on *instructional* practices. It should be stressed, however, that the physical and health needs of learners with multiple disabilities interact closely with their ability to acquire skills. This chapter presumes, for example, that the student is positioned comfortably and appropriately for a given activity (see Chapter 3).

Functional Tasks and Materials   It is assumed that a skill or activity selected through one of the approaches to curriculum described earlier will be one that the student and/or family will find functional to acquire. That is, the outcome will include a meaningful use in the person's daily life. It is possible, however, for a potentially functional skill to be taught in a nonfunctional manner. The skill of scanning, for example, is most useful in the context of searching for one's coat hook, but not very meaningful (or interesting) when the student is asked to scan three unrelated objects—especially if the task fails to lead to a choice.

One can generate possible functional activities and materials by asking: 1) What materials or activities do nondisabled people of the same age use or perform? and 2) What materials or activities are available for teaching the skill in the places where the student now goes or might be able to go? (Holvoet et al., 1982). Range-of-motion exercises for the wrist at school could include winding up toys, using a calculator, and opening magazines. At home, the child might perform such exercises by manipulating television knobs, lifting the telephone, or putting the toothbrush in the holder. By initially concentrating on *activities* in determining possible IEP content, one avoids many of the pitfalls of selecting nonfunctional, isolated skills.

Natural Settings and Cues   Because children with multiple disabilities often do not generalize skills across situations, it is important to teach functional activities in those settings in which the child is expected to perform them. Obviously, one teaches toileting skills in the bathroom (or, for very young children, in a portable potty chair). Similarly, hairbrushing should be taught at a sink or in front of a mirror, and eating lunch would be taught at a cafeteria table. Most activities that are traditionally therapeutic in nature can also be taught in classrooms, playgrounds, libraries, and other settings within and around the school.

By extension, the most natural environments for many skills lie outside the school. Thus, major parts of the instructional day can be spent in home, work, and community settings (Brown et al., 1983; Falvey, 1989; Sailor et al., 1986; Snell & Browder, 1986). It is also important that instructional objectives be practiced thoughout the day whenever natural opportunities arise, rather than learning being limited to structured teaching sessions only.

Functional cues are those verbal or gestural prompts or directions (or merely the stimuli present in the environment) that ultimately trigger the behavior. They can be determined in the same way in which skills are chosen, that is, by a survey of the environment for what people say and do.

Transdisciplinary Services and Integrated Therapy   As indicated in Chapter 1, successful programs are built on a team approach in which professionals (and parents whenever possible) share their knowledge and skills across disciplines. Students with multiple disabilities learn much less efficiently, if at all, when the school day is splintered into separate instructional and therapy sessions, which generally imply separate goals in each area. It is particularly important that communication and motor programs be incorporated into the daily routine throughout the day. This means less reliance on traditional, massed-trial sessions, in which students are taught to practice a response over and over within 20- or 30-minute periods. Similarly, strategies for reducing undesired, excess behaviors should be built around and into as many skill-building activities as possible.

Interaction with Individuals Who Do Not Have Disabilities   The evidence is clear that systematically arranged opportunities for interaction with peers who do not have disabilities have numerous benefits for the student with multiple disabilities (cf. Lipsky & Gartner, 1989; Sailor, Gee, Goetz, & Graham, 1988). This interaction dictates not only that physical integration take place, but that IEPs and instructional programs be purposefully directed towards similar outcomes.

Data-Based Instruction   It is clear that professionals who take data on a regular basis and use those data to make instructionally relevant decisions are more effective than their colleagues who do not. Data not only are essential to ensure accountability to the child and the parents, but also they provide a common language for discussion of student progress among team members.

Partial Participation   If one were to select for instruction only those skills or activities that a student could perform in their entirety, there would be few functional areas left from which to select. Some tasks demand performance that is simply beyond the student's physical ability, even with systematic and intensive instruction. Rather than dropping these skills automatically from the student's IEP, or providing endless skill training, it is helpful to allow the student to perform as much of these tasks as possible. This approach, termed the "principle of partial participation," is designed to enable students with significant disabilities to engage in parts of activities that are meaningful to them (Baumgart et al., 1982). Partial participation may be made possible through the creation and use of individualized adaptations. This process, along with examples, is described further in Chapter 8.

Teaching Within Activities

It should be clear that it is essential to stress the importance of teaching children in the context of typical routines or activities. Activity-based instruction facilitates learning and retention, promotes integration, and is more enjoyable for both staff and students. Teaching within activities implies two conditions: 1) IEP goals and objectives must be written in an activity-based format; and 2) instruction on a given activity must cut across traditional curricular domains, thus embedding social, communication, and motor skills within the activity.

Activity-Based Goals and Objectives   As discussed earlier in this chapter, all IEP goals and objectives should reflect the real needs and interests of the student and the family. Using a process such as the Home Activities Interview (Ferguson & Wilcox, 1988) will help to guarantee that these conditions are met. Once the team and the family have agreed on the outcomes, team members are faced with developing the actual IEP document.

While there are a variety of reasonable formats for writing goals, Ferguson and Wilcox (1988) suggested that well written goals conform to the following standards:

1. The goal is *measurable;* that is, it describes an observable, measurable behavior that the student (not the staff) will perform.
2. The goal is an *activity;* that is, it describes three phases: initiation or preparation, execution or doing, and resolution or ending. The activity must result in an outcome that is functional for the student.
3. The goal is *age-appropriate;* that is, it represents an activity that is typically performed by individuals of the same age who do not have disabilities.
4. The goal is *generalizable;* that is, it describes the range of natural settings in which the behavior is to be exhibited.

The following are examples of goals (developed by Ferguson & Wilcox, 1988) in the personal management domain for the student whose Home Activities Interview form was presented in Figure 7.3:

1. Sheila will participate in a personal hygiene routine daily after lunch in the girls' restroom for 3 consecutive days. She will be given physical assistance to complete this routine.
2. When accompanied by a trainer, Sheila will purchase one to two items at a grocery store, fast food restaurant, or school bookstore, 3 times per week using a picture list.

One way of developing IEPs is to describe the goal as the overall activity, and then to embed the social, motor, and communication skills within the short-term objectives. Following are several examples based on this approach:

Social
Goal   When positioned at her school locker (approximately four to five times daily), Mary will remove or replace her outer clothing and gather belongings to prepare for the next scheduled activity.
Objectives   Mary will request help opening her locker by gesturing to a familiar classmate.   When positioned at her locker before homeroom, Mary will greet familiar students nearby by smiling at them.

Motor
Goal   When packaging and labeling items in the central supply department of Mercy Hospital 2 afternoons per week, Mary will increase her rate and accuracy.
Objectives   When positioned standing with a belt supporting her hips, Mary will stand with her knees straight (for 12 minutes per hour, during 2 hours each day, for 3 out of 3 days).   After wearing a palmar splint for 20 minutes of packaging, Mary will maintain use of a pincer grasp (for the next two opportunities, three of four trials per day, for 2 days).

Communication
Goal   While participating daily in Art 8, Mary will express herself creatively by contributing to the completion of individual and group projects.
Objectives   Mary will greet classmates who share her table by seeking eye contact and smiling.   When a supply or assistance is needed, Mary will gesture to a classmate or point to her communication board to request help. (From St. Peter, S.M., Ayres, B.J., Meyer, L., & Park-Lee, S. "Social skills;" Rainforth, B., Giangreco, M., & Dennis, R. "Motor skills; and Mirenda, P. & Smith-Lewis, M. "Communication skills." In A. Ford, R. Schnorr, L. Meyer, L. Davern, J. Black, & P. Dempsey [Eds.], *The Syracuse community-referenced curriculum guide for students with moderate and severe disabilities* [pp. 183, 224, & 202]; reprinted with permission.)

Activity-Based Instruction   Developing activity-based goals and objectives requires that the instructional day be organized to take maximum advantage of the teaching opportunities within the activities for each student. This task requires planning and coordination. One strategy is to develop an "Activities Planning Matrix" for every child (Ferguson & Wilcox, 1988). Figure 7.4 presents an example of a completed matrix, once again for Sheila, the same student represented in Figure 7.3.

Once the school day has been scheduled for all students (see Davern & Ford, 1989a,b, for an excellent discussion of this process), it is time to prepare the instructional sessions. This is essentially a three-step process (Black & Ford, 1989):

1. *Conducting an initial activity-based assessment*   This is akin to the discrepancy analysis strategy described earlier in the chapter under the "Environmental Model" section.

2. *Determining the general instructional procedures*   This part, which often is quite detailed, includes concerns such as: 1) how students will be posi-

Activities Planning Matrix

Name: Sheila Chandler
Age: 14
School year: 1988-89

Priority areas:
Participation in reg. Activities Clubs
Meal/snack prep
Apprpo-Social Interaction
Arm/hand movement
Vocational Skills
Picture recognition

Activity Components Areas

Priority	Activities	Social/communication			Self support/ management	Motor			Academics				
		Public comm.	Training comm.	Behavioral support		Manipu-lation	Mobility	Health/ fitness	Reading	Time	Numbers	Writing	Money
1	Hygiene Routine		Sign to "sitdown"	✓		less resistance		✓	Photos for schedule	Picture schedule			
2	Food Prep.	Choice: what to cook	Sign to "eat"/"drink"	Give appropriate sign		Slicing eating				"			
3	Eating Routine	Choice: what to eat/drink	Sign to "eat"/"drink"	Take short break		Self-feeding	walking w/tray			"			
4	Bus Riding Grocery store	Pictures Pass	"sitdown" "standup" "stop sign"	grasping		Pincergrasp -Pushcart	walking w/cart arm movement		Bus I.D. Picture, Grocery list	"			Tokens purchase items
5	Adaptive P.E.	Choice: Activities		✓		holding balls -pass out equipment	walking	Increase endurance		"			
6	Recycling Crew		"sitdown" "stop" sign	✓	Checklist	Pick up papers	Walking		Sorting papers	"		Assist w/checklist	
7	Homeroom		"sitdown" "standup" sign	✓		Pass out materials	Walk to class		Look at magazines	"			
8	Activity Class	Choice: Materials projects	"sitdown" "stand up" sign	Tolerate noise, people, textures		-Projects -carry supplies	Walk to Class		Projects	"	Projects		

Figure 7.4. Sample Activities Planning Matrix. (From Ferguson, D.L., & Wilcox, B.B. [Eds.]. [1988]. *The elementary/secondary system: Supportive education for children with severe handicaps. Module I: The activity-based IEP.* Eugene: Specialized Training Program, University of Oregon, p. 124; reprinted with permission.)

tioned, 2) whether each student will perform all steps in a sequence or only part of a sequence, and 3) how the lesson will be brought to a close.

3. *Using a planning and data card system*   This is a tool to allow the team member to organize instruction by listing, for each activity, the instructional target, the planned instructional cue, and the cue actually used (see Black & Ford, 1989, for details on this system).

Delivering Antecedent Events

Antecedent events include cues or directions, the materials used in instruction, and the instructional arrangement itself. All of these stimuli exert a tremendous influence on the student's responses. This section examines several key elements of selecting, arranging, and delivering antecedents.

Types of Prompts   Prompts are stimuli added before or during a response that help make a correct response more likely. They are used only after the cue naturally present in an instructional situation fails to evoke a correct response. There are three major types of prompts: verbal, observational, and physical (Falvey, Brown, Lyon, Baumgart, & Schroeder, 1980).

Verbal prompts are statements designed to urge the student to respond. They can be a repetition of the original stimulus or, more commonly, an elaboration or clarification of the direction. One variation of verbal prompts is the auditory prompt, involving the use of supplemental speech or other sound cues different from the initial verbal cue. Verbal prompts are particularly useful in working with students with significant visual loss.

Observational prompts can be either models of the behavior itself (i.e., "Do this") that the student imitates, or gestures (e.g., pointing, leaning) that cue the student to the form or location of a response. One might also include in this category augmentative visual cues (e.g., shining flashlight on an item) that help call attention to an item for a learner with a visual impairment.

Physical prompts, usually considered to be the most intrusive (i.e., they interfere with the natural sequence), are commonly used with individuals with multiple disabilities. They can be partial (i.e., helping with part of the task or providing part of the total movement) or total (i.e., actually guiding the student through the task). They can also provide tactile input for students with visual impairments by providing manual assistance, for example, to a child trying to turn his or her head to track.

Prompting Systems   Typically, prompts are used in combinations to evoke correct responses while preventing continued dependence on the instructor. Two common systems are briefly described here.

Least intrusive prompts involve giving the student an opportunity to respond to the naturally occurring stimulus. If the student does not respond in a reasonable amount of time, the instructor adds a verbal prompt (assuming adequate hearing, of course). This process is repeated, as necessary, with a verbal plus observational prompt combination and, finally, a verbal plus a physical prompt. The concept is to allow the student to perform the behavior at the least intrusive/most natural level of prompt possible.

Graduated guidance uses a most-to-least prompt hierarchy. The instructor applies partial to full physical assistance and gradually reduces, or fades, the location or degree of assistance to allow the student to take over.

More information on these and other prompting strategies can be found in Schoen (1986) and Snell (1987). It should be noted that the necessity for adding prompt hierarchies and artificial prompts should be reduced through instruction on natural routines within natural environments.

Task Presentation There is mounting evidence that the way instructional trials or tasks are organized makes a difference in skill acquisition (Holvoet et al., 1982; Kayser, Billingsley, & Neel, 1986; Mulligan et al., 1980; Mulligan, Lacy, & Guess, 1982). One relevant variable is the spacing of trials. Mulligan et al. (1982) differentiated among three types of trial sequencing:

1. *Massed* trials are those presented so closely together that no other behavior can be expected to occur between them.
2. *Distributed* trial sequences have separated trials or periods of time between two trials from the same program, in which trials from one or more other programs are inserted.
3. *Spaced* trial sequences also have spaces between trials, but there is a rest or pause in those spaces instead of trials from other programs.

Although massed or spaced trial presentations are most commonly used with children with multiple disabilities, the research clearly demonstrates the superiority of distributed trial training.

Another aspect of task presentation that may have a significant effect on skill acquisition is the task format. Tasks can be taught: 1) one step at a time from start to finish, with the student reaching criterion at each level (forward chaining); 2) one step at a time from the end, sequentially working backward to the first step (backward chaining); or 3) all at once (total task). Little research is available in this area, although Kayser et al. (1986) demonstrated the superiority of total task, single-trial instruction over the backward chaining, multiple-trial format. "Single trial" means that students are exposed to instruction on the total task during each session, but on only one trial per session.

The major lesson from the research conducted on task presentation—and from what has *not* yet been done—seems to be to avoid becoming trapped in a traditional, step-by-step, massed-trial approach to every task. Teaching embedded skills in the context of functional routines or activities is one sure way of avoiding this problem.

Delivering Consequent Events

Students with multiple disabilities, like other people, learn from the consequences of their behaviors. When students are correct, or behave in desired ways, they are rewarded, either as a natural consequence of their actions or by a reinforcer dispensed by an adult. Incorrect responses or undesired behaviors are corrected and, it is hoped, correct or desired behaviors taught in their place.

Delivering Reinforcement   The idea that one's behavior needs to be reinforced (or to generate reinforcers) in order for one to continue to exhibit it is fundamental to almost all learning. It is also recognized that reinforcers have individualized effectiveness and are situation specific; what works with one student in one setting may not work with a different student or even with the same student in a different situation. Despite the almost endless possibilities for reinforcers (e.g., food, drink, praise, activities, toys), it is not uncommon for team members to report finding it impossible to discover a reinforcer that works.

The only true way to discover whether a stimulus works as a reinforcer is to deliver the stimulus immediately following, and contingent on, the behavior and see if the behavior then strengthens (e.g., becomes faster, more proficient). The mere delivery of praise or an edible after a response does not ensure that the praise or edible will have a positive effect on learning. They may, in fact, have the opposite effect in certain situations. Nevertheless, it can be frustrating to identify a true reinforcer for the student with multiple disabilities. One can ask the child who is verbal what he or she would like or give the student free rein over the classroom to point out a preference. The learner who cannot speak or move about freely, however, usually has more limited—or at least different—means of expressing preferences. There are several strategies for determining potential reinforcers:

1. Caregiver surveys can be used to discover what items or events the child seems to enjoy.
2. The environment can be structured for trying out possible items. In reinforcer sampling, the student briefly samples small groups of similar items and is then allowed to choose freely.
3. Several studies (Green et al., 1988; Gutierrez-Griep, 1984; Pace, Ivancic, Edwards, Iwata, & Page, 1985; Wacker, Berg, Wiggins, Muldoon, & Cavanaugh, 1985; Wacker, Wiggins, Fowler, & Berg, 1988) have described procedures for systematically assessing the reinforcement value of items for individuals with profound mental retardation who had restricted physical movement. This research clearly reveals how individualized and consistent the choice of reinforcers truly is.
4. The Comprehensive Communication Curriculum (Klein et al., 1981) describes an excellent process for establishing potential reinforcers for children with very limited motoric and communication repertoires. The techniques involve noting changes in facial expression, vocalization, and body movement upon presentation and withdrawal of stimuli. In a particularly interesting variation, the parent or professional repeatedly presents an item to the child over several days and then withholds it, looking for an anticipatory response from the child.

5. Shevin (1982) has described guidelines for selecting reinforcers, particularly food and drink, for students with severe disabilities. Figure 7.5 presents a checklist to help guide the selection process.

Correcting Errors   Although instruction is often arranged to prevent errors, they are an inevitable—and often constructive—part of learning. It is difficult to separate the correction aspect of a task (i.e., consequences) from the cues before the task (i.e., antecedents), particularly when a system of least prompts is used. Nevertheless, a few general guidelines may be helpful:

1. Errors should be corrected either immediately following the incorrect response or by interrupting the incorrect response. The student should be provided with another chance to respond correctly, with additional help if necessary.
2. Correction procedures that are as close as possible to those in the student's natural environments should be used.
3. Only the least help necessary to help the student to respond correctly the next time should be provided; one should avoid doing everything for the student. If total physical assistance is needed initially, it should be removed gradually to prevent the student's overdependence on the staff.
4. Partial participation should be considered if the task appears to be too difficult. Numerous errors may also suggest that the task needs to be reanalyzed or that antecedents or materials need to be modified.

Reducing Problem Behavior

The traditional approach to modifying undesired, excess behavior (e.g., aggression, stereotypic behavior) has been to treat it like an extra, useless appendage that can be cut off, thus restoring the person to "normal." In the 1980s analyses of behavior, however, have come to view undesired problem behaviors as serving important functions for the individual (e.g., Durand, 1986; Durand & Carr, 1987). Strategies for reducing these excess behaviors have focused on teaching acceptable alternatives that serve the same function. Moreover, relevant models for altering problem behaviors are committed to techniques that are positive and supportive of the person's rights and dignity (e.g., Meyer & Evans, 1989).

Meyer and Evans (1986, 1989) have described a model for determining which behaviors are a priority for intervention. In this model Level I represents "urgent behaviors requiring immediate attention." Examples typically include self-injurious behaviors that cause tissue damage. Level II behaviors are considered "serious, requiring formal consideration." Such behaviors either interfere with learning, are likely to become more serious if left alone, are dangerous to others, or are of great concern to caregivers. Level III behaviors "reflect normal deviance," and may or may not be serious enough to include in a student's program.

It is important for team members not to overreact to every annoying be-

1. Is the reinforcer under consideration known to be effective with this child, OR is it being paired with a known effective reinforcer? ___ YES ___ no
2. Has the program in which the reinforcer is to be used been designed to include:
    a. Concrete, attainable objectives? ___ YES ___ no
    b. Arrangement of the antecedent environment to make success likely? ___ YES ___ no
    c. Procedures for reinforcing successive approximations to the target behavior? ___ YES ___ no
3. Has more than one reinforcer been identified for this task? ___ YES ___ no
4. a. Is the reinforcer under consideration in the natural environment, OR can it be paired with a reinforcer available in the natural environment? ___ YES ___ no
    b. Are there prominent natural changes in the environment that will follow the display of the appropriate behavior by the student? ___ YES ___ no
5. a. Does the reinforcer under consideration decrease the likelihood of the behavior being displayed as the lesson goes on? ___ yes ___ NO
    b. Does the reinforcer under consideration slow the lesson down unacceptably? ___ yes ___ NO
6. a. Does the reinforcer under consideration include a high sugar content, suspect food additives, or psychoactive ingredients such as caffeine? ___ yes ___ NO
    b. Have the student's parents or guardians been consulted concerning food allergies or other food counterindicators? ___ YES ___ no
    c. Will the student's parents or guardians be informed concerning the types and quantities of food consumed in school? ___ YES ___ no
    d. Will food and drink be administered at a** leisurely pace in the lesson? ___ YES ___ no
    e. Will the teacher accompany edible reinforcers** with eye contact and conversation? ___ YES ___ no
    f. Will edible reinforcers be consumed with**appropriate utensils, in normative ways? ___ YES ___ no
    **g. (If the answer to 6d, 6e or 6f is no): Will the edible reinforcer be one which is unavailable in any setting other than the instructional setting? ___ YES ___ no

Capitalized answers represent optimum reinforcer selection and use.

Figure 7.5. Checklist for selecting reinforcers. (Capitalized answers represent optimum reinforcer selection and use.) (From Shevin, M. [1982]. The use of food and drink in classroom management programs for severely handicapped children. *The Journal of The Association for the Severely Handicapped,* 7[1], 43; reprinted with permission.)

havior. There are several relevant considerations. First, students often exhibit excess behaviors because they are bored, frustrated, or in some way reacting to a deficiency in their daily routine or instuctional program. It would be wrong (and ineffective) to blame the student for a behavior that is maintained by the program. Second, many students with multiple disabilities are in discomfort from improper positioning, poorly designed equipment, illness, medications, and so forth. This discomfort may result in vocalizations and other behaviors that are annoying. Again, however, the *cause* of these behaviors needs to be modified, not just the behaviors themselves. Third, learners may drool, exhibit tongue thrust, refuse food, and engage in other behaviors that directly or indirectly result from their physical condition and that may or may not be under their control. Alternative skills should be taught (e.g., to swallow saliva periodically to reduce drooling), and others in the school and community might be taught to accommodate some differences in individuals' appearance and behavior.

In helping to determine the purposes a behavior serves for an individual, the process of *functional analysis* is invaluable. Functional analysis is an assessment strategy that yields three major outcomes (O'Neill, Horner, Albin, Storey, & Sprague, 1990):

1. Description of the undesirable behaviors
2. Prediction of the times and situations when the behaviors will and will not be performed throughout the day
3. Definition of the maintaining reinforcers that the behavior produces for the person

Several authors have designed approaches to functional analysis. Touchette, MacDonald, and Langer (1985) proposed a scatter plot method of graphing data that provides a visual representation of the times and situations during which the behavior is most prevalent. Durand and Crimmins (1988) developed a Motivational Assessment Scale that assesses, through a simple interview technique, which of four major functions a behavior is most likely to serve. O'Neill et al. (1990) designed a more thorough and complex approach to functional analysis, incorporating in-depth interview and observation protocols, as well as a process of "systematic environmental manipulation" to provide clearer evidence of the role of variables suspected to support the behavior.

Once the purpose or function of an excess behavior is clear, it becomes easier to organize an approach toward reducing it and strengthening other, more positive, behaviors. It is beyond the scope of this chapter to detail the myriad strategies for accomplishing this. Readers are directed to Meyer and Evans (1989) for a good description of the philosophy and practices briefly sketched here. The point should be made, however, that any approach to dealing with undesired behavior should be constructive and positive. There is ample evidence—as well as the validation from the professional community—that aver-

sive strategies that go beyond mere corrective feedback (i.e., mild verbal reprimand, brief withdrawal of positive attention, and limited restricted access to
preferred materials and activities) are not necessary and, in fact, are harmful to
the overall goal of education and intervention.

CONCLUSION

This chapter has touched upon a variety of key elements in developing content
and teaching students with multiple disabilities. No chapter, no book, no manual, no matter how detailed, can ever teach all the subtleties needed to teach
these individuals. But it is also true that a professional may be an excellent
technician without possessing the value base for making important decisions. It
is hoped that this chapter provides enough of a flavor of some of these essential
values, and whets the reader's appetite for learning more and trying out some
new ideas.

REFERENCES

Baumgart, D., Brown, L., Pumpian, I., Nisbet, J., Ford, A., Sweet, M., Messina, R.,
    & Schroeder, J. (1982). Principle of partial participation and individualized adapta-
    tions in educational programs for severely handicapped students. *Journal of The Asso-
    ciation for the Severely Handicapped, 1,* 17–27.
Black, J., & Ford, A. (1989). Planning and implementing activity-based lessons. In A.
    Ford, R. Schnorr, L. Meyer, L. Davern, J. Black, & P. Dempsey (Eds.), *The Syracuse
    community-referenced curriculum guide for students with moderate and severe dis-
    abilities* (pp. 295–311). Baltimore: Paul H. Brookes Publishing Co.
Brown, F. (1987). Meaningful assessment of people with severe and profound handi-
    caps. In M.E. Snell (Ed.), *Systematic instruction of persons with severe handicaps*
    (pp. 39–63). Columbus: Charles E. Merrill.
Brown, F., Holvoet, J., Guess, D., & Mulligan, M. (1980). The Individualized Curricu-
    lum Sequencing Model (III): Small group instruction. *Journal of The Association for
    the Severely Handicapped, 5*(4), 352–367.
Brown, F., & Lehr, D.H. (Eds.). (1989). *Persons with profound handicaps: Issues and
    practices.* Baltimore: Paul H. Brookes Publishing Co.
Brown, L., Branston, M.B., Hamre-Nietupski, S., Pumpian, J., Certo, N., &
    Gruenewald, L. (1979). A strategy for developing chronological age appropriate and
    functional curricular content for severely handicapped adolescents and young adults.
    Journal of Special Education, 13, 81–90.
Brown, L., Nisbet, J., Ford, A., Sweet, M., Shiraga, B., York, J., & Loomis, R.
    (1983). The critical need for nonschool instruction in educational programs for se-
    verely handicapped students. *Journal of The Association for the Severely Handi-
    capped, 8*(3), 71–77.
Davern, L., & Ford, A. (1989a). Managing classroom operations. In A. Ford, R.
    Schnorr, L. Meyer, L. Davern, J. Black, & P. Dempsey (Eds.), *The Syracuse
    community-referenced curriculum guide for students with moderate and severe dis-
    abilties* (pp. 281–294). Baltimore: Paul H. Brookes Publishing Co.
Davern, L., & Ford, A., (1989b). Scheduling. In A. Ford, R. Schnorr, L. Meyer, L.
    Davern, J. Black, & P. Dempsey (Eds.), *The Syracuse community-referenced curricu-*

lum guide for students with moderate and severe disabilities (pp. 247–278). Baltimore: Paul H. Brookes Publishing Co.

Durand, V.M. (1986). Self-injurious behavior as intentional communication. *Advances in Learning and Behavioral Disabilities, 5,* 141–155.

Durand, V.M., & Carr, E.G. (1987). Social influences on "self-stimulatory" behavior: Analysis and treatment application. *Journal of Applied Behavior Analysis, 20,* 119–132.

Durand, V.M., & Crimmins, D. (1988). *The motivation assessment scale.* New York: University of Albany.

Falvey, M.A. (1989). *Community-based curriculum: Instructional strategies for students with severe handicaps* (2nd ed.). Baltimore: Paul H. Brookes Publishing Co.

Falvey, M., Brown, L., Lyon, S., Baumgart, D., & Schroeder, J. (1980). Strategies for using cues and correction procedures. In W. Sailor, B. Wilcox, & L. Brown (Eds.), *Methods of instruction for severely handicapped students* (pp. 109–133). Baltimore: Paul H. Brookes Publishing Co.

Ferguson, D.L., & Wilcox, B.L. (Eds.). (1988). *The elementary/secondary system: Supportive education for students with severe handicaps. Module 1: The activity-based IEP.* Eugene: Specialized Training Program, University of Oregon.

Ford, A., Schnorr, R., Meyer, L., Davern, L., Black, J., & Dempsey, P. (Eds.). (1989). *The Syracuse community-referenced curriculum guide for students with moderate and severe disabilities.* Baltimore: Paul H. Brookes Publishing Co.

Gaylord-Ross, R.J., & Holvoet, J.F. (1985). *Strategies for educating students with severe handicaps.* Boston: Little, Brown.

Goetz, L., Guess, D., & Stremel-Campbell, K. (Eds.). (1987). *Innovative program design for individuals with dual sensory impairments.* Baltimore: Paul H. Brookes Publishing Co.

Green, C.W., Reid, D.H., White, L.K., Halford, R.C., Brittain, D.P., & Gardner, S.M. (1988). Identifying reinforcers for persons with profound handicaps: Staff opinion versus systematic assessment of preferences. *Journal of Applied Behavior Analysis, 21,* 31–43.

Guess, D., Benson, H.A., & Siegel-Causey, E. (1985). Concepts and issues related to choice-making and autonomy among persons with severe disabilities. *Journal of The Association for Persons with Severe Handicaps, 10*(2), 79–86.

Guess, D., & Helmstetter, E. (1986). Skill cluster instruction and the individualized curriculum sequencing model. In R.H. Horner, L.H. Meyer, & H.D.B. Fredericks (Eds.), *Education of learners with severe handicaps: Exemplary service strategies* (pp. 221–248). Baltimore: Paul H. Brookes Publishing Co.

Guess, D., Horner, D., Utley, B., Holvoet, J., Maxon, D., Tucker, D., & Warren, S. (1978). A functional curriculum sequencing model for teaching the severely handicapped. *AAESPH Review, 3,* 202–215.

Guess, D., & Siegel-Causey, E. (1985). Behavioral control and education of severely handicapped students: Who's doing what to whom? and why? In D. Bricker & J. Filler (Eds.), *Severe mental retardation: From theory to practice* (pp. 230–244). Reston, VA: Council for Exceptional Children, Division on Mental Retardation.

Gutierrez-Griep, R. (1984). Student preference of sensory reinforcers. *Education and Training of the Mentally Retarded, 19*(2), 108–113.

Helmstetter, E. (1989). Curriculum for school-age students: The ecological model. In F. Brown & D.H. Lehr (Eds.), *Persons with profound disabilities: Issues and practices* (pp. 239–263). Baltimore: Paul H. Brookes Publishing Co.

Helmstetter, E., & Guess, D. (1987). Application of the individualized curriculum sequencing model to learners with severe sensory impairments. In L. Goetz, D. Guess,

& K. Stremel-Campbell (Eds.), *Innovative program design for individuals with dual sensory impairments* (pp. 255–282). Baltimore: Paul H. Brookes Publishing Co.

Helmstetter, E., Murphy-Herd, M.C., Roberts, S., & Guess, D. (1984). *Individualized curriculum sequence and extended classroom models for learners who are deaf and blind.* Lawrence: The Kansas Individualized Curriculum Sequencing Project, University of Kansas.

Holvoet, J., Mulligan, M., Schussler, N., Lacy, L., & Guess, P.D. (1982). *The KICS model: Sequencing learning experiences for severely handicapped children and youth.* Lawrence: The Kansas Individualized Curriculum Sequencing Project, University of Kansas.

Horner, R.H., Meyer, L.H., & Fredericks, H.D.B. (Eds.). (1986). *Education of learners with severe handicaps: Exemplary service strategies.* Baltimore: Paul H. Brookes Publishing Co.

Kayser, J.E., Billingsley, F.F., & Neel, R.S. (1986). A comparison of in-context and traditional instructional approaches: Total task, single trial versus backward chaining, multiple trials. *Journal of The Association for Persons with Severe Handicaps, 11*(1), 28–38.

Klein, M.D., Wulz, S.V., Hall, M.K., Waldo, L.J., Carpenter, S.A., Lathan, D.A., Myers, S.P., Fox, T., & Marshall, A.M. (1981). *Comprehensive communication curriculum guide.* Lawrence: Kansas Early Childhood Institute.

Lipsky, D.K., & Gartner, A. (Eds.). (1989). *Beyond separate education: Quality education for all.* Baltimore: Paul H. Brookes Publishing Co.

Meyer, L.H., & Eichinger, J. (1987). Program evaluation in support of program development: Needs, strategies, and future directions. In L. Goetz, D. Guess, & K. Stremel-Campbell (Eds.), *Innovative program design for individuals with dual sensory impairments* (pp. 313–353). Baltimore: Paul H. Brookes Publishing Co.

Meyer, L.H., Eichinger, J., & Park-Lee, S. (1987). A validation of program quality indicators in educational services for students with severe disabilities. *Journal of The Association for Persons with Severe Handicaps, 12*(4), 251–263.

Meyer, L.H., & Evans, I.M. (1986). Modification of excess behavior: An adaptive and functional approach for educational and community contexts. In R.H. Horner, L.H. Meyer, & H.D.B. Fredericks (Eds.), *Education of learners with severe handicaps: Exemplary service strategies* (pp. 315–350). Baltimore: Paul H. Brookes Publishing Co.

Meyer, L.H., & Evans, I.M. (1989). *Nonaversive intervention for behavior problems: A manual for home and community.* Baltimore: Paul H. Brookes Publishing Co.

Mirenda, P., & Smith-Lewis, M. (1989). Communication skills. In A. Ford, R. Schnorr, L. Meyer, L. Davern, J. Black, & P. Dempsey (Eds.), *The Syracuse community-referenced curriculum guide for students with moderate and severe disabilities* (pp. 189–209). Baltimore: Paul H. Brookes Publishing Co.

Mulligan, M., Guess, D., Holvoet, J., & Brown, F. (1980). The Individualized Curriculum Sequencing model (I): Implications from research on massed, distributed, or spaced trial training. *Journal of The Association for the Severely Handicapped, 5*(4), 325–336.

Mulligan, M., Lacy, L., & Guess, D. (1982). Effects of massed, distributed, and spaced trial sequencing on severely handicapped students' performance. *Journal of The Association for the Severely Handicapped, 7*(2), 48–61.

Neel, R.S., & Billingsley, F.F. (1989). *Impact: A functional curriculum handbook for students with moderate to severe disabilities.* Baltimore: Paul H. Brookes Publishing Co.

Nietupski, J.A., & Hamre-Nietupski, S.M. (1987). An ecological approach to curriculum development. In L. Goetz, D. Guess, & K. Stremel-Campbell (Eds.), *Innovative program design for individuals with dual sensory impairments* (pp. 225–253). Baltimore: Paul H. Brookes Publishing Co.

O'Neill, R.E., Horner, R.H., Albin, R.W., Storey, K., & Sprague, J.R. (1990). *Functional analysis of problem behavior: A practical assessment guide.* Sycamore, IL: Sycamore Publishing Co.

Orelove, F.P. (1991). Educating all students: The future is now. In L. H. Meyer, C.A. Peck, & L. Brown (Eds.), *Critical issues in the lives of people with severe disabilities* (pp. 67–87). Baltimore: Paul H. Brookes Publishing Co.

Pace, G.M., Ivancic, M.T., Edwards, G.L., Iwata, B.A., & Page, T.J. (1985). Assessment of stimulus preference and reinforcer value with profoundly retarded individuals. *Journal of Applied Behavior Analysis, 18,* 249–255.

Rainforth, B., Giangreco, M., & Dennis, R. (1989). Motor skills. In A. Ford, R. Schnorr, L. Meyer, L. Davern, J. Black, & P. Dempsey (Eds.), *The Syracuse community-referenced curriculum guide for students with moderate and severe disabilities* (pp. 211–230). Baltimore: Paul H. Brookes Publishing Co.

Reichle, J., York, J., & Eynon, D. (1989). Influence of indicating preferences for initiating, maintaining, and terminating interactions. In F. Brown & D.H. Lehr (Eds.), *Persons with profound disabilities: Issues and practices* (pp. 191–211). Baltimore: Paul H. Brookes Publishing Co.

Sailor, W., Gee, K., Goetz, L., & Graham, N. (1988). Progress in educating students with the most severe disabilities: Is there any? *Journal of The Association for Persons with Severe Handicaps, 13*(2), 87–99.

Sailor, W., & Guess, D. (1983). *Severely handicapped students: An instructional design.* Boston: Houghton Mifflin.

Sailor, W., Halvorsen, A., Anderson, J., Goetz, L., Gee, K., Doering, K., & Hunt, P. (1986). Community intensive instruction. In R.H. Horner, L.H. Meyer, & H.D.B. Fredericks (Eds.), *Education of learners with severe handicaps: Exemplary service strategies* (pp. 251–288). Baltimore: Paul H. Brookes Publishing Co.

St. Peter, S.M., Ayres, B.J., Meyer, L., & Park-Lee, S. (1989). Social skills. In A. Ford, R. Schnorr, L. Meyer, L. Davern, J. Black, & P. Dempsey (Eds.), *The Syracuse community-referenced curriculum guide for students with moderate and severe disabilities* (pp. 171–188). Baltimore: Paul H. Brookes Publishing Co.

Schoen, S.F. (1986). Assistance procedures to facilitate the transfer of stimulus control: Review and analysis. *Education and Training of the Mentally Retarded, 21*(1), 62–74.

Shevin, M. (1982). The use of food and drink in classroom management programs for severely handicapped children. *Journal of The Association for the Severely Handicapped, 7*(1), 40–46.

Shevin, M., & Klein, N.K. (1984). The importance of choice-making skills for students with severe disabilities. *Journal of The Association for Persons with Severe Handicaps, 9*(3), 159–166.

Snell, M.E. (Ed.). (1987). *Systematic instruction of persons with severe handicaps* (3rd ed.). Columbus: Charles E. Merrill.

Snell, M., & Browder, D.M. (1986). Community-referenced instruction: Research and issues. *Journal of The Association for Persons with Severe Handicaps, 11*(1), 1–11.

Touchette, P.E., MacDonald, R.F., & Langer, S.N. (1985). A scatter plot for identifying stimulus control of problem behavior. *Journal of Applied Behavior Analysis, 18,* 343–351.

Wacker, D.P., Berg, W.K., Wiggins, B., Muldoon, M., & Cavanaugh, J. (1985). Evaluation of reinforcer preferences for profoundly handicapped students. *Journal of Applied Behavior Analysis, 18,* 173–178.

Wacker, D.P., Wiggins, B., Fowler, M., & Berg, W.K. (1988). Training students with profound or multiple handicaps to make requests via microswitches. *Journal of Applied Behavior Analysis, 21,* 331–343.

White, O.R. (1980). Adaptive performance objectives: Form versus function. In W. Sailor, B. Wilcox, & L. Brown (Eds.), *Methods of instruction for severely handicapped students* (pp. 47–69). Baltimore: Paul H. Brookes Publishing Co.

White, O.R. (1985). The evaluation of severely mentally retarded populations. In D. Bricker & J. Filler (Eds.), *Severe mental retardation: From theory to practice* (pp. 161–184). Reston, VA: Council for Exceptional Children, Division on Mental Retardation.

Wilcox, B., & Bellamy, G.T. (1982). *Design of high school programs for severely handicapped students.* Baltimore: Paul H. Brookes Publishing Co.

Wilcox, B., & Bellamy, G.T. (1987). *A comprehensive guide to The Activities Catalog: An alternative curriculum for youth and adults with severe disabilities.* Baltimore: Paul H. Brookes Publishing Co.

Wuerch, B.B., & Voeltz, L.M. (1982). *Longitudinal leisure skills for severely handicapped learners: The Ho'onanea curriculum component.* Baltimore: Paul H. Brookes Publishing Co.

Chapter 8

Developing Instructional Adaptations

Jennifer York and Beverly Rainforth

An adaptation can be thought of as any device or material that is used to accomplish a task more efficiently. Most people use a variety of adaptations in everyday living. For example, datebooks and calendars are used for recording appointments, birthdays, holidays, and deadlines for various projects and commitments. Timers are used to indicate when food should be removed from the oven. Lists are used to remind shoppers of groceries or other items to be purchased. Each of these examples is an adaptation to assist with memory. Other adaptations simplify physical demands. Common examples are using an electric mixer instead of stirring batter by hand, or using an electric garage door opener instead of lifting open the door by hand. Another type of adaptation is used to serve as a model. A picture of a pineapple upside-down cake illustrates how the pineapple and cherries should be arranged; a picture of a completed needlework project shows the colors of thread to use and how various stitches should be made. An analysis of the daily activities performed by most people undoubtedly would reveal the use of numerous other adaptations.

The business world is replete with adaptations, many of which enhance the efficiency, accuracy, and speed of one's performance of various tasks. Automatic coin counters at banks are used to sort and stack coins. Cash register keys at fast food restaurants are color coded by food category (e.g., beverages, sandwiches, and side orders) to make locating keys easier for clerks. Frequently, the keys also have specific food or drink labels and, when pushed, automatically enter the price of the item to be purchased. This eliminates the need for clerks to remember the different prices, and decreases the time required to complete chases. Many businesses invest enormous amounts of money to research and develop adaptations that will increase productivity and efficiency while maintaining a high degree of quality.

Not surprisingly, the value of adaptations also has been recognized in the field of education, particularly for assisting students with multiple disabilities in participating more fully in home, school, and community activities. Parents and professionals have found that motoric, sensory, and intellectual disabilities presented by some students require creative approaches in which systematic instruction is augmented by the development and use of individualized adaptations. The "principle of partial participation" asserts that when systematic instruction and adaptation strategies are integrated and applied, "all students can acquire skills that allow them to function in a wide variety of least restrictive environments" (Baumgart et al., 1982, p. 19). (The principle of partial participation was described in greater detail in Chapter 7.) Certainly, this presents a significant challenge to educators, therapists, parents, and others involved in educational programming. Meeting the challenge of making adaptations to attain meaningful participation, however, is a cornerstone in educational service provision and, more broadly, community integration for persons with multiple and often complex learning needs.

This chapter presents a strategy for conceptualizing the development and implementation of individualized adaptations to increase the participation of students with multiple disabilities in educational activities. Examples are provided of domestic, recreation/leisure, and vocational adaptations that have been used in school, home, and community environments. The chapter finishes with a discussion of considerations, precautions, and resources related to effective use of adaptations as an instructional tool.

A STRATEGY FOR DEVELOPING INDIVIDUALIZED ADAPTATIONS

The need for adaptations is determined by a top-down analysis of individual student abilities and needs. That is, environments in which a student should learn to function are identified. Then, strategies for teaching successful participation in the selected environments are developed. Use of adaptations may be one instructional strategy employed. Figure 8.1 presents a flow chart of the steps involved in a top-down approach for developing adaptations. This strategy is based largely on the work of Brown and his colleagues (Brown et al., 1979; Brown et al., 1980; Brown, Shiraga, York, Zanella, & Rogan, 1984a; Brown, Shiraga, York, Zanella, & Rogan, 1984b). First, the actual school, domestic, recreation/leisure, vocational, and community environments in which a given student should learn to function are selected. Second, the activities and skills required for participating in the selected environments are delineated. Third, the ability of the student to engage in the required activities and skills is

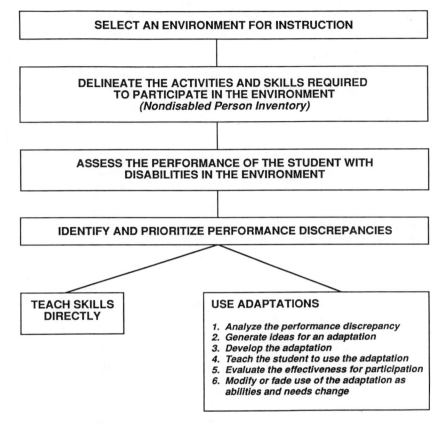

Figure 8.1. A flow chart of a top-down, environmentally referenced approach for developing individualized adaptations. (Based on Baumgart et al., 1982.)

assessed in the actual environments. Fourth, difficulty areas, or performance discrepancies, are identified and priority skills are targeted for instruction. Fifth, instructional solutions are developed.

Essentially there are two instructional options. One is to teach the student to perform the skill in the same way that a person who does not have a disability would perform the skill. For example, if a student is unable to carry his science lab materials to the lab table, he would be taught to do so in a way identical to the way his nondisabled classmates do. The other option is to generate an adaptation for accomplishing the task by modifying skill requirements or by developing an adaptive device. For example, the student might carry the lab items individually or use a carrying bag attached to his walker. Another example would be for a student who is unable to speak to present her report on leisure

Table 8.1. Example of a partial assessment conducted at a public library

Nondisabled person inventory	Student with disabilities inventory (assessment)[a]	Instructional solutions (teach directly or adapt)[b]
ACTIVITY: Choosing a tape		
Skills:		
Locate tape section.	− T pointed to audio-visual section, then to tapes.	D: S will look in direction of tape area once in visual field. (T/peer push wheelchair.)
Browse through tapes.	− T located age-appropriate tapes, then selected four.	A: S will look at tapes pulled from stack by T/peer.
Select one tape.	+ S looked at one tape after T presented four.	
ACTIVITY: Listening to tape		
Skills:		
Locate tape.	+ S scanned then located after T pointed to picture of tape player on communication board.	
Position self.	− T wheeled and positioned S.	A: S will be pushed by T/peer to tape section.
Open tape player lid.	− S initiated move toward eject button; T relaxed S's arm then primed reaching for and pushing button.	A: S will push on lever extended from eject button; T/peer positions tape player.
Insert tape.	− S pushed tape into place with back of wrist after T aligned tape in track.	A: S will push in tape after T/peer places tape player close to S's wrist and aligns tape.
Close lid.	− S initiated move toward lid; T relaxed S's arm then assisted to reach down and push closed.	D: S will push lid closed with forearm after T/peer places tape player near forearm.
Put on headphones.	− T places earphones on S's head.	A: T/peer will perform.
Turn on tape.	− S was unable to reach and exert enough pressure; T turned on.	A: S will turn on tape with hand/head using microswitch.

(continued)

Table 8.1.   *(continued)*

Nondisabled person inventory	Student with disabilities inventory (assessment)[a]	Instructional solutions (teach directly or adapt)[b]
Adjust volume.	− T moved volume dial; S frowned then smiled.	A: S will smile when appropriate volume dialed by T/peer.

ACTIVITY: Choosing a magazine
Skills:

Locate magazine section.	− T pointed to magazine section.	D: S will look in direction of magazines once in visual field (eventually S will choose between tapes and magazines).
Locate preferred magazines.	− T located age-appropriate and preferred content magazines.	A: S will scan magazine section with T/peer guiding by pointing.
Select one magazine.	+ S looked at one magazine and smiled after T presented three.	

ACTIVITY: Browsing through magazine
Skills:

Locate an area to sit.	− T pointed out several open spots then decided to go near window.	D: S will choose where to sit by looking at one area (window or lounge) pointed out by T/peer.
Position self.	− T wheeled and positioned S.	A: S will be positioned by T/peer (consider getting S out of chair to sit on carpet.)
Hold magazine.	− T positioned and held magazine on wheelchair tray.	A: T places magazine in magazine/book holder adaptation.
Read articles/look at pictures.	+ S looked at pictures.	
Turn pages.	− S initiated reaching to page but required T's assist to relax, reach, turn pages.	A: S will turn pages with hand/mouth using dowel rod with Plasti-Tac end.

[a]T = teacher; S = student; + indicates independent and acceptable performance; − indicates assistance was required to achieve acceptable performance.

[b]D = teach directly, A = adapt.

interests to social studies classmates using a slide projector. If a student lacks essential intellectual, motoric, or sensory abilities required for performing a skill in a typical manner, an adaptation is one way to accommodate the difficulties. The initial steps in an environmental model curricular approach were discussed in greater detail in Chapter 7; therefore, in this chapter emphasis is placed on the latter steps which specifically relate to developing adaptations.

Application of the process is illustrated through an example of a student using a public library for recreation/leisure purposes. The student, George, was 19 years old and had been labeled as having severe to profound mental retardation. He enjoyed community activities immensely and was beginning to be included in community activities with some of his senior classmates in high school. He had fair control over turning his head to each side when provided with a head rest for support. He could extend one elbow and exert pressure downward with the side of his hand. George's primary method of mobility was being pushed in a wheelchair by another person. He was not able to speak but readily communicated likes and dislikes through facial expressions and could indicate choices or direction with his eyes.

Select an Environment for Instruction

The first phase of an environmentally referenced individualized adaptation strategy is to select the natural environment in which the student must learn to function. Environments must be determined individually for each student. Some of the reasons for selecting the public library as a recreation/leisure environment for George included: 1) he enjoyed listening to music and looking at magazines, both of which activities were available at the library; 2) the activities were age appropriate; 3) George's family used the particular branch of the library in which instruction would take place; 4) the library was close to George's home; 5) the library was located near other community environments in which George might learn to function (e.g., a grocery store and clothing store); 6) use of the library required little or no money; and 7) the library was open much of the week, including weeknights and weekends. Although use of the library was not a preferred activity of nondisabled peers, current and future use of the library was determined to be a priority for George.

Delineate the Activities and Skills Required in the Environment

After selection of an environment, a nondisabled person inventory is completed; this involves delineation of activities performed and skills required for functioning within the selected environments (Brown et al., 1984a). A detailed breakdown of some of the activities and skills required at the public library is presented as the nondisabled person inventory in the first column of Table 8.1. For example, the activity of choosing a tape at the library required the following skills: locate the tape section, browse through the tapes, and select one tape. A nondisabled person inventory that specifies skills is used as the assessment tool for determining student abilities in a natural environment.

Assess the Performance of the Student with Disabilities

Next, an inventory of the student with disabilities is conducted through assessment of how the student performs within the designated environment (Brown et al., 1984b). Assessment requires taking the student to the specific environment and using the nondisabled person inventory as the assessment tool for recording performance. First, the response of the student to the natural conditions that should ultimately cue performance of specific skills within the environment is recorded. Independent and acceptable performance and the type and degree of any assistance required should be recorded also. An example of assessment information on George's performance at the library is provided in the second column of Table 8.1. There were four skills performed independently: looked at one tape, scanned then located one tape, looked at one magazine, and looked at pictures in magazine. Acceptable performance of all other skills required teacher assistance.

Identify Performance Discrepancies

After the assessment is conducted in the actual environment, student performance discrepancies, or problem areas, are identified in relation to how a person who does not have disabilities would function in the environment. In this way, specific activities and skills in which the student requires instruction are identified. From the identified discrepancies, priorities are selected and corresponding objectives written. The skills for which George required assistance in the tape playing activity were: locate the tape section, browse through the tapes, position self, open the tape player lid, insert the tape, close the tape player lid, put on the headphones, turn on the tape, and adjust the volume. Discrepant skills in the magazine activity were: locate the magazine section, locate the magazines, locate an area to sit, position self, hold magazine, and turn the pages. With performance discrepancies and priority objectives identified, instructional strategies can be developed.

Develop Instructional Solutions

The next step is for team members to decide how each of the discrepant skills will be addressed instructionally. Designing integrated instructional methods involves drawing upon the expertise of all team members. The decision is made whether to teach the skill directly (i.e., the way that a person who does not have disabilities would perform the skill) or to generate adaptations that will enable greater and more independent participation. When students are unable to engage in individually appropriate activities by typical means because of motoric, sensory, and/or intellectual disabilities, it is necessary to develop individualized adaptations that involve modifying the environment or teaching strategies to enhance participation.

The performance discrepancies of George at the library were noted previously. Analysis of these discrepancies resulted in instructional decisions either to teach the discrepant skills directly or to make an adaptation. The team decided on direct instruction for the following skills: locate the tape section, close the tape player lid, locate the magazine section, and locate an area to sit. It was decided that George would be taught to scan the library, then to indicate the appropriate locations by looking in one direction for a few seconds, and also to push the tape player lid closed with his forearm. The remaining discrepant skills required various adaptations.

Baumgart et al. (1982) conceptualized four categories of adaptations: 1) providing personal assistance, 2) modifying skills or activities, 3) using an adaptive device, and 4) modifying the physical and social environments. In the following sections these adaptation strategies are described, and examples specific to George are provided. The third column in Table 8.1 summarizes the instructional solutions decided upon for George.

Providing Personal Assistance Providing personal assistance is a familiar adaptation. Occasionally, educational team members decide to provide personal assistance on a long-term basis for skills that a student is very unlikely to learn using direct instruction or other adaptations. For example, a student who has not been successful learning to move between high school classes independently may require the assistance of a peer on a long-term basis. In the library example, it was decided that personal assistance would be provided, specifically, that a nondisabled peer accompany George and assist with mobility between areas of the library and with appropriate positioning for particular activities.

Modifying Skills or Activities The second type of adaptation, modifying skills or activities, involves changing typical skill sequences. A student who has difficulty managing her belongings and her dine-in meal at a fast food restaurant may be taught first to deposit her belongings at a table, then proceed to the counter to order and obtain her meal. Another example involves a student with severe disabilities in a middle school reading class. This student's primary reading class objectives were selecting a magazine from the school library, checking it out, browsing, and returning the magazine. While most of the students in the class used the library on a bi-weekly basis, this student used the library three times a week. In yet another reading class example, this time for an elementary school student with multiple disabilities, the student's reading routine deviated from that of her classmates because she remained in the quiet reading area of the room for all of the three reading periods. Her classmates rotated between the quiet reading area, independent seated work, and small group instruction.

In George's library example, use of an activity adaptation was an appropriate instructional strategy for him to learn to locate a set of tapes and magazines from which to select one. Because of inefficient arm use, George was not able to secure and browse independently through the magazines and tapes prior to making a selection. It was decided that a nondisabled peer would choose several tapes and magazines that were age-appropriate and interesting and George would then make a final selection by looking at or touching one of the options presented.

Using an Adaptive Device   The third type of an adaptation, using an adaptive device, was also employed in the library example. George was unable to depress the play button on the tape player using a controlled, desirable arm movement. Using a microswitch as an adaptation was considered appropriate. The switch was to be positioned for activation either by controlled arm or head movement. Another difficulty area indicated in the assessment was turning pages of a magazine. To adapt the physical skills required for holding a magazine and turning the pages, the magazine/book holder, illustrated in Figure 8.2, was made. This allowed George to browse independently through a magazine after a peer (or teacher) secured the magazine in the device.

When adaptive devices are used, it is important to remember that direct instruction for use of the device is necessary. Use of an adaptive device serves only to simplify the task in some way; it does not teach the student. Instructional programs that delineate systematic cueing and fading strategies should be designed and implemented.

Figure 8.2.   Magazine/book holder. (Developed by Jennifer York and Jo-Ann Schaidle.)

Modifying the Physical and Social Environments   The final category of adaptations, modifying the physical and social environments, includes changes such as making entryways to buildings accessible, rearranging furniture to create space for maneuvering a wheelchair, modifying public transportation vehicles, and creating space for wheelchairs to be positioned in movie theaters. An inventory of environmental modifications and examples can be found in Nordic Committee on Disability (1985) and Orelove and Hanley (1979). Such adaptations are encountered frequently in general education classes and vocational and domestic situations. Some examples include: rearranging desks so that wheelchairs can be maneuvered around them, rearranging bedroom furniture so that a wheelchair can be maneuvered close to at least one side of the bed; installing a sink that does not have a cabinet underneath so that a person who uses a wheelchair can be close enough to use the sink; and lowering a work surface so that a person seated in a wheelchair can work at a comfortable height.

Adapting the social environment to promote positive interdependence among classmates is being used to an increasing degree in classrooms that include students with multiple disabilities. A variety of peer support strategies for facilitating interactions among classmates with and without labels are presented in Stainback and Stainback (1990).

EXAMPLES OF DOMESTIC, RECREATION/ LEISURE, AND VOCATIONAL ADAPTATIONS

This section of the chapter provides examples of adaptations, specifically adaptive devices. The devices were developed by public school personnel in educational programs serving students with severe disabilities in Urbana, Illinois; Madison, Wisconsin; and Mansfield, Connecticut. Most were designed for use by specific students. The examples are simple and are intended to provide readers with ideas for adaptive devices that may enhance the participation of persons with disabilities elsewhere. However, appropriate use of these adaptations requires individual consideration of student needs and environmental demands. Most of the adaptive devices were developed to compensate for motoric and intellectual difficulties. For organizational purposes, the adaptation examples are categorized as domestic, recreation/leisure, and vocational adaptations, but they could be used in a variety of school, home, and community environments.

Domestic Adaptations

Pouring Adaptation   The pouring adaptation shown in Figure 8.3 was constructed with Plexiglas, a plastic pitcher, a wire hanger for the handle, and a metal band. It was made for a high school student to use during meal preparation. The student was able to flex and extend his left elbow slightly, approximately 30 degrees. The pouring adaptation was placed on his wheelchair tray so that the extended handle of the pitcher hooked around his forearm. After a

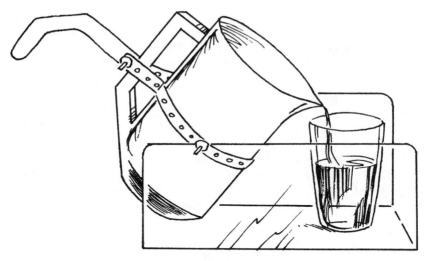

Figure 8.3. Pouring adaptation. (Developed by Nancy Caldwell.)

peer placed a glass on the plastic base of the adaptation, the student bent his arm, thereby pushing up on the handle, tipping the pitcher, and causing liquid to pour into the glass. He learned to judge when the glass was full and then relaxed his arm to right the pitcher.

Plate and Glass Holder The plate and glass holder shown in Figure 8.4 was made from wood and is covered with nonslip material. It was made for a

Figure 8.4. Plate and glass holder. (Developed by Nancy Caldwell.)

high school student to enable independent eating. The student demonstrated large, sweeping arm movement but had difficulty coordinating hand-to-mouth movement and bilateral hand use. The square surface of the adaptation was covered with a nonslip mat, and he learned to scoop his food independently and bring it to his mouth. The student's glass was placed in the cutout hole. The straw extended far enough that the student could lean his head and trunk forward, then close his mouth around the straw to drink. Previous attempts to teach bringing the glass to his mouth with his hand were unsuccessful and frustrating. The adaptation compensated for inadequate upper extremity and head coordination. Independence increased dramatically.

Spoon Splint and Plate Wedge Adaptations   The spoon splint and plate wedge shown in Figure 8.5 were used by a 4-year-old boy who demonstrated only fair control of full elbow flexion and near full extension. Range of motion

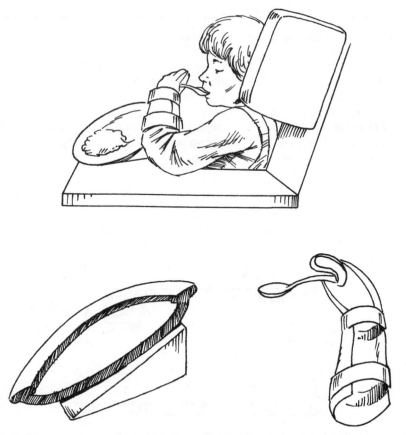

Figure 8.5.   Spoon splint and plate wedge adaptations. (Developed by Jennifer York.)

at his shoulders, elbows, wrists, and fingers was limited because of slight webbing (i.e., tight skin at the joints). The spoon splint was formed with plastic splinting material, and a spoon was molded into the splint under the palm area. The spoon protruded between the student's thumb and index finger. It was bent and angled to maximize the amount of food that could be scooped independently and remain on the spoon as it was moved to the mouth. The splint was secured at the upper forearm and wrist with narrow foam straps attached to Velcro on the splint. The plate wedge was made from cardboard and covered with nonslip material. The wedge angle was steep enough for the student to use vertical arm movement almost exclusively. Horizontal movement in toward the body was extremely difficult for this student and was minimized by use of these adaptations. The student learned to combine vertical forearm movement and forward head movement to achieve success and greater efficiency with placing food into his mouth.

Sandwich Clip   Illustrated in Figure 8.6 is a sandwich clip made for a 4-year-old girl who had only one finger on each hand. The child was unable to hold a sandwich, cookie, or other finger foods in her hand. Commercial sandwich clips proved unsatisfactory. Devising an alternative involved securing a large tension binder clip to a wooden platform. A butterfly barrette (hair clip) was held in the jaws of the binder clip and functioned as the sandwich clip or holder for other food. The sandwich clip was made removable for washing. An adult continued to provide assistance by placing the food item in the clip, but the child could eat the food independently by leaning forward to take a bite.

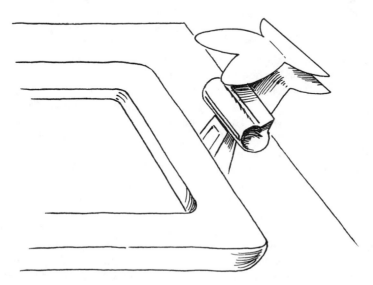

Figure 8.6.   Sandwich clip. (Developed by Barbara Williams and Debra Kohrs.)

Figure 8.7.   Extended-handle duster mounted to wheelchair. (Developed by Nancy Caldwell.)

Extended-Handle Duster Mounted to Wheelchair   The extended-handle duster shown in Figure 8.7 was mounted on the abductor of the wheelchair of a high school student. To extend the handle, a dowel rod was secured to the handle of an ordinary duster. (The student who used this duster also used the pouring adaptation described previously.) After positioning the student in the wheelchair and in front of a hard, flat surface (e.g., tables, counters, shelves) in need of dusting, the teacher adjusted the angle of the duster so it exerted slight pressure on the surface. The student then alternated pushing each side of the handle, causing the duster to move laterally over the surface to remove dust. The duster was used in home environments.

Dusting Mitt   The dusting mitt shown in Figure 8.8 was a very simple adaptation sewn of soft cloth with a Velcro closure that could be fastened across the palm or wrist. The dusting mitt was used by several high school students who had difficulty simultaneously holding onto a dust cloth and moving their arms in a dusting motion. Prior to use of the mitt, common problems were scrunching the dust cloth into a ball in the hand, leaving insufficient cloth protruding to dust with, and excessive muscle tension throughout the arm as a result of maintaining a fisted hand.

Toothpaste and Toothbrush Holder   Illustrated in Figure 8.9 is a toothpaste and toothbrush holder that was used by a high school student who had functional use of one arm only. The muscles in her other arm were contracted in a totally flexed position and she could not use that arm to assist in daily activities. The holder rested on the side of a sink. On the board was a rubber band that crossed over and secured a tube of toothpaste and a toothbrush. With the

Figure 8.8. Dusting mitt. (Developed by Nancy Caldwell.)

toothpaste tube secured, the student unscrewed the cap and pushed on the tube until a small amount of toothpaste protruded. Next, she removed the toothbrush and brushed its bristles over the protruding toothpaste. After brushing her teeth, the student rinsed her toothbrush and replaced it under the rubber band; she then screwed the cap back onto the toothpaste tube. Using of this adaptation required use of only one arm for the entire toothbrushing sequence.

    Toothpaste Pump Adaptation The introduction of toothpaste pumps to the general public has unintentionally assisted persons who have difficulty with fine movements of their hands. Figure 8.10 shows one such toothpaste pump that was screwed onto a piece of wood to prevent tipping. In addition, a thin piece of wood with a notch cut at one end was attached so that depressing the lever would place pressure on the push knob, thereby dispensing toothpaste. This adaptation was used by persons who demonstrated only gross arm movement.

    Hinged Tray The hinged tray is an adaptation attached to one armrest of a wheelchair (Figure 8.11). With the assistance of a local metalworking expert, a Plexiglas tray was mounted along one armrest using heavy piano hinges. The piano hinge allowed the tray to be lifted up from a horizontal position across the armrests and moved in a 270 degree arc to rest against the rim of one wheel. Prior to the development of this particular hinged tray, the only skill that prevented a high school student from total independence using restrooms was his inability to remove, then replace, his wheelchair tray. His tray was necessary for positioning purposes and because it held his communication board.

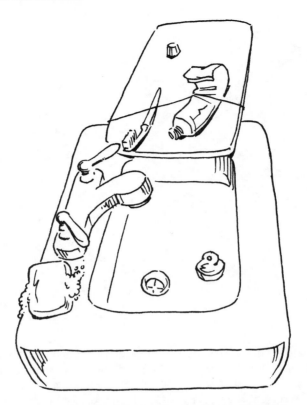

Figure 8.9.   Toothpaste and toothbrush holder. (Developed by Jennifer York.)

Prolonged removal of the tray, therefore, was not a reasonable option. The student required only a few weeks of instruction on removing and replacing the hinged tray. Most of the instruction was directed at teaching controlled lowering of the tray to the side of the wheelchair, instead of the student releasing the tray from its highest point and watching it crash into the side of the wheelchair.

Recreation/Leisure Adaptations

Needlework Holder   The needlework holder illustrated in Figure 8.12 was made of wood. Its width was adjustable to accommodate varying canvas or mesh dimensions. The mounting angle for the needlework was adjustable also. It was constructed for a junior high school student who demonstrated some functional use of her left arm but whose fine motor skills and rate were poor. The right arm could be relaxed and the elbow and forearm positioned on the wheelchair tray or table, allowing the student to lean on the arm to increase support. The student learned to keep her trunk forward and to lean on her right forearm independently. This placed her body in an efficient and stable position

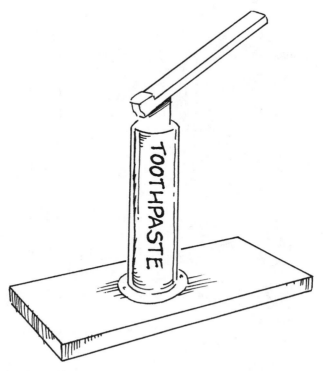

Figure 8.10.   Toothpaste pump adaptation. (Developed by Nancy Caldwell.)

in which with her left arm she could use the needle with reasonable control and efficiency. Initially, a mesh with large holes and rug yarn were used. Most of the resulting needlework projects were abstract and unique (i.e., wherever the student managed to place the needle through the mesh, the yarn was pulled through). When supervised closely, however, the student could place the needle more accurately in accordance with the colors on a mesh with a printed design.

Magazine/Book Holder   The magazine/book holder illustrated in Figure 8.2 and briefly discussed earlier was initially made for a 5-year-old girl who loved books. It was made of cardboard and ½ inch wide elastic straps to hold the books. The girl enjoyed looking through books and listening to the stories read by her peers, parents, or a teacher. She demonstrated full range, but uncontrolled, rigid, sweeping movements of both arms. There was no functional arm use. To use the holder, she was positioned in her wheelchair with her head totally supported in a neck collar support, and her wheelchair tray raised to give support to both arms. The magazine/book holder was made to hold books upright so that the student could see the material without looking down and losing control of her head position. She was taught to reach toward and push the right side of the book with her left hand. Then, she pushed against the book to

Figure 8.11.   Hinged tray. (Developed by Jane Barry and Jennifer York.)

achieve stability of her arm and turned pages by sliding her hand to the left, pulling a page along with this arm movement.

Card Holder   The card holder illustrated in Figure 8.13 was simply a 12-inch piece of 2 × 4 wood with a deep groove cut down the middle. With the same design but a wider groove, this adaptation was also used to hold needle-work projects that were purchased with the frames already in place.

Remote Control Car Adaptation   The remote control car and its control unit illustrated in Figure 8.14 were adapted for use by a 4-year-old boy who was able to fully flex and partially extend his left elbow. (This is the same student who used the spoon splint and plate wedge adaptation described previously.) The control unit lever was simply extended with a ¼-inch dowel rod attached with plastic splinting material. The student was positioned in a kneeler that was made for his body dimensions. The control unit was placed on a low and narrow table in front of him. In this stable, upright kneeling position, the student demonstrated an adequate amount of controlled elbow flexion and extension to push the lever. A particularly nice feature of this control unit was that it could be locked into one of three operating modes. One mode allowed the car to go only

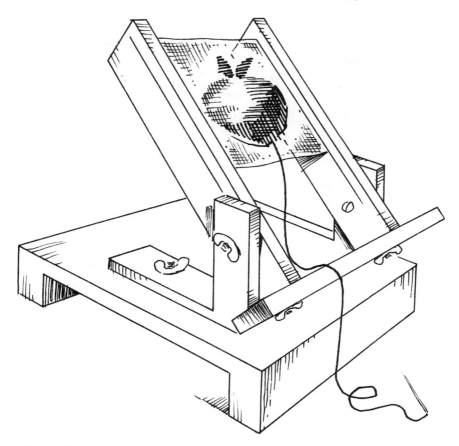

Figure 8.12.   Needlework holder. (Developed by Jennifer York and Rod Ivey.)

straight (forward or backward). Another mode allowed the car to go around in circles only. The third mode freed the car to go in whatever direction the lever was pushed. The straight or circle modes enabled the child to play independently for a longer time because the area in which the car could run had definite boundaries; in the free direction mode, it was not long before a peer needed to rescue the trapped car from a remote area of the room.

Pulley Adaptation   The pulley adaptation illustrated in Figure 8.15 was made of a wooden base, metal rod, plastic cup, rope, pulley, and cotton straps to attach the adaptation to the user's forearm and hand. It was made for a junior high school student who learned to isolate controlled elbow flexion, then to relax back to a natural position without her entire body becoming tense. The cuff was attached around her wrist and palm. When she flexed her elbow the string was pulled and the contents of the cup were dumped. Initially, the student

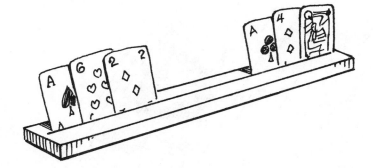

Figure 8.13.   Card holder. (Developed by Rod Ivey.)

Figure 8.14.   Remote control car adaptation. (Developed by Jennifer York.)

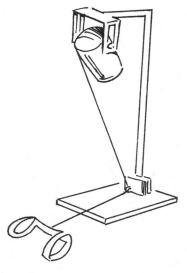

Figure 8.15.   Pulley adaptation. (Developed by Cheryl Moran-Behrens and Rod Ivey.)

used the pulley adaptation to throw dice. During cooking, the standard cup could be replaced with a measuring cup, so that after appropriate amounts of ingredients were measured into the cup, pulling on the string would dump the ingredients into a mixing bowl.

Grasping Mitten   Illustrated in Figure 8.16 is a grasping mitten that was made for a 4-year-old boy to use during a music class. Tracing the boy's hand produced a pattern for the mitten. A heavy-weight cotton fabric was used to construct the mitten and a T-shaped strap was sewn into the tip of the mitten. The mitten was placed on the student's hand, in which there was an item to be held. The fingers, inside the mitten, were passively flexed around the item and then maintained in a whole hand grasp by the strap being secured around the wrist. This particular student demonstrated no active muscle control for grasping. Use of this adaptation allowed him to participate in a regular kindergarten music class. He also used this adaptation to maintain a grasp on a joystick during initial training to operate a power wheelchair.

Wheelchair Putter   The wheelchair putter shown in Figure 8.17 was designed for the many children in wheelchairs at a local miniature golf course, who received total physical assistance to tee off. Very little active participation was possible for them. At this writing this adaptation is very new and has not yet actually been used at a miniature golf course. For the students who were unable to lean forward far enough to use a putter while seated in their wheelchairs, this adaptation may be useful. A spring clamp or regular metal clamp (used to hang brooms, rakes, or ski poles) was obtained from a local hardware

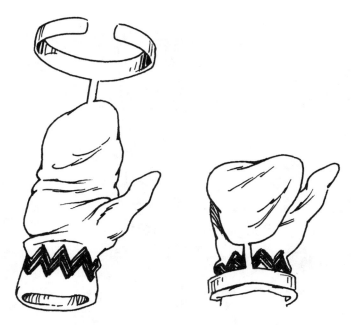

Figure 8.16.   Grasping mitten.

store. This was attached to the metal tubing of the wheelchair arm with a hose clamp. The putter was placed into the spring clamp and could move backward and forward with slight pushing on the handle. This adaptation may allow some children the opportunity to tee off more independently. However, peers may need to complete the putting for each hole, because it is difficult to maneuver wheelchairs on the putting greens.

Microswitch Mounts for Sidelying and Sitting   A common difficulty with the use of microswitches is mounting them securely but also in such a way that daily variability in a child's ability to control movement can be accommodated. Figure 8.18 shows two ways that microswitches were positioned to enable independent access to and control of a microswitch by two students. Figure 8.18a shows a 6-year-old boy who had very low underlying muscle tone and whose only arm movement was uncontrolled, rigid crossed extension with hands fisted. In a sidelying position, however, the student learned to control elbow flexion and extension of his lower arm (i.e., the arm that was very stable because of bearing the weight through the shoulder girdle). The microswitch that was used by this student required only slight pressure to push. It was mounted on its edge so that the push panel was perpendicular to the surface of the sidelyer. Mounted in this way, the student had only to slide his arm along the surface of the sidelyer to push the switch; no lifting the arm against gravity was necessary. During free time, the student chose a switch-operated toy he wished

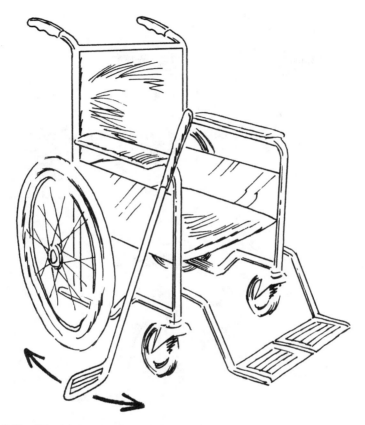

Figure 8.17.   Wheelchair putter. (Developed by Jennifer York.)

to operate by looking at the preferred item; he then proceeded to manipulate the toy through the switch as described above.

Figure 8.18b shows a microswitch that was mounted from the back of a chair made for a 4-year-old boy. Standard microphone equipment (e.g., a gooseneck, mounting flange, and microphone holder, all available at local radio equipment stores) was used. The microswitch was placed into the microphone holder and, because of the flexibility of the gooseneck, could be placed to the left or the right of the student's head. The student was placed in a supported sitting position with a neck collar supporting his head. He learned to drop his head slightly to the side to push the switch.

Vocational Adaptations

Stapling Adaptation   Illustrated in Figure 8.19 is a stapling adaptation that was first described by Nisbet et al. (1983). The adaptation was made of a

a

b

Figure 8.18. Microswitch mounting for (a) sidelying and (b) sitting positions. (Developed by Jennifer York.)

moveable tray that held letter-size paper and was mounted on a wooden base. An electric stapler was placed at the far end of the tray. Papers to be stapled were placed in the tray, which kept the pages collated and aligned appropriately. When pushed, the tray moved forward causing the top, left-hand corners of the papers to be inserted into the electric stapler, resulting in a staple being discharged. A spring was mounted under the tray so that the tray returned to its resting position after being pushed and released. This adaptation was made for a high school student for use at a community work site. The student demonstrated no purposeful arm movement but did occasionally move her arms ran-

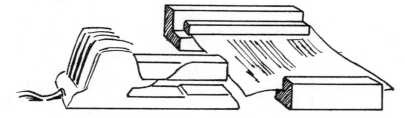

Figure 8.19. Stapling adaptation. (Developed by Alice Udvari-Solner.)

domly. A teacher, assistant, or another student placed papers to be stapled in the tray, and the student learned to push in the tray with firm, controlled movement. As the staple discharged, the adaptation provided immediate feedback to the student regarding the movement.

Stamping Adaptation   Illustrated in Figure 8.20 is a stamping adaptation that was developed for use by a middle school student to stamp brochures at a travel agency. Prior to development of this adaptation, the student learned to reach and hold a handle extended from a self-inking stamp, but was unable to apply sufficient pressure to stamp. The stamping adaptation shown here was made from Plexiglas. The top piece, to which the actual stamp was secured, was attached by two hinges to the base. The resting position for the adaptation was with the stamp raised. Very little pressure was required to depress the stamp onto the brochure. The two pieces of Plexiglas located on the base of the adaptation could be moved to form a guide to slide brochures of varying sizes into place to be stamped. The stamp position was adjustable also.

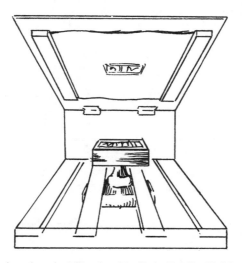

Figure 8.20. Stamping adaptation. (Developed by Kathy Zanella Albright.)

Collating Adaptation   The collating adaptation illustrated in Figure 8.21 employed use of two microswitches. It was made from Plexiglas, two lever microswitches, a metal track, and a control unit. The top part consisted of one tray divided into two compartments. The left compartment held the first page to be collated; the right compartment contained the second page. The top tray was mounted onto the base in two horizontal tracks. The tray could slide laterally in these tracks. One lever microswitch was placed under each compartment of the top tray and each was wired to the control unit located behind the device.

The collating adaptation was designed by a vocational teacher who was responsible for developing a community work site for a 21-year-old student with quite severe intellectual and physical disabilities. The student had to remain lying on his back in a reclined wheelchair for health reasons. His one reliable movement (besides that of opening and closing his mouth) was extension and flexion of his right elbow. The student wore a forearm and hand splint to keep his wrist near neutral and to prevent his fingers from curling into his palm.

In order to pick up the pages to be collated, Plasti-Tac (a sticky, putty type material) was placed on the tip of his hand splint. The collating procedure learned by the student was as follows: 1) extend the elbow so Plasti-Tac lands on the paper in the left compartment; 2) flex the elbow, thereby pulling the top page off the pile; 3) wait for the paper to fall off the splint onto the table in front of the device; 4) extend the elbow to press firmly over the microswitch under the left compartment; 5) flex the elbow and wait for tray to slide to the left (pushing of the microswitch resulted in the tray being moved by a chain through the horizontal tracks); repeat steps one through five for the second page. The ability of this student to collate afforded him the opportunity to work in the community for several mornings a week upon graduation from school. Otherwise, he would have remained home.

Figure 8.21.   Collating adaptation. (Developed by Alice Udvari-Solner.)

Bagging Adaptation   The bagging adaptation shown in Figure 8.22 was made for a high school student to use in the pharmacy department of a local hospital. The bottom section was a rectangular piece of pegboard with solid wood sides. Mounted on the pegboard were three sets of vertical metal rods with alligator clips welded at the top of each (only one pair of rods is illustrated in the figure). A plastic bag was clipped open between each pair of rods. A funnel attachment extended vertically from the end of the top section as illustrated. An opened bag was aligned under the funnel in a position to receive items that fell through the funnel. Metal drawer glides were mounted in the base to allow the pegboard section to slide laterally. The black handle was used to move the pegboard laterally to position the bags under the funnel.

The student who learned the bagging activity demonstrated gross arm movements and unrefined grasp and release. A variety of items were bagged (e.g., sodium chloride packets and plastic syringes). Each was bagged in groups of 30. (Another student with disabilities arranged the items in groups of 10 by placing one item in each compartment of a cardboard adaptation that had 10 divisions. Once this cardboard container was filled, all the items were removed and placed in one box. The student filled three of these boxes, making 30 items that were then bagged by the student using the bagging adaptation.)

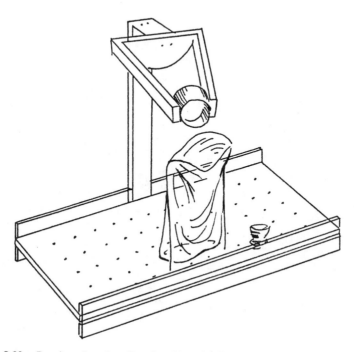

Figure 8.22.   Bagging adaptation. (Developed by Alice Udvari-Solner.)

The student using the bagging adaptation grabbed a handful of items from the first box of 10 and placed them in the funnel. The items then fell into the opened bag. This continued until all three boxes of 10 items (e.g., 30 items) were bagged. The student then pulled on the black handle until the next open bag was moved into place under the funnel. The bagging procedure continued until all three bags were full. The teacher then removed and sealed the bags and placed three more empty bags in the clips for filling.

Coffee Bagging Adaptation   The coffee bagging adaptation shown in Figure 8.23 is a funnel made of flexible sheet metal to which a hook was attached to the back and a clip attached to the bottom. The funnel was hooked onto the coffee bin as illustrated. A plastic bag was clipped open under the funnel. This adaptation was used by a junior high school student at a local bakery and health food store. She was not able to hold open the plastic bag and simultaneously scoop coffee, so the adaptation was made to require scooping only. The student stood in front of the coffee bin and scooped coffee beans into the funnel. She learned to stop scooping when the funnel began backing up. This indicated the bag was full, at which point she was assisted to remove and close the bag.

Plant Watering Adaptation   The plant watering adaptation illustrated in Figure 8.24 was made of wood, various pieces of hardware, a plastic watering

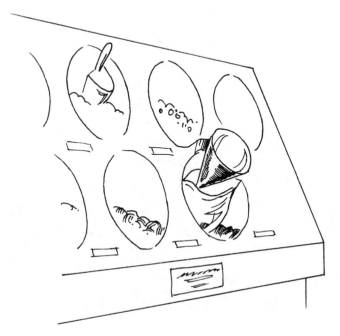

Figure 8.23.   Coffee bagging adaptation. (Developed by Renee Reif.)

can, and cord. The base of the adaptation extended the width of a wheelchair to clamp to the armrests. The same clamps used to secure trays to armrests were used here. A small triangular platform was added to the right side of the base to provide a place for the student using the device to stabilize her right elbow. A piece of wood extended vertically from the base and another piece extended horizontally from the top of this piece, forming an inverted "L" off the base. To this extension the watering can was attached in such a way that it was allowed to swing. A cord was attached to the front part of the watering can. On the other end of the rope was a 2-inch-wide cuff that was secured with Velcro around the wrist of the student using the device.

A student in junior high school used the device to water plants at the public library two afternoons each week. The student sat in the wheelchair with her right elbow supported on the triangle base and the cuff secured on her wrist. She was pushed through the library and learned to turn her head to identify the plants that she was responsible for watering. Once the plants were identified,

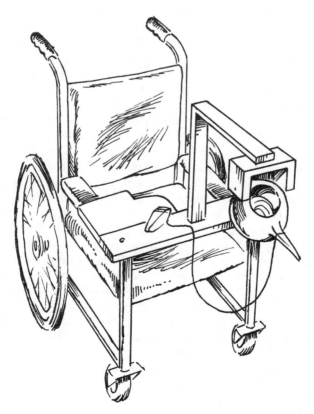

Figure 8.24.   Plant watering adaptation. (Developed by Jennifer York and Rod Ivey.)

the student's instructor would place the plant under the watering can. The student then pulled back on the rope by flexing her right elbow. This caused the can to tip and water to be poured onto the plant.

After a suggestion from the student's mother, use of a water meter to determine whether plants, in fact, needed to be watered was initiated. Although this student had never learned colors or numbers, she learned through this job that when the meter needle was on black, she pulled back the rope and held momentarily. This resulted in a large amount of water being poured. When the meter needle was on red, she pulled back then relaxed immediately, resulting in a small amount of water being poured. When the meter needle was on green, she did not water the plant. These were discriminations previously thought too difficult for the student to learn.

CONSIDERATIONS FOR USING ADAPTATIONS

There are numerous factors that team members should consider carefully before determining which adaptations should actually be used by individual students (Baumgart et al., 1982; Nisbet et al., 1983; York, Nietupski, & Hamre-Nietupski, 1985). First, use of an adaptation should increase *active participation* in an activity. This is important for many reasons. Active participation can increase responsibility, foster development of age-appropriate attitudes, and increase self-esteem. Increased active participation also can change the perceptions of students with disabilities that are held by persons who do not have disabilities. For example, active participation of students with disabilities in general education classroom routines and activities fosters perception of the students as doing the best they can do and making a contribution. Using an adaptation to achieve active participation without assistance from an adult can increase the opportunity for interaction with classmates. Adults assigned to support students in general education classrooms sometimes inhibit interactions between the student and classmates or even the classroom teacher (York, Vandercook, Heise-Neff, & Caughey, 1990). Postschool functioning in integrated community environments may occur more frequently if students learn partial participation and positive interdependence during their school years. If the goal of community integration for all persons with disabilities is to be achieved, the responsibility cannot rest solely on paid human services support personnel. During the school years, therefore, educational teams must systematically plan for more interdependent participation of students with disabilities with peers who do not have identified disabilities. Use of adaptations can be a tool for promoting interdependence.

A second consideration when contemplating use of an adaptation is *preference*. Would use of an adaptation allow a student to engage in an activity that he or she enjoys or finds interesting? Would use of an adaptation increase participation in activities that are preferred, enjoyed, or highly valued by family members and peers? Every effort should be made to facilitate participation in preferred, age-appropriate, and family activities. Students who have opportunities to indicate and engage in preferred activities sometimes enter into the learning process with greater enthusiasm. For example, for one student who was taught to choose preferred audiotapes and to activate the tapes with a microswitch, sharing this preferred musical activity with classmates was the highlight of her school day.

A third consideration is the anticipated *longitudinal use* of an adaptation. Will it be used in future as well as in current environments? Will the adaptation remain age-appropriate? For example, using the magazine/book holder, described earlier in the chapter, could remain appropriate throughout life if reading or browsing materials were changed in accordance with changing interests and age. However, an adaptation designed to assist a 2-year-old child to stack blocks would not remain age appropriate.

A fourth consideration concerns the amount of *instructional time* required for teaching the student to use the adaptation compared to the amount of time that might be required to teach participation *without* use of an adaptation. Sometimes team members resort to use of an adaptation before carefully considering or systematically implementing unadapted participation options. If, within a reasonable period of time, a student could learn to engage in an activity without using an adaptation, then the student should be taught to engage in the activity directly, and no adaptation should be used. Failure in direct approaches, however, would indicate the need to consider use of adaptations.

Fifth, *design and construction* characteristics are another consideration. Some adaptation ideas require more technical expertise than the team has. Is the design of an adaptation so complex or are the construction requirements so time-consuming that months will pass before the adaptation is developed? Will frequent repairs be likely? Complex adaptations have a greater likelihood of breakdown. Broken equipment can delay teaching students the skills that will enhance participation in home, school, and community environments.

A sixth consideration must be the *physical movement demands* required to use an adaptation. Some physical movements (e.g., excessive, rigid extension of the arm), if used to activate adaptations, can ultimately result in more restricted movement and loss of function. However, if using an adaptation promotes more efficient movement patterns, the likelihood of developing contractures and deformities is reduced, and long-term functional maintenance increased. Use of an adaptation sometimes can reduce the physical demands of an activity and enable the individual to move with greater ease and efficiency.

Given the characteristics and abilities of each individual student and the wide range of instructional priorities, the influence of each of the above considerations in the adaptation decision-making process will vary. Discussions regarding appropriate use of adaptations require active participation from parents, teachers, therapists, classmates, and others to ensure careful consideration of many factors. Appropriate decisions result from the expertise of all educational team members.

PRECAUTIONS FOR USING ADAPTATIONS

Precautions for the use of adaptations have been suggested by several authors (Baumgart et al., 1982; Davis, 1981; York et al., 1985) and are summarized here. First, perhaps the most common misuse of adaptations results from their mere existence. That is, because a particular adaptation exists or because it was successful and appropriate for one student, team members overgeneralize its use to other students for whom use is inappropriate. For example, the introduction of microswitches as valuable instructional tools has resulted in the overuse of microswitches to activate, for example, tape players. Many children can learn to operate tape players using a finger, toe, or pencil to depress the buttons, or pushing a tongue depressor that is extended from the buttons (York et al., 1985). Microswitches are unnecessary and, therefore, inappropriate in such cases. Furthermore, when microswitches are necessary, team members should consider that not all children need or can use the same type. There are many different microswitches, each requiring a different type of movement for activation. Also, not all children enjoy music, or the same music as their peers, or listening to the same songs throughout a week of instruction. During leisure time, some children may prefer listening to a talking book, watching battery-powered games and toys, or operating a slide projector to view slides of the family vacation. The use of any adaptation must be considered individually, based on the abilities of the student, preferences for activities, and specific demands of the activity.

A second precaution concerns the critical need for systematic instruction when using adaptations. Individualized adaptations do not replace the need for instruction. Just as placing a student in a sidelyer is not instruction, neither is providing a student with an adaptive device. One student for whom use of the magazine/book holder adaptation was appropriate required months of instruction using a mouthstick to become efficient at turning pages. Similarly, Maloney and Kurtz (1982) and Walmsey, Crichton, and Droog (1981) reported that proficiency in activating a microswitch to play music using efficient movement patterns required ongoing instruction. Adaptations are one means by which performance is enhanced and dependence is decreased. However, most students will require direct instruction to learn appropriate use of an adaptation.

A third precaution is to engage in ongoing evaluation of student performance with and without an adaptation. This will help ensure that appropriate decisions regarding the long-term use of an adaptation are made. Adaptations may be required for only short periods of time until student abilities improve. For example, if a student's arm and hand movement improves so that direct activation (i.e., without use of a microswitch) of a tape player is possible, the microswitch should be removed. Similarly, if a student learns to turn magazine pages independently, demonstrating controlled arm movement, the magazine/book holder adaptation should be removed. Adaptations must be modified, replaced, or eliminated based on changes in student abilities and/or task requirements.

A final precaution aimed at reducing frustration for team members and students is to expect that adaptations will require several modifications before an efficient match of student abilities and task demands is attained. Very rarely does the initial adaptation prove most functional. An example is the plant watering adaptation illustrated in Figure 8.24, which underwent more than 10 modifications over at least a 6-month period of time before optimal efficiency was attained.

ADAPTATION RESOURCES

Local Community Resources

Numerous local community resources can be invaluable in the design and construction of adaptive devices. Most average-size towns have professionals with expertise in the use of plastic, metal, wood, electronics, and upholstery. Frequently, these individuals can construct adaptive devices at a fraction of commercial cost and much more efficiently than educational team members. A situation involving one of the authors illustrates this point well. A 20-year-old man required a wheelchair tray hinged to one armrest that he could remove by lifting up the tray from one side, then lowering it alongside the wheelchair. (This hinged tray, illustrated in Figure 8.11, was discussed briefly earlier in this chapter.) Commercially available hinge mounting equipment was expensive and was not durable enough to withstand the repeated tray removal and twisting that occurred when the student was upset. This harsh use of the tray resulted in the metal being bent and the joint weakened. After many months of attempts at modification by several team members, a local metalworking company was contacted. The problem was described and the existing equipment was shown to one of the metal experts, who recommended that heavyweight metal piano hinges that extended the entire length of the tray be used. The expert reconstructed and mounted the hinge joint, which resulted in a more durable and functional tray. The process took about 2 hours and a nominal fee was charged. In the process of working with this metal expert, school staff learned that he had been involved previously with modifying wheelchairs. He designed and constructed fenders to prevent mud, rain, or snow from spraying onto the clothes of persons using the wheelchairs. He was a creative individual, quite willing and interested in providing expertise and, of course, developing a new clientele.

The time involved in the construction of devices can be minimized greatly if appropriate expertise and tools are available. In many situations it is more time- and cost-efficient to contract with local experts instead of purchasing all the necessary equipment required for construction and spending countless hours learning to use it proficiently.

A material that is very useful in adaptation development, particularly for constructing initial models, is Tri-wall cardboard. Tri-wall is a very sturdy material made of three layers of cardboard. It can be purchased in large sheets, approximately 3 feet by 4 feet. It is much less expensive than wood and working with it requires only basic design knowledge and the skills of using an Exacto knife, a saw, and glue. Tri-wall can be obtained through the central supply stores in many school districts. Workshops in the design and construction of devices and equipment using Tri-wall cardboard are available. In addition, several written resources are available on this subject (see Bergen & Colangelo, 1982).

One more resource possibility available in some communities is school district and university students or staff. Occasionally, students from industrial arts, architecture, and other design curricula can be recruited to assist with adaptive devices to fulfill one of their design project requirements. Additionally, some universities, clinics, or businesses devote a percentage of time to providing various services to the community at large. For example, one university-based center was developed primarily to provide service and support to university students with physical or sensory disabilities. This center was expected to allocate 10% of its time for community service as well. Persons working at this center provided repair and maintenance service of wheelchairs for some school-age students and also allowed school personnel to borrow various equipment to use on a trial basis.

Educational service providers are encouraged to develop cooperative working relationships with local community resource personnel. The time expended doing so will yield benefits for students and staff. These interactions also provide an opportunity to educate community members about school programs.

Written Resources

In addition to local human resources, numerous written resources are available that provide useful information regarding adaptations. Davis (1981), Finnie (1975), and Robinault (1973) are sources for ideas on relatively simple adaptations for daily living, house care, and leisure activities. They also include lists of local and national resources. Campbell (1977, 1982) provides specific teaching and adaptation strategies for mealtime and dressing activities; she also includes a list of local and national resources. Clothing adaptations to make dressing easier for persons with limited postural and movement abilities are described by Bowar (1978) and Hoffman (1979). Bigge (1991) presents communication, self-care, house care, and recreation/leisure strategies and adaptations useful for persons whose primary disabilities are motoric in nature. Vocational adaptations are described and illustrated in Nisbet et al. (1983). Kangas (1988) developed an excellent bibliography of seating, positioning, mounting, and physical access resources. Additional resources for obtaining positioning and communication adaptations are presented in this book (Chapters 3 and 9, respectively). Also, the reference list for each chapter contains resources.

In the area of electronic devices, Webster, Cook, Tompkins, and Vanderheiden (1985) provide an overview of current technology available to assist persons with motoric, visual, and hearing difficulties. Adaptations to assist with mobility, conversation, writing, manipulation, and work are covered particularly well. Specifically related to the use of microswitches, Burkhart (1980, 1982) and Campbell, McInerney, and Middleton (1982) provide information about construction and related hardware. They also present guidelines for using the equipment in instructional situations. York et al. (1985) present a step-by-step decision-making process for use of microswitches as an adjunct to educational programming for students with multiple disabilities.

One more resource for adaptations is equipment companies and manufacturers. One can obtain catalogs that illustrate a wide variety of products by writing to each company or manufacturer. Persons interested are warned that in order to obtain products it may be necessary to order through a local medical supplier since some companies do not accept orders directly from individual consumers or will not process small orders. While many useful ideas can be gleaned from these resources, more economical, individualized versions often can meet the particular needs of an individual student in a specific situation.

CONCLUSION

The use of individualized adaptations provides a creative and useful tool in educational programming for students with multiple disabilities. Adaptations present a means for increasing the interdependence and ease with which students engage in age-appropriate and functional activities in normalized school, domestic, community, vocational, and recreation/leisure environments. Central to an adaptive instructional approach is an affirmative, problem-solving, and nonexclusionary orientation to educational service provision for all students. Team members are encouraged to adopt enthusiastically the philosophy inherent in the principle of partial participation and to be optimistic about the possibilities afforded to students through use of individualized adaptations. Appropriate use of adaptations can allow all children, regardless of their disabilities, to participate and be fully included in regular family, school, and community life. The degree of participation is limited only by the bounds of the collective creativity of members of the educational team.

REFERENCES

Baumgart, D., Brown, L., Pumpian, I., Nisbet, J., Ford, A., Sweet, M., Messina, R., & Schroeder, J. (1982). Principle of partial participation and individualized adaptations in educational programs for severely handicapped students. *Journal of The Association for the Severely Handicapped, 7*(2), 17–27.

Bergen, A., & Colangelo, C. (1982). *Positioning the client with central nervous system deficits*. Valhalla, NY: Valhalla Rehabilitation Publications.

Bigge, J.L. (1991). *Teaching individuals with physical and multiple disabilities* (3rd ed.). Columbus, OH: Charles E. Merrill.

Bowar, M.T. (1978). *Clothing for the handicapped: Fashion adaptations for adults and children*. Minneapolis: Sister Kenny Institute.

Brown, L., Branston-McLean, M., Baumgart, D., Vincent, L., Falvey, M., & Schroeder, J. (1979). Utilizing the characteristics of current and subsequent least restrictive environments as factors in the development of curricular content for severely handicapped students. *AAESPH Review, 4*(4), 407–424.

Brown, L., Falvey, M., Vincent, L., Kaye, N., Johnson, F., Ferrar-Parrish, P., & Gruenewald, L. (1980). Strategies for generating comprehensive, longitudinal, and chronological age appropriate individualized education programs for adolescent and young adult severely handicapped students. *Journal of Special Education, 14*(2), 199–215.

Brown, L., Shiraga, B., York, J., Zanella, K., & Rogan, P. (1984a). Ecological inventory strategies for students with severe handicaps. In L. Brown, M. Sweet, B. Shiraga, J. York, K. Zanella, P. Rogan, & R. Loomis (Eds.), *Educational programs for students with severe handicaps* (Vol. XIV, pp. 33–41). Madison: Madison Metropolitan School District.

Brown, L., Shiraga, B., York, J., Zanella, K., & Rogan, P. (1984b). The discrepancy analysis technique in programs for students with severe handicaps. In L. Brown, M. Sweet, B. Shiraga, J. York, K. Zanella, P. Rogan, & R. Loomis (Eds.). *Educational programs for students with severe handicaps* (Vol. XIV, pp. 43–47). Madison: Madison Metropolitan School District.

Burkhart, L. (1980). *Homemade battery powered toys and educational devices for severely handicapped children*. Millville, PA: Author.

Burkhart, L. (1982). *More homemade battery devices for severely handicapped children with suggested activities*. Millville, PA: Author.

Campbell, P. (1977). Daily living skills. In N. Haring (Ed.), *Developing effective individualized education programs for severely handicapped children and youth* (pp. 115–138). Washington, DC: Department of Heath, Education and Welfare.

Campbell, P. (1982). *Problem oriented approaches to feeding the handicapped child* (2nd ed.). Akron: Children's Hospital Medical Center of Akron.

Campbell, P., McInerny, W., & Middleton, M. (1982). *A manual of augmental sensory feedback devices for training severely handicapped students*. Akron: Children's Hospital Medical Center of Akron.

Davis, W.M. (1981). *Aids to make you able: Self help devices for the disabled*. New York: Beaufort Books.

Finnie, N.R. (1975). *Handling the young cerebral palsied child at home*. New York: E.P. Dutton.

Hoffman, A.M. (1979). *Clothing for the handicapped, the aged and other people with special needs*. Springfield, IL: Charles C Thomas.

Kangas, K. (1988). *Bibliography: Seating, positioning, mounting and physical access*. Harrisburg: Pennsylvania Assistive Device Center.

Maloney, F.P., & Kurtz, P.A. (1982). The use of a mercury switch head control device in profoundly retarded, multiply handicapped children. *Physical and Occupational Therapy in Pediatrics, 2*(4), 11–17.

Nisbet, J., Sweet, M., Ford, A., Shiraga, B., Udvari, A., York, J., Messina, R., & Schroeder, J. (1983). Utilizing adaptive devices with severely handicapped students. In L. Brown, A. Ford, J. Nisbet, M. Sweet, B. Shiraga, J. York, R. Loomis, & P. VanDeventer (Eds.), *Educational programs for severely handicapped students* (Vol. XIII, pp. 101–146). Madison: Madison Metropolitan School District.

Nordic Committee on Disability. (1985). *The more we do together: Adapting the environment for children with disabilities.* New York: World Rehabilitation Fund.

Orelove, F.P., & Hanley, C.D. (1979). Modifying school buildings for the severely handicapped: A school accessibility survey. *AAESPH Review, 4*(3), 219–236.

Robinault, I.P. (Ed.). (1973). *Functional aids for the multiply handicapped.* New York: United Cerebral Palsy Association.

Stainback, W., & William, S. (Eds.). (1990). *Support networks for inclusive schooling: Interdependent integrated education.* Baltimore: Paul H. Brookes Publishing Co.

Walmsey, R.P., Crichton, L., & Droog, D. (1981). Music as feedback for teaching head control to severely handicapped children: A pilot study. *Developmental Medicine and Child Neurology, 23,* 739–746.

Webster, J.G., Cook, A.M., Tompkins, W.J., & Vanderheiden, G.C. (1985). *Electronic devices for rehabilitation.* New York: John Wiley & Sons.

York, J., Nietupski, J., & Hamre-Nietupski, S. (1985). A decision making process for using microswitches. *Journal of The Association for Persons with Severe Handicaps, 10*(4), 214–223.

York, J., Vandercook, T., Heise-Neff, C., & Caughey, E. (June, 1990). Does an "integration facilitator" facilitate integration? *TASH Newsletter,* p. 4.

Chapter 9

Communication Skills

Communication is the complex process of information transfer that individuals use to influence the behavior of others. It includes writing, speech, gestures, facial expression, body language, physical contact, and many other modes of behavior. Communication skills are critical for developing and maintaining social relationships, learning, community living, and meeting almost all human needs.

This chapter includes information on assessing communication and teaching communication skills to children with multiple disabilities and their communication partners. It is based on five fundamental principles: 1) maximization, 2) functionality, 3) individualization, 4) mutuality, and 5) normalization. These principles are relevant to each of the topics included in this chapter.

The principle of maximization dictates that intervention should aim toward the greatest possible increase in the frequency of appropriate communication and the utilization of all modes available to the child. This means that initial emphasis should be placed on acquisition and building fluency rather than quality. Since each attempt at communication also provides an opportunity to learn, refinements can be made more easily after frequency is increased.

The principle of functionality requires a focus on social outcomes: This dimension of communication is sometimes referred to as pragmatics. Thus, concerns about *how* a person communicates are considered important only to the extent that they contribute to or interfere with the purpose of the communication.

The principle of individualization, a central theme in all areas of education of children with multiple disabilities, requires a unique assessment of each child and his or her environmental requirements, and it requires a consideration of the context in order to determine appropriate intervention and support. No single approach, mode, or device can be expected to be ideal for all children with multiple disabilities or all children in any other category.

The principle of mutuality recognizes that all communication requires at least two partners. Therefore, all assessment and intervention must be aimed at both partners and the social and physical contexts that surround their interaction. It may be possible to teach individual words or gestures in isolation, but making sounds and handshapes is not communication unless it occurs as a functional part of a dynamic interaction.

The principle of normalization implies that unless a particular modification can be justified by an unequivocal benefit to the individual, the patterns of communication common to other people in the community should be the ones taught to children with multiple disabilities. Although normalization is a principle that should be considered in every aspect of educational programs for children with multiple disabilities, there are two reasons why it is particularly relevant to communication. First, this principle interacts directly with the principle of mutuality. Unless people with disabilities learn to use forms of communication compatible with those used by other members of the community who are their potential communication partners, communication will be difficult or impossible. Second, intensive study of language and communication, particularly as used by people with disabilities, tends to focus on highly technical approaches to teaching language; these methods sometimes alienate educators from simpler and more natural approaches. This often leads to an artificial and counterproductive emphasis on pathology and the differences between communication for people with disabilities and other communicators. People with disabilities are often viewed as users of augmentative systems and electronic devices, while others are viewed as speech users. Such distinctions are artificial and simplistic. More important, they often lead away from the most productive and most natural approaches to communication.

All of the five principles have implications for the following example of a mother and daughter. Mandy uses alternative communication modes and augmentative systems. She wakes up to the sound of a voice from her clock radio (electronic communication aid) and receives information on the day's weather before deciding what to wear. She hugs her children (tactile mode) before giving them breakfast and telephones (augmentative device) her neighbor to verify carpool arrangements. On the way to work, she carries on a conversation with her colleagues (vocal mode) riding with her while honking the car horn (augmentative device) and gesturing (gestural mode) to other drivers. On arriving, she shows her new family pictures (graphic mode) to her secretary and starts work. During her work day, she will use pen and paper, computers, fax machines, and a number of other communication aids. She will also talk, gesture, smile, rearrange environmental cues (e.g., leave something on her boss's desk that needs urgent attention), make and break eye contact, and employ a wide range of communicative behavior. Some of her communication is deliberate;

some of it is quite unintentional but equally important and effective. She chooses which mode to use according to the functional requirements of the situation, and she would feel constrained by the loss of any of these modes of communication.

Mandy's daughter, Candi, has an intellectual disability and athetoid cerebral palsy. Because she can make only a few discriminable speech sounds and has poor finger control, the team of experts evaluating her communication prescribed a communication board (graphic) system and suggested focusing on the board as a sole mode of communication since they believed that Candi might be confused by exposure to a mixture of modes and systems. Like most children with multiple disabilities, Candi will never communicate as easily or proficiently as Mandy does, but her mental and physical disabilities may not be the greatest obstacle to her success.

The primary handicap that Candi faces in developing improved communication skills may be the rigid and artificial nature of the decisions guiding her training. Restricting her to a single mode of communication will place an unnecessary limitation on the size of her total communication repertoire, and, perhaps more important, it will ensure failure in functional areas that are poorly suited to graphic communication. Furthermore, it will likely reduce her frequency of communications by prohibiting some natural communication alternatives, and this reduction in frequency will reduce natural opportunities for her and her communication partners to learn. It seems absurd to imagine her mother trying to communicate about the physical appearance of her children by honking her car horn or holding up pictures to attract the attention of other drivers. Restricting her to any single communication mode, regardless of the communication context and function, would necessitate such obvious and ridiculous mismatches of mode and function. Nevertheless, the devastating effects of placing the same kind of restrictions on her daughter seem less obvious to the team of experts making this decision. Keeping the expectations for Candi's communication close to the normal expectations for her mother's communication might help avoid such counterproductive approaches to intervention. Decisions about how Candi communicates must consider her communication partners, the context, and, most important, the potential function of her communications.

COMMUNICATION FUNCTIONS

Pragmatics is the study of communication in a social context, emphasizing the functional nature of communication to achieve goals through social interaction (Donnellan, Mirenda, Mesaros, & Fassbender, 1984; Doss & Reichle, 1991). Thus, it is less concerned about the content (semantics) or form (syntax) of a message than about its effects on other people. The messages "Give me some soup," "That soup smells good," and "Do you have any extra soup?" are all different, but all of them may serve the same function (prompting the listener to give some soup). Some communications, called performatives, primarily direct social interactions (e.g., requesting attention or assistance), while others, called propositionals, primarily make declarative statements (e.g., naming objects), although these also must have some social component in order to be useful (Bates, Camaioni, & Voltera, 1979). Many communication programs for children with severe language deficits concentrate on propositional content (e.g., object labeling); however, the early communications of most children appear to lack propositional content and to be pure performatives (Greenfield & Smith, 1976). A pragmatic focus suggests that more emphasis on communication function (why children communicate) and structure (how children communicate) would result in faster and more relevant progress (MacDonald, 1985).

The discussion of the power of a child's communication behavior to control others might seem to imply that they preconceive the desired effects on their audiences and plan their communications to produce these effects. This would require intent prior to communication (illocution). Communication partners may be influenced by the child even before intent develops (perlocution). For example, the crying or smiling of infants may not be intended to make caregivers attend to their needs, but caregivers consistently respond to this behavior as if intent were present. Through these consistent responses, real intent eventually develops (MacDonald, 1985). Such interpretation of communicative intent and its role in developing communication skills suggests the power of the expectations of caregivers. When potential respondents in the child's environment assume intent, they react to communication and help develop language. When potential respondents assume the child lacks intent or the capacity to communicate and subsequently fail to respond, development of language is impeded. This means that caregivers' expectations of communication from children and consistent responses to possible attempts at communicating are critical to acquisition of functional language by children with severe and multiple disabilities.

Relatively little information is available regarding the communication functions of children with disabilities, and, to date, the most current information comes from data gathered on the development of infants who do not have disabilities (Leonard, 1984). Experience in other curricular areas with attempting to apply developmental models to individuals with severe or multiple disabilities suggests that great caution should be used when applying such information to these learners. Often, developmental sequences: 1) fail to correspond with the typical order in children with multiple disabilities, 2) fail to include age-appropriate skills for individuals with severe delays, and 3) lack functional value (Guess & Noonan, 1982). These potential difficulties, however, do not invalidate all developmental tasks. They simply require that developmentally generated goals and objectives be validated as age appropriate and functional in current and potential future environments. Since pragmatic communication acts are defined by their effects rather than by the forms of the behaviors, they typically have functional value (by definition) and can be acquired in an age-appropriate form. For example, attracting the attention of others is functional for everyone. Crying to receive attention is age appropriate for an infant but not for an adult. In the rare pragmatic assessments of communication among people with severe disabilities that have been published (Cirrin & Rowland, 1985; Owings, McManus, & Scherer, 1981), there is empirical support for the role of similar communications functions (e.g., requesting objects, protesting, asking for information). More research is needed in this area to further validate functions and to help determine the relative importance of specific functions. Although specific functional categories of communication have been proposed by many authors (e.g., Halliday, 1975; Karlan & Lloyd, 1983; McShane, 1980; Waterson & Snow, 1978), many functions identified by specific investigators have no precise equivalents in alternative communication systems, and no universal classification system exists.

An analysis of the communication functions of one 14-month-old child is illustrated in Table 9.1. This analysis is based on careful observation of the child and her communication partners. In addition to the function, information regarding mode (the general response category), form (the specific response), and content (a basic translation) is included. This child already has at least 10 communication functions, and several of these are expressed in more than one mode and form. It is important to note the diversity of modes used; limiting this child to a single mode (e.g., vocal) would severely restrict communication. It is also significant (and typical) that although this child is an active communicator, she can name only two items. Many language programs focus on naming objects; however, this skill may have little functional value to the beginning communicator when compared to more general communication acts (e.g., generalized attention or item requests).

Waterson and Snow (1978) report that the most common communication functions (in order of frequency) in a nondisabled infant (12–16 months old) were: 1) requesting items, 2) directing other's attention to objects, 3) calling attention to self, 4) requesting exchanges of objects, and 5) protesting situations. These five functions made up 94% of all communication acts. The only labels used were caregivers' names used to attract their attention. Cirrin and Rowland (1985) reported that the most common communication functions (in order of frequency) in a group of 15 nonverbal youths (10–18 years old) living in a facility for persons with mental retardation were: 1) requesting items, 2) requesting actions, 3) protesting, 4) directing attention to self, and 5) directing attention to communication. Again, these functions were typically produced without the use of object labels.

Further information on pragmatic functions is provided along with discussions of assessing and teaching communication skills, in the "Assessment, Planning, and Intervention" section of this chapter. Pragmatic functions pro-

Table 9.1 Language functions of a basic communicator

Function	Mode	Form	Content
Request attention	1. vocal 2. proximity 3. contact	1. "aaanhh" 2. moves closer 3. touch	(pay attention to me)
Request item or event (general)	1. gesture 2. vocal	1. open hand extended toward item 2. "mawh"	(give me)
Reject item or event (specific)	1. mixed 2. proximity	1. "na" plus horizontal head nod 2. moves away	(no/leave me alone/take it away)
Request information	1. mixed	1. touch (or point to) item plus "doht" with raised pitch	(what is that?)
Direct attention to object or event	1. mixed 2. environmental modification	1. point to or touch item or event plus "nuh" 2. bring object to respondent	(look at this/ listen to this)
Request event (specific)	1. vocal	1. "utt"	(pick me up/ take me out of this chair)
Initiation/greeting	1. gestural 2. vocal	1. wave 2. "hiyah"	(hello)
Name/label	1. vocal	1. "dawh" 2. "nana"	1. (dog) 2. (banana)
Turn-taking	1. gestural 2. vocal	1. imitates raising and lowering of hands 2. attempts to duplicate words	(my turn, your turn/do it again)
Reinforce	1. vocal 2. gestural 3. mixed	1. laughs 2. smiles imitates	(I like that/do it again)

vide essential guidance for determining what to teach and assist in planning how to teach it. Before covering these areas, however, some consideration of communication modes and systems may be helpful.

COMMUNICATION MODES AND SYSTEMS

Communication modes refer to general categories of behavior used to communicate. Vocal, gestural, and graphic modes have been identified as communication alternatives for children with multiple disabilities (Musselwhite & St. Louis, 1988; Silverman, 1980). Other modes include physical contact with the respondent, environmental modification, augmentative systems (often grouped within graphic systems but with distinct response requirements and output options), simultaneous modes (presenting the same parts of a message in two or more modes), and mixed modes (presenting different parts of a message in two or more modes). *Communication systems* refer to specific sets of responses used to communicate within a mode. For example, American Sign Language is a communication system in the gestural mode.

Although modes and systems might be considered for both reception and production of communication, more emphasis has traditionally been placed on production. Although greater consideration probably should be given to reception in communication intervention, data generally support the development of receptive skills that surpass productive skills (e.g., Leonard, 1984; Oviatt, 1980; Terrace, 1979), and direct instruction on production of signs was shown to lead to the emergence of reception of signs in an adult with multiple disabilities (Kleinert & Gast, 1982). In spite of these general assurances that current emphasis on production in training is justified, reception must be verified carefully in communication assessment. Intervention that considers both partners and the interactive process avoids the artificial isolation of reception and production in training (MacDonald, 1985).

Combining Modes

Before discussing individual modes, it may be helpful to consider the multimodal options. Vanderheiden and Lloyd (1986) recommended designing communication systems for people with disabilities that utilize a combination of the most accessible and effective graphic symbols. They suggest that dependence on a single communication strategy is limiting, and effective communicators must be able to adjust their communication strategy to the context. Elements from different specific systems within modes may be used in combination (e.g., photographs, PIC symbols, and Rebus symbols from within the graphic mode) in addition to combinations that use elements from different modes (e.g., photos from the graphic mode, pointing from the gestural mode, and words from the vocal mode). These combined modes can be categorized as simultaneous, mixed, or duplicated.

Simultaneous modes, which concurrently duplicate the same message in two individual modes, have been used with many children. For example, total communication (simultaneous speech and sign) has been used in training (Silverman, 1980). Its potential advantages include: 1) providing communication to both signers and listeners concurrently, 2) providing extra cues to interpretation when either speech or signing is not completely intelligible, and 3) providing more easily acquired signs to learners having difficulty with speech, while maintaining their exposure to speech and working toward its acquisition in the longer term. Unfortunately, empirical support for such advantages has been mixed (Mustonen, Locke, Reichle, Solback, & Lindgren, 1991). For example, total communication has been shown to have few advantages over signing without speech for children with autism (Carr & Dores, 1981; Remington & Clarke, 1983). The simultaneous mode probably has its greatest utility when used by teachers working with groups that include verbal and nonverbal students, and it may also be useful during initial training to help assess which of two modes a student responds to best.

Mixed modes use different modes for different communications or different parts of the same communication (e.g., vocalizing to attract attention and gesturing to obtain an object) (Mustonen et al., 1991). Although the possibility of combining modes is generally recognized, the fact that interventionists are encouraged to make decisions regarding modes before function and content decisions (e.g., Musselwhite & St. Louis, 1988; Shane & Bashir, 1980; Silverman, 1980) discourages use of mixed modes. Postponing the decision regarding mode until content is selected and making individual modal decisions for each communication objective encourages mixed modes. Bricker (1983) pointed out that early communication of persons who do not have disabilities typically has gestural and vocal components. Similarly, the data displayed in Table 9.1 reveal the use of several modes, the students with disabilities studied by Cirrin and Rowland (1985) used mixed modes, and casual observation of most communicators who do not have disabilities will reveal a similar mix. Reichle and Keogh (1986) pointed out the confusing and contradictory nature of decision-making rules for selecting modes, recommended mixed modes as the best alternative for most learners with severe disabilities, and suggested that mixed modes improve intelligibility. Similarly, MacDonald (1985) supported multiple modes because they: 1) allow intervention to begin at the current level of function; 2) allow intervention with every child; and 3) allow analysis of all current behavior, permitting access to current semantics and pragmatics. Thus, mixed modes allow the interventionist to take advantage of the full spectrum of behavior in the individual's repertoire. For children who can produce a limited number of discriminably different classes of response within different modes, using as many modes as possible greatly increases the number of items in their general repertoire. For example, if a child can vocalize three distinct words, form four signs, point to five pictures, and communicate two concepts through touch, this child can communicate 14 items by mixing modes.

Mixed modes also allow fitting the mode to the function and content of communication as well as to learner characteristics. For example, pointing to pictures in a book may be an excellent means of identifying objects for some learners, but it is a poor way of attracting someone's attention from across the room. Even gestures (as anyone who has had difficulty attracting a server's attention in a restaurant can attest) are poorly suited for attracting the attention of another person. Not surprisingly, although Cirrin and Rowland (1985) found that signs and other gestures accounted for most of the communications used by nonverbal youths with severe disabilities, signs and other gestures were not used to request attention. Attention was requested almost exclusively by physical contact. Similarly, other functions or specific vocabulary items may be better suited to other modes.

Mixed modes allow the child, family, and educational team to take advantage of the best components of vocal, gestural, and graphic modes (Mustonen et al., 1991). Since the mixed mode is normalized, allows for maximum use of the student's entire behavioral repertoire, and allows matching modes to communicative function, it is strongly recommended. The proportion of the individual modes within the mix, however, will vary for each child based on his or her abilities and communication needs. Therefore, each individual mode requires discussion.

Duplicated modes of communication require the child to learn to represent the same vocabulary or function in more than one mode (Mustonen et al., 1991). Unlike simultaneous modes, however, only a single mode is typically used during a communication interaction, and the mode of expression selected for a particular interaction is chosen according to appropriateness to the communication partner and context.

Vocal Mode

Speech is the most commonly used individual mode of communication in this society. In addition to its normalization value (Musselwhite & St. Louis, 1988), it is portable, rapid, and precise when used by a proficient communicator. Unfortunately, speech demands good auditory discrimination, extremely fine motor control of oral and respiratory structures, and considerable cognitive development. These (and probably other) factors account for the fact that many children with multiple disabilities do not develop speech or develop only very limited speech. For example, S.E. Morris (1978a) reported that 75%–95% of people with cerebral palsy have speech disturbances. Problems with head control, respiration, phonation, or eating skills typically suggest potential difficulty acquiring speech (Love, Hagerman, & Taimi, 1980). In a mixed mode system, however, it is not necessary to select or reject vocal expression totally. Thus, potential limitations may influence the extent of vocal communication, but they should not eliminate its use as long as a child can make at least a single vocalization. For example, if a child can cry, this cry typically can be shaped into a reliable (and more socially acceptable) attention signal, first by consistent responses to the cry as a request for attention and second by differential responses to more socially acceptable occurrences of the cry.

Even when children have developed considerable vocal skills, augmenting their vocal skills with gestural and graphic components can enhance the functional communication repertoire. Furthermore, considerable evidence suggests that learning other modes of communication enhances acquisition in the vocal mode rather than competing with vocal communication (Reichle, 1991).

Gestural Mode

Some gestures accompany the words of most speakers, and for many communicators with hearing impairments, gestural language is the primary communication mode. Although signing has been criticized as a primary mode of communication because it is not understood by many potential communication partners (Sailor & Guess, 1983), it is a useful component of a mixed mode system and may be an appropriate primary mode when speech and other alternatives are ruled out or when communication occurs in a gestural language environment. Evidence suggests that some learners acquire language more easily through gestures than speech (Carr & Dores, 1981), although which learners will benefit remains somewhat unpredictable (Creekmore, 1982).

Reichle, Williams, and Ryan (1981) suggested that signs should be taught when: 1) the age and history of the learner suggest a poor prognosis for speech, 2) there are signing communication partners in the environment, 3) arm, hand, and finger dexterity is adequate (relative to oral-motor skills), 4) adequate cognitive skills are present (Piaget's stage VI), and 5) a portable system is desirable. When initial goals require acquisition of only a few gestures rather than a large repertoire, even these basic requirements may be relaxed. Other discussions of entry level skills cast significant doubt on the reality of cognitive prerequisites (Reichle, 1991).

Similarly, a number of criteria have been identified for selecting initial signs, including: 1) ease of production (Dennis, Reichle, Williams, & Vogelsberg, 1982); 2) iconicity (extent of resemblance between sign and the object or action represented) (Reichle et al., 1981); 3) topographical dissimilarity (ease of distinction from previously or concurrently trained signs) (Musselwhite & St. Louis, 1988); 4) potential frequency of use (Reichle et al., 1981); 5) familiarity of work or object (Reichle et al., 1981); and 6) functionality across settings (Reichle et al., 1981). Without question, it is the last criterion, functionality, that is most important. The pragmatic function of each individual communication act should be considered first, and decisions about modes or systems should be considered only after the purpose of the communication is determined. If the communication serves an important function, some effective means of expressing it to the appropriate communication partners should be found. If the function is unimportant, it may not be worth training simply because of ease of acquisition. Still, once communication functions are targeted, the remaining criteria can be useful in determining whether the gestural mode is suitable to serve this function and, if so, what form the gesture might take.

Gestural Systems   Musselwhite and St. Louis (1988) grouped sign systems into four basic categories: 1) sign languages (e.g., American Sign Language) having their own structure and rules; 2) educational sign systems using standardized gestures to represent spoken English or some other spoken language; 3) gestural language codes using signs to represent letters or sounds of a language; and 4) other unaided gestural systems, which include a wide range of systems that fall outside of the three previous categories. Gestural language codes and sign languages have limited application with children with severe and multiple disabilities since the cognitive and motor requirements are quite demanding and they require communication partners with considerable signing skills. Although some specific signs or gestures from these systems may be useful as part of a mixed mode system, educational sign systems and other gestural systems are more likely to prove useful than complete sign languages or gestural codes.

Educational Sign Systems   Educational sign systems, also called pedagogical sign systems (Allaire & Miller, 1983), use signs to substitute for or sometimes accompany their English equivalents. They are especially well suited to a simultaneous (speech and sign) mode and also work well in a mixed mode. Some examples include Signing Exact English, Paget-Gorman Systematic Sign, Linguistics of Visual English, and Duffy's System (Musselwhite & St. Louis, 1988). Duffy's System is inherently a mixed mode since it uses some vocalization along with gestures.

These systems differ in their motor requirements, transparency (ease of interpretation by an untrained observer), and the number of signs available. For example, Signing Exact English has enough similarity to American Sign Language (ASL) to be interpreted fairly well by ASL signers. This might be an advantage if potential communication partners already are familiar with ASL. Duffy's system requires less fine motor skill, but it includes fewer than 500 signs and may require creation of new signs for some learners (Musselwhite & St. Louis, 1988).

Other Gestural Systems   Among other gestural systems, Amer-Ind is not considered a language because the gestures have broader conceptual interpretations rather than single-word equivalents. It has been shown to be more transparent than ASL to trained and untrained observers (Kirschner, Algozzine, & Abbott, 1979). While it is unclear if this transparency to persons who do not have disabilities implies transparency to children with multiple disabilities, transparency to potential communication partners may be of equal importance. Amer-Ind gestures also typically use more gross motor and fewer fine motor skills than ASL, and, as a result, they may be more easily acquired by individuals with motor limitations.

Natural gestures are also included under the general category of other gestural systems, and, although they have received relatively little attention from interventionists and researchers until now, they are an important alternative to other gestural systems. Natural gestures refer to actions that are generally understood by most untrained observers. Some researchers believe these gestures are inborn traits (Morris, 1982). They represent an important part of the mainstream of human communication and have several advantages: 1) they are understood by a wide variety of communication partners; 2) they require no special equipment; 3) they appear normal since they are in common usage; 4) they have many models in the natural environment to aid in instruction; 5) they have a high potential for being part of the learner's entry-level repertoire; 6) they typically involve simple gross motor movements; and 7) they often include two or more alternative forms, which increases the probability that one of the alternatives will be suited to the learner (e.g., raising hands palm out and pushing away or horizontal head nod for "no").

Idiosyncratic gestures are actions (which are not shared by the majority of communicators) that a specific individual uses to communicate specific content or functions. In some cases, they are easily interpreted and are therefore also natural gestures. In many other cases, however, they are not easily interpreted. Of course, when a gesture is both easily interpreted and already present in the individual's repertoire, it is ideal, but when a choice must be made between an idiosyncratic or a natural gesture, the alternatives must be considered carefully. For the child with a limited repertoire and infrequent communication, it may be more important to reinforce current (idiosyncratic) communication efforts than to attempt to teach a more widely understood gesture. For the more advanced communicator who already can communicate with a few significant others but lacks the ability to communicate with a larger audience, the natural gesture will be more useful.

Graphic Mode

The graphic mode of communication has also received considerable attention as an alternative to speech (Mustonen et al., 1991). The graphic mode has frequently been labeled the symbolic mode (e.g., Musselwhite & St. Louis, 1988).The term graphic is used here because all modes of communication (e.g., vocal, gestural, graphic) are symbolic. Graphic systems may use: 1) actual objects, 2) photographs, 3) drawings, 4) iconic graphics (which share at least some characteristics with the item they represent), 5) abstract graphics (which have no resemblance to the items they represent), or 6) combinations of two or more of the others (Allaire & Miller, 1983). Of course, this type of categorization of graphic systems is based on the representation of objects rather than actions, relationships, or conditions, which are typically more difficult to represent directly. The fact that graphic systems are typically classified in this way may reflect a specific suitability for object labels.

Graphic communication systems may be homemade or purchased. Homemade systems typically: 1) are less expensive, 2) provide easier control of symbol size, 3) allow a better fit of content to the learner's needs, and 4) are easy to update or expand. However, they may also be time consuming, require special design or construction skills, and cause difficulty when replacing unique graphics or pictures (Mirenda, 1985). Drawings, photos, magazine clippings, and product labels are good sources of visual symbols for homemade systems (Mirenda, 1985).

Some attempts have been made to compare commercial systems. Generally, systems that are more abstract appear to be more difficult for learners with severe and multiple disabilities. For example, Hurlbut, Iwata, and Green (1982) found (more abstract) Blissymbols required four times as many trials for acquisition as a (less abstract) iconic alternative, and that the iconic symbols were retained better. While pointing out these general advantages of the (more iconic) Rebus System over Blissymbolics, Clark (1984) noted that each system has some advantages and that decisions on suitable systems are best made after consideration of the needs of each individual learner. Mirenda (1985) further stressed this need for matching the system to the communicator on the basis of the multiple dimensions of the task. She pointed out that black-and-white line drawings may require less advanced discrimination skills since they present fewer stimulus dimensions than color photographs, but, even so, they may require more advanced graphic language skills than photographs. Therefore, graphic system selection requires the formulation of a hypothesis (based on the learner's environments and characteristics) regarding what systems might be suitable, and it requires empirical support for those systems based on a limited field test with the learner.

Augmentative Systems   Since most electronic communication systems use graphic symbols, they have traditionally been considered part of the graphic mode. As an increasing number of input (e.g., photoelectric, myoelectric) and output (e.g., printing, synthesized speech) options become available with various electronic systems, their relationship to graphic systems weakens; consequently, augmentative systems should probably be considered a separate mode.

Augmentative systems take movements already in the communicator's repertoire and transform them to more interpretable communication responses. For example, a series of puffs and sucks on a mouth tube may be electronically transformed to a written or spoken word. Some individuals are assisted greatly by these devices, particularly people with very limited motor skills but good sensory, receptive language, and cognitive skills. For many others, particularly those with very limited cognitive skills, these augmentative devices provide few advantages. For this reason, augmentative devices will not be discussed in this chapter. Some information regarding specific aspects of these devices is included in Chapter 8, and much of the information that follows on selection methods and communication board design is also suitable for augmentative devices.

Graphic Arrays   For graphic communication, an array of graphic symbols must be available to the learner and the communication partner, and the learner must have a reliable method of indicating which symbol is chosen. The physical arrangement of this array must consider the sensory, cognitive, and motor characteristics of the communicator in order to maximize the speed and reliability of communication. The simplest method of indicating the chosen symbol is direct selection, which requires the learner to touch, point to, look at, or otherwise indicate one symbol at a time with each selection.

For children with limited movement, suitable arrays may be determined by: 1) range of motion (areas through which they can move in various planes); 2) resolution of motion (smallest movement reliably differentiated); 3) control (reliability, speed, freedom from involuntary movement for a given location); 4) endurance (length of time a movement can be maintained or repeated); and sometimes, 5) force (amount of pressure that can be exerted) (Capozzi & Mineo, 1984). York and Weiman (1991) recommended eight principles of designing, positioning, and handling to help maximize the performance of children with limited movement. These include: 1) using one's own movements as reference models for planning, 2) using dynamic rather than static assistance whenever possible to minimize dependency, 3) controlling position and movements from key points, 4) increasing time and frequency of practice, 5) normalizing muscle tone, 6) providing a stable base of support, 7) working toward symmetrical alignment, and 8) using a variety of positions. (More detailed information on handling and postioning is included in Chapters 3 and 8.) Graphic symbol size must be based on visual acuity as well as motor accuracy. Placement of individual symbols within the array may be based on a number of factors. For example, frequently used symbols are typically placed in the most accessible positions in order to minimize the effort and time required for communication, but frequently used symbols associated with high levels of reinforcement are sometimes placed in peripheral positions to encourage learners to reach farther toward their limits. When the number of selections increases beyond six or so, it typically becomes helpful to group them into categories by content or function (Musselwhite & St. Louis, 1988).

Many factors should be considered in the design of communication boards (Baumgart, Johnson, & Helmstetter, 1990). Figure 9.1 illustrates the top view of a communication board on a young girl's lap tray mounted on her wheelchair. Although some machines and computers move easily across rows and down columns, children do not. Since this child uses one hand for direct selection, one must consider the arc of movement of that arm across the lap tray in planning the location of symbols on the board. The white area represents the area of the board that allows best access and accuracy for this child. As illustrated, some other areas of the board are inaccessible, limit accuracy, cannot be seen, or require maladaptive positioning or movement patterns to reach. Some areas of the board can be reached but require extra effort. If the child is being encouraged to use these areas, symbols associated with highly reinforcing items or events may be placed in these areas. Symbol size is determined primarily by visual abilities and accuracy of selection. It may be desirable to elongate symbols in one dimension since accuracy may differ from the vertical to

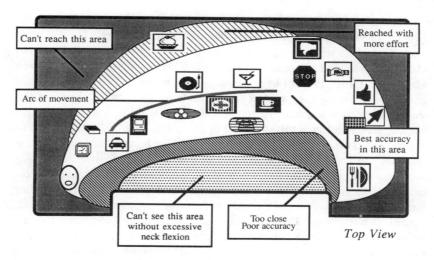

Figure 9.1. A communication board individualized to the movement patterns and visual abilities of one child with multiple disabilities.

the horizontal axis. The size and distance between symbols may also be varied according to accuracy in each particular area of the board. Usually, accuracy is best near the center of the arc of movement and worsens as distance increases from the arc. Placing conceptual classes of symbols and related pragmatic functions close together is desirable for some students, but placing them farther apart is often better when accuracy is an issue. For example, if "yes" and "no" symbols are close together and the child is asked a "yes/no" question, great accuracy is required to answer. If these symbols are far apart, however, communication partners can more reliably discriminate the intended answer despite some inaccuracy. Physical therapists and occupational therapists can be extremely useful team members in helping to map a child's movement patterns and determining the best placement of symbols.

The space between graphic symbol locations must be wide enough to ensure reliable discrimination between responses. A raised divider between symbols may be useful for eliminating borderline responses. Building a confirmation exchange into each selection may be necessary to ensure reliable selection with some learners, particularly those using gaze (eye pointing) for selection. For example, when the learner appears to be looking at a specific symbol, the partner touches that selection (as if saying, "This one, right?"), and the communicator signals "yes" or "no" with a nod or other reliable movement or vocalization. When eye gaze is the best selection mode, an ETRAN (a clear, vertical, Plexiglas rectangular board with an open center), which is placed between the communicators, improves discriminability of gaze direction (Bigge, 1991). Still, only about 8–10 items can be displayed and reliably selected in this manner.

Scanning and encoding provide alternatives when the number of graphic symbols needed exceeds the number that can be indicated reliably. Scanning presents symbols sequentially to the communicator, who indicates selection by some predetermined response when the appropriate symbol appears (Musselwhite & St. Louis, 1988). Linear scanning presents every item in order, while group item scanning first presents categories (e.g., rows on the chart, content areas) for selection and then presents specific items within a category only after that category is selected (Musselwhite & St. Louis, 1988). Directed scanning can be controlled by the communicator proceeding horizontally, vertically, or diagonally in order to shorten the path to a desired item (Silverman, 1980). Since linear scanning is the simplest method, it probably has the greatest potential for most learners with severe and multiple disabilities. Similarly, encoding methods probably will be useful only with communicators with relatively advanced cognitive skills. Encoding uses a series of simpler selections to indicate an item (Bigge, 1991). For example, selecting one of six shapes may indicate a row, and selecting one of six colors may indicate a column. Thus, 36 items may be encoded, but the learner need only reliably select from an array of six.

Piché and Reichle (1991) recommended four major steps for students who are learning scanning: 1) selecting the signaling response, 2) learning to use this response selectively, 3) increasing selectivity to larger arrays of items, and 4) generalizing the response across different types of arrays. Scanning involves an elaboration of a confirmation function since items are presented sequentially until one is confirmed as the correct selection. Therefore, indicating "yes" may be viewed as an essential initial step.

Physical Contact and Environmental Modification

While vocal, gestural, and graphic modes are the predominant elements of mixed mode systems, other communication modes also can be identified. Two of these modes that play an important role in basic communication are physical contact and environmental modification. Physical contact is often used to attract attention (e.g., tap on shoulder), to display affection (e.g., hug), or to reject another (e.g., push away). Modification of the environment (e.g., placing a coat by the door to indicate wanting to leave) may be a similarly useful mode of communication. Although neither of these modes can easily serve as the sole mode of communication, each can be an important element in a mixed modal system.

ASSESSMENT, PLANNING, AND INTERVENTION

Before an effective and functional communication training program can be implemented, four basic decisions must be made. First, there must be a decision as to which communication functions would be most useful to the individual. Second, the specific content or messages to be communicated must be determined. Third, the form of the communication (which includes mode and system decisions) must be selected. Fourth, the way in which each item will be taught must be chosen.

Figure 9.2 illustrates a decision-making process for determining the functions and modes to be taught and the kinds of training that may be required. The process starts with an ecological assessment (Sigafoos & York, 1991) to determine what behaviors are required in the current environment and also potentially in future less restrictive and age-appropriate environments. Priority may be placed on skills essential to maintaining a placement in current desirable environments or critical to placement in a future desirable environment. Functions that are already present need not be taught, but they may require fluency training or topographical refinement to improve understanding by communication partners. Functions that are easily understood, fluent, and appropriate should be supported by maintenance and generalization programming that takes advantage of natural reinforcers to the greatest extent possible. If functions are present in socially inappropriate forms, pragmatic functional alternatives should be taught. Any required function that is absent needs to be taught in a mode and form that considers the context, partners, production abilities of the child, and the best fit between mode and function. The new forms and functions taught become the focus of the child's communication acquisition program. Early in the process of acquisition, fluency training should begin. For low frequency communicators, it is typically desirable to stress fluency rather than topographical refinement since increased use of communication will provide more opportunities for feedback and subsequent refinement.

Assessment

Traditional assessment has emphasized decisions of candidacy for communication training (Musselwhite & St. Louis, 1988). Mirenda and Iacono (1990), however, suggested that the participation model first proposed by Rosenberg and Beukelman (1987) is more appropriate for individuals with severe and multiple disabilities. This model assumes that all individuals are candidates for communication intervention and focuses on development of opportunity and access rather than candidacy for intervention. Standardized assessments of language and communication skills are typically inappropriate for children with severe and multiple disabilities for at least six reasons (Correia & Sobsey, 1984):

1. They typically emphasize more advanced skills and fail to evaluate adequately very basic skills.
2. They generally assume the child understands that a task is being presented and is motivated to perform as well as possible.
3. They often focus on the individual rather than the communication dyad and environment.

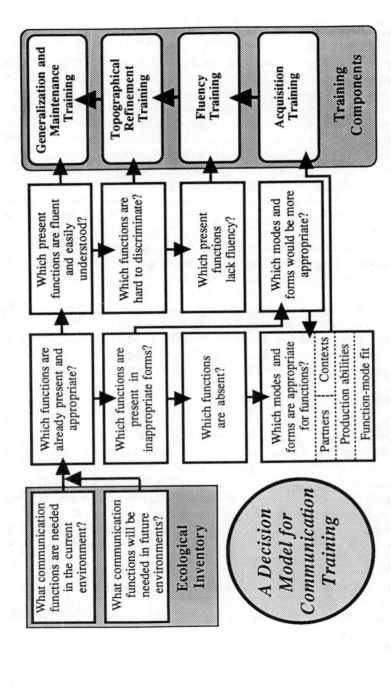

Figure 9.2. A decision model for communication training. Ecological inventory is used to determine the functions, modes, and forms to be taught. Analyses of these content components are used to determine instructional program components.

4. They commonly require demonstration of specific skills and fail to allow for functional alternatives.
5. Many depend on too small a sampling of target behavior.
6. Most are designed to determine how the child compares with some reference group, which is not useful information (when the individual obviously differs from the norm) for planning and intervention.

Since such standard assessments measure communication responses to test stimuli, they are particularly poor indicators of children's behavior in natural environments and of skills used in initiating communication (Reichle & Yoder, 1979). Although more time consuming, a flexible, natural communication sample provides a more accurate indication of such behavior. This individualized approach to assessment also permits greater consideration of the environmental requirements when determining appropriate program content.

In view of their deficiencies, standard assessments of communication have only limited application to children with multiple disabilities and should only be used to help answer specific program decisions. For example, the Pre-Speech Assessment Scale (Morris, 1978b) may be very useful for identifying the specific oral-motor skills that need improvement for speech.

Assessment must include consideration of communication partners and context (Rogers-Warren, 1984). Sigafoos and York (1991) outlined procedures for ecological inventories of communication behavior. This process considers communication demands and opportunities along with communication intents, modes, and vocabulary.

Correia and Sobsey (1984) suggested a flexible evaluation process that combines: 1) identifying information, 2) relevant data from physical and learning histories, 3) information gathered in an interview with significant others, 4) results of a natural communication sample, 5) results of an elicited communication sample, 6) a description of the physical and social environment, 7) a summary, and 8) program recommendations. Although suggested interview questions are included, evaluators are advised to select those that seem relevant and to supplement them with their own questions. Both natural and elicited communication samples are potentially useful since data collected during the natural sample can be used to formulate interventions that can be field tested during the elicited sample. Similarly, an interview with significant others before the natural sample is collected may help suggest the best times, places, and communication partners for the natural sample. Assessment information can help interventionists with each of the four decisions (functions, content, form, intervention) they face, but it may be necessary to do additional assessment after each decision before the next one can be made.

Olswang, Stoel-Gammon, Coggins, and Carpenter (1987) have prepared a structured yet flexible assessment designed to assess prelinguistic and early linguistic communication responses in children who are at early developmental stages. This comprehensive package evaluates cognitive antecedents, play behavior, communicative intent, language comprehension, and language production. Even though considerable modification is necessary in most cases, some components of this assessment instrument can be useful in designing individualized assessments for children with severe and multiple disabilities.

Determining Communication Functions, Content, Form, and Interventions

The discussion of functional communication that appeared earlier in this chapter mentioned that no generally agreed upon, comprehensive list of pragmatic functions is available. Therefore, in generating the list of functions most useful to a specific child, the interventionist must depend on his or her observations of current communication behavior and the child's current and potential future environments. Environmental information reveals why and what the child needs to communicate. Information regarding the child's behavior in the environment tells what communication functions the child currently fulfills and what skills the learner may be able to use for additional communication. Parents, other team members, and all who regularly interact with the child can provide a great deal of information about current communication, reducing the amount of time required for direct observation by the interventionist.

Attention   One basic function in all communication is to draw the attention of a potential communication partner to oneself. Without this skill, a communicator is restricted to the role of passive respondent and cannot initiate interaction. Although this function is so basic that it may be taken for granted, Light, Collier, and Parnes (1985) found that 15% of initiation attempts by the physically disabled children they studied failed because the children did not have the attention of their communication partners. Similarly, Reichle, Rogers, and Barrett (1984), in teaching a student with severe, multiple disabilities to make requests, found that requests were often nonfunctional because they were made prior to having another person's attention.

More complex functions may direct the communication partner's attention to an object or event, but the attention must be drawn to the communicator before it can be directed elsewhere. Therefore, if a reliable method for attracting attention is not already in the individual's repertoire, this should probably be one of the first functions taught. The graphic mode is generally poorly suited for attracting attention. The gestural mode can be more effective in some contexts, especially with gross-motor gestures (e.g., waving, hand-raising). The vocal mode is often the most effective mode for attracting attention since the communication partner need not be looking at the communicator to receive this message. Augmentative devices with auditory output (e.g., ringing telephone, buzzer, bell) are also well-suited to this task. Sobsey and Reichle (1989) suggested that the auditory feedback of a buzzer may act as an intermediate conditioned reinforcer and facilitate the acquisition of single switch activation as an attention signal.

After a basic attention signal is taught, it may be differentiated into various forms with more specific content (e.g., "Look at me," "Listen to me," "Look at that"), but to start with, a single message (e.g., "I need you") is the only content required. If the child has an existing behavioral form for the attention function, its effectiveness and appropriateness should be examined; if it is currently working well, it should be preserved and other functions targeted for training. The behavioral form used for the attention function must be easily discriminable at a distance. If the potential communication partner must already be paying attention in order to receive the message, it has no functional value. Therefore, although some gross motor gestures may be useful, the graphic mode and much of the gestural mode are poorly suited to this communication function. Moving into proximity or touching another may be useful for some learners. If the learner can produce adequate volume, even though articulation may be poor, vocalization is well suited to this function. For individuals without a suitable response in their repertoire, a buzzer system is a simple and typically effective alternative (Sobsey & Reichle, 1989).

Teaching the individual to request attention is generally easy to accomplish. The primary teaching method involves consistent responding to the learner's use of the signal. If initial signaling rates are low, it may be necessary to build high rates by adding instructional reinforcers to the attention response or through prompting and reinforcing signal production during massed trial instruction. Once high rates of signaling have been developed, the artificial reinforcers can be faded, and attention can take over as the reinforcer.

Occasionally, signaling rates may be too high. The learner may request attention so frequently that communication partners consider these repeated requests to be disruptive and stop responding to them. Such situations should be carefully evaluated. Often, the number of requests for attention is not as high as believed. Although potential communication partners may subscribe, in theory, to the importance of encouraging initiation, they may not be prepared to allow the learner to control their interactions. An adjustment in the attitudes of these partners may be required before successful training can take place. It is pointless to attempt to teach requests for attention if they will be ignored when made. In other cases, requests for attention temporarily reach disruptively high levels but return to more acceptable levels as the learner becomes more accustomed to this new power. If signaling levels do not become normalized, raising the signal requirements (e.g., moving buzzer switch to a location demanding more reaching) or adjusting the reinforcement schedule (e.g., to a fixed interval) may help bring the signaling rate to a normal level.

Requesting Items and Events Requests are an important part of early communication and continue to be important to communicators at every level. Reichle and Keogh (1985) noted that early requests are typically undifferentiated and require the communication partner to use contextual cues (e.g., history of learner's previous requests, presence of possible referents in the environment) to determine what is requested. Only later, when more advanced communication skills develop, does the ability to request specific items or events emerge. Requests also appear to generalize from the training to the natural environment better than naming or question-asking responses (Warren & Rogers-Warren, 1983). At this basic level, communication content might be interpreted as "I want something." This allows one communication form to request many different items and events (Reichle & Sigafoos, 1991). Once generalized requests are taught, item-specific content may be considered.

The form selected for teaching depends mostly on learner characteristics. Graphic, gestural, and vocal modes are equally suited to the task, and many learners have some form of requesting in their natural repertoire. If such a response can be identified, it should be used in current or modified form rather than being discarded for a new form.

Keogh and Reichle (1985) taught generalized requesting in a massed trial format. They presented an array of choices to the learner to reinforce communicating "want." To ensure that the communication did not become bound to a single reinforcer, they suggested rotating the reinforcers in the array or replacing any item that the learner selected three times in a row. This method has led to rapid acquisition of requesting by learners with severe and multiple disabilities. Reichle and Sigafoos (1991) provided detailed procedures for teaching generalized requests for items and events.

Rejection and Protest   Just as the ability to request items and events is important for establishing control over the environment, the ability to reject or protest against them may be equally important. Cirrin and Rowland (1985) found this protest function particularly common among infrequent communicators. Often, natural gestures (e.g., moving away, turning one's face away) are already available in the learner's repertoire and require only improvement of reliability through standardization or minimal modification to more acceptable forms. The basic message of these protests might be interpreted as "No" (Sigafoos & Reichle, 1991). As with requests, their form is best determined on the basis of learner characteristics.

As with attention signals, the success of training depends largely on the willingness of communication partners to accept the message and allow learners to refuse the things they attempt to reject. If communication partners refuse to take "no" for an answer, communication of rejection has no functional value. Of course, there may be some instances that require ignoring the learner's protests. For example, most people would feel justified in saving a child from drowning even though the child struggled against (protested) the effort. The rationale for many other things (e.g., eating the last bite of liver) that are imposed on protesting learners with severe and multiple disabilities, however, is much less clear. Any attempt to increase functional communication skills requires empowering the learner with greater control over the social environment, and, therefore, it requires communication partners to relinquish some of their control. Before overriding the protests of the learners he or she serves, one must carefully examine the reasons for one's restrictive response. Such an imposition on the freedom of the individual is not justified simply because one judges something to be good for that person. After all, people in general can think of things that would be good for them but that they refuse because they simply do not like them. Such intrusions can be justified only if the consequences of the learner's refusal would be catastrophic. An extremely important by-product of empowering the learner to refuse or protest unwanted items and events is the subsequent need for caregivers and interventionists to ensure that activities are adequately reinforcing to make certain that participation is voluntary.

Confirmation/Negation For some learners, particularly those with relatively advanced receptive skills but limited productive communication, confirmation/negation responses are particularly useful (Bigge, 1991). Since these "yes" and "no" responses may require frequent usage, a set of responses that can be discriminated from each other quickly and reliably is desirable. Vertical and horizontal head nods are often used. The same responses used as request and reject signals may also be generalized to this purpose.

Often, confirmation or negation is used when the communication partner repeats the message received from the learner. Examples of the form that this communication might take include vocal repetition or touching the symbol of an ETRAN on which the learner's gaze seemed to focus. If the message repeated back by the respondent is correct, the learner confirms it and proceeds with the conversation. If the message repeated back is incorrect, the learner communicates negation and tries again to communicate the original message.

Reference and Description Many programs designed to train children with severe or multiple disabilities to use language focus on identification or naming of objects or events. These reference and description functions no doubt are important, but they are difficult ones (Light et al., 1985), and they require relatively large amounts of learned behavior for more limited functional value (i.e., learning a generalized requester can be useful in requesting anything, whereas learning an object name is useful for requesting only one thing). Such advanced communication behavior should not be considered for training until most of the basic communication functions described above have been mastered. Providing training in early forms of establishing joint reference, including touching, pointing, and looking at objects, can be accomplished through modeling and prompting methods. The graphic mode can be especially useful for object identification when specific labels are required. Once a general match-to-sample (picture-to-object) strategy is learned, new labels can often be learned with relative ease.

Questions Another advanced communication function is requesting additional information about an object, event, or previous communication. In speech, questioning is often indicated by changes in pitch and rhythm of the voice (sometimes called prosodic features) rather than by the content or sequence of the utterance. Such an add-on feature also can be devised for graphic, gestural, and mixed modes. For example, a child may add the vocalization "Nuh?" to pointing to something in order to indicate more information is desired about that thing. Although training in questioning behavior should probably be reserved until more basic communication functions are mastered, it is a function that becomes increasingly useful as communication progresses.

The Interactive Process   In considering the various ways that communication functions to control and modify the environment, it is easy to miss one of the most basic. The very process of communication requires interaction between participants. This interaction is the basic medium upon which all other functions and content are overlayed, but to overlook the funtional significance of the medium would be a grave mistake. As suggested by McLuhan (1964), "the medium is the message" (p.9). In much of communication, the primary function is to interact. It is the medium that MacDonald (1985) considers to be the primary target of communication intervention. Thus, conversational functions might be viewed as fundamental acts that maintain and regulate communication. They allow communication of specific content, but often "the 'content' of any medium blinds us to the character of the medium" (McLuhan, 1964, p.9), and we remain unaware of these conversational functions. Nevertheless, these functions are among the most valuable both because of their vital role in transmitting other content and because of the inherent value of interaction. Pragmatic conversational functions have been taught to students with severe disabilities in structured learning contexts and have generalized well to natural communication contexts (Hunt, Allwell, Goetz, & Sailor, 1990).

McLean and Snyder-McLean (1978) identified some basic behaviors that support early language transactions: 1) receiving reinforcement from social attention, 2) enjoying the presence of others, 3) benefiting from others' assistance, 4) showing objects to others, 5) offering objects to others, and 6) participating in reciprocal exchanges. Others might be added to this list, for example, providing reinforcement to communication partners may be as important as receiving reinforcement from them. The learner who smiles or entertains communication partners is often much more successful in maintaining interaction.

Developing simple turn-taking routines between communicators is one essential interaction behavior required for all communication. Participants must attend to their partners' behavior and then, on cue, fill their turns with related behaviors while their partners attend to them. Traditionally, imitation has been the primary form of turn-taking routine taught in early communication (Sailor et al., 1980). Imitation is believed to help develop the skills required for production of spoken or gestural language; also, it has been theorized that imitation assists in acquisition (Leonard, 1984); however, empirical evidence has not supported its necessity for either.

Sternberg, Pegnatore, and Hill (1983) described a progression of behaviors that help develop imitation and more general turn-taking. The first, resonance, uses physical contact and motion to coordinate the behavior of the learner with that of the interventionist. The second, coactive behavior, inter-rupts physical contact but maintains the simultaneous coordination between learner and interventionist. The third, deferred imitation, delays the learner's response until the interventionist finishes, which establishes turn-taking.

These and other turn-taking routines can often be taught through play. Stacking blocks for the learner to knock over, give-and-take games, and danc-ing can be simple and effective methods of establishing turn-taking routines. Siegel-Causey and Ernst (1989) emphasized early interactive patterns, stress-ing five essential instructional strategies for developing interaction: 1) develop-ing nurturance, 2) enhancing sensitivity of communication partners, 3) se-quencing experiences, 4) increasing opportunities for communication, and 5) utilizing movement. Similar strategies are recommended by van Dijk (1986) for developing communication with children who are deaf and blind.

No doubt additional valuable communication functions could be identi-fied, and some of those discussed may be unsuitable for some learners because they are too advanced or because the learners already have the response func-tion in their repertoire. In general, however, determining program content by pragmatic function is a relatively simple and extremely productive process.

Initiation During the 1980s, there has been an increased emphasis on training the learner in initiating communication, rather than solely in respond-ing to the initiations of others. The lack of initiation and control that has been demonstrated by children with physical disabilities during their interaction with nondisabled caregivers is not surprising since caregivers seldom have afforded these children sufficient time to respond or to initiate their own topics (Light et al., 1985). Instructional programs that train students only in responding to teachers or peers, while ignoring initiation, may actually make matters worse. For example, the findings of Kohl, Moses, and Stettner-Eaton (1983) that non-disabled schoolchildren assumed more dominant roles over their disabled peers after being trained to provide them with instruction, suggest the need for the utmost care in training. Current efforts to better conceptualize and implement initiation training provide valuable suggestions for all who design programs, but further efforts are needed to determine which methods actually encourage initiation. Kaczmarek (1990) suggested that careful analysis of the communica-tion context is essential. To begin with, spontaneous requests should be devel-oped through delay procedures and faded prompting with the desired object in full view, proximity to the communication partner, and the full attention of the communication partner. Once requests occur under these conditions, one in-creases task requirements by reducing the visibility of the object and by reduc-ing proximity to or initial attention of the communication partner.

Teaching Methods

Most of the instructional methods described in this chapter are generic and can be applied to a variety of modes or systems of communication. A generic ap-proach has been selected because it is consistent with the mixed-mode approach recommended in this chapter and with the principle of individualization emphasized throughout this book. Despite this generic approach, some specific methods have particular application to specific modes. For example, molding a child's hand around an object to teach the shape of a gesture may be useful, but directly applying this method to vocal or graphic modes is impossible.

Three basic approaches can be easily identified for teaching communication: 1) intensive, structured programs; 2) planned instruction, integrated into normal activities throughout the day; and 3) environmental intervention to increase exposure to speech and/or reinforcement for vocalization. These should not be viewed as alternatives since good teaching often requires the use of all three. These three basic approaches also can be used for training in other communication modes, but they have most often been used in teaching speech.

Intensive Programs   Musselwhite and St. Louis (1988) discussed 20 vocal language programs for use with children with severe and multiple disabilities that share four common stages originally identified by Harris (1975): 1) attention, 2) nonverbal imitation, 3) verbal imitation, and 4) functional language. Establishing the child's attention is essential in training all communication. Evidence suggests that generalized imitation is not required to teach communication functions (Reichle et al., 1984), and its value as an intermediate step is questionable (Sailor et al., 1980). Even the inclusion of verbal imitation might be questioned since imitation, in itself, is not typically a functional skill. There is some evidence, however, that verbal imitation helps develop language production and may facilitate acquisition of spontaneous language (Leonard, 1984). Problems with structured programs typically include: 1) requiring steps that are too large for students with very severe disabilities, 2) lacking flexibility to be individualized to each learner, 3) encouraging the learners only to respond and ignoring training in initiation of conversation, 4) failing to generalize outside the lesson, and 5) failing to teach the skills most functional for the individual. Many of these problems are partially solved through the use of integrated instruction and environmental intervention along with intensive programs. Advantages of structured intensive programs include: 1) providing a vastly increased number of learning trials, which reduces acquisition time; 2) structuring instruction to increase the probability of correct responses; and 3) providing a turn-taking format that teaches a basic interaction pattern required in all communication. These advantages are particularly important for response acquisition (e.g., learning to say words), but they are less valuable for training in the functional use of words in appropriate situations.

Integrated Instruction   Planned instruction, integrated into normal activities, includes: 1) incidental teaching, 2) the delay procedure, 3) the mand-model procedure, and 4) the interrupted behavior chain procedure. Additional procedures could be identified or devised in this category, but these four are representative.

Incidental Teaching   In incidental teaching, the interventionist selects appropriate occasions within ongoing activities for a prespecified communication behavior. If the learner fails to respond appropriately, natural cues are strengthened (and additional prompts are added only if necessary). Natural reinforcers (items or events that would be likely consequences in the noninstructional environment) are used whenever possible (Halle, 1982). Incidental teaching has been demonstrated to be more effective than a less structured approach during free play (Cavallaro & Bambara, 1982).

Delay Procedures In the delay procedure, the interventionist creates or selects a situation that calls for communication from the child, then stops for a few seconds to encourage the learner to communicate (Halle, 1982). For example, the teacher or parent might bring the child's plate of food, but delay just before putting it down, hoping to evoke communication of "eat" or "want" from the learner. This technique has been demonstrated to be effective both when the delays between natural cues and prompts have been gradually increased and when these delays have been held constant (Kleinert & Gast, 1982).

Mand-Model Procedure The mand-model procedure is similar to incidental teaching in selecting appropriate teaching moments. If learners fail to respond, however, they are prompted by a direct question (e.g., as "What do you want?"), and if they still fail to respond, the correct response is modeled for them (Rogers-Warren & Warren, 1980). Like incidental teaching and the delay procedure, the mand-model procedure may be particularly useful in helping to generalize speech learned in structured lessons to functional times and places.

Interrupted Behavior Chain Procedure The interrupted behavior chain procedure goes a step further in actually integrating structured training and the natural environment. The interventionist interrupts a partially completed task and teaches a brief (one-trial), but complete lesson before the task is resumed (Goetz, Gee, & Sailor, 1985). Thus, it is possible to begin training in the natural environment without prior training in a massed trial format (i.e., concentrating a large number of training trials in a block of instructional time). Interrupted behavior chains have been shown to be effective in teaching communication and also in developing generalization to new environments (Alwell, Hunt, Goetz, & Sailor, 1989).

Environmental Intervention Both intensive programs and integrated instruction differ from the informal interactions between children and their caregivers that teach communication skills to most people who do not have disabilities. Although structured intervention is desirable and probably necessary to assist many children with multiple disabilities to acquire communication skills, providing a social environment that fosters communication skill acquisition is probably of equal or greater importance.

General Principles Many of the environmental interventions described in Chapter 12 will contribute substantially toward building communication skills. Although there is inadequate space here for a full discussion of environmental interventions, some general principles follow:

1. Family members and other primary caregivers must have a major role in developing communication skills (Bloom & Lahey, 1978). Isolated intervention is unlikely to produce changes in functional communication without this participation.
2. The interaction between the learner and primary caregivers, rather than the behavior of the individual, should be seen as the target of intervention (MacDonald, 1985). The interventionist's failure to recognize or respond to initial efforts and expectations that are too low or too high often teach children with multiple disabilities not to communicate.
3. Siblings, peers, and others should be considered and included along with parents and caregivers in enhancing the communication environment (Allaire & Miller, 1983; Sobsey & Bieniek, 1983). The nature as well as quality and number of interactions should be considered. Children with severe disabilities sometimes interact primarily with caregivers and less frequently with peers (Hill & Whitely, 1985), but attempts to increase peer interaction by training peers as caregivers or instructors may not increase true peer interactions (Kohl et al., 1983).
4. Care must be taken not to anticipate all of children's needs. If all their needs are met before being communicated, there will be little motivation for them to communicate (Silverman, 1980).
5. Adequate time must be provided by communication partners for the individual to respond. Memory and processing are often slower among people with disabilities (Merrill, 1985).
6. Intervention (e.g., suggestions, demonstrations, and guided practice) during play has been shown to facilitate communication interactions between mothers and their children (Rosenberg & Robinson, 1985). Play in which the child and caregiver actively participate and enjoy interaction may be an important medium for building communication skills.
7. Both the child and the communication partner must use feedback mechanisms to let the other know that the message is understood (Snyder & McLean, 1976). This feedback may be simple confirmation or reinforcement. Reinforcement should be functional rather than instructional. For example, if a child says "Look," and points toward a dog, the respondent should look and comment on the dog rather than failing to look and telling the child, "Nice talking" (Bottorf & De Pape, 1982).
8. A rich communication environment should be provided (Allaire & Miller, 1983). Often potential communication partners fail to talk to minimally responsive children. The result is reduced opportunity for language learning. Selecting topics of potential or known interest and using simple vocabulary and construction are also important.
9. Any structured language programs must be integrated with events in the natural language environment (Nietupski, Scheutz, & Ockwood, 1980). This means that information from the natural environment (e.g., what

and how the learner currently communicates; what the learner needs or wants to communicate) must be considered in the design and implementation of the structured program and that information from the program (e.g., functions and forms of communication) must be communicated to and considered by communication partners in the natural environment.

10. Children must be encouraged to actively initiate communication, not only passively respond (Kaczmarek, 1990). This requires allowing the learner to exercise as much control and make as many decisions as possible (Shevin & Klein, 1984) during daily activities.

Educational and Social Integration The decreased use of segregated living and learning environments by children with multiple disabilities means greater participation in the mainstream of society. As these children enter regular classrooms and integrated activities, their opportunities for interaction change in character and frequency. These changes facilitate learning age-appropriate, functional communication skills (Stremmel-Campbell, Campbell, & Johnson-Dorn, 1985). Research suggests that peer interactions occur more frequently and that more advanced patterns of communication are used by children with disabilities in integrated settings (Guralnick & Groom, 1988). Brinker (1985) studied the interactions between students with severe disabilities in segregated and integrated settings. Students with disabilities made significantly more social bids to their peers and received more social bids from their peers in integrated settings. Students who did not have disabilities also responded more frequently to the social bids from students with severe disabilities. Integration by itself, however, is not usually adequate to produce major effects on interaction (Guralnick, 1984). It is most useful when used in conjunction with good instructional programs and, when required, with intervention to encourage peer interaction.

A communication program that combines structured language programs, integrated instruction, and environmental modification is ideal for teaching vocal language, but it is also suited for teaching communication in other modes or mixed modes, as previously suggested. For this reason, discussion of these modes will not duplicate the previous information; instead, it will add other information and issues relevant to the mode discussed.

Teaching Gestural Communication The training interventions discussed for the vocal mode are also useful for gestural communication, but there are some important differences. First, gestural systems frequently require more special training of families, interventionists, peers, and other potential respondents who are more likely to use the vocal mode for most of their communication. Coordinated efforts of all involved are essential to generalizing gestures to new communication contexts (Kollinzas, 1983). Second, since there likely will be fewer natural models in the learner's environment (especially if gestures are being used exclusively as the learner's output mode and communication partners use speech for the learner's reception), more instructional models may be necessary. Third, unlike the vocal mode, gestures are often taught through the use of physical prompts.

Two physical prompting methods are commonly used (Musselwhite & St. Louis, 1988). Handshaping uses physical contact, with the trainer positioning the learner's hands appropriately. Molding positions the learner's hands by placing them around an object and is useful when the gesture being taught resembles the shape of the hand formed by grasping the object (e.g., cup).

Teaching Graphic Communication   Many of the same methods used to teach speech or gestures can be adapted to teach graphic communication. Most often, learners who use graphic symbols for production use speech for receptive communication. Keogh and Reichle (1985) suggested a basic training sequence for labeling photographs. First, the learner is taught to touch the object when its name is spoken. Second, the learner is taught to touch a photograph of the object when the object's name is spoken. Third, the learner is taught to select the photograph out of an array when its name is spoken. Fourth, the learner is taught to touch the photograph from the array to request the item. Fifth, the learner is taught to touch the photograph from the array when the object is presented along with the question, "What is this?" (Keogh & Reichle, 1985). Empirical evidence suggests that teaching only one object at a time produces faster acquisition but that concurrent teaching of items produces better discrimination among these items (Waldo, Guess, & Flanagan, 1985). Graphic symbol systems can provide the primary mode of communication for learners with severe disabilities and play an important part in many mixed mode approaches.

Generalization and Maintenance

Closely associated with the concern for developing initiation are the generalization and maintenance of communication behaviors. Warren, Baxter, Anderson, Marshall, and Baer (1981) observed that while the need to address generalization and maintenance in training has been acknowledged, the manner of addressing them often has questionable application to the natural environment. This implies, for example, that even though multiple trainers may be used, there is no certainty that the behavior will generalize to the natural environment. This is part of the reason that structured programs often fail to produce generalization. Reichle and Keogh (1985) recommended the integration of structured and incidental approaches to overcome this problem.

In considering generalization, it is important also to consider its limits. The effective use of communication in the natural environment requires the learner not only to generalize across appropriate partners and situations, but also to discriminate inappropriate ones. For example, it may be appropriate to request help in toileting from family members and caregivers but not from bus drivers or cashiers in the grocery store. The ability to use communication discriminatively is as important as the ability to generalize it.

It is often true that communication behavior is not maintained over time because it is not functional for the learner. It is important to remember that no attempt to communicate is functional unless communication partners respond to it appropriately. For example, requesting foods or beverages would generally be considered a functional communication skill, but, in fact, it is functional only if, at least to some degree, it can be used to control access to food or beverages. If the learner requests something, but the responses to the request are "Not now, I'm busy," "You just ate," "It's almost lunch time," and so forth, the communication will not be maintained because it is not functional. Before attempting to teach any communication act, the communication partner must be prepared to respond to it.

Communication Functions and Problem Behavior

One of the most rapidly growing subjects in educating children with multiple disabilities is the emerging model of problem behavior as a form of communication (Donnellan et al., 1984). In this model, bizarre, disruptive, or destructive behavior is analyzed in terms of its pragmatic function (i.e., control over environmental events). It may serve as a request for attention, assistance, a desired item, or relief from an unpleasant situation. Using this paradigm, interventionists have provided training in more appropriate methods of communicating the same function and thereby reduced the inappropriate behavior (e.g., Carr & Durand, 1985). Many issues still need to be resolved before the full impact of such findings can be known. Whether this model can be applied to all problem behavior has not yet been determined, but it does work in many cases, and provides the opportunity for intervention through reinforcement of the adaptive behavior, rather than mere suppression of the inappropriate behavior.

From a communication perspective, this has another interesting implication. When problem behavior serves an identifiable pragmatic function, it is likely that the learner has been unable to master a more appropriate form for that function (Doss & Reichle, 1991). Therefore, behavior problems may help to identify communication functions for which the child needs training. For example, if it is determined that a learner bangs his or her head on the floor in order to obtain the attention of caregivers, it is likely that no appropriate attention-requesting response is available in the learner's repertoire or that caregivers ignore more appropriate requests and respond to the inappropriate behavior. In either case, the learner's investment of energy and pain reveal that this function is important to him or her. If the learner has no more appropriate requesting form in his or her repertoire, he or she should be taught one. If the learner already has one, he or she must be prompted to use it, and caregivers must be trained to respond to it. Doing so will improve both communication and behavior.

Basic steps in application of pragmatics to improving inappropriate behavior include:

1. Conducting a functional analysis of the behavior to determine the contexts in which it occurs and the environmental responses to the behavior
2. Hypothesizing the pragmatic function that the behavior may serve
3. Determining an appropriate mode and form for an alternative behavior to serve the same function
4. Prompting and functionally reinforcing the new behavior
5. Differentially reinforcing the appropriate behavior over the inappropriate behavior
6. Maintaining data on both the appropriate and the inappropriate behavior (and modifying the program if progress is not apparent)
7. Providing for generalization and maintenance of the new behavior to prevent regression

Transdisciplinary Teamwork

The need for an environment responsive to the child's communication is just one important reason for close cooperation among parents, teachers, therapists, and all other members of the transdisciplinary team. Isolated communication therapy is unlikely to: 1) provide adequate training time, 2) provide consistent responses from communication partners, 3) generalize to the natural environment, or 4) provide an appropriate communication context (Nietupski et al., 1980). Integrated assessment, program development, and intervention efforts contribute toward elimination of all of these problems.

In addition to providing some specific training to the learner, locating resources (e.g., assessment instruments, training programs, adaptive communication equipment), and maintaining progress records (Silverman, 1980), within integrated systems, the communication therapist may act as a consultant sharing his or her expertise with all other team members (Musselwhite & St. Louis, 1988). Occupational and physical therapists can be extremely helpful in evaluating motor function for gestural and augmentative systems of communication. Often, they are helpful in designing or modifying equipment to suit the child's capabilities or in helping the child develop the motor control required for a specific communication system (Silverman, 1980).

Increasingly, biomedical and electrical engineers are participating on the team when specialized electronic equipment is required (Silverman, 1980). Their expertise allows for design and construction of equipment that meets the requirements identified by other team members.

Family members and other caregivers play a vital role on this team, helping to identify the functions and content for training. Their interactions with the learner are critical to the development of functional communication. They are the primary communication partners with the child. Their responses can make the child's communication meaningful or futile in the child's current environments, and their interactions provide a model for potential future environments.

The teacher's role overlaps that of many other team members. He or she is often caregiver, evaluator, and interventionist, but the teacher typically has the additional role of coordinator. In discussing the need for integrated services, it is important to point out that, while the integration process need not be a struggle, it does require active and ongoing efforts to facilitate communication and ensure smooth transdisciplinary coordination. Most often, the teacher takes a major role in this.

This list of team members is far from complete. Teacher's associates may provide much of the instruction in structured and natural environments. Audiologists, physicians, and others may provide important assessment of sensory abilities or limitations. The communication team must not be a fixed entity with prespecified members. It must be flexible enough to alter its membership based on the current decisions to be addressed for the individual child.

SUMMARY

This chapter has provided information related to training in communication functions for children with severe and multiple disabilities. In doing so, it has concentrated on very basic communication. A pragmatic focus, in which the purpose (social effectiveness) of communication is emphasized, provides the major framework for program content. Eclectic training methods that are not restricted to a single communication mode are strongly recommended because they place the fewest restrictions on the child and most closely approximate normal communication. Finally, the need to consider the interaction between communication partners, rather than only the behavior of the individual in isolation, has been stressed.

REFERENCES

Allaire, J.H., & Miller, J.M. (1983). Nonspeech communication. In M.E. Snell (Ed.), *Systematic instruction of the moderately and severely handicapped* (2nd ed., pp. 289–311). Columbus: Charles E. Merrill.

Alwell, M., Hunt., P., Goetz, L., & Sailor, W. (1989). Teaching generalized communicative behaviors within interrupted behavior chain contexts. *Journal of The Association for Persons with Severe Disabilities, 14*, 91–100.

Bates, E., Camaioni, L., & Voltera, V. (1979). The acquisition of performatives prior to speech. In E. Ochs & B.B. Schieffelin (Eds.), *Developmental pragmatics* (pp. 111–130). New York: Academic Press.

Baumgart, D., Johnson, J., & Helmstetter, E. (1990) *Augmentative and alternative communication systems for persons with moderate and severe disabilities*. Baltimore: Paul H. Brookes Publishing Co.

Bigge, J.L. (1991). *Teaching individuals with physical and multiple disabilities* (3rd ed.). Columbus: Charles E. Merrill.

Bloom, L., & Lahey, M. (1978). *Language development and language disorders*. New York: John Wiley & Sons.

Bottorf, L., & De Pape, D. (1982). Initiating communication systems for severely speech impaired persons. *Topics in Language Disorders, 2*, 55–71.

Bricker, D.D. (1983). Early communication: Development and training. In M.E. Snell (Ed.), *Systematic instruction of the moderately and severely handicapped* (2nd ed., pp. 269–288). Columbus: Charles E. Merrill.

Brinker, R.P. (1985). Interactions between severely mentally retarded students and other students in integrated and segregated public school settings. *American Journal of Mental Deficiency, 89,* 587–594.

Capozzi, M., & Mineo, B. (1984). Nonspeech language and communication systems. In A.L. Holland (Ed.), *Language disorders in children: Recent advances* (pp. 173–209). San Diego: College-Hill.

Carr, E.G., & Dores, P.A. (1981). Patterns of language acquisition following simultaneous communication with autistic children. *Analysis and Intervention in Developmental Disabilities, 1,* 347–361.

Carr, E.G., & Durand, V.M. (1985). Reducing behavior problems through functional communication training. *Journal of Applied Behavior Analysis, 18,* 111–126.

Cavallaro, C.C., & Bambara, L.M. (1982). Two strategies for teaching language during free play. *Journal of The Association for the Severely Handicapped, 7*(2), 90–92.

Cirrin, F.M., & Rowland, C.M. (1985). Communicative assessment of nonverbal youths with severe/profound mental retardation. *Mental Retardation, 23,* 52–62.

Clark, C.R. (1984). A close look at the standard Rebus System and Blissymbolics. *Journal of The Association for Persons with Severe Handicaps, 9,* 37–48.

Correia, L.M., & Sobsey, D. (1984, May). *Assessing communication and precommunication skills in clients with severe multiple handicaps.* Paper presented at the Annual Meeting of the American Association on Mental Deficiency, Minneapolis. (ERIC Document Reproduction Service No. ED 252 032)

Creekmore, N. (1982). Use of sign alone and sign plus speech in language training of autistic children. *Journal of The Association for the Severely Handicapped, 6*(4), 45–55.

Dennis, R., Reichle, J., Williams, W., & Vogelsberg, R.T. (1982). Motoric factors influencing the selection of vocabulary for sign production programs. *Journal of The Association for the Severely Handicapped, 7*(1), 20–32.

Donnellan, A.M., Mirenda, P.L., Mesaros, R.A., & Fassbender, L.L. (1984). Analyzing the communicative functions of aberrant behavior. *Journal of The Association for Persons with Severe Handicaps, 9,* 201–212.

Doss, L.S., & Reichle, J. (1991). Replacing excess behavior with an initial communicative repertoire. In J. Reichle, J. York, & J. Sigafoos, *Implementing augmentative and alternative communication: Strategies for learners with severe disabilities* (pp. 215–237). Baltimore: Paul H. Brookes Publishing Co.

Goetz, L., Gee, K., & Sailor, W. (1985). Using a behavior chain interruption strategy to teach communication skills to students with severe disabilities. *Journal of The Association for Persons with Severe Handicaps, 10,* 21–30.

Greenfield, P., & Smith, J. (1976). *The structure of communication in early language development.* New York: Academic Press.

Guess, D., & Noonan, M.J. (1982). Curricula and instructional procedures for severely handicapped students. *Focus on Exceptional Children, 5,* 1–12.

Guralnick, M.J. (1984). The peer interactions of young developmentally delayed children in specialized and in integrated settings. In T. Field, J. Roopnarine, & M. Segal (Eds.), *Friendships in normal and handicapped children* (pp. 139–152). Norwood, NJ: Ablex.

Guralnick, M.J., & Groom, J.M. (1988). Peer interactions in mainstreamed and specialized classrooms: A comparative analysis. *Exceptional Children, 54,* 415–425.

Halle, J.W. (1982). Teaching functional language to the handicapped: An integrative model of natural environment teaching techniques. *Journal of The Association for the Severely Handicapped, 7*(4), 29–37.

Halliday, M. (1975). *Learning how to mean: Explorations in the development of language.* New York: Elsevier.

Harris, S.L. (1975). Teaching language to non-verbal children—with emphasis on problems of generalization. *Psychological Bulletin, 82,* 565–580.

Hill, C.A., & Whitely, J.H. (1985). Social interactions and on-task behavior of severely multihandicapped and non-handicapped children in mainstreamed classrooms. *Canadian Journal for Exceptional Children, 1,* 136–140.

Hunt, P., Alwell, M., Goetz, L., & Sailor, W. (1990). Generalized effects of conversation skill training. *Journal of The Association for Persons with Severe Handicaps, 15,* 250—260.

Hurlbut, B.I., Iwata, B.A., & Green, J.D. (1982). Non-vocal language acquisition in adolescents with severe physical disabilities: Blissymbols versus iconic stimulus formats. *Journal of Applied Behavior Analysis, 15,* 241–258.

Kaczmarek, L.A. (1990). Teaching spontaneous language to individuals with severe handicaps. *Journal of The Association for Persons with Severe Handicaps, 15,* 160–169.

Karlan, G., & Lloyd, L.L. (1983). Considerations in the planning of communication intervention: Selecting a lexicon. *Journal of The Association for the Severely Handicapped, 8*(2), 13–25.

Keogh, W.J., & Reichle, J. (1985). Communication intervention for the "difficult-to-teach" severely handicapped. In S.F. Warren & A.K. Rogers-Warren (Eds.), *Teaching functional language: Generalization and maintenance of language skills* (pp. 157–194). Baltimore: University Park Press.

Kirschner, A., Algozzine, B., & Abbott, T.B. (1979). Manual communications systems: A comparison and its implications. *Education and Training of the Mentally Retarded, 14,* 5–10.

Kleinert, H.L., & Gast, D.L. (1982). Teaching a multihandicapped adult manual signs using a constant delay procedure. *Journal of The Association for the Severely Handicapped, 6*(4), 25–37.

Kohl, F.L., Moses, L.G., & Stettner-Eaton, B.A. (1983). The results of teaching fifth and sixth graders to be instructional trainers with students who are severely handicapped. *Journal of The Association for Persons with Severe Handicaps, 8*(4), 32–40.

Kollinzas, G. (1983). The communication record: Sharing information to promote sign language generalization. *Journal of The Association for the Severely Handicapped, 8*(3), 49–55.

Leonard, L.B. (1984). Normal language acquisition: Some recent findings and clinical implications. In A.L. Holland (Ed.), *Language disorders in children: Recent advances* (pp. 1–36). San Diego: College-Hill.

Light, J., Collier, B., & Parnes, P. (1985). Communicative interaction between young nonspeaking physically disabled children and their primary caregivers. *Augmentative and Alternative Communication, 1,* 74–83.

Love, R.J., Hagerman, E.L., & Taimi, E.G. (1980). Speech performance, dysphagia, and oral reflexes in cerebral palsy. *Journal of Speech and Hearing Disorders, 45,* 59–75.

MacDonald, J.D. (1985). Language through conversation: A model for intervention with language-delayed persons. In S.F. Warren & A.K. Rogers-Warren (Eds.), *Teaching functional language: Generalization and maintenance of language skills* (pp. 89–122). Baltimore: University Park Press.

McLean, J., & Snyder-McLean, L. (1978). *A transactional approach to early language training.* Columbus: Charles E. Merrill.

McLuhan, M. (1964). *Understanding the media: The extensions of man.* New York: McGraw-Hill.

McShane, J. (1980). *Learning to talk.* London: Cambridge University Press.

Merrill, E.C. (1985). Differences in semantic processing speed of mentally retarded and nonretarded persons. *American Journal of Mental Deficiency, 90,* 71–80.

Mirenda, P. (1985). Designing pictorial communication systems for physically able-bodied students with severe handicaps. *Augmentative and Alternative Communication, 1,* 58–64.

Mirenda, P., & Iacono, T. (1990). Communication options for persons with severe and profound disabilities: State of the art and future directions. *Journal of The Association for Persons with Severe Disabilities, 15,* 13–21.

Morris, D. (1982). *A pocket guide to manwatching.* London: Triad/Panther Books.

Morris, S.E. (1978a). Sensorimotor prerequisites for speech and the influence of cerebral palsy. In J.M. Wilson (Ed.), *Oral-motor function and dysfunction in children* (pp. 123–128). Chapel Hill: University of North Carolina, Division of Physical Therapy.

Morris, S.E. (1978b). Pre-speech assessment scale. In J.M. Wilson (Ed.), *Oral-motor function and dysfunction in children* (pp. 133–488). Chapel Hill: University of North Carolina, Division of Physical Therapy.

Musselwhite, C.R., & St. Louis, K.W. (1988). *Communication programming for persons with severe handicaps* (2nd ed.). Boston: Little, Brown.

Mustonen, T., Locke, P., Reichle, J., Solbrack, M., & Lindgren, A. (1991). An overview of augmentative and alternative communication systems. In J. Reichle, J. York, & J. Sigafoos, *Implementing augmentative and alternative communication: Strategies for learners with severe disabilities.* Baltimore: Paul H. Brookes Publishing Co.

Nietupski, J., Scheutz, G., & Ockwood, L. (1980). The delivery of communication therapy services to severely handicapped students: A plan for change. *Journal of The Association for the Severely Handicapped, 5,* 13–23.

Olswang, L.B., Stoel-Gammon, C., Coggins, T.E., & Carpenter, R.L. (1987). *Assessing prelinguistic and early linguistic behaviors in developmentally young children.* Seattle: University of Washington Press.

Oviatt, S. (1980). The emerging ability to comprehend language. An experimental approach. *Child Development, 51,* 97–106.

Owings, N., McManus, M., & Scherer, N. (1981). A deinstitutionalized retarded adult's use of communication functions in the natural setting. *British Journal of Disorders of Communication, 16,* 119–128.

Piché, L., & Reichle, J. (1991). Teaching scanning and selection techniques. In J. Reichle, J. York, & J. Sigafoos, *Implementing augmentative and alternative communication: Strategies for learners with severe disabilities* (pp. 257–274). Baltimore: Paul H. Brookes Publishing Co.

Reichle, J. (1991). Defining the decisions involved in designing and implementing augmentative and alternative communication systems. In J. Reichle, J. York, & J. Sigafoos, *Implementing augmentative and alternative communication: Strategies for learners with severe disabilities* (pp. 39–60). Baltimore: Paul H. Brookes Publishing Co.

Reichle, J., & Keogh, W.J. (1985). Communication intervention: A selective review of what, when, and how to teach. In F.S. Warren & A.K. Rogers-Warren (Eds.), *Teaching functional language: Generalization and maintenance of language skills* (pp. 25–59). Baltimore: University Park Press.

Reichle, J., & Keogh, W.J. (1986). Communication instruction for learners with severe handicaps: Some unresolved issues. In R.H. Horner, L.H. Meyer, & H.D.B. Fredericks (Eds.), *Education for learners with severe handicaps: Exemplary service strategies* (pp. 189–220). Baltimore: Paul H. Brookes Publishing Co.

Reichle, J., Rogers, N., & Barrett, C. (1984). Establishing pragmatic discriminations among communicative functions of requesting, rejecting and commenting in an adolescent. *Journal of The Association for Persons with Severe Handicaps, 9,* 31–36.

Reichle, J., & Sigafoos, J. (1991). Establishing an initial repertoire of requesting. In J. Reichle, J. York, & J. Sigafoos, *Implementing augmentative and alternative communication: Strategies for learners with severe disabilities* (pp. 89–114). Baltimore: Paul H. Brookes Publishing Co.

Reichle, J., Williams, W., & Ryan, S. (1981). Selecting signs for the formulation of an augmentative communicative modality. *Journal of The Association for the Severely Handicapped, 6*(1), 48–56.

Reichle, J.E., & Yoder, D.E. (1979). Assessment and early stimulation of communication in the severely and profoundly mentally retarded. In R. York & G. Edgar (Eds.), *Teaching the severely handicapped* (Vol. IV, pp. 180–218). Columbus: Special Press.

Remington, B., & Clarke, S. (1983). Acquisition of expressive signing by autistic children: An evaluation of relative effects of simultaneous communication and sign-alone training. *Journal of Applied Behavior Analysis, 16,* 315–328.

Rogers-Warren, A.K. (1984). Ecobehavioral analysis. *Education and Treatment of Children, 7,* 283–303.

Rogers-Warren, A., & Warren, S. (1980). Mands for verbalization: Facilitating the display of newly trained language in children. *Behavior Modification, 4,* 361–382.

Rosenberg, S., & Beukelman, D. (1987). The participation model. In C.A. Coston (Ed.), *Proceedings of the National Planners Conference on Assistive Device Service Delivery* (pp. 159–161). Washington, DC: RESNA, The Association for the Advancement of Rehabilitation Technology.

Rosenberg, S.A., & Robinson, C.C. (1985). Enhancement of mothers' interactional skills in an infant education program. *Education and Training of the Mentally Retarded, 20,* 163–169.

Sailor, W., & Guess, D. (1983). *Severely handicapped students: An instructional design.* Boston: Houghton-Mifflin.

Sailor, W., Guess, D., Goetz, L., Schuler, A., Utley, B., & Baldwin, M. (1980). Language and severely handicapped persons: Deciding what to teach whom. In W. Sailor, B. Wilcox, & L. Brown (Eds.), *Methods of instruction for severely handicapped students* (pp. 71–108). Baltimore: Paul H. Brookes Publishing Co.

Shane, H.C., & Bashir, A.S. (1980). Election criteria for adoption of an augmentative communications system: Preliminary considerations. *Journal of Speech and Hearing Disorders, 45,* 408–414.

Shevin, M., & Klein, N.K. (1984). The importance of choice-making skills for students with severe disabilities. *Journal of The Association for Persons with Severe Handicaps, 9,* 159–166.

Siegel-Causey, E., & Ernst, B. (1989). Theoretical orientation and research in nonsymbolic development. In E. Siegel-Causey & D. Guess (Eds.), *Enhancing nonsymbolic communication interactions among learners with severe disabilities* (pp.15–51). Baltimore: Paul H. Brookes Publishing Co.

Sigafoos, J., & Reichle, J. (1991). Establishing an initial repertoire of rejecting. In J. Reichle, J. York, & J. Sigafoos, *Implementing augmentative and alternative communication: Strategies for learners with severe disabilities* (pp. 115–132). Baltimore: Paul H. Brookes Publishing Co.

Sigafoos, J., & York, J. (1991). Using ecological inventories to promote functional communication. In J. Reichle, J. York, & J. Sigafoos, *Implementing augmentative and alternative communication: Strategies for learners with severe disabilities* (pp. 61–70). Baltimore: Paul H. Brookes Publishing Co.

Silverman, F.H. (1980). *Communication for the speechless.* Englewood Cliffs, NJ: Prentice-Hall.

Snyder, L.K., & McLean, J.E. (1976). Deficient acquisition strategies: A conceptual framework for analyzing severe language deficiency. *American Journal of Mental Deficiency, 81,* 338–349.

Sobsey, R., & Bieniek, B. (1983). A family approach to functional sign language. *Behavior Modification, 7,* 488–502.

Sobsey, D., & Reichle, J. (1989). Components of reinforcement for attention signal switch activation. *The Mental Retardation and Learning Disability Bulletin, 17*(2), 46–60.

Sternberg, L., Pegnatore, L., & Hill, C. (1983). Establishing interactive communication behavior with profoundly mentally handicapped students. *Journal of The Association for the Severely Handicapped, 8*(2), 39–46.

Stremmel-Campbell, K., Campbell, R., & Johnson-Dorn, N. (1985). Utilization of integrated settings and activities to develop and expand communication skills. In M.P. Brady & P. Gunter (Eds.), *Integrating moderately and severely handicapped learners: Strategies that work* (pp. 185–213). Springfield, IL: Charles C Thomas.

Terrace, H.S. (1979). *Nim.* New York: Alfred A. Knopf.

Vanderheiden, G.C., & Lloyd, L.L. (1986). Communication systems and their components. In S.W. Blackstone (Ed.), *Augmentative communication: An introduction* (pp. 49–161). Rockville, MD: American Speech-Language-Hearing Association.

Van Dijk, J. (1986). An educational curriculum for deaf-blind multihandicapped persons. In D. Ellis (Ed.), *Sensory impairments in mentally handicapped people* (pp. 374–382). San Diego: College-Hill.

Waldo, L., Guess, D., & Flanagan, B. (1985). Effects of concurrent and serial training on receptive labeling by severely retarded individuals. *Journal of The Association for the Severely Handicapped, 6*(4), 56–65.

Warren, S.F., Baxter, D.K., Anderson, S.R., Marshall, A., & Baer, D.M. (1981). Generalization of question-asking by severely retarded individuals. *Journal of The Association for the Severely Handicapped, 6*(3), 15–22.

Warren, S.F., & Rogers-Warren, A.K. (1983). A longitudinal analysis of language generalization among adolescents with severely handicapping conditions. *Journal of The Association for Persons with Severe Handicaps, 8*(4), 18–31.

Waterson, N., & Snow, C. (1978). *Development of communication.* New York: John Wiley & Sons.

York, J., & Weiman, G. (1991). Accommodating severe physical disabilities. In J. Reichle, J. York, & J. Sigafoos, *Implementing augmentative and alternative communication: Strategies for learners with severe disabilities* (pp. 239–255). Baltimore: Paul H. Brookes Publishing Co.

Chapter 10

Mealtime Skills

Probably no single activity cluster is as critical to the health, education, and happiness of children with multiple disabilities as mealtimes. In the best instances, meals combine the nutrition needed for growth and survival; the pleasure of enjoyable tastes, aromas, and textures; the opportunity for positive social interaction; and the chance to increase independence in eating and feeding skills. Such mealtimes are undoubtedly among the most pleasant times spent by children and their caregivers. For others, however, mealtimes are stressful and unpleasant. Some children struggle through seemingly endless meals with little opportunity for positive social interaction or learning, desperately trying to obtain adequate foods and fluids without choking or gagging. Caregivers struggle to overcome the children's abnormal movement and behavior problems. For many children, the mealtime experience falls somewhere in between these two extremes; but what are the factors that determine whether meals will be more like the positive or negative extreme? Can caregivers intervene to alter some of these factors, and if so, how?

Although complete answers to all these questions are not available at this writing, research and clinical experience in a number of disciplines has provided at least partial answers. Some factors that influence mealtime performance are related to the characteristics of the child who is eating (e.g., muscle tone, reflex patterns). Other factors are related to the physical environment (e.g., food texture, types of utensils provided). Still other factors are related to the social environment (e.g., pace of feeding, noise and disruption in the dining area). Although some factors may be easier to control than others, intervention can produce significant improvements in performance regardless of whether internal or external factors must be addressed.

This chapter describes common mealtime concerns and discusses methods for intervening to achieve specific objectives. Both eating and feeding skills are included. Although these two closely related skills are often grouped together, they are treated separately here to ensure that each receives adequate coverage. *Eating* refers to accepting and processing food in the mouth and to swallowing food. *Feeding* refers to bringing food to the mouth. Two other topics, nutrition and dentistry, are also considered here because of their close relationship with eating and feeding skills. Finally, this chapter discusses the roles of various members of the transdisciplinary team in assessing performance and planning programs. Prevention and treatment of airway obstruction is an essential topic for all staff involved in eating and feeding activities, and information on this topic is included in Chapter 6.

EATING AND DRINKING SKILLS

Many children with multiple disabilities have difficulty eating their food. Disorders of muscle tone may make lip closure difficult, interfering with the child's ability to take food from a spoon or hold liquids in the mouth. Primitive reflexes (e.g., tonic bite reflex) may make chewing difficult or impossible. Inappropriate selection of food textures and utensils, poor positioning, improper presentation of foods, or stress factors in the mealtime environment can aggravate these problems or cause additional problems. Structural abnormalities (e.g., cleft lip, cleft palate) can further complicate eating, and oral-motor patterns that develop to help compensate for these impairments (e.g., excessive neck extension to keep food from falling out of mouth) may create secondary problems. Compounding all of these problems, dysfunctional eating patterns are inadvertently taught to some children by their caregivers in well-intentioned attempts to improve eating (e.g., feeding the child in a supine position). Often, many of these factors interact in the same child, and it is difficult to determine which factor is primarily responsible for a given problem.

Of course, each child is an individual, and it is impossible to describe a general pattern of eating and drinking for all children with disabilities or even for all children with any specific category of disability. Similarly, normal eating and drinking includes a wide range of behavior. Notwithstanding this variability, some general patterns of eating and drinking behavior are described here along with intervention methods.

Oral Motor Patterns

Normal Development   Eating and drinking are complex physiological processes (Morris & Klein, 1987). Three major body systems make major contributions to the process:

1. The skeletal system provides underlying structural support, anchors muscles, and provides the cutting and grinding surfaces on the teeth required to chew food.

2. The muscular system provides additional structure as well as movement required to accept, retain, chew, and mix food with saliva, which lubricates and begins to digest food in the mouth. The muscular system also moves food into the esophagus and closes off the airway to allow its safe passage.
3. The nervous system directs and coordinates these activities.

Although eating and drinking are generally considered to be under voluntary control, experimental evidence indicates that much of oral-motor behavior is primarily reflexive or patterned by neural circuits. Biting, chewing, licking, and sucking all follow the same rhythmic pattern for each individual (Campbell, 1978). Each movement in the cycle results in sensory stimulation that influences the next response in the cycle. For example, the closing of the jaws during chewing stimulates pressure receptors. The pressure receptors signal the jaws to open, and so on. A central neural pattern generator controls the pace and coordination of movements. Voluntary control can modify activity of this generator but cannot replace its function. So the responses involved in eating behavior are a combination of reflexes, more complex (reflex-like) patterns, and voluntary movements.

Newborns who do not have related impairments obtain nourishment through sucking or suckling patterns. *Sucking* refers to obtaining liquid as a result of the suction created by raising and lowering the tongue after sealing the oral cavity by pressing the lips against the nipple. *Suckling* refers to obtaining liquid as a result of a rhythmic licking of the nipple and does not require lip seal for suction (Morris, 1978a). Although some investigators have reported observing early sucking patterns, suckling is generally considered the predominant pattern in young infants. Swallowing is integrated with both of these patterns.

For most children, the next stage of eating occurs when semisolid foods are introduced at about 6 months. The exact age varies greatly since it depends more on the caregivers' decision to introduce semisolids than the child's ability to handle them. In fact, the handling of semisolid food as a developmental stage is highly questionable since children in many parts of the world routinely progress directly from liquids to solids with no apparent difficulty (Sobsey, 1983). Initially, babies respond to semisolids with the same suckling pattern used for liquids. Much of the food is pushed back out of the mouth by the tongue at this stage. Gradually, babies learn to keep their tongues in their mouths and to use their lips to take food from the spoon.

As more solid foods are introduced, children learn to bite and chew. At about age 5 months, *munching* is exhibited by most infants. Munching combines vertical jaw movements with a flattening and spreading of the tongue. *Rotary chewing,* which combines lateral tongue and rotary jaw movements, replaces munching as increasingly more solid foods are presented over time (Morris, 1978a). The emergence of teeth makes chewing more effective, but the chewing pattern is normally fully or nearly fully developed by the age of 6–9 months, well before the molars emerge.

Drinking from a cup is also commonly introduced at this time. Again, the child typically responds with a suckling pattern, but, gradually, he or she learns to control excess tongue movements and to accept and hold liquids in the mouth before swallowing them.

Although suckling, sucking, munching, rotary chewing, and drinking are all distinct patterns, common components can be seen in all of these actions, and each subsequent pattern integrates elements of the earlier patterns. The rhythmic signature of each individual's neural pattern generator leaves little doubt that all these behaviors are under the control of the same mechanism.

The basic facts about normal oral-motor development have important implications for understanding the abnormal oral-motor patterns encountered among children with multiple disabilities, and this knowledge may help to suggest appropriate intervention strategies (Morris & Klein, 1987). Since many basic patterns are not under voluntary complex control, intervention that can evoke or facilitate more normal reflexive patterns is desirable. Similarly, intervention that inhibits or blocks abnormal patterns could be equally useful. Since the mechanisms that generate these patterns are not directly accessible (or even clearly identified), intervention must influence these patterns indirectly by altering their environment (e.g., positioning, food texture). Since it is clear that voluntary responses play some role and that all responses are influenced to some degree by learning experiences, traditional teaching methods may also play an important role. Finally, since it is known that normal eating patterns typically emerge in the first few months of life, intervention should begin as soon as possible.

Common Difficulties   Most children with multiple disabilities have problems eating (Gallender, 1979). As the number and severity of disabilities increase, so does the likelihood of eating problems. These problems fall into five general categories, depending on their origin: 1) disorders of muscle tone, 2) abnormal reflexes or dysfunctional primitive reflexes, 3) problems associated with structural abnormalities, 4) learning problems, and 5) combinations of these four. Each category is briefly discussed below.

Disorders of Muscle Tone   As discussed in Chapter 3, inadequate muscle tone (hypotonicity) or excessive muscle tone (hypertonicity) are frequent problems among children with multiple disabilities. These problems often affect the oral musculature as well as many other parts of the body and result in significant eating problems.

Generalized hypotonicity may result in drooping of the head, jaw, and lips and weak and futile attempts at chewing. Inadequate tone is likely to lead to secondary problems since inability to maintain stability of the trunk, neck, and head makes control of fine oral-motor movements impossible (Morris & Weber, 1978).

Generalized hypertonicity, however, may result in extreme rigidity that severely limits any movement of the oral structures and may deform some of these structures as a result of constant pressure. Since increased tone may be present in the muscles controlling movement in opposing directions, great effort may be required for any movement.

Making matters more complicated, abnormalities of muscle tone do not typically affect all muscles in the same manner or to the same extent. Most children with disorders of muscle tone exhibit uneven tone across muscle groups. Typically, patterns of extension or of flexion predominate as a result of uneven tone. This may result in the chronic retraction of lips, protrusion of the tongue, limited voluntary control, or a number of other problems. Unfortunately, the dominant muscles grow stronger as a result of continual contraction, and their antagonists grow weaker as a result of disuse. This leads to further restriction of movement and more difficulty with voluntary control.

Some children have fluctuating muscle tone that may result in involuntary movements of oral structures or make precise coordinated movements of lips, tongue, and jaws impossible (Morris & Weber, 1978). All of these disorders of muscle tone have adverse effects on eating skills, and intervention to normalize tone is an important component of an eating skills program. Some of the positioning and stimulation procedures described under the "Intervention Techniques" section of this chapter are useful in normalizing muscle tone, but, before intervention is considered, other problems that affect eating skills are presented.

Abnormal Reflexes or Dysfunctional Primitive Reflexes   Several types of involuntary motor patterns (discussed in Chapter 3) can create eating problems for children with multiple disabilities. *Abnormal reflexes* are involuntary responses to stimuli that do not occur in nondisabled children of any age. *Primitive reflexes* are involuntary responses to stimuli that are normal (and appear to be functional) in very young children, but that may persist in children with multiple disabilities well beyond the time of normal integration or disappearance. *Hypersensitive reflexes* are involuntary responses to stimuli that are normal in all children, but that may require much higher levels of stimulation (or are totally absent) in children with disabilities. Although not all authors and clinicians agree on which reflexes are normal, abnormal, primitive, or hypersensitive, or even on whether some response patterns should be considered reflexes, all of them agree that the control of these patterns is important for improving eating skills.

Following are descriptions of several specific reflexes: The *rooting reflex* is normal soon after birth and helps the infant orient his or her mouth toward a food source. The head turns toward any stimulus that lightly touches either cheek (Gallender, 1979). When this persists beyond the first few months of life, it interferes with voluntary head control, especially during meals. The *tonic bite reflex* is exhibited when stimulation in the mouth produces a forceful, involuntary, and generally prolonged clamping of the jaws (Palmer & Horn, 1978). This response pattern obviously interferes with spoon-feeding and also often makes chewing extremely difficult. *Tongue thrust* or *tongue protrusion* may not be a true reflex (Morris & Weber, 1978), but it still occurs involuntarily in some children. Each attempt to chew or swallow results in the tongue pushing forward against or between the teeth. Often, this pushes food or fluids back out of the mouth, and, over time, this may also push the teeth out of position. Similar movements are also described in a *generalized infantile suck-swallow pattern* (Gallender, 1979; Morris & Weber, 1978). Although the tongue does not typically protrude for as long as it does with tongue thrust, each swallow is followed by an infant sucking or suckling pattern. Although it is often most evident during drinking, it may also occur during the eating of solids. Although an *asymmetrical tonic neck reflex* (ATNR) affects the whole body, it creates specific problems for eating and feeding (Gallender, 1979). As the head rotates to one side, the arm on that side involuntarily extends, and the other arm flexes in a "fencing pose." The legs may be similarly affected when the reflex is strong (Fraser & Hensinger, 1983). Not only does the turning head make it difficult to put food into the mouth, but muscle contractions generalize to the tongue and jaw, interfering with normal oral-motor control.

In addition to the problems caused by abnormal or dysfunctional primitive reflexes, problems may also be associated with normal, age-appropriate reflexes that are hyperactive or hyporeactive (Morris & Klein, 1987). A *gag reflex* is normal in children and adults, and it protects against the inadvertent swallowing of things that might obstruct the windpipe. When hypersensitive, it causes difficulties because chewing and swallowing become difficult. Hyporeactive gag reflexes are also problematic because they do not protect against the swallowing of large pieces of food or foreign objects (Palmer & Horn, 1978). Hypersensitivity of the *startle reflex* may also create problems. Any loud noise, change in position, or sudden movement may result in total flexion or extension patterns (Gallender, 1979). These patterns interfere with voluntary movements, and they may also contribute to excessive muscle tone. Generally, hypersensitivity of oral and facial areas may exaggerate these and other reflexes. Such hypersensitivity is frequent among children with multiple disabilities, especially in children with excessive muscle tone or severe visual impairment. These children are often reluctant to accept new textures, tastes, or temperatures in food, and, often, they resist any feeding or eating intervention that results in even minimal facial contact.

Structural Abnormalities Abnormal formation of the oral structures may cause or complicate eating problems. Some of the more common problems are cleft lip, cleft palate, high-arched palate, and missing or displaced teeth. Uncorrected cleft lip and cleft palate make sucking and swallowing difficult. This may require the infant to develop abnormal patterns (e.g., increased use of the tongue to obtain milk from the nipple) that lead to secondary eating problems (e.g., tongue thrust) later in life. Tongue thrust as well as sucking and swallowing abnormalities occur frequently (Kalisz & Ekvall, 1978; Springer, 1982).

Surgical correction, as early as possible, is the best treatment for these conditions. High-arched palates are also common. Food may collect on the roof of the mouth and be impossible for the child to reach. Such deformities may result from a lack of appropriate oral stimulation or from abnormal muscle tone during infancy and childhood rather than from genetic factors (Goose & Appleton, 1982), and, therefore, they are partially if not entirely preventable. Similarly, missing and/or displaced teeth are largely preventable and contribute significantly to eating problems. Methods of preventing or treating dental conditions are discussed in the "Dental Concerns" section of this chapter.

Learning Problems   Many eating problems experienced by children with severe disabilities are not the result of anatomical or physiological defects; instead, they result from not learning to perform eating skills properly or from learning inappropriate eating behaviors. Often, these learning problems are mistaken for physical problems. Some examples include: 1) refusing to accept solid foods, 2) swallowing with little or no chewing, 3) eating too rapidly or too slowly, 4) not closing the lips completely, and 5) allowing food to fall back out of the mouth. Of course, any of these examples may have a physiological basis in some children, and, conversely, many other eating problems with physiological causes may also have significant behavioral components.

Combinations   In fact, while discussed as separate factors, disorders of muscle tone, abnormal reflexes, dysfunctional primitive reflexes, structural abnormalities, and learning problems most commonly interact to produce eating difficulties encountered by children with multiple disabilities and their caregivers. To be successful, intervention need not be based on a precise diagnosis of the cause; rather, it needs to focus on determining how to bring about desired changes.

Intervention Techniques

A large number of intervention techniques have been proposed to improve eating skills. Some of these techniques have been demonstrated to be effective in clinical practice or structured research. Entire books (e.g., Campbell, 1982; Gallender, 1979) have focused on this topic, and the limited length of this chapter will not permit the same comprehensive treatment of these techniques. Therefore, nine major categories of intervention are discussed below, with some specific examples included in each: 1) modifying the position of the student, 2) modifying foods, 3) modifying utensils, 4) modifying feeding schedules, 5) modifying presentation of foods, 6) modifying the mealtime environment, 7) providing physical assistance, 8) providing sensory stimulation, and 9) providing specific training.

Modifying Positioning   The importance of positioning for performance of eating skills cannot be overemphasized. The optimal position for eating varies from student to student (Mueller, 1975; Utley, Holvoet, & Barnes, 1977), but certain principles remain constant. First, one should provide as much support as required to ensure stability (Utley et al., 1977). This may require lateral supports in the chair, a firm table or tray surface to rest the elbows on, and/or foot supports at the appropriate height. The finer muscle coordination required for eating and feeding is impossible unless larger muscle groups provide a stable base (Campbell, 1987). Second, the child should be kept as near to upright as possible (Palmer & Horn, 1978). Recumbent or semirecumbent positions encourage infantile feeding patterns. Third, positioning should be normalized as much as possible (Stainback, Stainback, Healy, & Healy, 1980). Providing more support than is needed can be restrictive, discourage independence, and actually weaken muscles that the student would otherwise use for support. Dynamic or temporary support is often adequate and makes more restrictive, static support unnecessary. Most children will do best if the neck is slightly flexed, but the degree of flexion required must be determined individually through careful observation. It is important to position many children (especially those with excess tone) 10 or 15 minutes before the meal begins in order to allow time to relax and adjust to the new position. For some children, it will be important not to position them too far ahead of time, so that they will not become fatigued. The great majority of children will eat best if positioned in a manner as nearly symmetrical as possible (Cautner & Penrose, 1983). For some children with unilateral reflex patterns, slightly asymmetrical postures may work better. The key to determining the best position for each student is careful transdisciplinary assessment and planning.

Modifying Foods Changes in food selection and preparation also influence performance of eating skills. Often, students with multiple disabilities are given diets that consist wholly or primarily of pureed foods. Although some of the literature suggests using soft or pureed foods with students at early developmental levels (e.g., Blockley & Miller, 1971), later empirical studies suggest that many children given pureed foods would do as well or better with whole or coarser textured foods (Jones, 1983; Sobsey, 1983). A study of adults with swallowing disorders found that those receiving pureed diets were significantly more likely to suffer episodes of aspiration pneumonia than those fed a soft diet with thickened liquids (Groher, 1987). The rate in the group receiving pureed foods was more than five times as high as that of the group receiving a soft diet. Alexander (1991) recommended avoiding thin purees whenever possible and using more coarsely ground table foods if the child cannot chew solids. Since many normal eating skills (e.g., chewing) require the stimulation of having solid food in the mouth, pureed foods do not allow the development of some skills. Pureed foods also contribute to constipation, dental caries, weakened and deformed oral structures, and vitamin deficiencies (Sobsey, 1983). Unfortunately, many children who are not exposed to whole foods in infancy may resist them later in life. Although gradual increments in introducing more solid foods are most typically recommended (Morris, 1978b; Stainback et al., 1980),

Jones (1983) found more rapid adjustment with rapid transitions to whole foods. Although a few children may never learn to eat whole foods and transitions must be carefully supervised and evaluated, most students will eat whole foods better than puree, and the transition to coarser textures is generally accomplished with little difficulty (Jones, 1983; Sobsey, 1983).

Similarly, the choice of foods needs consideration. Since not all solid foods have the same consistency, careful matching of the food to the current abilities of the child is essential (Alexander, 1991). Foods that combine liquid and solid components (e.g., soup, fruit cup) may cause particular problems. Some children may exhibit better performance if hot or cold foods are avoided. Careful selections must be made, and they should consider nutritional concerns and child preferences.

Modifying Utensils   Most often, utensils are modified to assist with self-feeding, but some modified utensils also help with the performance of eating skills. The cutaway cup is used to allow drinking without hyperextension of the neck (Morris, 1978b). Normal glasses and cups require hyperextension because when they are tipped up far enough for the contents to pour into the mouth, the rim hits the drinker's nose unless the head is tipped back. Unfortunately, many children with multiple disabilities choke, gag, exhibit infantile suck-swallow patterns, or have other difficulties when they tip their heads back to drink. Cutting away part of the rim of a cup or glass allows it to be tipped up farther without hitting the child's nose or requiring the head to be tipped back. For children who are being fed, clear, plastic cups are best. These allow the person doing the feeding to observe the fluid in the cup and the child's mouth without having to move to an inappropriate position for presentation.

Some children with hypersensitive bite or gag reflexes may do better with modified spoons. Trefler, Westmoreland, and Burlingame (1977) suggest a spatula-spoon to minimize stimulation within the mouth for individuals with extreme intraoral hypersensitivity. Nylon, plastic, or rubber-coated spoons may work well for children with hypersensitivity, especially those who react strongly to hot or cold stimuli, because metal utensils conduct heat to or from the oral structures very rapidly. Non-metal spoons are also useful for children who bite down on utensils, since they are generally softer and are less likely to cause injury. Although small, disposable, plastic spoons are excellent for some children because they minimize stimulation, they are not suitable for a child who may bite down on them because they break, often leaving sharp splinters of plastic in the mouth.

Modified utensils can be extremely useful for many children with disabilities when used in combination with other interventions. Other children, however, eat as well or better with regular utensils. It is important to remember the normalization principle and to use specialized eating utensils only when a clear benefit over the more normal alternative can be demonstrated. Careful, ongoing assessment is the best method for determining whether modified utensils have value for a specific student, and it allows planning for their introduction and use as well as planning for a return to more normal alternatives.

Modifying Feeding Schedules   Snell (1983) points out that considerable controversy exists regarding the best times and places to teach eating skills. Some researchers suggest that frequent small meals provide faster acquisition of skills than just three meals per day (Azrin & Armstrong, 1973). Others suggest that quiet times and places may produce better acquisition than busy lunchrooms at mealtimes (Wilson, 1978). It also may be argued that skills taught in a natural setting, under typical conditions, are most likely to generalize and maintain over time. In view of the apparent disagreement, it is difficult to see how all of these points of view could be correct unless the individual nature of each child is taken into account. Again, if no clear benefit can be demonstrated as a result of using modified times or places, the normalization principle dictates that meals be provided at typical times in the normal environment. Several reasons can be identified, however, for providing at least part of a child's eating skills training at specialized times and/or in specialized places. In general, when specialized training times and places are used, they should supplement rather than substitute for regular mealtime training.

One important reason for supplementing regular mealtimes with specialized training sessions is to allow for a temporary reduction in function that may occur during acquisition of a new behavior. For example, a child with cerebral palsy may exhibit an infantile suck-swallow pattern when drinking from a cup. Although he or she uses an inefficient pattern and has difficulty obtaining adequate fluids, it is the most efficient drinking pattern currently in his or her repertoire. Teaching the child a more efficient and more mature drinking pattern will be extremely useful, but during the initial acquisition phase, it will be much less efficient than his or her current pattern. Requiring the child to use the new pattern at his or her regular meal and drink times has two major disadvantages. First, it will reduce fluid intake and may threaten his or her health. Second, the child will almost certainly resist since using the new pattern at first will lessen fluid intake. By teaching initial acquisition outside regular meal and drink times, more fluids are provided instead of less, and the additional fluids provided at these special times reinforce the newly acquired pattern. When the new pattern becomes as efficient as the old one, it can be introduced (and reasonably required) at regular meal and drink times. Acquisition of new eating and drinking patterns typically leads to such temporary reductions in efficiency. The addition of specialized training times can be useful to overcome the problems associated with these temporary reductions.

Another reason for providing training in eating and drinking skills outside of regular mealtimes is to overcome resistance by the child. Many parents report that their children will not accept new tastes and textures at home, but quickly accept them in a new environment. Therefore, it is not surprising that researchers have found a similar increase in willingness to accept new foods among children with developmental disabilities when they are placed in a new environment (Linschied, Oliver, Blyer, & Palmer, 1978).

Providing small meals for training purposes in addition to regular mealtimes may also be useful for training in eating skills because this provides distributed rather than massed practice (Snell, 1983). While this has learning advantages for all learners, it may be particularly useful for children who tire quickly or become distracted or disruptive during longer meals. Other children may benefit from additional or alternative eating and drinking times because they take advantage of their peak learning times. Peak learning times are easily identified for many students who may be active, alert, and attentive at some times during the day and may be lethargic, unresponsive, or irritable at other times. Finally, it should be noted that snacks are normal in this society, and few people restrict their eating to only three meals a day. Using snacks for either structured or incidental learning is consistent with normal patterns of everyday life.

Modifying Food Presentation   The manner in which food is presented to the child is extremely important, especially when the child is being fed by another individual. If food or drink is presented from above, it will encourage extension patterns. If it is presented from below, it will encourage flexion patterns. If it is presented from either side, it will encourage the child to turn to that side. The pace and cues provided with presentation can enhance relaxation or increase tension in the child. As with other interventions, presentation must be individualized for each child, but some general strategies will be useful for most children with eating problems.

The person feeding the child should be seated on a low chair so that the food is well below the child's face and the feeder's face is at or below eye level when the child is properly positioned (Stainback et al., 1980). This encourages a slightly flexed neck, which makes swallowing easier and minimizes abnormal reflexes. Exceptions may be when the child has excess flexion and encouraging extension is desirable, or when the feeder must be positioned behind the child to provide physical assistance.

The person feeding the child and the food itself should be positioned as closely as possible to directly in front of the child (Stainback et al., 1980). This encourages symmetrical positioning and discourages asymmetrical reflex patterns (e.g., asymmetrical tonic neck reflex). Exceptions may be when the need to provide physical assistance requires that the feeder be positioned behind or alongside the child, or when the child's posture and reactions are so strongly oriented toward one side that food presented from the opposite side brings the child's position closer to midline and reduces asymmetrical patterns.

Similar attention must be given to the way in which the spoon or cup comes into contact with the child's mouth. The bowl of the spoon should be inserted only partially into the mouth. If the entire bowl of the spoon is inserted, it may cause gagging, and it will be difficult to tip the spoon up to transfer its contents without scraping the spoon against the upper teeth. For the great majority of children, food should be placed in the middle of the mouth on the tongue, but a few children with very limited tongue movement may require food to be placed directly between the teeth.

The rim of the glass or cup should be placed on the child's lower lip, encouraging good lip seal and avoiding stimulation of the bite reflex, which often occurs if the rim is placed between the teeth. Cups and glasses must be tipped up just far enough to allow a controlled flow from the vessel to the mouth. If the cup or glass is tipped up too far, it will encourage the child to use an extension pattern to compensate or to assume a sudden and extreme flexion posture. Either of these extremes will interfere with drinking.

The timing of presentation also is extremely important. Individuals must coordinate eating and drinking behavior with their breathing patterns. Failure to do so will result, at least, in increased difficulty eating or, at most, in life-threatening aspiration or airway obstruction.

Modifying the Mealtime Environment   For most children, especially those with excess tone and/or hypersensitive reflexes, providing a relaxing mealtime environment can help greatly with the performance of eating skills (Stainback et al., 1980). At the same time, providing a training environment that is as close as possible to the child's natural environment (or the environment that the child will progress to) is consistent with the normalization principle and provides the best possibility for maintenance and generalization. This means that sources of stress should be identified and eliminated from both the natural and the training environments. This requires careful attention to the attributes of both the child and the environment. Sources of excessive noise and other disruption in the environment must be controlled. Children who may be aggressive or steal food must be controlled or separated from children with severely limited movement. Of course, some children are more sensitive to specific environmental stimuli that others. These stimuli must be identified for each individual and modifications made where necessary.

Not all environmental modifications require the elimination of problem stimuli. Perhaps even more emphasis should be placed on developing a supportive and relaxing environment. Lighting should be adequate but not harsh. Neither child nor feeder should be backlighted because each must carefully observe the details of the other's movements in order to coordinate the feeding and eating processes. Acoustical dampening will soften the sounds of large dining areas, and the addition of soft music is sometimes helpful. Maintaining a comfortable air temperature is also important. Uncomfortable temperatures (especially cold) increase muscle tone and may increase abnormal reflex activity. Attention to these and other environmental factors will improve the performance of eating skills by most children with multiple disabilities.

Providing Physical Assistance   Physical assistance, especially head and jaw control, is an important component of many eating skill programs (e.g., Alexander, 1991; Morris, 1978b; Stainback et al., 1980; Utley et al., 1977). One may provide head control by placing the feeder's hand on top of the child's head or on the neck area. Pushing the head forward at the occipital area (back of the head) is not recommended since it is believed to stimulate an increased extension reaction (Stainback et al., 1980). Static positioning of the head is best accomplished through positioning aids (e.g., cushions) rather than physical assistance; however, intermittent positioning is a more desirable alternative children who need positioning help only part of the time since it allows for greater independence. For example, many children with cerebral palsy have particular difficulty swallowing liquids (Logemann, 1983). These children may need help keeping their heads in a flexed position when drinking but have adequate head control for the rest of the meal. The feeder may physically assist with head flexion by placing a hand on top of the child's head during drinking but still allowing the child to exercise independent head control at other times during a meal.

Direct control of the jaw, lips, and tongue may be accomplished through manual guidance, but it should be considered only when minimally adequate performance is unattainable through other methods (Alexander, 1991). Although application from the front is typically suitable only for minimal assistance, jaw control may be applied from the front, back, or side of a child. Usually, the feeder uses the nondominant hand to control the jaw and the dominant hand to feed, but, depending on the amount of control required and the position the feeder finds most comfortable and effective, this may change. Although opinion still differs, most authors agree that jaw control should not involve control of the upper lip since pulling down the upper lip will stimulate more lip retraction. Morris (1978b) suggests that the feeder place the middle finger under the child's chin just behind the bony part, placing the index finger between the tip of the chin and the lips, and placing the thumb on the side of the face near the eye. This allows the feeder to assist and control considerably the opening and closing of the jaw.

These procedures can be very helpful with some students, but extreme caution should be exercised in their use. It must be remembered that one develops muscle strength and tone by working against resistance. External control may produce the movements required, but it will not contribute to movements developing by themselves. Worse yet, it may strengthen and increase tone in overdeveloped and hypertonic muscles, while further weakening the underdeveloped muscles that work in opposition to them. This may be a particular problem for the hypertonic child since considerable force may be required to produce the desired movements. Therefore, external jaw control is not recommended if it is possible to use other methods that allow the child to produce the desired movements for himself or herself. When jaw control must be used, it is essential that the minimum effective force be used and that other procedures (e.g., exercises outside of mealtime) be used to develop the independent responses in the child.

Similarly, tongue protrusion is sometimes controlled by the feeder pushing the tongue back in the mouth with the spoon or fingers. This external control may also strengthen the muscles that produce the inappropriate movement (protrusion) and weaken the muscles that produce the desired movement (retraction). Again, this procedure is not recommended if alternatives that require the child to exert his or her own efforts to retract the tongue are available.

One alternative to using external control is to stimulate the child to produce the desired response. While these elicitation procedures are much more effective with some students than others, the appropriateness of these procedures for a specific child can be quickly assessed. Generally, these procedures exert pressure or apply resistance *against* the direction of the desired movement. For example, upward pressure briefly applied against the bony part of the chin will stimulate some children to open their jaw. Upward pressure briefly applied to the soft area beneath the chin at the root of the tongue will stimulate some children to retract a protruding tongue. This type of stimulation acts to elicit desired responses with the child's own muscles rather than through external control. When using these procedures, it is also important to use the minimum effective level of stimulation. This will make it easier to transfer control of the desired behaviors from the training stimuli to normal stimuli, leading to complete voluntary control. Such eventual transfer to voluntary control by the child should be considered and planned for in the use of any physical assistance techniques.

Providing Sensory Stimulation   In addition to the stimulation procedures mentioned above that elicit immediate responses, stimulation that is intended to produce longer lasting changes in tone, movement, and control are often included in eating skill training programs. Various stimulation procedures have been used by many therapists and teachers to reduce oral-facial hypersensitivity (e.g., Alexander, 1991; Campbell, 1982), facilitate appropriate movement patterns (e.g., Utley et al., 1977), and/or inhibit dysfunctional movement patterns (e.g., Gallender, 1979). Empirical evidence supports the use of these procedures for improving eating skills (Sobsey & Orelove, 1984). Such procedures may include general relaxation procedures: stroking the lips, face, and cheeks; rubbing the gums and hard palate; brushing the skin over muscles involved in chewing, swallowing, and lip closure; applying ice to these areas; applying "stretch pressure" to the areas around the lips and cheeks; vibrating oral and facial muscles; and "walking" a tongue blade back on the tongue. The specific procedures appropriate for a particular child must be determined by the service team, including an appropriately trained therapist. Ongoing evaluation is required to determine whether the treatment is producing the desired results for the child, especially since results appear to be inconsistent among different children.

At least two theories have been used to explain the effects of stimulation procedures. One theory suggests that increased sensory input increases motor output and control by lowering the threshold for motor neuron firing. Another theory suggests that the threshold for hypersensitive oral and facial reflexes can be raised through increased sensory input. In any case, exteroceptive (through superficial skin receptors) and proprioceptive (through deeper muscle receptors) stimulation have been shown to be useful for improving lip closure and chewing in some children (Sobsey & Orelove, 1984) and may also prove useful for training in other eating skills.

Alexander (1991) suggested that when a child has extreme hypersensitivity, desensitization needs to begin with less sensitive areas of the body before proceeding to the mouth and other sensitive surrounding areas. She also points out that oral stimulation can be provided in a variety of ways (e.g., using a soft toy, the child's fingers, a toothbrush) and that careful attention to the child's preferences is helpful in increasing tolerance.

Providing Specific Training   Most of the methods for improving eating skills discussed so far have been highly specialized, but many of the most useful procedures for teaching eating skills are basically the same procedures as those used to teach any other skill. Campbell (1982) stresses the need for careful assessment, establishing reasonable and measurable objectives, and collecting regular progress data. These three elements should be included as parts of any eating skills training program, regardless of the intervention techniques used. Other specific training components that should be considered in planning eating skills programs include reinforcement, shaping, chaining, prompting, modeling, and response-cost procedures.

Reinforcement   Reinforcement procedures, which reward target behaviors, are a natural way of teaching eating skills for children. Food and drink, which are integral parts of these programs, are powerful reinforcers for most children. Programs should be structured so that children obtain food more efficiently when they use the desired eating behaviors. Care must be taken to ensure that the specific food or drink used is an effective reinforcer for the particular child involved. Using social reinforcers in addition to edible reinforcers may be desirable or even necessary with some children, especially if these children do not respond positively to edibles. The combination of reinforcers may also be useful during acquisition and early fluency-building stages, when the target behaviors may be less efficient than current inappropriate eating patterns. The natural reinforcement power of food and drink is a valuable component of almost any mealtime program. In addition to its effectiveness with most children, it has the additional advantage of providing for excellent maintenance and generalization since it is common to the natural mealtime environment as well as to the training situation.

Shaping   Shaping, a specific reinforcement method, is extremely useful in eating and drinking programs. When the child cannot perform a target behavior exactly as it should be performed, the child's best approximation of that behavior can be reinforced. As performance improves, the criterion for reinforcement becomes stricter. Shaping must be used to make reinforcement an effective part of almost any eating or drinking training since the amount of food and drink used must remain fairly constant throughout training. If this were not so, children would be undernourished during early stages of the program and overnourished during later stages. Shaping the criterion to the child's current level of performance allows contingent delivery of food without resulting in significant changes in total intake. It also allows the child to experience success no matter how low his or her current skill level may be.

Chaining   Chaining, the assembling of separately taught discrete responses into a more complex behavior, may also have a part in training in eating and drinking skills. Although eating and drinking skills typically require whole-task presentation, task analysis can be extremely useful in pinpointing which step or steps need work, and focusing training on a single or only a few steps often provides the best results.

Prompting   Prompting, which involves providing extra cues or assistance to the child, is also useful for training in eating skills. Although physical prompts are often impossible or too disruptive for eating or drinking skills (e.g., reaching into a child's mouth to help position his or her tongue properly), many of the physical assistance procedures described above might be considered physical prompts. Verbal and gestural prompts are also commonly useful.

Modeling   Modeling, which involves demonstrating the appropriate behavior, is also extremely useful for training in eating and drinking skills. Most commonly, the trainer models the behavior for the child to imitate, but peers also can be powerful models.

Response-Cost Procedures   Response-cost procedures, which penalize the child for inappropriate behavior, may occasionally be needed if reinforcement of the correct responses is not adequate enough to eliminate the less desirable alternative. Since deprivation of food and drink would rarely be ethically justified, most response-cost procedures in eating skills training programs are delay procedures. If the child responds inappropriately, the opportunity to obtain food or drink is withheld for a brief period (e.g., 15 seconds). For example, after a child has acquired a mature drinking pattern, he or she may occasionally revert to a primitive suck-swallow pattern. The trainer may immediately withdraw the cup for 15 seconds each time the primitive behavior is demonstrated. This delay in reinforcement will often discourage the inappropriate behavior.

All of the specific training strategies discussed above and other basic teaching techniques can be used as part of a training program in eating and drinking skills. The other training techniques described above, which focus on physiological responses, can be used in conjunction with these specific behavioral methods. Together, they provide a wide range of alternatives that can be employed by the service team in designing effective programs.

Those involved in teaching eating skills to children with multiple disabilities, along with all who are involved in mealtime routines, need to be prepared to prevent, recognize, and treat airway obstruction. Airway obstruction is a serious threat to all young children and to older children and adults with disabilities. Total airway obstruction typically occurs without warning and requires immediate action. Chapter 6 includes information on how this emergency occurs, how it can be prevented, and the first aid procedures that can save the life of the victim.

Preventing Aspiration   Aspiration, the inhalation of fluids or food particles into the lungs, is one of the major risks for children and adults with multiple disabilities (Chaney, 1987; Chaney, Eyman, & Miller, 1979). Aspiration can occur when food or fluids are on their way down to the stomach or when the contents of the stomach reflux up the esophagus. Reflux aspiration is likely to occur when the individual is in a supine or semi-recumbent position and often is associated with nasogastric tube or gastrostomy feedings. Aspiration problems are different from total airway obstruction, described in Chapter 6. In airway obstruction, the lower airway and lungs are often free of foreign material but occluded by food stuck in the throat which restricts the epiglottis from opening. No air can move in or out, the victim is silent and rapidly turns blue and loses consciousness. In aspiration, smaller particles or liquid enter the lower airway and lungs. Typically, there is severe coughing, wheezing, or there are gurgling sounds, but sometimes, particularly if the victim is not fully conscious, there may be no immediate signs of difficulty. Reflux occurs when the contents of the stomach flow up the esophagus. Vomiting involves active pushing of these contents of the stomach up the esophagus by the muscles of the gastrointestinal tract, and normally a protective closing of the airway. Unlike vomiting, reflux usually involves the passive flow of these contents, often without the airway being closed off, and so creates greater risk.

In some cases, there are immediate signs of aspiration. The individual may cough or gag. Although air can move into and out of the lungs, it is difficult for the person who has aspirated to vocalize because reflexes protecting against further aspiration create spasms in the airway and vocal cords. There may be wheezing or gurgling sounds. In severe cases or when the victim of aspiration already has some difficulty receiving adequate oxygen into circulation, lips, nailbeds, and face may turn blue. In some cases, however, especially if protective reflexes are inadequate, "silent aspiration" occurs without any of these signs (Groher, 1988).

Incidents of suspected aspiration should be recorded and reported to the health care team. The report should include the signs of aspiration that were observed and how long they lasted. Second, information should be included regarding conditions before and during the incident. If the aspiration incident occurs during eating or drinking, the report should include: 1) positioning, 2) feeding procedures, 3) foods and fluids involved, 4) texture of foods and fluids involved, 5) when during the meal aspiration seemed to occur (e.g., the beginning, middle, near the end, several minutes after), 6) any treatment that was given, and 7) any other factors that might be useful for future prevention. If only a few drops are aspirated and the individual is alert, the body's natural defenses (e.g., constriction of the airway, increased mucus production, coughing) often will resolve the problem in a few minutes. For an individual who is unconscious, positioning in the seizure recovery position described in Chapter 6 may facilitate drainage. If gurgling or wet breathing sounds are present, if the individual has significant difficulty breathing, or if signs of oxygen deficit appear (e.g., blue tint of nailbeds or lips), health care professionals should be notified immediately. In some cases, suctioning or other procedures can be useful, and the administration of oxygen is useful in severe cases. If the airway is completely obstructed, the Heimlich maneuver (described in Chapter 6) can open the airway and save the person's life, but most cases of aspiration do not result in complete airway obstruction.

Every episode of aspiration produces discomfort, and severe episodes result in immediate danger of oxygen insufficiency. The worst effects of aspiration, however, are often delayed. Aspiration pneumonia often occurs after a day or more, and, frequently, it is aggravated by secondary infection. Chronic aspiration results in scarring of the lungs, which impairs breathing and makes the individual more vulnerable to future aspiration episodes. These effects are life-threatening and treatment is limited; consequently, prevention is essential.

Fortunately, many aspiration problems are preventable, and aspiration prevention should be a major goal for every child with increased risk for aspiration or a history of aspiration problems. Evaluation of the success of prevention programs may be based on the reduction in the number of incidents, normalization of breathing sounds and rate, or other objective data (Sobsey, 1988).

Some drugs that are commonly taken by people with disabilities increase the risk of aspiration by relaxing the muscles that keep the stomach contents from entering the esophagus or inhibiting reflexes that protect the airway. These drugs include phenobarbital, Valium, Dantrium, Cogentin, and other tranquilizers and anticonvulsants (Karb, Queener, & Freeman, 1989). Reducing these medications, if possible, will reduce the risk of aspiration. If the medication is necessary, the effects may be counteracted through the use of other drugs that stimulate the depressed gastrointestinal function (e.g., Duvoid, Clopra, Reglan), which can reduce reflux in some individuals. Unfortunately, children with epilepsy often cannot take these drugs because they increase seizure activity (Karb et al., 1989).

Aspiration problems occur more frequently with tube feedings than with oral feedings. Whenever possible, use oral feedings and avoid nasogastric or gastric tube feedings. If tube feeding is a temporary measure, work to restore oral feedings as quickly as possible. If tube feeding will be used for an extended period of time, fundoplication, a surgical procedure that alters the connection between stomach and esophagus, may be needed to reduce the risk of aspiration (Groher, 1988).

Rapid or forced entry of food into the stomach may result in pressure that pushes food up the esophagus and into the lungs. Tube feedings should use small portions, every few hours, and be given slowly over 30 minutes to an hour to prevent overfilling the stomach and the subsequent pressure, which may result in reflux aspiration (Groher, 1988).

Normal peristalsis keeps food moving down the esophagus. It prevents reflux and helps maintain muscle tone in the upper gastrointestinal system. Since people being tube fed do not swallow food normally, they lack peristalsis and are more likely to aspirate. Maintaining some oral feedings of solid foods may decrease reflux from tube feedings by stimulating normal peristalsis. If no food can be taken by mouth, oral stimulation before or during tube feeding may help to stimulate peristalsis and muscle tone (Sobsey, 1988).

Whether feeding occurs orally or by tube, positioning is an essential prevention strategy. While one is in an upright position, gravity helps prevent reflux of food out of the stomach; but the reclining position allows the contents of the stomach to flow easily into the esophagus. Tube feeding the individual in an upright position or with the head elevated 45 degrees helps prevent reflux. Those receiving their meals by mouth should be fed in an upright position with their heads flexed slightly forward, which encourages active swallowing and prevents food from passively running down their throats. Since reflux may occur after the meal is finished, the individual should remain in an upright to semireclining position for at least 45 minutes after finishing a meal (Groher, 1988).

There are several other factors to be aware of. Constipation may block the intestinal system. As a result, the contents of the stomach cannot move down and are more likely to be pushed up. Taking precautions to prevent constipation, watching carefully for signs, and treating it quickly help to ensure that food in the stomach is free to move into the intestines, which helps reduce the risk of aspiration (Sobsey, 1988). Pureed foods and thin liquids increase the risk of aspiration because they can easily run down the throat without stimulating a true swallow response, which closes the airway and protects against aspiration. Using solids, soft solids, or coarsely ground foods and thickened liquids may provide better stimulation for swallowing and reduce the risk of aspiration (Sobsey, 1988). Children should be relaxed but alert when they eat. Feeding someone who is stuporous is very risky. Waiting until children recover fully from seizures before giving anything by mouth and stimulating children with activities before meals can help ensure alertness and decrease the risk of aspiration (Sobsey, 1988). Children sometimes aspirate their own secretions while unconscious. Placing them in the seizure recovery position described in Chapter 6 until they are fully conscious helps to reduce this risk (Sobsey, 1988). The best combination of prevention and treatment procedures for each individual should be identified by the health care and educational teams. No prevention program can totally eliminate risk, but a well-designed program can reduce substantially the risks associated with feeding.

FEEDING SKILLS

Every child who eats and drinks must feed himself or herself or be fed by caregivers. The ability to feed oneself is an important step toward independence. For the individual who seems far from total independence, partial participation may be an important intermediate goal. Even for the child who continues to require feeding by a caregiver, the way in which feeding is carried out will have a major effect on the quality of his or her life. Some methods of feeding and of providing training in self-feeding are discussed in this section. These include passive feeding alternatives, cooperative feeding skills, and self-feeding skills.

Passive Feeding Alternatives

Passive feeding alternatives are methods of providing nutrition without any active participation on the part of the child being fed. Methods of passive feeding include intravenous feeding, enteral feeding (e.g., nasogastric tube, gastrostomy), and bird-feeding (a term used for pouring liquified food into the child's throat).

Intravenous Feeding   Intravenous feeding does not provide total nutrition, and, therefore, it can be considered only as an extremely short-term alternative. It should not be considered for children with multiple disabilities, except under the same conditions that it would be used for individuals who do not have disabilities (e.g., to maintain blood volume, electrolyte balance, and/or glucose levels following surgery).

Enteral Feeding   Enteral feeding—nasogastric tube feeding (through a tube inserted into the stomach via the nose and throat) and gastrostomy feeding (through a direct opening in the stomach)—has been used frequently for a number of reasons. Often, the reasons for using any of these procedures with a child with multiple disabilities are not clearly identified, but the procedures may be started during a specific illness or simply because less intrusive feeding methods are of little effectiveness.

Nasogastric tube feeding should not be used for long-term treatment. Bastian and Driscol (1984) suggested a maximum of 4–8 weeks. At least 28 negative effects of nasogastric tube feeding have been identified, including pulmonary aspiration, depressed cough and gag reflexes, dysphagia, otitis media, diarrhea, vitamin deficiencies, and chronic vomiting (Silberman & Eisenberg, 1982). Infants who are not given solid foods by mouth by the age of 6 or 7 months are at risk for chronic rumination, have more difficulty learning to chew, may refuse solids, and may be at increased risk for choking as a result of a permanently depressed gag reflex (Kennedy-Caldwell & Caldwell, 1984). Recognizing these problems, the team should make every effort to avoid using nasogastric tube feeding. If nasogastric tube feeding must be used, several measures can be taken to minimize their negative effects. First, the period for which they will be used should be kept as short as possible. Second, nasogastric tubes should not be left in place between feedings. Third, any feeders must be adequately trained by a nurse specialist or another appropriately trained individual. Fourth, each time the tube is passed, its location must be checked carefully by x-ray or other adequate method before feeding begins (Silberman & Eisenberg, 1982). Fifth, nasogastric tube feeding should not be used for unconscious, sleeping, or stuporous individuals. Sixth, if possible, some oral feedings should be given between tube feedings to help normalize oral responses. Seventh, intraoral stimulation (e.g., pacifiers for infants) should be provided if no oral feedings are possible. Eighth, even before starting the first nasogastric tube feeding, a plan should be developed by the team for transition to oral feeding.

Gastrostomy or jejunostomy (tube directly enters the small intestine) may initially seem more intrusive than nasogastric tube feeding because it requires surgery, but for many children with multiple disabilities, these procedures have several advantages. First, they greatly reduce the risk of aspiration. Second, they do not irritate the throat or depress the gag or cough reflexes. Third, they may typically be used concurrently with oral feedings and so allow eating and feeding skill training along with their use. The gastrostomy button is easily inserted into the abdominal stoma (surgical opening) (Gauderer, Picha, & Izant, 1984). This device means that tubes do not have to be reinserted and no dangling feeding tube needs to be left in place, which makes gastrostomy more compatible with normal activities. Since 1980, many gastrostomies have been done with a punch procedure that does not involve major surgery (Gauderer, Ponsky, & Izant, 1980). These procedural changes make gastrostomy less intrusive and available to some children who might have been excluded from the older procedures.

While oral feedings are preferred whenever possible, some children's nutritional status is greatly improved with tube feeding. Families and other caregivers as well as the children involved sometimes also benefit from stress reduction since unsuccessful attempts at oral feedings can produce great frustration (Campbell, 1988). It is important that parents and others involved in decisions about feeding alternatives have full information about the potential benefits, costs, and risks of all possible alternatives.

Those administering tube feedings should carefully follow procedures. General procedures for administering these feedings are available from a number of sources (e.g., Graff, Ault, Guess, Taylor, & Thompson, 1990), but it is important to individualize the procedures (e.g., positioning, rate of flow) to each child.

One of the most challenging aspects of tube feeding is the transition back to oral feeding. These transitions are often difficult for six reasons. First, the problems that led to the initial decision to use tube feeding are often still present. Second, the initial problem is often aggravated by a weakening of the oral structures as a result of disuse. Third, because the oral structures lack stimulation normally provided by feeding, they may be hypersensitive. Fourth, while some oral reflexes become hypersensitive, others may become hyposensitive. For example, children who frequently have a nasogastric tube in place may have hyposensitive swallow reflexes because they are desensitized to feeling something in the back of their throats. Fifth, children who become accustomed to tube feeding sometimes resist the reintroduction of oral feedings. Sixth, the motivation of family and team members may be reduced because the availability of tube feeding makes oral feeding less vital.

Programs to reinstitute oral feedings must be individually developed. Usually, the best time to begin the program is as soon as the child starts tube feedings or even before tube feedings are started. Blackman and Nelson (1985) described a program designed to reduce resistance to feeding, tasting, and swallowing food that is often present in children without oral feeding experiences. Some children were served on an outpatient basis, but those with more intensive medical needs were hospitalized for the transition. Praise and other reinforcement procedures for accepting food orally were used, and initial protest behavior was ignored. Nine of 10 children made successful transitions to oral feedings, while the tenth had aspiration problems associated with swallowing and was returned to tube feedings. Blackman and Nelson (1987) subsequently reported data from another eleven children placed in a rapid transition program. Ten of the 11 children made a transition from tube feeding to total oral feeding in 2–3 weeks.

Morris and Klein (1987) described many stimulation procedures designed to ease the transition to oral feedings. Often, the mouth, tongue, lips, and other oral structures are hypersensitive as a result of deprivation of the stimulation normally involved in eating. They suggested encouraging or assisting the child to explore the environment with the tongue and lips. Voice and sound play are also useful components of a transition program. Stimulating the child with smells and tastes throughout the tube feeding phase may also be useful, even if the child cannot be allowed to actually swallow food during this time. If it is possible to allow some oral feedings concurrently with the tube feeding phase, this should be done with an emphasis on making the experience as pleasant as possible for the child.

Bird Feeding   Bird feeding merits little discussion here. This method of pouring food into the throat of a person whose head is extended back, lying in a semirecumbent position, can only serve to interfere with the acquisition of appropriate eating and feeding skills. Children who have been fed in this way may have difficulty adapting to more normal methods, but almost all of them will attain more functional eating skills as feeding methods are normalized.

Cooperative Feeding Skills and Development of Communication

Cooperative feeding skills are needed by individuals being fed and by their caregivers. These skills allow the coordination of movements and the smooth transition of food or drink from the feeder to the person being fed. Both members of this dyad must work together to develop these skills. In addition to their obvious help in the feeding process, these basic turntaking and coordinated movement skills may be useful in many other activities of daily living.

Coactive movement refers to the coordination of movements between two individuals who are not in direct physical contact. It has been recognized and trained as an early communication skill (Sternberg, Pegnatore, & Hill, 1983). If the ability to coordinate movements at the coactive level is not present, it may be necessary to start resonance, which develops coordination through physical contact as well as movement, at an even earlier level. In addition to mealtime, coordinated movement is developed through affectionate contact, play, and physical prompting procedures.

Other measures can also facilitate coordination. First, the feeder should watch and listen carefully to the child and coordinate presentation of food with the child's natural breathing and movement patterns. Second, lighting and positioning should ensure a clear view of food or drink as it approaches the mouth. Third, the feeder should establish a smooth and predictable pace. Fourth, for many children, a verbal (or tactile) ready signal from the feeder is helpful. It should be pointed out that many children will not require this signal and some hypertonic children may respond with a countertherapeutic increase in tone (Campbell, 1982). Fifth, some children may be able to signal (e.g., look up, grunt) when they want the next bit of food or drink. One should encourage this by attending carefully to these signals and responding to them. Sixth, distractions and interruptions (to feeder and child) need to be minimized. Most feeders will find it impossible to coordinate their movements with the children they are feeding and carry on a conversation with a third party since each activity involves coordination with a different person.

The turntaking behavior developed in feeding builds an essential foundation for more advanced communication skills. Feeding is also one of the important interactive contexts for the development of attachment between children and their caregivers, and attachment is also a powerful force in the development of communication (Alexander, 1991). The oral-motor skills that are refined in eating are fundamental to the development of speech (Alexander, 1991). These influences on the development of communication skills make mealtimes an important context for teaching early communication. Teaching more advanced communication and social skill objectives is also easily integrated into meal-time activities because these behaviors are natural elements of mealtime routines.

Self-Feeding Skills

Probably much more has been written about training in feeding skills than training in eating skills. Basic self-feeding skills may include handling finger foods, drinking from a self-held cup, and eating with a spoon. More advanced skill training may include using other utensils, table manners, serving foods, food preparation, and food purchasing skills.

Finger Foods   Generally, teaching children to feed themselves with their fingers is best accomplished at the beginning of a meal when they are hungry (Snell, 1983). Some children, however, may become easily frustrated at this time and tolerate training better after having something to eat. The trainer must be certain that the child knows and likes the foods (in the forms provided) to ensure reinforcement value. Many children need little more than this opportunity to begin self-feeding, and their training may focus primarily on improving dexterity or establishing a suitable pace. For other children, movement difficulties or skill deficits may make acquisition more difficult. Modeling the desired behavior may be helpful, but graduated guidance is the most common training method. Generally, the trainer will find it easiest to work from behind the child. The child is guided through the required movements with as little assistance as is required. Assistance is gradually withdrawn over time as independence increases.

Drinking from a Self-Held Cup   Learning to drink from a cup is a messy but rewarding experience for almost any child. For many children, only the willingness of caregivers to provide ample learning opportunities is required. For others, the coordination of arm, hand, head, and mouth movements is extremely challenging. Good, stable positioning will help. For some, thickened liquids may be easier to control at first. Selecting a cup or glass with the best shape and weight for the specific child will often be helpful. Although spout cups reduce spilling, they are not generally recommended since they may encourage dysfunctional drinking patterns. For many children, the goal may be limited to partial participation until they develop adequate enough oral skills to handle their first imprecise independent attempts to transfer fluids into their own mouths.

Eating with a Spoon   Graduated guidance is also a common method of teaching children with disabilities to eat with a spoon. Since spoon-feeding involves a fairly long chain of discrete responses, task analysis may be useful in determining exactly which steps need work. Adaptive spoons will be helpful for some children who have difficulty gripping, bringing the spoon into the mouth at the appropriate angle, or keeping food balanced on the spoon while bringing it to the mouth. For many children, spoon-feeding is possible but less efficient than eating with their fingers. For children who revert to finger-feeding, a delay or interruption procedure may be useful (Snell, 1983). Interruption to attempts at finger-feeding causes spoon-feeding to become more efficient and differentially reinforcing.

Advanced Mealtime Skills   For children who master basic self-feeding skills, training in more advanced mealtime skills will increase their level of independence and allow them to function in a wide array of environments. The selection and order of skills taught will not be the same for all students. They should be selected on the basis of the needs and skills of the child and requirements of his or her current and potential future environments. For example, tray carrying skills may not be relevant for children who eat only family-style meals at home and in their classrooms, but these same tray carrying skills may be extremely important for children who eat in a school cafeteria. Some advanced skills include table manners, mealtime social skills, food serving, table setting, food preparation, selecting nutritious foods, requesting desired foods, ordering in restaurants, and food shopping. Many more skills could be added to this list. Few children with multiple disabilities can be expected to master all these skill areas, but many of them can be expected to master at least some basic goals in several of these areas. Since advanced mealtime skills include so many areas and this chapter focuses on more basic skills, only a brief discussion of mealtime social skills is included here.

Mealtime social skills programs are often viewed as fitting into two categories: 1) building desirable behaviors, and 2) eliminating undesirable behaviors. In practice, the development of desirable social behavior at mealtime is often adequate to control or eliminate inappropriate behavior, which, in turn, eliminates the need to institute direct intervention to reduce inappropriate behavior. This focus on building appropriate behavior is consistent with the increasing awareness that behavior that is inappropriate (in the eyes of caregivers) is typically extremely functional for the child and that teaching a more appropriate functional alternative may be the best means of behavioral control (Evans & Meyer, 1985; Meyer & Evans, 1989). For example, if a child finishes his or her food and then grabs food off other children's plates, this behavior may function to satisfy the child's continuing hunger. The intervention team might try to use punishment procedures to eliminate food stealing, but such procedures probably have little chance for success if the child has no more acceptable way of asking for a second helping. If the child is taught to obtain food through an acceptable requesting behavior (e.g., hand raising, standing in line), the unacceptable behavior may be eliminated with no other intervention or with less intrusive intervention than otherwise might be required.

Of course, the success of this type of training procedure depends on correctly identifying the function of the undesired behavior. Certainly, attaining food is the most obvious function one might ascribe to food grabbing. If the child does not really want the food and instead grabs food to attract the caregiver's attention, teaching the child more appropriate requesting behavior may do little to control food grabbing. Therefore, the success of these programs depends upon careful analysis of behaviors, consequences, and antecedents and upon careful ongoing evaluation of behavioral changes, all of which will confirm or rule out the hypothesis developed regarding behavioral function.

Eliminating problem behaviors is only one aspect of mealtime social skills. Perske, Clifton, McLean, and Stein (1986) estimate that "better than eighty percent of . . . severely handicapped persons do not experience relaxed, human-communion types of meals" (p. xix). Programs that focus on the mechanical process of efficient eating and feeding fail to meet emotional human needs. A physical and social environment must be created that meets these needs.

No single recipe will work for every child in every environment, but a number of measures are worth consideration. Caregivers should normalize the dining room environment to the greatest extent possible. Communication between caregivers and the children they feed is desirable, but communication among caregivers that excludes the children they feed is undesirable and potentially dehumanizing. Such communication may include verbal, touch, and/or visual components. Whenever possible, children should be allowed to make choices for themselves. Mealtimes should be long enough to avoid the need for rushing. The room should be fairly quiet and relaxed. These and other simple measures can do much to provide a positive mealtime social environment.

NUTRITIONAL CONCERNS

Any discussion of eating and feeding skills training for children with multiple disabilities should consider nutrition. After all, one of the major goals of teaching eating and feeding skills is to help ensure adequate nutrition, and any intervention that affects what or how children eat also affects their nutrition.

Of course, for the most part, children with multiple disabilities have the same nutritional needs as other children, and normalization suggests that the same methods be used to maintain good diet and nutrition. Unfortunately, children with multiple disabilities appear to be at far greater risk for nutritional deficits than their nondisabled peers, and a number of factors can be identified that demand special consideration (McCamman & Rues, 1990; Sobsey, 1983). Comprehensive discussion has been devoted to these special considerations elsewhere (e.g., Palmer & Ekvall, 1978; Springer, 1982), and they merit some discussion here.

Signs and Symptoms

One of the difficulties of providing better recognition of nutritional deficits in children with multiple disabilities is that signs and symptoms of these deficits are often ascribed to other causes. Lethargy and poor resistance to infection, major signs of anemia, and other nutritional deficiency diseases are often considered to be due to the child's primary diagnosis or to the medication given the child. Retarded growth and scoliosis, which may be signs of inadequate calcium and/or vitamin D, are often seen as resulting from some genetic syndrome or disorders of muscle tone and posture. Thus, nutritional problems may be masked by other risk factors. Of course, this does not mean that the non-nutritional factors never play a role in these problems. Rather, it means that maintaining adequate nutrition is even more important because any nutritional risk factor is likely to interact with a number of other risk factors to produce potentially devastating results. It also means that nutritional assessment must be particularly thorough to avoid the masking of signs and symptoms by other risk factors in children with multiple disabilities.

Some Nutritional Risk Factors

Some nutritional risk factors are associated with the specific disability (McCamman & Rues, 1990). Children with increased tone and limited movement normally require fewer calories than their peers. Since their needs for protein and vitamins do not decrease proportionally, their diets may require more of these (Sobsey, 1983b). Children with PKU (phenylketonuria) cannot eat foods with phenylalanine, including foods with the artificial sweetener aspartame, which is being used with increasing frequency. When specific foods are eliminated from the diet, it is important to assess the effects of the restriction on the entire diet to ensure balance. Children with Prader-Willi syndrome typically eat to excess and often become obese, causing secondary health problems (Lupi & Porcella, 1987; McCamman & Rues, 1990). Frequently, the diet consumed is high in caloric value but low in other essential nutrients. Even with normal caloric intake, these children gain weight, and a diet very low in calories is needed to normalize weight (Lupi & Porcella, 1987). In order to maintain adequate nutrition with reduced caloric intake, the diet must include a higher ratio of vitamins, minerals, and protein to calories.

Oral-motor problems that affect eating directly affect nutritional status. Children with cerebral palsy and oral-motor involvement have been shown to be shorter in stature and weigh less for their height when compared to children with cerebral palsy who do not have oral-motor involvement (Krick & Van Duyn, 1984).

Other risk factors may be related to problems that affect all children, but they may be less frequently noticed in children with multiple disabilities. Although congenital lactose intolerance (lactase deficiency) is usually detected in infancy, late-onset lactose intolerance may begin gradually as the child approaches adulthood (Springer, 1982). Gradual onset makes detection more difficult, and the child's inability to communicate discomfort will further complicate detection. Inability to communicate and dependence on others to meet one's needs can also lead to serious problems with maintaining adequate hydration, another nutritional concern. Although people generally require about 1 ml of water for each calorie consumed (Batshaw & Perret, 1986), differences in air temperature, electrolyte intake, and other factors can greatly influence these requirements. For most people, adjustment to these altered requirements occurs spontaneously through increased intake, but for the child who lacks the mobility to obtain fluids without assistance and lacks the communication skills to request fluids, caregivers must carefully monitor signs of hydration status.

Other nutritional problems may be related to the methods used to feed children. Pureed diets tend to be high in carbohydrates and low in protein, vitamin C, and fiber, and, as discussed under the "Modifying Foods" section of this chapter, they should be replaced whenever possible by diets more normal in texture. Similarly, nasogastric tube feedings are often nutritionally inferior, and children maintained on enteral feedings for extended periods may lose interest in resuming normal diets, which can cause additional nutritional problems (Hargrave, 1979).

Nutritional problems can also develop as a result of medication side effects (McCamman & Rues, 1990). Many drugs have nutritional side effects, but the significance of these side effects may be small with short-term usage. For example, the effects of an occasional aspirin in depressing vitamin C and folic acid (Crump, 1987) are probably unimportant, but individuals receiving daily doses of aspirin may be significantly affected. Since children with multiple disabilities often take medications with known nutritional side effects for extended periods, they are more likely to be affected. Crump (1987) pointed out that drugs may affect nutrition in six ways: 1) increasing or decreasing intake, 2) inhibiting synthesis of nutrients, 3) interfering with absorption, 4) altering transport of metabolites, 5) blocking storage or utilization of metabolites, and 6) increasing excretion of nutrients.

As regards specific drugs: many anticonvulsants irritate the stomach lining and may interfere with the general absorption of nutrients (Hargrave, 1979). Some anticonvulsants also interfere with vitamin D and calcium metabolism, and they also cause depletion of folic acid (Sobsey, 1983). Careful consultation with a physician, nutritionist, and other team members is required to eliminate or at least minimize these potential problems, especially since attempts to supplement folic acid can precipitate seizures if not properly carried out. Tranquilizers tend to reduce caloric requirements and increase caloric intake, which leads to weight gain. Stimulants, conversely, decrease intake and increase activity, which may result in growth retardation as well as weight loss (Lucas, 1981). Laxatives, another category of medications used frequently with children with multiple disabilities, also have nutritional side effects. They decrease absorption of most nutrients and some specifically interfere with particular nutrients. For example, mineral oil decreases absorption of fat-soluble vitamins (Sobsey, 1983). Whenever possible, reducing or eliminating the use of medications is the simplest method of eliminating nutritional side effects.

When medication is essential, however, carefully assessing and controlling diet and nutrition helps to minimize these drug side effects.

The lack of mobility associated with many disabilities also contributes to nutritional concerns in several ways. First, decreased mobility reduces caloric requirements. This means less food with higher proportions of protein and vitamins is needed. Second, decreased mobility often leads to constipation, which can impair absorption of nutrients. Third, decreased mobility leads to decalcification of bones and atrophy of muscle, which requires nutritional intervention (Hargrave, 1979). Finally, lack of mobility often results in less time outdoors and, therefore, less exposure to the sun, the major source of vitamin D for most children (Batshaw & Perret, 1986). All of the risk factors described above contribute to nutritional problems for a large percentage of children with multiple disabilities. Awareness of these concerns by all team members and careful periodic evaluation by a professional in dietetics and nutrition are important components of total service delivery to each child. Improved nutrition can make a major contribution to health, learning, and quality of life for children with multiple disabilities.

Diet and Behavior

Much has been written about specific dietary interventions that aim to produce substantive changes in behavior and learning potential. These include megavitamin or orthomolecular therapy to reduce hyperactivity and improve learning, reducing sugar intake to eliminate hyperactivity, eliminating common food allergens to eliminate hyperactivity, and the Feingold diet (eliminating natural salicylates, artificial colors and flavors, and certain preservatives). Some published research has supported these kinds of intervention, but the great majority of carefully controlled research has demonstrated that they have little or no effect (Lucas, 1981). Such conflicting results suggest that some small subgroup of children may be helped by these interventions, but only a small number. Therefore, whenever such therapy is considered for a child, it must include careful, systematic, criterion-based evaluation. If it helps the child, it should be continued as one element of the child's program, but not as a substitute for other intervention. If clear benefits for the individual are not demonstrated, the intervention should be abandoned.

DENTAL CARE

Dental care is another area of concern closely related to feeding, eating, and nutrition. Like many services for children with multiple disabilities, dental care has evolved through fairly distinct stages. Lange, Entwistle, and Lipson (1983) described the first stage as supervised neglect. Few services were available, and, often, the services that were available were of poor quality. Restraints and sedation characterized the next phase. During the early 1970s, increasing concern was demonstrated through the development of specialized dental techniques and equipment. Later in the 1970s and during the 1980s, the trend toward normalization and increased training efforts resulted in fewer specialized and more generic services. The traditional reluctance of many dentists to treat patients with disabilities has been eliminated or greatly reduced as a result of efforts to shape more positive attitudes in dental schools (Gurney & Alcorn, 1979) and through public education.

These changes in attitude have resulted partly from the efforts of specific organizations. The Academy of Dentistry for the Handicapped and the National Foundation of Dentistry for the Handicapped along with the American Academy of Pediatric Dentistry have promoted high quality dental care for children with disabilities, preparation of dentists to work with patients with disabilities, and research relevant to these goals. They also serve as useful resources to the public, assisting in locating dentists with appropriate skills in patients' geographical areas. With funding from the Robert Wood Johnson Foundation, the American Fund for Dental Health coordinated development of dental school program components during the 1970s to prepare graduating dentists to work with people with a wide range of disabilities (Walker, 1979). For example, all students at the University of Minnesota Dental School complete a course in handicapping conditions and have optional practicum experience with patients who have disabilities.

Special Dental Concerns

Although dental care for children with multiple disabilities is not much different from dental care for other children, some special concerns exist. Children with cerebral palsy often have more cavities, more periodontal disease, poor occlusion, and damaged teeth due to bruxism (grinding of the teeth). Children with Down syndrome appear to have fewer cavities than other children, but they often have increased periodontal disease and poor occlusion (McIver & Machen, 1979). Children with epilepsy are at risk for damaging teeth in a fall, may have gingival hyperplasia (abnormal overgrowth of the gums), and may have poorly developed teeth due to calcium and vitamin D metabolism disturbances caused by their medication. Difficulty in communicating the reason for dental procedures may make some children fearful and difficult to manage during dental treatment (Burkhart, 1984). Children with mobility problems have difficulty cleaning their own teeth and gums thoroughly. Many children are not taught to brush their teeth adequately. Soft, sticky diets provided to some children are cariogenic (promote cavities) and increase the need for brushing (Albertson, 1974). Abnormal reflexes and limited ranges of motion may make dental treatment more difficult for some children with multiple disabilities. All of these factors contribute to the need for ongoing, high-quality dental services. These services can best be provided through close cooperation between dental specialists and other service team members.

Dental Care and Prevention

Good dental care requires the teamwork of dentists, dental assistants, dental hygienists, parents, teachers, and other caregivers. Introducing solid foods as early as possible and avoiding soft and pureed foods can reduce cavities (Coffee, 1986) and encourage normal development of oral structures (Goose & Appleton, 1982). Avoiding the use of sweets as reinforcers and snacks will reduce cavities (Sobsey, 1983). Perhaps most important, regular brushing and flossing are major preventors of both cavities and periodontal disease (Coffee, 1986). Whenever possible, children should be taught to brush their own teeth, but there may be a need to supplement this with cleaning by caregivers until proficiency is developed. Oral irrigators, disclosing solution, and electric toothbrushes may help ensure the quality of cleaning for some children.

Regular dental care is also essential. Visits to the dentist three or four times per year may be required for some children. In addition to allowing for early treatment of cavities and preventative care, regular visits to the dentist provide opportunities to build a history of positive interactions without the stress of a toothache or invasive procedures. Also, fluoride treatments are a valuable part of this preventative care. Careful observation for signs of cavities can help to ensure early treatment. This is particularly important since early treatment of cavities can normally be accomplished through single-surface fillings. More advanced decay often requires treatment of two or more tooth surfaces. These reconstructions of multiple surfaces are extremely difficult to accomplish if the patient cannot or will not hold extremely still in the position required. This may require general anesthesia and hospitalization for some children with multiple disabilities.

Specific dental problems can often be ameliorated through team intervention. For example, about half of children who receive Dilantin (phenytoin) have significant gum overgrowth (Lange et al., 1983). If tolerated, a reduction in phenytoin can reduce this overgrowth. If phenytoin cannot be reduced, ascorbic acid may be prescribed to reduce this effect (Lange et al., 1983). Such intervention will require careful consultation with the physician, who must assess the potential effects on seizure activity. If overgrowth of gums cannot be prevented, careful and frequent cleaning of teeth and gums will reduce the infection and irritation that can lead to serious dental disease, and periodic surgical removal of excess tissue can keep the overgrowth in check.

Modern dental procedures allow for the elimination of almost all pain and discomfort. Every effort should be made to minimize discomfort and the need for restraint. This is not only important for ethical reasons, but it is crucial for encouraging patient cooperation. Every effort should be made to let the child know what will be done and why. Efforts to communicate must also include making every attempt to understand and respond to the child's concerns and desires.

This list of measures to enhance dental care for children with disabilities is not comprehensive, but their application can make a significant difference in dental health. Improved dental health, in turn, can contribute significantly to better eating skills, nutrition, and feeding procedures. Together, these components can improve quality of life throughout the day, including mealtimes.

ASSESSMENT AND PROGRAM PLANNING

This chapter has presented a discussion of many of the factors and concerns related to the mealtime skills of children with severe disabilities. Developing and implementing mealtime programs that consider these factors require transdisciplinary assessment and planning. This process is described briefly below.

The Mealtime Program Team

Many people have expertise that should be considered in mealtime planning. Some disciplines will be more important to include on the team for some children than for others, depending on the child's individual needs. Some team members may contribute to assessment and planning in only a few specific areas, based on their expertise in their disciplines. Other team members may contribute to more decisions because of their knowledge of the child.

One person, commonly the teacher, must take overall responsibility for integrating input from the entire team. This client coordinator (or educational synthesizer) organizes the assessment and planning processes as well as program implementation. The teacher also brings expertise in training methods to the team. The physical therapist can contribute valuable information about motor skills, reflexes, and therapeutic interventions. The occupational therapist's skills may partially overlap, but they are typically applied more to functional activities. The occupational therapist is often also an excellent resource for adaptive utensils and furniture. The speech therapist can contribute expertise that will help with potential speech use as well as eating skills since motor patterns developed in eating will influence those used in speech (Alexander, 1991). The nurse may help train staff to prevent choking and recognize signs of discomfort. Parents and other primary caregivers must be included for two reasons. First, they typically know the child and history of interventions better than any other team member. Second, they generally participate in feeding the child the major part of his or her meals. Aides and any other caregivers involved in feeding also should be included. The nutritionist or dietitian has important expertise that should be included in planning. Failure to include someone with expertise in nutritional planning can have disastrous consequences. Similarly, the dentist should be part of mealtime planning. Many decisions made by these professionals and other members of the feeding team interact with the physician's treatment decisions. Therefore, the physician should also be included. When it is not possible to have all these professionals attend team meetings, input should be gathered from them prior to team planning, and programs should be circulated to them for approval prior to implementation.

The Assessment Process

Assessment of eating and feeding skills requires both a determination of what the child can and cannot do and a determination of what skills are critical to improving the child's functioning in current and potential future environments. Assessment of nutritional concerns requires careful recording of daily intake, measures of physical characteristics, and measures of physiological functions. Assessment of dental status requires a physical examination and a review of risk factors.

Each child's evaluation must be individualized. Although some may prove useful, no specific assessment protocol is required. Ekvall (1978) included two assessment protocols that evaluate both eating skills and nutritional status in her thorough discussion of assessing nutritional status. Schmidt (1976) provided a concise format for evaluating feeding and eating skills. Several curricula (e.g., Tawney, 1979) provide skill sequences for eating and feeding that are appropriate for assessment. Elements that seem most relevant to the child being evaluated can be selected from these and other assessment instruments, or evaluation can proceed without the use of any specific instrument as long as the assessment collects and organizes the information required to set measurable and realistic objectives.

Setting objectives is a key step in program planning (Campbell, 1982). Vague goals such as "to improve nutritional status" or "will chew better" defy evaluation and make training extremely difficult. Typically, objectives should have criteria that reflect a level of performance sufficient for independent function in a normal environment. Occasionally, setting intermediate objectives with criteria at lower levels may be desired, especially if intervention techniques will be modified after the intermediate objective is mastered.

SUMMARY

This chapter has presented information and discussed issues concerning mealtime skills and related concerns for children with multiple disabilities. Mealtime skills are essential for survival, health, and good quality of life. Interventionists can do much to promote these by providing training in eating and feeding skills, by creating a normal and relaxed mealtime environment, by protecting against the danger of airway obstruction, and by ensuring good nutrition and dental care. Transdisciplinary teamwork is required to assess the child's level of functioning and the demands of the environment and to implement effective mealtime programming.

REFERENCES

Albertson, D. (1974). Prevention and the handicapped child. *Dental Clinics of North America, 18,* 595–608.

Alexander, R. (1991). Prespeech and feeding. In J.L. Bigge, *Teaching individuals with physical and multiple disabilities* (3rd ed., pp. 175–198). New York: Macmillan.

Azrin, N.H., & Armstrong, P.M. (1973). The "Mini-Meal"—a method of teaching feeding skills to the profoundly retarded. *Mental Retardation, 11,* 9–13.

Bastian, C.H., & Driscoll, R.H. (1984). Enteral tube feeding at home. In J.L. Rombeau & M.D. Caldwell (Eds.), *Enteral and tube feeding* (pp. 494–512). Philadelphia: W.B. Saunders.

Batshaw, M.L., & Perret, Y.M. (1986). *Children with handicaps: A medical primer* (2nd ed). Baltimore: Paul H. Brookes Publishing Co.

Blackman, J.A., & Nelson, C.L.A. (1985). Reinstituting oral feedings in children fed by gastrostomy tube. *Clinical Pediatrics, 24,* 434–438.

Blackman, J.A., & Nelson, C.L.A. (1987). Rapid introduction of oral feedings to tube-fed patients. *Developmental and Behavioral Pediatrics, 8*(2), 63–67.

Blockley, J., & Miller, G. (1971). Feeding techniques with cerebral palsied children. *Physiotherapy, 57,* 300–308.

Burkhart, N. (1984). Understanding and managing the autistic child in the dental office. *Dental Hygiene, 58,* 60–63.

Campbell, A.L. (1988, April). Tube feeding: Parental perspective. *Exceptional Parent,* pp. 36–40.

Campbell, P. (1982). *Problem-oriented approaches to feeding the handicapped child* (rev.). Akron: Children's Hospital Medical Center. (ERIC Document Reproduction No. ED 231 127).

Campbell, P.H. (1987). Physical management and handling procedures with students with movement dysfunction. In M.E. Snell (Ed.), *Systematic instruction of persons with severe handicaps* (3rd ed., pp. 174–187). Columbus: Charles E. Merrill.

Campbell, S.K. (1978). Oral sensori-motor physiology. In J. M. Wilson (Ed.), *Oral-motor function and dysfunction in children* (pp. 1–11). Chapel Hill: University of North Carolina, Division of Physical Therapy.

Cautner, M., & Penrose, J. (1983, December 21). Solving feeding problems. *Nursing Times, 51,* pp. 24–26.

Chaney, R.H. (1987). Risk of pulmonary edema in mentally retarded persons. *American Journal on Mental Deficiency, 91,* 555–558.

Chaney, R.H., Eyman, R.K., & Miller, C.R. (1979). Comparison of respiratory mortality in the profoundly mentally retarded and the less retarded. *Journal of Mental Deficiency Research, 23,* 1–7.

Coffee, L. (1986). Planning daily care for healthy teeth. In R. Perske, A. Clifton, B. M. McLean, & J. I. Stein (Eds.), *Mealtimes for persons with severe handicaps* (pp. 119–122). Baltimore: Paul H. Brookes Publishing Co.

Crump, I.M. (Ed.). (1987). Interactions and influences on nutrient function. In I. Crump (Ed.), *Nutrition and feeding of the handicapped child* (pp. 19–28). Boston: Little, Brown.

Ekvall, S. (1978). Assessment of nutritional status. In S. Palmer & S. Ekvall (Eds.), *Pediatric nutrition in developmental disorders* (pp. 502–550). Springfield, IL: Charles C Thomas.

Evans, I.M., & Meyer, L.H. (1985). *An educative approach to behavior problems: A practical decision model for interventions with severely handicapped learners.* Baltimore: Paul H. Brookes Publishing Co.

Fraser, B.A., & Hensinger, R.H. (1983). *Managing physical handicaps: A practical guide for parents, care providers and educators.* Baltimore: Paul H. Brookes Publishing Co.

Gallender, D. (1979). *Eating handicaps.* Springfield, IL: Charles C Thomas.

Gauderer, M.W.L., Picha, G.J., & Izant, R.J. (1984). The gastrostomy "button." A simple, skin-level, non-refluxing device for long-term enteral feedings. *Journal of Pediatric Surgery, 19,* 803–805.

Gauderer, M.W.L., Ponsky, J.L., & Izant, R.J. (1980). Gastrostomy without laparotomy: A percutaneous endoscopic technique. *Journal of Pediatric Surgery, 15,* 872–875.

Goose, D.H., & Appleton, J. (1982). *Human dentofacial growth.* Oxford: Pergamon.

Graff, J.C., Ault, M.M., Guess, D., Taylor, M., & Thompson, B. (1990). *Health care for students with disabilities: An illustrated medical guide for the classroom.* Baltimore: Paul H. Brookes Publishing Co.

Groher, M. (1987). Bolus management and aspiration pneumonia in patients with pseudobulbar dysphagia. *Dysphagia, 1,* 215–216.

Groher, M. (1988, January). *Approaches in the evaluation of swallowing disorders.* Paper presented at the Current Concepts in Mealtime Management for Neurologically Impaired and Mentally Retarded Clients: Special Topics Symposium, Dallas.

Gurney, N.L., & Alcorn, J. (1979). The concept of attitudes. In K.E. Wessels (Ed.), *Dentistry and the handicapped patient* (Postgraduate Dental Handbook Series, Vol. 5, pp. 1–19). Littleton, MA: PSG Publishing.

Hargrave, M. (1979). *Nutritional care of the physically disabled.* (Publication No. 719). Minneapolis: Sister Kenny Institute.

Jones, T.W. (1983). Remediation of behavior-related eating problems. A preliminary investigation. *Journal of The Association for Persons with Severe Handicaps, 8(4),* 62–71.

Kalisz, K., & Ekvall, S. (1978). Cleft palate. In S. Palmer & S. Ekvall (Eds.), *Pediatric nutrition in developmental disorders* (pp. 36–41). Springfield, IL: Charles C Thomas.

Karb, V.B., Queener, S.F., & Freeman, J.B. (1989). *Handbook of drugs for nursing practice.* St. Louis: C.V. Mosby.

Kennedy-Caldwell, C., & Caldwell, M. (1984). Pediatric enteral nutrition. In J.L. Rombeau & M.D. Caldwell (Eds.), *Enteral and tube feeding* (pp. 434–479). Philadelphia: W.B. Saunders.

Krick, J., & Van Duyn. (1984). The relationship between oral-motor involvement and growth: A pilot study in a pediatric population with cerebral palsy. *Journal of the American Dietetic Association, 84,* 555–559.

Lange, B.M., Entwistle, B.M., & Lipson, L.F. (1983). *Dental management of the handicapped: Approaches for dental auxiliaries.* Philadelphia: Lea & Febiger.

Linschied, T.R., Oliver, J., Blyer, E., & Palmer, S. (1978). Brief hospitalization for behavioral treatment of feeding problems in the developmentally disabled. *Journal of Pediatric Psychology, 3,* 72–76.

Logemann, J. (1983). *Evaluation and treatment of swallowing disorders.* San Diego: College-Hill.

Lucas, B. (1981). Diet and hyperactivity. In P.L. Pipes (Ed.), *Nutrition in infancy and childhood* (2nd ed., pp. 236–248). St. Louis: C.V. Mosby.

Lupi, M.H., & Porcella, J.E. (1987). Some considerations in the education and management of the child with Prader-Willi syndrome in the special education classroom. *Techniques: A Journal for Remedial Education and Counseling, 2,* 230–235.

McCamman, S., & Rues, J. (1990). Nutrition monitoring and supplementation. In J.C.

Graff, M.M. Ault, D. Guess, M. Taylor, & B. Thompson, *Health care for students with disabilities: An illustrated medical guide for the classroom.* Baltimore: Paul H. Brookes Publishing Co.

McIver, F.J., & Machen, J.B. (1979). Prevention of dental disease in handicapped people. In K. E. Wessels (Ed.), *Dentistry and the handicapped patient* (Postgraduate Dental Handbook Series, Vol. 5, pp. 77–115). Littleton, MA: PSG Publishing.

Meyer, L.H., & Evans, I.M. (1989). *Nonaversive intervention for behavior problems: A manual for home and community.* Baltimore: Paul H. Brookes Publishing Co.

Morris, S.E. (1978a). Oral-motor development: Normal and abnormal. In J.M. Wilson (Ed.), *Oral-motor function and dysfunction in children* (pp. 114–122). Chapel Hill: University of North Carolina, Division of Physical Therapy.

Morris, S.E. (1978b). *Program guidelines for children with feeding problems.* Edison, NJ: Childcraft.

Morris, S.E., & Klein, M.D. (1987). *Pre-feeding skills.* Tucson: Therapy Skill Builders.

Morris, S.E., & Weber, S.S. (1978). Problems of cerebral palsy and oral-motor function. In J.M. Wilson (Ed.), *Oral-motor function and dysfunction in children* (pp. 163–166). Chapel Hill: University of North Carolina, Division of Physical Therapy.

Mueller, H. (1975). Feeding. In N.R. Finnie (Ed.), *Handling the young cerebral palsied child at home* (2nd ed.) (pp. 113–132). New York: E.P. Dutton.

Palmer, S., & Ekvall, S. (Eds.). (1978). *Pediatric nutrition in developmental disabilities.* Springfield, IL: Charles C Thomas.

Palmer, S., & Horn, S. (1978). Feeding problems in children. In S. Palmer & S. Ekvall (Eds.), *Pediatric nutrition in developmental disorders* (pp. 107–129). Springfield, IL: Charles C Thomas.

Perske, R., Clifton, A., McLean, B.M., & Stein, J.I. (Eds.). (1986). *Mealtimes for persons with severe handicaps.* Baltimore: Paul H. Brookes Publishing Co.

Schmidt, P. (1976). Feeding assessment and therapy for the neurologically impaired. *AAESPH Review, 1,* 19–27.

Silberman, H., & Eisenberg, D. (1982). *Parenteral and enteral nutrition for the hospitalized patient.* Norwalk, CT: Appleton-Century-Crofts.

Snell, M.E. (1983). Self-care skills. In M.E. Snell (Ed.), *Systematic instruction of the moderately and severely handicapped* (2nd ed., pp. 358–409). Columbus, OH: Charles E. Merrill.

Sobsey, D. (1988, January). *Mealtime skills cluster: Bringing it all together.* Paper presented at the Current Concepts in Mealtime Management for Neurologically Impaired and Mentally Retarded Clients: Special Topics Symposium, Dallas.

Sobsey, D. (1983a). A comparison of feeding pureed and whole foods to a multihandicapped adolescent. *Mental Retardation and Learning Disabilities Bulletin, 11,* 85–91.

Sobsey, R.J. (1983b). Nutrition of children with severely handicapping conditions. *Journal of The Association for Persons with Severe Handicaps, 8*(4), 14–17.

Sobsey, R., & Orelove, F.P. (1984). Neurophysiological facilitation of eating skills in children with severe handicaps. *Journal of The Association for Persons with Severe Handicaps, 9,* 98–110.

Springer, N.S. (1982). *Nutrition casebook on developmental disabilities.* Syracuse, NY: Syracuse University Press.

Stainback, S., Stainback, W., Healy, H., & Healy, J. (1980). Basic eating skills. In J. Umbreit & P.J. Cardullias (Eds.), *Educating the severely physically handicapped: Basic principles and techniques* (Vol. I, pp. 16–30). Reston, VA: Council for Exceptional Children, Division on Physically Handicapped.

Sternberg, L., Pegnatore, L., & Hill, C. (1983). Establishing interactive communication behaviors with profoundly mentally handicapped students. *Journal of The Association for the Severely Handicapped, 8*(2), 39–46.

Tawney, J.W. (1979). *Programmed environments curriculum.* Columbus, OH: Charles E. Merrill.

Trefler, E., Westmoreland, D., & Burlingame, D. (1977). A feeding spatula for cerebral-palsied children. *American Journal of Occupational Therapy, 31,* 260–261.

Utley, B. L., Holvoet, J. F., & Barnes, K. (1977). Handling, positioning and feeding the physically handicapped. In E. Sontag, J. Smith, & N. Certo (Eds.), *Educational programming for the severely and profoundly handicapped* (pp. 279–299). Reston, VA: Council for Exceptional Children.

Walker, P.O. (1979, January–March). The patient with a handicap—Are we adding insult to injury? *Dental Dimensions,* pp. 9–12.

Wilson, J.M. (1978). Helpful hints for feeding children with oral-motor dysfunction. In J.M. Wilson (Ed.), *Oral-motor function and dysfunction in children* (pp. 198–202). Chapel Hill: University of North Carolina, Division of Physical Therapy.

Chapter 11

Self-Care Skills

One area of the curriculum for students with multiple impairments that everyone agrees is important is self-care skills. In fact, many educational programs focus almost solely on teaching students to become more proficient in taking care of their own hygiene and appearance. In addition to mealtime skills (discussed in Chapter 10), toileting, dressing, grooming, and personal hygiene are viewed as particularly important self-care skills for several reasons. First, individuals use toileting, dressing, and grooming skills every day, and these skills are used for a lifetime. Second, helping children to void and to undress, dress, and tend to the rest of their personal care requires much time and energy from parents, teachers, and other caregivers. Teaching students to perform even parts of these skill sequences is helpful to caregivers. Third, the ability to dress and groom and, especially, handle self-toileting is a badge of independence. The performance of these tasks not only serves to make individuals feel better about themselves, but often creates a perception in others that the students are more competent and capable of learning. Fourth, in the case of toileting and personal hygiene, learning appropriate techniques can improve the student's health by reducing the rashes, sores, and, in some cases, bladder and kidney infections (Gallender, 1980; Stauffer, 1983).

This chapter discusses approaches to teaching students with multiple disabilities to become more independent in toileting, dressing, grooming, and personal hygiene. Suggestions are provided for assessing students' behavior and for adapting materials and instructional approaches to accommodate children with severe physical involvement. Emphasis is given throughout to a team approach in all of these important skill areas.

TOILETING SKILLS

Normal Development of Voiding and Toileting Skills

Urinary System and Urination   The urinary system consists of two kidneys, two ureters, one bladder, and one urethra (Gallender, 1980) (see Figure 11.1). These organs excrete, store, and eliminate urine as waste, thus maintaining the body's fluid and electrolyte balance. Their functions are as follows:

- Kidneys: Extract urea and other substances from the blood
- Ureters: Tubes that transport urine from kidneys to bladder
- Bladder: Stores urine until it is voided
- Urethra: Tube that carries urine from bladder to the exterior to be expelled

The process of urination is basically a reflex act under voluntary control. When the bladder fills to a certain extent, the reflex is initiated and the person has a desire to urinate. The restraint or inhibition is voluntarily removed and urination follows automatically (Gallender, 1980; Yeates, 1973). This voluntary control, of course, does not develop in the normally developing child until between 2 and 3 years of age.

Gastrointestinal Tract and Defecation   The gastrointestinal tract consists mainly of the stomach, small intestine, and large intestine (see Figure 11.2). The food in the stomach mixes with gastric juices and enters the duodenum, or the first part of the small intestine (Schaefer, 1979). Much of the food mixture, now in a semiliquid state, is absorbed by the large intestine (colon). The remainder is formed into feces or stools. The colon pushes the stool to the lower part of the intestine and into the rectum to be evacuated.

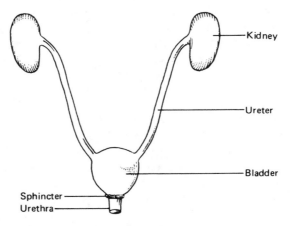

Figure 11.1.   The urinary system. (From Schaefer, C.E. [1979]. *Childhood encopresis and enuresis: Causes and therapy.* p. 99. New York: Van Nostrand Reinhold; reprinted with permission.)

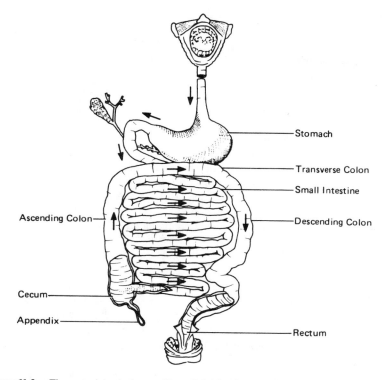

Stomach

Transverse Colon

Small Intestine

Descending Colon

Ascending Colon

Cecum

Appendix

Rectum

Figure 11.2. The gastrointestinal tract. (From Schaefer, C.E. [1979]. *Childhood encopresis and enuresis: Causes and therapy*, p. 12. New York: Van Nostrand Reinhold; reprinted with permission.)

The ability to control bowel movements is related to tightening and relaxing two circular muscles (sphincters) that circle the anus. The muscle near the outside, the external sphincter, comes under voluntary control around age 2 or 3 years (Myers, Cerone, & Olson, 1981). The internal sphincter usually opens automatically when a stool fills the rectum.

Toileting Skills   The ability to urinate or defecate at appropriate times and places involves more than voluntarily constricting or relaxing certain muscles. The nondisabled child follows a predictable developmental sequence, as depicted in Table 11.1. Two points, however, should be noted. First, several of the more advanced toileting skills, such as managing clothes and seating oneself on the toilet, may never be possible for many students with multiple disabilities because of their pronounced motor deficits. Even more basic skills (e.g., signaling the need to go) may be difficult for some children. It is important to avoid requiring of the child too many nonphysiological, developmental prerequisites before initiating a training program.

The second point concerns the age at which an individual with disabilities is ready for toilet training. Surprisingly, there is no empirical evidence to an-

Table 11.1.   Normal developmental sequence of toileting skills

Approximate age	Toileting skill
10 months	Child indicates when wet or soiled
12 months	Regularity of bowel movements
15 months	Child will sit on toilet when placed there and supervised (short time)
18–21 months	Regularity of urination
20 months	Toileting becomes regulated
22 months	Child indicates need to go to toilet
24 months	Daytime control with occasional accidents Must be reminded to go to bathroom
30 months	Child tells someone he or she needs to go to bathroom
34 months	Child seats self on toilet
3–4 years	Goes to bathroom independently May need help with clothing
4–5 years	Completely independent

swer this question. Lohmann, Eyman, and Lask (1967), in a review of institutional records, concluded that residents around 6 years old with an IQ of 20 or greater had a better chance of being toilet trained than older residents with lower (between 10 and 20) IQ scores. Smith and Smith (1977) found that institutional residents under age 20 progressed faster than adults over 25 and that children with milder mental disabilities did better than residents with more severe mental disabilities. Foxx and Azrin (1973a) also suggested that their procedures might work best for individuals with severe mental disabilities who are over age 5 years. No study, however, reports an attempt to train younger (2½ –5 years) persons with multiple disabilities, so an answer is not available for them. A prudent course would be to follow Snell's (1980, 1987) advice to provide training regardless of level of mental disability, assuming the child is medically sound and physiologically mature.

Assessing Toileting Skills

Assessment in toileting encompasses three areas: determining readiness, determining elimination patterns, and assessing related skills.

Assessing Readiness   It was intimated in the previous section that children who are candidates for toilet training should exhibit certain essential prerequisites. In addition to a suggested minimum chronological age of 2½ years, Snell (1987) listed two others: 1) a stable pattern of elimination, such that voiding occurs within certain daily time periods; and 2) daily stable patterns of dryness. Campbell (1977) also included: 1) freedom from medical problems that preclude training, 2) adequate liquid intake, and 3) ability to be properly positioned on a potty chair. Once the student has a thorough medical examination to rule out any obvious organic problems, his or her patterns of elimination and dryness are easily determined through use of a simple chart.

Determining Elimination Patterns   A chart of the child's toileting behavior proves helpful to detect when the child: 1) is wet or dry, 2) has urinated or defecated, and 3) has voided in a toilet rather than elsewhere. (Since many students with multiple disabilities are nonambulatory, they will be unable to take themselves to a toilet facility.) A sample chart, constructed for one child for 1 week, is presented in Figure 11.3. The child should be checked at half-hour intervals and the appropriate notation marked. This particular chart covers a 24-hour period and can be marked by both parents and school staff. A small period that includes only the school day can be used instead. Daytime regulation and training typically precede nighttime training, although it is possible for a child to be dry at night but not during the day (MacKeith, Meadow, & Turner, 1973). How long the charting of elimination patterns should continue will vary, depending on the student's regularity and the type of training to be done. It is important to take enough data upon which to base a training program (usually between 7 and 15 days). It is also essential to change students' clothing after detecting accidents to avoid confusing new accidents with earlier ones (Snell, 1987).

Assessing Related Skills   It is helpful to the toilet training process if the student can perform parts or all of such related skills as adjusting clothing,

toilet training schedule

Date: from _____ to _____

		Mon.	Tues.	Wed.	Thur.	Fri.	Sat.	Sun.
A.M.	12–2							
	2–4							
	4–6							
	6–7							
	7–8							
	8–9							
	9–10							
	10–11							
	11–12							
P.M.	12–1							
	1–2							
	2–3							
	3–4							
	4–5							
	5–6							
	6–7							
	7–8							
	8–9							
	9–10							
	10–12							
Total hits								
Total misses								

Hit–went in toilet   U–urine   S–sleep or school
Miss–went elsewhere   B–bowel movement

Figure 11.3.   Chart for determining toilet training.

flushing, wiping, and washing hands. As indicated earlier, however, students unable to perform these skills should not be kept from a toilet training program. More specific information on dressing is covered later in this chapter. Other skills can be assessed through a task-analytic format, in which the skills are broken down into steps and the student's performance on those steps is recorded. The child with limited use of motor or sensory systems can be taught to do parts of related skills or alternatives to traditional methods of performing those skills through individualized adaptations and the use of partial participation (see Chapters 7 and 8).

Positioning for Toileting

Prior to beginning training, it is important to establish a comfortable position for the student on the toilet. Ideally, the head and shoulders should be slightly forward and in midline, the arms relaxed and close to the body, the hips at approximately a 90 degree angle, the knees bent, and the feet supported (Finnie, 1975; Gibson, 1980) (refer to Figure 11.4). Many children with multiple

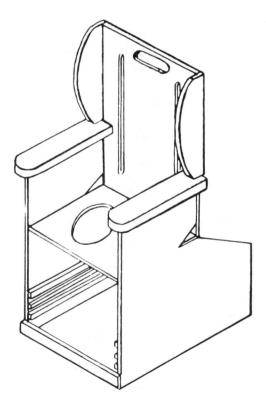

Figure 11.4. Box-type potty chair.

disabilities are unable to assume this exact sitting posture, but approximations to it should be attempted. It is important for the student's own sense of comfort and well-being and for the success of the program that the student be relaxed and secure. Voiding requires voluntary relaxation of muscles, which is difficult when the body is struggling to maintain balance.

Toileting adaptations for young children with cerebral palsy are depicted in Finnie (1975). The student with severe involvement might benefit from the box-type potty chair shown in Figure 11.4. This chair provides support at the front, back, and sides as well as at the head and feet. (Bergen, 1974, provides procedures for constructing this chair.)

Several other possible adaptations for the training area include: 1) a stepping stool to help a small child get on the toilet, with rubber matting on the stool and underneath it to prevent slipping; 2) nonslippery floor, with either well-fastened carpeting or a rubber mat around the toilet; and 3) removing the bathroom door to allow the child using a wheelchair, walker, or crutches to enter more easily (Calkin, Grant, & Bowman, 1978). In a school setting, the occupational or physical therapist can provide a great deal of help in determining and fashioning specific adaptations.

Methods of Toilet Training Students

The zero-reject principle, put into practice by Public Law 99-457, the Education of the Handicapped Act Amendments, terminated the common practice of refusing to accept children with enuresis or encopresis (involuntary urination or defecation) into public school programs. (Unfortunately, some community-based vocational and residential programs still refuse to accept individuals who are not toilet trained.) Numerous studies in the 1970s and 1980s have demonstrated that persons with severe or profound disabilities can be taught to regulate their toileting behaviors and to decrease their rate of accidents (e.g., Foxx & Azrin, 1973b; Lancioni, 1980).

Several cautions are in order, however. First, although individuals with profound disabilities were studied in much of the research, experimenters frequently excluded persons who were nonambulatory (e.g., Baumeister & Klosowski, 1965; Hundziak, Maurer, & Watson, 1965). Since many students with multiple disabilities are nonambulatory and have additional sensory, behavioral, and medical problems, it is not always possible to apply procedures in their entirety from one population to another. Second, the great majority of studies were performed in institutional settings, where the environment, staffing, and motivation to train typically differ from that in public school programs. This is especially true of the studies in the 1960s and early 1970s, when educational programs in residential facilities were not required. Third, the exact procedures for toilet training are not detailed in many studies and the degree of experimental control is often slight. It is therefore hard to tell what part of a package of procedures made the difference. (One early study [Bensberg, Colwell, & Cassel, 1965] even speculated that all or part of their success may have been due to the increased amount of personal attention given the resident.)

Despite these caveats, however, there is sufficient evidence, including hundreds of successful cases, that individuals with multiple disabilities can be toilet trained with thoughtfully designed and executed programs. This section describes several of the techniques that have been included in successful programs.

Early Research on Toilet Training   Ellis (1963) presented a 15-step plan for a toilet training program, which detailed who should be included, what they should be given to eat, on what schedule the program should be conducted, and even what the attendants should wear. The model and plan, although theoretical in nature, stimulated research with individuals with mental retardation in institutions with varying degrees of success (Baumeister & Klosowski, 1965; Bensberg et al., 1965; Dayan, 1964; Giles & Wolf, 1966; Hundziak, Maurer, & Watson, 1965; Kimbrell, Luckey, Barbuto, & Love, 1967; Levine & Elliott, 1970; Lohmann et al., 1967; Roos & Oliver, 1969). None of these studies, however, included individuals with severe physical impairments. Many of them were designed to reduce administrative costs and attendant care. The major measure of success in two of the studies, in fact, was a decrease in the amount of soiled laundry (Dayan, 1964; Levine & Elliott, 1970). Even studies that were relatively well designed (e.g., Giles & Wolf, 1966) suffered from ethically questionable procedures, including restraining residents in jackets and tethering them with ropes.

Foxx and Azrin Procedures   Azrin and Foxx (1971) toilet trained nine adults with profound mental retardation and 34 nondisabled children (Foxx & Azrin, 1973b). Their procedures, detailed in an often-cited book (Foxx & Azrin, 1973b), ushered in the modern era of toilet training research and practice. This section describes the main components of the Foxx and Azrin program.

Increased Fluid Consumption   Toilet training requires that individuals have numerous opportunities to practice and to be reinforced. As a way of increasing elimination, Foxx and Azrin (1973b) gave residents extra fluids (e.g., coffee, tea, soft drinks, water) to induce more frequent urination, a technique referred to as rapid toilet training. It should be noted that the Foxx and Azrin procedures were developed with adult residents in a state school for persons with mental retardation. School staff contemplating using a rapid technique for children with multiple disabilities should consult with a nurse or physician to determine an appropriate liquid to use. It is best to avoid giving children large amounts of caffeine and sugar or other fluids (e.g., apple juice) that might cause or aggravate constipation or other health problems. Perhaps more important, forcing liquids over an extended period may lead to a condition called *hyponatremia*. Marked by nausea, vomiting, seizures, and even coma, hyponatremia requires emergency medical care (Thompson & Hanson, 1983).

Bladder Training   The first phase of the toilet training program, bladder training, is designed for the person to gain control over his or her bladder and bowel muscles so that elimination occurs only on the toilet. The sequence for this phase is presented in Table 11.2. A prompting-fading procedure is used throughout bladder training. Prompts appropriate to the learner's skill level (verbal, gestural, and/or physical) are provided to teach approaching the toilet, pulling down pants, and so forth, and are faded as soon as possible. Obviously, many students with severe physical impairments may require help with some or all of the steps, even after bladder control has been achieved.

Dry Pants Inspection   As Table 11.2 indicates, individuals are checked every 5 minutes to detect whether they are wet or dry. The procedure includes: 1) asking the person, "Are you dry?", using gestures if appropriate; 2) prompting the person to feel his or her crotch area; and 3) reinforcing the person for dry pants or admonishing for wet pants and withholding reinforcement. Dry pants inspection can be used as part of any toilet training program, and would be performed less frequently in programs that did not increase fluids. Step 2 (feeling the crotch area) could also be modified for students lacking the necessary arm movements.

Accident Treatment   During bladder training, Foxx and Azrin (1973b) used a "brief cleanliness training procedure" when an individual had an accident. The procedure consists of grasping the person and stating, "No, you wet your pants," and requiring him or her to wash the chair and floor. During self-initiation training (see the following section), accidents are followed by the "full

Table 11.2.   Sequence of steps in bladder training procedure

(Step one is begun exactly on the half-hour)
1.   Give as much fluid to the resident as he will drink while seated in his chair.
     a.   Wait about 1 minute
2.   Direct resident to sit on toilet seat using the minimal possible prompt.
3.   Direct resident to pull his pants down using the minimal possible prompt.
4.   a.   When resident voids, give edible and praise while seated, then direct him to stand.
     b.   If resident does not void within 20 minutes after drinking the fluids, direct him to stand.
5.   Direct resident to pull up his pants using the minimal possible prompt.
     a.   If resident voided, direct him to flush the toilet using the minimal possible prompt.
6.   Direct resident to his chair using the minimal possible prompt.
7.   After resident has been sitting for 5 minutes, inspect him for dry pants.
     a.   If pants are dry, give edible and praise.
     b.   If pants are wet, only show him the edible and admonish him.
8.   Check resident for dry pants every 5 minutes.
9.   At the end of 30 minutes, begin the sequence of steps again.

From *Toilet Training the Retarded* (p. 45) by R. M. Foxx and N. H. Azrin, 1973, Champaign, IL: Research Press. Copyright 1973 by the authors; reprinted with permission.

cleanliness" procedure. The individual must secure a mop and bucket, wipe up the area, clean and return the materials, change his or her clothes, and wash the wet clothes. Following this procedure, the individual is made to practice the toileting procedure (walk to commode, lower pants, sit, arise, raise pants, and so forth) six times. Most children with multiple disabilities are physically unable to perform such a procedure, and the time it takes the staff member to complete it renders it impractical in school settings. Smith (1979) discovered that a reprimand and a 10-minute timeout from reinforcement worked equally as well as the cleanliness training for children with severe disabilities.

Self-Initiation Training   Once the learner initiates toileting without prompting, self-initiation training begins. Table 11.3 presents this procedure. Note that many individuals with multiple disabilities will be unable to initiate ambulating to the toilet. Others may ambulate to the proper location, but find it difficult to move themselves onto the commode. Gibson (1980) described several types of techniques children can use to transfer to and from a toilet, both with and without assistance. As with all physical care procedures, proper body mechanics and handling techniques are essential (see Chapter 3).

Moisture Signaling Devices   Foxx and Azrin (1973b) used two special devices that detect moisture and emit an auditory signal (Azrin, Bugle, & O'Brien, 1971). The function of these devices is to alert the trainer at the moment of voiding, thus facilitating implementation of reinforcement and cleanliness training procedures. One such device is a pants alarm (depicted in Figure 11.5), which signals the presence of wetness. The other device is a urine alert (Figure 11.6), which fits into a toilet bowl and signals urination or defecation.

Other researchers have used similar signaling devices. Van Wagenen and associates (Van Wagenen, Meyerson, Kerr, & Mahoney, 1969; Van Wagenen &

Table 11.3.   Self-initiation training procedure

1.   Give fluids immediately following an elimination.
2.   No further toilet-approach prompts are given.
3.   Continue to provide guidance and prompts for dressing and undressing and for flushing the toilet, if necessary, but never at a level greater than that needed on previous toiletings.
4.   Move resident's chair farther from the toilet after each successful self-initiation.
5.   Gradually lengthen the time between dry-pants inspections.
6.   Intermittently reward correct toileting.
7.   When resident is self-initiating from the area where he spends most of his time, remove urine alert from the toilet bowl, pants alarm from resident's briefs, and the chair.
8.   Require resident to show you that he can find the toilet from various areas on the ward.
9.   Include resident on the Maintenance Program after 9 self-initiations.

From *Toilet Training the Retarded* (p. 54) by R. M. Foxx and N. H. Azrin, 1973, Champaign, IL: Research Press. Copyright 1973 by the authors; reprinted with permission.

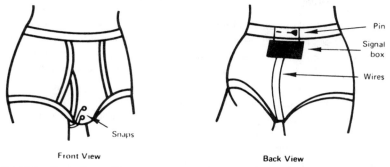

Figure 11.5. Pants alarm. (From *Toilet training the retarded* [p. 32] by R.M. Foxx & N.H. Azrin, 1973, Champaign, IL: Research Press. Copyright 1973 by the authors; reprinted with permission.)

Murdock, 1966) fitted children with auditory signal generators that sounded a tone while the child was urinating. A later study (Mahoney, Van Wagenen, & Meyerson, 1971) used a modified device by: 1) adding a miniature transistor radio receiver through which an audio alert was triggered by an FM transmitter, and 2) replacing speakers with earphones. These devices were used to prompt correct responding toward the toilet, rather than to signal the trainer when reinforcement or punishment was needed. Herreshoff (1973) provided schematics for constructing electronic devices that operate a relay switch to activate a light or any electric appliance, rather than sounding a tone. A list of commercially available antienuretic devices has been compiled by Mountjoy, Ruben, and Bradford (1984).

The use of electronic devices may facilitate toilet training, but cannot be viewed as an essential part of a training procedure. They certainly should never

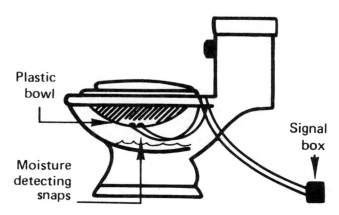

Figure 11.6. Urine alert. (From *Toilet training the retarded* [p. 30] by R.M. Foxx & N.H. Azrin, 1973, Champaign, IL: Research Press. Copyright 1973 by the authors; reprinted with permission.)

be used to replace techniques of systematic prompting and reinforcement. It is also extremely unlikely that technology in the form of automated elimination signaling devices (Watson, 1968) will ever replace a caring teacher or parent.

Other Training Procedures   This section examines other training procedures, many based on Foxx and Azrin (1973b), and their applications to other populations and settings.

Variations of Foxx and Azrin   Several individuals have toilet trained children or adults with moderate to profound mental retardation with procedures based largely on those used by Foxx and Azrin (1973b). Williams and Sloop (1978) trained six institution residents using all these procedures except for moisture signaling devices. Smith, Britton, Johnson, and Thomas (1975) taught five adults with profound mental retardation, using shorter timeout periods and less intense cleanliness training procedures. Full cleanliness procedures were used to treat encopresis in an 8-year-old boy with moderate mental retardation (Doleys & Arnold, 1975). Finally, Trott (1977) reported successful application of the Foxx and Azrin procedures with an 11-year-old boy in a public school setting.

Mahoney et al. (1971) Procedure   Mahoney et al.'s technique is distinctly different from the Foxx and Azrin procedure. The learner is taught to approach the toilet in response to an auditory signal (see the earlier section, "Moisture Signaling Devices"). Training proceeds through six phases:

1.   The student walks to the toilet in response to an auditory signal.
2.   The student lowers his or her pants after a signal.
3.   The student sits on or stands at the toilet.
4.   The student drinks liquids. (The student voids in the toilet.)
5.   The student pulls up his or her pants.
6.   The student practices the preceding steps without a signal.

Although the authors found their technique successful, it is somewhat limited for children with multiple disabilities, who often lack the ability to walk independently or to manipulate their clothing. Moreover, a study that compared these procedures to the Foxx and Azrin procedures revealed that the transistorized equipment used with the latter was difficult for staff to maintain and use, in addition to being expensive (Smith, 1979).

Training with Other Populations   Two studies reported attempts to toilet train children with autism. The earlier study (Marshall, 1966) used salt to reinforce initial toileting plus punishment (slap on the buttocks) for accidents after 2 weeks. Five children with autism in Japan were given similar reinforcement and punishment, with varying degrees of success (Ando, 1977). (No study has isolated the effectiveness of aversive techniques in toilet training. Physical punishment for accidents is not only likely to lose its effectiveness over time, but is ethically questionable.)

Finally, nine deaf-blind students were toilet trained with a variation of the

Foxx and Azrin procedures (Lancioni, 1980). Treatment was conducted for only 4 hours daily. To accommodate the students' sensory impairments: 1) they were taught to touch the toilet stall door on their way to the commode, 2) edible reinforcers were brought into contact with their lips, and 3) tactile reinforcement (rubbing students' backs) was used. The researchers also found that cleanliness training was not feasible, since the total physical guidance necessary to help students clean the urine was reinforcing to them.

Irregular Enuresis Irregular enuresis, or wetting on a sporadic basis, was treated in three boys with severe to moderate mental retardation (Barmann, Katz, O'Brien, & Beauchamp, 1981). Procedures included a shortened version of the Foxx and Azrin program, with verbal praise for staying dry and cleanliness training for having accidents. A unique feature of this study was its implementation in the boys' homes, with parents as trainers, and with data recorded concurrently at school. The children reduced their accidents to zero, even when teachers only performed dry pants checks and praised the children for staying dry.

Nighttime Toilet Training The preceding material concentrated on daytime toilet training programs. A common problem among persons with multiple disabilities (and in children who do not have disabilities) is nocturnal enuresis, or bed-wetting. This section briefly examines procedures that have proven successful in nighttime toilet training.

Traditional Procedures Snell (1980) summarized the following components of traditional nighttime procedures:

1. Reducing fluids 1½–2 hours before bedtime
2. Toileting just before bedtime
3. Giving simple instructions to the child about receiving a reward for a dry bed in the morning
4. Performing regular awakenings and recording of accidents and successes every 1–1½ hours during the parents' or caregivers' working hours
5. Guiding the child to the toilet for 5 minutes without allowing sleeping
6. Praising on-toilet eliminations and recording them
7. Changing wet linens, with awakening of child at an earlier time the next night

Bed-Wetting Equipment The use of signaling devices to awaken the person who wets the bed goes back to the 1930s. Much of the research of the 1970s and 1980s on nocturnal enuresis has examined procedures that include use of a bed pad that sets off a buzzer when wet (Azrin, Sneed, & Foxx, 1974; Baller, 1975; Bollard, 1982; Bollard & Nettelbeck, 1982; Bollard, Nettelbeck, & Roxbee, 1982; Bollard & Woodroffe, 1977; Lovibond, 1963). Sloop and Kennedy (1973) used such a device for night training of residents with mental retardation in a state training facility. Slightly over half of the individuals were successfully trained, with a relapse rate of 36%.

Rapid Training Procedures   As with rapid training procedures for daytime toilet raining, rapid nighttime training procedures include increased fluid consumption. One specific rapid procedure designed by Azrin, Sneed, and Foxx (1973) also includes components similar to those used by Foxx and Azrin (1973a, 1973b) in their daytime training protocol. Table 11.4 outlines their dry-bed procedure as used in the home with enuretic children who do not have disabilities (Azrin et al., 1974). This procedure (in a slightly different format, to accommodate institutional staff) significantly reduced nighttime accidents in 12 residents with profound mental retardation (Azrin et al., 1973).

Smith (1981) used a modified version of the Azrin et al. (1973, 1974) program to train successfully five residents in England with severe or profound disabilities. Given that many early toilet training studies purposely excluded persons with such problems, it is notable that three of these individuals had behavior problems described as fairly major. Although Smith used the alarm, reinforcement, and increased fluids, she reduced the degree of punishment for accidents, using only a verbal reprimand and requiring the person to feel the "nasty wet bed." Day staff also expressed disapproval to the residents the day after an accident. No cleanliness training was used, as opposed to the procedure used by Azrin et al. (1973). It is clear that reinforcement for a dry bed was designed for the individual, including "tea and biscuits; long lie in bed; new trendy clothing to wear that day; and access to the juke box." Smith's (1981) nighttime procedure is important for individuals with multiple impairments, since it demonstrates—as did the Smith (1979) study of daytime training—that complicated, aversive punishment techniques may not be essential to the success of a program.

Alternative Toileting Techniques

Some children with multiple disabilities are physically unable to control the muscles that contribute to the normal processes of urination and defecation. These individuals cannot be toilet trained in the ways described in the previous sections of this chapter. However, their bladder and bowel care are important for cleanliness, comfort, and overall health (Bigge, 1982). This section describes several of the alternative techniques for managing bladder and bowel functions. It should be stressed that general descriptions of procedures should never be substituted for individualized physical care protocols developed by medical personnel and implemented by trained practitioners in the educational setting.

Bladder Management   Often because of injuries to or maldevelopment of the spinal cord or for other medical reasons, children are left with partial or total loss of bladder control. One of the most common causes in children with multiple disabilities is a condition in which the nervous system fails to form properly in the developing embryo. The infant is born with the spinal cord severed and partially enclosed in a sac along the back. This condition, known as

Table 11.4. Dry-bed procedure

I. Interview training (one night)
  (A) One hour before bedtime
    1. Child informed of all phases of training procedure
    2. Alarm placed on bed
    3. Positive practice in toileting (20 practice trials)
      (a) child lies down in bed
      (b) child counts to 50
      (c) child arises and attempts to urinate in toilet
      (d) child returns to bed
      (e) steps (a), (b), (c) and (d) repeated 20 times
  (B) At bedtime
    1. Child drinks fluids
    2. Child repeats training instructions to trainer
    3. Child retires for the night
  (C) Hourly awakenings
    1. Minimal prompt used to awaken child
    2. Child walks to bathroom
    3. At bathroom door (before urination), child is asked to inhibit urination for one hour (omit for children under 6)
      (a) if child could not inhibit urination
        (i) child urinates in toilet
        (ii) trainer praises child for correct toileting
        (iii) child returns to bed
      (b) if child indicated that he could inhibit urination for one hour
        (i) trainer praises child for his urinary control
        (ii) child returns to bed
    4. At bedside, the child feels the bed sheets and comments on their dryness
    5. Trainer praises child for having a dry bed
    6. Child is given fluids to drink
    7. Child returns to sleep
  (D) When an accident occurred
    1. Trainer disconnects alarm
    2. Trainer awakens child and reprimands him for wetting
    3. Trainer directs child to bathroom to finish urinating
    4. Child is given Cleanliness Training
      (a) child is required to change night clothes
      (b) child is required to remove wet bed sheet and place it with dirty laundry
      (c) trainer reactivates alarm
      (d) child obtains clean sheets and remakes bed
    5. Positive Practice in correct toileting (20 practice trials) performed immediately after the Cleanliness Training
    6. Positive Practice in correct toileting (20 practice trials) performed the following evening before bedtime

(continued)

Table 11.4.   *(continued)*

II. Post training supervision (begins the night after training)
     (A) Before bedtime
          1. Alarm is placed on bed
          2. Positive Practice given (if an accident the previous night)
          3. Child is reminded of need to remain dry and of the need for
              Cleanliness Training and Positive Practice if wetting occurred
          4. Child is asked to repeat the parent's instructions
     (B) Night-time toileting
          1. At parents' bedtime, they awaken child and send him to toilet
          2. After each dry night, parent awakens child 30 minutes earlier than
              on previous night
          3. Awakening discontinued when they are scheduled to occur within
              one hour of child's bedtime
     (C) When accidents occurred, child receives Cleanliness Training and
          Positive Practice immediately on wetting and at bedtime the next day
     (D) After a dry night
          1. Both parents praise child for not wetting his bed
          2. Parents praise child at least 5 times during the day
          3. Child's favorite relatives are encouraged to praise him

From Azrin, N. H., Sneed, T. J., & Foxx, R. M. (1974). Dry-bed training: Rapid elimination of childhood enuresis. *Behaviour Research and Therapy, 12,* 150–151; reprinted with permission. Copyright 1974, Pergamon Press, Ltd.

myelomeningocele (a form of spina bifida or open spine), causes a neurogenic bladder, because of the loss of connections of nerves to it (Myers et al., 1981). There are two types of neurogenic bladders—flaccid and spastic. Flaccid (limp or relaxed) bladder muscles cannot be tightened completely to force out all of the urine, which often results in continual leakage. Spastic (tight) bladders cannot store urine because even small amounts cause the bladder to tighten, causing leakage. The child with myelomeningocele needs a permanent alternative means of voiding. Three different bladder management strategies are: 1) external catheters, 2) clean intermittent catheterization, and 3) surgical intervention.

External Catheters   Used with males, a urinary collection device (condom catheter) is placed over the penis. A tube drains into a collection bag, which is fastened to the child's leg with Velcro straps. It is important that the device fit well to avoid leakage or backflow of urine into the condom (Jones, 1985). Staff and parents can consult local surgical supply stores for help.

Clean Intermittent Catheterization (CIC)   This technique for emptying the bladder has gained wide acceptance since the mid-1970s. Children with neurogenic bladders can be tested to determine their eligibility for CIC. The purposes of CIC are: 1) to prevent bladder distention through regular voiding, 2) to prevent kidney infection by controlling bladder infection, and 3) to reduce the social distress caused by wet clothes and odor (Stauffer, 1983). The technique involves inserting a catheter into the urethra to the bladder in order to drain off urine and collect it in a basin. The key to preventing infection is not the sterility, but the frequency, of catheterization (Altshuler, Meyer, & Butz, 1977). Children who are capable of performing CIC themselves are encouraged to do so, although few individuals for whom this book is intended will be able to be totally independent. Fortunately, school staff and parents can be taught CIC quite successfully (Wolraich, Hawtrey, Mapel, & Henderson, 1983). Children are sometimes given medications in conjunction with catheterization to prevent infections, relax the bladder, minimize irregular bladder contractions, or tighten the bladder sphincter (Taylor, 1990). Consultation with a urologist before and during CIC training is essential.

Surgical Intervention   Occasionally surgery is required to redirect the normal course of urine flow. One such intervention, designed to prevent progressive kidney disease, is the ileal conduit. The ureters are disconnected from the bladder and implanted in a segment of the small bowel, which is brought out to the surface of the abdomen. The segment is sutured there to form a hole, or stoma, through which urine passes. The child is fitted with a pouch to collect the urine. Medical specialists, called enterostomal therapists, can provide information and support before and after the operation on physical care and diet.

Bowel Management   In a way similar to having a neurogenic bladder, children may also possess a neurogenic bowel. Individuals with myelomeningocele often experience an absence of tone in their sphincter muscles, a loss of the sensation of fullness or need to evacuate, and sluggish bowel contractions. They may also have constipation, diarrhea, and impaction; each of these conditions is discussed later in this section. Other persons require surgery to facilitate removal of wastes. Any bowel management program should be designed for regular emptying of the bowels with no leakage of stool in between (Myers et al., 1981). It should be noted that many children with multiple disabilities have bowel movements less frequently and less regularly than the average individual. It is common for students with multiple disabilities, in fact, not to have bowel movements during the school day. Bowel management programs in the school, therefore, should be coordinated carefully with home interventions.

Bowel Evacuation   One of the keys to helping students regulate their bowel movements is to help ensure a stool consistency that is fairly firm without being too hard. Two important factors that contribute to stool consistency are food and water intake. High-fiber foods should be included in the diet daily; these include whole grain products and edible skins of fruits and vegetables. Consultation with a dietitian can prove very helpful. Water is also essential to prevent stools from becoming too hard. If stools become loose, adjusting the diet should involve a change in foods rather than reduction of fluids.

Bowel evacuation can take advantage of the peristaltic action of the stomach occurring after meals. This action can be triggered by digital stimulation, that is, the stimulation of the anal sphincter with one's finger (Jones, 1985). It is possible to check for the presence of a stool inside the rectum by using a gloved lubricated finger. (This should be done only by a parent, nurse, or other qualified professional.)

Occasionally a large mass of hard stool will collect in the rectum, creating an impaction (Myers et al., 1981). The child with this impaction often has frequent soft stools in small amounts, because the mass holds the sphincters open and allows the liquid stool to slip around and pass through. Impactions must be removed, often with an enema to help soften the stool. Sometimes glycerin suppositories are used to help evacuate a normal stool that does not move (Jones, 1985).

Finally, laxatives often are administered to facilitate bowel evacuation. There are four basic types: 1) a stool softener with a substance designed to break surface tension and keep the stool moist; 2) a bulk former, which absorbs water and keeps the stool soft; 3) an irritant to stimulate peristalsis; and 4) a purgative, usually used to empty the bowel before testing or surgery. Many laxatives are combinations of any of these four types. Physicians and pharmacists should be consulted for the correct type and form for a given child (Jones, 1985). Laxatives should not substitute for a regular bowel management program, including exercise when possible (Cheever & Elmer, 1975).

Constipation and Diarrhea   Constipation is a common problem in children with multiple disabilities because they are inactive, eat inadequate amounts of fiber, do not drink enough fluids, and often are in poor health. Preventing constipation through a sensible and individualized bowel management program is the best approach to this problem. Otherwise, removing stools can be done through the techniques described in the preceding section. Prolonged constipation can lead to urinary tract infections, especially in girls (Graff, Ault, Guess, Taylor, & Thompson, 1990).

Diarrhea, an intestinal disorder characterized by soft or watery bowel movements, is often a symptom of an illness or food intolerance (Jones, 1985). Because the stools are watery, diarrhea can be confused with impactions. The most serious consequence of diarrhea is the loss of water, which normally is reabsorbed into the body during the passage of feces through the colon. Water loss can lead to dehydration, a serious condition needing prompt medical care (Graff et al., 1990). Mild diarrhea can be controlled by a diet of clear liquids such as apple juice, with the gradual addition of foods like bananas, rice, applesauce, and toast (Jones, 1985). A child unable to eat these foods should be taken to a doctor for possible medications. Very young children and infants with diarrhea should see a physician regardless.

Surgical Intervention   Because of certain diseases or conditions that involve the small or large intestine or the rectum, some individuals require surgery to create an alternative method of removing bowel contents. When the end of the small intestine (ileum) is brought out through the abdominal wall, the procedure is termed an ileostomy. When a portion of the large intestine (colon) is involved, the procedure is call a colostomy. In both cases, the patient discharges fecal matter through a hole, or stoma, in the abdominal wall. School personnel who work with a student with an ileostomy or colostomy need to understand how to handle the external collecting appliances. Also, the student will be placed on a specific diet, which needs to be followed carefully. Typically, this involves a progression from a clear liquid to a low fiber diet, in small quantities (Graff et al., 1990). Teachers, therapists, school nurses, and others are encouraged to consult a book written for parents of children who have had ostomies, *These Special Children* (Geter, 1982).

DRESSING SKILLS

This section of the chapter focuses on strategies for selecting, assessing, and teaching dressing skills. The final section discusses selecting and adapting clothing, both closely linked to success in dressing.

Normal Development of Dressing Skills

It is helpful to remember that dressing skills require relatively sophisticated and coordinated movements of almost every body part. A child who does not have disabilities is about 12 months old before he or she cooperates in even a simple way with dressing and is age 5 years or older before becoming completely independent (Finnie, 1975). Table 11.5 presents the order in which children who do not have disabilities acquire dressing and undressing skills. This information should not suggest that children with multiple disabilities will or should learn these skills in the same sequence or in the same fashion. Nor should the chronological ages listed in the table be used to exclude children at given "functioning levels" or "mental ages" from participating in dressing programs. It is apparent from a normal developmental sequence, however, that certain skills (e.g., undressing, using gross motor actions) tend to be easier and learned faster than others (e.g., dressing, fastening buttons). This information can be useful in developing general guidelines for selecting target skills for instruction.

Table 11.5.   Normal developmental sequence of dressing skills

Approximate age	Dressing skill
12 months	Begins to cooperate by holding out foot for shoe, arm for sleeve
12–18 months	Begins to remove hat, socks, mittens
2 years	Removes unlaced shoes, socks, and pants
2½ years	Removes all clothing Can put on socks, shirt, coat
3 years	Undresses rapidly and well Dresses, except for heavy outer clothing
4 years	Dresses and undresses with little assistance

Selecting Dressing Skills for Instruction

A glance at commercially published curricula for students with severe disabilities (e.g., Tawney, Knapp, O'Reilly, & Pratt, 1979; Williams & Fox, 1979) quickly reveals a wide range of dressing and undressing skills from which to choose. It becomes clear that no child with multiple disabilities could learn all of the possible skills at one time. Moreover, most curricula fail to organize the various skills in a sequence designed for the individual with severe physical impairment. Table 11.6 presents a sequence based on the complexity of motor acts required for dressing, from easier to more difficult (Campbell, 1977). This progression, as with others, serves as a rough guide only; the physical and cognitive abilities of individual students must be assessed to help determine individualized teaching targets. Furthermore, the complexity of a specific dressing skill can be reduced by modification of the materials.

Decisions on selecting dressing skills should also reflect the following considerations:

1. The wishes of the parents or caregivers for the student to learn specific skills
2. The frequency with which the student needs to use the skill during the day
3. The importance of learning the skill for moving into a less restrictive vocational or residential setting
4. An analysis of the features of the student's clothing
5. The degree to which learning the skill would facilitate acquiring other important skills (e.g., toileting)

Table 11.6.   Sequence of dressing based on motor complexity

Removing clothing
Removes hat, mittens
Removes socks from toes
Takes arms from sleeves of garment with front opening
Takes legs from pants when pants have been pulled to knees
Takes arms from sleeves of pullover garment
Removes shoes (laces untied)
Removes socks
Removes pants
Removes pullover garment
Putting on clothing
Puts arms through large armholes on front-opening garment
Puts head into pullover garment
Pulls pants on
Puts on shoes
Puts on socks

Adapted from Campbell (1977).

In short, the student should be taught simpler, less complex, undressing and dressing skills first, but not at the expense of learning *meaningful* skills.

Assessing Dressing Skills

Assessment is done for two purposes. First, an overall evaluation of the student's dressing abilities can be used to help determine a starting point for instruction and to gain information on how the student moves to perform various tasks. Second, ongoing assessment of performance on specific dressing tasks is used to monitor progress and to make decisions about possible changes in instructional procedures.

The first type of assessment, the overall evaluation, is best achieved through criterion-referenced checklists. Figure 11.7 presents an example (Copeland, Ford, & Solon, 1976). Note that space is provided for recording information on how the child attempts each item. A physical or occupational therapist, working with a teacher, can gain valuable information on the *quality* of a student's movements, which is equally important as knowing whether a student did or did not perform a particular action. Remember that commercially published checklists typically fail to yield specific information on individual students that can be readily translated into instructional objectives.

The second type of assessment, ongoing assessment, is used to determine the performance of a student on a particular skill both before and throughout instruction. Figure 11.8 depicts a data sheet used to assess a child's ability to remove a coat. This format reflects a task-analytic approach to data collection. Performance on each of the steps is recorded with a simple plus or minus. The data sheet depicts the cues given to the student, the materials, the response latency (the time allowed between the initial cue and the beginning of the student's response), and the criterion for success. The student in Figure 11.8 has just completed his fifth instructional session on this task.

Strategies for Teaching Dressing Skills

Positioning   As with all other activities, dressing is facilitated when the student has been properly positioned. The choice of position is largely determined by the individual's postural tone and movement patterns and by the actions required in the specific dressing task. Thus, consultation with a therapist is strongly encouraged. Parents also can provide helpful information, since they have more practice than anyone and often develop useful tricks.

Following are guidelines for positioning children with neuromotor involvement for dressing activities (Connor, Williamson, & Siepp, 1978; Copeland & Kimmel, 1989; Finnie, 1975).

1. Dressing children when they are supine (on their backs) should be avoided. Most children in this position have a tendency to push their head and shoulders back and to straighten and stiffen their hips and legs. Children on their backs also are unable to see and are likely to become uninterested in the

activity. (It is sometimes necessary to dress older, heavier children in this position. In these cases, put a hard pillow under the child's head and raise his or her shoulders slightly.)

2. Children should be dressed while they are sitting, if possible. They should be made to feel secure in this position. Children who cannot sit and maintain their balance unsupported are easier to dress if they sit with their backs to you and lean forward. Children who can sit supported can use hard surfaces, such as walls, for stability.

Child's name: Date: Pretest of dressing skills	Independent	Verbal assistance	Physical assistance	Description of method child uses to complete the task
Undressing trousers, skirt 1. Pushes garment from waist to ankles 2. Pushes garment off one leg 3. Pushes garment off other leg				
Dressing trousers, skirt 1. Lays trousers in front of self with front side up 2. Inserts one foot into waist opening 3. Inserts other foot into waist opening 4. Pulls garment up to waist				
Undressing socks 1. Pushes sock down off heel 2. Pulls toe of sock pulling sock off foot				
Dressing socks 1. Positions sock correctly with heel-side down 2. Holds sock open at top 3. Inserts toes into sock 4. Pulls sock over heel 5. Pulls sock up				
Undressing cardigan 1. Takes dominant arm out of sleeve 2. Gets coat off back 3. Pulls other arm from sleeve				
Dressing cardigan flip-over method 1. Lays garment on table or floor in front of self 2. Gets dominant arm into sleeve 3. Other arm into sleeve 4. Positions coat on back				
Undressing polo shirt 1. Takes dominant arm out of sleeve 2. Pulls garment over head 3. Pulls other arm from sleeve				
Dressing polo shirt 1. Lays garment in front of self 2. Opens bottom of garment and puts arms into sleeves 3. Pulls garment over head 4. Pulls garment down to waist				
Undressing shoes 1. Loosens laces 2. Pulls shoe off heel 3. Pulls front of shoe to pull shoe off of toes				
Dressing shoes 1. Prepares shoe by loosening laces and pulling tongue of shoe out of the way 2. Inserts toes into shoe 3. Pushes shoe on over heel				

Figure 11.7. Checklist of dressing skills. (From Copeland, M., Ford, L., & Solon, N. [1976]. *Occupational therapy for mentally retarded children*, p. 95. Baltimore: University Park Press; reprinted with permission of author.)

Teacher: Lesley Bain

Target Behavior: Remove the jacket and hang it up

Student: Christina

Instructional Cue: "Take off your jacket and hang it up."

Setting: Near coat hooks Times: After all trips outside

Assessment Procedure: Single opportunity

DATE	9-10	9-11	9-12	9-13	9-14
1. Grab the jacket (both zipper edges at waist)	+	−	+	+	−
2. Pull up and back	−	−	+	+	−
3. Let go	−	−	−	−	−
4. Straighten arms (at sides)	−	−	−	−	−
5. Grab the cuff (behind back, opposite hand)	−	−	−	−	−
6. Pull your arm out (straighten both arms)	−	−	−	−	−
7. Let go (of cuff)	−	−	−	−	−
8. Grab the other cuff (with other hand)	−	−	−	−	−
9. Pull your arm out (don't drop jacket)	−	−	−	−	−
10. Grab the collar (other hand)	−	−	−	−	−
11. Let go (of cuff)	−	−	−	−	−
12. Grab the collar (turn inside away, then grab collar)	−	−	−	−	−
13. Hang it on the hook (no falling)	−	−	−	−	−
Total %	8%	0%	8%	8%	0%

Materials: Jacket (unbuttoned, unzipped) on student

Response Latency: 3 seconds

Recording Key: + correct / − incorrect

Criterion: 3 consecutive days 100% performance

Figure 11.8. Data sheet for removal of a jacket. (From Snell, M.E. [1987]. Basic self-care instruction for students without motor impairments. In M. Snell [Ed.], *Systematic instruction of persons with severe handicaps* [3rd ed.], p. 378; reprinted with permission.)

3. Children should be dressed on their sides when sitting is not possible. Side-lying often relaxes children, makes bringing their shoulders and head forward easier, facilitates bending their legs and feet, and enables them to see.
4. Infants should be dressed in prone (on their stomachs) across one's lap. Sometimes diapering can be performed in this position, as well, especially if the infant tends to push his or her head back or his or her body backward with the feet.

General Teaching Strategies   Dressing skills can be taught in the same general manner as any other skill. One breaks down the specific task (e.g., putting on hat, fastening snaps) into its component parts, decides upon a teaching approach (e.g., backward chaining, whole task), selects a system of prompts, reinforces correct responses, and remediates errors.

In light of the importance of dressing skills in the curriculum, surprisingly few studies have examined the effects of specific techniques with individuals with severe disabilities. Two relatively early studies (Martin, Kehoe, Bird, Jensen, & Darbyshire, 1971; Minge & Ball, 1967) failed to describe their teaching methods in sufficient detail for replication of the procedures. Later studies (Azrin, Schaeffer, & Wesolowski, 1976; Diorio & Konarski, 1984) employed a broad package of techniques to teach persons with profound mental retardation how to dress, making it impossible to tease apart specific aspects of the package that may have contributed to success. Moreover, Diorio and Konarski (1984) failed to replicate the success of the Azrin et al. (1976) study. Finally, all of these studies were conducted in institutional settings and purposely excluded individuals with severe motoric impairments. Thus, their applicability to students with multiple disabilities in public schools is questionable.

Despite the absence of applied research data, it is clear that many students who experience significant physical restrictions in movements will be unable to complete most dressing tasks with total independence. It is also clear that these students usually can perform at least part of most tasks. The principle of partial participation (described in Chapters 7 and 8) can be especially useful in dressing and undressing tasks. For example, an adult (e.g., teacher, therapist, or parent) might have to position the shirt sleeve for a child and let the child lift his or her arm. Later in the session, the teacher may insert the child's arm halfway through the sleeve and encourage the child to extend his or her arm the rest of the way. Partial participation in dressing often refers to personal assistance, as in the preceding example.

Another form of assistance is the use of specialized adaptive devices or dressing aids. Many of these devices require sufficient upper extremity strength or dexterity to use, but can be modified by a clever therapist or teacher to suit an individual child's needs. Some common dressing aids include: dressing sticks to help persons pick up, pull up, and push off clothes; stocking aids to help pull up stockings; adapted shoe horns; and buttonhooks (Hale, 1979; Kreisler &

Kreisler, 1982; Ruston, 1977). Sokaler (1981) described a simple-to-make buttoning aid, in which a small button is attached to a crocheted loop of elastic thread, enabling the person to slip a hand through the sleeve without unbuttoning the cuff. Specialized companies, including Fred Sammons (in Brookfield, IL), Maddak (in Pequannock, NJ), and Cleo (in Cleveland, OH), offer many clothing aids through their catalogs. One more type of partial participation, adapting clothing, will be discussed later in this chapter under "Specific Guidelines for Selecting and Adapting Clothing."

Campbell (1987), Finnie (1975), and Ruston (1977) offered the following general strategies for dressing the child with cerebral palsy:

1. Dress the more disabled arm or leg first and undress it last.
2. Straighten the arm before putting the sleeve on.
3. Do not pull on the child's fingers.
4. Bend the child forward at the hips to enable you to bring his or her arms forward.
5. Bend the child's leg before putting on socks and shoes.
6. Guide the extremities *slowly* through the clothing.
7. Place seams on a garment correctly before putting on the garment, to prevent having to pull them into position later.

Specific Teaching Techniques A variety of strategies for putting on and removing specific articles of clothing have been developed. Often there are three or four methods of accomplishing the same task, depending on the abilities and disabilities of the student. Several particularly good sources that describe these techniques are Copeland et al. (1976), Orelove and Gibbons (1981), Ruston (1977), and Tawney et al. (1979). Each reference includes diagrams or photographs that accompany the narrative. Interestingly, the authors of these books or articles come from various backgrounds, including education, occupational therapy, and nursing.

Before considering any teaching strategy, one must give thought to the article of clothing to be used in the program. Although the goal of dressing programs is to teach students to put on and remove their own clothing, it may prove helpful to use oversize shirts, sweaters, and so forth to allow easier movement and greater success in early phases of training. Similarly, the size, shape, and location of fasteners may facilitate speed of learning. Kramer and Whitehurst (1981), for example, found that children with mental retardation did better with larger buttons at the top of the garment (that were not visually accessible) than with smaller buttons situated lower. Special, permanent modifications of clothing and fasteners may be required (e.g., Velcro for buttons). It is easier to justify altering the task or materials to speed up learning than it is to spend months or years teaching a minute step of a dressing skill. When use of permanent adaptations is not anticipated, however, materials that resemble the student's own clothing in size and orientation are best used whenever possible.

Thus, a button vest that fits over the student's clothes, with temporarily oversize buttons, is preferable to a buttoning board or doll (Adelson-Bernstein & Sandow, 1978).

Selecting and Adapting Clothing

As the preceding material suggests, the ease with which children learn to dress (or to be dressed) is linked to the type of clothing they will wear. Of particular importance are the garment design features (e.g., cut, sleeve style, fabric) (Levitan-Rheingold, Hotte, & Mandel, 1980). The choice of clothing not only can facilitate dressing but also can make the student feel better and look better. This section presents both general and specific guidelines for selecting clothing.

General Guidelines for Selecting Clothing   The following guidelines can be used as general rules of thumb in selecting clothing (Bigge, 1991; Convenience clothing and closures, n.d.; Finnie, 1975; Hale, 1979; Hoffman, 1979; Jones, 1985; Reich, 1976; Ruston, 1977).

Fabric   The choice of fabric influences comfort, durability, and ease of care. Comfort is affected by what fibers the material is made of and how they are woven into fabric. Loosely woven natural fibers (e.g., cotton, wool) or blends that breathe can help with regulation of body temperature. Synthetic insulators (e.g., Thinsulate) can provide warmth without weight and bulk. Slippery fabrics (e.g., nylon) may make it harder for students to maintain balance or for staff to pick up and carry students. Some stretch fabrics, which expand somewhat, may increase comfort by not binding the student.

Durability is greater in more tightly woven or knit fabrics. Many synthetic fibers are stronger than natural fibers. Ease of care is enhanced with synthetics that can be machine washed and dried. Print, textured, and dark fabrics show stains less than light, solid color fabrics. This is especially important for parents and other caregivers of children with multiple disabilities, since these children often drool, have food on their clothes, and are incontinent.

Construction   How a garment is constructed helps determine the student's comfort and the garment's durability. Several desirable design features include:

1. Double-stitched seams
2. Adequate seam allowance with small, even stitches
3. Reinforcement of all openings (e.g., pockets, fly)
4. Reinforcement with double fabric on areas of heavy wear

Fastenings   Buttons are more easily manipulated if they are medium size and sewn onto a shank; flat and concave buttons slip through holes more easily, although rims may make the buttons easier to hold. Zippers are easier than buttons for children with the strength and coordination to pull them up. Larger-toothed zippers and zipper pulls facilitate zippering. Most hooks, clasps, and buckles are difficult for persons with multiple disabilities. Velcro is an ideal solution to most fastening problems. It is sold by the foot in various widths and also comes as precut fasteners in specific sizes and strengths. Velcro should be fastened before laundering to prolong its life.

Specific Guidelines for Selecting and Adapting Clothing The abilities of children with multiple impairments vary markedly. This variability demands that clothing be chosen and adapted to meet the needs of the individual. Sometimes the student's use of mobility aids (e.g., crutches) and orthoses (e.g., braces) also requires special clothing accommodations. Table 11.7 presents some specific suggestions for selecting or modifying garments based upon students' physical needs. Jones (1985) also offers practical suggestions to parents and caregivers for buying specific articles of clothing for their children with disabilities.

Occasionally a child will present a unique challenge to the designer of specialized clothing. For example, White and Dallas (1977), an occupational

Table 11.7. Specific suggestions for modifying clothing

Problem or disability	Suggested solutions
Difficulty with pullover shirts or sweaters	Use garments of stretchable knits
	Use elasticized necklines
	Open seams under arms and at sides
	Use Velcro dots along seam lines
	Use large sleeve openings
Difficulty with cardigans, jackets, or front-opening shirts	Use garments of stretchable knits
	Select styles with fullness in back (add gathers, action pleats, gussets)
	Use large sleeve openings
	Use smooth, nonslippery fabrics
Difficulty with pants or pull-on skirts	Sew loops at waistband
	Use elasticized waistbands
Difficulty with socks	Use tube socks
	Sew loop tabs at top sides of socks
Crutches	Add fabric patches to underside
	Line garment
	Choose knit or stretch fabric
	Select longer shirt tails
	Use overblouses or sweaters
Long leg braces or cast	Choose pants legs loose enough to fit over braces/cast
	Apply long zipper to inside seam

Adapted from *Convenience clothing and closures* (n.d.) and Orelove and Gibbons (1981).

therapist and a university instructor in textiles and clothing respectively, designed attractive, practical clothing for a 7-year-old girl who was a congenital, quadruple amputee. School personnel confronting similar situations might consult university clothing and textiles departments, home economics teachers, or state Cooperative Extension programs. In addition, many home dressmakers are skilled at altering patterns or ready-to-wear clothing (Ahrbeck & Friend, 1976). Finally, a variety of mail order businesses produce and sell adapted clothing. Fraser, Hensinger, and Phelps (1990) provided a partial list of those companies.

GROOMING AND PERSONAL HYGIENE SKILLS

Many individuals may consider grooming skills as less critical instructional targets than toileting and dressing. Part of the reason may be that many grooming skills—especially showering and bathing—are viewed traditionally as the responsibility of the parents or primary caregiver and lend themselves less easily to school instruction. There is also a limit on the degree to which individuals with multiple disabilities can participate in grooming activities, and therefore, learners often become passive recipients of caregiving.

While both of these points may have merit, there are at least three reasons why it is valuable to work on grooming and personal hygiene skills. First, being and feeling clean makes most people feel better about themselves generally. Second, a well-groomed appearance makes individuals more approachable by others, which is vitally important for establishing and maintaining friendships. Third, cleanliness and good personal hygiene help prevent illness and infection, already a concern among individuals with multiple disabilities.

This section of the chapter briefly explores the instruction of grooming and personal hygiene skills. It focuses on assistive devices that can be used in school and at home to help the teacher and caregiver.

Grooming Skills

Grooming skills consist of basic routines such as hand and face washing, showering and bathing, and hair washing and hair care. (Dental care, a vital grooming area, was discussed in Chapter 10.) Some adolescent boys, of course, may also need to add shaving to their daily grooming routine. For the most part, grooming skills can be taught through the basic principles of systematic instruction that were described in Chapter 7. (Snell [1987] also does a nice job of detailing instructional strategies and applying them to teaching selected grooming skills.) The concept of partial participation becomes especially salient, since the average child with multiple disabilities lacks the motor skills necessary to complete most grooming tasks independently.

The most common application of partial participation in daily practice no doubt is personal assistance, whereby the instructor or parent performs major parts of the grooming tasks for the child. For many children, this is quite appropriate, and these individuals may always require some form of personal assistance. Instruction can be provided in accomplishing tasks that the child is able to learn to perform. As noted in Chapter 3, however, even a relatively simple task like face washing requires sophisticated coordination of positioning and movement skills. Before beginning instruction on any grooming task, the reader is cautioned to take into consideration the principles relevant to the sensorimotor systems and handling and positioning, described in Chapters 2 and 3 respectively.

One method of facilitating the completion of grooming routines is the use of assistive devices and equipment. Some of these, such as liquid soap in a pump dispenser substituted for bar soap, and a self-soaping, long-handled bath sponge, are used increasingly by people in general. (Of course, the soap dispenser may require further modification, such as extension of the handle and more secure mounting to the sink or wall. See Chapter 8 for additional ideas.) Other assistive devices require more individualization, such as creating special splints and cuffs to allow someone to use a hairbrush or razor.

Special devices and equipment for bathing and showering may be less familiar to school personnel. However, children who participate in physical education classes, especially at the secondary level, should be allowed the opportunity to shower after exercising. Some of the following items may prove useful (Hale, 1979; Jones, 1985):

1. Safety stripping for the bottom of the tub or shower
2. Permanent safety guard or grab rails
3. Bath mats made from the foam pads that are used for backpacks
4. Hand-held shower head
5. Bath seats, usually constructed of tubular metal with plastic seat
6. Wooden ramp built up to the shower stall
7. Shower caddy to hold soap, shampoo, and other items

A variety of companies manufacture and sell, through catalogs, adaptive devices that facilitate grooming skills. Professionals might also wish to consult local specialty stores and pharmacies that sell items to individuals who are elderly or convalescing. Naturally, nothing can replace the work of a transdisciplinary team that coordinates efforts to devise effective and normalized strategies for accomplishing tasks.

Personal Hygiene Skills and Menstrual Care

An important area of personal hygiene is menstrual care. The benefits of teaching menstrual hygiene to girls and young women are obvious. Unfortunately, few individuals have published in this area. In one of the few data-based studies available, Richman, Reiss, Bauman, and Bailey (1984) taught menstrual skills to four women with severe mental retardation. The study has limited direct relevance to individuals with multiple disabilities, however, since the authors selected participants who were ambulatory and proficient in toilet training. Many of the steps in the menstrual training package, in fact, involved gross and fine motor skills akin to those involved in toileting and would be too difficult for the typical female with multiple disabilities. As with grooming skills, instruction on menstrual hygiene should not be avoided simply because a particular person has motor and sensory impairments. Rather, an attempt should be made to involve the learner in as many aspects of the routine as practicable.

SUMMARY

This chapter has presented strategies for assessing and teaching toileting, dressing, grooming, and personal hygiene skills to students with multiple disabilities. It is undoubtedly apparent that the specialized skills of many persons are needed to provide these students with a full range of services. Occupational and physical therapists play major roles in ensuring proper positioning, adapting materials, and so forth. Other specialists—including urologists, nurses, dietitians, and home economics teachers, among many others—can provide important consultation and direct services. Clearly, in self-care skills, as in all other parts of the curriculum, team efforts are essential.

REFERENCES

Adelson-Bernstein, N., & Sandow, L. (1978). Teaching buttoning to severely/profoundly retarded multihandicapped children. *Education and Training of the Mentally Retarded, 13*, 178–183.

Ahrbeck, E.H., & Friend, S.E. (1976). Clothing—an asset or liability? Designing for specialized needs. *Rehabilitation Literature, 37*(10), 295–296.

Altshuler, A., Meyer, J., & Butz, M.K.J. (1977). Even children can learn to do clean self-catheterization. *American Journal of Nursing, 77*, 97–101.

Ando, H. (1977). Training autistic children to urinate in the toilet using operant conditioning techniques. *Journal of Autism and Childhood Schizophrenia, 7*(2), 151–163.

Azrin, N.H., Bugle, C., & O'Brien, F. (1971). Behavioral engineering: Two apparatuses for toilet training retarded children. *Journal of Applied Behavior Analysis, 4*, 249–253.

Azrin, N.H., & Foxx, R.M. (1971). A rapid method of toilet training the institutionalized retarded. *Journal of Applied Behavior Analysis, 4*, 89–99.

Azrin, N.H., Schaeffer, R.M., & Wesolowski, M.D. (1976). A rapid method of teaching profoundly retarded persons to dress by reinforcement—guidance method. *Mental Retardation, 14*, 29–33.

Azrin, N.H., Sneed, T.J., & Foxx, R.M. (1973). Dry-bed: A rapid method of eliminating bed-wetting (enuresis) of the retarded. *Behaviour Research and Therapy, 11*, 427–434.

Azrin, N.H., Sneed, T.J., & Foxx, R.M. (1974). Dry-bed training: Rapid elimination of childhood enuresis. *Behaviour Research and Therapy, 12*, 147–156.

Baller, W.R. (1975). *Bed-wetting: Origins and treatment.* New York: Pergamon Press.

Barmann, B.C., Katz, R.C., O'Brien, F., & Beauchamp, K.L. (1981). Treating irregular enuresis in developmentally disabled persons. *Behavior Modification, 5*(3), 336–346.

Baumeister, A.A., & Klosowski, R. (1965). An attempt to group toilet train severely retarded patients. *Mental Retardation, 3*, 24–26.

Bensberg, G.J., Colwell, C.N., & Cassel, R.H. (1965). Teaching the profoundly retarded self-help activities by behavior shaping techniques. *American Journal of Mental Deficiency, 69*, 674–679.

Bergen, A. (1974). *Selected equipment for pediatric rehabilitation.* Valhalla, NY: Blythedale Children's Hospital.

Bigge, J. (1982). Self-care. In J.L. Bigge, *Teaching individuals with physical and multiple disabilities* (2nd ed.) (pp. 290–313). Columbus: Charles E. Merrill.

Bigge, J.L. (1991). *Teaching individuals with physical and multiple disabilities* (3rd ed.). Columbus: Charles E. Merrill.

Bollard, J. (1982). A 2-year follow-up of bed-wetters treated by dry-bed training and standard conditioning. *Behaviour Research and Therapy, 20*, 571–580.

Bollard, J., & Nettelbeck, T. (1982). A component analysis of dry-bed training for treatment of bed-wetting. *Behaviour Research and Therapy, 20*, 383–390.

Bollard, J., Nettelbeck, T., & Roxbee, L. (1982). Dry-bed training for childhood bed-wetting: A comparison of group with individually administered parent instruction. *Behaviour Research and Therapy, 20*, 209–217.

Bollard, R.J., & Woodroffe, P. (1977). The effect of parent-administered dry-bed training on nocturnal enuresis in children. *Behaviour Research and Therapy, 15*, 159–165.

Calkin, A.B., Grant, P.A., & Bowman, M.M. (1978). *Toilet training: Help for the delayed learner.* New York: McGraw-Hill.

Campbell, P.H. (1977). Daily living skills. In N.G. Haring (Ed.), *Developing effective individualized education programs for severely handicapped children and youth* (pp. 115–138). Washington, DC: Department of Health, Education, and Welfare, Office of Education, Bureau of Education for the Handicapped.

Campbell, P.H. (1987). Physical management and handling procedures with students with movement dysfunction. In M.E. Snell (Ed.), *Systematic instruction of persons with severe handicaps* (pp. 174–187). Columbus: Charles E. Merrill.

Cheever, R.C., & Elmer, C.D. (1975). *Bowel management programs.* Bloomington, IL: Accent Press.

Connor, F.P., Williamson, G.G., & Siepp, J.M. (Eds.). (1978). *Program guide for infants and toddlers with neuromotor and other developmental disabilities.* New York: Teachers College Press.

Convenience clothing and closures. (n.d.). New York: Talon/Velcro Consumer Education.

Copeland, M., Ford, L., & Solon, N. (1976). *Occupational therapy for mentally retarded children.* Baltimore: University Park Press.

Copeland, M.E., & Kimmel, J.R. (1989). *Evaluation and management of infants and young children with developmental disabilities.* Baltimore: Paul H. Brookes Publishing Co.

Dayan, M. (1964). Toilet training retarded children in a state residential institution. *Mental Retardation, 2*, 116–117.

Diorio, M.S., & Konarski, E.A. (1984). Evaluation of a method for teaching dressing skills to profoundly mentally retarded persons. *American Journal of Mental Deficiency, 89*(3), 307–309.

Doleys, D.M., & Arnold, S. (1975). Treatment of childhood encopresis: Full cleanliness training. *Mental Retardation, 13*(6), 14–16.

Ellis, N.R. (1963). Toilet training the severely defective patient: An S-R reinforcement analysis. *American Journal of Mental Deficiency, 68*, 98–103.

Finnie, N.R. (1975). *Handling the young cerebral palsied child at home.* New York: E.P. Dutton.

Foxx, R.M., & Azrin, N.H. (1973a). Dry pants: A rapid method of toilet training children. *Behaviour Research and Therapy, 11*, 435–442.

Foxx, R.M., & Azrin, N.H. (1973b). *Toilet training the retarded: A rapid program for day and nighttime independent toileting.* Champaign, IL: Research Press.

Fraser, B.A., Hensinger, R.N., & Phelps, J.A. (1990). *Physical management of multiple handicaps: A professional's guide* (2nd ed.). Baltimore: Paul H. Brookes Publishing Co.

Gallender, D. (1980). *Teaching eating and toileting skills to the multihandicapped.* Springfield, IL: Charles C Thomas.

Geter, K. (1982). *These special children.* Palo Alto, CA: Bull Publishing.

Gibson, B.D. (1980). Adaptive toilet training. In J. Umbreit & P.J. Cardullias (Eds.), *Educating the severely physically handicapped: Basic principles and techniques* (Vol. I, pp. 31–47). Reston, VA: Division on Physically Handicapped, Council for Exceptional Children.

Giles, D.K., & Wolf, M.M. (1966). Toilet training institutionalized, severe retardates: An application of operant behavior modification techniques. *American Journal of Mental Deficiency, 70,* 766–780.

Graff, J.C., Ault, M.M., Guess, D., Taylor, M., & Thompson, B. (1990). *Health care for students with disabilities: An illustrated medical guide for the classroom.* Baltimore: Paul H. Brookes Publishing Co.

Hale, G. (Ed.). (1979). *The source book for the disabled.* New York: Paddington Press.

Herreshoff, J.K. (1973). Two electronic devices for toilet training. *Mental Retardation, 11*(6), 54–55.

Hoffman, A.M. (1979). *Clothing for the handicapped, the aged, and other people with special needs.* Springfield, IL: Charles C Thomas.

Hundziak, M., Maurer, R.A., & Watson, L.S. (1965). *American Journal of Mental Deficiency, 70,* 120–124.

Jones, M.L. (1985). *Home care for the chronically ill or disabled child.* New York: Harper & Row.

Kimbrell, D.L., Luckey, R.E., Barbuto, P.F.P., & Love, J.G. (1967). Operation dry pants: An intensive habit-training program for severely and profoundly retarded. *Mental Retardation, 5,* 32–36.

Kramer, L., & Whitehurst, C. (1981). Effects of button features on self-dressing in young retarded children. *Education and Training of the Mentally Retarded, 16,* 277–283.

Kreisler, N., & Kreisler, J. (1982). *Catalog of aids for the disabled.* New York: McGraw-Hill.

Lancioni, G.E. (1980). Teaching independent toileting to profoundly retarded deaf-blind children. *Behavior Therapy, 11,* 234–244.

Levine, M.N., & Elliott, C.B. (1970). Toilet training for profoundly retarded with a limited staff. *Mental Retardation, 8,* 48–50.

Levitan-Rheingold, N., Hotte, E.B., & Mandel, D.R. (1980). Learning to dress: A fundamental skill toward independence for the disabled. *Rehabilitation Literature, 41*(3–4), 72–75.

Lohmann, W., Eyman, R.K., & Lask, E. (1967). Toilet training. *American Journal of Mental Deficiency, 71,* 551–557.

Lovibond, S.H. (1963). The mechanism of conditioning treatment of enuresis. *Behaviour Research and Therapy, 1,* 17–21.

MacKeith, R., Meadow, R., & Turner, R.K. (1973). How children become dry. In I. Kolvin, R.C. MacKeith, & S.R. Meadow (Eds.), *Bladder control and enuresis* (pp. 3–21). London: William Heinemann.

Mahoney, K., Van Wagenen, K., & Meyerson, L. (1971). Toilet training of normal and retarded children. *Journal of Applied Behavior Analysis 4,* 173–181.

Marshall, G.R. (1966). Toilet training of an autistic eight-year-old through conditioning therapy: A case report. *Behaviour Research and Therapy, 4,* 242–245.

Martin, G.L., Kehoe, B., Bird, E., Jensen, V., & Darbyshire, M. (1971). Operant conditioning in dressing behavior of severely retarded girls. *Mental Retardation, 9,* 27–31.

Minge, M.R., & Ball, T.S. (1967). Teaching of self-help skills to severely retarded patients. *American Journal of Mental Deficiency, 71,* 864–868.

Mountjoy, P.T., Ruben, D.H., & Bradford, T.S. (1984). Recent technological advancements in the treatment of enuresis. *Behavior Modification, 8*(3), 291–315.

Myers, G.J., Cerone, S.B., & Olson, A.L. (Eds.). (1981). *A guide for helping the child with spina bifida.* Springfield, IL: Charles C Thomas.

Orelove, F.P., & Gibbons, S.J. (1981). A guide to independent dressing. *Exceptional Parent, 11,* 50–53, 55–56.

Reich, N. (1976). Clothing for the handicapped and disabled. *Rehabilitation Literature, 37*(10), 290–294.

Richman, G.S., Reiss, M.L., Bauman, K.E., & Bailey, J.S. (1984). Teaching menstrual care to mentally retarded women: Acquisition, generalization, and maintenance. *Journal of Applied Behavior Analysis, 17,* 441–451.

Roos, P., & Oliver, M. (1969). Evaluation of operant conditioning with institutionalized retarded children. *American Journal of Mental Deficiency, 74,* 325–330.

Ruston, R. (1977). *Dressing for disabled people.* London: The Disabled Living Foundation.

Schaefer, C.E. (1979). *Childhood encopresis and enuresis: Causes and therapy.* New York: VanNostrand Reinhold.

Sloop, E.W., & Kennedy, W.A. (1973) Institutionalized retarded nocturnal enuretics treated by a conditioning technique. *American Journal of Mental Deficiency, 77*(6), 717–721.

Smith, L.J. (1981). Training severely and profoundly mentally handicapped nocturnal enuretics. *Behaviour Research and Therapy, 19,* 67–74.

Smith, P.S. (1979). A comparison of different methods of toilet training the mentally handicapped. *Behaviour Research and Therapy, 17,* 33–43.

Smith, P.S., Britton, P.G., Johnson, M., & Thomas, D.A. (1975). Problems involved in toilet training profoundly mentally handicapped adults. *Behaviour Research and Therapy, 13,* 301–307.

Smith, P.S., & Smith, L.J. (1977). Chronological age and social age as factors in intensive daytime toilet training of institutionalized mentally retarded individuals. *Journal of Behavior Therapy and Experimental Psychiatry, 8,* 269–273.

Snell, M.E. (1980). Does toilet training belong in the public schools? A review of toilet training research. *Education Unlimited, 2*(3), 53–58.

Snell, M.E. (1987). Basic self-care instruction for students without motor impairments. In M.E. Snell (Ed.), *Systematic instruction of persons with severe handicaps* (3rd ed.) (pp. 334–389). Columbus: Charles E. Merrill.

Sokaler, R.A. (1981). A buttoning aid. *American Journal of Occupational Therapy, 35,* 737.

Stauffer, D.T. (1983). A spina bifida student? You may have to catheterize! *DPH Journal, 7*(1), 14–21.

Tawney, J.W., Knapp, D.S., O'Reilly, C.D., & Pratt, S.S. (1979). *Programmed environments curriculum.* Columbus: Charles E. Merrill.

Taylor, M. (1990). Clean intermittent catheterization. In J.C. Graff, M.M. Ault, D. Guess, M. Taylor, & B. Thompson. *Health care for students with disabilities: An illustrated medical guide for the classroom* (pp. 241–252). Baltimore: Paul H. Brookes Publishing Co.

Thompson, T., & Hanson, R. (1983). Overhydration: Precautions when treating urinary incontinence. *Mental Retardation, 21,* 139–143.

Trott, M.C. (1977). Application of Foxx and Azrin toilet training for the retarded in a school program. *Education and Training of the Mentally Retarded, 12,* 336–338.

Van Wagenen, R.K., Meyerson, L., Kerr, N.J., & Mahoney, K. (1969). Field trials of a new procedure for toilet training. *Journal of Experimental Child Psychology, 8,* 147–159.

Van Wagenen, R.K., & Murdock, E.E. (1966). A transistorized signal-package for toilet training of infants. *Journal of Experimental Child Psychology, 3,* 312–314.

Watson, L.S. (1968). Applications of behavior shaping devices to training severely and profoundly mentally retarded children in an institutional setting. *Mental Retardation, 6,* 21–23.

White, L.W., & Dallas, M.J. (1977). Clothing adaptations: The occupational therapist and the clothing designer collaborate. *American Journal of Occupational Therapy, 31*(2), 90–94.

Williams, F.E., & Sloop, E.W. (1978). Success with a shortened Foxx-Azrin toilet training program. *Education and Training of the Mentally Retarded, 13,* 399–402.

Williams, W., & Fox, T. (Eds.). (1979). *Minimum objective system for learners with severe handicaps.* Burlington: University of Vermont.

Wolraich, M.L., Hawtrey, C., Mapel, J., & Henderson, M. (1983). Results of clean intermittent catheterization for children with neurogenic bladders. *Urology, 22*(5), 479–482.

Yeates, W.K. (1973). Bladder function in normal micturition. In I. Kolvin, R.C. Mac-Keith, & S.R. Meadown (Eds.), *Bladder control and enuresis* (pp. 28–36). London: William Heinemann.

Chapter 12

Working with Families

Irene H. Carney

The transdisciplinary model enjoys acceptance and support within a variety of human service fields. The preceding chapters cited such support within the professional literature in early childhood education, medicine, nursing, occupational therapy, physical therapy, and special education.

Parent participation in team decision-making is also generally accepted among service providers. With the Education for All Handicapped Children Act (EHA) of 1975 (PL 94-142), parents gained the right to help shape the nature of their children's education. PL 94-142 has allowed parents to contribute to, or at least to review and agree or disagree with, their children's individualized education program (IEP). The law also provides procedural safeguards so that children and families are guaranteed due process of law. The 1986 amendment to the EHA, the Education for All Handicapped Children Act Amendments, 1986 (PL 99-457), expanded parents' roles. Part H, the section of the bill pertaining to infants and toddlers, dictates that services be delivered according to an individualized family service plan (IFSP). In this radical departure from many professionals' established practices, multidisciplinary decision-making teams must consider not only the concerns and preferences, but also the service and support needs, of parents and other family members as well as those of the infant or toddler receiving services. In many states, implementation of the law is exceeding the letter of the law by means of policies that give parents the option to exercise substantial control over the answers to questions such as: Who will constitute the family's team? Who will provide the service coordination required by the law? Will the child and family, in fact, participate in early intervention? In spite of these legislative landmarks, however, and in contrast to a wealth of arguments in support of parent involvement, few parents experience full membership in the teams with which they are involved. In an excellent review and discussion of parent participation in IEP development, Turnbull and Turnbull (1990) noted that, while some parents are active participants, the majority are not. They based this conclusion on their review of research on parent involvement in IEP planning. They cited, for example, Lynch and Stein's (1982) finding that, of 400 parents of students with disabilities, only 71 or 18% reported participating in the development of their child's IEP. This study reported differences among parents in terms of their racial or ethnic group, their child's age, and the nature of the child's disability. Worth noting here is the fact that parents of students with physical disabilities reported significantly less participation than parents of children with other disabling conditions.

Turnbull and Turnbull (1990) listed several barriers to parent participation, including logistical problems, communication problems, lack of understanding of the school system and parents' rights within that system, feelings of inferiority, and uncertainty about their child's disability. The authors also examined barriers that teachers have identified, including parental apathy, professional time constraints, and lack of professional training for collaboration with parents.

This chapter proposes an alternative explanation for the discrepancy between the *ideal* of parent involvement and the *reality* of parent participation in the team process. The chapter also describes a model for team decision-making based on the practices of principled negotiation (Fisher & Ury, 1983). This discussion will include a consideration of the interests that parents bring to the team process in general and at different stages of family life.

AN ALTERNATIVE HYPOTHESIS
REGARDING PARENTAL NONINVOLVEMENT

Chapter 1 noted that it is difficult to organize a truly effective team. Among the factors that contribute to team effectiveness are team size (relatively small teams being preferable), the degree to which team members adhere to group norms, clear and frequent communication, leadership, and a shared framework for making decisions and resolving conflicts.

The present chapter suggests that discomfort with disagreement, and the lack of a constructive means for resolving differences, detract from the functioning of many transdisciplinary teams and, in particular, inhibit parent involvement in team development and team process. Discomfort with conflict, for example, may keep parent or professional team members from acknowledging and exploring their differences of perspective or opinion.

Disagreements and differences are natural and inevitable features of interdisciplinary or transdisciplinary team discussions. Even more marked than the expected differences among professional team members is the difference between professionals and parents. Ruppman (1990) explained, from a parent's point of view, why this is true:

I don't get paid for what I do and I didn't choose to do what I do. I didn't choose to go to IEP meetings. I didn't choose to become a physical therapist. I didn't choose to become a behavior management expert. I didn't choose to become a language therapist. . . . Most of you chose what you do, and this is a very big difference. I am the reluctant, uneasy . . . IEP team member. I'm the one who doesn't get paid for my time, and I'm the one who doesn't want to be there. . . . That's a very essential difference between us. . . . (not paginated)

Ruppman further explains tensions between parents and professionals by noting that teams seldom can deliver all the services and experiences that parents would like for their sons and daughters to have: "What do parents want? They want everything! They want every service their child needs. They want people to be competent. They want people to be sensitive. . . . We want everything, and you can't give it to us" (not paginated).

Ruppman is emphatic, however, in her assertion that inevitable tensions between parents and professionals can be helpful by keeping all parties attentive to what they do and why they do it. She maintains that properly directed tension can "improve what I do as a parent and improve what you do as a professional" (not paginated).

In contrast to Ruppman's perspective, however, many people see conflict as necessarily negative. More important, perhaps, relatively few people have information about or experience with confronting conflict and dealing with it in a constructive way.

Team decision-making is one of many areas to which a conflict resolution framework can be and has been applied. Variously referred to as conflict resolution, mediation, and negotiation, constructive approaches to resolving differences are now practiced in labor relations, divorce proceedings, child custody decisions, family violence interventions, and parent-child disputes (Girdner & Eheart, 1984). A number of specific paradigms have been developed and demonstrated. One of those most widely used is principled negotiation.

PRINCIPLED NEGOTIATION

Principled negotiation is the term that Fisher and Ury (1983) have used to describe one approach to conflict resolution. Through their work with the Harvard Negotiation Project, these authors have applied this approach to diverse disagreements such as tenant-landlord deputes, conflicts between local governments and their citizenry, and international tensions such as the Middle East Crisis of the 1970s. Fisher and Ury's approach addresses actions or decisions that are stalemated by conflict. Their approach could also be adopted in a proactive way, however, as a general approach to decision-making.

The basic elements of principled negotiation include:

1. Separating the people from the problem
2. Focusing on interests, not on positions

3. Creating options for mutual gain
4. Using objective criteria to evaluate outcomes

Separating the People from the Problem

Bailey (1984) suggested that in an ideal team conflict is not necessarily absent, but stems from substantive issues. Conflict rooted in personality differences, however, threatens the team's effectiveness. Fisher and Ury substantiated this observation and asserted that decision-makers will be unable to generate effective decisions if they blame problems on individual participation in decision-making.

As noted earlier, one of the explanations teachers give for lack of parental involvement on IEP teams is parental apathy (Turnbull & Turnbull, 1990). If a teacher were to apply the "separate the people from the problem" approach in this case, the problem might be stated not as the parents' lack of concern, but as the teacher's frustration with the difficulty of obtaining information from parents that might aid in planning. With the problem restated in this way, the potential for solving the problem is greatly improved. The teacher is unlikely to change a parent or the parents' investment in the team. However, the teacher could very well find a means of obtaining needed information from parents such as removing logistical barriers to parents' attending meetings or securing information by means other than the team meeting.

Fisher and Ury suggested several ways out of the trap of blaming another person for difficulties in the decision-making process. They highlighted the need for clear and consistent communication. They also advocated the practice of recognizing and acknowledging the emotional by-products of conflict such as anger, distress, frustration, and confusion. Finally, they emphasized the importance of checking perceptions rather than making assumptions about why people behave as they do or believe what they profess. Fisher and Ury proposed that by transcending personality differences, parties involved in conflict can begin to view one another as allies in the effort to solve a difficult problem.

Focusing on Interests, Not on Positions

One of the most logical yet novel features of principled negotiation is the emphasis on *interests* rather than on positions. Fisher and Ury provided a succinct description of the difference between the two when they noted, "Your position is something you have decided upon. Your interests are what caused you to decide" (p.42). A parent team member, for example, may advocate for direct occupational therapy for his son, arguing that the indirect or integrated therapy model that the rest of the team supports does not provide sufficient structure or intensity. Upon exploration, it may become apparent that the father has taken this position because his child, at age 9, does not yet demonstrate the strength and dexterity necessary to manage snaps and zippers and is, therefore, still dependent on others for dressing. The father took a position on a model for service delivery. His real interest, however, had to do with his concern that his son needed to become more independent. With this additional information on the table, the team has the opportunity to construct a plan in which the team's service delivery preference is adopted, but the fathers' priorities for instructional goals are respected and addressed.

Fisher and Ury observed that this approach is very effective in resolving disagreements for two reasons. First, focusing on interests helps parties in conflict to find a common ground. In the example above, the parent and professional team members upheld opposing positions regarding the appropriate and desirable model for occupational therapy services. All teams members, however, could agree that independent dressing was an appropriate goal. They all shared an interest in seeing this student develop the skills he needed to dress himself.

Second, focusing on interests helps team members to identify different paths to the desired end. In the example, the team could elect to find or create more frequent opportunities for the student to practice snapping and zipping throughout the school day. They could also choose to modify the child's clothing, for example, with Velcro closures, so that the elusive snapping and zipping skills would no longer be necessary.

On the subject of how to identify interests, Fisher and Ury suggested taking the others' perspectives and trying to imagine or understand why they take the positions they do. The authors recommended making a list of interests that might be influencing all parties. They also emphasized that the most powerful and influential interests reflect basic human needs such as security, recognition, and control over one's life. (The interests that parents have identified as determinants of their preferences and priorities for their children's education are discussed under subsequent sections of this chapter.) Once team members are aware of the interests at work in their decision-making, they are able to generate options among which they ultimately will choose.

Creating Options for Mutual Gain

"The key to wise decision making," Fisher and Ury (1983) asserted, "lies in selecting from a great number and variety of options" (p. 68). A team can best generate a large menu of options through the process of brainstorming. Brainstorming is an approach with which most team members are likely to have experience. The steps in brainstorming include:

1. Defining your purpose
2. Choosing participants and a facilitator
3. Creating an informal and relaxed atmosphere
4. Seating participants side by side, facing a flipchart or chalk board
5. Clarifying ground rules including the rule that no idea is to be criticized
6. Brainstorming
7. Selecting the most promising ideas and then inventing improvements on them

In the context of transdisciplinary team work, these activities would most likely take place in preparation for a program planning meeting such as an IEP meeting. A more formal meeting, however, could be the setting in which the final decision is discussed and agreed upon. Fisher and Ury listed several considerations that can enhance the effectiveness of brainstorming. Three of their suggestions may be particularly useful for transdisciplinary teams.

First is the idea of making sure that parties who hold different positions, particularly parties who disagree with one another, participate in brainstorming together. In the case of parent and professional team members, this implies that both groups should create the list of options that the team will finally consider. Program planning, as it is most frequently practiced, is characterized by professionals determining what recommendations they will make to parents. Parents are, in fact, often unaware of any options other than those that are pre-selected and presented to them. The process of reviewing all options together gives all participants equal access to information in addition to ownership of the problem.

A second and related consideration is that brainstorming groups look through the eyes of different experts. A transdisciplinary team has the resources, in the form of its members, to consider possibilities from the perspectives of several professional fields as well as through the parents' expertise.

Third, Fisher and Ury caution that there may not be one best answer. Teams may find their best and most creative plans by selecting combinations or parts of several different options. Once the team has reached consensus on how they will proceed, they can complete the process of principled negotiation by identifying what objective criteria they will use to evaluate their decision.

Using Objective Criteria To Evaluate Outcomes

Transdisciplinary teams traditionally have been concerned with criteria that indicate whether or not a student is achieving or progressing toward specific goals and objectives. These criteria can also be the means by which team members choose to evaluate their plans.

When plans have been constructed through principled negotiation, however, teams might also wish to evaluate their plans in terms of whether the interests of team members have been met. This approach is illustrated in the case example that follows.

Principled Negotiation: A Case Example

How can principled negotiation work in the instance in which a decision cannot be made or implemented because of disagreement between a parent and the professional members of the team? This example will apply the components of principled negotiation to such a scenario.

Caitlin is a 6-year-old student with spastic quadriplegic cerebral palsy. Her standardized tests scores indicate mental retardation in the moderate range. She attends elementary school where she receives services from a first grade teacher, a special education teacher, and a teaching assistant. The classroom staff members receive consultation from a language and communication specialist, an occupational therapist, and a physical therapist. Caitlin lives with her parents, an 8-year-old brother, and an 18-month-old sister. Her mother does not work outside the home. Caitlin's IEP includes a goal that she will self-initiate toileting by the end of the school year. All team members, including Caitlin's parents, agreed to this goal.

During the mid-year parent-teacher conference, the teachers suggest that it is time to begin toilet training and they review a Foxx and Azrin procedure (Foxx & Azrin, 1973; see Chapter 11). They suggest that they will start the training at school, then schedule a home visit to help Caitlin's family begin the highly structured intervention there. Once training is underway, Caitlin's parents have a hard time making a commitment regarding a date for a home visit. The teachers begin to feel frustrated, confused, and a bit angry. Caitlin's parents feel harassed.

Separating the People from the Problem   It would be easy and not unusual for this type of situation to become bogged down at this point with each party blaming the other for the stalemate. The teachers, for example, might make assumptions about Caitlin's parents' behavior and label them, for example, overprotective, apathetic, or uncooperative. The parents might see the school staff as being unrealistic about Caitlin's abilities and insensitive to the demands of their home life.

In order to move beyond this impasse, it will be important for all participants to attribute the problem to something other than the other people involved. If the teachers were to explore why Caitlin's parents are unavailable, they might learn that they are ambivalent about starting training. If the team accepts that position, training will not proceed as planned. Team members adhering to the elements of principled negotiation, however, will try to discern the interests that contribute to the parents' ambivalence.

Focusing on Interests, Not Positions   In shifting their focus from differing positions to interests, teachers could acknowledge their frustrations and explore the parents' perspectives on the situation. Thereby, teachers might discover that a number of interests, some of them competing with others, influence Caitlin's parents' feelings about toilet training. These hypothetical interests are listed in Table 12.1.

Once the professionals understand the interests at work, they have many more options to explore in order to reach agreement about whether and when training will begin at home. They also have a way to restate the problem: the difficulty of finding a training method and a schedule that are equally appropriate for the home and the school settings.

Creating Options for Mutual Gain   Creating options for mutual gain re-

Table 12.1. Interests that influence parents' position on toilet training

Interests that support training
Ceasing Caitlin's use of diapers in order to save on expense
Completing Caitlin's toilet training before her younger sister is ready to be trained

Interests that interfere with training
Concern that training will take time away from the other children
Interest in not having to do a great deal of additional laundry
Concern about inconvenience of traveling around community if Caitlin is not in diapers

quires that all parties engage in brainstorming to identify all possible paths to a solution. Following is a list of options that could be included in reaching a mutually satisfactory decision:

1. Identify school staff who can help conduct training at home so the mother will be available to her other children.
2. Start training at home during the school day when at least one child is away from home at school.
3. Dress Caitlin in skirts and dresses so only underwear will have to be changed in case of accidents, and put waterproof cloths under her on upholstered furniture.
4. Allow Caitlin to wear diapers when not at home or at school.
5. Start training during a vacation when both parents are home.
6. Identify a neighbor, relative, or babysitter who can help with the other children until the father comes home so the mother can attend to toilet training.

Using Objective Criteria To Evaluate Outcomes Even decisions that result from careful and creative discussion can yield disappointing results. For this reason, it is important to have a means by which participants can evaluate their decision. Agreeing upon objective evaluation criteria and the time at which the decision will be evaluated acknowledges that the decision can be renegotiated. The more fundamental the conflict, the more important this assurance may be.

For this step in the example, the concern is not whether Caitlin has achieved the toilet training goal, but whether the agreed upon approach to training satisfies the interests of the team members. Say, for example, the team agreed upon options 3, 4, and 6. The criteria could include: 1) no more than one additional load of wash every 2 days, 2) Caitlin making as many trips outside home as she did before training, and 3) the mother consistently having a second adult at home during training.

Summary

In summary, principled negotiation provides a framework that confronts and makes constructive use of differences among team members. In groups that adopt this approach, individual members:

1. View one another as allies in the challenge of fashioning a mutually agreeable and effective plan.
2. Explore one anothers' perspectives in order to better understand differences and to find shared interests.
3. Map several different paths to a solution.
4. Use objective criteria to ensure the effectiveness of the plan.

The following section provides perspectives on interests that parents bring into the team process.

CONSIDERING PARENTS' PERSPECTIVES IN TEAM DECISION-MAKING

In order for principled negotiation to succeed in the transdisciplinary team context, participants must develop a curiosity about and a sincere interest in the perspectives of other team members. Particularly in regard to the steps of separating the people from the problem, and focusing on interests rather than positions, team members must attempt to stand in each other's shoes in order to understand the behavior and the opinions of individual participants. This section describes parental interests and perspectives that may influence team decision-making.

This discussion of parental perspectives should not be construed to say that families of children with multiple disabilities have a uniform set of beliefs, opinions, experiences, and needs. Quite to the contrary, families differ from one another on several dimensions. Ethnicity, religion, economic resources, family size, and coping styles all combine to distinguish families from one another (Turnbull & Turnbull, 1990). These characteristics influence a family's values, beliefs, and needs. Families are further influenced by the changes they experience over the course of their family life. These changes have been studied and described as a series of events and stages that constitute a family life cycle.

The Family Life Cycle

Sociological writings on the individual life cycle (Erikson, 1959) established the logic of the family life cycle concept (Carter & McGoldrick, 1980; Duvall, 1957). These theories assert that individuals or families progress through a series of predictable stages, and that each stage introduces new developmental tasks. Where the family life cycle is concerned, stages are determined by the changing constitution of the family (as with the birth of a child, or an adult child's departure from home), by the family's changing relationship to social institutions (e.g., entering the school system, or retiring from the work force); and by family members' experiences of important individual stages (e.g., adolescence).

Several authors have theorized about the nature of the family life cycle in typical families (Carter & McGoldrick, 1980; Duvall, 1957; Solomon, 1973). Others have mapped the course of change in families of children with disabilities (Carney, 1987; Suelzle & Keenan, 1981; Turnbull, Summers, & Brotherson, 1986; Turnbull & Turnbull, 1990).

Turnbull and Turnbull (1990) cautioned that the family life cycle is a theoretical structure based on broad generalizations. The generalizations that follow are organized by three life cycle stages that appear salient in a discussion of educational teams: birth and early childhood, childhood, and adolescence and young adulthood.

Family Life Cycle Stages

Birth and Early Childhood

Stage Characteristics   A baby's birth and infancy is generally portrayed as an emotionally warm and happy time in parents' lives and relationships. Magazine pictures and television advertisements portray visions of quietly joyous adults caring for an attractive and responsive newborn. Warmth and happiness may accurately characterize parents' experience, in part. Parents of a newborn, however, also face several subtle but critical challenges. A new baby's inclusion in the family, whether the child is the firstborn or has one or more siblings, forces change in all other family relationships. The time and attention involved in an infant's care necessarily shift energy away from other children, or from the parents' relationship with one another.

Regaining Balance in Family Life   For new parents, one of the central dilemmas of this period involves establishing a balance between their absorption in their child and the energy and attention still required by the other parent, their own personal needs, and by other members of the family, particularly if the family includes older children. This balance clearly is elusive. It is essential, however, if families are to preserve their integrity and carry on the work of family life. This is a critical adjustment that each family confronts during a child's infancy and early childhood. The challenge may be particularly great, however, if the new baby has a health condition or disability that necessitates the family's involvement with extraordinary caregiving routines and specialized professionals and services. In other words, parents of children with special needs not only must re-establish the equilibrium in family life that a new baby disturbs, but must achieve this with a number of additional weights on one side of the balance.

Developing a Relationship with the New Family Member   The presence of a disability may also complicate what is, perhaps, the most important task of infancy—the development of a positive, reciprocal relationship between the parents and the child. Trout and Foley (1989) described this process and the potential impact of a child's delayed development:

Successful and supportive interactions between infant and caregiver occur when both parent and infant are maximally available, emotionally and physically, and when a pattern of contingent, attuned responsiveness is developed that helps them to "fit" together. Handicapped infants may not be available in these ways, and the fit does not come easily. (pp. 39)

In describing her first year as the mother of a premature and medically fragile child, Ann Oster (1984) related the pain and confusion of adjusting to her son's birth:

During much of Nick's early life the successes in coping with his problems belonged to professionals. Only the failures were mine. I hadn't had a healthy baby, couldn't seem to get him healthy, couldn't comfort him, and most painful, I didn't feel connected to him. I believed that I wasn't capable of doing him any good. (p.30)

The author acknowledges that, after a year, a positive parent-child relationship began to take root.

Sometime after Nicholas had started nursery school, I saw a videotape that demonstrated what Dr. [T. Berry] Brazelton calls the irresistible responsiveness of a premature baby. I almost cried while I watched as a 3 lb. preemie slowly followed a ball with his eyes, looked for the sound of his mother's voice, and with heroic effort, finally turned his head and reached for her. A nurse practitioner had taught that mother to read the subtle clues that would have drawn me to my son so much earlier. It was a piece of information, a teachable skill, that might have changed the course of our lives. (p. 31)

This experience identifies a skill that enabled a parent to become more responsive to her baby. With the following example, Trout and Foley (1989) emphasized that sensitivity to the parent-child relationship should guide team members in identifying goals for the child:

When a blind child fails to develop language because he or she lacks the object constancy necessary to suggest the existence of objects "out there" that might be labeled, it may well be that the child is not saying "Mama". To go about the job of language development with such a child without attending to how it feels to the mother not to be named may well invite failure, not only in the area of language work, but also with respect to establishing the bonds that are essential to both the child's and mother's development. (pp 61–62)

Greenspan (1988) also emphasized the need to design therapeutic interventions so that they support positive parent-child interactions. This author suggested that educators and therapists must understand the emotional milestones of infancy and early childhood and promote emotional growth by integrating motor, sensory, and cognitive goals with age-appropriate social behaviors. Greenspan suggested, for example, that an 8-month-old infant who needs practice on reaching can be taught to reach out to touch her father's face or reach up to signal to her mother that she wants to be picked up. Such an approach emphasizes the interdependence of transdisciplinary team members in understanding the child and parent in relationship to one another, and in designing and implementing activities that maximize the child's own development as well as his or her fit within the family.

This is an area in which it is particularly important for team members to be aware of and responsive to cultural values and patterns of interaction. As Trout and Foley (1989) noted, the family's cultural context will influence parents' concerns and preferences regarding such patterns as involvement of the extended family, the appropriateness of contact comfort, the duration of breast feeding, and promotion of the child's independence. Team members will need to consider patterns of social and emotional behavior through the filter of the family's racial, ethnic, and religious culture, and promote developments that support and respect these characteristics.

Implications/Summary The general picture of a family into which a new child has come is one of intense involvement with the simultaneous tasks of establishing a new relationship while adjusting and balancing the patterns and relationships of the family as a whole. Olson and his colleagues (1983) described the early childhood years as a time of intense absorption with the inner workings of the family. If the child has a special need, however, children and parents are thrust from the privacy of the family environment into a world of professionals, services, and bureaucracies. Parent involvement on early intervention teams requires parents to confront other tasks and challenges in addition to the stage-specific tasks described above. As team members, parents must come to terms with the diagnosis of their child's disability. This process involves both understanding the practical implication for the child's behavior and development and experiencing the emotional aftermath of the diagnosis. It is a process that requires the understanding, respect, and support of the professional members of the team.

It is also a process, as several parents have noted, that is facilitated by accurate information and honest communication. Ruppman described those situations in which professionals have to communicate information that may be difficult for parents to hear. She recalled:

> The first tough love I ever received was from my son's first principal who (stopped) me in the hall one day . . . and he just quite simply said, "[Y]ou haven't asked me this, but I'm going to tell you—you and [your husband] need to gird yoursel[ves] for the long haul here. This boy's doing real well. They could call him autistic . . . they could call him mentally retarded . . . what they call him doesn't matter. . . . What you and [your husband] need to know is that physically, emotionally, financially you need to gird yourselves for the long haul with this young man—it's not going away." And I cried, but it was love. (not paginated)

In summary, the professional members of transdisciplinary teams can promote involvement of parent team members by:

1. Appreciating and valuing parents' involvement in the team
2. Remembering that the family is in the midst of a normal process of change and adjustment

3. Recognizing that the child's fit within the family might be a priority concern
4. Respecting the family's cultural patterns and beliefs
5. Communicating accurately and honestly with parents

Childhood

Adjusting to the Child's Involvement in the School System   At some point early in childhood, each child becomes part of a system other than, and in addition to, his or her family. The most universal example of this transition is the child's entry into elementary school. Many children, with or without disabilities, also attend preschool programs, and thereby experience dual system membership at an earlier age. At either point of entry, a child's introduction to the system of education presents novel challenges and tasks for the family. A subtle but important challenge, for example, is the parents' adjustment to sharing their authority with professional educators. Once in school, a child's teacher exerts a major influence over his or her routine activities, behavior, peer relationships, learning experiences, and development of beliefs and values. Teachers also contribute to students' assessment of their own competence as individuals. For parents, many of whom hold strong personal beliefs about teaching and child rearing, their children's school years require a balance of entrusting their child's care to the schools and monitoring that trust to ensure the child's well-being and appropriate development. Maintaining this balance requires vigilance and energy.

An additional challenge relates to the fact that a child entering the school system enters, along with the family, the public eye. Preschool and school programs, even when they emphasize individualized education, have as their basis a set of norms and ideals for students' behavior and achievement. Whether the norm relates to a grade level, developmental status, personal appearance, or a standard of independence and normalization, parents and teachers use comparisons to place an individual child on the continuum of strengths and deficits. Concern about how their children measure up and represent the family to the outside world is characteristic of parents' reactions to the transition to school-based services, whether on the preschool or early elementary level.

Also, mothers and fathers are subject to comparison with other parents. Parents are judged on the basis of how well they uphold mainstream social and cultural mores, determined by, for example, the degree to which they teach their children manners, whether they send their children to school when sick, and whether they pack a nutritious lunch. Professionals also evaluate parents by appraising the extent to which they are interested in, and involved with, their children's education.

Professionals' tendency to evaluate parents may be particularly evident with regard to parents whose children have disabilities, since the professionals' involvement is specified and mandated by federal law. Furthermore, parents of children with disabilities have long been seen as critical contributors to their children's ability to learn and change.

The relationship between parent involvement and teacher attitude is reflected in a study by Fuqua, Hegland, and Karas (1985). These authors surveyed teachers of preschool students with disabilities regarding their ideals for, and assessment of, parents' involvement with the school. Respondents reported that their satisfaction with parents increased as a function of: 1) teachers visiting the home, 2) parents attending parent group meetings, and 3) parents showing they could teach their children at home.

Home visits, parent group meetings, and home-based teaching do not, however, appear in reports on parents' preferences for involvement. Winton and Turnbull (1981) conducted one of the earliest investigations of parents' preferred means of working with school personnel. Their sample consisted of 31 mothers whose children had mild or moderate disabilities. The mothers, during structured interviews, identified all the involvement opportunities to which they had access, and specified which among those they preferred. The medium for involvement that these parents clearly preferred was informal contact with the child's teacher. Other available activities (listed in decreasing order of importance) included: parent training opportunities, opportunities to help others understand their child, and volunteering inside or outside of class.

Carney, Snell, and Gressard (1986) also assessed parents' actual means of involvement, as well as preferences, in various parent-professional activities. Thirty-seven parents of students of various age and disability groups participated in a structured telephone interview. Frequency data indicated that informal communication with the teacher and participation in the individualized education program (IEP) meeting were considered the most heavily used and preferred forums for parent-teacher interaction. Activities in which parents expressed less interest included those related to observing or volunteering in the classroom, receiving the teacher into the home for information or skill exchange, and participating in parent group activities.

The degree and nature of parents' involvement may vary in relation to a number of influences. Sloper, Cunningham, and Arnljotsdottir (1983), for example, found an inverse relationship between the number of children in the family and the extent to which parents participated in one child's special education program. Other authors have noted that parents from low-income groups are less likely to take an active part in their disabled children's schooling (Cone, DeLawyer, & Wolfe, 1985; Leyser & Cole, 1984). Lynch and Stein (1982) concluded that parents whose children had physical disabilities were less actively involved than parents of students with mental retardation or other mental disabilities.

Vincent and Salisbury (1989) referred to changes in the American family that are likely to influence parents' participation in their child's education. These authors noted that 10% of the households in the United States use a language other than English, 67% of American children will be raised by a single parent at some point in their lives, and increasing numbers of children are raised in poverty.

Whatever the reason for individual differences among parents, the differences should inform professionals' expectations for parent involvement in team meetings and other school related activities. As Kaiser and Hayden (1984) admonished their constituents:

> Special educators must appreciate that parenting can be every bit as important and helpful a thing to do as teaching or therapy. The parent role must not be inadvertently disparaged on the basis of its departure from standard professional trappings. A parent's effectiveness must not only be judged through criteria measuring his or her successive approximations to the professional therapists and teachers providing treatment. (p. 311)

Stage Characteristics By the time a child with multiple disabilities enters school, his or her parents are usually veterans of assessments, planning meetings, progress reports, and parent training activities. When the child and family enter the educational system, however, they enter a model that is fundamentally different from the early intervention program they leave behind. Turnbull and Turnbull (1990) listed some of the features of this model to which parents must adjust when the child enters school. These include a lessened commitment to family support activities and a shift to a categorical model within which their child will receive a classification and, too often, an accompanying label. Other factors that parents encounter anew at this point are the reactions to disability from the child's peer group, and the parents' need to clarify preferences regarding self-contained, integrated, or inclusive schools (Turnbull et al., 1986).

The roles of occupational, physical, and speech therapy in the child's IEP can also change radically with the transition to school-based services. In the early intervention program, the family's primary contact and service provider might be, for example, an occupational therapist. Under the provisions of PL 99-457, this therapist might be not only the conduit through whom other members of the team funnel their recommendations, but also the service coordinator who links the family with other agencies and assists them with their transition to public school. Once in school, however, occupational therapy is a related service for which the child is eligible only if it relates to the child's attainment of other educational goals. If delivered through a transdisciplinary or integrated therapy model, moreover, occupational therapy may involve little or no direct contact between the child and the occupational therapist. Given this scenario, parents might well feel that the school is failing to provide a needed service and is falling short of its commitment to meeting their child's needs.

Implications/Summary As Turnbull and Turnbull (1990) noted, the childhood stage of the family life cycle is the stage at which parents begin the process of letting go. It is at this point that parents begin to share responsibility and control with the professionals with whom their child interacts every day. Turnbull and Turnbull also described this stage as an era during which parents may become concerned for the first time about their child's interactions and relationships with other children.

These adjustments do not generally entail the emotional turbulence of the infancy and early childhood period. Parents are, however, accommodating a variety of changes as the child becomes increasingly involved with a system outside of the family, and as parents become familiar with all of the implications of the educational model.

As parents experience this transition, they will need to come to terms with an educational classification, clarify their attitudes and preferences regarding their child's involvement with peers who do not have disabilities, and, perhaps, revise their understanding of the need for and delivery of therapy services. Parents' positions on program placement, integration, and related services needs may well differ from those of other team members. In this case, it is particularly important for the professional members of the team to seek out and understand the interests that underlie parents' stated preferences. Such exploration may be the only way in which the team will be able to identify common interests and create a mutually agreed upon plan.

Differences such as those described above sometimes lead to professionals labeling parents as overprotective, apathetic, hostile, or uncooperative. Such explanations for parents' behaviors are, at best, nonconstructive. Under these circumstances, the practice of separating the people from the problem will be necessary in order to direct the team's problem-solving in a productive way.

The differences that parents and professionals encounter during the childhood years provide the opportunity for both groups to assess why they believe what they do and whether their approaches are serving the best interests of the child in question. In this way, teams can follow Ruppman's (1990) advice to make constructive and creative use of the natural tensions between parents and professionals.

Adolescence/Young Adulthood

Stage Characteristics   Adolescence is widely regarded as a troublesome period for both teenagers and their families. This stage is characterized by a struggle between the adolescent's competing needs for personal autonomy and continued dependence on the family. As they respond to this struggle, parents are challenged by their child's need for sensitivity and flexibility. Mothers and fathers may be further challenged by issues related to their individual lives, such as diminished energy, career developments and disappointments, and satisfaction with their own relationship (Kraft, 1985).

These same parental issues are likely to accompany a child's transition to young adulthood. The challenges implicit in the child's development are quite different, however, from those that characterize adolescence. At this point, the move toward independence typically acquires more momentum. Parents are called upon to help their sons and daughters establish a life, and perhaps a family, of their own. The transition to young adulthood requires both parents and children to adjust to new roles relative to one another.

The changes implicit in adolescence and young adulthood are difficult for many families. These stages appear to be particularly stressful for parents of young men and women with disabilities. Kraft (1985), for example, reported a direct relationship between stress measured by the QRS-R (Questionnaire on Resources and Stress–Revised) and the age of a family member with a moderate or severe disability. Other authors suggested that parents experience the most sadness in response to a disability soon after a disability is identified, during early childhood, and during early adulthood (Wikler, Wasow, & Hatfield, 1981). There are several plausible explanations for the relative difficulty of adolescence and young adulthood. Among these are discrepancies between the experience of families with a member who has a disability and typical families; changing physical characteristics of the adolescent child; and differences between parents' and professionals' attitudes regarding appropriate services for adults.

Discrepancies Between Typical Families and Families with a Member Who Has a Disability   In some families following a predictable life course, adolescence and young adulthood represent times in which parents and children revise their relationships to accommodate the child's decreasing dependence on the family. Sons and daughters become self-sufficient in functions once served by their parents. Young adults, for example, assume some measure of financial responsibility. Their needs for affection, guidance, and recreation are likely to be met, in large part, by individuals outside of the family. Young men and women may demonstrate further independence by living on their own or by starting a new family, thereby maintaining their domestic routine outside of their parents' home.

For the young adult with multiple disabilities, however, the family is not likely to experience any such relief from responsibility. Once the son or daughter has graduated from high school, in fact, the parents may have to adjust in the direction of satisfying more, rather than fewer, of their child's needs. Particularly in cases where employment or day activity options are limited, parents face a substantial increase in the amount of time during which they must offer supervision, activity, or company for their adult child.

It is often the case, unfortunately, that as demands on parents increase, their resources diminish. It may be that other children who have helped with social and caregiving routines, for example, no longer live in the parents' home. Brothers and sisters who do not have disabilities may take with them an important source of assistance and support when they leave home. Retirement, too, may imply diminished financial flexibility.

It is important to note that families of adults with disabilities have varied, often effective, means of coping (Brotherson, 1984). The circumstances with which they cope, however, are undeniably different from the trials experienced by families who are not affected by members with disabilities.

Changing Physical Characteristics of the Child   The physical changes that accompany adolescence and young adulthood introduce an unfortunate paradox. As parents become older and usually less strong and healthy, their children become taller and heavier and generally more difficult to lift, carry, and position. Some of the accompanying strains can be alleviated with building modifications and special equipment. On a very basic level, however, strong arms, legs, and back muscles are irreplaceable machines.

Puberty may entail hormonally induced seizures or changes in behavior (DeMyer & Goldberg, 1983). These new characteristics can be confusing and difficult to manage. Puberty also introduces the issues of sexuality, reproduction, and menstrual hygiene.

Differences with Professionals   Trends in the field of disability promote integration of people with disabilities with nondisabled people. The emphasis on normalization, furthermore, suggests that all adults be permitted and encouraged to experience the privileges of adulthood. This logic implies independence and self-determination in as many respects as possible, including choices regarding sexual expression.

Parents may not, however, be aware of or agree with such philosophical and practical trends. Research with parents of individuals with mental retardation, in fact, indicates that parents of adults with mental retardation are more conservative regarding normalization than parents of their younger counterparts (Suelzle & Keenan, 1981). Respondents in this study reported concerns about their child's isolation and vulnerability as reasons for preferring more sheltered options for adult services.

Ferrara (1979) found that even parents who agreed theoretically with the principle of normalization were conservative about the extent to which the principle should be applied to their own son or daughter. Hill, Seyfarth, Orelove, Wehman, and Banks (1985) documented similar conservatism among parents of children enrolled in sheltered workshops. The parents in their sample asserted that they were not particularly interested in having their child work alongside nondisabled peers. Moreover, they were not dismayed by their childrens' low rate of pay or lack of fringe benefits.

These differences may stem, in part, from what Turnbull et al. (1986) term transitional resistance. These authors coined this term to describe families they had studied who appeared to resist their young adult child's potential independence. Turnbull and her colleagues concluded that the continued presence of their adult child in their home might contribute to parents' socialization and self-definition. This conclusion is supported by Seltzer's (1989) finding that mothers caring for an adult child with mental retardation compared favorably to their counterparts without such responsibilities. Caregiving mothers fared better on measures of health and depression than women who did not have an ongoing mothering role.

Implications   In short, the situation that many parents encounter during their child's adolescence and young adulthood is one of increasing demands and diminishing resources. As parents become older, they may become less strong, energetic, and financially flexible. At the same time, however, they face the challenge of providing care for an older, heavier individual. Furthermore, in the absence of jobs or other opportunities for their adult sons or daughters parents may find themselves in the position of being the only caregivers. And in the midst of coping with such daily demands, parents may realize the need to make important and difficult decisions about their child's future. The most important work of transdisciplinary teams serving adolescents and young adults relates to this need for future planning and decision-making. Team members can best support and collaborate with parents by recognizing parents' concerns regarding their sons' and daughters' futures.

Current model programs have demonstrated the feasibility of training students with multiple disabilities on competitive jobs, and of securing employment for those students following their graduation from high school. This kind of demonstration points the way to a future in which competitive or supported employment might constitute a realistic option for persons with multiple disabilities.

In most areas, however, students with multiple disabilities are presently transitioned to sheltered work or day activity programs. And in many areas, unfortunately, students are barred from even those opportunities because of architectural barriers, motoric requirements of jobs or training for other programs, entry criteria such as independent toileting, and inadequate client-staff ratios. For many families, then, the only certainty they feel about the future is its absolute uncertainty. In response to this dilemma, families may, at one or more points during adolescence and adulthood, desire assistance with the task of future planning.

The need for assistance should be easy to understand. Making decisions about future circumstances requires gathering information about available resources, identifying which agencies and individuals should be included in the search, assessing the match among students' skills and preferences and availability of local programs, articulating the family's priority concerns, and reaching consensus between the family and relevant professionals. Each of these steps calls for an investment of time, energy, and skill. Together, the components constitute a major commitment of personal, professional, and family resources.

Families and professionals can now refer to a number of resources developed specifically to facilitate parent access to, and progress through, future planning activities. One such resource is a family guide compiled by Goldfarb, Brotherson, Summers, and Turnbull (1986). This volume provides information and strategies pertaining to practices including, but not limited to, planning for the future. The guide covers such topics as coping, sources of formal and informal support, family communication, brainstorming, and taking action. Through reading and structured exercises, the authors invite family members to assess their needs and resources, and to apply a problem-solving approach to their own situation and concerns.

Turnbull, Turnbull, Bronicki, Summers, and Roeder-Gordon (1989) compiled a guide to decisions specific to adulthood. Their comprehensive volume covers such issues as the participation of adults with disabilities in making decisions (including mental competence and consent), guardianship, financial planning, relevant government benefits, advocacy, and planning for life in the community. These authors emphasized the importance of long-range planning but acknowledged the difficulty this process can involve for parents. They observed, for example, that future planning activities might elicit painful memories or issues such as parents' fears regarding their children's loneliness and vulnerability. Looking toward the future also requires parents to face their own mortality—a specter that can invite anxiety or depression.

Several authors have developed programs for involving parents in planning for post-school employment. (Halvorsen, Doering, Farron-Davis, Usilton, & Sailor, 1989; Morton, Everson, & Moon, 1987; Sowers, 1989). Their collective suggestions include providing in-service training for parents; using examples or videotapes of people working to illustrate models; visiting prospective job sites, and inviting veteran employers, workers, and parents to describe their experiences. Most important, perhaps, is the assertion that professional team members must listen more carefully to parents' needs and desires regarding employment (Morton et al., 1987; Sowers, 1989). Morton et al. (1987) quoted a parent as follows, "Professionals need to let parents get through the 'feeling part' of transition instead of getting bogged down in solving problems. If professionals let parents express their feelings and talk it out, then they'll be able to work together" (pp. 130–131).

SUMMARY

This chapter has suggested that parents and professionals bring fundamental differences to the transdisciplinary team process and that those differences, if properly explored and directed, can result in more appropriate and effective plans for students with multiple disabilities. The first section presented a framework for team decision-making and problem solving. The second section summarized experiences that may influence parents' interests and preferences at three different life stages.

This discussion presented the possibility that an alliance of parents and professional team members will yield more creative and meaningful plans, services, and, ultimately, lives. Wiegle's (1990) comments provide a closing reflection:

> What I ask for from professionals is that you stand next to me, that you believe that those kids that you work with are O.K. Too often I feel that the professionals who

are working with me pity me, they pity my child. I do not want to have to fight against the people who are here to help my children. I want you to know that they were born with the same rights and responsibilities as every child born within our country. I want you to help me help them lead the best lives they possibly can. I want you to value them. I want you to value me. (not paginated)

REFERENCES

Bailey, D.B. (1984). A triaxial model of the interdisciplinary team and group process. *Exceptional Children, 5*(1), 17–25.

Brotherson, M.J. (1984, October). *Future planning in families of adolescents with severe disabilities.* Paper presented at the meeting of the Association for Persons with Severe Handicaps, Chicago.

Carney, I.H. (1987). Working with families. In F.P. Orelove & D. Sobsey, *Educating children with multiple disabilities: A transdisciplinary approach* (pp.315–338). Baltimore: Paul H. Brookes Publishing Co.

Carney, I.H., Snell, M.E., & Gressard, C.F. (1986). *Parent involvement in IEPs: The relationship between student age and parent preferences.* Unpublished manuscript, University of Virginia, Charlottesville.

Carter, E.A., & McGoldrick, M. (Eds.). (1980). *The family life cycle: A framework for family therapy.* New York: Gardner Press.

Cone, J.D., DeLawyer, D.D., & Wolfe, V.V. (1985). Assessing parent participation: The parent/family involvement index. *Exceptional Parent, 51*(5), 417–424.

DeMyer, M.K., & Goldberg, P. (1983). Family needs of the autistic adolescent. In E. Schopler & G.B. Mesibov (Eds.), *Autism in adolescents and adults* (pp. 225–250). New York: Plenum Press.

Duvall, E. (1957). *Family development.* Philadelphia: Lippincott.

Erikson, E. (1959). *Identity and the life cycle.* New York: International Universities Press.

Ferrara, D.M. (1979). Attitudes of parents of mentally retarded children toward normalization activities. *American Journal of Mental Deficiency, 84*(2), 145–151.

Fisher, R., & Ury, W. (1983). *Getting to yes.* New York: Penguin Books.

Foxx, R.M., & Azrin, N.H. (1973). *Toilet training the retarded: A rapid approach for daytime and nighttime independent toileting.* Champaign, IL: Research Press.

Fuqua, R.W., Hegland, S.M., & Karas, S.C. (1985). Processes infuencing linkages between preschool handicap classrooms and homes. *Exceptional Children, 51*(4), 307–314.

Girdner, L.K., & Eheart, B.K. (1984). Mediation with families having a handicapped child. *Family Relations, 33*(1), 187–194.

Goldfarb, L.A., Brotherson, M.J., Summers, J.A., & Turnbull, A.P. (1986). *Meeting the challenge of disability and chronic illness—A family guide.* Baltimore: Paul H. Brookes Publishing Co.

Greenspan, S.I. (1988). Fostering emotional development in infants with disabilities. *Zero to Three, 9*(1), 8–18.

Halvorsen, A.T., Doering, K., Farron-Davis, F., Usilton, R., & Sailor, W. (1989). The role of parents and family members in planning severely disabled students' transitions from school. In G.H.S. Singer & L.K. Irvin (Eds.), *Support for caregiving families* (pp.253–267). Baltimore: Paul H. Brookes Publishing Co.

Hill, J., Seyfarth, J., Orelove, F., Wehman, P., & Banks, D. (1985). Factors influencing parents' vocational aspirations for their mentally retarded children. In P. Wehman & J.W. Hill (Eds.), *Competitive employment for persons with mental retardation* (pp.315–331). Richmond: Virginia Commonwealth University, Rehabilitation Research and Training Center.

Kaiser, C.E., & Hayden, A.H. (1984). Clinical research and policy issues in parenting severely handicapped infants. In J. Blacher (Ed.), *Severely handicapped young children and their families* (pp.275–318). New York: Academic Press.

Kraft, S.P. (1985, November). *Family adaptation to severely handicapping conditions.* Paper presented at the meeting of The Association for Persons with Severe Handicaps, Boston.

Leyser, Y., & Cole, K.B. (1984). Perceptions of parents of handicapped children about school and parent-teacher partnership. *The Exceptional Child, 31*(3), 193–201.

Lynch, E.W., & Stein, P. (1982). Perspectives on parent participation in special education. *Exceptional Education Quarterly, 3*(2), 56–63.

Morton, M.V., Everson, J.M., & Moon, S. (1987). Guidelines for training parents as part of interagency transition planning teams. In J.M. Everson, M. Barcus, M.S. Moon, & M.V. Morton (Eds.), *Achieving outcomes: A guide to interagency training in transition and supported employment* (125–142). Richmond: Rehabilitation Research and Training Center.

Olson, D.H., McCubbin, H.I., Barnes, H., Larsen, A., Muxen, M., & Wilson, M. (1983). *Families: What makes them work.* Beverly Hills: Sage Publications.

Oster, A. (1984). Keynote address. In *Equals in this partnership: Parents of disabled and at-risk infants and toddlers speak to professionals* (pp.26–32). Washington, D.C.: National Center for Clinical Infant Programs.

Ruppman, J. (1990, June). *What parents have to teach professionals.* Paper presented at the conference "Where the Heart Is: Home, Family, and People with Disabilities," Richmond.

Seltzer, M.M. (1989, Spring). Lifelong care,aging family study yields new data. *Newsletter of the University Affiliated Program for Persons with Developmental Disabilities.* (Available from the University of Georgia UAP, Athens, GA).

Sloper, P., Cunningham, C.C., & Arnljotsdottir, M. (1983). Parental reactions to early intervention with their Down syndrome infants. *Child: Care,Health, and Development, 9*(6), 357–376.

Solomon, M. (1973). A developmental, conceptual premise for family therapy. *Family Process, 12,* 179–188.

Sowers, J. (1989). Critical parent roles in supported employment. In G.H.S. Singer & L.K. Irvin (Eds.), *Support for caregiving families* (pp. 269–282). Baltimore: Paul H. Brookes Publishing Co.

Suelzle, M.J., & Keenan, V. (1981). Changes in family support networks over the life cycle of mentally retarded persons. *American Journal of Mental Deficiency, 86,* 267–274.

Trout, M., & Foley, G. (1989). Working with families of handicapped infants and toddlers. *Topics in Language Disorders, 10*(1), 57–67.

Turnbull, A.P., Summers, J.A., & Brotherson, M.J. (1986). Family life cycle: Theoretical and empirical implications and future directions for families with mentally retarded members. In J.J.Gallagher & P.M. Vietze (Eds.), *Families of handicapped persons: Research, programs, and policy issues.* (pp.45–65). Baltimore: Paul H. Brookes Publishing Co.

Turnbull, A.P., & Turnbull, H.R.(1990). *Families,professionals, and exceptionality: A special partnership.* Columbus, OH: Charles E. Merrill.

Turnbull, H.R., Turnbull, A.P., Bronicki, G.J.,Summers, J.A., & Roeder-Gordon, C. (1989). *Disability and the family: A guide to decisions for adulthood.* Baltimore: Paul H. Brookes Publishing Co.

Vincent, L.J., & Salisbury, C.L. (1989). Changing economic and social influences on family involvement. *Topics in Early Childhood Special Education, 8*(1), 48–59.

Wiegle, L. (1990, June). *What parents have to teach professionals.* Paper presented at the conference "Where the Heart Is: Home, Family, and People with Disabilities," Richmond.

Wikler, L., Wasow, M., & Hatfield, E. (1981). Chronic sorrow revisited: Parents' vs. professionals' depiction of the adjustment of parents of mentally retarded children. *American Journal of Orthopsychiatry, 51*(1), 63–70.

Winton, P., & Turnbull, A.P. (1981). Parent involvement as viewed by parents of preschool handicapped children. *Topics in Early Childhood Special Education, 1,* 11–19.

Chapter 13

Trends and Issues

The preceding 12 chapters should make the reader appreciate that there is much known about educating children with multiple disabilities. From designing instructional strategies and adaptations to determining appropriate therapeutic positions for eating, dressing, and other activities, school personnel and others have a wide array of techniques and principles to guide them. Moreover, this book has tried to make clear certain values in providing services to individuals with multiple disabilities. Perhaps the value that has been most clearly articulated embraces an approach in which professionals share with one another their knowledge and skills in meeting the needs of the children with whom they work.

A transdisciplinary approach, however, no matter how faithfully it is implemented, cannot by itself guarantee a good education for learners with multiple disabilities. Students who continue to be educated apart from their typical peers, for example, are receiving an education that is inherently unequal and inappropriate. Similarly, students whose behavior problems are met with unpleasant, punishing consequences are not receiving an appropriate education.

Unfortunately, children with multiple disabilities have been—and often continue to be—discriminated against on many levels. As suggested above, many of these students are served in segregated settings, and many are punished for engaging in aggressive, stereotypic, and self-injurious behavior (see Chapter 6). More revealingly, there has been heated debate over the degree to which individuals with the most severe disabilities should be provided medical treatment and whether they should be allowed to receive a public education.

This chapter examines these issues, each of which goes to the heart of the values underlying service. The emphasis is on those students with the most severe disabilities, as defined by Sailor, Gee, Goetz, and Graham (1988):

Many of these students have various orthopedic and sensory disabilities and may have little or no voluntary control over their movements. Many are medically at risk, chronically ill, or medically dependent, while others have extremely severe behavior disorders. These students often do not demonstrate any obvious choice or preferences, may show no signs of anticipation, or show very little affect. Their self-injurious or assaultive behavior may be so severe that they are restricted from participation in many environments. (p. 89)

The medical treatment of infants and older individuals with significant disabilities is covered first, followed by issues relevant to individuals with multiple disabilities within school settings.

TREATING INFANTS WITH DISABLING CONDITIONS

Nature and Extent of Practice

The practice of infanticide for economic, social, and other reasons has a long history that extends across centuries and cuts across cultures (John Fletcher, 1974). The contemporary practice of selective nontreatment of newborns with disabilities is, as Weir (1984) stated, a continuation of these historical practices of infanticide. Rather than parents engaging in physical abandonment, drowning, or smothering—to name just a few of the past methods of infanticide—decisions to treat or withhold treatment now are usually made in neonatal intensive care units.

It is very difficult, of course, to determine the prevalence of withholding treatment to infants with disabilities. The most famous documentation of this practice is a 1973 article by Duff and Campbell, physicians in the special care nursery at the Yale-New Haven Hospital. The authors examined the records of all 299 infants who died in a 30-month period and classified the deaths into two categories. Deaths in Category 1 (86%) resulted from pathological conditions in spite of treatment. Deaths in Category 2 (14%) resulted from discontinuation of treatment. Medical problems in this category included multiple anomalies, trisomy (three chromosomes, instead of the usual pair), and myelomeningocele. As Duff and Campbell concluded, "that decisions are made not to treat severely defective infants may be no surprise to those familiar with special-care facilities" (p. 892).

A decade later, four physicians and a social worker reported on their decision to withhold surgery from 24 infants born with myelomeningocele at the University of Oklahoma Health Services Center (Gross, Cox, Tatyrek, Pollay, & Barnes, 1983). All 24 babies, given only "supportive care" (with no treatment for infection or acute illness), died; the oldest lived about 6 months. All of the 36 babies who received vigorous treatment survived.

Other information on the extent to which treatment is withheld is largely anecdotal. A summary of four survey studies, however, showed that most physicians sampled would prefer that life-sustaining treatment for infants with

Down syndrome be withheld in certain instances (Affleck, 1980). The important point in these samples of nontreatment is that the presence of (or the anticipation of) significant cognitive impairments played a major role in the decision to treat or to withhold treatment.

Medical practices with newborns with disabling conditions have included: 1) withholding (or withdrawing) treatment that is necessary to prolong life, and 2) withholding of sustenance. These practices became visible to the public in the 1980's through two heavily publicized cases, commonly referred to as Baby Doe and Baby Jane Doe. Each is briefly discussed in turn.

Baby Doe Case   The Baby Doe case centered around an infant born on April 9, 1982, in Bloomington, Indiana. The child, known as "Infant Doe," had Down syndrome, plus esophageal atresia with associated tracheoesophageal fistula. This meant that the esophagus ended in a blind pouch, rather than connecting with the stomach, and that an abnormal passage connected part of the trachea with the esophagus.

The physicians in this case were divided regarding treatment or nontreatment (the surgery was considered routine), but the parents chose to withhold surgery and intravenous feeding. Various legal hearings supported the parents' decision, including the Indiana Supreme Court. Baby Doe died on April 15 before an emergency stay could be requested of U.S. Supreme Court Justice Paul Stevens (Weir, 1984). (For details of the situation and insight into the emotional effects on the physicians, nurses, and others present, see Koop [1989] and Schaffer & Sobsey [1991].)

The Baby Doe case was not the first to confront withholding sustenance and treatment from a disabled baby. The case is significant, however, in the degree of attention it received from the press and the federal government (e.g., Hentoff, 1985; "Private Death," 1982). The legislation that followed in the ensuing months, in fact, was popularly called the "Baby Doe Regulations." This legislation is discussed under the "Federal Executive and Legislative Action" section of this chapter.

Baby Jane Doe Case   Baby Jane Doe was born October 11, 1983, on Long Island, New York, with myelomeningocele, hydrocephaly, and microcephaly. Her physicians told her parents that, without surgery, life expectancy ranged from a few weeks to 2 years (Steinbock, 1984). Baby Jane Doe's parents declined to agree to surgery, and they were supported by the Court of Appeals.

The case was a complex one, involving suits by a "right-to-life" lawyer and the federal government, which wanted to examine Baby Jane Doe's hospital records. This case, as with Baby Doe, generated debate in the media, this time over the role of government in protecting newborns with disabilities (e.g., "Baby Jane's Big Brothers," 1983; Will, 1983). The situation resolved itself, because the parents agreed to have a shunt implanted in their child, reducing the hydrocephaly. They brought their daughter, Keri-Lynn, home in April, 1984 (Kerr, 1984).

Ethical and Moral Dilemmas

When the legal and purely medical issues are stripped away, the core of the debate to withhold treatment involves professional ethics and personal moral values. As would be expected, the debate is emotionally charged and often engenders individual stress and anguish among professionals, parents and family members, and other concerned parties (e.g., clergy, advocates, ethicists). Some individuals have compared the modern practices of withholding and withdrawing treatment to those used in the Nazi Holocaust (e.g., Lifton, 1986; Neuhaus, 1990; Wolfensberger, 1981). Medical organizations have fought to retain control of decisions to treat certain newborns with significant disabilities. This section delineates several major ethical positions that individuals have taken (based on an analysis by Weir [1984]).

Treat All Nondying Newborns Some individuals believe that decision-makers in neonatal intensive care units should focus solely on the medical indications for treatment. The likelihood of success of surgery, for example, would have been the only relevant consideration in the Baby Doe case; the presence or absence of Down syndrome would not have been a factor. Ramsey (1978) summarized this position: "We have no moral right to choose that some live and others die, when the medical indications for treatment are the same" (p. 192).

Decisions about treatment or nontreatment, moreover, should not be made on the basis of quality-of-life judgments. Rather, physicians should determine which infants are dying and which are not and should vigorously treat the latter group. Individuals who espouse this viewpoint differ in their allowance of exceptions. Ramsey (1978), for example, feels that infants with Tay-Sachs disease and Lesch-Nyhan syndrome, two genetic conditions, may best be left untreated. Others allow no exceptions to this principle.

Coulter (1991) suggests that medically indicated treatment is in the best interest of the infant, except when any of the following cannot be ensured:

1. Freedom from intractable pain and suffering ("suffering" *not* being defined as the mere presence of a disability)
2. The capacity to experience and enjoy life, defined very broadly as including "anyone who is consciously aware of other people and the environment"
3. Expectation of continued life

Terminate the Lives of Selected Nonpersons At the opposite extreme from the preceding category, some ethicists find nontreatment to be morally justifiable, because some newborns do not count as persons. The argument centers on what psychological criteria make up personhood. Tooley (1977), for example, has stated that "an organism possesses a serious right to life only if it possesses the concept of a self as a continuing subject of experiences and other mental states, and believes that it is itself such a continuing entity" (p. 59).

Equally controversial, Joseph Fletcher has described indicators of "humanhood." Pared from an original list of 15 positive and five negative human criteria, Fletcher (1974) claimed the following four features to define persons: neocortical function, self-consciousness, relational ability, and happiness. In an application, Fletcher (1972) stated: "Any individual of the species *homo sapiens* who falls below the I.Q. 40-mark in a standard Stanford-Binet test, amplified if you like by other tests, is questionably a person; below the 20-mark, not a person" (p. 4). Similarly, Singer (1979) believes that "killing a defective infant is not morally equivalent to killing a person" (p. 138).

   Withhold Treatment According to Parental Discretion   This view holds that parents, who are the persons with the greatest emotional involvement in the birth, should decide to treat or to withhold treatment. The great majority of newborns should be given care, and cure, whenever possible (Fletcher, 1979). Nontreatment is sometimes justifiable, however, for reasons of mercy to the infant and relief of meaningless suffering of the parents and medical team.

   Garland (1977) agreed that parents have the right to avoid severe and unnecessary familial burdens that their children, if treated, would bring upon them. He proposed that infants be divided into three categories: duty to treat (vast majority), duty not to treat (infants for whom there is no hope), and option to treat. The last category involves parental discretion on treatment, based in part on quality-of-life issues that generate family burdens. In their model for selecting infants with myelomeningocele for treatment, Gross et al. (1983) admitted that they took into consideration the potential contribution of the home and family, based upon a "formula" proposed by Shaw (1977, 1988).

   There is a problem, however, with giving parents complete decision-making authority. As one group of individuals summarized this problem, "even if parents sincerely believe themselves incapable of caring for a child with an impairment, such a belief is insufficient for allowing efficacious medical treatment to be withheld or withdrawn. The interests of parents ought not to be allowed to override the fundamental principle of respect for the best interests of the child" (Imperiled newborns, 1987, p. 17).

   Moreover, Turnbull and Turnbull (1986), among others, have questioned the assumption that children with disabilities are a drain or burden on the family. Certainly, many families who care for a child with a serious illness or disability experience stress related to: 1) providing home health care, 2) being fatigued, and 3) feeling socially isolated. However, many such families find meaning and satisfaction in their lives, despite the obstacles. At the very least, the literature on the impact of the person with a disability on the family unit is conflicting (Guess et al., 1984).

   Withhold Treatment According to Quality of Life   Some individuals hold that the potential for a meaningful life should influence decisions to treat infants with severe disabilities. Some factors used to determine the quality of a person's life include the severity of the disability, the prognosis for development and a prediction of future suffering, and the cost to society of supporting the individual (Lusthaus, 1985a). The quality-of-life formula mentioned in the preceding section, in addition to using family contributions, includes the new-born's physical and intellectual endowment and society's contribution. As Lusthaus (1985b) observed, "lives that are seen as not worthwhile are thought to be less than fully human, for fully human lives have potential worth" (p. 149).

There is another, more practical, concern with making quality-of-life decisions. There often is simply great uncertainty in determining a diagnosis and prognosis for a particular individual (Coulter, 1991; Steinbock, 1987). This is especially true for an infant of very low birthweight. "When the outcomes for a child are known to be death or devastating handicap, decisionmaking by doctors and parents is ethically relatively unproblematic. But if there is uncertainty about outcome for the infant, termination of treatment may cause a death that is difficult to justify" (Imperiled newborns, 1987, pp. 11–12).

Withhold Treatment Judged Not in the Child's Best Interests   In this option, the choice may be made to withhold treatment based on a projected burden of continued existence for the infant. Weir (1984) stated the central question: "Given the possibility that a handicapped infant will not have a meaningful life by normal (nonhandicapped) standards, is that life likely to represent a fate worse than death or a life worth experiencing even with the handicaps?" (p. 171). Who makes this determination, and against what criteria, naturally pose difficult problems. It might be relatively clear to suggest that this option be invoked in cases in which the infant is likely to suffer intractable pain or to be permanently unconscious (cf. Coulter, 1991). Less clear, however, might be situations in which adults judge that the infant's future experiences will be negative or without value, especially since these judgments are typically made from the adults' own sensibilities. A special report on newborns with disabilities stated the issue well: "An infant-centered quality of life standard should be as objective as possible, in an attempt to determine whether continued life would be a benefit, from the child's point of view. An impaired child does not have the luxury of comparing his life to a 'normal' existence; for such a child, it is a question of life with impairments versus no life at all" (Imperiled newborns, 1987, p. 15).

Summary of Ethical and Moral Dilemmas   It is impossible to summarize or analyze the various ethical positions in a simple manner. One report (Imperiled newborns, 1987), however, offers several conclusions and directions for future investigations:

1. Disabilities, in and of themselves, do not provide a basis for failing to accord children born with them the same access to medical and social services that would be given to any other child with a problem requiring medical intervention.

2. The concerns of premature newborns and those children born with injuries as a result of the birth process need greater attention. For example, how should physicians and nurses cope with uncertain prognoses for extremely

premature infants? What ethical norms ought to guide the continuation of treatment efforts once they have been initiated in an intensive care unit?
3. Insufficient attention has been paid to the moral responsibility that families and the community have to ensure that infants with special needs do not become the victims of discrimination, abuse, or neglect by the community.
4. A "best interests" standard that focuses exclusively on the interests of the child is the most appropriate moral norm to use when deciding whether to withdraw or withhold treatments.
5. Actively killing children conflicts with standards protecting the best interests of children.
6. Most decisions concerning treatment for children are best handled by informed, open, and frank discussions among health care professionals and the families of children with medical needs.

Legal Issues

Assuming one could accept selectively withholding treatment from both personal moral and professional ethical perspectives, a question still remains: Are there not legal sanctions against directly causing or contributing to the death of an infant, disabled or not? The brief answer is yes. The intentional taking of a human life is defined by criminal codes as homicide (Guess et al., 1984; Robertson, 1975). Depending on the means and intent of actions leading to the death, other charges might be brought, including first- or second-degree murder or involuntary manslaughter. Other possible criminal charges resulting from withholding needed medical care include child abuse or neglect, conspiracy, and being an accessory before the fact.

Despite the relatively clear legal consequences for withholding treatment, no parents or physicians have been successfully prosecuted for neonatal euthanasia in the United States (Imperiled newborns, 1987). Why is this? The first, and, perhaps, major reason is the strong legal doctrine that parents are the appropriate decision-makers for their infants (President's Commission, 1983). In the Baby Jane Doe case, for example, the appellate court held that the parents chose between two medically valid approaches (Steinbock, 1984). In general, the law has traditionally been sensitive to the parent-child relationship in matters of state interference (Guess et al., 1984).

In spite of this strong familial bias, the law also recognizes that the parents' rights are not absolute. In a case similar to Baby Jane Doe, a girl was born with myelomeningocele (*Cicero,* 1979). The father refused the life-saving surgery that the doctor recommended. The New York State Supreme Court rejected the parents' right to decide and appointed the executive director of the hospital as the infant's guardian *ad litem* (Steinbock, 1984).

There are other, more subtle, reasons for the absence of criminal indictments in infant nontreatment situations (Weir, 1984). Decisions to withhold treatment are made in the quasi-privacy of neonatal intensive care units. Often, all parties agree to the decision. In other cases, physicians may conceal their actions by claiming to administer "pain-relieving" medications. Such low-visibility cases rarely are reported to legal authorities.

In addition, prosecutors may decline to file charges, even if informed anonymously. They may respect parental authority, agree with the parents' position, choose not to take a politically unpopular stand, feel that the presiding judge would be sympathetic with the hospital, or conclude that the evidence would be too difficult to obtain to secure a conviction, among other practical reasons.

Case law in this arena has been overshadowed in the 1980s by federal legislation. The following section briefly examines the federal role in guiding decisions about treatment of newborns with disabilities.

Federal Executive and Legislative Action

As mentioned earlier in this chapter, the Baby Doe case in Bloomington, Indiana prompted action at the federal level. On March 7, 1983, the Department of Health and Human Services (HHS) issued an interim final rule to all hospitals receiving federal funds. The hospitals were to post warning signs in delivery rooms, pediatric wards, nurseries, and neonatal intensive care units that stated: "Discriminatory failure to feed and care for handicapped infants in this facility is prohibited by federal law." The sign also listed a "handicapped infant hotline" for individuals to report instances of withholding of sustenance or medical care. Following a suit from the American Academy of Pediatrics and several other medical associations, a federal judge struck down the interim rule as invalid.

Two more sets of rules were issued by HHS: a proposed rule (July 5, 1983) and the final rules (January 12, 1984) (Hardman, 1984; Murray, 1984). The final rule encouraged hospitals to establish Infant Care Review Committees, which should: 1) set hospital policy for types of cases, 2) give advice in specific cases, and 3) perform retrospective reviews of cases of nontreatment. Once again, these rules were contested in federal court (*Bowen v. American Hospital Association et al.*, 1986). The U.S. Supreme Court, in a 5–3 decision on June 9, 1986, affirmed the ruling of the U.S. Court of Appeals that the regulations were invalid. The majority opinion basically held that HHS had failed to offer evidence of discrimination under Section 504 of the Rehabilitation Act of 1973. The court did not hold, however, that parents had a right to refuse treatment for their disabled babies, but held that, ordinarily, review of such parental decisions belongs to the states (Imperiled newborns, 1987).

As a compromise measure, Congress subsequently passed amendments to the Child Abuse Prevention and Treatment Act. Signed by President Reagan in October, 1984, Public Law 98-457, the Child Abuse Amendments of 1984, extended the meaning of the term "medical neglect" to include "the withholding of medically indicated treatment from a disabled infant with a life-threatening condition" (U.S. Code [1988], Title 42, Chapter 67, Subchapter IV, Section 5106g). The rule also designated the State Child Protective Service Agency as the authority to ensure that no infant is the victim of medical neglect (Murray, 1985).

The specific definition for withholding medical treatment is:

> The failure to respond to the infant's life threatening conditions by providing treatment (including appropriate nutrition, hydration, and medication) which, in the treating physician's . . . reasonable medical judgment, will be most likely to be effective in ameliorating or correcting all such conditions. . . . (Child Abuse Prevention and Treatment Act, Child Abuse Amendments, 1984, U.S. Code [1988], Title 42, Chapter 67, Subchapter IV, Section 5106g)

The rule goes on to list three exceptions. Withholding of treatment is not "medical neglect" when:

> (1) the infant is chronically and irreversibly comatose; or
> (2) the provision of such treatment would merely prolong dying, not be effective in ameliorating or correcting all of the infant's life-threatening conditions, or otherwise be futile in terms of the survival of the infant; or
> (3) the provision of such treatment would be virtually futile in terms of the survival of the infant and the treatment itself under such circumstances would be inhumane. (Child Abuse Prevention and Treatment Act, Child Abuse Amendments, 1984, U.S. Code [1988], Title 42, Chapter 67, Subchapter IV, Section 5106g)

The amendments have been taken to indicate that all infants who are born with disabilities, such as Baby Doe, should receive treatment for life-threatening conditions, although infants whose immediate prognosis is dismal and for whom treatment is inhumane need not be treated (Imperiled newborns, 1987). Despite this positive direction, some individuals have been critical of the amendments. Some (e.g., Coulter, 1991) cite the weak provisions for enforcement (withholding of selected federal funds). Partly as a result, Coulter asserts, there is no process to ensure that treatment decisions do in fact conform to the rules. Nolan (1990) suggests that the law has resulted in *overtreatment* of some infants. More important, religious exemption clauses in state child abuse statutes have legally allowed parents and religious "healers" to avoid obtaining medical treatment (Nolan, 1990). Finally, there is confusion over the terminology used in the amendments. Of special concern is the phrase "chronically and irreversibly comatose," a condition cited as one of the exceptions to treatment. As Cranford (1988) noted, however, this class of patients "simply does not exist in any meaningful sense" (p. 32). The life span of a truly comatose patient is limited to weeks or months, rarely years. In one case, an infant was ruled by the judge to be protected by the Child Abuse Amendments, but he was in a persistent vegetative state, not in a coma (Bermel, 1986).

While clarifying terms and securing consistency in state statutes would be helpful, the central issues around treatment of infants with significant disabilities will remain essentially moral and ethical. Parents, physicians, lawyers, advocates, and others will continue to debate the issues of life and death, issues which will become even thornier as technology becomes more sophisticated. At least one major professional organization, The Association for Persons with Severe Handicaps (TASH), has taken a strong policy stance against withholding medical treatment to infants when the decision is based upon the diagnosis of, or prognosis for, a specific disability. The TASH resolution appears on page 441. Each person who works with individuals with multiple disabilities needs to take a position with which he or she can live.

OTHER BIOETHICAL ISSUES

In addition to the concerns revolving around the treatment of newborns with disabilities, two other current bioethical issues are relevant: the removal of organs for transplant from anencephalic infants; and continuing life support, nutrition, and hydration for individuals in a persistent vegetative state. Each issue, which touches on familiar ethical themes and introduces new ones, is discussed briefly in this section.

Anencephalic Infants as Sources of Transplantable Organs

Many newborns require replacement of vital organs, such as hearts, kidneys, and livers for survival. Unfortunately, the supply of organs is insufficient to meet the need. Consequently, some individuals have suggested that organs be taken from babies with anencephaly, a congenital condition characterized by the absence of skull, scalp, and forebrain (Shewmon, 1988). Individuals born with anencephaly typically have only their brainstem present, and that is often malformed or incomplete (Coulter, 1988). Most of these infants die within a few days, although questions remain about actual life expectancy (Shewmon, 1988).

Given the short life span and the limited potential of infants with anencephaly, some individuals believe they would make ideal candidates for sources of transplantable organs. Indeed, such procedures have already been undertaken in Canada (Annas, 1987) and in the United States, most notably at Loma Linda University in California (Walters & Ashwal, 1988). The procedure has been justified through utilitarian reasoning (i.e., it is appropriate to use the organs to benefit another individual in need) and through the belief that it would help give meaning and comfort to the parents of these children who are certain to die soon.

Despite these "advantages," using babies with anencephaly as donors is fraught with ethical dilemmas and practical problems. The issue foremost among them concerns the definition of "death" and the status of the infant with anencephaly. Organ donors, by law, must be dead, which currently is defined as irreversible cessation of all functions of the entire brain, including the brain stem. Removing organs from an infant with anencephaly, who, in fact, has brain stem function, is thus tantamount to active euthanasia, which is illegal.

Resolution on Infant Care

TASH opposes the withholding of medical treatment and/or sustenance to infants when the decision is based upon the diagnosis of, or prognosis for, retardation or any other disability. TASH affirms the right to equal medical treatment for all infants in accordance with the dignity and worth of these individuals, as protected by federal and state laws and regulations. TASH acknowledges the responsibilities of society and government to share with parents and other family members the support necessary for infants with disabilities. Finally, TASH acknowledges the obligation of society to provide for life-long medical, financial, and educational support to persons with disabilities extending to them opportunities offered to all members of society.

The rationale for this resolution is as follows.

- The right to life and liberty is guaranteed by our Constitution, Bill of Rights, and federal and state laws and regulations.
- The life and liberty of persons with disabilities are threatened by the prejudice which results from the ignorance generated by segregation and separation.
- This prejudice can only be overcome when the next generation of children born without disabilities grow up, play with, go to school with, and live and work with their peers with disabilities.
- TASH is extremely concerned with the practice of withholding medical treatment and/or sustenance from infants based upon the diagnosis of, or prognosis for, disability.

ORIGINALLY ADOPTED APRIL 1983
AMENDED APRIL 1989

441

To circumvent this dilemma, individuals have recommended various solutions, mainly that of redefining "death" or redefining the status of infants with anencephaly (Fost, 1988).

These solutions have included the following:

1. Amend current brain death laws to include "anencephalics."
2. Redefine brain death to permit "cortical death" only.
3. Redefine persons with anencephaly as a special category of "brain-absent."
4. Amend the Anatomical Gift Act to permit organ harvesting from "anencephalics."

A second concern, which grows out of attempts to redefine death and the status of a certain class of people—those with anencephaly—is the familiar "slippery slope" argument. That is, once we begin to make exceptions for one group, when do we stop? (Capron, 1987; Coulter, 1988; Willke & Andrusko, 1988).

Third, there is a question about the degree of certainty with which one can make a definitive diagnosis of anencephaly. As Shewmon (1988) stated, "The commonly encountered contention that 'anencephaly' is so well-defined and so distinct from all other congenital brain malformations that misdiagnoses cannot occur and that organ-harvesting policies limited to 'anencephalics' cannot possibly extend to other conditions, is simply false" (p. 12).

Fourth, putting ethical questions aside, some doubt remains about the practical impact of using newborns with anencephaly as sources of organs. Walters and Ashwal (1988), for example, claim that "hundreds of fatally ill babies may be saved if organs from anencephalic newborns can be utilized" (p. 24). Shewmon (1988), however, has suggested that the "yearly number of patients in the country actually benefiting from anencephalic kidneys, hearts, and livers optimistically projects to zero, nine, and two, respectively" (p. 17).

Summarizing the concerns involved in this issue, Coulter (1988) suggested that the following conditions be adhered to:

a. Society respect the worth of the infant with anencephaly;
b. All active euthanasia be prohibited;
c. Mechanical ventilation be permitted only if adequate steps are taken to minimize harm and prevent suffering;
d. Brain death is diagnosed according to currently accepted medical criteria . . .; and
e. Removal of organs for transplantation is permitted only after a diagnosis of brain death has been made according to these criteria. (p. 75)

As in the treatment of newborns with other disabilities, the issue of removing organs from newborns with anencephaly reveals various competing interests among parents, medical professionals, society at large, and, of course, the infants involved. There does not promise to be a clear resolution in the very near future. In weighing the concerns, one would do well to listen to the words of one individual: "Whether anencephalic infants can be used as organ donors will depend not on the law, however, but on our ability to deal with them as members of the human race, and to safeguard them from harm as we try to turn their plight (and their bodies) to the benefit of others" (Annas, 1987, p. 38).

Supporting Individuals in a Persistent Vegetative State

Approximately 5,000–10,000 individuals in the United States are in a persistent vegetative state (Cranford, 1988). The most well-known person in this condition, of course, was Karen Ann Quinlan. Patients in a persistent vegetative state are unconscious; they are unaware of themselves or the surrounding environment. Unlike comatose patients, though, they are awake. In this respect (eyes-open consciousness), individuals in a persistent vegetative state are like people with anencephaly. However, unlike people with anencephaly, individuals in a persistent vegetative state have relatively intact brain stems and, with appropriate food, water, and care, can survive for a long time. Therefore, as Cranford (1988) takes pains to observe, it is important to appreciate that the persistent vegetative state is quite distinct from coma (which is "eyes-closed unconsciousness" and often leads to frequent and fatal respiratory infections) and from brain death (in which all brain stem functions are lost). Patients in a persistent vegetative state are neither dead nor terminally ill so that death would be expected in a few months to a year. Except for a few documented instances, however, the condition of such individuals is irreversible. Moreover, it is important to appreciate that most medical professionals believe that persons in a persistent vegetative state cannot experience pain and suffering (Cranford, 1988).

Some of the bioethical questions posed in the debates about treating babies with disabilities and using organs from newborns with anencephaly are also appropriate to issues concerning individuals in a persistent vegetative state. Of course, there are some salient differences. Primary among these, perhaps, is that individuals in a persistent vegetative state can survive for years, with virtually no chance of improving. This situation can and often does result in a drain on family members and health care professionals. Moreover, there is the central question of the dignity and rights of the patient to not be kept alive through artificial means. One ethicist has even likened prolonging the lives of patients in a persistent vegetative state to the archaic practice of banishment from the community, and suggested that withdrawing life-supporting treatment is "not merely ethically permissible, but an obligatory act of beneficence" (Schneiderman, 1990, p. 5).

Clearly, deciding not to maintain treatment in patients in a persistent vegetative state has increasingly become an ethically accepted practice. One ethicist even entertains (but does not endorse) the idea of redefining death to include "permanent loss of sentience" (Wikler, 1988, p. 44). Under this definition, health care providers would not be required to treat individuals in a persistent vegetative state and, except in unusual circumstances, all life supports (including nutrition and hydration) would be withdrawn. Thus, terminating treatment under a revised definition of death would not require prior agreement of the patient.

In most situations, however, life supports are withdrawn only when it is clear that the patient would not want further treatment (giving rise to the increased awareness of "living wills"). What about people with severe disabilities? As Coulter (1991) observed, such individuals "have never had the opportunity to express a clear and competent desire regarding their care" (p. 557). For such individuals, Coulter argues, there is no justification for denying nutrition and hydration. The Association for Persons with Severe Handicaps has taken the same stand on this issue. Through a formal resolution, the organization "opposes any cessation of nutrition and hydration for people who are incapacitated." The resolution further "strongly opposes approaches . . . which authorize third parties exercising substitute judgment to decide 'on behalf' of a person who has been labeled incapacitated that the person's life is no longer 'worth' living, and strongly opposes any position that it would be in the best interests of a person to die rather than to live with a disability" (TASH Resolution on Nutrition and Hydration, 1986).

The bioethical issues discussed thus far are truly "life and death" concerns. Fortunately, they are issues that most people will not have to deal with directly in their lifetimes. Nevertheless, they force people to think through concepts such as the dignity and worth of individuals with multiple disabilities, people who typically are unable to speak for themselves.

EDUCATING ALL STUDENTS

Historically, society has excluded certain classes of individuals from public education. At the beginning of the twentieth century, a distinguished pioneer in the field of mental retardation declared: "The great majority of the thirteen hundred children whom we have seen in special classes have been tried in the ordinary schools, and have been shown to be incapable of receiving any proper benefit from the instruction, having for the most part learned little or nothing beyond certain habits of discipline" (Fernald, 1903, p. 26).

Much later, after special education had become an established profession, another noted educator argued against serving children with severe mental retardation in the schools: "Public schools were established to educate those who have the ability to learn, and the severely retarded are unable to benefit from education. . . . There is no real advancement possible either for individual children or for society as a whole in providing public school education for the severely retarded"(Cruickshank, quoted in Kirk, 1962, p. 138).

The status of special education, of course, has changed considerably since 1962. Right-to-education cases and subsequent federal legislation guaranteeing a free, appropriate education to all handicapped children have changed the focus of the debate. Since then attention has been placed on the "appropriateness" of educating children with the most severe disabilities in public schools. The concern pivots around the degree to which it is perceived that certain children are capable of being educated. Kauffman and Krouse (1981) articulated the "ineducability" viewpoint: "The position that all children are educable may be indefensible on philosophical grounds, undesirable as a social policy, and questionable as a moral precept or ethical standard" (p. 54). They continue: "There are some children so severely handicapped that no program now available can be expected to produce significant improvement in their behavior" (p. 55).

Kauffman and Krouse and others in the early 1980's were referring to what is thought of as a surprisingly "high functioning" type of student, relative to what is known today. Kauffman (1981) described the following primary characteristics of "this extremely debilitated group" (p. 1):

1. All function is at the extreme lower levels of cognitive attainment and adaptive behavior.
2. Most have not acquired basic self-care skills.
3. Most are permanently nonambulatory.
4. Most show extremely little promise of becoming creative, productive citizens.

A more representative description of the type of child embodied by what is to date the latest version of the educability debate can be found in the case, *Timothy W. v. Rochester, New Hampshire, School District* (1989). Timothy W., who was almost 9 years old when his parents filed a suit against the school district in 1984, was born with severe respiratory problems. Shortly thereafter, he experienced an intracranial hemorrhage, subdural effusions (leakage and accumulation of fluids between the skull and the brain cortex), seizures, hydrocephaly, and meningitis. The court summary showed that Timothy had multiple disabilities and profound mental retardation; he had cerebral palsy (spastic quadriplegia) and a seizure disorder and was cortically blind. The Rochester, New Hampshire school district denied Timothy an education because they believed him to be incapable of benefiting.

Although the district court supported the school district, the United States Court of Appeals reversed the decision and issued an important ruling:

> The statutory language of the [Education for All Handicapped Children] Act, its legislative history, and the case law construing it, mandate that all handicapped children, *regardless of the severity of their handicap* [italics added], are entitled to a public education. The district court erred in requiring a benefit/eligibility test as a prerequisite to implementing the Act. School districts cannot avoid the provisions of the Act by returning to the practices that were widespread prior to the Act's passage . . . of unilaterally excluding certain handicapped children from a public education on the ground that they are uneducable. (*Timothy W. v. Rochester, New Hampshire School District*, 1989, pp. 972–973)

This ruling entitled Timothy to attend school, but it left open the question as to what an appropriate program for Timothy should look like. In defining "appropriateness," it is necessary first to define the terms *education, meaningful skill,* and *significant progress.* The remainder of this section is devoted to this task.

What Is "Education"?

The definition of education will forever be debated by academicians, educators, philosophers, and citizens. Predictably, each successive generation of legislators and educators has assumed responsibility for another previously disenfranchised group. The late 1970's and the 1980's gave birth to public education for (among others) learners with severe mental retardation and other significant disabilities. Society is now witnessing the schools' attempts to adjust to the needs of students with the most severe disabilities, individuals like Timothy W.

The *Timothy W.* case has, in a legal sense, answered the question, "What is education?" It is what happens in and through school programs for individuals who have been labeled as "handicapped." The official document within each state in the United States for describing those agreed upon elements of education is the individualized education program (IEP). For a particular child, such a plan might consist of predominantly teaching self-care skills. For another, it may consist solely or primarily of accelerating operant responses. Education is defined by teachers, related service and other professionals, and parents *for each individual child.*

What Are "Meaningful Skills"?

In choosing goals and objectives for the IEP, the team of professionals and parents is implicitly claiming those goals to be meaningful. Meaningful to whom? Certainly not necessarily to society at large, since it would be difficult to explain to the average citizen why teaching a student to swallow after receiving a taste on her tongue (Bostrom, 1983) is a valuable thing for society. It is assumed that the citizens will entrust educational planning and teaching to the educators who are hired through the local school boards (Orelove, 1991).

Skills, then, should be selected primarily for their meaning to the learners themselves. Thus, the emphasis should be on what is important to the *student,* not to *others* (Holvoet, 1989). Accordingly, it is necessary to rethink choosing goals and objectives for students with the most severe disabilities that try to make them more like "normal" people. Thus, an ecological inventory approach (Brown et al., 1979) probably cannot be relied upon completely in the design of a curriculum (see Chapter 7). Some students have response repertoires so limited as to render a straight skill development approach impractical (Orelove, 1991). Using partial participation has similar limits, often resulting in acquisition of slices of behavior that are too fine to have any clear function remaining for the learner.

One possible alternative is to focus on developing a repertoire of *effective* behaviors, which produce an effect upon the social environment (Evans & Scotti, 1989). The value of effective behaviors is their influence on a range of individuals and situations. As Dunst, Cushing, and Vance (1985) demonstrated in a study with infants with multiple disabilities, a small behavior (in this case, fixated head turning) had the important effect of exciting and engaging parents, who previously felt frustrated by their childrens' apparent lack of ability and awareness.

Indeed, meaningfulness can, and should, extend beyond the learner to the parent or caregiver. Hawkins (1984), a professional and the parent of a child (Karrie) with a disability, defined meaningfulness as the *"functionality* of [a] behavior for *someone"* (p. 284). He goes on to state:

> Furthermore, if anyone were to be the judge of whether a particular behavior change is "meaningful" it should certainly not be the general taxpayer alone, who has no idea how rewarding it is to see your retarded 19 year old acquire the skill of toilet flushing on command or pointing to food when she wants a second helping. . . . It is functional for the taxpayer even though his or her answer to the question, "Is this meaningful?" might well be, "No" or, "Not enough to pay for." And, although we cannnot readily say how much Karrie's being able to flush the toilet enhances her personal reinforcement/punishment ratio, I can testify that it enhances mine as a parent. (p. 285)

What Is "Significant Progress"?

Assuming "significant" can be thought of in the same fashion as the term "meaningful," "progress" is still left to be determined. Evans and Scotti (1989) have suggested several outcome measures applicable to learners with the most severe disabilities. First, a decrease in the level of a learner's excess (i.e., inappropriate) behavior may signal an improvement in the educational program or indicate a positive change in the individual. Second, selected indices reflective of learners' emotional states can be examined, including facial expression, vocalization, and physiological measures such as pulse. Third, the amount of time an individual spends continuously involved in an (unforced) activity could indicate the degree to which the person is enjoying the activity.

There may also be motor measures available to determine significant progress. Landesman-Dwyer and Sackett (1978) measured increases in eye movement, head and facial movement, and trunk and limb movements in persons with multiple disabilities. To the degree to which improvements in these movements made individuals more comfortable or gave them greater access to people, directly or indirectly, they could be said to be "significant." Evans and Scotti (1989) also suggested two measures: 1) endurance of simple to complex motor actions to enable individuals to gain physical benefits; and 2) eye movements, which might be measured electronically.

Finally, teachers would do well to place value on observing their students closely and to notice small changes in appearance, expression, and movement.

Interviewed in a qualitative study, teachers of learners with the most severe disabilities talked about placing great value on increasing levels of awareness in their students, and about looking for indications that the students were reacting to environmental input (Thompson & Guess, 1989).

Teachers are at the very heart of the issues surrounding the educability of students with multiple disabilities. Blatt (1981) eloquently explained:

> The "educability" hypothesis has a pervasive fascination that sustains the researcher, for the concept includes all people and so many things that it can easily intrude into every nook and cranny of our time and energy; the hypothesis refers not only to children, not only to the mentally retarded, not only to those in the inner city or those in the institution; but, to the degree it has relevance for those groups, it has relevance for all of us—not only for children, but for their teachers, not only for their teachers, but for the teachers of their teachers. For a child to change, his teacher has to change. (p. 29)

INTEGRATING STUDENTS WITH MULTIPLE DISABILITIES

While some individuals continue to debate whether all children with multiple disabilities are deserving of or capable of benefiting from an education, many professionals are working diligently to determine ways to include these children as fully as possible into the educational and social life of the school (e.g., Gaylord-Ross, 1989; Lipsky & Gartner, 1989; Sailor et al., 1989; Stainback, & Stainback, 1990; Stainback, Stainback & Forest, 1989). The authors of this book believe that while integration is a trend, it is not *trendy*; rather, it is a long overdue practice that recognizes the essential equality of all pupils. Moreover, to adopt the practices and procedures suggested throughout this book in a context of segregated service delivery would be, in our belief, a serious error. Learning how to communicate and eat are important, but these skills should not be taught at the expense of the child being physically and socially separated from his or her peers. Indeed, integration itself *makes possible* the more rapid development of a repertoire of functional skills and the reduction in the effects of physical disabilities (cf. Sailor, 1989; Sailor et al., 1988).

In fact, the superiority of integrated over segregated services for students who do *and who do not* have disabilities has been demonstrated repeatedly across a variety of critical dimensions. The outcomes are so clear and convincing that this chapter does not attempt to summarize them. Readers wishing to examine this literature are urged to consult several excellent reviews and meta-analyses of the research: Carlberg and Kavale (1980); Gartner and Lipsky (1987); Halvorsen and Sailor (1990); and Wang and Baker (1985–1986). In addition, Dreimanis et al. (1990) have compiled an annotated bibliography on integration with over 400 entries.

Despite this overwhelming evidence in favor of integration, many states or individual school districts within states continue to place students in segregated centers (Danielson & Bellamy, 1989; Laski, 1991). Halvorsen and Sailor (1990) identified 20 variables that appear to be predictive of student placement. These variables are grouped within five categories: student issues, family issues, instructional issues, administrative issues, and logistical issues. While it cannot be stated with certainty why a particular student is segregated, Snell and Eichner (1989) suggested two key barriers to full inclusion: philosophical inertia and nonacceptance, and territorial self-interest.

These and many other barriers to integration (e.g., general intolerance towards others, inequitable funding formulas) affect all students with disabilities. Some barriers, however, have particular relevance for students with multiple disabilities. For instance, specialized services for students labeled "medically fragile" often have not been put in place. Moreover, misunderstandings arise about the role of schools in providing certain types of therapies or medical procedures. Some in the educational system question the real benefits of integrating learners who do not appear to be aware of their environment. Parents also may have become accustomed to, or even come to expect, separate and specialized services through their experiences with segregated early intervention programs.

Of course, these issues, rather than being viewed as barriers, may instead be viewed as challenges. Numerous school divisions, many of them large and rooted in decades of providing separate services, have successfully tackled difficult problems. The remainder of this section describes some possible steps members of transdisciplinary teams can take to enhance integrated opportunities for learners with multiple disabilities. Before considering these suggestions, two pieces of advice are in order. First, while many of the elements of putting an integrated service delivery system in place are technical—that is, they involve logistics and coordination—the *decision* to integrate is not. Integration should not depend on data proving that it is cost effective. Rather, integration should be implemented because it is *right* for all children. Second, integration is not a "special education" issue. It is a matter of creating schools that are effective and that care about all students. Readers are advised to consult Sailor et al. (1989) and Sapon-Shevin (1990) for strategies for achieving this goal.

The strategies for promoting integration recommended here are geared primarily towards teachers and related services staff, who make up the nucleus of most transdisciplinary teams. It is recognized that many vital components of integrated programs—proximity of classrooms, school schedules, transportation arrangements, and so forth—are under the control of building principals or district level personnel. Nevertheless, mere physical presence of students, while necessary, is not sufficient to guarantee a quality integrated program. It is toward the realization of high program quality that the following practices are offered (based on Campbell, 1989; Hamre-Nietupski & Nietupski, 1985; Sailor et al., 1989; and Wolfe & Snell, 1990).

1. *Carefully select materials, toys, and activities.* Activities and materials that are age appropriate and that can be used and enjoyed by both students with disabilities and typical students facilitate interactions among peers.
2. *Conduct activities with age-appropriate peers.* Students are more likely to interact with one another when there are structured opportunities to do so. It is important that the activities be conducted with peers, that is, students of the same approximate chronological age. Participation in integrated, age-appropriate activities should be written into each student's IEP.
3. *Use the entire school and community.* It helps to take advantage of the facilities that most schools have. This includes not only the cafeteria and gymnasium, but the library, home economics room, and computer lab. In doing so, "handicapped only" times should be avoided. Thus, schedules must be coordinated with the regular education staff. Moreover, physical proximity alone does not promote integration. Students should be mixed throughout the cafeteria, for example, not segregated by classes at different tables.
4. *Establish IEP goals for each student on social interactions.* Many learners with multiple disabilities are nonverbal and may not have reliable means of expressing thoughts, which is both challenging to and a critical issue of social integration. Part of the strategy must be to offer numerous natural *opportunities* for interactions to be taught. Then, systematic prompting, modeling, rehearsal, and other techniques can be used throughout the interaction. In addition, typical children need to be taught ways in which nonverbal peers communicate. Naturally, this argues that the team develop a systematic means of communication for every child (see Chapter 9).
5. *Work with colleagues to develop a "special friends" program.* "Special friends" programs have two major goals: 1) to develop positive, mutually rewarding personal relationships between students with severe disabilities and typical students; and 2) to support the development of social competence in both groups of students to allow them to interact in integrated settings (cf. Forest & Lusthaus, 1989). Clearly, there are other, less structured means of allowing friendships to occur. The important point is that if interactions and friendships do not occur naturally, then team members need to facilitate their occurrence. In doing so, however, it is often best to "get out of the way" and let the children come to know one another (Strully & Strully, 1989).
6. *Participate in the life of the school.* For too long, special educators segregated themselves from their colleagues. Integration for students is greatly facilitated when staff participate in extra-curricular activities, faculty meetings, lunch duty, and so forth.
7. *Talk to and about students respectfully.* Students need to be treated and spoken to with respect. This includes not ridiculing a student and not talking about students as if they were not present.

8. *Use behavior change strategies that are normalized.* Apart from the ethical and educational concerns about using aversive strategies to reduce inappropriate behaviors (see Chapters 6 and 7), such procedures damage efforts at integrating students by calling attention to the *differences,* rather than the similarities between learners who do and learners who do not have disabilities.

9. *Operate within the transdisciplinary model.* When assessment, instruction, and therapy are coordinated and delivered throughout the day in natural environments (including regular education classrooms, the playground, the gymnasium, and so forth), integration is enhanced.

CONCLUSION

This chapter has touched on just a few issues concerning the treatment and education of individuals with multiple disabilities. Other concerns have been discussed in preceding chapters. Chapter 5, for example, explored some of the issues in providing school health care services, and Chapter 6 briefly examined the problems of aversive treatment of undesired behaviors.

The issues discussed in this and previous chapters reveal a common theme: individuals with multiple disabilities should be afforded equal treatment and equal opportunity. It is hoped that the instructional strategies and team process described in this book will assist professionals in achieving this goal for the students they serve. Thus, although good technical skills for therapists, teachers, nurses, and so forth, are important, it is at least equally important that these skills be rooted in a solid foundation of values.

REFERENCES

Affleck, G.G. (1980). Physicians' attitudes toward discretionary medical treatment of Down's syndrome infants. Mental *Retardation, 18,* 79–81.

Annas, G.J. (1987). From Canada with love: Anencephalic newborns as organ donors? *Hastings Center Report, 17*(6), 36–38.

Baby Jane's big brothers. (1983, November 4). *The New York Times.*

Bermel, J. (1986). Confusion over the language of the Baby Doe regulations. *Hastings Center Report, 16*(6), 2.

Blatt, B. (1981). *In and out of mental retardation: Essays on educability, disability, and human policy.* Baltimore: University Park Press.

Bostrom, S. (1983). Jennifer. *TASH Journal, 8*(1), 58–62.

Bowen v. American Hospital Association et al., 106 S. Ct. 2101 (1986).

Brown, L., Branston-McLean, M.B., Baumgart, D., Vincent, L., Falvey, & Schroeder, J. (1979). Using the characteristics of current and subsequent least restrictive environments in the development of curricular content for severely handicapped students. *AAESPH Review, 4*(4), 407–424.

Campbell, P.H. (1989). Students with physical disabilities. In R. Gaylord-Ross (Ed.), *Integration strategies for students with handicaps* (pp. 53–76). Baltimore: Paul H. Brookes Publishing Co.

Capron, A.M. (1987). Anencephalic donors: Separate the dead from the dying. *Hastings Center Report, 17*(1), 5–9.

Carlberg, C., & Kavale, K. (1980). The efficacy of special versus regular class placement for exceptional children: A meta-analysis. *Journal of Special Education, 14,* 295–309.

Child Abuse Amendments to the Child Abuse Prevention and Treatment Act, Sect. 102, 121, 42 U.S.C. Sec. 1750, 1752, (1984).

Cicero, 421 N.Y. Supp. 2d 965, New York State Supreme Court, Bronx County (1979).

Coulter, D.L. (1988). Beyond Baby Doe: Does infant transplantation justify euthanasia? *Journal of the Association for Persons with Severe Handicaps, 13*(2), 71–75.

Coulter, D.L. (1991). Medical treatment. In L.H. Meyer, C.A. Peck, & L. Brown (Eds.), *Critical issues in the lives of people with severe disabilities* (pp. 553–558). Baltimore: Paul H. Brookes Publishing Co.

Cranford, R.E. (1988). The persistent vegetative state: The medical reality. *Hastings Center Report, 18*(1), 27–32.

Danielson, L.C., & Bellamy, G.T. (1989). State variation in placement of children with handicaps in segregated environments. *Exceptional Children, 55,* 448–455.

Dreimanis, M., Sobsey, D., Gray, S., Harnaha, B., Uditsky, B., & Wells, D. (1990). *Integration and individuals with moderate to profound intellectual impairment: An annotated bibliography.* University of Alberta, Edmonton.

Duff, R.S., & Campbell, A.G.M. (1973). Moral and ethical dilemmas in the special-care nursery. *The New England Journal of Medicine, 289*(17), 890–894.

Dunst, C.J., Cushing, P.J., & Vance, S.D. (1985). Response-contingent learning in profoundly handicapped infants: A social systems perspective. *Analysis and Intervention in Developmental Disabilities, 5,* 33–47.

Evans, I.M., & Scotti, J.R. (1989). Defining meaningful outcomes for persons with profound disabilities. In F. Brown & D.H. Lehr (Eds.), *Persons with profound disabilities: Issues and practices* (pp. 83–107). Baltimore: Paul H. Brookes Publishing Co.

Fernald, W.E. (1903). Mentally defective children in the public schools. *Journal of Psycho-Asthenics, 8,* 25–35.

Fletcher, John. (1974). Attitudes towards defective newborns. Hastings Center Studies, 2(1), 21–32.

Fletcher, John C. (1979). Prenatal diagnosis, selective abortion, and the ethics of withholding treatment from the defective newborn. In A.M. Capron, R.F. Murray, & S.B. Twiss (Eds.), *Genetic counseling: Facts, values, and norms* (pp. 239–254). New York: Alan R. Liss.

Fletcher, Joseph (1972). Indicators of humanhood: A tentative profile of man. *Hastings Center Report, 2,* 1–4.

Fletcher, Joseph (1974). Four indicators of humanhood—the inquiry matures. *Hastings Center Report, 4,* 4–7.

Forest, M., & Lusthaus, E. (1989). Promoting educational equality for all students: Circles and maps. In S. Stainback, W. Stainback, & M. Forest (Eds.), *Educating all students in the mainstream of regular education* (pp. 43–57). Baltimore: Paul H. Brookes Publishing Co.

Fost, N. (1988). Organs from anencephalic infants: An idea whose time has not yet come. *Hastings Center Report, 18*(5), 5–10.

Garland, M.J. (1977). Care of the newborn: The decision not to treat. *Perinatology/Neonatology, 1*(2), 14–21, 43–44.

Gartner, A., & Lipsky, D.K. (1987). Beyond special education: Toward a quality system for all students. *Harvard Educational Review, 57*(4), 367–395.

Gaylord-Ross R. (Ed.). (1989). *Integration strategies for students with handicaps.* Baltimore: Paul H. Brookes Publishing Co.

Gross, R.H., Cox, A., Tatyrek, R., Pollay, M., & Barnes, W.A. (1983). Early management and decision making for the treatment of myelomeningocele. *Pediatrics, 72*(4), 450–458.

Guess, D., Dussault, B., Brown, F., Mulligan, M., Orelove, F., Comegys, A., & Rues, J. (1984). *Legal, economic, psychological, and moral considerations on the practice of withholding medical treatment from infants with congenital defects* (Monograph #1). Seattle: The Association for Persons with Severe Handicaps.

Halvorsen, A., & Sailor, W. (1990). Integration of students with severe and profound disabilities: A review of research. In R. Gaylord-Ross (Ed.), *Issues and research in special education* (Vol. 1, pp. 110–172). New York: Teachers College Press.

Hamre-Nietupski, S., & Nietupski, J. (1985). Taking full advantage of interaction opportunities. In S. Stainback & W. Stainback (Eds.), *Integration of students with severe handicaps into regular schools* (pp. 98–112). Reston, VA: The Council for Exceptional Children.

Hardman, M.L. (1984). The role of Congress in decisions relating to the withholding of medical treatment from seriously ill newborns. *TASH Journal, 9*(1), 3–7.

Hawkins, R.P. (1984). What is "meaningful" behavior change in a severely/profoundly retarded learner: The view of a behavior analytic parent. In W.L. Heward, T. Heron, D. Hill, & J. Trap-Porter (Eds.), *Behavior analysis in education* (pp. 282–286). Columbus, OH: Charles E. Merrill.

Hentoff, N. (1985, January). The awful privacy of Baby Doe. *The Atlantic Monthly,* 54–58, 61–62.

Holvoet, J.F. (1989). Research on persons labeled profoundly retarded: Issues and ideas. In F. Brown & D.H. Lehr (Eds.), *Persons with profound disabilities: Issues and practices* (pp. 61–82). Baltimore: Paul H. Brookes Publishing Co.

Imperiled newborns (Special Report). (1987). *Hastings Center Report, 17*(6), 5–32.

Kauffman, J.M. (1981). Are all children educable? Editor's introduction. *Analysis and Intervention in Developmental Disabilities, 1,* 1–3.

Kauffman, J.M., & Krouse, J. (1981). The cult of educability: Searching for the substance of things hoped for, the evidence of things not seen. *Analysis and Intervention in Developmental Disabilities, 1,* 53–60.

Kerr, K. (1984). Reporting the case of Baby Jane Doe. *Hastings Center Report, 14*(4), 7–9.

Kirk, S.A. (1962). *Educating exceptional children.* Boston: Houghton Mifflin.

Koop, C.E. (1989). Life and death and the handicapped newborn. *Issues in Law and Medicine, 5*(1), 101–113.

Landesman-Dwyer, S., & Sackett, G.P. (1978). Behavioral changes in nonambulatory, profoundly mentally retarded individuals. In C.E. Meyers (Ed.), *Quality of life in severely and profoundly mentally retarded people: Research foundations for improvement.* Monograph of the AAMD, No., 3 (pp. 55–144). Washington, DC: American Association on Mental Deficiency.

Laski, F.J. (1991). Achieving integration during the second revolution. In L.H. Meyer, C.A. Peck, & L. Brown (Eds.), *Critical issues in the lives of people with severe disabilities* (pp. 409–421). Baltimore: Paul H. Brookes Publishing Co.

Lifton, R.J. (1986). *The Nazi doctors: Medical killing and the psychology of genocide.* New York: Basic Books.

Lipsky, D.K., & Gartner, A. (Eds.). (1989). *Beyond separate education: Quality education for all.* Baltimore: Paul H. Brookes Publishing Co.

Lusthaus, E. (1985a). "Euthanasia" of persons with severe handicaps: Refuting the rationalizations. *Journal of The Association for Persons with Severe Handicaps, 10*(2), 87–94.

Lusthaus, E.W. (1985b). Involuntary euthanasia and current attempts to define persons with mental retardation as less than human. *Mental Retardation, 23*(3), 148–154.

Murray, T. (1984). At last, final rules on Baby Doe. *The Hastings Center Report, 14*(1), 17.

Murray, T.H. (1985). The final, anticlimactic rule on Baby Doe. *The Hastings Center Report, 15*(3), 5–6.

Neuhaus, R.J. (1990, March). The way they were, the way we are: Bioethics and the Holocaust. *First Things,* 31–37.

Nolan, K. (1990). Let's take Baby Doe to Alaska. *Hastings Center Report, 20*(1), 3.

Orelove, F.P. (1991). Educating all students: The future is now. In L. H. Meyer, C.A. Peck, & L. Brown (Eds.), *Critical issues in the lives of people with severe disabilities* (pp. 67–87). Baltimore: Paul H. Brookes Publishing Co.

President's Commission for the Study of Ethical Problems in Medicine and Biomedical and Behavioral Research. (1983). *Deciding to forego life-sustaining treatment.* Washington, DC: Author.

Private death. (1982, April 27). *The New York Times,* p. 22.

Ramsey, P. (1978). *Ethics at the edge of life.* New Haven: Yale University Press.

Robertson, J.A. (1975). Involuntary euthanasia of defective newborns: A legal analysis. *Stanford Law Review, 27,* 213–269.

Sailor, W. (1989). The educational, social, and vocational integration of students with the most severe disabilities. In D.K. Lipsky & A. Gartner (Eds.), *Beyond separate education: Quality education for all* (pp. 53–74). Baltimore: Paul H. Brookes Publishing Co.

Sailor, W., Anderson, J.L., Halvorsen, A.T., Doering, K., Filler, J., & Goetz, L. (1989). *The comprehensive local school: Regular education for all students with disabilities.* Baltimore: Paul H. Brookes Publishing Co.

Sailor, W., Gee, K., Goetz, L., & Graham, N. (1988). Progress in educating students with the most severe disabilities: Is there any? *Journal of The Association for Persons with Severe Handicaps, 13*(2), 87–99.

Sapon-Shevin, M. (1990). Initial steps for developing a caring school. In W. Stainback & S. Stainback (Eds.), *Support networks for inclusive schooling: Interdependent integrated education* (pp. 241–248). Baltimore: Paul H. Brookes Publishing Co.

Schaffer, J., & Sobsey, D. (1991). A dialogue on medical responsibility. In L. H. Meyer, C.A. Peck, & L. Brown (Eds.), *Critical issues in the lives of people with severe disabilities* (pp. 601–606). Baltimore: Paul H. Brookes Publishing Co.

Schneiderman, L.J. (1990). Exile and PVS. *Hastings Center Report, 20*(3), 5.

Shaw, A. (1977). Defining the quality of life: A formula without numbers. *Hastings Center Report, 7*(5), 11.

Shaw, A. (1988). QL revisited. *Hastings Center Report, 18*(2), 10–12.

Shewmon, D.A. (1988). Anencephaly: Selected medical aspects. *Hastings Center Report, 18*(5), 11–19.

Singer, P. (1979). *Practical ethics.* Cambridge: Cambridge University Press.

Snell, M.E., & Eichner, S.J. (1989). Integration for students with profound disabilities. In F. Brown & D. H. Lehr (Eds.), *Persons with profound disabilities: Issues and practices* (pp. 109–138). Baltimore: Paul H. Brookes Publishing Co.

Stainback, S., Stainback, W., & Forest, M. (Eds.). (1989). *Educating all students in the mainstream of regular education.* Baltimore: Paul H. Brookes Publishing Co.

Stainback, W., & Stainback, S. (Eds.). (1990). *Support networks for inclusive schooling: Interdependent integrated education.* Baltimore: Paul H. Brookes Publishing Co.

Steinbock, B. (1984). Baby Jane Doe in the courts. *Hastings Center Report, 14*(1), 12–19.

Steinbock, B. (1987). Whatever happened to the Danville Siamese twins? *Hastings Center Report, 17*(4), 3–4.

Strully, J.L., & Strully, C.F. (1989). Friendships as an educational goal. In S. Stainback, W. Stainback, & M. Forest (Eds.), *Educating all students in the mainstream of regular education* (pp. 59–68). Baltimore: Paul H. Brookes Publishing Co.

TASH Resolution on Nutrition and Hydration (1986, November). Seattle: The Association for Persons with Severe Handicaps.

Thompson, B., & Guess, D. (1989). Students who experience the most profound disabilities: Teacher perspectives. In F. Brown & D.H. Lehr (Eds.), *Persons with profound disabilities: Issues and practices* (pp. 3–41). Baltimore: Paul H. Brookes Publishing Co.

Timothy W. v. Rochester, New Hampshire, School District, 875 F.2nd 954 (1st Cir., 1989).

Tooley, M. (1977). Abortion and infanticide. In M. Cohen, T. Nagel, & T. Scanlon (Eds.), *The rights and wrongs of abortion* (pp. 52–84). Princeton, NJ: Princeton University Press.

Turnbull, A.P., & Turnbull, H.R. (1986). *Families, professionals, and exceptionality: A special partnership.* Columbus, OH: Charles E. Merrill.

Walters, J.W., & Ashwal, S. (1988). Organ prolongation in anencephalic infants: Ethical and medical issues. *Hastings Center Report, 18*(5), 19–27.

Wang, M.C., & Baker, E.T. (1985–1986). Mainstreaming programs: Design features and effects. *Journal of Special Education, 19,* 503–521.

Weir, R. (1984). *Selective nontreatment of handicapped newborns.* New York: Oxford University Press.

Wikler, D. (1988). Not dead, not dying? Ethical categories and persistent vegetative state. *Hastings Center Report, 18*(1), 41–47.

Will, G.F. (1983, November 14). Protecting handicapped infants' rights. *Pittsburgh Post-Gazette.*

Willke, J.C., & Andrusko, D. (1988). Personhood redux. *Hastings Center Report, 18*(5), 30–33.

Wolfe, P.S., & Snell, M.W. (1990). *Program packet on the facilitation of social interactions between persons with severe disabilities and their nondisabled peers in school and community settings.* Charlottesville: Virginia Statewide Systems Change Project, University of Virginia, Charlottesville.

Wolfensberger, W. (1981). The extermination of handicapped people in World War II Germany. *Mental Retardation, 19,* 1–7.

Index

Abnormal reflexes, defined, 339
ABR (auditory brainstem response), in hearing
    assessment, 133
Absence seizures, 199
    see also Seizure *entries*
Abuse, 221–226
Academy of Dentistry for the Handicapped,
    364
Accident treatment, in bladder training,
    381–382
Acquired immunodeficiency syndrome (AIDS),
    189–190
    communicable disease susceptibility in,
        193–195
        chicken pox, 193
        transmission of, 194
Activities Planning Matrix, 246, 247
Activity(ies)
    age-appropriate peers and, 450
    for alternative positions, 108
    deaf-blind children and, 146
    functional tasks and, 243
    hazardous, seizures and, 203–204
    instructional adaptation and, 264–265,
        266–267
    modification of, 266–267
    selection of, 450
    in structured curriculum, 237, 240–242
    teaching content and, 19
    teaching within, 245–248
    see also Task *entries*
Activity/skills matrix, 236, 238–239
Activity-based goals and objectives, 245–246
Activity-based instruction, 245, 246–248
Acuity, *see* Visual acuity; Visual impairment
Acute otitis media, 161, 162
Acute viral rhinitis, 190
Adaptation(s)
    clothing, 399–400
    defined, 259
    domestic, 268–274
    positioning, determining need for, 103–104
    recreation/leisure, 274–281

toileting, 378, 379
types of, 56, 259–260
    see also Instructional adaptations
Adaptive approaches, 56–57
Adaptive equipment, 267
    for dressing, 396–397
    for positioning, 95–96
        chairs, 96–104
    for visual impairments, 136–137
Adaptive responses, in sensory integration, 55
Administrative challenges to implementation,
    26–27
Administrative guidelines for health care,
    157–159, *see also* Health care services
Administrative reform, in abuse prevention, 225
Administrator(s), 6–7
    failure to understand transdisciplinary model,
        26–27
    steps in facilitation of implementation, 27
Adolescence stage in family life cycle,
    422–426
Age
    dressing skills and, 391
    at onset of hearing loss, 123
    readiness for toilet training and, 375–376
Age-appropriate peers, 450
Aggression, epilepsy and, 209
AIDS, *see* Acquired immunodeficiency
        syndrome
AIDS-related complex, *see* ARC
Air temperature, eating and, 346
Airway, seizures and, 205
Airway obstruction, 215–218
    aspiration versus, 351
Akinetic seizures, 199, *see also* Seizure *entries*
Alcohol, abuse and, 221
Alerting stimuli, *see* Arousal/alerting stimuli
Alignment, *see* Positioning
Alphabet gloves, 146
Alphabet methods, 146
American Academy of Pediatric Dentistry, 364
American Academy of Pediatrics, 158, 438
American Federation of Teachers, 158

457